D0278964

TERENCE
RATTIGAN
THE MAN AND HIS WORK

TERENCE
RATTIGAN
THE MAN AND HIS WORK
MICHAEL DARLOW

 QUARTET BOOKS

This revised and updated edition published in 2010 by
Quartet Books Limited
A member of the Namara Group
27 Goodge Street, London W1P 2LD

Previous revised edition published by Quartet Books Ltd in 2000
Original edition of *Terence Rattigan: The Man and his Work* by
Michael Darlow and Gillian Hodson published in 1979

Copyright © Michael Darlow 2000, 2010

The moral right of Michael Darlow as author of this
work has been asserted by him in accordance with
the Copyright, Designs and Patents Act 1988

All rights reserved. No part of this book may be
reproduced in any form or by any means without
the prior written permission of the publisher

A catalogue record for this book is available
from the British Library

ISBN 978 0 7043 7197 2

Printed and bound in Great Britain by
TJ International, Padstow, Cornwall

Contents

In memory of the late Professor Susan Rusinko, whom I met through Rattigan, through whom I gained many valuable insights into the man and with whom I shared many great evenings at the theatre, in both Britain and America.

Acknowledgements

It is now well over thirty years since I first became involved in enquiring into and writing about the life and work of Terence Rattigan. In that time an enormous number of people have helped, guided and encouraged me. They are so numerous, and their help has been so extensive, that I can never adequately acknowledge my debt to them all. Out of literally hundreds of individuals, institutions and other authors I can therefore only mention here those to whom I owe an extra-special debt of gratitude. In doing so, I am conscious that I must overlook many others. To these people I can only apologize and hope that they will forgive me.

First and foremost I must acknowledge the help of the late Sir Terence Rattigan, who gave me and Gillian Hodson permission to write the first edition of this book; without his enthusiastic help and encouragement we would certainly never have been able to complete it, and without the memory of his determination and courage I would not, during the more than thirty years between the appearance of that first edition and this new one, have continued to collect information and deepen my knowledge of his work. Although mortally ill and in continuous pain when Gillian and I first met him in 1977, he gave generously of his time and encouragement, advising us about where to look and whom to contact for the truth behind many crucial events in his life.

I also wish to acknowledge my special debt to Peter Carter-Ruck, Lee Penhaligan and the Trustees of the Rattigan Estate for their unstinting help during the preparation of this new and revised edition.

Gillian and I would never have been able to write the first edition of this book without the help and unfailing support of Michael Imison, Sir Terence's agent. Throughout the more than thirty years between that first edition and this, Michael in particular and the staffs of Dr Jan van Loewen Ltd and Alan Brodie Representation Ltd have continued to encourage me and to provide vital information and advice. I also wish to acknowledge the help of the British Broadcasting Corporation which brought me to Rattigan in the first place and gave Gillian Hodson and me permission to quote from broadcasts made by Sir Terence and others. This book originally came about as a result of a BBC Television programme and I owe a special debt of gratitude to James Cellan-Jones, then Head of BBC Television Plays, and Graham Benson, the producer who first asked me to write and direct a programme about Sir Terence. Both have continued to encourage me in the intervening years.

I also acknowledge my debt to the many authors and publishers from whose work I have quoted. Their works are listed in the Bibliography and are specifically acknowledged in the text. I am also indebted to the Trustees of the Rattigan Estate, to Hamish Hamilton Ltd and to Alan Brodie Representation for permission to quote from the plays, both published and unpublished, from the prefaces to Sir Terence's *Collected Plays* and from his other works. In acknowledging my debt to other authors who have written specifically about Sir Terence's life or work, I wish in particular to pay tribute to Holly Hill. In interviewing Sir Terence in the mid-1970s and writing a postgraduate dissertation, in the face of opposition from her academic supervisor, followed by a series of articles, she blazed a trail towards a critical reappraisal of the work of Rattigan which I, and all other writers about Rattigan since then, have followed. Over the years she has remained a true friend and sound adviser. Others who have followed that trail include Rattigan's friend, the critic B. A. Young, who in 1978 wrote the introduction to the fourth volume of Rattigan's *Collected Plays* and in 1986 was the author of a uniquely personal memoire and critical evaluation of him and his work – *The Rattigan Version*. In 1995, Geoffrey Wansell produced a new biography of Rattigan, the first which drew on all the papers lodged by the Rattigan Estate in the British Library. He uncovered important new pieces of information and provided valuable insights into a number of things, in particular into Sir Terence's many involvements in films.

In recent years other critics and writers have contributed major essays and articles on Rattigan or his work. Two have written with perhaps unique insight – Michael Billington in numerous articles in the *Guardian* and Sean O'Connor in his 1998 book *Straight Acting: Popular Gay Drama from Wilde to Rattigan*. To each of these writers I acknowledge my special indebtedness.

This book is dedicated to the late Susan Rusinko. In 1983 she wrote an outstandingly perceptive study – *Terence Rattigan* – aimed mainly at American undergraduate students of English literature, in which she analysed in detail Rattigan's play-writing techniques. I am indebted not only to Susan's book, but to her friendship, continuing enthusiasm for Rattigan and to the many insights she provided me with during numerous conversations about Rattigan over almost twenty years. Tragically, Susan died shortly before I started detailed work on the 2000 edition, but my debt to her remains immeasurable.

Since 1976 I have interviewed an enormous number of Rattigan's friends, professional colleagues and people with a special insight into or knowledge of him or his work. I have also been in correspondence with many more. A list of the most important is included in the Bibliography at the end of this book. I am indebted to each and every one and thank them all. I fear I may have missed some out, and if so I apologize. It is invidious to single out any individuals, but I must thank in particular just seven people from the legion who have helped me. Each has given me quite exceptional amounts of their time, allowing me to go back to them to check facts and details repeatedly over the years, or has told me about particularly important, sometimes intimate or emotional events in Rattigan's life. They are Adrian Brown, Jean Galitzine (née Dawnay), David Heimann (son of the co-author of Rattigan's first performed play, *First Episode*, with whose permission quotations from the unpublished text are included) and the late Peter Glenville and John Perry; also John Montgomery and Peter Osborn, who wrote to me at length and with exceptional candour about critical events in their own and Rattigan's lives. This book could not have been written without their assistance.

I would like to thank the following institutions for help during my research: the British Library, and in particular Sally Brown, Curator of Modern Manuscripts, Chris Fletcher and the unfailingly helpful staffs of the Humanities Reading Rooms; the London Library; St Pancras Public Library; the Public Record Office at Kew and the staff there who guided me through the maze of Foreign Office Papers and Service Records; the Family Records Centre; Claire Hudson and the staff of the Theatre Museum, Raymond Mander and Jo Mitchenson; the Imperial War Museum; the British Film Institute; New York Public Library Theatre Collection; Thames Television; ATV; *Spotlight*; Sony Classics Film Distribution; Diana Carter and the staff of St Mary Abbots Church, Kensington; Roger D. Dark of The Old Manor House, Combe Florey; Harrow School and Sandroyd School.

I would also like to thank the many correspondents who have contacted me with new information since the appearance of the 2000 edition, especially Gerald Campion and Linnet Allardyce who brought to my attention valuable material which has a bearing on two of his most important plays.

Gillian Hodson and I would never have embarked on our book without the enthusiasm and encouragement of Naim Attallah, the chairman of Quartet Books, and I would never have written this revised edition without his continued confidence and prompting. I am similarly indebted to Piers Blofeld and David Elliott, my editors at Quartet Books, for all their patience and tolerance. My heartfelt thanks also go to my assistant Debbie Slater, who not only computed my often unruly manuscript but was tireless in digging up obscure facts and tracing tenuous contacts.

It is a source of regret to me that my original co-author during the preparation of the first edition of this book, Gillian Hodson, was not available because of her other commitments to work with me on the present edition. But my debt to her, as my co-author, for all the work and research that she undertook between 1977 and 1979, and for her continuing support and encouragement when I embarked on this new edition, cannot be overestimated. However, any mistakes or false conclusions in this new edition are mine, and mine alone.

Finally, I wish to pay a special tribute to my wife, Sophie. She has not only borne with my sometimes near obsessive pursuit of the facts behind Rattigan's life and my determination for a proper recognition of his special genius, encouraging me when I was discouraged, but it was she who kept together all my notes, interview transcripts, letters from Rattigan's friends and colleagues and early manuscript drafts of this book for over thirty years and through successive moves of house. Without her dedication these papers, many of them irreplaceable, would have become dispersed and this author would probably have given up.

Michael Darlow
Bradford-on-Avon, Spring 2010

Introduction

Shortly before Sir Terence Rattigan's death, I was asked by the BBC to prepare his television obituary. Almost my first question was could I be critical? In those days, in the mid-1970s, it was more or less axiomatic, especially for anyone who, like me, had marched to 'Ban the Bomb', protested against the government during the Suez Crisis in 1956 and cheered at the original Royal Court production of John Osborne's *Look Back in Anger*, to regard Rattigan as the epitome of a tired, slick, uncommitted and conservative theatre that had rightly been swept away.

In 1973, when Frank Dunlop, Artistic Director of the Young Vic, had suggested that his company should revive Rattigan's first successful comedy, *French Without Tears*, he had received a typically adverse reaction:

> I put it to the Arts Council, who had hysterics. They said, 'You've got to be mad. This is just trash.'
>
> But I remembered seeing a production of *French Without Tears* and finding it very entertaining. Then I read it, and found it absolutely smashing – wonderfully constructed, very funny, and very moving because all of the characters are very, very true. In it you see people behaving the way you did when you were young and felt desperate about a lot of things . . .
>
> Rattigan knows about love, and that's in *French Without Tears* in the most delicate way. He knows about friendship and relationships between people too, and I don't know any other playwright but Osborne who understands relationships between people in such a subtle way.
>
> I thought the play just as relevant in 1973 as when Rattigan had written it almost forty years before. The hero is fighting to write and get out of his social class and into contact with other

people. That is still very relevant in England – breaking out of one's class, doing some sort of job, making connections between people from different strata of society. Rattigan does it very delicately and implicitly, rather than with some big message.[1]

Frank Dunlop's youthful Young Vic audiences had been enthralled by the play and it had stayed in the company's repertoire for almost a year. Dunlop told that story to an American, Holly Hill, while she was preparing her postgraduate degree dissertation at Columbia University on the plays of Terence Rattigan. In 1969 she had been greeted with derision when she had suggested Rattigan as a subject. Her professor had dismissed the idea out of hand: 'Nobody takes Rattigan seriously.' Yet only twenty-five years earlier Rattigan had dominated the British theatre. One of the most financially successful English playwrights who had ever lived, he was only the third playwright in the twentieth century to receive a knighthood.

When we started work on our television obituary early in 1977, Gillian Hodson and I asked the BBC Library to dig out every book and every article about Rattigan. It was then that we discovered that there was not one single book about him. Such articles as there were had been written more than twenty years previously or were damning. One from 1970 by Albert Hunt, headed 'Danger. Craftsman at Work', was typical: 'It's facile knowingness that's at the heart of Rattigan's theatre ... Every complexity can be explained away, every facet of human experience reduced to a simple matter of manipulation ... '[2] But that view of Rattigan's plays did not accord with my memory of them. Despite my initial desire to criticize their conservatism and conventional construction, my memory from seeing them at school and appearing in them as a young repertory-theatre actor was of the precisely created atmosphere and true emotions of *The Browning Version*, *The Deep Blue Sea* and *Separate Tables*, and of the infectious humour of *While the Sun Shines*. Rereading them, Gillian and I found, like Frank Dunlop, that they remained relevant and engaging. In the words of an American academic, Professor Susan Rusinko, these comedies and dramas 'about flawed or failed characters course their way unerringly down the moral and emotional mainstream of their troubled times'.[3]

Gillian and I came to believe that a serious injustice had been done to Rattigan. Not simply in the years after the Royal Court revolution of 1956, but even in his heyday. The critics, suspicious of his commercial success, seemed rarely, if ever, to have accorded Rattigan the recognition which he deserved. That sense of injustice provided the initial impetus for the first edition of this book. We wanted to fuel a reassessment. Our television programme might help, but to achieve all that we had in mind required more space and freedom than was available in a broadcast obituary.

It is now more than thirty years since Rattigan's death and that re-evaluation has taken place. Gillian Hodson and I can claim no credit; it has been the enduring quality of the plays themselves that has wrought the transformation. There are more revivals of his work around the world now than at any time since the 1950s; more new productions for television and even new feature films based on his plays. Many of the major plays are back in print and, since our book in 1979, there have been no less than three more books devoted entirely to Terence Rattigan, plus essays about him and his work in numerous others, together with a continuous flow of articles in magazines and newspapers. Today Rattigan's place in the canon of British drama seems more secure than at any time since he started writing.

But our purpose in writing went well beyond a critical reappraisal of Rattigan's work (there were others better qualified than us to undertake that). In our work on the television programme we had come to suspect a striking and perhaps distinctive relationship between Rattigan's life and his writing. Investigation, especially of the less well-known aspects of his life which did not fit the public image of the unruffled, establishment-minded English gentleman, tended to confirm this. Rattigan himself had said that if a playwright was honest he had to admit that he was 'compelled' to write the same play over and over again. That did not sound like the cool craftsman of conventional opinion; but it did accord with the evidence of the plays themselves.

In 1976, in a radio programme about Rattigan, Anthony Curtis had quoted from a letter by the playwright David Rudkin:

I detect in his plays a deep personal, surely sexual pain, which he manages at the same time to express and disguise. The craftsmanship of which we hear so much loose talk seems to me to arise from deep psychological necessity, a drive to organize the energy that arises out of his own pain. Not to batten it down but to invest it with some expressive clarity that speaks immediately to people, yet keeps himself hidden. I really think the Aunt Edna business and the ethic of the well-made play are but the most outward social manifestations of this and because it is possible, if one is very innocent, inattentive or self-dishonest, to sit right through a Rattigan play and not have the ghost of an idea what is going on ... I think Rattigan is not at all the commercial middlebrow dramatist his image suggests but some-one peculiarly haunting and oblique who certainly speaks to me with resonance of existential bleakness and irresoluble carnal solitude.[4]

Rattigan heard Curtis's radio programme and confirmed the truth of what Rudkin had said: 'He's quite right, of course ... but I never thought my slip showed as much as that.' Curtis himself detected 'a deeply Proustian ambivalence at the heart of Rattigan that needs, as they say, to be gone into'.[5] Gillian and I became convinced that not only was there a special relationship between Rattigan's life and its visible reflection in his work, but that it was only through understanding more about his life, and in particular those elements of it that had been kept hidden, that it would be possible to achieve a full appreciation of his plays.

It was always going to be a delicate task. We were charting uncharted or deliberately concealed territory. Many of the people who had been closest to him were still living so there were bound to be limits to what we could say. Our first task was to approach Rattigan himself. He not only agreed, he encouraged us. 'Go to those who know the truth and will be least discreet,' he told us, and gave us names and addresses. Almost all agreed to talk. A few, however, for reasons which we understood even though we disagreed with them, tried to change Rattigan's mind. They were worried that any discussion of his homosexuality or his sometimes fraught personal relationships might harm Rattigan's reputation and the public's willingness to accept his plays. Despite the advances in sexual freedom in the 1960s and relaxation of the law relating to homosexual acts in private, in the late 1970s Gay Liberation had made far less progress than it has today.[6] But Rattigan's mind was not changed and we were given a unique opportunity to talk in depth to many of the people who had been closely involved in the most significant events of his life.

As one might expect with a playwright whose recurring themes are the difficulty and pain of love and sex, emotional repression and the agony of self-awareness, concealment and evasion, the problem for a biographer is not only one of finding the evidence but of knowing how to read it. The evidence is often contradictory. Depending on the circumstances and to whom he was talking, Rattigan frequently gave more than one version of the same event or conflicting explanations for his actions. With Rattigan this seems to go beyond the old adage that 'there is no story that cannot be improved by a bit of judicious exaggeration'. As a result, over the years a number of myths and misunderstandings have grown up about some of Rattigan's actions and intentions. However, it is significant that the more one studies the plays, the more one finds that where there is a conflict of evidence it is in the plays themselves that one can often find the most revealing clues about where to seek the truth. Through the act of writing his plays, Rattigan is working through his most deeply felt concerns and emotions. This is not to suggest that the plays are directly autobiographical in the way that, for instance, the early chapters of *David Copperfield* are for Dickens. Rattigan's method is more akin to the action of a kaleidoscope. A myriad of bright shards of truth or emotion is endlessly rearranged until the pieces make up the pattern he finds most satisfying.

In revising and updating the book for this new edition, not only have I been able to gain access to most of the papers that were withheld from Gillian Hodson and myself thirty years ago, but more of Rattigan's unperformed and unpublished work has come to light, together with earlier drafts and notes for some of his best known plays. Not only have I had years more in which to live with and study the plays, I am now able to make fuller use of material originally collected in the 1970s which it would have been inappropriate to make public while the people concerned were still alive. In addition, over the years since the book first appeared a number of people whom we were unable to trace or of whose existence we simply did not know have approached me with valuable new information. As a result I hope that I have been able to deepen and improve this portrait of a writer who, in the words of the young critic and theatre director Sean O'Connor writing in 1998, 'as the century turns, seems to have finally confirmed his status as one of the great British dramatists of the century'.[7]

Notes

1   Quoted in *A Critical Analysis of the Plays of Sir Terence Rattigan* by Holly Hill, University Microfilms International, 1977.
2   *New Society*, 12 November 1970.
3   *Terence Rattigan* by Susan Rusinko, Twayne Publishers, Boston, 1983.
4   *Rattigan's Theatre*, Radio 3, 30 March 1976.
5   Anthony Curtis, *Plays and Players*, November 1978.
6   I have generally opted to use the terms 'homosexual' and 'homosexuality' as they were the terms which during most of Rattigan's lifetime carried the least implication of moral disapproval. For much of the period covered by this book words such as 'gay' conveyed an entirely different meaning from that understood today. In justifying my decision to those who may disagree with it, I can do no better than cite Anthony Grey's justification for using it in his book about his involvement in the fight for homosexual law reform, *Quest for Justice*, where he reminds his readers that the word homosexual originated in 1869 'as a scientifically neutral medical description', which Grey regards as 'an adequate working tool' for the purposes of his book.
7   *Straight Acting: Popular Gay Drama from Wilde to Rattigan* by Sean O'Connor, Cassell, London, 1998.

1

Entrances

The power of Rattigan's best plays comes from the implicit rather than the explicit, from unspoken feelings, buried emotions and hidden truths. So too with his life. Rattigan's public persona of the effortlessly successful, unfailingly cool and well-mannered popular playwright concealed a much less confident, more tormented and private Rattigan. He or members of his immediate family often deliberately hid or distorted key events in his life or about himself. Yet his most powerful work comes straight from that hidden part of himself. Equally, the best of the work provides the least distorting window into the real man.

The first uncertainty about Terence Rattigan is the date of his birth. The most likely date, 10 June 1911, was a wet and blustery Saturday. A long spell of sweltering heat had ended abruptly the day before. A rain storm had settled the eye-pricking dust of London's pavements and soaked those taking part in the full-scale rehearsal of the Coronation. George V was to be crowned in twelve days' time.

Most of the visitors who already thronged the capital were relieved at the sudden drop in temperature, but not Terence Rattigan's father Frank, home on leave from North Africa, nor the royal guest who had been put in his charge for the duration of the celebrations – Sid Menebhi, ex-Grand Vizier of Morocco. Frank Rattigan was thirty-two, a qualified Arabic speaker (for which he received an additional salary allowance from the Foreign Office) and on his own admission an unconventional diplomat. He seemed to have a brilliant career in front of him. He had entered the Diplomatic Service in 1902, at the age of twenty-three, after leaving Oxford without taking a degree and going abroad to study languages. Since May 1909 he had been Second Secretary on the staff of the British Legation in Tangier; an important position because Morocco had recently been the focus of international tension between France and Germany.

It was typical of Frank Rattigan that in taking leave with his beautiful young wife Vera in May 1911 he should combine professional advantage with domestic convenience. Many other British colonial administrators, diplomats and officers serving overseas arranged their annual leave that year to coincide with the Coronation. Unlike Frank Rattigan, however, few of them managed to get themselves a role in the ceremony itself. Escorting his Arab charge to meet Lord Derby, the Duke of Rutland and senior officials at the Foreign Office was good for Frank Rattigan's career; accompanying him to the ball at Derby House, playing tennis with him at Belvoir Castle, with Lady Anglesey and the seventeen-year-old Lady Diana Manners (later Lady Diana Cooper), helped his social standing; arranging the provision of amenable young ladies for the Grand Vizier's off-duty hours provided him with the opportunity to indulge his own taste for fluffy blondes.

Frank and Vera Rattigan had been married for five and a half years. Vera was strikingly beautiful, erect with a perfect figure and gently curling fair hair. The wedding had taken place shortly after Frank's appointment to the staff of the British Embassy in The Hague. At first Vera had been nervous of the social duties entailed in being a diplomat's wife, but being a young woman of energy and character, she entered easily into her husband's hectic life. With the help and guidance of other wives in the diplomatic circle in The Hague, she soon mastered the complex etiquette and rules governing the round of functions and entertaining that made up diplomatic existence in the capitals of Europe. Frank was lax in these matters almost to the point of eccentricity. While on the embassy staff in Vienna he had sent other dancers flying at a court ball in honour of the Prince of Wales by a wild performance of the polka when partnering Princess Mary. On another occasion he had been rebuked by the court chamberlain for dancing a Boston with the daughter of an ambassador when the orchestra had been playing a waltz. In breach of every rule of etiquette Frank Rattigan had sneaked away from the ballroom on yet another state occasion because he was bored by the slow rigidity of the dancing. In the refreshment room he was joined by an Austrian, resplendent in a general's uniform, who asked him why he was not dancing. He replied, with undiplomatic honesty, that he was bored. The general, whom Rattigan did not recognize, laughed and suggested an inspection of the palace's collection of sporting trophies might be more amusing. The identity of the general, who was by then showing Frank Rattigan round the gun rooms, was only revealed when an aide-de-camp clicked his heels and approached them saying: 'Your Imperial Highness, some of the important guests are about to leave!' The 'general' had been Frank Rattigan's host, the Archduke himself.[1]

Vera provided a steadying influence on Frank. She was also an asset in her own right. Vivacious, but at the same time assiduous in the duties of an embassy wife, she was well able to hold her own in the most exalted company. Both Vera and Frank came from distinguished families of Irish lawyers. Frank's grandfather, Bartholomew Rattigan, seems to have moved from County Kildare in the 1840s to practise as an advocate in India.[2] His son William in turn practised at the bar in India, becoming the greatest authority of his day on Indian law and publishing numerous books on the subject. He also produced a short book entitled *Events to be Remembered in the History of India from the Invasion of Alexander to the Latest Times*. In his first chapter, he said he was trying to rescue the story of Alexander from 'the enveloping dark and filmy haze of mythological story', an enterprise to be undertaken later by his grandson Terence in his own, rather different, way. At the time of Frank's birth, William Rattigan was Chief Justice of the Punjab. When he retired with a knighthood and returned to Britain, Sir William became Member of Parliament for North-East Lanarkshire. Another Rattigan, Sir Henry Adolphus Rattigan, followed in his footsteps and became Chief Justice of the Punjab.

In spite of the social position they had achieved, the Rattigans were not wealthy. Frank's father, Sir William, believed in the virtues of self-reliance. When he was six, Frank, who spent his early childhood in India, was presented by his father with a saloon rifle and a daily ration of six cartridges and told to roam about and fend for himself. Later, as a young man studying for the Diplomatic Service entrance exam at a crammer in France, Frank was short of money, and kept himself in funds by regularly winning a weekly sweepstake on a pigeon-shooting competition at the local country club. Frank, who undoubtedly loved and respected his father, would in his turn expect the same self-reliance and ingenuity from his sons Brian and Terence.

There was nothing in either Frank's or Vera's family background that would have led anyone to expect that their second child would turn out to be a dramatist. The only evidence of an interest in the theatre was on Vera's side of the family, and that was tenuous. Her family, the Houstons, included a professor of political economy at Trinity College, Dublin – Arthur H. Houston. He was a noted authority on English drama and in 1863 gave a public lecture, which was subsequently published, entitled 'The English Drama – Its Past History and Probable Future'. The lecture contained one sentiment which his descendant Terence Rattigan would endorse a century later: 'The highest type of dramatic composition is that which supplies us with studies of character, skilfully worked out, in a plot not deficient in probability and by means of incidents not wanting in interest.' However, Arthur Houston's prognosis for the future of drama was not encouraging – he predicted that the drama would 'languish as a literary production' and that 'whatever power of depicting character and describing incidents as exists today...will be diverted into novel-making'.

The Rattigans' first child, Brian, had arrived after three years of marriage. He had been born with a deformity in one leg. A major reason for the Rattigans' return to England on leave in 1911 was that Vera was due to be delivered of a second child that summer. This is where the first ambiguity surrounding the facts of Terence Rattigan's life occurs. On what date was he born? The Births column of *The Times* for Monday, 12 June 1911 carries this announcement: 'Rattigan on 9th inst. at Lanarkslea, Cornwall Gardens, the wife of Frank Rattigan, Second Secretary in H.M. Diplomatic Service, of a son'. Clear enough; yet throughout his life Terence Rattigan and his family would celebrate his birthday on 10 June and in every public document or authorized account of his life he would record his date of birth as 10 June 1911. Why? At this distance in time it is hard to be certain. The one person, apart from Terence himself, who we can be absolutely sure was present at the birth was Vera Rattigan and, there being no complications during the birth itself, she seems likely to be the most reliable witness to when it actually happened. And she seems never to have so much as considered suggesting that her son's date of birth was other than 10 June.

By contrast it seems improbable that Frank Rattigan was in the house when his second son Terence was born. The duties and social functions arising from his minor role in the Coronation and attending on his royal guest would have seen to that, with the result that he probably had only a hazy idea of whether his son had been born shortly before midnight on Friday, 9 June, or sometime early in the morning of Saturday, 10 June. However at some point on that Saturday, or possibly on the Sunday, he took a few moments between his duties as official host and minor ceremonial coronation official to contact *The Times* and place the birth announcement or to give a servant instructions to do so. The wording of the actual announcement, when compared to others appearing on the same day and in the preceding and following weeks, with its emphasis on Frank's official station in life, reads even in these formally constrained circumstances as a characteristically Frank Rattigan production. He did not get around to registering the birth officially for another month, no doubt reasoning that there were far more pressing and rewarding matters to occupy his time. Frank's attitude can be gauged from the fact that in the autobiography which he wrote a few years later he records the official visits he made in those weeks in the company of his Arab guest, the balls he attended and even the results of the tennis matches he played with his visitor, but he does not so much as mention the birth of his son. In the same book, covering his life until 1920, Frank Rattigan includes such minutiae as his school cricket scores and the number of birds he bagged on various hunting expeditions, but alludes to his children only once, and then not by name.

The address recorded by Frank Rattigan as Terence's birthplace was 'Lanarkslea', Cornwall Gardens; that is to say, just off Gloucester Road, in Kensington. Lanarkslea was the house of his mother, Lady Rattigan, where Frank and Vera were staying for their leave. Lady Rattigan was now a widow; Sir William had been killed in a motor accident in 1904. This formidable Victorian lady started to play a large part in Terence Rattigan's life from the moment of his birth. Although Vera was not sufficiently recovered from the confinement to attend the Coronation ceremony itself on 22 June, she was soon up and about again, taking her place at the diplomatic receptions and magnificent balls that continued to be given in the weeks after the Coronation was over. As a result, baby Terence was left in the care of Lady Rattigan and the family servants.

Dennis Potter once referred to 'the lost but still dangerous land from which every writer is in exile: Childhood'. Over the years, as we shall see, many people were to remark on the direct influence Vera Rattigan exerted on what her son wrote, but missed the less immediately obvious, but equally important, presence of his father in almost all his work. Many of his most deeply felt plays are about relationships between fathers and sons. They are, at only a slight remove, about his relationship with his own father.

The first few months of Terence Rattigan's life are of particular interest, not only because of their presumed subconscious psychological effect on him, but because in his writing he would return over and over again to events that occurred during these early weeks.

In a general sense all Rattigan's writing can be seen as probing the uneasy translation of his class and generation out of the comfortable certainties of the days immediately before the First World War into the uncertainties and self-doubts of the period after the end of the Second War – the years of Rattigan's most consistent strength and maturity as a writer. The reason that the years before 1914 are generally seen as a golden age may, in part at least, be that it was the period of the greatest advance and influence of the middle class. Rattigan's writing is exclusively concerned with the lives of the middle class – their loves and laughter, problems and disillusionments. The values he inherited, and reacted against, were those of the successful middle class whose apotheosis came in the years immediately before the First World War.

Frank had been educated at Harrow and expected his children to be so too; in addition to the family house in Kensington, there was a rambling Tudor house in the country. He spent his annual leave on the Continent or at shooting parties. His father had received a knighthood; Frank and other members of the family were well placed to be similarly honoured.

Serving abroad, Frank and Vera Rattigan may have been cut off from the true nature of affairs back in England, but a look at the newspapers on the first day of Terence Rattigan's life reveals that public events were just as threatening as the storms which had swept away the recent spell of fine weather. In Germany, yet another battleship was launched on that day. The naval armaments race between Britain and Germany had been unconcealed for almost five years. The news from the East on 10 June 1911 was of the barbarous way in which the Sultan of Turkey had put down a rebellion in Albania. This was just one of a succession of revolts against the Ottoman Empire. A major European conflict was creeping inexorably nearer.

At home the Liberals, led since 1908 by Mr Herbert Asquith (whose relationship with his favourite son Raymond would one day be the subject of a long-nurtured but never completed Rattigan play and another of whose sons, Anthony, was to become one of his closest friends), had been in office for five years. To date the chief beneficiaries of Mr Asquith's policies had been the burgeoning professional class, people such as the Rattigans, but the Liberals promised to spread the benefits of the wealth and commercial power accumulated during the previous century of industrial and overseas expansion beyond the families of wealthy industrialists, landowners and colonial entrepreneurs not only to the middle class but to the working class as well. On that day, 10 June 1911, the ebullient Chancellor of the Exchequer, David Lloyd George, made a stirring speech in Birmingham in support of his new National Insurance Bill, by which he proposed a supertax on high incomes to pay for sickness and un-employment benefits as well as for old-age pensions for the needy. But on that day also the Seamen's Union announced its intention to call an all-out strike. In 1911 there were national strikes not only of seamen, but on the railways and in the docks. The women's movement erupted into violence. It was probably the worst year of civil and industrial unrest the nation had ever known.

For those members of the middle and upper classes who did not like the Liberal government there was at least one notable victory to celebrate that summer. In July 1911, the government finally paid compensation of three thousand pounds to Colonel Archer-Shee for the wrongful expulsion of his son from Osborne Naval College for the alleged theft of a five-shilling postal order. This seemingly trivial case had become inflated into a public trial of strength between the government and those who proclaimed that they were defending the rights of the individual against the growing and unbridled power of the state.

Nevertheless, the news which dominated the week of Terence Rattigan's birth concerned the preparations for the Coronation of George V and Queen Mary (who had once been Frank Rattigan's partner in the wild polka in Vienna). Capital and Empire were set for an interlude of complacent rejoicing. The celebrations surrounding the Coronation lasted until well after the ceremony itself. As a result it was not until the second week in July 1911 that Frank and Vera Rattigan got round to dealing with the formalities relating to the birth of their second son. On Monday, 10 July, a full month after the event, Frank Rattigan at last found time to go down to the Kensington Register Office to register the birth. Again, possibly using a copy of the *The Times* birth announcement to check, he recorded the date of birth as 9 June

1911. On the following Saturday, 15 July, they held a family christening at the old parish church of Kensington, St Mary Abbots, off Church Street. Here, in the imposing church rebuilt in the 1870s to designs by Sir George Gilbert Scott to have the highest spire in London, the newest member of the Rattigan family was baptized into the Church of England with the Christian names Terence Mervyn. But the ceremony, despite the impressive surroundings, seems to have left as little mark on the baby as the water from the font, as, apart from compulsory attendances at services at school and while he was in the RAF, Terence Mervyn Rattigan would show almost no interest in religion or matters spiritual.

Days later Frank Rattigan uprooted his family and returned to his post in Morocco. It is not clear whether Terence actually accompanied his parents when they returned to Morocco in the summer of 1911 or whether he was left in the care of his grandmother Lady Rattigan. However, the evidence does point strongly to him being with his parents at various times during their overseas postings in the years between his birth and the outbreak of the First World War. This period marked the start for Terence Rattigan of what was to become a lifetime of travelling and removals from one home to another.

Hardly had Frank and Vera begun to settle back into legation routine at Tangier than a message arrived from the Foreign Office in London informing them that, with effect from 30 January 1912, Frank was appointed Second Secretary in Cairo. As they packed their household possessions for the P.&O. steamer voyage that would take them dog-legging across the Mediterranean via Gibraltar, Marseilles and Malta to Egypt, Frank and Vera were sorry to be leaving Morocco. They would look back on their years in Tangier as the best, the most carefree and harmonious, of their married life. But the posting to the British Agency in Cairo was a golden opportunity for an aspiring diplomat. Not only did it represent an advance in Frank Rattigan's career, it meant serving under the legendary Lord Kitchener, hero of Omdurman and Commander-in-Chief in the Boer War.

For some weeks after their arrival in Cairo, while they looked for a flat, the family lived close to the British Agency in the Semiramis Hotel, overlooking the Nile. Kitchener had a reputation for being cold, hard and inhumanly efficient. Frank was dumbfounded when, the morning after his arrival, he was summoned by his new chief and told he was to write the annual report on the Sudan, a massive document detailing the work of every branch of that country's administration. Kitchener asked sharply, 'Have you any comment to make?' Rattigan replied, 'No, sir, except that for the moment I know nothing about the Sudan.' 'Then you are in luck,' retorted Kitchener, 'for when you have finished you should know everything that can be known about it. I can give you exactly a fortnight to finish the draft report!'

Frank Rattigan accomplished the task and the two men subsequently became friends, Kitchener being a frequent and welcome guest in the Rattigan household. Frank's hours in Egypt were long and the work arduous. He had little time to spend with his wife and children, but in his few free hours Kitchener fostered Frank's interest in antiques by taking him on forays into the bazaars of Cairo. He also encouraged Frank's interest in excavating archaeological sites. The Rattigans' flat soon became fairly encrusted with small statuettes, bronze cats and other priceless objects of ancient Egyptian origin. These exercised an irresistible fascination over young Terence. His father describes how his younger son, aged about two, 'if left to himself for one moment', would reach up to any he could get his hands on and hurl them to the floor with excited cries of, 'Teeka, teeka!'[3]

Frank Rattigan's greatest friend in Cairo was Ronald Storrs, the Oriental Secretary at the Agency, later described by T. E. Lawrence in Seven Pillars of Wisdom as the most brilliant Englishman in the Near East, 'always first and a great man among us'. Storrs, as much as anyone else, was to be the instigator of the Arab Revolt, and Lawrence's foremost champion and advocate. Although young Terence Rattigan cannot then have been aware of the identity of the public figures around him, and can hardly have remembered Ronald Storrs when he came to portray him as a character in Ross, such 'famous characters' were to bulk large in family reminiscences in later years. By the time Terence was an adolescent, Frank Rattigan's own career had come to an abrupt end, but the 'great days' and characters of his successful diplomatic past remained a part of the family consciousness. Frank, by then denied the opportunity to consort with the famous or be personally involved in momentous events, would endeavour to sustain his own self-respect by keeping alive in his family memories of former times. Many families develop what could be called a family myth – memories of hard or successful, happy or anxious times shared which, through being repeatedly recalled over the years, take on a legendary character. The Rattigan 'family myth' covered the time from just before Terence's birth until immediately after his tenth birthday.

At the end of 1913, Frank Rattigan was posted from Egypt to Berlin; as a result, young Terence, now two and a half years old, was unable to be with his parents for much of the first six months of 1914. This was probably because Frank and Vera were uncertain as to where they would live in Berlin. They must also have known that there would be a heavy load of work and formal engagements for both of them. Terence's elder brother Brian was now old enough to go to school and, although one cannot be absolutely certain, it seems very probable that both boys were once again left in the care of Lady Rattigan in Kensington.[4]

The children were not reunited with their parents until late July 1914, when Vera and Frank returned to England to take a family seaside holiday. However, hardly had their holiday begun than the confrontation between Austria and Serbia, following the assassination of the Archduke Franz Ferdinand at Sarajevo, erupted, threatening a European war. Reading the news, Frank Rattigan realized he was needed back at his post. He telephoned the embassy in Berlin direct from the seaside resort and offered to return.

On 31 July, leaving his family to continue their holiday, he succeeded in boarding the last boat-train through to Berlin, which was packed with Germans returning in response to their government's order of general mobilization. When he arrived the next day it was to find that Germany had already declared war on Russia.

On 9 August, Vera and Lady Rattigan, who were still holidaying by the sea, were startled to receive a telegram from Frank summoning them and the children to London. He had already returned home again, having been forced to abandon their collection of furniture and antiques to the mercies of an angry anti-British mob raging through the streets of Berlin. He had applied in person to his old mentor and friend Lord Kitchener, now Secretary for War, for a post in the army, and was leaving next day for France.

When the women and children arrived back in Kensington they were dismayed to find Frank already kitted out in khaki, wearing the uniform of a captain which he had bought ready-made from a military tailor that morning. He was full of enthusiasm for his new role. He tried to allay their fears by explaining that because of his linguistic skills he had been loaned by the Foreign Office to the War Office to do a staff job with the British Mission to the French and Belgian armies. This could not entail the slightest danger. Next morning he left for France and a series of characteristically eccentric adventures. Terence and Brian were again in the care of their mother and grandmother.

A month later, despite the assurances he had given to Vera, Frank Rattigan was near enough to the fighting for a German shell to land only yards away from him. It blew him into the air and ruptured both his eardrums. On 17 September he was hospitalized in Paris. Frank Rattigan's brief military career was effectively over. At the end of 1914 he was recalled to the Foreign Office to work night shifts. It seems to have been at about this time that Frank and Vera Rattigan decided that they ought to have a permanent base of their own in England, rather than having to spend their leaves in Lady Rattigan's home in London. They bought the Old Manor House at Combe Florey, a very pretty village in a fold of the Quantock hills a few miles north-west of Taunton. Modest, low-roofed but charming, the building dated from 1450, its grounds, which included a trout stream, extended to seven acres. With characteristic enthusiasm, Frank Rattigan set about restoring the house, installing fine oak panelling, Tudor roses and gryphons, generally bringing it to 'a style much grander than even its wealthiest previous owners probably enjoyed'.[5]

In March 1915, coinciding with the disastrous British campaign in Gallipoli, Frank Rattigan was posted as Second Secretary to the British Legation in Romania. Vera, as usual, accompanied him and Terence was once again entrusted to the care of Lady Rattigan. Although Romania was still neutral, it was likely to be engulfed in the war at any moment and was not therefore a safe place to take the children. This posting marked the beginning of a separation between Terence Rattigan and his parents which was to last for almost three years. Now nearly four, he had already seen little enough of his father because of his absences from home caused by work or sporting activities. Already much under the influence of the powerful personalities of his mother and grandmother, he would now be almost totally bereft of adult male company for three more formative years. During these impressionable years he was brought up by a grandmother, whom he increasingly grew to dislike, and by various well-intentioned aunts and friends. Rattigan claimed later that while his grandmother spoilt her other grandchildren, especially his elder brother Brian, she was hard on him.

But he was not short of companionship during these years. His grandmother's household seems to have been constantly full of a changing assortment of relatives' children deposited on Lady Rattigan whenever their parents became victims of the chaos and separation of war. In November 1916, Frank Rattigan's younger brother was killed in France. Cyril Rattigan had caused a family scandal some years earlier by marrying a Gaiety Girl – Barbara. Their three young children now came to live with Lady Rattigan, and seem to have spent the rest of their childhood in her care. It is not clear why Barbara Rattigan should have consented to allow Lady Rattigan to become entirely responsible for the upbringing of her children after her husband's death, but it was probably because of the combination of comparative poverty and Lady Rattigan's continuing disapproval of the marriage. Rattigan would later recall a mysterious and much-disapproved-of Aunt Barbara lurking in the family background. He also mentions in his prefaces an indulgent Kensington aunt who fostered his interest in play-making by taking him to London theatres. Aunt Barbara seems to have been the only person in the family directly connected with the theatre, and it would be nice to think that Barbara Rattigan was that 'indulgent aunt'. Most of the details now seem irrecoverably lost, but what is certain is that when, towards the end of his own life, Rattigan discovered that his Aunt Barbara was still alive and living in straitened circumstances in Penzance, he took immediate steps to help her.

In the meantime, and largely unknown to Lady Rattigan and the other members of the family in London, events were taking place in Frank and Vera's life in Bucharest which were to have a lasting effect on their son Terence. In May 1916, Frank had been promoted to First Secretary. With his chief, the Ambassador, his task was to further the British policy of persuading the Romanians to enter the war on the Allied side. In Bucharest, Frank and Vera had become great favourites at the Romanian court. In particular they had gained the confidence of Queen Marie, a granddaughter of Queen Victoria, the most influential figure in the country and widely recognized as the power behind the Romanian throne. As a result Frank was able to provide first-hand information for inclusion in embassy dispatches back to the Foreign Office in London of long conversations with the queen, outlining in minute detail the power struggles raging in the Romanian government. In August 1916, encouraged by a powerful Russian offensive, the Allies had succeeded in persuading the Romanians to enter the war on their side. Frank Rattigan's role in this achievement was duly recognized by the ambassador and reported back to London.

However, the Germans counter-attacked and inflicted a massive defeat on the Romanian army, sweeping it from the field. In December 1916, Bucharest fell and Frank and Vera made a hurried retreat, together with the rest of the diplomatic corps and the Romanian government, to the provincial city of Jassy.

Conditions were catastrophic, hunger and disease widespread. While Frank and the Ambassador, with the depleted legation staff, set about improvising new offices in a commandeered mansion,

Vera, with Queen Marie, her two eldest daughters, Princesses Elisabetta and Mignon, and such other embassy wives as remained, worked in the local hospitals looking after the sick and wounded. Vera became a great support to the queen, using the diplomatic bag to organize the collection and shipment of medicines and bandages from England to the beleaguered Romanians. As conditions deteriorated during the first half of 1917, Frank Rattigan became ill, struck down by septicaemia from a knee injury. By late summer Frank was no longer able to move. It was clear that it could only be a matter of weeks before Romania would be forced to surrender. On Sunday, 12 August 1917, Vera sought a formal audience with Queen Marie and asked for her assistance in trying to get Frank out of the country by train through Russia. Queen Marie recorded in her diary that '. . . if worst came to worst they would have to contemplate being taken prisoner by the Germans; awful thought!'[6] Early in September, Vera and Frank boarded a train crowded with deserting Russian soldiers, on the start of their escape back to England. By the time they arrived in Petrograd, Frank was no longer fit to travel and, although the city was by then in the throes of the Revolution, Vera had no alternative but to put him into a hospital.

It took Frank and Vera until November 1917 to complete their journey back to London. By then Frank was so ill that he would be unfit for service for a whole year. Vera had cared devotedly for her injured husband throughout their hair-raising adventures in Romania and their protracted and dangerous journey home across Russia. Yet on their arrival home there was an unmistakable change in the relations between them – a change which Terence undoubtedly detected and which in turn affected his own relations with each of them. It subsequently loomed large in his writing.

It is hard at this distance to pin down the precise details of what had happened, but it seems that Frank Rattigan had had an affair with a Romanian countess. Whether she was the first of a succession of ladies with whom Frank would enjoy himself or simply the first that Vera found out about it is impossible now to say. In Frank Rattigan's book there is a photograph of the wife of a Romanian cabinet minister, Vera Rattigan and a third lady described only as 'Countess'. There is no reference anywhere in the text to this 'countess'. Whether or not this is the lady with whom Frank Rattigan had the affair is unknown, but she bears a striking similarity to the succession of bubbly blondes with whom he later did have affairs. Over the years rumours about the liaison have multiplied, most of them owing their origin to stories told later by Terence Rattigan. So far as I can discover, nothing survives in the Foreign Office papers or the diaries of Queen Marie (who records many pieces of discreditable scandal concerning her own family and others in Romanian court circles) to support the more colourful embellishments on the basic story: that the affair became so public as to threaten a diplomatic scandal and the possible recall of Frank Rattigan to London or that it involved a member of the Romanian royal family. As we shall see, the most colourful of all, which involved Queen Marie's own solemn and sexually unattractive twenty-year-old daughter, Princess Elisabetta, was almost certainly founded less on fact than on Terence Rattigan's own schoolboy needs when he was at Harrow.

The important fact is that from late 1917 onward, throughout the rest of his childhood, Rattigan was aware of 'atmospheres' between his parents, half-concealed rows and outbursts, often suppressed into 'not-in-front-of-the-children' whispers or conducted in diplomatic French. His mother recalled that one morning during the last year of the war, when his parents were both at home, Rattigan, then aged seven, wandered into his mother's bedroom and announced that he would never marry – 'Wives can be an awful handicap to writers. They are constantly telling their husbands to do this, fetch that, and ordering them from the house.'[7]

From his earliest schooldays, Terence Rattigan's contemporaries remarked on his lonely, self-possessed air. It was not that Terry, as he was known, was unpopular or did not join in whatever games and activities were going on. Far from it. But behind the pretty blue eyes, fair hair and perfect manners, children and adults alike sensed a premature reserve. Even as quite a little boy, he was possessed of exceptional charm and gentleness. When asked, in later life, what made him a playwright, he would reply that it was a misguided question and ask in return, 'What makes a man start doing anything – building bridges or making candlesticks?' He repeated many times that he could not remember a time when he did not want to be a writer. Certainly by 1918, before his seventh birthday, the idea of becoming a writer (not necessarily solely a playwright but a storyteller) was fixed and would never change. It was at about this time that he was taken to the theatre for the first time. He saw *Cinderella*. He was thrilled, transported out of himself. 'It was important to me, as a member of that audience, that Cinderella should go to the ball and marry the prince.' The little boy found himself caught up in a quite new kind of excitement: 'I believed implicitly in everything I saw on that stage.'[8]

By November 1918 Frank Rattigan was fit enough to be sent to Scandinavia as King's Messenger with dispatches. He returned in time for Christmas and then, in the spring of 1919, he and Vera set out again for war-ravaged Bucharest. The good work he had done there between 1915 and 1917 was recognized and he was now British Chargé d'Affaires. His task was to develop a lasting understanding between the new Romanian administration and the Allies. Frank Rattigan's dealings with the Romanian royal family, and, according to his son's later account with Princess Elisabetta in particular, were dramatically to change his father's life and the family's fortunes.

On his return to Romania Frank Rattigan found Bucharest even more full of Ruritanian intrigue and scandal than when he left it. The previous year the Crown Prince had eloped with a commoner, but had been forced to divorce her and marry someone 'more suitable'. As a result the royal princesses were largely confined to the palace while the king and queen tried to arrange politically advantageous royal marriages for them. Elisabetta stood accused by her mother of pursuing men with 'cold-blooded persistence', though with apparently limited success. She was regarded by her mother as a particularly difficult proposition in the marriage stakes as she had become 'tremendously fat and lazy'.

When Queen Marie left Romania to represent her country at the Peace Conference in Versailles she took the royal princesses with her, and on her return left Princess Elisabetta behind in Paris to look for a suitable husband. In August 1919 Romania again got itself involved in a war, this time with Bela Kun's Hungary, and stood accused by the Allies of the loot and rape of thousands of innocent Hungarians. In this crisis Queen Marie turned to Frank Rattigan. 'She appealed to me,' he told his Foreign Office masters in a dispatch to London, 'as an Englishwoman turning to me for help and advice.'[9] Once the crisis had passed, Frank Rattigan continued to advocate the Romanian cause with London, telling the new Foreign Secretary, Lord Curzon (who two years later would be his nemesis), that Romania, despite being 'exploited by a gang of unscrupulous politicians is the most reliable friend of British interests and policy in the Near East'.[10]

For the moment young Terence was unaware of the significance of these events. For him his parents' posting to Bucharest meant yet another long separation from them and a further sojourn in the care of his unloving grandmother. In May 1920, Rattigan was sent away to school, at Mr W. M. Hornbye's preparatory boarding school 'Sandroyd', near Cobham in Surrey. Sandroyd was a very grand school which prepared the sons of the richest and most distinguished families for entry to Harrow, Eton and Winchester. It was, of course, assumed that Terence and Brian would follow their father by going to Harrow.

Rattigan distinguished himself early at Sandroyd. Because his elder brother Brian was already there, he was automatically known when he arrived as Rattigan Minor. But, even at the age of nine, surnames were not his style. He told everyone his name was 'Terry' and insisted on calling everyone else by their Christian names – in those days a virtually unheard-of thing at a private preparatory school. Contemporaries remember him as a rather inky little boy, with two consuming interests – the theatre and cricket.[11]

Rattigan next saw his parents in the Christmas holidays of 1920. During that holiday he regularly pestered one or the other of them to take him to the theatre. His mother later commented,

'If he had had his way he would have got there long before the dust sheets were removed from the seats.' That Christmas the Rattigan family had every cause to celebrate. In November 1920, Frank had been promoted to the rank of Counsellor of Embassy in the Diplomatic Service, and moved up into the second-highest salary band for a diplomat, starting at twelve hundred pounds a year (equal to more than forty thousand pounds today). With allowances on top, this represented comparative affluence. In January 1921, Frank set off for his new posting, as number two to Sir Horace Rumbold in another international hot spot – Constantinople.

Left on his own again, Terence's passion for the theatre continued to grow. When he accepted a part in a school play, his work fell off so badly that the headmaster offered him the choice of abandoning the part or taking a beating.[12] Rattigan chose the beating. At school and home alike he rapidly became accepted as the resident theatre expert, entertaining everyone with names, dates and places connected with the most obscure productions. He devoted all his pocket money to playgoing – taking gallery seats at a shilling or one-and-sixpence a time. He kept the extent of his compulsive playgoing a secret from the family and school authorities alike, sneaking out of the house, and sometimes out of school also, it seems, without telling anyone. In middle age he recalled the excitement of those stolen afternoons and evenings in the theatre:

By the age of eleven I was already a confirmed and resolute playgoer . . . If my neighbours gasped with fear for the heroine when she was confronted with a fate worse than death, I gasped with them, although I suppose I could have had but the haziest idea of the exact nature of the lady's peril; when my neighbours laughed at the witty and immoral paradoxes of the hero's bachelor friend, I laughed at them too, although I could have appreciated neither their wit nor their immorality; when my neighbours cheered the return of some favourite actor I cheered with them, even though at the time of his last appearance in London I had, quite possibly, not been born.

All of which, no doubt, sounds very foolish – seemingly no more than an expression, in a rather absurd form, of the ordinary child's urge to ape the grown-ups. Yet I don't think it was only that. Up in my galleries (or, as my pocket money increased proportionately with my snobbishness, down in my pits), I was experiencing emotions which, though no doubt insincere of origin in that they were induced and coloured by the adult emotions around me, were none the less most deeply felt.[13]

One is struck by the similarity of Rattigan's experience to that of other artists who have felt neglected by their parents during childhood. Charles Dickens recalled that as a boy he would sneak upstairs to a room and shut himself up for hours 'keeping alive my fancy and my hope of something beyond that place and time... reading as if for life!' As a boy François Truffaut would sneak out of the house to go to the cinema, and for the rest of his life would ascribe his sense of delinquent excitement about every aspect of film-making to the thrill associated with those clandestine visits to local cinemas. Rattigan's lifelong obsession with the theatre, the way in which everything else in his life was subordinated to it, echoes the experience of Dickens and Truffaut.[14]

Until he was ten years old the most notable feature of Terence Rattigan's relationship with his father was separation, owing to Frank's long absences abroad. But the summer of 1921 changed all that for ever. Late in May 1921, Frank Rattigan's boss in Constantinople, Sir Horace Rumbold, returned to London for ten weeks for talks at the Foreign Office and his annual leave. Frank Rattigan was left in charge of a volatile situation. Following the end of the 1914–18 war, Allied troops still occupied Constantinople, but Turkey had a new popular national leader, Kemal Pasha, Atatürk, committed to restoring his country's territorial integrity and full independence. Old animosities between Turkey and Greece had flared into armed conflict. There was the real possibility of a full-scale war involving the whole region. But back in London Lloyd George's coalition government was openly divided, with Lloyd George pro-Greek and Lord

Curzon, the Foreign Secretary, eager to come to a lasting settlement with Turkey. It was a situation which called for cool heads, especially from Britain's man in the crisis centre itself, Constantinople. In the summer of 1921 that man was Frank Rattigan.

As we have seen, Frank Rattigan was an impetuous diplomat and during his time in Romania had developed strongly pro-Balkan and anti-Turkish sympathies. Early in July, without waiting for instructions from London, he told the Turkish Foreign Minister that there was no way that the British government could agree to Turkish demands for full independence. This was clearly inflammatory and Frank Rattigan was immediately contacted by London and left in no doubt of Lord Curzon's displeasure. Curzon felt equally strongly about the Turkish question and saw himself as locked in a Homeric single-handed struggle against a treacherous Prime Minister for control of British foreign policy. He was certainly not going to tolerate subordinates in the field pre-empting his policy. Frank Rattigan hastily penned a grovelling personal apology to Lord Curzon. But deliberately or otherwise, Frank Rattigan's apology was both grovelling and cocky at the same time. It survives among Curzon's personal papers, a measure of how important this issue was to him. Dated Constantinople, 11 July 1921, Frank Rattigan starts by saying that he is writing '... to express to you in person my regret for having gone too far in informing Izzet Pasha [the Turkish Foreign Minister] that HMG could not accept Mustafa Kemal's [Atatürk's] pre-emptory demand for initial recognition of entire independence... I would only wish to say that I had no idea of prejudging by local action the decision of HMG...' He goes on to try to justify his action, saying that to have waited for instructions would have wasted four days. He ends by alluding to previous government policy statements in a way that points to the fact that Lloyd George's preferred policy on the Turkish Question differed from Curzon's, and might be taken to imply that Lloyd George's policy was preferable to Curzon's. Diplomatically worded as it is, Frank Rattigan's apology can be read as a veiled act of defiance. Curzon certainly seemed to read it that way.

The undiplomatic diplomat had spoken his mind once too often. Frank Rattigan was allowed to stay in post until the Ambassador, Sir Horace Rumbold, returned to Constantinople on 1 August. But shortly afterwards, Frank Rattigan was called back to London, never to return to Constantinople, nor to any other post in the Diplomatic Service. Lord Curzon could not afford loose cannons. By the end of October 1921, although Frank Rattigan's term in Constantinople was not up, he was no longer listed as holding any position in the Foreign Office. In the book he published three years later, Frank Rattigan says of these events simply that he stayed on in Constantinople until the signing of the Lausanne Treaty at the end of July 1923. He did not. The Foreign Office List records him as officially 'Unemployed' from 1 June 1922 and 'Retired on a pension' from 1 December 1922. Frank Rattigan was forty-three. It was an inglorious end to a promising career.

In later years the exact circumstances of Frank Rattigan's demise as a diplomat would become the subject of conflicting accounts and not a little romanticization by both Frank Rattigan and his younger son. The different versions given by Terence Rattigan and Frank Rattigan at different times almost certainly tell us more about their own inner conflicts at the time of their telling and about their relationship with each other than about what actually happened. Frank Rattigan increasingly came to maintain, and in time perhaps even to believe, that the sole reason for him leaving the Diplomatic Service was his principled objections to appeasement of the Turks and that, as he could not conscientiously carry out Curzon's policy, he resigned. Terence, as we shall see, would at various times give totally different accounts of what had happened, depending on whom he was trying to impress or what daemons within himself he was trying to slay.

One year after Frank Rattigan's departure from Constantinople, while he was still receiving a Foreign Office salary, but with a dark shadow hanging over the family's future, Vera Rattigan took her two boys away for a quiet holiday alone to a country cottage owned by a drama critic called Hubert Griffiths. In later years Terence Rattigan was to say that this summer holiday was the turning point in his progress towards becoming a playwright. The only books in the cottage were plays, and for three weeks he read nothing else. He found himself fascinated by how plays were written, how character and situation were established and how stories were told through dialogue. At the age of eleven he was becoming immersed in the techniques of playwriting.[15]

By 1922 the post-war economic boom had bust and the government was looking for cuts in all departments. With his career as a diplomat now clearly damaged beyond repair, Frank Rattigan was probably relieved to get an offer of early retirement on a Foreign Office pension, even though it would not be enough for him to maintain his family in the style to which they had become accustomed. While they did not have to endure anything that approximated to poverty – Frank Rattigan had some investments and was able to play the stock market, though sometimes with catastrophic results – they all had to make adjustments. Frank tried to increase the family income by developing his interest in antiques into a business. He also settled down to write a highly coloured account of his adventures in the Diplomatic Service. Neither venture seems to have been particularly successful. In 1925 the Rattigans sold the house at Combe Florey which they had restored at such expense. A few years after that Frank Rattigan sold most of his collection of antiques at an auction in New York. Terence Rattigan would later estimate that his parents' total family income never again rose above a thousand pounds a year until that time came when he himself was able to supplement it from his own earnings.

Although Terence Rattigan was kept on at Sandroyd, he was not immune to the pressures of his father's changed circumstances. From now on, he knew that if he was to take his place at Harrow he would have to earn it by winning a scholarship. For the next fifteen years he was never as well off as his friends at school or university. His social position was never as secure. Everything that he coveted had to be won. Yet there were still reminders of the 'good old days', which perhaps only served to make the contrast with the family's new circumstances all the sharper. When Queen Marie of Romania paid an official visit to

Britain, she sought out the Rattigans and made time for a private visit with Vera to meet Terence at Sandroyd. To Rattigan's intense embarrassment he was presented to Queen Marie in front of the assembled school.

Vera could hardly have asked Queen Marie back to the family's London home, even had protocol permitted it. The family now lived in a rather poky flat at the top of a terrace house in Stanhope Gardens, Kensington, on the other side of Gloucester Road from Lady Rattigan's home in Cornwall Gardens. Rattigan's school friends who lived near by noticed that although he was always invited to their birthday parties, they were never invited to his home. One who did manage to get himself invited in after a visit to the cinema was intrigued to discover how small the flat was when they reached it after climbing to the fourth floor.[16]

Later, people could not understand how Rattigan, who had apparently come from such a comfortable background and had always appeared to possess such social poise, could write with such sympathy and precision about the feelings of social misfits and emotional failures. For many years he took steps to conceal the difficulties of his own childhood. His plays abound in characters who hide their insecurity and feelings of inadequacy behind a veneer of extrovert confidence and bluff social conformity. Towards the end of his life he would confirm that his interest in, and even self-identification with, such characters was already present by the time he came to move from Sandroyd to Harrow.

The drop in the family's income was not the only aspect of his father's resignation from the Diplomatic Service which affected Rattigan. It must be reckoned that once any sense of self-righteousness about the circumstances of his resignation had evaporated, his father increasingly came to see himself as a failure. He found himself entering what should have been the prime of life at a loose end – a middle-aged man with a brilliant future behind him. Perhaps to bolster his self-esteem he styled himself 'Major', the rank to which he was entitled as a result of his brief war service in France, and took to reminiscing about his great days shooting with European royalty or adventuring in the mysterious East. His one remaining hope was his sons. It was not realistic to hope that Brian, with his disability, could emulate his father's schoolboy prowess at games, and Frank Rattigan seemed to give up on him. Instead, he concentrated all his own frustrated ambitions on Terence. He was determined that his son should follow in his footsteps and become a diplomat and a sportsman. The previously absent father became a pressurising father.

Despite the fact that he was now at home, Frank Rattigan's casual affairs with unsuitable young blondes continued, and even increased in number. Relations between Frank and Vera continued to deteriorate and there are grounds for supposing that the possibility of divorce arose more than once during the years that followed.

Vera Rattigan put her own rather different kind of pressure on her son. Her demands were emotional. 'That poor lost boy, Terry Rattigan' was how at least one family of friends referred to him in his early teens: gentle, polite but sad, the second son of what those close to the family knew to be an unhappy marriage. Vera was still a beautiful woman and not a few men were attracted to her, but she was not the sort of person to permit herself to enter into an affair. Hurt and disappointed in her relationship with her husband, she turned, like so many mothers before and since, to her children for emotional compensation. It was perhaps inevitable that her prime target should be her younger son. She was, as we already know, a strong personality and must have fairly smothered Terence with possessive emotion. She did more than show a consuming interest in all he did: she demanded an exclusive filial affection. Whether she could help herself or not, she vilified Frank Rattigan to his sons and tried to focus all their love on to herself, building up the impression of how unfairly and unfeelingly he had treated her. From this, plus occasional explosive outbursts and an all-pervading 'atmosphere', Rattigan grew up to side with his mother against his father.

Notes

1   Much of the information for the early life of Frank and Vera Rattigan is taken from Frank Rattigan's autobiography *Diversions of a Diplomat*, Chapman & Hall, London,

1924, editions of The Foreign Office List for relevant years and the Foreign Office Papers held in the Public Record Office.

2   The precise circumstances of Bartholomew Rattigan's emigration to India are unclear. Early editions of *The Dictionary of National Biography*, not always a reliable source, suggest he got a job in the Ordinance Department of the East India Company, while B. A. Young tells us in his biography of Rattigan (*The Rattigan Version*, Hamish Hamilton, 1986) that he may have gone to India as a private soldier.

3   Frank Rattigan, op. cit.

4   Terence Rattigan may have been with his parents for some of their time in Berlin, if only on a visit. Many years later in a radio talk which he gave he claimed to 'vaguely remember' being given a gift of sweets by Crown Prince William.

5   Truman Press, *Somersetshire Country Houses and Villages*, printed by Walker & Co. for the sole Editor – Proprietor, T. Press, 1931.

6   *The Story of My Life* by Marie, Queen of Romania, Cassell, London, 1935.

7   Vera Rattigan interviewed in *John Bull* magazine, 6 December 1952.

8   Radio talk by Terence Rattigan entitled *Theatre Sense*, BBC Home Service, 22 March 1949.

9   Foreign Office Papers, Public Record Office, dispatch from Frank Rattigan dated 15 August 1919.

10   Ibid., dispatch dated 8 October 1919.

11   In addition to the records of Sandroyd School itself, my sources for Rattigan's time at Sandroyd include interviews conducted in 1978 with Rattigan's school contemporary A.J.H.Benn and the reminiscences of Roger Machell in Anthony Curtis's BBC Radio 3 programme *Rattigan's Theatre*, op. cit.

12   Told by Rattigan to Kenneth Tynan and reproduced in an article in the London *Evening Standard*, 1 July 1953.

13   Preface to *Collected Plays of Terence Rattigan*, Volume II, Hamish Hamilton, London, 1953.

14   Charles Dickens in *David Copperfield* and his unpublished autobiography; François Truffaut interviewed by the author for BBC Television in 1973.

15   Rattigan interviewed by Sheridan Morley for BBC Radio 4's *Kaleidoscope*, July 1977.

16   Source interview with A.J.H. Benn, 1978.

2

Boy Dramatist, Self-Dramatist

Rattigan had been saying he wanted to be a playwright since he was seven, but when the time came for him to leave Sandroyd and sit the scholarship examination for Harrow, his parents were becoming seriously alarmed that he might really mean it. They warned him that no one could make a career by simply writing plays – which prompted him to try writing novels as well. One attempt, started when he was about ten but abandoned halfway down page three, and called *Self-Sacrifice – An Enthralling Novelette by the Famous Playwright and Author T. M. Rattigan*, survived among his papers into adult life.[1]

His earliest completed play to survive was probably begun in his last term at Sandroyd and finished during his first year at Harrow. Inspired by reading Raphael Sabatini, it was a blood-curdling story about the Borgias called *The Parchment*. It had two acts and a playing time of about ten minutes. It opened with a prologue set in a contemporary English drawing-room and then flashed back to the palace of the Borgias in Rome in 1549. The finished work was carefully put into covers, which were then decorated with a variety of coloured inks. On the front, in green ink, 'The Author' made it clear that he wished to apologize for any historical inaccuracies. He continued: 'He wishes it known that the following cast would be eminently suitable for a presentation of this work.' The names that followed included Godfrey Tearle, Gladys Cooper, Marie Tempest, Matheson Lang, Isobel Elsom, Henry Ainley – the most famous stars of the day.

Rattigan later claimed he had actually sent it to Marie Tempest, whose part consisted of just one line, 'Milk and sugar, Mr Fortesque?' with the accent firmly on the 'and'. She does not seem to have replied. Another innovative piece of casting was the selection of Noël Coward, then a rising young star, for the part of a velvet-jacketed poet. At about the time of the play's composition Rattigan's parents had prevented him from seeing Coward's *The Vortex* because they considered it 'unsuitable'.[2]

Rattigan once described himself at this period as lying on his hard school bed, his soul split between rival dreams of making witty first-night speeches to wildly cheering houses (after being kissed by Marie Tempest and Gladys Cooper simultaneously) and of bowling out the entire Australian eleven for thirteen – 'eight of which I usually conceded to my hero, Macartney, the rest being byes'.

Rattigan entered Harrow in 1925, having won a scholarship with credits in Latin and French. The parents of most boys who won scholarships to Harrow did not accept the money. Rattigan's did. During his first year two incidents occurred, one of which Rattigan later cited as evidence that by the age of fourteen he had two of the essentials for a playwright – a sense of theatre and a compulsion to keep writing plays. Mr Laborde, the French master, set Rattigan's form to compose a one-act playlet during prep. While the others composed uneventful little dramas whose dialogue was within the scope of their severely limited French, Rattigan plunged straight into the climax of a full-blown tragedy, without regard for his total inability to render the words of his emotion-torn characters into correct French. The Comte de Boulogne, driven mad by his wife's passion for a handsome young gendarme, rushes into the countess's boudoir where she sits at her dressing-table having her hair done by three maids (Rattigan commented that he had not yet become as economical with the small parts as he would later) and announces that her gendarme (who is all along hidden in a cupboard) is none other than her long-lost brother, Armand. The heroine faints – or, as T. M. Rattigan put it, 'mesure son longueur'. Curtain! Mr Laborde awarded Rattigan only two marks out of ten, commenting in angry red ink – 'French execrable: theatre-sense first class'.

The second incident, recalled by a friend who had come up to Harrow with him from Sandroyd, tends to confirm Rattigan's own assessment of the significance of the first. Given the task of working on a Latin set text, Rattigan spotted that the story would make a good play and proposed to the friend that each of them should submit a short play as their work, which they did, although the friend could not recall whether their Latin was any better than their French.[3]

In his first two years at Harrow, one master had a particular fascination for Rattigan – an ageing, dry-as-dust Greek teacher, who taught the high-flying young classicists of the lower fifth, Mr Coke Norris. A rigid disciplinarian who never showed a lighter side, he was very unpopular with the boys. During Rattigan's second year Coke Norris retired, probably because of ill health. It seems that one of the boys gave him a leaving present (it may have been Rattigan himself, but fifty years later Rattigan was not sure).[4] Coke Norris received this small gift, almost certainly a book, with hard words rather than any apparent pleasure. Rattigan could not understand how anyone could return kindness with unkindness. Knowing nothing about Coke Norris's personal life, not even whether he was married, he invented a number of different life stories and family backgrounds for him. These imaginary broodings produced nothing, but Rattigan put them into what he came to call his 'writer's cupboard'. One of the things that had provoked Rattigan's brooding about Coke Norris was the boredom of his classes. One of the set Greek texts Coke Norris used was the *Agamemnon* of Aeschylus. Somewhere beneath the repetitious parsing, scansion and insistence on grammatical exactitude of Coke Norris' Greek lessons Rattigan detected that they were being made to read, fragment by dead fragment, a living play. His Greek was not good, but the theatre enthusiast in him recognized a good scene when he saw one. Frustrated, he went to the school library and read the play in translation. He found that indeed this was no dead text, but an exciting, emotion-packed drama. He was furious. Why did Coke Norris, who must presumably once have loved Aeschylus, use the *Agamemnon* as a Greek translation excercise, but pay no attention to the fact that it was a play? Spurred on by this realization, Rattigan read more plays in the library. He started with the 'dangerous' modern playwrights who were represented on the shelves – Pinero, Barrie, Galsworthy. These playwrights influenced him before the English classical dramatists. He at first ignored Shakespeare and only came back to him later. Shaw he found disappointing because he was not moved by his plays. By the time he left Harrow he had read all the plays in the library and many more acquired from outside.

As he progressed through school he continued to write plays of his own, even though there seems to have been no intention of having them performed, even by his friends. He himself described the progress of his theatre craft by the time he came to leave school:

> ...my heroines had ceased to measure their lengths at moments of crisis. I had found other ways of bringing down the second-act curtain. My heroes and my villains had stopped glaring at each other, boldly on one side and malevolently on the other. They had merged gradually into one and had become much the same person. Impossibly happy endings and convenient last-act suicides had been, or at least were in process of being, eliminated. Now self-discipline began to tighten even more, and those grandly built-up entrances for the star, together with those comic or dramatic exit lines to take them off to applause... were sadly but ruthlessly included in the list. Curtains no longer fell slowly. They simply fell.[5]

Evidence of the manner of that progress is to be found in a schoolboy play which has survived in two copies. The original, written in black ink on the ruled sheets of a school exercise book and bound with a dark blue ribbon, was called *Integer Vitae*. Among Rattigan's papers there is also a later, typed copy, on which someone has written 'age 15'. It has a new title. *Integer Vitae* has been inked out and *The Pure in Heart* written in. It is in two acts and the credit is, 'By T. M. Rattigan, author of *The Consul's Wife, King's Evidence* &c.' It is set in the drawing-room of a suburban house and deals with relationships under stress in a family where the parents have used their savings to send their son to a public school in the hope that he will make a good career and 'earn a salary of a £1,000 a year' to keep them in their old age. He has disappointed them by becoming a wastrel.

Although this is a schoolboy melodrama, hinging on a murder, the themes and even some of the dramatic method already bear the characteristic imprint of the playwright Rattigan was to become. The play's central preoccupation is deception – suppressing awkward truths about oneself – and the corrosively evil results of an all-consuming pursuit of keeping up social appearances. The theme is private guilt and personal responsibility. Although the plot is heavily indebted to adolescent readings in the school of John Buchan or Dornford Yates, the focus is mainly on the interaction of the three central characters rather than stage action.

There are also some amusing clues as to life *chez* Rattigan. The room where the action takes place is, we are told, 'scrupulously neat and has that air of shabby gentility that is usually to be found in middle-class homes'. The play opens with mother and father in armchairs; father is reading the paper and grunting angrily.

THE FATHER (to his paper)   What rot!
THE MOTHER (used to this)   The socialists again, dear?
THE FATHER: Yes, the swine!

In 1924 Ramsay Macdonald's Labour Party had formed a government for the first time. In the second act a lady visitor arrives who, we are told, is 'a shopworker's wife' but pretends her husband works in the city. She is planning to send her son to Eton or Harrow, probably Harrow as it is '... the more expensive, and so there is probably a better class of boy there...'

Rattigan first saw his name in print in the school magazine – *The Harrovian*. In an article on modern drama which appeared in 1929, his theme was: 'The ceaseless conflict being waged in the drama today, "Entertainment versus Instruction".' This theme too foreshadowed much that he would write and say later. In the same article he prophesied 'a mechanized drama of the future', which might replace the theatre. In another edition of the magazine he had a short story published – *The Laughter of the Gods*. The story's theme is archetypal Rattigan. It concerns a circus trapeze act and the vengeful emotions provoked in the catcher, David, when a powerful impresario entices his beloved, but more talented, youthful partner, Luigi, away from him with offers of money and fame. Significantly Rattigan describes David as 'universally popular with his colleagues, and indeed all who met him', but then goes on to show that this ease and confidence is an illusion. When David overhears Luigi accept the impresario's offer and say that he has no scruples about deserting his partner, his world crashes – 'He had not known what misery was until that moment.' Climbing up to the trapeze to begin their act, David finds himself elated by the idea of paying Luigi back. As he looks down at the crowd of white faces below him, 'he wondered were they all as vile as this boy whom he had loved, who had been a part of himself?' He determines to kill him.

Writing was not Rattigan's only concern at Harrow. He had entered a fiercely masculine and competitive world, and public schools were harsh places at the time. N.M.V. Rothschild, a classmate of Rattigan's, remembers 'many hideous aspects of life at Harrow',[6] including being compelled to walk barefoot on freezing stone floors, not being allowed a hot bath until your third year nor to close the lavatory door (as a result one boy did not go to the lavatory for a whole term, he claimed). To win the approval of the masters was not enough; a boy had to win the acceptance of his fellows. Academic ability alone, which Rattigan had in abundance, counted for little with the other boys. They demanded conformity, toughness, a British stiff upper lip. Those who excelled at sport were worshipped as heroes. Those who did not conform, or were regarded as sissies, were bullied – in ways which we would now find incredible and would almost certainly consider criminal. Rothschild records being beaten for 'lip' (being intellectually precious) by two larger boys who excelled at sport. It is true that most of the worst nineteenth-century excesses had disappeared, but public schools in the 1920s were still brutal and intolerant, breeding grounds of the worst kind of male chauvinism.

Confine more than six hundred boys together in a school that contains no girls at just the time when their sexuality is awakening and no matter how fervently the masters encourage their charges to take cold baths whenever they detect the onset of 'urges', nor how dire the threats against giving way to 'sin', some will succumb. Lord Rothschild records that eleven boys in his house alone were fired in his first term at Harrow. But, he admits, at the time he did not know why. He quickly found out. 'There is more immorality here than at any other school except Harrow' an Etonian informed a new boy a few years before Rattigan and Rothschild went to Harrow.

Sex, however fumbling, between boys seems to have been even more frowned upon than it would have been, were it possible, between a boy and a girl: hence the strictly enforced rule about open lavatory doors. Even looking at a boy too intently could bring down the most draconian punishments on a culprit's head. In the 1930s, when the future writer George Hayim was caught by his housemaster staring too intently towards another boy's door, and confessed to a platonic fondness for the boy, he was accused by his housemaster of being 'perverted, twisted, filthy and depraved... how could I be allowed to sleep under the same roof as his respectable wife?'[7]

Rattigan, although very sophisticated for his age, was, as we have seen, by nature a gentle boy, not muscular or hard. He had no inclination towards athletics, football, boxing or the games of contact.[8] His reserve could have made him a misfit, but he compensated through his wit, his charm and, above all, his natural eye for games like cricket, racquets and squash. It was, perhaps, fortunate for Rattigan that the boys did not sleep in communal dormitories. Even as juniors they were given rooms which they shared with one other boy. The more senior boys had a room of their own, but still the cult of toughness continued to be promoted and senior boys were not allowed to have armchairs or fires in their rooms even on the coldest winter days.[9]

His impoverished family circumstances, his own sense of not really belonging, but perhaps above all the need to live up to his father's expectations, sharpened Rattigan's competitive streak at

Harrow and at the same time caused him to disguise it under a cloak of elegant detachment. He never seemed to do any work, yet his academic brilliance got him moved into higher forms ahead of his contemporaries.

Rothschild found that being good at cricket was an automatic passport to popularity at Harrow and by 1929 he and Rattigan had become established as the school's opening batsmen. Rattigan was a graceful stroke-maker whose timing rather than strength enabled him to hit many boundaries that season. His trademark was a sliced off-drive to the left of cover. He was selected for the team to meet Eton at Lord's, the highlight of the school's sporting and social year. Rattigan's father and mother were among the fashionably dressed crowd at Lord's on Friday, 12 July 1929, a grillingly hot day, when he took his place in the slips at the start of the Eton innings. Harrow had not won since 1909 (while Rattigan's father had been in the team, in the 1890s, Harrow were never defeated). It was to prove an historic match.

Before lunch he took a very good slip catch to dismiss one of Eton's top batsmen, but during the afternoon he dropped an easier ball. By late afternoon Eton were all out for a formidable 347. It was now up to Rattigan and Rothschild to lay the foundations for a winning Harrow innings. By then the heat had abated and a wind had got up. Rattigan seemed a little shaky and snicked one to the wicket-keeper. Luckily for him the catch was missed and went on to the boundary. Having taken the first shine off the ball, Rothschild started to hit out, while Rattigan was content to play more cautiously, keeping the bowling at bay while his partner made the runs. The score was 67 for no wicket, of which Rothschild had scored 43, when an event occurred that went down in the annals of cricket. It was the last ball of the over and Rattigan was facing the Eton medium-fast bowler Franks. He played the ball to extra cover, who was fielding deep. After some hesitation he called for a single. The ball was thrown in hard and chanced to hit one of Rothschild's pads: deflected out of the wicket-keeper's reach it ran all the way to the boundary: five runs to Rattigan! But the umpires were not satisfied and halted play while they consulted together. They decided to disallow the four extra runs and in the confusion sent the batsmen back to the wrong ends. When the new over commenced, with Rothschild facing the bowling, he mistimed his stroke and played the ball on to his wicket. By rights it should have been Rattigan who faced that ball; but the umpires had made a mistake and they could not go back on it. Rothschild was given out. It was now up to Rattigan to justify himself by making a good score, but after keeping his end for a while he was out for a disappointing 29. Rattigan's, and his father's, disappointment was sharpened next day when he was out for only one run in the second innings, and Harrow had to struggle for a draw.

Despite this disappointment, Rattigan often looked back on 1929 as the happiest year of his life. As well as being in the cricket eleven he was in the school racquets and squash teams. He was more than just another member of the school hierarchy; because of his gentleness and wit he was a hero to many of the junior boys. He had grown into a tall and strikingly handsome boy, with wavy, light brown hair, smooth skin and regular features. That summer, although he still had a full year to go in the sixth form, he won the Bourchier History Prize and second place in the St Helier English Literature Prize. For most people who are successful at school their last year is the happiest, because it is the one that brings the greatest rewards and the most freedom. That it was not so for Rattigan was due to a number of factors that all came to a head in 1929–30. The gap between the generations was unusually wide in the 1920s. To Rattigan and his friends, people of his father's generation, those who had fought in the Great War, with their ideas of patriotism and their moral and political conservatism, seemed not so much out of touch with the post-war world as relics of a bygone age who had been preserved by some accident of time; comic-opera figures, good only for laughter. 'Major' Frank Rattigan, with his ramrod back, moustaches and reminiscences, seemed a particularly ripe example. Rattigan's emotional ambivalence towards his father and antagonism to all he stood for, fostered by his unhappy mother, was increased by Frank Rattigan's habit of turning up at Harrow to visit his son, complete with sharp-cut suit and red carnation in his buttonhole, with his latest mistress on his arm. Frank Rattigan would invent elaborate covers for this string of improbable young ladies, who typically came from dress shops and had names like Cora, claiming they were cousins or nieces he had brought down to meet his son. Behind his father's back Rattigan laughed and told his friends the embarrassing truth.

The turbulent state of Rattigan's feelings about his father almost certainly explains why, one day in his last year at Harrow, he made an extraordinary visit to the room of another boy to whom he had not previously been particularly close. Swearing him to secrecy, Rattigan told the boy that he 'wanted to get something off his chest'. Rattigan then proceeded to explain that the real reason behind his father's early retirement from the Diplomatic Service was that while he was serving in Bucharest he had got Queen Marie's daughter Princess Elisabetta pregnant and that she had to have an abortion. Rattigan went into elaborate detail about the special contraceptive precautions his father took, two rubber sheaths not just one. Unfortunately, he said, they burst. Not long afterwards, Princess Elisabetta had been married off to Prince George of Greece. But in October 1922, as a result of an unexpected turn of political events, Prince George had become King of Greece. King George, who had been told about the burst sheaths and the unwanted pregnancy, now 'let his objections be known in London'. That, Rattigan continued, explained why his father was no longer a diplomat.[10] Sadly, for reasons we have already explored, this splendid fantasy almost certainly tells us more about the fertility of the eighteen-year-old Rattigan's imagination, and the state of his own feelings, than it does about Frank Rattigan or the real reasons for the abrupt end to his diplomatic career.[11]

What then was Rattigan up to? As he had become more senior at Harrow, his father had steadily become an ever greater embarrassment to him. It was not only the girls, the out-dated blimpish attitudes and stories of the great old days 'out east' that made his father an embarrassment. In such a status-ridden institution as Harrow it was also that his father did not have a job, an important position, status in fact. Frank Rattigan was still

51

in his forties when Rattigan went to Harrow, clearly too young to have retired by reason of age. Among the closed circle of the upper class who sent their children to Harrow in the 1920s it would have been well known that the Rattigans did not have inherited wealth. So, while affecting an impeccably mannered modesty and detachment, Rattigan craved success, recognition and to be wanted. Sensitive, vulnerable and unloved as he secretly felt, status mattered to him terribly. How then was he to explain his father to his Harrow friends? As we have seen, he often made a joke of him. But that was not really satisfactory. He must have felt that some of the humiliation rubbed off on to him too. Again, as we have seen, while he had been at Harrow Rattigan had cultivated an air of sophisticated raffishness, of a superior worldliness. So what better way of explaining his father, as well as simultaneously enhancing his own air of mystery and knowing worldliness, than revealing the sensational 'truth' about his father. An affair with a queen; an accidental pregnancy. And an abortion! In a perverted kind of way that had real cachet, especially among a group of teenage schoolboys. Swearing his confidant to secrecy only added to the effect, and at the same time Rattigan possibly thought that by doing so he might increase the likelihood of the story spreading in mysterious whispers. As we know, Rattigan hated his father for the unhappiness he had caused his mother by his genuine affairs. Here was a way of paying him back.

To Rattigan and his friends, the ideals proclaimed by his father's generation were so much humbug. In 1929, the headmaster of Harrow, Dr Cyril Norwood, brought out a book on public-school education:

What has happened in the course of the last hundred years is that the old ideals have been recaptured, the ideal of chivalry which inspired the knighthood of medieval days, the ideal of service to the community which inspired the greatest of the men who founded schools for their day and for posterity, have been combined in the tradition of English education which holds the field today. It is based upon religion, it relies largely upon games and open-air prowess, where these involve corporate effort... [12]

Rattigan's attitude to that sort of sentiment can be gauged by the fact that he clandestinely passed round the works of Bertrand Russell and the Huxleys, which were banned at Harrow. He and his friends were inspired by Marx and Freud rather than by the ideals of medieval chivalry. Before he left Harrow he had adopted a philosophy that was broadly rational and socialist, liberal and humanist. To these principles was added a youthful delight in anything that shocked the older generation.

At Harrow, as in many public schools, homosexuality became positively fashionable precisely because it was forbidden. [13] To affect 'a foppish demeanour and a licentious tongue' became chic. However, the headmaster of Harrow, Cyril Norwood, left no room for doubt about what happened if a boy was caught in 'active immorality'. He, like many of his contemporaries, regarded homosexuality as contagious:

Expulsion is not only necessary but just. Medical men... would never leave a patient with smallpox in a dormitory of healthy people, and it has always been somewhat astonishing to me that they should think that a schoolmaster should think twice about permitting a detected corrupter to range free inside a school. [14]

But despite the vigilance of the masters, sexual curiosity continued to draw a substantial number of boys into their first adolescent homosexual encounters. Whether Rattigan's first experience came about in this way or as a result of the sort of homosexual bullying and blackmail reported by Rattigan's contemporaries at Harrow and other public schools it is impossible to know. In later years he remembered one serious 'crush' (his own word) on another boy at Harrow, but whether it was, or was not, requited goes unrecorded. [15] But by the time that Rattigan was a senior boy he regularly and quite openly eyed juniors entering his house at Harrow, pointing out to his friends the ones he found attractive. Many boys pass through a homosexual phase in adolescence, but for Rattigan to advertise it so openly must also have been a piece of deliberately unconventional behaviour. At the end of his life Rattigan told Robin Midgley, the director, that the sub-plot of his last play, *Cause Célèbre*, was largely autobiographical, probably the most directly autobiographical that he ever wrote. In it two seventeen-year-old public schoolboys, Tony and Randolph, discuss their feelings about being forced to relieve their sexual frustrations with other boys, not because they want to, but because of the attitude of their parents and teachers:

> TONY I wonder what our parents think we do between thirteen and twenty-one.
> RANDOLPH What we do, I imagine...solo...they hope of course, but if it's the other – better than with some nasty woman.
> TONY It's such damn humbug. No female of our age will look at us, and any female older than us isn't allowed to have us.

Later, when Tony suggests that Randolph will still be 'doing it' with a boy when he is eighty, Randolph concedes that he is not sure, concluding, 'It'll do till something better comes along. It's got to anyway.' During his last year at Harrow the daughter of one of the staff seems to have developed a crush on Rattigan. This he played up for all it was worth, regaling his friends with hilarious accounts of each new attempt by the girl to corner him while he was alone, and his own successful escapes.[16] Predatory young women in pursuit of sexually gauche and inexperienced young men had long been a staple of British comedy and would later be the subject of Rattigan's first big success in the theatre.

Brought up by a family and educated in schools with such an ostentatiously heterosexual ethos, in which 'unnatural practices' were associated with guilt and ostracism, it is not surprising to find that Rattigan continued to expect that he, like the majority of his contemporaries, would grow out of his schoolboy homosexuality into what was regarded as 'a normal man'. Even so, though most of the other boys passed over his publicly flaunted homosexuality as defiance of adult authority, there still remained a risk that his slightly fey and detached manner, his graceful movements, feminine gentleness and rather nasal voice could, in the exaggeratedly masculine atmosphere of Harrow, make him a target for the more conventional bully-boys were it not for his prowess at games. That he was liable to such attacks became apparent in his last year at school.

A strand of Rattigan's radical beliefs that particularly shocked his parents' generation and his more conformist contemporaries was his anti-militarism. Between 1927 and 1930 a spate of books and a play, *Journey's End*, had appeared, dealing with life in the trenches during the Great War. The work of Blunden, Sassoon, Graves and R. C. Sherriff affected Rattigan and his friends deeply. By portraying the futility and horror of war, these authors confirmed the new generation's determination that it should not happen again. They embraced the ideals of the Kellogg Pact, whereby the nations of the world had renounced war as an instrument of policy, and placed internationalism and pacifism above what they regarded as short-sighted nationalism. For this the conventionally minded branded them unpatriotic.

An obvious target for their pacifism was the Officer Training Corps. Whether boys should be made to undergo basic military training at school was the subject of repeated political controversy throughout the late 1920s. The government claimed that recruitment to the Officer Training Corps was voluntary, and a matter for the school authorities. At most of the public schools, however, joining the Officer Training Corps was compulsory. At Harrow there were two compulsory OTC parades each week. One, held at lunchtime on Fridays, was particularly irksome, so Rattigan and a group of protesters tried to get it stopped. One of them, possibly Rattigan himself, wrote a letter signed 'Sufferer' to *The Harrovian*, asking by what right boys could be compelled to join the corps. The letter declared that it was an out-of-date institution and that compulsion was illegal. This provoked sneering replies about the writer's effeminacy, suggesting that if he did not accept what happened at Harrow he could always leave. The issue took on some of the character of a national scandal when Rattigan wrote a letter to *The Times* which was noticed by the Prime Minister, Baldwin, who was an old Harrovian, and who brought it to the attention of the House of Commons. The protest had little effect and compulsory OTC parades continued. Michael Denison, a junior boy at the time and Rattigan's fag, remembers mistakenly applying far too much polish to Rattigan's Sam Browne in the belief that the more applied the greater the shine. When Rattigan appeared on corps parade with his belt a sticky mess he was reprimanded. Later he called Denison to his study. 'Look, old boy, I don't care about the OTC, but I do care about getting ticked off for something you are supposed to have done. So just learn how to do it, will you?'[17]

Rattigan had already been in trouble over his relationship with a local bookie and with Geoffrey Gilbey, the horse-racing correspondent of the *Daily Express*. As a journalist, Gilbey also had a role in whipping up the press furore over the Harrow OTC 'mutiny'. Gilbey, an old Etonian, seems to have been a friend of Frank Rattigan's and that is almost certainly how Rattigan first met him. Rattigan and a Harrow friend, John Bayliss, were in the habit of betting, and Bayliss's expertise with the form book ensured that they won regularly, thus providing a much needed supplement to Rattigan's schoolboy finances. In itself Rattigan's betting would not have caused trouble. But the fact that the bookie and Gilbey seemed always to be hanging round Rattigan became the subject of gossip and then scandal which looked as though it might escalate to the point where he might be expelled. Rattigan claimed the bookie was collecting his debts and that Gilbey was giving him tips. His detractors suggested that, in view of Rattigan's sexual proclivities, there was more to his relationship with the two men than an interest in gambling.[18]

One other adult friendship towards the end of his time at Harrow also caused raised eyebrows. This was with the actor Douglas Byng, who was best known for his appearances as a dame in pantomime and as a 'drag' artiste, performing risqué material in sophisticated West End reviews. Rattigan took some school friends along with him to meet Byng at the Café Royal. Rattigan's Harrow contemporary Jimmy Stow recalled that 'Terry rather liked all that, the groups of homosexual men'.[19] Of course, for Rattigan to be able to show that he was a friend of a 'notorious' person like Byng had definite cachet and served to enhance the reputation he had cultivated at Harrow for worldliness and sophistication.

All these things clearly upset Frank Rattigan, as indeed they were meant to. But the greatest bone of contention between father and son was his choice of career. Trouble had been brewing for some time over this, but as Rattigan entered his last year at school his father wanted a clear decision. Frank Rattigan was as determined as ever that his son should follow him into the Diplomatic Service; Rattigan was just as determined to be a playwright. There were endless rows over the next few years: father insisting that no one could support himself by playwriting and that Terence should get himself into 'the Diplomatic' and do his playwriting in his spare time; son insisting that he wanted playwriting to be his life, not his hobby. They remained at an impasse, except that Rattigan conceded that, if need be, he would be a journalist until such time as he could support himself from his plays alone.

The hardest blow of Rattigan's final year at Harrow fell only weeks before he was due to leave. He was now nineteen. He had already won a string of academic prizes and been recommended for the School Leaving Scholarship Examination. But this meant less to him, and to his father, than that he should do well in the Eton and Harrow cricket match at Lord's. It was his third season in the eleven and everyone expected him to open the Harrow batting. He had begun the season well, being top scorer in the matches played in May. However, in the trial match in mid-June against Harlequins, he had made a surprisingly sleepy stroke to a half-volley and was out for a duck. In the final trial before the match itself, against an Old Harrovian eleven which contained many of his old team-mates from the previous two seasons, he was moved down the batting order. But he was out of form; in neither innings did he reach double figures. To the joy of those who had jeered at him, the captain decided to drop him and replace him with a younger boy from the same house.

He seems to have been broken-hearted by the decision. He went up to his room and wrote a telegram to his father, who was naturally planning to be at Lord's, to warn him of what had happened. After that he could control his tears no longer and sat with his head on his desk, sobbing. A few doors away in the same corridor a friend, Dorian Williams, heard sobs coming from Rattigan's room and then his name being called. Williams went in, and through his tears Rattigan asked if he would go to the post office and send a telegram for him. Williams agreed, but when he was at the door Rattigan stopped him: 'You'd better read it first.' That was the first Williams knew of what had happened. The mask of ease and apparently effortless nonchalance had slipped and for a moment the true strain and emotional investment Rattigan had in being a success was revealed. As if to increase his humiliation, his father, having received the telegram, rushed down to Harrow and started to lobby all and sundry to have his son reinstated. Even worse was to come. On the second morning of the match Geoffrey Gilbey, possibly at the instigation of Rattigan's father, ran an article in the *Daily Express* under the heading 'Eton and Harrow Hate'. In it he said that no matter which side won the match or who were the outstanding players in it, Rattigan's would be the performance that all Harrovians would remember. He said that before the match, knowing he was off form, his young friend Rattigan had done 'what not one in a thousand would have done', he had offered to be dropped from the team.[20] This indeed may have been true, but to blazon Rattigan's self-effacing gesture abroad in the sporting pages of a national newspaper, and in such gushingly embarrassing terms (Gilbey even offered to give his fee for the article to charity, so touched did he claim to be by the nobility of his 'young friend's' gesture), was, amid the stiff-upper-lip ethos of 1930s' Harrow, simply to leave him wide open to the derision of his enemies.

Although Rattigan would look back on his days at Harrow as among the best of his life, they had afforded him the taste of humiliation, deepening his need for concealment, simultaneously making him distrust his own popularity and yet making him crave it as a substitute for the security of knowing he was wanted.

Throughout his life he would suffer from a feeling of not really belonging.

Notes

1 Unfortunately *Self-Sacrifice* seems subsequently to have vanished. I was unable to find it among the Rattigan Papers in the British Library in 1999.

2 *The Vortex* had been regarded as very shocking when it first opened in London in 1924 because of the picture it presented of the futility of life, the rootlessness of the young and the use of drugs as a means of escape.

3 Interview with A. J. H. Benn.

4 In his biography of Rattigan (*Terence Rattigan*, Fourth Estate, London, 1995), Geoffrey Wansell has pointed out that Rattigan was not in Coke Norris's class. However, when Gillian Hodson and I spoke to Rattigan in 1977 he was quite convinced that he had been taught by him. Perhaps this occurred when another master was absent. In any case, Coke Norris was a well-known character in the school and Rattigan would certainly have run into him and heard him preach at school services. At Harrow, unlike other schools, the lower fifth was a class for academically bright pupils.

5 Preface to *Collected Plays*, Volume II, op. cit.

6 *Meditations of a Broomstick* by Lord Rothschild, Collins, London, 1977.

7 Quoted in *The Poisoned Bowl: Sex, Repression and the Public School* by Alisdare Hickson, Constable, London, 1995.

8 At Sandroyd, where football was compulsory, he had played in goal.

9 *Our Age: Portrait of a Generation* by Noël (Lord) Annan, Weidenfeld & Nicolson, London, 1990.

10 This version was told to Geoffrey Wansell, op. cit., by an unnamed informant who was a contemporary of Rattigan's at Harrow.

11 Even if one knew nothing about the facts behind the end to Frank Rattigan's career as a diplomat, the whole tone of the story, and particularly the colourful details such as the twin layers of rubber his father employed as extra contraceptive precautions, would make one suspect the possibility of this being a schoolboy production. In addition, there is a series of facts that undermines this version of what happened. By the time King George became King of Greece in October 1922, Frank Rattigan had already been without a post in the Foreign Office for over a year and his career was effectively over. In any case, we know from Queen Marie of Romania's private diaries that her daughter Princess Elisabetta had a lover, a Romanian nobleman. If Frank Rattigan got Princess Elisabetta pregnant, it would almost certainly have had to be during his first posting in Bucharest, as Princess Elisabetta was out of the country or confined under close supervision in a royal palace during most of his post-war posting. If he did get her pregnant during his first posting it is probable that at least a few senior people in court circles would have known, the king and queen being the most likely. Yet when Frank Rattigan returned as the number two man in the British Embassy after the war the Romanian government and court, and Queen Marie in particular, far from objecting to his presence, welcomed him back as a particularly trusted friend, ally and confidant. There is absolutely no hint of Frank Rattigan doing anything that incurred the Romanian royal family's displeasure during his second term

in Bucharest. Far from it. In fact, so successful was his time there that he was promoted and sent to the diplomatic hotspot of the region, Constantinople. As we have seen the Romanian royal family continued to befriend the Rattigan family even after Frank Rattigan's career in the Foreign Office had ended. Queen Marie made positive references to both Frank and Vera Rattigan in her book published in the 1930s, an indiscretion she would certainly not have permitted herself had she even the slightest reason for suspicion of Frank. Finally, so far as I can discover, no hint of any complaint of this nature against Frank Rattigan survives in the Foreign Office or the Curzon Papers, although plenty of other references to Frank Rattigan do survive (both to his valued services in Romania and to the row with Curzon). There is also a question. If the story were true, who provided young Terence Rattigan with the intimate details? The only possible candidates are his parents. But is it conceivable that either would do so? What motive could Frank or Vera have for revealing to their son intimate details of a story which they must have found not only indecent and embarrassing, but personally demeaning?

12 *The English Tradition in Education* by Dr Cyril Norwood, John Murray, London, 1929.

13 See Alisdare Hickson, op. cit., Noel Annan, op. cit., and *The Thirties And The Nineties* by Julian Symons, Carcanet, 1990.

14 Dr Cyril Norwood, op. cit.

15 See *Exit Praying* by Peter Osborn, Peacock Publications, Norwood, South Australia, 1995.

16 Geoffrey Wansell, op. cit.

17 *Overture and Beginners* by Michael Denison, Gollancz, London, 1973.

18 Geoffrey Wansell, op. cit., is in no doubt that Gilbey and Rattigan had a full-blown affair and this is quite probable; however, as both men are now dead one cannot be absolutely certain.

19 Geoffrey Wansell, op. cit., and *As You Were* by Douglas Byng, Gerald Duckworth & Co. Ltd, London, 1970. In his reminiscences Byng said that he first met Rattigan at a fancy-dress party which he attended as an elderly dowager kitted out in full court dress complete with a flowing robe. According to Byng, Rattigan was already an Oxford undergraduate, but Stow seems in no doubt that Byng met Rattigan while he was still at school.

20 *Daily Express*, 12 July 1930.

3

First Episode

On 10 October 1930, Rattigan entered Trinity College, Oxford. He had won a minor scholarship to read history, thus relieving his father of some of the strain of supporting him through university.

Rattigan was not the sort of person to push himself forward, yet he was one of those in his generation who, his contemporaries agree, made an impression while still at Oxford. This was not through any particular achievement as an undergraduate, but through a combination of immaculate good looks, perfect manners, sophistication, elegant wit and the declared and unswerving determination to become a playwright. Rattigan was distinguished too through his circle of friends, who included many of the most colourful characters in the literary and theatrical life of the university during the early 1930s. Paul Dehn, Angus Wilson and Peter Glenville went on to become famous; others disappeared or were killed in the war. Tony Goldschmidt, who had been one of the outstanding characters at Harrow with Rattigan, was widely considered one of the most brilliant young men of his generation. Another outstanding Harrovian friend who went up to Oxford at the same time was Rattigan's school expert with the horse-race form book, John Bayliss.

The university was divided, as it had been through much of the 1920s, into two, often mutually hostile, camps – Aesthetes and Hearties. Rattigan was unusual in that he managed to keep a foot in each. He shared the enthusiasm of the Aesthetes for writing, the arts, acting, the theatre; he went to their parties and enjoyed their company; yet he was quieter, more reserved. He did not show off, talk too much or too loud. He stayed in the background at their gatherings, a quietly amused observer who made witty asides and did not push himself to the centre of the stage. Despite prejudice to the contrary, being an Aesthete did not necessarily mean being a homosexual. Often it went little further than a rather outrageous affectation of homosexual manners, part of the familiar juvenile attempt to shock their elders. Questioned about homosexuality at Oxford at this time, one of Rattigan's friends said, 'We might have worn a purple hat or a green cloak, but as far as doing anything – really – almost nothing. It wouldn't have occurred to most of us.' The extent of most people's general unknowing innocence about homosexuality in the 1930s can perhaps be gauged by the comment of an elderly actress who as a young woman lived in Oxford at the time that Rattigan was there and appeared in undergraduate productions with him: 'If you'd told me at the time that Terry Rattigan was a homosexual I wouldn't have known what you meant. You see, I didn't even know the word.'[1]

The other group, the Hearties, were the sporting, beer-drinking upholders of unchanging undergraduate convention: the players of team games and their supporters. They were also raggers and practical jokers, although their idea of a joke often seemed perilously close to vandalism or bullying. One of their favourite diversions was to corner some unsuspecting Aesthete who was out on his own and taunt him, finally attacking him and stealing some part of his clothing, usually his trousers, and running off whooping with joy. Rattigan, although identified with the Aesthetes, won acceptance among the Hearties because of his excellence at games, his conventional dress, good manners and modesty.

During his first year at Oxford, Rattigan lived in college at Trinity. He said he was not going to make the mistake of working. He was determined to be a writer and did not want to be marked out for life by getting a degree.

Then, as now, Oxford could be used as a stepping stone to the professional theatre. The Oxford University Dramatic Society put on an important annual production attended by the London critics. Many who later went on to successful theatrical careers first made their mark in OUDS. The 'star' members when Rattigan joined included George Devine, Hugh Hunt and Giles Playfair. The society's club rooms, where members could read, eat and drink, were a convivial meeting place for kindred spirits, and Rattigan was soon enjoying the long lazy Sunday breakfasts.

Rattigan first made his mark in OUDS through his contributions to their 'smokers'. The smoker was a revue performed in the club room for members and their guests. The sketches were often risqué, even lewd by the standards of the day. They usually abounded in in-jokes about events and characters in OUDS and the university. Many famous wits first drew blood and felt the intoxication of provoking laughter at smokers. Rattigan developed a celebrated turn for these occasions, delivering a stream of catty comments on his contemporaries in the guise of an outrageous female character he created for himself called Lady Diana Coutigan (a play on a disparaging phrase commonly used to describe homosexuals as 'queer as a coot'). This creation may have owed something to the drag act of Douglas Byng, which Rattigan knew and admired, although the male dressed up as a woman to deliver a stream of more or less risqué asides and jokes stretches back into the mists of showbusiness time and forward to our own day with performers such as Barry Humphries and Les Dawson.

Rattigan's father was still determined that his son should go into the Diplomatic Service and had decided that he would spend his long summer vacations at crammers in France and Germany, getting his languages up to the required standard. He accordingly arranged for him to stay in the house of Monsieur Martin at Wimereux, near Boulogne, for the long vacation of 1931.

Monsieur Martin had written to Frank Rattigan saying that he would meet his son off the steamer at Boulogne. He would, he said, 'be extremely distinguishable' from all the others on the quay by having a white handkerchief which he would be holding in his right hand. As the steamer drew alongside on the afternoon of 17 July 1931, Rattigan, now twenty years old, spotted among the small crowd on the quay a man with a high domed forehead, grey hair, jutting beard and ferocious expression, holding a far from clean white handkerchief rigidly above his head. On shore, Rattigan advanced to meet his new French tutor and host. Holding out his hand and smiling, he asked politely, 'Monsieur Martin?' The reply was a grim nod. Rattigan continued in his best undergraduate French: 'Comment allez-vous?' There was a long pause while Monsieur Martin stuffed the off-white handkerchief back into his pocket. Then he took Rattigan's hand in a vice-like grip and, speaking very slowly and loudly, with exaggeratedly perfect pronunciation, said: 'Enchanté de faire votre connaissance, Monsieur.' Rattigan smiled politely, but Monsieur Martin did not release his hand. Instead he repeated very slowly, 'Enchanté de faire votre connaissance, Monsieur.' Rattigan was confused – why, he wondered, should Monsieur Martin keep on saying 'How do you do?' By now they had been shaking hands for some time and were attracting the attention of others in the crowd on the quayside. As Monsieur Martin was about to go into the routine for a third time, Rattigan realized that he was trying to tell him what *he* should have said. Nervously, he tried out the formula for himself. 'Accent abominable,' Monsieur Martin growled, but after a moment let go of his hand and turned to look for a porter. Rattigan had had his introduction to Monsieur Martin's teaching method.[2]

Monsieur Martin's house turned out to be a rambling villa where six or seven other young men were spending the summer polishing their French. Each had a bedroom to himself for private study. The only language permitted in the house was French. Meals were taken together in the company of Monsieur Martin, and each had a daily tutorial with him, in addition to having to write French essays, stories and letters. Despite a good deal of high-spirited horseplay, Rattigan did not enjoy himself much that summer. He was the youngest there and everyone else seemed far more proficient in French than he was. He squirmed under Monsieur Martin's daily cries of, 'Ah, mon Dieu! Entendez, messieurs, cette nouvelle abomination de Monsieur Rottingham!'

He was lonely, in spite of being with young men of his own age. The others were essentially conformist, working to better their chances in the very career he had decided to reject. He saw himself as a rebel, and these young men were in no way kindred spirits. While everyone else worked diligently at French exercises, Rattigan brooded in his room about the plays he would write, including the soul-searing tragedy that was taking shape in his head, based on the glum experience he was living through at that moment.

When he returned to Oxford in October, he stopped living in at Trinity and moved into digs. 'Canters', Canterbury House in King Edward Street, was a fashionable address among undergraduates and Rattigan did well to get rooms there. Another who moved in at the same time was a fair-haired, athletic-looking South African, Philip Heimann. A year older than Rattigan, Heimann had already taken a general degree at Witwatersrand University and was at Oxford to read law. Like Rattigan, he was in revolt against his father over the choice of his career. Heimann's father owned a business in South Africa, but Heimann had refused to go into it and intended to practise at the bar instead. The two young men rapidly became very close friends.

Another undergraduate who followed Rattigan into Canters was Peter Glenville. He came from a theatrical background, and he and Rattigan quickly established a reputation for throwing elegant, often hilarious, parties in their rooms. The biggest party of all was for Rattigan's twenty-first birthday. There were more guests than could be squeezed into Canterbury House and it was held at the Randolph Hotel. A notable guest and the star attraction was Douglas Byng, who convulsed the revellers by appearing in drag to perform some of his best known and most risqué songs. Rattigan's scholarship and the allowance from his father did not stretch very far, so he had to pay his share of the costs of these sometimes wild and invariably alcoholic functions from winnings on the horses. John Bayliss was still his tipster, devising ever more ingenious ways of laying out a few shillings against the possibility of bringing in pounds. His schemes came good with surprising frequency and he managed to pick two Derby winners, April the Fifth and Windsor Lad.

To those who did not know what he was doing, Rattigan

seemed studious, spending much of his time alone working in his room, but he was writing plays rather than history essays. One of these, a one-acter which Rattigan described as 'a highly experimental piece rather in the vein of Constantin's effort in *The Seagull*', Rattigan submitted for production to the OUDS president, George Devine. Devine turned it down, telling him that some of it was absolutely smashing 'but it goes too far'.

From the autumn of 1931 he wrote cinema and theatre reviews for one of Oxford's leading university papers. His friend Tony Goldschmidt had become co-editor of *Cherwell*. Rattigan's first piece as a critic appeared on 31 October 1931 and was headed 'George Street Cinema'. It did not mention the title of the film, a western, probably because Rattigan did not know it. He had arrived towards the end in time to see only the final shoot-out: 'a most glorious battle in which every one of the twenty or so combatants were wiped out except the hero. Even he must have been pretty badly wounded, seeing that he seemed to have been shot through the heart. However, these heroes (I could not make out if he was a bandit or a ranger) are notoriously tough.' He must also have seen the final clinch because he devoted most of his two-hundred-word article to praising Mary Pickford.

A week later *Cherwell* dispatched him to London to cover Noël Coward's *Cavalcade*, which had just opened at Drury Lane. Before he left, Tony Goldschmidt took him on one side and pointed out that as the rival undergraduate paper *Isis* had just printed an article headed: 'Noël Coward: Genius and Prophet', the policy of their paper demanded that he be not over-generous in his praise. *Cherwell* paid for his return rail fare and an upper-circle seat. On his return from the matinée performance he began his review with the heading: 'No, No, Noël'. This, it seems was too racy even for *Cherwell* and they did not use it. However, they did print the long article that followed. Rattigan argued that whereas Coward's early plays had led serious students of drama to believe that a young revolutionary dramatist of immense promise had emerged, he had now, alas, succumbed to the lure of commercial success and sold his soul to the devils of Shaftesbury Avenue. *Cavalcade* was merely a parade of sentimentalized popular emotion. It eulogized the generation that fought the Great War in order to damn the current gutless generation. T. M. R., as Rattigan signed himself, compared Coward unfavourably with Bernard Shaw, and castigated those who had recently hailed him as a genius. Coward was merely a skilful follower of the public mood – 'He has the happy knack of feeling strongly what other people are feeling at the same time. If he has the ability to transform this knack into money and success, we should not begrudge them to him. But such cannot be the qualities of genius.' The irony of Rattigan's attack on Coward is that it was identical to the one that would one day be launched against him.

T. M. R. sharpened his pen on less well known writers as well. In December he reviewed Lionel Hale's *Passing Through Lorraine*: 'Mr Hale has determined to let no chance slip of making the most of his plot [which was about a resurrected St Joan] and he has consequently taken it upon himself to be tragedian, comedian, satirist, romanticist and philosopher at one and the same time. The inevitable result is that his play is formless, dull, insincere and trivial.' After exonerating the actors he ends by telling the luckless Mr Hale that one day perhaps he '...may write a successful comedy. But first he must learn the bitter lesson of his own limitations.' More than thirty years later, when a new generation of young critics was having fun attacking his own plays, Rattigan invested money in a production of a new play by Lionel Hale. It sank without trace.[3]

But Rattigan's undergraduate theatregoing experiences could be uplifting as well as dispiriting. Forty years later he ascribed his final decision to reject a career in the Diplomatic to seeing Sybil Thorndike as Mrs Alving in Ibsen's *Ghosts* during his first year at Oxford. Rattigan had been in awe of actors since he was a small boy. In his first few terms at Oxford he seems to have entertained some thoughts of trying to become an actor himself.

The OUDS major production of the 1931–2 season was to be *Romeo and Juliet*. George Devine, the president of the society, invited John Gielgud to direct. Although Gielgud was the rising poetic actor of his generation, this was to be his first production as a director. OUDS did not have women members, and the society therefore persuaded professional actresses to appear in their major productions. Devine managed to get Peggy Ashcroft to play Juliet.

The allocation of the male parts among the students in OUDS, as in many amateur dramatic societies, was traditionally based on the status and seniority of the members and a consensus view of their acting ability. Gielgud, however, took a more professional approach and held readings to determine the casting. As a result, Christopher Hassall was selected to play Romeo, George Devine Mercutio, William Devlin Tybalt and Giles Playfair was awarded the part of Friar Laurence. Rattigan got one line as one of the musicians who discover Juliet's body at the end of Act IV. In the text this musician has nine lines, but either Gielgud did not trust Rattigan to deliver them all adequately or the society wanted to share the lines out equally because of the number of aspirants for a place in this prestigious production. With only fourteen days to go before the production opened, Gielgud managed to persuade Edith Evans, who had just returned from America in low spirits after a Broadway flop, to play the Nurse.

Meantime, trouble had broken out among the student members of the cast. George Devine and Giles Playfair had recently contested an acrimonious election for the presidency of OUDS. Rehearsals began in an atmosphere of chaos and high excitement. Gielgud, full of bounding enthusiasm and nervousness, was too preoccupied with the problems of the production to take any notice of the partisan rivalries which obsessed his young cast off-stage. Playfair withdrew, and his part was taken over by Hugh Hunt. After rehearsal each day, when Gielgud had gone back to London (where he was appearing in J. B. Priestley's *The Good Companions*), rival factions were locked in fierce argument over drinks in the club room. Sometimes Edith Evans, who, like the other ladies in the production, was staying in Oxford, would burst into the smoke-filled room crying in Lady Bracknell-like tones, 'All this frousting about!' She would then lead one faction out on a bracing walk along the Oxford Canal, while Peggy Ashcroft would soothe another party over an omelette at the George. Awed though the boys were by Gielgud, Edith Evans and

Peggy Ashcroft, there was great competition for their attention. They inundated them with invitations to parties, dinners and tête-à-têtes. Rattigan watched all these rivalries, manoeuvrings, politickings, romances and theatrical affectations with amusement. He took no very active part himself but as usual noted everything and stored it away in his 'writer's cupboard'.

The first night itself was a splendid undergraduate occasion. The large and excited audience at Oxford's New Theatre included critics from most of the London papers. Gielgud had been given the night off from the production in which he was appearing in London and sat shaking with nerves in the pit. It was a free-flowing production without breaks and all went well until towards the end, when Rattigan produced a roar of quite the wrong sort of laughter by the way he played his single line: 'Faith, we may put up our pipes and be gone.' In spite of Gielgud's patient help, he had struggled with the line throughout rehearsals. The roar of laughter on the first night was mortifying. His embarrassment became still worse when he thought he detected in Edith Evans' playing of her next line an extra edge aimed at him: 'Honest good fellows, ah, put up, put up! For well you know, this is a pitiful case.' The last phrase in particular could have been designed as a comment on his performance. In this hypersensitive moment he imagined he saw a look of disapproval on Peggy Ashcroft's face too, although in reality she was concentrating so hard on keeping still as the dead Juliet that she was oblivious to Rattigan's contortions. At each succeeding performance Rattigan tried a different inflection of the line in order to try to kill the laugh, but to steadily worsening effect. Gielgud later recalled having given Rattigan 'endless demonstrations of disapproval.' But Rattigan did not manage to stop the audience from laughing at him until the last performance, when he spoke his line so softly that no one heard it.[4]

The production had lasting results for Rattigan. It checked a sneaking, but strengthening, desire to become an actor. It also introduced him to Gielgud and to John Perry, the two people to whom he attributed his eventual success in the theatre. Perry, an actor and writer, was only a little older than Rattigan, and had recently taken a house with Gielgud in the hills above Henley-on-Thames. He visited Oxford with Gielgud during the rehearsals and performances and continued to visit Rattigan once the production was over. Rattigan regarded Gielgud as 'the greatest man alive'. He was far too much in awe of him to approach him directly. A brasher young man, fired with Rattigan's single-minded ambition, might have turned his failings as an actor to his advantage, using them as an excuse to approach Gielgud under the guise of asking for correction and advice. However much he might have wanted to, Rattigan could not have brought himself to do this. Meeting John Perry presented an alternative way of getting closer to Gielgud and being introduced into theatrical circles.

Even though Rattigan's friendship with Perry may have been tinged with opportunism at the outset, it quickly developed into something more important. Their mutual admiration and respect lasted for the rest of Rattigan's life. Rattigan became a regular visitor in the Gielgud/Perry household. There were frequent high-spirited house parties. Perry and Rattigan shared a boyish enthusiasm for poker schools and exuberant ping-pong. Both were addicted to betting, and Rattigan would take days off from Oxford to go to race meetings with him. Rattigan remained too overawed to get very close to Gielgud. He was coltishly, unashamedly, star struck. So grown-up and sophisticated among his undergraduate friends, he was almost gauche when faced by Gielgud, Perry and their friends. Perry, although nothing like so well known as Gielgud, was to him a dazzling figure – 'He was God!' He had almost everything Rattigan dreamed of – he moved among a glittering circle of actors who seemed able to choose their own productions and parts, to control their own careers and destinies. This was, of course, largely illusory, but Rattigan did not realize this. He was particularly impressed one day when Perry, having lost about a hundred pounds in their poker school, wrote a cheque for the full amount. Rattigan and his undergraduate friends rarely paid their debts.

Rattigan was moving into circles which were frankly homosexual. To these people, homosexuality was not a game or an affectation as it was among many Oxford Aesthetes. The theatre is one of the few professions in which it has almost never been a disadvantage to be homosexual. But it must not be supposed that this homosexuality was in any sense public knowledge. It had to remain the darkest of secrets, acknowledged only among close friends. Public admission of their sexual preferences would have ruined the careers of many theatre stars. Taboos against being 'queer' or 'degenerate' were absolute. The liberalizing influence of Edward Carpenter and Havelock Ellis had so far produced no effect on public or legal attitudes. E. M. Forster could not publish even the most discreet stories in which one man loved another. The Lord Chamberlain would not license any play which contained a tacit, let alone explicit, homosexual relationship. Noël Coward's 1926 play *Semi-Monde* remained unperformed until 1977. In many countries, the 1920s had seen an intellectual association of socialism with pacifism, free thinking, and liberal sexual attitudes which included homosexuality. In Germany in particular a more liberal attitude prevailed briefly, at least in large cities and among the political and creative avant-garde.

But these liberal views had never won general public acceptance, and by 1930 a massive reaction had set in. Public toleration of homosexuality was widely associated with national degeneration. A feature of fascist movements in all countries was their 'queer-bashing' mentality. Fascists promised to end national decline by, among other things, restoring moral discipline and ending sexual chaos. In Britain, homosexual acts, even between consenting adults in private, were illegal. Every year more than three hundred people were convicted for 'gross indecency'.

Outside hostility led inevitably to mutually protective homosexual in-groups. The accusation was made, and has been made at regular intervals ever since, that such groups controlled the theatre, or at least had a disproportionate influence over which plays and authors were encouraged, which actors, directors and designers were used in the most prestigious productions; that no man could make a successful career in the theatre unless he was 'bent', prepared to humour the powerful homosexuals with whom he came into contact. This was wild exaggeration in the early 1930s. The truth is that the theatre was more tolerant than society at large, and theatre people more liberal in their attitudes than people in other professions.[5]

Rattigan was now almost twenty-one. As we have seen, he had suspected that his homosexual escapades at Harrow might simply be a passing phase 'until something better comes along'. He had been brought up to believe in the inevitability of marriage and children – even if his father's example suggested there might be a succession of 'right girls' rather than just one. While his friends were busy competing for the attentions of the limited number of girls at Oxford, he was still not really at ease with women and found men, rather than women, sexually attractive.[6] The homosexual escapades did not cease when he got to Oxford, they continued. People have said, 'Terry was homosexual at Oxford, that's all there is to it.'[7] But that is to overlook something that Rattigan was to be at pains to hide for years to come, perhaps from his homosexual contemporaries above all – his guilt and pain. 'Coming out' as a homosexual is almost never easy, even in the most sympathetic circumstances. One only has to consider Rattigan's background and the public attitude of the period to appreciate how difficult he must have found it to come to terms with the realization that he was a homosexual. One can get some sense of that pain from a heart-rending entry in the private diary of another former Harrow schoolboy who was to become a friend and colleague of Rattigan's: 'My friendships with men are much more wonderful than with women. I've never been in love with women and I don't think I ever shall be in the way that I have been in love with men. I'm really a terrible, terrible homosexualist and try so hard not to be. I try so terribly hard to be good and not cheap and horrid.' In the same passage he wrote that he would be '...horrified and I'd quiver inside ever afterwards if some friend or relation read it'.[8] That was Cecil Beaton, a man who perhaps managed eventually to come to terms with his sense of sexual guilt more openly than Rattigan. Yet that description gives an inkling of the kind of thing Rattigan himself felt and of his deep need to hide his true feelings, particularly from those closest to him. Feelings of guilt about homosexuality arose not only from public attitudes, the pronouncements of moralists like Dr Cyril Norwood, Rattigan's headmaster at Harrow, or reactionary politicians, but even from the writings of one of Rattigan's own heroes, whose work he had clandestinely passed round at Harrow, Sigmund Freud. The man who had done so much to lift the worst Victorian taboos about sex had, by dethroning the notion of heterosexuality's inevitability and naturalness, and replacing it with the idea that it is a learned or developed response, led many leading psychoanalysts to interpret homosexuality as either a psychiatric problem or else a learned or willed deviancy; if not sin, then a disease or problem requiring 'cure'. Those who could accept their homosexuality without self-doubt, self-hate or regret, were either exceptionally well adjusted or very lucky.

His homosexuality was obviously a subject that Rattigan could never broach at home. This led on one occasion to a situation worthy of farce: while accompanying his father for a weekend in a hotel, he was surprised to discover that his father had registered them with the hotel as a family of three, the third member of the party being a fluffy blonde, another in the succession of such young ladies. Frank Rattigan had signed her into the hotel register as Rattigan's sister. Matters threatened to get out of hand when the girl started to make advances to Rattigan in preference to his father. Hints of the incident would later appear in more than one of Rattigan's plays.[9]

Although Rattigan's friends at Oxford were tolerant, he did not like the sense of being different. Despite his ostentatiously camp performances at OUDS 'smokers', these did not of themselves label him as a 'queer'. Rattigan increasingly tried to keep knowledge of his homosexuality a secret from all but his closest friends and began to be careful not to do things that might give him away. He seems still to have entertained some faint hope that his homosexuality might not be final and might in some way be reversed. The sense of guilt about his sexual feelings was never to leave him. His visits to John Perry and his circle of theatrical friends were a relief. It was no secret that they found him attractive – 'He was wonderfully good-looking. Very much the school cricket captain, you know. Very attractive,' Perry remembered. Weekends away from Oxford lengthened and grew in number.

During this period, although he never specified the exact date, Rattigan contracted venereal disease. He later claimed that this finally put him off women. A psychologist might interpret this as a rationalization, adduced to justify a sexuality he was reluctant to accept. In *Cause Célèbre*, Rattigan's last play, the boy Tony contracts a venereal disease from a prostitute and great play is made of the 'filthy, disgusting cure' he has to undergo as a result of this 'filthy, disgusting disease'. Rattigan claimed that he himself contracted VD as a result of an experiment with a prostitute. However, the radio and stage versions of *Cause Célèbre* are contradictory over this episode. In the earlier, and probably more autobiographically reliable, radio version, Tony tries but fails to make it with a prostitute. He leaves, ashamed and disillusioned. Whichever is closer to the true version of what happened, it is clear from what Rattigan said about the play that he had felt driven to try a sexual experiment with a woman while attempting to come to terms with his sexual inclination.[10] *Cause Célèbre* conjures up a picture of youthful desperation. The real-life consequences were disastrous, confirming feelings about himself which he wanted to avoid. In the long summer vacation of 1932, Rattigan had again been sent to a French crammer, this time at La Baule in Brittany. There is some evidence to suggest that the episode with the prostitute occurred while he was there.

'In the thirties the cult of homosexuality met a competitor for shocking the older generation. You could choose between joining the Comintern or the Homintern – unless, like Guy Burgess, you joined both.'[11] As we have seen, even at Harrow Rattigan was interested in politics and the ideal of world peace. So at Oxford, just as his homosexuality became more adult, so did his interest in socialism. Rattigan's friend John Bayliss actually went on to join the Communist Party and Tony Goldschmidt became an active member of the Labour Party. Rattigan was content to remain an interested observer, but there is no doubt about where his sympathies lay. A hunger march passed through Oxford and made a profound impression on all thoughtful undergraduates. Like many of his friends, the nearest Rattigan had come to real slums or factories was probably the view of smoking chimneys and rows of tiled roofs seen from the window of the train from Paddington to Oxford or on journeys to stay with friends near Liverpool. This lack of personal experience of deep poverty did not mean that he lacked feeling for the suffering of others. Nevertheless, it was inevitable that his concerns remained essentially middle class, and his most passionate political feelings were directed mainly towards international affairs.

In January 1933, Hitler came to power in Germany. Although with hindsight we may judge Rattigan's generation as naïve because they did not grasp the nature of Hitler's military intentions, the Nazi takeover strengthened their belief in the necessity for pacifism. World peace was a higher loyalty than narrow patriotism. Pacifism and disarmament were the best policy for Britain because they were the only hope for the world. Such was the reasoning behind a motion that came up for debate in the Oxford Union in February 1933: 'That this House will in no circumstances fight for its King and Country'. Its supporters, who included Rattigan and his friends Tony Goldschmidt and Philip Heimann, did not see themselves as disloyal, but as more far-sighted than their blinkered opponents.

To Rattigan and the four hundred and fifty or so others who attended the debate it did not seem a particularly notable occasion. C. E. M. Joad, as the main speaker for the motion, made a brilliantly emotive pacifist speech, and Tony Goldschmidt spoke in his support in the general debate that followed. Rattigan was one of two hundred and seventy-five who voted in favour of the motion, which was carried by a hundred and twenty-two votes. But those who supported the motion had reckoned without the campaigning zeal of the *Daily Telegraph* and the Beaverbrook press. A few days later these newspapers orchestrated an outcry which reverberated around the world. Those who had voted for the motion were branded as 'woolly-minded Communists, practical jokers and sexual indeterminates'. They were indecent and decadent; they had proved that Britain had 'gone soft'.

As early as 1931, Philip Heimann had himself proposed a motion in the Oxford Union, which had been carried, but which had caused no stir at all. It had claimed that 'Pacifism is the only true form of Patriotism'. Among Rattigan's papers survives an unpublished short story which he wrote at Oxford called 'Life and Soul'. It is about a young man's encounter with an older man, a typical Hearty, who has fought in the First World War. It is told from the point of view of the young man and contains this passage:

'Do you know,' he said, 'I sometimes wish there'd be another war.'

'You liked the last one, then?'

He didn't answer.

'War brings out the best in people,' he said.

'The worst too, surely.'

'What the hell do you know about war?'

'Only what I've read about it.'

He laughed contemptuously. 'You youngsters believe everything you read in books, don't you?'

'No,' I said, 'not everything.'

'The trouble with you and your crowd of whining little pacifists is that you think of war only in terms of mud and blood. You don't think of the other side of it.'

As the young first-person narrator of the story comes to know the older man better, and witnesses the lingering effect of an injury and the shell shock which he suffered during the war, he comes slowly to understand and then to sympathize.

The importance of Rattigan's closeness to Tony Goldschmidt and Philip Heimann at this period cannot be overstated. It was his involvement with Heimann that provoked his first mature play. For over a year Heimann had been embroiled in a romance with a woman undergraduate called Irma Basilewich. There were five Basilewich sisters. John Bayliss had fallen for another sister, Lydia. In 1933 the eldest of the five, Irma, who had married an Indian Army officer at the age of sixteen, left her husband and returned to England. She was twenty-six. In Oxford she met Philip

Heimann and, despite recriminations and complications with the other sisters, they had fallen in love.

Rattigan was attracted to Heimann himself. He watched his friend, as he saw it, making a fool of himself over a woman who seemed far older than he was. He asked himself why Heimann and his other friends made their lives so difficult for themselves over women. At least one of his companions had been sent down for being found with a woman in his room. In spite of the prejudice and penalties imposed by the outside world, in his experience sex was easier between men. They did not make the mistake of confusing physical need with love.

He and Heimann spent hours discussing the possible consequences of Heimann's involvement with Irma. As he watched the development of his friend's relationship and monitored his own reactions to the feeling that she was coming between them, he began to conceive the idea for a play. As Heimann was so deeply involved in its conception, it was only logical that they should work on it together. The plot of 'Embryo', as they provisionally called it, was hammered out on spring-morning walks in Christ Church Meadow. They decided to set it in an undergraduate lodging house in a university town thinly disguised as other than Oxford. It concerned four young men during a production of *Antony and Cleopatra* by the university dramatic society. Their lives are upset by the introduction into their midst of two very attractive professional actresses, one of whom is a star and quite a lot older than themselves. A love affair develops between her and one of the boys. A triangle situation is created when she finds she is competing for her young lover's affections with his closest friend – another of the boys living in the digs.[12]

Some months previously Rattigan had been left a thousand pounds by his grandmother. He and Heimann had decided to invest it in putting on plays. They had advertised in the *Morning Post* for scripts and had received one they liked from a successful author. However, when they met him they were unimpressed and decided that they themselves must be able to do better than this 'uneducated second-rater'.[13]

They had a lot of fun satirizing the antics of their friends – they packed their play with betting, casual bedding, parties and in-jokes. Their animated conversations, interrupted by shrieks of laughter as they walked round the Meadow, were followed by more intense bursts of writing back at Canterbury House, but their play was still not complete by the end of the 1933 summer term.

Although Rattigan still had another year to do at Oxford, Heimann completed his law degree that summer and was due to return to South Africa. Rattigan's father had arranged for him to spend that summer polishing up his German at a crammer in a village in the Black Forest, so Heimann decided to go to Germany with Rattigan so that they could complete their play. In July 1933, Heimann left Irma Basilewich behind in England, and the two young men set off alone for a small village in the hills above Karlsruhe. The weeks in Germany were happy. There seemed little compulsion to study German seriously and Heimann was allowed to put up in the house itself, sharing Rattigan's room. Everyone in the village soon knew about the two fair-haired young Englishmen who were writing a play. From the screams of laughter, they guessed it must be a comedy. One day Rattigan was delighted to hear the Germans speaking of their *lustige Schauspiel.* Thinking *lustige* meant 'lusty' rather than 'merry' he ran out into the garden, throwing sheets of manuscript into the air.

The two young men found a good deal to laugh at about the Germans, and planned to include in their play a skit on Hitler. Their German hosts were not amused – the *Hausfrau* was herself a Nazi. A few nights later Philip woke up in the middle of the night to find a member of the Hitler Youth in their bedroom. He had found the manuscript of 'Embryo' and was about to steal and destroy the blasphemous document. They managed to retrieve the precious manuscript and bundle the zealous youth out of the room. The skit on Hitler did not appear in their finished manuscript, but Rattigan, as always, stored away his impressions of Germany during the first months of Nazi rule. When the play was at last finished they parcelled it up and sent it to a manager with a reputation for putting on new work. Heimann returned to South Africa.

The loss of one friend was soon made good by the appearance of another. John Perry travelled out from England and took over Heimann's vacant place. The two friends were much amused by the antics of the other students. The small party of young men had been cooped up together for some weeks and must by now have been getting on each other's nerves. In the evenings Rattigan and Perry were also entertained by frantic arguments between the Nazi *Hausfrau* and her non-Nazi spouse. Hitler had consolidated the seizure of power that summer by removing his political opponents and was now opening a new phase – the psychological mobilization of the German masses. One night there was a massive torchlight rally in Karlsruhe, which Rattigan and Perry travelled down from their remote mountain village to see. 'Very pretty,' was their reaction. Despite his deepening involvement with the left, to Rattigan Hitler and the Nazis still seemed mainly a joke, something to be laughed into oblivion.

After five days away from the crammer, playing truant together in Salzburg, Rattigan and Perry returned to the Black Forest to find a message from Mr Rose, a theatre manager, suggesting an immediate production of 'Embryo'. Borrowing the money for the air fare from Perry, Rattigan set out for Croydon. He described the excitement of that flight, with its free champagne and his first sight of London from the air, in the radio version of *Cause Célèbre*. In an unusually long stage direction, he begged the producer to select background sounds for the arrival at Croydon Aerodrome which would 'point up the extreme contrast between the leisurely sounds of Croydon in 1933 and Heathrow in 1975, when passengers have been transformed into so many cubic centimetres of idiot animal but insensate matter, to be mistreated, mishandled and misdirected at electronic will'. Travelling to Croydon in the 1930s, he added, was 'gentle and as comfortable a process as can never now be imagined'.

Back in London he put up two hundred pounds towards the production, which was to open at a small experimental theatre near Kew Bridge – the Q – on 11 September. The play was retitled *First Episode*. Although the play is in places not fully realized, it is a truly remarkable first effort, especially when one considers that Rattigan was barely twenty-two at the time of its composition. With the benefit of hindsight, one can read in it an announcement of the themes that Rattigan would return to over and over again in his work. He shows a touching concern for incompatible lovers, in this case the actress Margot who falls victim to an uncontrollable passion, but finds the youthful object of that passion unable to make an adequate or enduring response. Inequality between lovers and the betrayal or humiliation fostered by such situations are an enduring motif in Rattigan's work. With Margot, too, we encounter the first of a series of portraits, seen largely from the perspective of the awe-struck male, of predatory and intimidating females. Among the students in *First Episode* we meet prototypes of characters who will be repeated and developed in later plays: the guileless Hearty, who seems impregnable to the envious, troubled and emotional intellectual; the apparently confident, but inexperienced, younger man who finds it difficult to articulate his emotions but who nevertheless triggers off a passion he cannot fully return and finds himself trapped thereby.

The American critic and champion of Rattigan, Holly Hill, has defined what she calls 'the mind–body dichotomy' as a major theme running through Rattigan's work. This she describes as 'the assumption that man's spiritual and physical natures are irreconcilable and that one can only be satisfied at the expense of the other'. *First Episode* is the first of a long line of plays in which the characters are caught up in a conflict between physical desire and the dictates of reason. Repeatedly Rattigan's characters find themselves driven by bodily craving – normally sex – to act in ways which they know are against their own best interests, ways which are contrary to the prompting of their reason, and which defeat the power of their own wills. Even if some of the clumsier lines in the scenes in which the undergraduates in *First Episode* philosophize about the difference between mind and body are not Rattigan's but Heimann's, as suggested by John Barber, the critic and Oxford contemporary of Rattigan, the conflict between reason and desire which Margot, Tony and his best friend David each experience in their own ways is mainstream Rattigan.

In the relationship between Tony and David, we touch the element in the play which not only put it ahead of its time for a 1930s' audience, but made it premature in Rattigan's development. Rattigan would portray many rewarding and sustaining friendships between men, but he steered away from openly depicting homosexual characters or relatiᴜnships for almost thirty years after *First Episode*. In the intervening plays, as we shall see, he did sometimes covertly depict homosexual relationships, but under the guise of heterosexual ones. He was unwilling to risk either a clash with the Lord Chamberlain or too much self-revelation. Even in this play, the homosexual implications of the relationship between Tony and David are oblique rather than explicit. Their relationship can be played as an extension of the wholesome *Boy's Own* tradition of friendship between pure-minded men which dominated the Edwardian fiction of Rattigan's youth and which was still a feature of the lives of many young men. But we know that, even at Harrow, Rattigan and his friends were scornful of that tradition and rejected the ideals it stood for. The necessary ambiguity in David and Tony's relationship is one of the unfolding strengths of the play; Rattigan portrays the two men becoming aware of the underlying nature of their feelings in a way that befits the early 1930s and his own post-Freudian generation.

The other Rattigan trademark which is already clearly in evidence is the economy of the dialogue. At first sight, Rattigan's dialogue is guilelessly realistic, simply a reproduction of everyday speech. Closer examination reveals the layers of unspoken meaning behind even quite simple exchanges. With no apparent skill or contrivance, Rattigan achieves extraordinary conden-sation. *First Episode* is uneven compared to later work, but there are already some dialogue sequences of surgical economy. In the second act Tony tries to persuade Margot to go away with him, and Rattigan conveys a host of meanings, which would take many dramatists a full emotional outburst or a torrent of explanatory dialogue, in just three lines. Margot says that she is 'so very much more in love with you than you are with me'. Tony objects: 'That's not true, Margot; I do love you passionately.' And Margot replies: 'That's just it, and it may only be passion.' The last line in particular is not just the simple retort which at first it seems. It opens up a whole range of possibilities about both Tony's feelings and Margot's previous experience.

Again, early in the play Margot says to David: 'The friendship of young men can be very selfish.' David replies in three words: 'But so impregnable.' This looks effortless and in David's mouth simply glib, yet those two lines act like a depth-charge whose shock waves spread out through the play until in the last act the full explosive impact is realized by the reiteration of almost exactly the same words just as Margot is about to make her final exit, humiliated and defeated by a friendship between the boys, the depth of which the rest of the play has slowly revealed.

When analysed, his economy of dialogue can be seen as a skilful device, but Rattigan seems to have used it, at least in his most important scenes, almost unconsciously. It is a measure of his remarkable natural talent for theatre. What had interested Rattigan from his boyhood beginnings as a playwright was the drama of the implicit. In *First Episode*, as in so many of the plays that were to follow, he goes to tortuous lengths to set up a situation where there is a confrontation redolent with meanings and emotions which gain their full power from not being directly expressed. This central dramatic device in Rattigan's work is very closely bound up in his own rather elusive personality, and it is striking when reading his manuscripts to see how confidently written are these central, multi-layered scenes, with hardly a change between first draft and final text. The crossings out and changes of mind occur in the more consciously manipulated establishing scenes. Having arrived at his play's emotional centre, he writes with unwavering confidence dialogue which conveys depths of unspoken meaning.

Another similarly economic device was to become a characteristic of Rattigan's comedy writing, but in *First Episode* it is absent to such an extent that one is forced to the conclusion that most of the comedy either is Philip Heimann's or is an uneasy afterthought inserted to meet the demands of the play's commercial producer. *First Episode*'s greatest weakness to the modern reader is the obviousness of the comedy characters and situations.

The extent to which *First Episode* is drawn directly from Rattigan's and Heimann's own experience of Oxford is obvious. When they portray and explore their own emotional experiences, their escapades with bookies, proctors, parties and girls, the Gielgud production of *Romeo and Juliet*, they are not behaving so very differently from other writers. But the extent to which Rattigan would follow this format throughout his career is unusual. The core of *First Episode* is the adjustment of two young men to an essentially homosexual, if ambiguous relationship: the effect on them of coming to terms with adult emotions and the fact that they do not reciprocate those emotions in equal measure. Rattigan's plots almost never exactly parallel the events of his own life. However, the fulcrum of the plot, the essential underlying issues, will always be close to his deepest concerns; and his plays' themes can usually be seen as working out or coming to terms with an emotion, a problem, a piece of self-revelation. In the same way, no one character can be said to stand for Rattigan, but the central characters may each contain aspects of his own personality, and the plot will contain elements of his own experience.

In a passage quoted in the Introduction, David Rudkin spoke of Rattigan's writing arising from a 'deep psychological necessity, a drive to organize the energy that arises out of his own pain', to express his own inmost feelings, yet keep himself hidden. The unique feature of *First Episode* is that Rattigan does not disguise what he is doing. Later in his life Rattigan more or less disowned the play and claimed to have burned his own copy. It had revealed with touching, but to him embarrassing, clarity his own homosexuality and the inner struggle connected with it.

Notes

1   In describing Rattigan's time at Oxford, in addition to the conversations which Gillian Hodson and I had with Sir Terence himself in 1977 and published sources, I have drawn on interviews conducted from 1977 onwards with Dame Peggy Ashcroft,

A. J. H. Benn, William Devlin, Sir John Gielgud, Peter Glenville, Philip Heimann, Lady Kaldor, John Perry and Valery Skardon.

2   Rattigan in an introduction to a season of his plays on BBC Radio in 1957.

3   Lionel Hale's play was also known under the title *Passing Through Europe*. The sharpness of Rattigan's attack may, as with his attack on Coward's *Cavalcade*, have owed something to the editorial policy of *Cherwell* – Lionel Hale was the editor of the rival magazine *Isis*.

4   The account of the OUDS production of *Romeo and Juliet* is based on interviews done with many of those involved, including Rattigan himself, Peggy Ashcroft, William Devlin and Valerie Skardon. See also *Peggy Ashcroft* by Michael Billington, John Murray, London, 1988, *The Secret Woman: A Life of Peggy Ashcroft* by Gary O'Connor, Weidenfeld & Nicolson, London, 1997 and *OUDS: A Centenary History of Oxford University Dramatic Society* by Humphrey Carpenter, Oxford University Press, 1985.

5   There were some notable exceptions to this tolerance – the popular West End star Gerald du Maurier was an instance. He announced that he would have no homosexuals in his company and that if he discovered any he would throw them out. 'Little did he know!' was John Perry's gleeful comment years later when I talked to him for this book.

6   Today it is easy to overlook the extent of most middle-class boys' general ignorance about both sex and girls in the 1930s. Coming from homes where sex was usually a completely taboo subject and sent away to boarding schools where they never came into contact with girls of their own age or class, unless they had sisters, most middle-class boys never really had any chance to mix socially with girls of their own age until they got to university or started work. The unease of young men with young women, regardless of sexual orientation, frequently persisted well into adulthood.

7   Bunny Roger to Geoffrey Wansell, op. cit.

8   *Cecil Beaton: The Authorised Biography* by Hugo Vickers, Weidenfeld & Nicolson, London, 1985; Beaton's diary entry for 9 October 1923.

9   P. Osborn, op.cit., suggests Rattigan never got to grips with the tragi-comedy he mapped out to him years later based on this incident but sees hints of the event in *French Without Tears*, *Who Is Sylvia?* and *Man and Boy*.

10 Rattigan talked extensively to Robin Midgley about the autobiographical nature of sections of *Cause Célèbre* and I am grateful to Robin Midgley for the many insights he gave me. However, I should stress that any errors in interpretation are mine alone and not Robin Midgley's.

11 *Our Age: Portrait of a Generation* by Noël Annan, Weidenfeld & Nicolson, London, 1990

12 As the *Sunday Express* recalled when the play was eventually produced in London, a similar situation had in fact arisen during an earlier OUDS production when its visiting West End star, Cathleen Nesbitt, playing Cleopatra, had had an affair with her young undergraduate Antony, Cecil Ramage. Years later Rattigan got to know Cathleen Nesbitt and she told him that she was convinced that he had based the actress in his play on her. He assured me that this was not so; neither he nor Heimann knew of the story: 'It just seemed a good idea. I wanted an older Shakespearean heroine, you know, and a younger actor.' Cathleen Nesbitt actually married her Antony.

13 In addition to the recollections of Rattigan himself, John Perry and the stories later told by Philip Heimann to his son David, the description of the composition of *First Episode*, as it came to be called, is taken from an article in the *Daily Telegraph*, 18 July 1977.

4

French Without Tears

First Episode opened at the Q Theatre, near Kew Bridge, for a one-week run on 11 September 1933. It was directed for laughs, and the more serious side of the play, especially the homosexuality, was cut and toned down drastically. Even so, local reviewers found it a disturbing picture of university life, which would have been impossible to stage even as recently as the 1920s. The betting, the drinking, above all the casual sex, all came in for comment. It was perhaps lucky for Rattigan that news of the play did not reach the Oxford proctors. However, the main effect of the small storm of controversy was to make the play seem a possibility for a transfer, perhaps with some alterations and strengthening of the cast, to a commercial theatre in the West End.

In the meantime Rattigan returned to Oxford. There he found many of his friends were frankly envious. John Bayliss in particular tried to discourage him from working on changes to the play in preparation for a West End opening. He told him that the whole thing was doomed to failure anyway. Later Bayliss confessed that he was furious with himself for not thinking of using the same idea for a play of his own. Jealousy perhaps motivated the new president of OUDS when he attacked Rattigan and his play for concentrating on one small, unpleasant and, he claimed, unrepresentative section of the undergraduate community. His attack was somewhat undermined, however, when it was pointed out that the characters in the play were clearly based on known real-life undergraduate originals and that, while the president might disapprove of Rattigan and Heimann's depiction of late-night drinking sessions and liaisons between undergraduate actors and visiting actresses, it was well known that such things did actually happen.

For the West End opening, the play was thrust even more firmly, by producer Muriel Pratt, in the direction of comedy than it had been at the Q and the cast was strengthened, again with comedy in mind. A musical comedy actress called Barbara Hoffe was brought in to play Margot. The little Comedy Theatre in Panton Street was packed on Friday, 26 January 1934. Philip Heimann had returned from South Africa to be present at the West End first night, and in addition to many Oxford friends there was a full turn-out of critics from the national and provincial press, including the most revered and hated critic of the day, James Agate. Also in the ranks of critics that night was Rattigan's Oxford friend and rival John Bayliss, who had got himself a commission to review the play from the magazine *Everyman*. He sat with pencil sharpened, intending to tear it apart.

In the event the first night was a success. For most of the play's duration, the audience roared with laughter. While most of them appeared to find the play shocking, they felt able to forgive it because of the production's infectious youthfulness. The evening's biggest successes were Patrick Waddington's display of drunken acting in the role of David and the earnest buffoonery of Max Adrian as the bespectacled Bertie. The extent of the rewrites and the substitution of comedy for the play's original more serious content can be gauged perhaps by the removal of a short and serious bedroom scene at the start of the third act between Joan and David in which David tells her of his ambition to become a campaigning journalist, attacking wealth and privilege. It was completely rewritten to allow the actor playing David to deliver a bravura turn as a comedy drunk, during which he falls out of bed.

Patrick Waddington, who played David, scored a personal triumph, not only falling out of bed, but continuing to speak as if nothing had happened and delivering a long speech while lying with his head on the floor and his feet still on the bed. Far from feeling that this damaged his intentions as a playwright, Rattigan was clearly impressed and grateful for what an experienced and talented actor could bring to a play. It was a lesson that stayed with Rattigan, not always with happy results. Rattigan's gratitude to Waddington certainly endured. Years later he gave generous financial support to a society devoted to staging new plays which was run by Waddington.

At the end of the performance, Rattigan and Heimann took a shy curtain-call together, one wearing a white rose in his button-hole, and the other a red. After the first-night party, they went down to Fleet Street to buy the first editions. To their excitement, most of the critics were backing *First Episode* to run. The *Daily Telegraph* headlined its piece 'Success of *First Episode*', and their critic, W. A. Darlington, called it 'an exceedingly cheerful entertainment, full of youthful high spirits'. Most of the reviewers saw it purely as a comedy, and where they detected a more serious side to the play either congratulated the authors on not dwelling on it or regretted that they had dragged it in at all. Even James Agate predicted that the play would run if its title was altered to 'When Children Wake'. He told his readers that the play was 'remarkable for the avenues which it declines to explore' – he was not to know that all the author's excursions down more serious avenues had been ruthlessly cut out. John Bayliss, in his piece in *Everyman*, confessed himself to have been completely won over. Admitting that the author's were his friends and that he was reluctant to believe that they were capable of anything, he said their first play demonstrated that they had 'all the talents necessary to the dramatist; their wit, their construction and their characterization are all of the highest class ... ' Over one thing the reviews were unanimous – the play was shocking, dirty, naughty; most identified the unnamed university as Oxford. The *News Chronicle* carried the headline: 'STAGE SHOCK FOR OXFORD. Lurid Picture in New Play'. In *First Episode*, Oxford had once again lived up to the 'degenerate' label attached to it after the 'King and Country' debate. A self-appointed watchdog group, of the kind familiar to anyone who has studied the antics of Mary Whitehouse and her friends in recent years, which gave itself the pompous title the Public Morality Council, went so far as to make angry representations to the Lord Chamberlain's office.

In Oxford itself the proctors took a perhaps understandably dim view. As well as press enquiries they received letters from all over the country complaining about this 'disgusting new play about Oxford life'. Just how seriously they took the sensation that had been caused was gauged when they summoned Paul Dehn, the editor of *Cherwell* and one of Rattigan's friends, and issued an edict forbidding the paper from printing any review of the play. But when the proctors summoned Rattigan himself he simply told them that he had already left the university.[1]

By early March, *First Episode* had notched up fifty performances. Philip Heimann had decided to stay on in London and moved into a flat on the corner of Half Moon Street to be near Irma, who lived just across Green Park in Catherine Place. He announced to the world that he and Rattigan were planning a series of plays. In fact he and Rattigan were getting no money from *First Episode*. They had discovered that under the terms of the contract they had signed the play had to take an impossibly high figure at the box office before they were entitled to any royalty payments. In spite of the encouraging reviews, *First Episode* was limping rather than running at the Comedy. In its best week it had taken barely fifteen hundred pounds. Rattigan and Heimann had received a hundred pounds advance between them before the transfer to the West End, but nothing more – not even repayment of the two hundred pounds Rattigan had put into the original production.

Rattigan did not notice, however, that he was receiving no money. He was too intoxicated with the excitement of simply having a play running in the West End. He began to believe the eulogizing quotes from the press posted up outside the theatre. His fate was sealed when the management put up a notice announcing: '50th Performance. Great Success!' Oxford was tame after this. He had known all along that he wanted to be a writer. He would leave Oxford without a degree. In doing this he was in any case only emulating his father, who had also left Oxford without taking his degree. But, bolder, he would not sit the

Diplomatic Service entry exam. Instead he would embark upon his career as a playwright at once.

With great dramatic flourish he wrote to his father from Oxford. The great divide had been reached; he was going to be a playwright, not a diplomat; he was going to live on his own and his father would not know where to find him. Next, he went to the proctors and told them peremptorily that he was leaving. Rattigan seems to have overlooked the fact that only a few weeks earlier he had told them that he had already left. But so, it seems, had the proctors, as they pointed out to Rattigan the consequences of such a step. However, he remained adamant. Rattigan then returned to London and moved in with Philip Heimann in Half Moon Street – in those days an area much favoured by impecunious but aspiring young men.[2]

It was a riotous life while it lasted, despite their lack of money. Wild schemes for plays, restaurants and parties every evening, betting on account and praying a winner would come in at good odds before Friday. In the mornings, a glass of tonic at Perkin's the chemist on the corner of Piccadilly to chase the hangovers away.[3] Rattigan felt he would be happy to live with Heimann in this way for ever; but in real life, unlike the theatre, Irma's claims on Heimann outweighed his. Before long, Heimann returned to the family business in South Africa, taking Irma with him as his wife. There he wrote an unpublished novel about the triangular relationship between Irma, Rattigan and himself and then stopped writing. Although he and Rattigan remained friends, they did not complete another successful play together.

After receiving his son's letter from Oxford, Frank Rattigan very quickly found out where he had gone to live. He telephoned Heimann's flat and told his son that if he had absolutely decided to leave Oxford it might be wiser to live at home where he would at least have to pay no rent. But even if Rattigan did not like that argument, he was left with little alternative when *First Episode* closed at the beginning of April and left him without even the hope of an income. He was now completely broke and could not expect to go on living indefinitely off gambling and the hospitality of his friends. He returned home to face his father.

It seems probable that a number of people had approached Frank Rattigan and pointed out that his son did have real potential as a playwright. Vera almost certainly sympathized with her son's ambitions, and Frank cannot have been wholly unimpressed with the fact that his son had succeeded in getting his first play produced in London. The reviews had been generally favourable, the play had staggered on for three months, and everyone conceded that he had promise. For whatever reasons, and they may have been no more than paternal affection, Rattigan found his father much more understanding than he might have expected. He offered him an allowance of two hundred pounds a year for two years, during which time he could stay at home and write. If, after that time, he had not succeeded to the point where he could support himself, he would be directed into whatever safe job his father could find, for by then he would be too old to enter the Diplomatic Service.

A worldly twenty-three-year-old, Rattigan felt humiliated at the prospect of having to live at home, supported by his parents, yet it was a generous offer and not one he could afford to refuse. Thus began a desperate race against time for success. A desk was moved into his upstairs room at the back of his parents' flat at 19 Stanhope Gardens, and every morning, with the regularity of a junior clerk in an office, he sat down to confront the blank pages of an exercise book. Looking back on it, he found it incredible that he should have embarked on his career in this way – the daily confrontation with the blank sheet and more often than not no idea what he was going to write about. As a student he had always been so full of ideas. Now, faced with two clear years and the need to produce work that would succeed, they seemed to evaporate. His desk overlooked a mews. From his window he could see chauffeurs hosing down cars on the cobbles; dogs being taken for walks; butcher's boys arriving on their bicycles; anything, in fact, but the plot of a play. Yet despite distractions he persisted. There was no turning back – 'I just kept on writing until somehow I had finished a play. Then I started the next one.' Each one he parcelled up and posted in the pillar box at the corner to a theatrical manager; but they all came back, some with polite notes of rejection, some with no note at all. Out they went again to another management and back they came again. Round and round until each play had been to all the managements he could find in the telephone directory.

During that two year period he wrote, and then rewrote, six plays in all. Comedies, plays aping the style of favourite dramatists – O'Neill and Chekhov. Most have disappeared without trace, but two at least survived. One, *Black Forest*, was probably completed in the autumn of 1935 in Denmark, where he went for a holiday after receiving a nominal fee of fifty pounds from Bronson Albery for his part in making an adaptation of *A Tale of Two Cities* and a payment for an unsuccessful New York production of *First Episode*.[4]

Black Forest was an earnest effort which Rattigan himself later described as 'a ghastly item...a turgid drama about tangled emotions'. At the most obvious level it is clearly the product of the weeks he had spent with Philip Heimann and John Perry at the crammers in Germany during the summer of 1933. Although more even in tone than *First Episode,* the play is a backward step. Yet here again we see Rattigan, albeit at a rather crude level as compared with the plays he would write only a few years later, exploring his deepest concerns. Set in a small hotel in the Black Forest, it concerns the rivalry of three young men over two girls. John, the youngest, is twenty-two and described by Rattigan as 'very hearty'. He plans to become a soldier. The oldest, David, is thirty and a master at a public school. He is expecting to marry John's sister Mary. David is described as wearing 'leather shorts and a tweed coat ... he has an air of spurious manliness about him, which suggests effeminacy'. John, the Hearty, calls him 'a complete wet...If he was at Cambridge we'd have his bags off him before he could turn round.' The equilibrium of the party's family holiday with John and Mary's parents is upset by the arrival of a young writer, Edward. With him is a German girl, Toni, with whom he is 'living in sin'. Edward 'has a past' in that he was expelled from the public school where David teaches by John and Mary's schoolmaster father when he was found 'with a girl of the servant class behind a tombstone in the college chapel'.[5]

Black Forest, like *First Episode*, deals with different kinds of love, the conflict between reason and emotion, the power of sexual need and, like his schoolboy effort *Integer Vitae*, with the desperate, sometimes comic, sometimes tragic, middle-class need to keep up respectable appearances – themes that were to become Rattigan's hallmark.

Early in the play we learn that, until he was 'found behind the tombstone' with the college kitchen maid, Mary was in love with, Edward. Thrown together in the small hotel they confront each other for the first time since Edward was expelled:

EDWARD   You implied that because I was found in a compromising situation with Elsie the kitchen maid I couldn't be in love with you.

MARY   Is it very stupid to imply that?

EDWARD   Of course it is. I was eighteen at the time. Like all schoolboys I had a dirty mind. I don't think I particularly wanted the wretched Elsie – in fact I remember rather disliking the whole business. Still it was an adventure. It was something to talk and boast about to my friends. But that's all it was.

MARY   And that's all I was, I suppose.

EDWARD   No, Mary. What I felt for you was a sort of sentimental worship. There was never anything consciously physical in it. In fact I think I'd have died if I thought there was. That's why it never occurred to me that you'd think that my affair with Elsie meant that I didn't love you. To my mind there was never any connection between the two.

Later, Mary asks David, the man she is supposed to be going to marry, to go to bed with her. When he is shocked and declines she tells him that she believes he is incapable of falling genuinely in love with anyone. She accuses him of not loving her:

MARY   Have you ever thought honestly about why I should want to marry you?

DAVID   But Mary I hoped it was because –

MARY Because I was in love with you? [She laughs shortly.]
Do you think that's the only reason a woman ever wants to
marry a man?

In the mid-1930s it was still far from generally accepted that
nice girls could want sex and remain 'nice girls'. Rattigan was
ahead of his time not so much because he wrote good leading
parts for women, which he did with a consistency matched by
few other English dramatists in the middle years of the century, as
for his understanding of the unspoken needs of women. Even in
a play as flawed as *Black Forest* the two young women, Mary and
Toni, are more interestingly drawn characters than the three
young men.

Later in the play, when Edward protests to Mary that he loves
her, she replies in a particularly Rattiganesque sally, 'Oh yes, Teddy,
you do in a way, but not in the way I love you.' Towards the end
of the play, Edward dismisses the whole unhappy tangle of
emotions that envelop them: 'It is silly what incredible
commotion we all make for ourselves by the perversion of a
natural and ordinary and rather boring desire to mate with each
other, isn't it?'

The play includes one other notable Rattigan first, a portrait of
an energetic schoolboy trying with little success to fathom the
standards of the adults around him. When his family are indignant
about the fact that Edward and Toni are living together while
unmarried, he asks: 'You mean if a clergyman came along and
married them today, they'd suddenly change from nasty people to
nice people?'

During his race against time at the writing-desk overlooking
the mews in his parents upstairs room, Rattigan returned more
than once to plots inspired by his experiences at the language
crammers in both Germany and France. One was a comedy
which he called *Joie de Vivre*. But it too failed to produce any
favourable response from the managements he sent it to. Early in
1935 he completely rewrote it and sent it out again under two
new titles: the first was *French Chalk*, the second *Gone Away*. It was
a comedy based on life at a French crammer very similar to the

one he had been to in 1931 at Wimereux. The proprietor was firmly based on Monsieur Martin, and the plot grew out of imagining what would happen if a good-looking, man-hunting blonde with similarities to Philip Heimann's fiancée Irma was introduced into the circle of sex-starved young men incarcerated at the crammer.

Cooped up at home with his parents, surrounded by manuscripts and rejection slips, and generally rather ashamed of himself, Rattigan was glad to escape when he could. On one occasion he escaped as far away as Copenhagen. Denmark was the only country in Europe where illiberal laws against homosexuality had been repealed, the Danes taking the sensible view that what people did together freely and in private was none of the state's business. But although Copenhagen was a welcome release from the constraints of home, Rattigan sat around nursing his beer to make it last longer and brooding over his latest tragedy of tangled emotions. In England he spent the weekends as often as he could with John Perry, who now had a house with John Gielgud at Fowlslow, near Finchingfield, in Essex. There he could be himself, free of the constraints and pretence of life in Stanhope Gardens. He was among friends, theatre people who shared his tastes and enthusiasms.

Fowlslow became a refuge also from the company of a detested collaborator, Hector Bolitho. Bolitho was a middle-aged New Zealander who wrote rather old-womanish travel books and novels. He was, however, successful, with a series of royal biographies to his name. When he invited Rattigan to collaborate on a stage adaptation of one of his novels, it was not the sort of opportunity Rattigan could afford to turn down. The introduction to Bolitho and the suggested collaboration very probably came about through Rattigan's father. Bolitho and the Rattigans had a number of friends in common and Frank seems to have been diligent in his efforts to find his son commissions. The story to be adapted was a turgid melodrama set in a Cambridgeshire farm. A possessive father goes steadily mad because his nineteen-year-old son has fallen in love with a girl undergraduate. In a fit of manic rage at what he sees as rejection by his son, the father strangles the maid and then goes upstairs to blow his own brains out. Bolitho and Rattigan no doubt thought that the father would provide a fine show part for a dramatic actor, and their main theatrical device was to have him stare broodingly at his upturned and flexing thumbs at regular intervals throughout the three acts, building up to a climactic outburst of mania and strangulation.

At the outset there was a certain kudos for Rattigan in being associated with Hector Bolitho, but it was not long before he discovered that his lack of enthusiasm for the plot of their play was more than matched by his growing dislike for his co-author. However, there was no getting out of it, and he had to keep his feelings to himself. The best he could do was to move out of Bolitho's Tudor country house at Hempstead whenever he was not actually working with him and concentrate on his own writing in a nearby inn on the banks of the Cam. Better still, he could escape to Perry and Gielgud's house which was only eight miles away. This resulted in another, still more important, commission. Gielgud was under contract for a number of productions to Bronson Albery, and had conceived the idea of adapting Dickens's *A Tale of Two Cities* in such a way that he could play both Sidney Carton and the wicked Marquis de St Evremonde. Gielgud too was looking for a collaborator, and it was almost certainly John Perry who suggested asking Rattigan. Years afterwards, Rattigan recalled Gielgud saying to him vaguely: 'I can't find anyone to do this *Tale of Two Cities*. You're not doing anything – I'm sure you're not doing anything. Would you like to do it?' and then wondering out loud, 'I wonder if it's all right to have someone without any experience?' It was a great opportunity for Rattigan and he accepted with alacrity.

For most of the summer of 1935 they worked together, Gielgud shaping the scenario and Rattigan writing the dialogue. When the first two acts were complete, they showed it to Albery, who promised that if the third act was equally good he would stage it in the autumn. They rushed back to the country and completed the script in a little over a week. Albery liked it and plans for the production went ahead. It was to be staged at Drury

Lane, and a trio of young lady designers, called Motley, who had first worked with Gielgud on the Oxford *Romeo and Juliet*, were brought in to design a composite set on which the complex succession of short scenes could alternate from one side of the stage to the other, using an upper stage that was reached by a central stairway for some of the intermediate episodes. Casting began immediately.

Gielgud and Rattigan's *A Tale of Two Cities* is inevitably a simplification of the original. It concentrates on the adventure-story aspects of the novel, omitting much of Dickens's richness and density of texture. A 1930s English jokiness is introduced, and some of the lines are so un-Dickensian that one is tempted to believe that they strayed in unnoticed while Rattigan's mind was on his comedy about the French crammer. The brooding quality of the novel and the depth of the characters are diminished thereby. An example of the way in which Rattigan's dialogue fails Dickens's darker purpose is to be found in the treatment of one of the central motifs in all Dickens, the hero Sidney Carton's deadness of heart. This is reduced to Lucie saying to Carton after the trial, 'I think at heart you're a very different person from what you'd have us believe;' and Carton's reply, 'That's impossible. At heart I don't exist.' Rattigan's inability, or unwillingness, to match in his dialogue Dickens's elemental and heroic intentions in *A Tale of Two Cities* can be seen as an early indication of later more serious failures by Rattigan when, at the height of his career, he came to write plays of his own which dealt with epic events. What Rattigan and Gielgud appear to be doing in their adaptation of *A Tale of Two Cities* is to mount a liberal defence – inside a popular theatrical entertainment – of British democratic values set against the dictatorship and tyranny to be found abroad. In 1935 that was a valuable thing to attempt. Yet a closer adherence to Dickens's original might have served that purpose even better. Dickens's horrifying picture of mob terror feeding on a taste for blood and violence would have been an appropriate parable for the 1930s and should have been a timely condemnation of Nazism. Sadly, Gielgud and Rattigan's version reduces Dickens's original to little more than a polite expression of distaste for tyranny. Dickens's emotional power and ability to plumb the depths of human drudgery was outside Rattigan's range and would always be so.

However, if this version of *A Tale of Two Cities* was short on spirituality, it was strong on sweep and gusto. With the production that was being lined up it seemed certain to succeed and to establish Rattigan's reputation. So one can imagine Rattigan's shock when in September 1935, only two weeks before *A Tale of Two Cities* was to go into rehearsal, Gielgud said to him, as if he already knew what had happened, 'It's a pity about Martin Harvey, isn't it? But it's lucky that the design works for *Romeo and Juliet*, so we can do that instead. Larry says he'll do Mercutio. Isn't it marvellous?' Thus, without so much as an apology, Rattigan discovered that the production of *A Tale of Two Cities* had been dropped.[6] Gielgud had received an emotional letter from the ageing actor-manager Sir John Martin Harvey begging him not to put the play on since it was a part he was still playing successfully in numerous farewell performances in an adaptation entitled *The Only Way*. To put on a rival production would be disgraceful, he said, like putting on *The Bells* while Irving was still alive. It would be taking the bread out of an old man's mouth. Gielgud had taken the letter to Albery and together they met the veteran actor at the Garrick Club. Then, after consulting some critics, including James Agate, they decided reluctantly to drop the production. Albery and Gielgud needed an alternative production quickly. As he had wanted to have another go at *Romeo and Juliet* ever since the Oxford production, and realizing that he already had the services of a powerful cast, Gielgud proposed this instead.

The set the Motleys had designed for *A Tale of Two Cities* would, with a minimum of modification, serve perfectly for *Romeo and Juliet*. The crowning stroke was discovering that Laurence Olivier was prepared to drop a production he was planning to come into Gielgud's, so that the two of them could alternate the roles of Romeo and Mercutio. Gielgud was not deliberately unfeeling towards Rattigan; he simply did not see it from his point of view and was delighted that it had been possible to salvage a potentially disastrous situation. To Gielgud, 'what was good for the theatre was good, full stop!' Rattigan managed to conceal his feelings during the interview with Gielgud, but he went away and, alone in his room, he wept.[7]

The Gielgud–Olivier *Romeo and Juliet*, which opened on 17 October 1935, was of course one of the theatrical landmarks of the inter-war years. But Gielgud did not forget Rattigan. He persuaded Bronson Albery to send him a cheque for fifty pounds in appreciation of his work on the adaptation of *A Tale of Two Cities*. With the cheque arrived a letter saying that Albery would be interested to read any other play he might have written. After eighteen months of frustration and rejection slips, at last a manager had asked him to submit a script. Rattigan debated long and earnestly which of his scripts to send. Albery had already received a number of Rattigan scripts, so the choice was limited to those he had not already rejected. This left two possibilities: one which Rattigan described as 'a rather turgid and ultra-serious psychological drama after Eugene O'Neill, an extremely long way after, I'm afraid' – this was probably *Black Forest* – or the comedy *Gone Away*. Albery's reputation was for serious plays rather than comedies, and Rattigan decided to send him the pseudo-O'Neill. At this point his mother intervened. 'Terence,' she said, 'better let him read a good farce than a bad drama!' Despite his protestations that eight other managements had already turned it down, she put the copy of *Gone Away* into an envelope and grimly sealed it.

Despite his new circle of friends and the areas of his life which he had kept carefully concealed, Rattigan and his mother had grown ever closer. Vera Rattigan was very interested in everything her son wrote. He had always enjoyed reading aloud what he wrote, and while he lived at home he had taken to trying out on her each new scene or important section of a play as he finished it. He found her reactions useful and increasingly he acted on her advice and criticism. For more than twenty years she would be the first audience for almost every play he wrote.

Bronson Albery read *Gone Away* on a train journey, laughing out loud at some of the lines. For a few pounds he bought a nine-month option. Gielgud also read a copy and he, too, liked it. He urged Albery to produce it quickly and suggested putting it on at the Embassy Theatre in Swiss Cottage with Jessie Matthews as the girl. However, Albery did not like the play so much that he was prepared to give it precedence over other more ambitious productions he had in the pipeline. *Gone Away* was put to one side.

1936 opened with Rattigan not really much further forward. The two years during which, according to his agreement with his father, he was to prove himself were almost up. Despite being asked to collaborate with Gielgud and Bolitho, he was no nearer being able to support himself. Apart from *Gone Away*, all the other plays he had completed had gone the rounds of the managements and had all been rejected, eight or nine times in most cases. His confidence was beginning to flag, yet he doggedly continued to write and rewrite. Another young writer, Emlyn Williams, told him, 'You just have to get over your disappointment and sit down and get on with it. Pick yourself up like we all have to do.'[8]

During the summer of 1935, a sensational trial had caught his attention, the Rattenbury murder case, in which a middle-aged woman and her young lover, who was the family chauffeur, were accused of murdering her husband. Rattigan followed the case in the newspapers day by day as it unfolded. Alma Rattenbury had taken her young lover, Stoner, because of her husband's failure as a sexual partner, but had soon found herself sexually as well as emotionally dependent on him. When Mr Rattenbury was found brutally beaten to death with a mallet, Mrs Rattenbury and young Stoner were jointly charged with the murder. Popular prejudice held that the boy must have been under Mrs Rattenbury's influence because she was so much older, and there was a public outcry when the jury found only Stoner guilty. On 5 June 1935, a few days after the end of the trial, Rattigan was on a London bus when he saw an evening newspaper headline – MRS RATTENBURY: SUICIDE. He jumped off the bus and bought the paper. Despite being acquitted, she had stabbed herself to death, leaving a note which implied that everything beautiful in her life had been destroyed. Even as he read it, he thought – there's a play there! For months he brooded, but a full year later he had still not managed to organize the story into a play.

As 1936 drew on Rattigan became steadily more discouraged. He wondered if he should give up the idea of being a playwright and find some other way of making his living in the theatre. He wrote to St John Ervine, who was both a critic and a playwright, telling him that he had written several plays but they had all been rejected, and asking if he should give up playwriting. He wondered if he should try turning his hand to criticism. St John Ervine replied that he must press on. Although he had not read any of his plays and expected that they were pretty awful, it was better to be a creative writer than a critic.

That summer Albery's option on *Gone Away* ran out and he had still not produced it. Dispirited, Rattigan showed the script to a friend, Norman Hast. 'Don't worry,' Hast told him after reading it. 'Within three years you will have a successful play running.' Encouragement of this sort was by now about the only thing that helped to keep Rattigan going. When a play had been rejected by every management he could think of, sometimes more than once, he would parcel it up and send it to a succession of stars in the hope that one of them might agree to play in it. But nevertheless Rattigan's two years were up. He now had no alternative but to accept whatever job his father could find for him.

The problem of his son's career had never been far from Frank Rattigan's mind. Although his son had disappointed all his hopes and seemed to be turning out to be the sort of young man he most disapproved of, he still did not desert him. He turned to a film producer he had met to see if he might find him some sort of job in a film studio. Through the producer's influence, and on the strength of *First Episode*, Rattigan was eventually given a job by Warner Brothers as a scriptwriter at their Teddington Studios. It was a seven-year contract with yearly options on the management side but none on his. At the end of that time the studio had the option to renew for an indefinite period. They could loan him out to other studios as they saw fit. In the unlikely event of their wanting to send him to Hollywood, they could do so for only a fifteen-per-cent increase in his salary. The salary was fifteen pounds a week, going up to twenty pounds at the end of two years and thereafter increasing at yearly intervals until it reached forty-five pounds a week in the seventh year – not a bad living wage by the standards of the time.[9]

At this time, each of the major studios had a number of writers on their payroll. These writers were expected to clock on and off each day even when there was nothing for them to do. They sat in the writers' room waiting for a scenario to be assigned to them or for a scene that needed knocking into shape for whatever picture was on the floor. For the first three months of his contract Rattigan sat in the writers' room doodling or playing noughts and crosses. One of the studio's other contract writers was not fooled by Rattigan's nonchalance, detecting the bitterness beneath: 'He was a thrusting young man whose primary concern was to make himself financially independent, not interested in "art" so much as immediate effect. Rattigan would talk entertainingly about how plays are written, always consciously from a "non-artist" angle, though never in a manner to bring in doubt his own grasp and intelligence.'[10]

After he had been at Teddington a few months, Rattigan approached the head of the studio, Irving Asher, with a proposition. He would be prepared to sell Warner Brothers the rights to *Gone Away* for a single lump-sum payment. Asked how much he wanted, Rattigan did a rapid calculation: 'You can have the whole thing – world rights, everything, all for two hundred pounds. I need the money.' Asher agreed to read it. Later, Rattigan got a message, passed down through his head of department – Asher was sorry but his script was no good, either as a film or a play.

His first major assignment at the studio finally came in the autumn of 1936. He was given two weeks to prepare a script from Eleanor Smith's novel of gypsy life, *Tzigane*. He sweated away and by the end of the fortnight congratulated himself that he had done a pretty good job. He sent it to Irving Asher and sat back confidently. Next day Asher summoned him. Crossing the pile carpet towards the vast desk, Rattigan was dismayed to see his boss pick up the script by one corner like a dirty handkerchief. 'Did you write this?' Asher asked. 'Well, yes, as a matter of fact I did,' replied Rattigan, still believing that if there was any justice in the world congratulations would follow. 'I thought so,' said Asher. Then he took the script firmly in both hands, tore it in two and dropped it in the waste-paper basket. Next he rang the bell and asked his secretary to send in another scriptwriter who had been with the company for some time. This character speedily appeared and Asher told him, 'I want you to take this young man Terence Rattigan away, and show him how to write scripts *properly*.'

In later years Rattigan conceded that the soulless regime of the studio was of value to him. It taught him a still more ruthless economy: 'There was no time for frills. The plot had to be told in three lines.' The experience purged him of any lingering pretensions towards fine writing acquired at Oxford. How his work read was unimportant; it was how it played that mattered. Nevertheless, his true feelings about work in the studio were graphically revealed shortly after he left. A fellow writer who inherited his desk in the writers' room found a studio list of dos and don'ts for scriptwriters in one of the drawers. At the bottom Rattigan had scrawled, 'Look behind radiator.' The newcomer did. He found a large sheet of cardboard. Scrawled boldly across it was a single word: 'Balls'.

Unknown to Rattigan, while he was undergoing the humiliations of being a studio writer, things were moving in his favour. Rattigan's policy of sending the plays that had been rejected by managements to actors bore fruit. He had sent one of his rejected plays, *Gone Away*, to a rising young actress called Kay Hammond. She liked it, and had mentioned it to Bronson Albery. Bronson Albery's 1936 autumn schedule of productions had just run into trouble. A major production had unexpectedly flopped, and in late September the play he had put into the Criterion, *The Lady of La Paz* starring Lilian Braithwaite, started to lose money. Albery desperately needed a cheap production to put in as a six-week stop-gap until his next big production was ready. The play that Kay Hammond had sent him was the same one that had made him laugh on the train journey. *Gone Away* called for only one set and a young cast – it would be cheap to put on. He remembered also that John Gielgud had mentioned it to him and had even offered to direct it himself.

Unfortunately, at the moment when *The Lady Of La Paz* failed, Gielgud was away in New York. Kay Hammond suggested a young actor she knew who had recently started directing called

Harold French. In urgent need of a replacement Albery sent it to him, with a note asking him to read it overnight. French loved it.

As a new young author, Rattigan found he was not consulted, but it did not matter – having the play produced was excitement enough. During the next two weeks Albery and French set about rapidly assembling a cast. Albery fixed the top salary at twenty-five pounds a week. Kay Hammond was an obvious choice in view of her role in bringing the play to Albery's and French's notice. Jessica Tandy and Robert Flemyng were both young actors who were beginning to attract attention in the business and Harold French already knew Roland Culver, as he was a fellow member of a club where actors gathered, the Green Room. Rattigan suggested a young actor whom he had seen in a recent comedy called *Heroes Don't Care*, which mocked 1930s' conventions of stage heroics, Rex Harrison. However Harrison was already under contract for forty-eight pounds a week to the film producer Alexander Korda and any money he received from outside work, no matter how much, went to Korda. Harrison and Korda asked for fifty pounds per week, plus a percentage of the box-office takings, but seem to have settled for less. These five were the only actors that anyone outside the theatre had heard of – and none of them was a big enough name to be a draw. No one could be found to play the youngest of the students. At the last moment Rattigan's agent, A. D. Peters, who had demonstrated his faith in his client by putting five hundred pounds of his own money into the production, suggested a twenty-year-old called Trevor Howard.

The first reading of *Gone Away* was in Bronson Albery's office at the New Theatre on the evening of 15 October 1936. These readings are always dry-mouthed occasions. No one quite knows how much is expected of him, and yet there is a feeling of being watched and judged. Even the most struttingly confident actors can be reduced to the edge of incoherence. For the author it is worst of all. When Rattigan entered Albery's office, high above St Martin's Lane, just before 7.30 that Wednesday evening, he had not so much as been introduced to the director, Harold French. Overloud and rather too enunciated conversation, the trademark by which any group of actors is immediately recognizable in a crowd, filled the room. Actors and actresses were catching up on each other's gossip. No one noticed Rattigan, a conventionally dressed young man hovering in a corner outside the animated group.

The stage-manager called everyone to order. The cast took their places on chairs arranged in a semi-circle facing a small table, where Harold French sat with Albery and the stage-manager. Rattigan found a chair in a corner.

The reading began. Harrison mumbled, Culver put in an 'er' before almost every line and Kay Hammond kept losing her place. However, there was an occasional chuckle from the cast and Rattigan himself could not help smiling at some of the lines. At the end of the second act there was a break while coffee was served. He was too shy to push himself forward and get a cup, so he hovered empty-handed on the edge of the group discussing the play. Then Kay Hammond spotted him, realized who he was, and approached with the director. French apologized for having ignored him and produced a cup of coffee. The reading resumed, and when it was over there was fuller discussion of the play. Then French asked Rattigan if he would care to join him for a drink at the Green Room Club. His eyes lit up – at the time Harold French thought it was the prospect of a drink that appealed to him, but on the way there Rattigan shyly confessed that he had always wanted to enter that theatrical holy-of-holies, ever since he had heard of its existence as a stage-struck schoolboy.

It was an evening Rattigan would never forget. Harold French was a rising director and to Rattigan appeared some kind of king. This impression grew as he plied Rattigan with dry Martinis, and club members – most of them household names – strolled past. Rattigan tried hard not to stare but to keep his mind on the suggestions that French was making about the play. Even so, from time to time he could not help interrupting to ask if that wasn't this or that famous star? Always the answer was, 'Yes'. It was a dream come true. French could have asked him to change anything in the play and he would have agreed. Here he was, with a distinguished director treating him as an equal, asking his opinion on possible changes with charming deference, calling him 'old fellow', 'dear chap' and on one occasion even 'my dearest charming boy'. He feared that such endearments between men in a public place might get them thrown out, but no moustache bristled, no irate eyebrow was raised. From time to time, one of the passing gods stopped to exchange a word with French and Rattigan was introduced – 'The author of the new play I'm directing at the Criterion. Brilliant work – I only hope I don't let it down.'

After the third Martini, French broached the most serious topic he wanted to discuss: the play's title. *Gone Away* suggested a hunting background, pink coats, horses and hounds. Rattigan saw what he meant: as a title, it raised false expectations; 'Would you mind awfully if I gave it some thought?' One more drink and he left. Back at home, through a haze of drink and excitement, he racked his brains for a new title. Then he remembered a popular little French primer by Lady Bell – *French Without Tears*. It was 1.30 in the morning but he telephoned Harold French. 'This is Terry Rattigan here. I'm terribly sorry to disturb you, but I've been thinking, and you're quite right . . . er . . . This is only an idea. Kick it out if you don't like it . . . but would *French Without Tears* be any good?' French liked it at once. The new title was fixed.

When rehearsals got underway French quickly realized that the actor he and Albery had chosen to play Brian, the most detached of the students at the crammers, the one who successfully divorces sex from emotion, was miscast. A few days into rehearsal Alec Archdale was replaced by Guy Middleton. This was an improvement. Yet as Rattigan lurked around the theatre unobtrusively watching rehearsals he had become growingly aware that the final twist he had given to his light plot did not produce quite the effect he had intended. Having been rejected by all the other young men at the crammer, the man-hunting girl, played by Kay Hammond, waits expectantly for the arrival of a new student, the titled heir to a fortune, Lord Heybrook. When he appears, he is an effeminate young man trailing a Borzoi dog. The man-hunter is confounded. Rattigan now sensed that this might leave a bad taste in the mouth, sending the audience out of the theatre in the wrong mood. So one day after rehearsals Rattigan invited French to have dinner with him at the Public Schools' Club. But as they ate Rattigan hesitated about revealing what was troubling him. Finally, he blurted out in a voice that made him sound angry, 'You know, Harold, I don't like the end of the play.' French started to protest, but Rattigan hurried on, 'What I don't like is that blond, swishy queer coming in with his dog and that fatuous dragged-in line, "Come along, Alcibiades." It's sort of . . . out of character with the rest of the play. Do you see what I'm getting at?' French was silent. Rattigan continued: 'It might easily kill Kay's and Rex's lines afterwards . . . or am I being a bloody fool?'

There was a silence. Eventually French asked, 'Have you any alternative in mind?' Rattigan had to confess that he hadn't. More silence. Then an idea began to form in Rattigan's mind. A title can be inherited at any age. Why couldn't Lord Heybrook be a little boy of thirteen or fourteen? Enthusiasm growing, he hurried on: 'It would be just as big a smack in the eye for Kay; the twist to the play would be there, without the unpleasant taste. What do you think?'

French obviously liked the idea, but this far into rehearsal a dislocation of this sort would risk upsetting the cast. Bronson Albery would have to be told, a boy would have to be found and a loyal actor fired. Yet, Harold French agreed. It would make a much better ending to the play.

Next morning, Albery was bearded in his office. He finally dropped his objections when French pointed out that not only would a boy's salary be smaller than a grown actor's, but that he would not have to pay for the hire of the Borzoi dog. Then, by chance, as French and his stage manager were setting about auditioning boys from stage schools to play Lord Heybrook, French bumped into a playwright friend of his in the Green Room Club. The playwright had a son who had just started training at the Royal Academy of Dramatic Art. The boy was auditioned and offered the part at a salary of four pounds a week. The boy's name was Gerald Campion.

Five days before the play was due to open, French called the first complete cast run-through. It was only then that ' . . . it was discovered that the play was at least twenty minutes below the minimum playing time that an English audience will regard as its money's worth. It was decided to send the curtain up at 8.40 instead of 8.30, which seemed to everybody a rather daring innovation, and the sulky author was sent off to his garret to write ten minutes into the last act. . .'[11]

The first dress rehearsal at the Criterion Theatre was on Wednesday, 4 November. Apart from the usual problems with missed lighting cues, some ill-fitting costumes and the unfamiliarity of the cast with the set and furniture, it was not too bad. Rattigan lurked unobtrusively in the dress circle, and at the end of the rehearsal French asked him to go round with him while he gave 'notes' to the cast. Backstage the mood was good, morale was high, yet Rattigan was uneasy – the ending of the play was still not right. Young Gerald Campion, playing the boy Lord Heybrook, did not really look quite young enough to guarantee getting the vital final laugh at the end of the play.

That evening French and Rattigan again had dinner together. They agreed. Young Campion would have to be replaced. In the one day remaining before the play opened another, younger-looking, actor would have to be found and rehearsed to take his place.

At ten o'clock the next morning the phone rang in the Campions' Covent Garden flat and young Gerald heard his father answer it. 'And you want me to tell him?' he heard his father say. Gerald sensed at once what was happening. Later that day, when he went round to the theatre to collect his make-up box and other belongings from his dressing-room, he found a rehearsal was going on. Gerald burst into tears.

As a consolation Gerald was offered the grey flannel suit and straw boater the management had made for him for the part and told he could continue as Lord Heybrook's understudy. Gerald rejected both the suit and boater. On his behalf his father rejected the offer of understudying, demanding instead that his son receive a payment of twenty pounds. The management agreed.

At 6.15 p.m. on 5 November the final dress rehearsal began, now with a new young actor called William Dear in the part of

Lord Heybrook. As the lights went down there were a dozen or so people dotted about the box-like, plush and gilt theatre. Apart from Harold French, Rattigan and his mother, who French had agreed could watch the rehearsal after Rattigan had given his word that she would not get in the way, there were the people who had put up the fifteen hundred pounds for the production, A. D. Peters and Alban Limpus, the man who had put on many of Noël Coward's successes. Among the few friends and other interested parties present were Ralph Lynn, the famous *farceur*, and Rattigan's film-studio boss, Irving Asher. Sitting far apart in a dark auditorium, this handful of people felt isolated and constrained. They were in no mood to laugh. The result, added to by uncertainty about the new boy as Lord Heybrook, was disastrous. The actors were slow, and 'dried'. Someone had had a row with Kay Hammond and it showed. Harrison was forced and Culver put in even more 'ers' than he had at the first read-through. There was not so much as a titter from 'the house'.

The moment the final curtain came down, Albery and Alban Limpus hurried out. Albery telephoned his office and made immediate arrangements to bring in another show which he had in the provinces, as soon as it could be moved. He gave *French Without Tears* a week. Limpus made a series of phone calls and off-loaded his share of the production to a big theatrical agency called O'Brien, Linnett and Dunfee.

While Harold French still sat frozen with misery in the stalls, A. D. Peters had gone backstage and was offering his share in the production to any of the actors for a hundred pounds. No one would take it. Ralph Lynn was also talking to the cast: 'Don't open! It's simply dreadful. Don't open!' he told them. Rattigan packed his mother off home and waited miserably by the stage-door to see what would happen. There Irving Asher found him: 'Don't worry too much, Terry,' he said gently, 'everyone has these flops!' Rattigan knew he was trying to comfort him in preparation for the bashing he was going to get from the critics.

Suddenly Harold French appeared backstage, galvanized into action. He called the disconsolate cast together and gave them the most terrible dressing down: 'That was the most disgusting performance I have ever seen from actors who call themselves professionals. How bloody dare you!' One or two started to protest, saying they could not open. But French would have none of it: 'I don't want any excuses.' He ordered them to go back to their dressing-rooms to get ready for another dress rehearsal immediately. The curtain would go up in fifteen minutes. He ordered that the set, which was a nasty dark green, was to be repainted before the next day's opening. The only member of the cast who remained at all confident was Roland Culver. He told Jessica Tandy to stop worrying – the play would be a great success.

Fifteen minutes later, French and the front-of-house manager found Rattigan in the foyer, head down, apparently studying the pattern in the carpet. French said, 'Terry, I don't know if anyone has told you, but we are having another full rehearsal right away.' Rattigan looked up and said slowly, 'I don't think I could stand it again.' 'Balls,' said French, grabbing his arm, and the three men went down the stairs into the stalls. French sat near the front while Rattigan and the front-of-house manager sat farther back. This time the run went smoothly. Afterwards the front-of-house manager reassured Rattigan and French: 'The show's fine. Bronnie Albery must be potty, and I'm going to tell him so first thing in the morning.'

It was now ten o'clock and Rattigan decided to go to the Savoy for supper. Perhaps he hoped to cheer himself up. He was still convinced his career as a playwright was finished. Entering the restaurant, he spotted Irving Asher and told him he could still buy the play. Asher politely declined. Another diner at the Savoy that evening was one of his friends from Oxford, Peter Glenville, who was now embarked on a successful theatrical career and had just returned from playing Romeo, Petruchio and Mark Antony at Stratford. They exchanged gossip, Rattigan bemoaning the fact that fame and fortune had eluded him. Later they drove home together. Turning into Piccadilly, Rattigan pointed to the Criterion and said casually, almost as an afterthought, 'They're doing a play of mine there tomorrow night. Don't congratulate me. They're only running it as a stop-gap because another play has folded.'

That was the first mention he had made to Glenville of the production of *French Without Tears*.

Friday, 6 November, was a wet and gloomy day. Finding himself with nothing that he could usefully do and desperate to keep his mind off what was going to happen that evening, Rattigan went out and walked round London. Then he turned into a barber's shop and had his hair cut.

That evening, before the performance, he and his parents went out to dinner. They had a bottle of champagne in an attempt to celebrate, but it was a glum meal. Although they were too polite to say so, they all privately felt that it was going to be a disastrous evening. After the meal, Vera slipped the champagne cork into her purse as a souvenir. When they reached the theatre, their spirits sank still lower. It was still raining and there were two other first nights in London that evening: opera at Covent Garden and the première of a Marlene Dietrich film. The West End was choked with traffic and the audience was coming into the theatre soaked and bad tempered.

The curtain went up to reveal Trevor Howard, as the youngest of a group of students at a French crammer, eating his breakfast and trying to finish his French composition in time for a tutorial. He was joined immediately by another student, played by Guy Middleton, whose first lines consisted of ordering bacon and eggs in loud but appalling French. The sublime over-confidence with which he did it produced a peal of infectious laughter from Cicely Courtneidge, the musical-comedy star, who was sitting a few rows back in the stalls. That set the tone for the rest of the audience and, a few lines later, when Middleton translated, 'She has ideas above her station,' as, 'Elle a des idées au-dessus de sa gare,' the audience gave a full-throated roar of delight. Only a page into the play and they were off to a good start.

The cast did not seem able to believe their ears. Still tense and nervous, they hurried on, without waiting for the laughs or timing their lines so as to build them. Hovering at the back of his box, Harold French was uneasy. If the cast did not calm down and play the audience accurately they would lose their sympathy. The rush continued for fifteen or twenty minutes, until Roland Culver came on. A few seconds after his entrance, he played a line he knew should get a laugh; it came. Then with the self-assurance built of experience and his faith in the play, he waited. The laugh grew. There was applause. Only then, with perfect timing, did he complete the line. He had steadied the anxious cast and now they all started to play with that confidence and touch which is the greatest joy of an actor's craft. The evening developed into one of the most magical first nights of all time.

As the final curtain rattled down, there was a storm of applause and people rose in their seats calling, 'Author, Author!' Harold French dived backstage looking for Rattigan, who had vanished from his place at the back of the dress circle. When he found him, in white tie and tails, he was green-faced and leaning for support against the back wall of the theatre. French virtually threw him on to the stage. The cheering grew louder. The success of the play was so unexpected that no one had arranged for the customary first-night speeches. As Rattigan stepped forward to thank the audience the curtain unceremoniously came down on his head.

In the small hours of the next morning, Rattigan lay, with the rest of the cast, on the floor of Kay Hammond's sitting-room reading the first editions of the morning newspapers. With the exception of the *Daily Herald* ('It has no conceivable relation to British Drama, and is a depressing commentary on the West End Theatre'), they were falling over themselves with praise. 'This brilliant little comedy' – 'Full marks' – 'Joyous jest'. In the *Daily Telegraph*, W. A. Darlington hailed Rattigan as a young author with the rare gift of lightness, while the *Morning Post* said his play was 'gay, witty, thoroughly contemporary without being unpleasantly "modern", brisk without blather and with a touch of loveable truth behind all its satire'. As the first light of dawn crept into the sky and the other guests started to tiptoe away, Rattigan was still stretched out on the floor, the papers strewn round him. He turned on his back and, staring up at Kay Hammond, whispered in blank and awestruck amazement: 'But I don't believe it. Even *The Times* likes it.'

Yet, even in this his first delicious moment of complete triumph, Rattigan remembered the disappointment that the young actor

Gerald Campion must be feeling at not being part of it. On the morning after the first night there was a knock on the front door of the Campions' flat. When young Gerald opened it there on the mat was a huge box of Fuller's chocolates with a letter of encouragement and commiseration from Rattigan. A few days later a silver cigarette case was also delivered, inscribed: 'To Gerald, from the Members of the *French Without Tears* Company – 1936'. Twenty years later Gerald Campion himself became famous, playing Billy Bunter, the fat boy of Old Greyfriars School, in the long-running BBCTV series.

When Harold French had first read *French Without Tears*, the thing that appealed to him particularly was a quality of tenderness which showed through the humour. It is this survival from the play's serious beginnings in Rattigan's own, at times painful, experience which gives the play its ultimate durability. Since the initial idea for the play, five years previously, Rattigan had rewritten and refined his material many times, but the essential core of feeling, which is necessary for any comedy to be other than merely empty and transient, remained. Although everything in the play was now seen for its humour, and each comic permutation was exploited to the full, both situation and characters were still rooted in real experience. People who knew the background to the story thought the characters too lifelike. Rattigan's mother was concerned right up to the first night that the real people on whom the characters were based would recognize themselves and sue. Indeed, after that first night Irma Basilewich's sister cornered Rattigan and accused him of modelling Kay Hammond's character, the man-hunting girl, on Irma. 'That was a bit near the bone,' she said. 'The nearer the bone the sweeter the meat,' he replied gracefully.

The action of *French Without Tears* is set in the living-room of Monsieur Maingot's cramming establishment in a small seaside town on the west coast of France. There are five students in residence, and the plot traces the comic results of the man-hunting activities of a beautiful young woman, Diana, who contrives in turn to hook each of the young men incarcerated in the crammer, and then unscrupulously attempts to play them all simultaneously.

French Without Tears is a comedy in which the humour and the emotion are inseparably blended, each arising naturally from the other. Such serious ideas as there are in the play seem for the most part to belong to it. *French Without Tears* can lay claim to being the best, as well as the best-known, comedy of the 1930s, and the representative British play of that decade. Noël Coward wrote nothing to compare with *French Without Tears* between 1930 and the war; Shaw wrote nothing of importance for the theatre during the decade; the work of Auden and Isherwood was not in the mainstream of popular theatre; and it is arguable that, although it only deals with the antics of a few privileged young people, *French Without Tears* touches more precisely on the central concerns of the generation that was rising to confront the onset of the Second World War than any of Auden and Isherwood's more obviously committed plays. J. B. Priestley produced four good plays in the 1930s: *Dangerous Corner*, *Laburnum Grove*, *When We Are Married* and *Johnson over Jordan*, but none of them has the combination of tenderness and humour which pervades *French Without Tears.*

Rattigan himself said that his model while writing *French Without Tears* was Chekhov. He cited the succession of short scenes between different groups of characters, and the way the central situation is built up almost imperceptibly through an accumulation of small events and revelations. The characters are all fully developed and of almost equal importance. There is another sense in which, with the benefit of hindsight, the play can be seen as belonging in the Chekhov tradition. Where Chekhov conveys the mood of uneasiness and underlying tension in middle-class Russian society in the years leading up to the 1905 and 1917 Revolutions, Rattigan seems to achieve something of the same effect in *French Without Tears.* Today, one cannot fail to be aware that behind the apparently empty-headed exuberance of his young people, their love affairs and petty squabbles, lurks a sense of futility, of being at the mercy of outside events. Beyond the set there lies a world of political violence which is not subject to reason or argument.

The most obviously political passage in the play is a long section in the second act where Alan, a student who is at the crammer at the insistence of his father but who really wants to be a novelist, not a diplomat, describes a novel he has just had rejected by yet another publisher. The plot of his novel concerns two pacifists who desert their country rather than fight in a new war. In exile they, like the boys in the play, come to blows over a woman. Nevertheless, Alan tells the vehemently patriotic Commander, their saving grace is that they have the honesty to accept that the instinct to fight, either each other or a war, is something to be ashamed of; they do not rationalize it as patriotism or manliness. They go back to fight for their country only because they admit that their reason is not strong enough to stand up against this ignoble instinct. The Commander says triumphantly that they were proved wrong in the end, but Alan tells him that because they were unable to live up to their ideal, that does not prove it was wrong. Another student asks, 'What's the use of an ideal, if you can't live up to it?' Alan replies: 'In a hundred years' time men may be able to live up to our ideals even if they can't live up to their own.' This belief in the eventual painful triumph of reason over instinct is one of the consistent hopes of Rattigan's life and work.

The conflict between emotion and reason, which is a motif in all Rattigan's plays, surfaces repeatedly through *French Without Tears*. In one scene the Commander and a younger student, Kit, are struggling to subdue their urge to fight over Diana. Kit asks, 'I wonder why it's such a comfort to get away from reason?'

COMMANDER   Because in this case reason tells us something our vanity won't let us accept.
KIT   It tells us that Diana's a bitch. [The Commander's belligerent instincts rise again.] Reason!
COMMANDER   You're right.

In Rattigan's plays the consequence of giving way to over-powering emotions is almost always shame. The tension lies in the struggle of his characters to resist the demands of such emotions. The most envied of the students is Brian. He manages to remain detached while the others suffer and squabble over the beautiful Diana. He relieves his frustrations by saving up to purchase the favours of a local prostitute. His fellow students concede that he has solved the problem of living better than any of them by the simple expedient of paying for sex rather than feeling love. It is Brian who finally opens their eyes to the way to deal with Diana by making them see that all they have to do is to ask her directly for sex. When she refuses they are free of her.

Even in this lightest of comedies Rattigan is preoccupied with the results of unequal love and love which goes unspoken, with painful consequences for the lovers. Kit and the Commander both love Diana, but she does not really love them – and the result is hilarious. Diana secretly loves Alan, but in vain. She dare not risk the humiliation of letting him know her feelings. When she does, it is hilariously too late. Again the results are disastrous. Jacqueline, the long-suffering daughter of the proprietor of the crammer, loves Kit but won't tell him, and so is unhappy because he does not notice her. 'Once someone else has told Kit how Jacqueline feels, the way is open for them to come happily together. In *French Without Tears*, the inequalities of love and the failure to express hidden feelings are worked out lightly. In the plays which followed, they are worked out in steadily more passionate earnest.

Notes

1   I am indebted to Geoffrey Wansell, op. cit., for the information about the proctors' interview with Rattigan.

2   Various myths have grown up about the circumstances of Rattigan's departure from Oxford and his decision to take up a full-time career as a playwright. In addition to various published accounts by Rattigan and others, I have drawn heavily on Gillian Hodson's and my interviews with Rattigan himself and with Philip Heimann's son David, on interviews both Rattigan and Heimann gave to journalists at the time and on an interview Rattigan gave in New Zealand to the *Auckland Daily News* in 1946.

3   It was not until years later, when a habitual customer was convicted of drunken driving, that it was discovered that the contents of Perkin's 'tonic' was sixty-per-cent medical alcohol, No wonder successive generations of West End partygoers found that a call on the way to work for a glass drunk at the shop counter was the only way they could face the day.

4   Writing of the New York production of *First Episode*, Brooks Atkinson called the production very crude and complained that had the theme been earnestly pursued the play might well have made a 'disarmingly poignant drama'. He and other New York critics strongly condemned the over-obvious farce that had been introduced to the

detriment of the play underneath. But the lesson was not learned. Another farcical production of the play was tried at the Garrick Theatre, London, in December 1934, and again it failed.

5   This may echo the circumstances of Rattigan's elder brother Brian's premature departure from Harrow. For a while Rattigan certainly propagated a rumour that Brian had to leave because of 'getting a girl into trouble', but this may have been another of his tall stories.

6   This is how Rattigan remembered the conversations with Gielgud when talking to Gillian Hodson and me in 1977.

7   Although there were a number of proposals to produce Gielgud and Rattigan's *A Tale of Two Cities* in the years immediately before the Second World War, including a production with music and lyrics, the play was not staged until 1950, when it was given an amateur production by St Brendan's College Dramatic Society in Bristol. This was followed later in the same year by a radio production, starring Eric Portman as Sydney Carton.

8   Emlyn Williams interviewed by the author in 1977 for the BBC Television obituary of Rattigan.

9   Details of Rattigan's contract with Warner Brothers were provided to Gillian Hodson and me in 1977 by Rattigan himself.

10 Anthony Powell in *Faces in My Time.*

11 From manuscript notes to a talk given by Rattigan, *c.*1941. My account of how *French Without Tears* came to be produced is taken from various descriptions by Rattigan himself, on radio, in published form or in his interview with me, from interviews I did with Sir John Gielgud, Robert Flemyng, Peter Glenville, John Perry, Rex Harrison and Roland Culver in 1977/8, from correspondence with Gerald Campion since 2000 and from published accounts by Harold French, Rex Harrison and Roland Culver. In talking to Geoffrey Wansell in the early 1990s, Harold French seems to have remembered his own role in some of the events rather differently from in the account given to me or in that given by him in his own books, *I Swore I Never Would* and *I Thought I Never Could*, Secker and Warburg, London, 1970 & 1973. Many of the versions conflict.

12 Some of the actual description of the novel may have been added by Rattigan during rehearsals as a result of the need to get the play up to an acceptable length. Rattigan himself suggested that most of the additional material went into Act III. If so, it seems likely that some of the material in the scene between Alan, Kit and Rogers at the start of the act, before Diana comes on, was added later.

5

After the Dance

'I no more understand this sort of play and acting than my cat understands Euclid,' wrote James Agate in his *Sunday Times* review of *French Without Tears*. The posh Sundays brought a douche of cold water after the elation of the daily-paper reviews. In the *Observer*, Ivor Brown also did not rate Rattigan as a writer: '... his play, brief and brittle, with little construction and no freshness or fun...' had, Brown claimed, only been saved by the director and cast.

Agate's outspoken criticism caused an uproar. He was accused of having arrived at the theatre fifteen minutes late, of staying only thirty minutes, and of spending most of this time looking at the audience rather than the stage. But Agate was unrepentant and continued to attack the play in his column. The row rumbled on, bursting into a final conflagration in March 1938, when Agate disparagingly named *French Without Tears* last in a list of plays running in the West End. John Gielgud, at some risk to himself, sprang to Rattigan's defence. He protested, in an open letter to the *Sunday Times*, that he had read Rattigan's play in manuscript and thought it 'particularly delightful and original both in conception and execution'. He reprimanded Agate for ignominiously baiting a promising young playwright, and reminded him that the theatre was in great need of young writers.

Agate used his speech at the annual Gallery First Nighters' dinner, on the same day that Gielgud's letter appeared, to attack both Gielgud and the notion that popular success could be equated with quality – which was hardly Gielgud's point. Percy Walsh, a member of the original cast who was a guest at the dinner, was so incensed that he jumped to his feet in protest. There was uproar. Shouts of, 'Sit down.' Cheers and counter-cheers. Percy Walsh was escorted from the room by a steward, while James Agate said that he would maintain to the grave a critic's duty to condemn work he dislikes no matter how popular it may be. A week later, Agate returned to the attack in a long reply to Gielgud in the *Sunday Times*. His central point was that plays such as *French Without Tears* are not harmless. The critic who endorsed such poor-quality work, he argued, discouraged and delayed the day when a finer theatre based on true critical standards would come into its own. Popular Piccadilly knick-knacks only encouraged the mindless, perfunctory, popular audience in its laziness.

Adverse criticism is often more deeply felt by those who receive it than is praise. Rattigan was no exception. He had ambition as a writer, and broadsides like this, especially from such respected quarters, reinforced his determination to be taken seriously. But the three-year struggle for financial success, the daily confrontation with the blank sheets of paper in an upstairs backroom, the stream of finished plays and answering rejection slips, had combined to deplete his stock of creative fuel. The sudden and wholly unanticipated popular success of *French Without Tears*, and the resulting transformation of his financial situation, produced an inevitable reaction – something very like a breakdown.[1]

He abandoned himself to a life of pleasure and gave up any attempt at serious writing. With his income rising overnight to more than a hundred pounds a week, he moved out of his father's home into a high-ceilinged flat in Hertford Street, Mayfair, where he started repaying some of his friends' hospitality. His drink and gambling bills rose in proportion to his income. Always a fastidious dresser, he now indulged his taste for Savile Row tailoring and took to having his hair cut by the king's barber. He bought a motor car and formed himself into a limited liability company for tax purposes. But his accountant was soon chiding him for his extravagance, and when, a year or so after the play had opened, he went out and bought a Rolls Royce, his accountant remonstrated: 'But you don't have that sort of money.' Rattigan replied that since everyone thought he had, 'It's your responsibility to see I do have!'

The first-night success of *French Without Tears* was immediately confirmed. Delighted audiences packed the theatre every night and the play settled down to a record-breaking run. Reports of the extraordinary sums it was taking at the box office and exaggerated stories of how much Rattigan was earning from it appeared regularly in the newspapers. *French Without Tears* became the most talked-about hit of the day.

Within a year of its London opening there were productions of *French Without Tears* in the provinces, in New York and Paris. In February 1937, Queen Mary made her first theatre outing since the death of the king to the London production of *French Without Tears*. Marlene Dietrich took Douglas Fairbanks to see it and soon the papers were reporting that both she and Carole Lombard wanted to play Diana in the film. Paramount was reported to have bought the film rights at Miss Dietrich's instigation for ten thousand pounds. (In fact, the film was not made until 1939 and it starred neither of these ladies.) Von Ribbentrop, the German Ambassador, was a fan of *French Without Tears*, seeing it five or six times with a series of Nazi dignitaries. It was thought that he used the play as a demonstration of how decadent the British had become – young men mocking the nation's most sacred institutions, the Diplomatic Service and the Navy.

Another regular attender, sitting proprietorially in a stage box, was Frank Rattigan. He unashamedly used his position as father of the author of the most fashionable play in London to impress young ladies he took a fancy to, and was escorted to the theatre by a succession of nubile blondes. He quite unscrupulously promised pretty young actresses parts in his son's future plays. Although he was well into his fifties his vigour was in no way impaired. He became well known to the cast from his frequent appearances both front and backstage. He took to challenging the more athletic members of the cast to games of squash, which he still played extremely well. As the run of *French Without Tears* progressed, a succession of different actresses took over the part of Diana. On the night when one of these young ladies played the part for the first time, the men in the cast had laid bets as to which of them would be the first to take her out to dinner. After the performance the young men came out of their dressing-rooms to see her walking down the corridor on the arm of Frank Rattigan.

Rattigan was now able to repay the years of subsidy from his father. He could hardly pay him an allowance, so he bought pictures and antiques and sold them to his father, who still ran an antique business, at prices far below the market value. Relations between Rattigan and his father received a rude jolt, however, when Frank Rattigan by mistake opened a letter to his son from a Paris hotel manager. The letter complained of Rattigan's improper behaviour with a man in the hotel and asked him in future to take his custom elsewhere. Frank wrote his son a two-page letter to tell him how shocked he was. But the solemnity of this missive was undermined somewhat by a postscript in which he added that he hoped he wouldn't mind but he had taken the liberty of giving his son's gramophone to a lady friend, and would he please on no account mention this to his mother.

One inevitable consequence of Rattigan's new found fame was the string of compliments he received. These he could normally accept with modesty and charm, but he had to develop a style of dealing with the more gushing adulation. Thus a débutante who approached him at a garden party and said, 'I think yours is the best play that's ever been written!' was parried with a smile and a question: 'Have you ever seen *King Lear*?'

Yet while the exciting new world of success and fame whirled around him, Rattigan still remained under contract in his fifteen-pounds-a-week day job with Warner Brothers at Teddington Studios. His boss Irving Asher might still not think much of him as a writer, but with his new found success young Rattigan might at last become something of an asset. Rattigan was now chafing at the bit but the studio were in no hurry to let him go. Perhaps in an effort to slap his young contract writer down, early in March 1937 Asher instructed Rattigan to take out to dinner the author of London's 'best and brightest comedy, George Savory'. Savory's *George and Margaret* had just opened and was vying with *French Without Tears* as the most fashionable hit in London. Next morning, an uncowed Rattigan reported back to his boss by letter. Pointing out that the author's name was Gerald not George Savory, Rattigan continued, 'I gathered a lot of valuable information from him, the most important of which being that he is twenty-seven and that he was unable to get seats for *French Without Tears* last week. These two facts I shall have pleasure in incorporating in my next script for Warner Brothers.'[2]

In September 1937, Rattigan went to America for the New York opening of *French Without Tears*. The production was again by Harold French but with a largely new English cast. The reviews were mixed. The New York *Herald Tribune* greeted the play as 'the first pleasure of the harassed new dramatic season ... it possesses gaiety, high spirits and an air of good-humoured freshness'. Brooks Atkinson in the *New York Times*, complimenting Rattigan on his attractive style and capricious gaiety, said the play was so light that it 'almost floats out of the theater'. *Variety* predicted that it was too light 'to stay anchored for long on Broadway'.

Rattigan had only intended a short visit to New York, but he so much enjoyed the hospitality and attention paid to him by Americans that he stayed on as *French Without Tears* settled down to a respectable New York run. Surprisingly, amid the New York parties he rediscovered the urge to write. It was well over a year since he had written anything more sustained than snippets of film dialogue. Nagging at the back of his mind had been the problem of how to follow his first success. He was afraid of anticlimax, and this had contributed to his creative paralysis. His mother had warned him: 'The poorhouses are full of people who have written one successful play.'

He was all too aware of the number of playwrights who had written one spectacular success and spent the rest of their careers writing sequel after sequel. He had to make a leap right away from comedy, to produce a play which would be taken seriously by the critics who, he suspected, would be gunning for him after such a commercial success. In the unlikely surroundings of the Waldorf

Astoria Hotel in New York, where he was staying, he took the plunge and started to map out a new play – *After the Dance*.

He was immediately interrupted. Irving Asher, his English studio boss, arrived and put up in an adjoining hotel. With the success of *French Without Tears*, Warner Brothers realized they could now hire Rattigan out to other producers for large sums, while Rattigan was still only entitled to his salary of fifteen pounds a week, plus a small percentage increment. Rattigan was only in New York under leave of contract and Asher announced he was going to take him to Hollywood, for which he would receive just fifteen per cent extra on his salary. Rattigan was adamant: he wasn't going. The final confrontation took place in Asher's hotel suite, which Rattigan noted gleefully was rather smaller than his own. Rattigan had had a lot to drink and, in his own words, proceeded to 'behave like an absolute shit'. Although he privately conceded that at fifteen pounds a week they had been over-paying him, he made it plain that he would not work for them for fifteen pounds a week any longer. Asher reminded him of the terms of his contract and said that he was taking him with him to Hollywood that very evening; he had already booked sleepers for them on the train. But Rattigan retorted hotly that he wasn't going anywhere and that if Asher didn't like it he could sue him. When Asher left on the train Rattigan remained behind and continued to write his play. Luckily, Asher was a benign boss. Rattigan was allowed to return to England and, although he was put on a number of assignments, the studio did not treat him harshly. Eventually, Warner Brothers British went out of business and their writers' contracts were nullified.[3]

The play which Rattigan brought back with him in outline from New York at the end of 1937 was about a high-living, hard-drinking successful author and his involvement with two women – his wife and an earnest-minded younger woman. Rattigan told journalists that it was intended as a firm statement that another war was coming and that the people responsible for it were the people who had been young just after the Great War: 'It was an indictment of that generation by the younger generation.' But once he settled down to write, he found that his sympathies drifted towards the older generation: 'With all their faults, they were less stupid, less boring and less priggish.'

After the Dance is set in the top-floor Mayfair flat of David Scott-Fowler, a successful thirty-eight-year-old writer of history books. The other principal male characters are John, a fat contemporary and friend of David's who lives as a parasite on his wealth, and Peter, David's idealistic young cousin and secretary, just down from Oxford, fresh and eager to make his way in the world, but unable to find a job 'because they are all filled, mostly by people who started at the top of something and worked their way to the bottom'.

The plot hinges on Peter's young fiancée Helen, who falls for David and makes it her mission to save him from drink, laziness and his wife Joan. Helen tells him that he and his generation have been spoiled by the war, even though they were too young to be part of it. She declares her love for him by vowing to help him back to the disciplines of writing and scholarship, so that he can realize his potential talent to the full.

Again Rattigan was clearly using a play to work through his own immediate preoccupations. At the time that he was working on *After the Dance*, the Civil War between fascism and socialism was raging in Spain. At the same time he was also reworking recurrent themes: inequality of love, feelings hidden until too late, the conflict between instinct and reason. It is only after Helen has come between them that Joan admits to the true strength of her feelings about her husband – and then only to a mutual friend, John. John calls her a fool for not telling David how much she really loves him – 'That's all he really wants – someone to be in love with him.'

JOAN   Not me. He doesn't want me to be in love with him. I'd have bored him to death if I'd ever let him see it. I know that.

JOHN   It's awful how two people can misunderstand each other as much as you and David have over twelve years.

Later Joan weakens and shows David her real need for him; she confesses that she has all along only pretended to enjoy the high life to please him, not realizing that he secretly craved someone more serious like Helen. In return, David confesses that he was ashamed to show the more serious side of himself. But it is too late, their marriage is over. During a party, brilliantly handled by Rattigan, Joan commits suicide by throwing herself from the balcony of their flat.

The play ends in disillusion. Peter, once the high-principled young idealist, becomes a shameless parasite. David and Helen are clearly incompatible, their relationship cannot work no matter how much they may want it to – instinct is stronger than reason or willpower. David, too, sets about killing himself. Not with a spectacular gesture like Joan, but by returning to his former life and the round of parties and drinking – which we realize will ultimately be just as effective a way of killing himself as throwing himself off the balcony.

After the Dance is in some ways reminiscent of Scott Fitzgerald. Rattigan, who had himself only narrowly escaped Hollywood, undoubtedly knew that Fitzgerald, now a hopeless alcoholic, was at that time trapped in Hollywood and condemned to writing material unworthy of the talent which only a decade before had dazzled the world. The moral could not have escaped anyone with Rattigan's underlying determination and self-knowledge about his own weakness for high living, drink and idleness. The parallels between Rattigan's fictional author and the real Scott Fitzgerald are underlined by his choice of the name Scott-Fowler.

The other writer called to mind by *After the Dance* is Noël Coward. Rattigan's student contempt for Coward had been replaced by respect for his craftsmanship, though not yet with approval of his use of it. The play seems to be as much an attack on the attitudes of Coward's 1920s' bright young things as on Fitzgerald. In later years, Coward and Rattigan were bracketed together, but Rattigan always firmly, though politely, dissociated himself from the connection, pointing out that they wrote different plays and that Coward belonged to an earlier generation. *After the Dance* can be read as a reproof to Coward, the brightest talent of the previous generation, from the rising hope of the new one, implying that Coward had broken faith with his talent by not producing work worthy either of himself or of the momentous times in which he lived. Yet Rattigan's claim that in *After the Dance* he was warning that another war was coming and that the previous generation was responsible is not borne out by the play itself. All that does emerge from the text is that the older generation cannot escape the consequences of clinging for too long to the values of their misspent youth. The play may show us the triumph of the puritanical attitudes of the new generation, but it also reveals their disastrous results. Helen's attitudes may roughly parallel some of the attitudes of Rattigan and his more earnest-minded friends – he himself claimed that the two young people in the play were 'more or less Communists' (although the text provides no evidence for such a claim) – yet the fruit of their new found seriousness is at best a mixed blessing.

It is characteristic of Rattigan that having recently experienced such a dramatic alteration in his own style of life he should write about people living that same life. He looks not only at the wealthy people in the centre of the circle, but at the parasites who hang round the periphery; not so long ago he had himself been a hanger-on, but he was now increasingly finding himself the target of parasites and flatterers. In the play Rattigan can be seen casting an eye on both his former situation and his new one. Among the characteristic in-jokes is a delicious side-swipe at a little-liked erstwhile collaborator. David, having reread some of the material which he has dictated, tells Peter that it stinks:

PETER   I thought it read rather well.
DAVID   That's just the trouble with it. It reads too well – imitation Hector Bolitho.
PETER   Well, you're writing it to be read, aren't you?
DAVID   Not by the sort of people who read Hector Bolitho.

Rattigan's work on *After the Dance* seems to have dragged on for over a year. This may have been due in part to the lingering effects of his earlier 'breakdown' and of Rattigan indulging his new found wealth and celebrity to the full. But the main cause was that by early March 1938 Rattigan had become deeply involved, with Tony Goldschmidt, in writing an openly propagandist political farce.

Rattigan, Goldschmidt and the rebellious circle from their Harrow and Oxford days had remained friends. As the 1930s progressed they had shifted further to the left. A *Daily Telegraph* reporter who interviewed Rattigan at this period formed the impression that he was 'an almost complete pacifist'. The hardening of their positions was, of course, a direct consequence of outside events. As Western governments failed to stand up to the dictators or give substance to the ideal of collective security through the League of Nations and settled for appeasement, the Communist Party seemed increasingly attractive as the only opponent of fascism. Although, unlike some of his friends, Rattigan did not join the Party, he certainly flirted with it. Goldschmidt joined the Labour Party and became very active in the Holborn constituency.

The catalyst for their feelings was the Spanish Civil War. Although they still denounced arms for Britain as immoral, they turned out to demonstrate for 'Arms and Food for Spain'. To them there was no inconsistency in this. Britain was a great power which had to set a moral example and work through the League of Nations; Spain was a small country in which democracy was being crushed by force of arms supplied to Franco by Hitler and Mussolini. So Rattigan, while enjoying the first flush of success and extravagant living, found himself increasingly in the company of such unlikely comrades as Michael Foot, being held back by the police outside No. 10 Downing Street. On one occasion, he found himself in a crowd being charged by mounted police, and the terror he felt then etched itself for ever in his mind.[4]

By the time Rattigan returned from America at the end of 1937, Hitler was once again making aggressive noises about the need to incorporate all people of German blood into one unified Nazi state. Rattigan, who had been contemplating for some time an idea for a satire on Hitler, was now galvanized into action. The problem was that he could no longer be sure what was funny in his idea and what was not. He needed someone like-minded to work with. Philip Heimann was no longer around, so he called in

Tony Goldschmidt, whose wit he knew from their time together at Harrow and Oxford. Goldschmidt would, he felt sure, draw the best out of him.

They secluded themselves in Shiplake so that they could concentrate undisturbed. As they wrote, Hitler stepped up his propaganda campaign for the incorporation of Austria within Germany. By mid-March the newspapers were full of the *Anschluss* and Hitler's triumphant reception in Vienna. Working together, Rattigan and Goldschmidt soon found themselves transported back to their larkish times together at Oxford, writing sketches for 'smokers' and articles for *Cherwell*. Their play, set in a country called Moronia, took the form of a decidedly unsubtle lampoon of the excesses of Hitler and the Nazis and Mussolini and the Italian fascists, and of the antics of the British government in trying to appease them. The idea of satirizing Hitler and the Nazis was by no means a new one for Rattigan. He and Philip Heimann had tried to incorporate the idea into *First Episode* in 1933, straight after Hitler came to power. *Follow My Leader*, Rattigan and Goldschmidt's new play, followed the rise to power of a plumber called Hans Zedesi. The national slogan of Moronia becomes 'Up Zedesi' – pronounced 'upsy-daisy' – accompanied by a Hitler salute. Having come to power through blowing up Moronia's parliament building and blaming the explosion on 'the cowardly liberals', Zedesi's party is sustained in power through organized 'spontaneous displays of devotion and love'. Further parallels with Hitler's Germany and Mussolini's Italy include frequent military displays to show off the power of the new regime's bombs and the magnificence of its poison gas. Zedesi boasts that on the 'constructive side' his party has 'abolished the constitution, eliminated the trade unions and resigned from the League of Nations!'

Satirizing Hitler's most notorious foreign-policy ploy, Rattigan and Goldschmidt have Zedesi invade a neighbouring small country called Neurasthenia which, conveniently, boasts a Moronian minority. This tactic, was extremely topical at the time when Rattigan and Goldschmidt were writing, following Hitler's recent reoccupation of the Rhineland, 'union' (*Anschluss*) with

Austria and Mussolini's invasion of Ethiopia. It is aimed at enhancing the party's prestige, while quelling the opposition and solving the nation's dire economic problems at a stroke (a tactic not unknown to dictators even in our own day). Unfortunately the plan misfires when the man hired to stage a bomb outrage, Riszki, sets his watch 'by Big Benito' and blows up the British Embassy. In the best scene in the play, the British Ambassador, Sir Cosmo Tate-Johnson, appears, his face blackened, striped trousers torn, top hat battered and morning coat in tatters, to protest in the true appeasing tones of Neville Chamberlain's government. Struggling to maintain his dignity at all costs, he tells Zedesi that unfortunately he has 'to draw the attention of your Government to certain – er – well – er – untoward circumstances that have just arisen in connection with my Embassy!' He explains that he and his secretary have been blown into the street and that, 'speaking entirely unofficially and without prejudice', the British Embassy has been 'more or less completely, well – disintegrated'. He regrets that he will have to inform His Majesty's Government and that, while they will make no hasty decisions and will view the matter from every angle, 'it is conceivable that they may instruct me to deliver a formal protest'. The play ends with the triumphant Zedesi taking a congratulatory phonecall from Adolf Hitler himself. In the intervals between the acts, Goldschmidt and Rattigan planned to show newsreels showing the recent sensational rise to power of the European dictators.

By the time Rattigan and Goldschmidt had finished *Follow My Leader*, Hitler had another campaign in full swing. His target this time was Czechoslovakia and the Sudetenland. As the Munich crisis loomed and the British government shilly-shallied about standing up to Hitler, Rattigan and Goldschmidt wanted to rush their play into immediate production. With the help of Rattigan's loyal agent A.D. Peters they found an impresario, Gilbert Miller, who was willing to put it on. However, the idea got no further than the Lord Chamberlain's office. The Lord Chamberlain referred the script to the Foreign Office. As a result, after an agonizing delay, it was banned. The Foreign Office, from which Anthony Eden had recently resigned in the wake of a largely semantic disagreement with Neville Chamberlain over the government's appeasement of Italy, felt that a production of the play would not be 'in the nation's interest'. It might offend Hitler.

Working with Goldschmidt on their extended skit against appeasement, Rattigan's private life seemed to regain some of the carefree abandon of his Harrow and Oxford days. While at Shiplake with Goldschmidt, Rattigan embarked on an affaire with a boyish-looking actor called Peter Osborn. Rattigan marked what Osborn later referred to as their first coming together, by presenting him with a signed copy of *French Without Tears*. His dedication read: 'For Peter Osborn, who will surely be responsible for a better one.' Osborn, described by a contemporary as 'one of the most strikingly beautiful actors ever seen', was a year or two younger than Rattigan and had recently started to make his way in the theatre. He had had a walk-on part as a footman in a production which Rattigan had seen, of *The Admirable Crichton* at the Embassy Theatre in 1935 and had later played a leading part in the touring production of Dodie Smith's *Call It a Day*. Although Osborn conformed physically to the type to which Rattigan was repeatedly attracted – small, trim, wide-eyed, neat (a kind of male equivalent to Frank Rattigan's succession of unsuitable bubbly blondes) – Osborn would turn out to be a much more substantial figure, both in terms of character and intellectual accomplishment, than many of the other young men that Rattigan would go for over the coming years. The relationship with Osborn would last, albeit through many vicissitudes, for the rest of Rattigan's life. For the moment their relationship seemed to be all champagne, parties and nights at the Ritz.[5]

In the summer of 1938 after Rattigan and Goldschmidt had finished their work on *Follow My Leader*, Rattigan decided that the time had finally come to move out of his parents' flat in South Kensington. He took a flat in Hertford Street in Mayfair, close to the one that he and Philip Heimann had rented in the heady days immediately after the West End opening of *First Episode*. Just as he and Heimann had then, Rattigan gave a series of optimistic interviews to journalists announcing his new ventures. In June, the *Daily Telegraph* reported that Rattigan had written a new play 'tentatively called *After the Dance*' which he hoped would be presented in the West End in September. In early August he was telling the *Daily Express* that his new play *After the Dance* was 'about post-war disillusionment'.[6]

Rattigan's affaire with Peter Osborn continued to progress idyllically in a whirl of glamorous first nights and parties. One of these was Ivor Novello's forty-fifth birthday party, at which Arthur Marshall, then a frightened young schoolmaster, was due to do a comic turn for the guests after dinner. He recalled meeting Rattigan: 'Terry, slim and neat and what fashion writers will call "well groomed"...might have been somebody from Lloyd's perhaps, or from an ancient and highly respected City firm of wine shippers.' Rattigan assured Marshall, who was terrified at the prospect of the performance ahead of him, that he at least would laugh. Marshall remembered that:

> We were of an age and, though he had by then met the world, he was still as stage-struck as I and together we goggled at the splendid creatures before us – Zena Dare, Beatrice Lillie, Dorothy Dickson, Leslie Henson and almost every other star then in London. There was an up-and-coming couple, who had just fallen desperately in love with each other, and their names were Laurence Olivier and Vivien Leigh.[7]

Peter Osborn later remembered it because he and Rattigan were given their own bedroom 'with a deep delicious double bed'.

There was an upstairs flat vacant in the same house as Rattigan's in Hertford Street and he prompted Peter Osborn to take it. Rattigan offered to pay the rent, at least until Osborn could afford to pay him back. This was a departure for Rattigan. Except at parties, or on short holidays away from London, trips abroad or one-night stands in adjacent rooms in hotels, he had always been careful not to live with his lovers under the same roof. Almost all of his emotional capital continued to go into his writing and into being a success. Where sex and love were concerned he followed the precepts of one of his own characters – Brian in *French*

Without Tears – he never mistook the desire for the one for the feeling of the other. So when Peter Osborn moved into the upstairs flat in Hertford Street, Rattigan made it clear that there were to be strict conditions. They were to keep up the appearance of two normal 'straight' young men about town, friends and no more. Osborn was to make himself scarce whenever Rattigan's grander straight friends turned up, and especially when Frank Rattigan breezed in, which he was wont to do unannounced. Rattigan seems to have allowed his father to make use of his flat for carrying on his own *affaires*.

The year 1939 opened with Rattigan facing the same kind of depression that had assailed him in the months after the first flush of excitement had worn off following the success of *French Without Tears*. Although Gilbert Miller, the impresario who had put on *French Without Tears* in New York, had commissioned him to adapt an Italian and a French play, Rattigan had nothing original on the stocks. He sank again into fits of black depression. In January he had finally to admit to journalists, who continued to enquire when they were going to see his new anti-appeasement play, that the Lord Chamberlain had banned *Follow My Leader*. At the same time a 'Last Weeks' notice was posted up outside the Criterion Theatre for *French Without Tears*. Rattigan tried to get round the ban on *Follow My Leader* by arranging a club performance, but to no avail. His spirits were somewhat lifted when the 'Last Weeks' notice outside the Criterion dramatically came down. It had boosted business and the management decided to continue the run with a transfer to the Piccadilly Theatre 'At Popular Prices'. This had a particular piquancy as Rattigan's play would replace its long running rival as 'the most popular comedy in the West End' – Gerald Savory's *George and Margaret*.[8] By early 1939, too, it was plain that Peter Osborn's feelings for Rattigan were much stronger than Rattigan's were for him. Osborn wanted to be able to be with Rattigan all the time. By now he was finding his evenings of waiting at the top of the stairs in Hertford Street to see if Rattigan would return alone from dinner, and if he did, waiting to see if he would be invited down to Rattigan's flat, unbearable. As were his banishments whenever Frank Rattigan or some other 'respectable' friend turned up. In years to come, Osborn would look back on his time in Hertford Street as 'those dreadful days'. Such inequality of feelings between Rattigan and his lovers would come to haunt much of his emotional life. It was already a leitmotif in his work, a leitmotif that would grow in depth and complexity.

Rattigan's difficulties were temporarily forgotten when he started to work with Anthony Asquith and Anatole de Grunwald on the film adaptation of *French Without Tears*. This was a new world for Rattigan. Although he had been a screenwriter, he had never been allowed to become involved as a collaborator among equals and, moreover, he was now working on his own material. It was suggested, apparently seriously, that Rattigan himself should play the Rex Harrison role, Alan. He wisely declined. Eventually the British actor, Ray Milland, returned from Hollywood to play it. Roland Culver and Guy Middleton remained from the original stage cast, and a promising twenty-one-year-old actor, Kenneth Morgan, came in as Babe Lake, the youngest of the students. He eventually won the Best British Screen Newcomer Award for his work in the film. Morgan was another trim, wide-eyed young man and, unknown to Peter Osborn, Rattigan embarked on a casual *affaire* with him.[9] Later this talented and very attractive young man was to play an even more crucial role in Rattigan's life than Peter Osborn.

By the summer of 1939 Rattigan was almost broke again. He had made more than thirty thousand pounds from *French Without Tears*, including the sale of the film rights. But he had spent heavily throughout the run, and lost still more by investing in his father's tips on the Stock Exchange. When *French Without Tears* finally closed at the beginning of May, after 1,030 performances, he went to France and in three weeks lost the remainder of his accumulated savings in the casinos.[10] But that summer *After the Dance* was at last about to open at the St James's Theatre. Rattigan knew it was unrealistic to expect the same sort of financial reward as from *French Without Tears*; even so he hoped he might get a six-month run out of it. That it was to be produced so soon after the closure of *French Without Tears* was due once again to the tireless efforts and faith of his agent, A. D. Peters. As with *French Without Tears*, Peters put some of his own money into the production. In addition he enlisted the support of another client of his, J. B. Priestley, who was at that time running the Westminster Theatre. Priestley approached Michael Macowan to direct, and a strong cast was assembled, headed by Robert Harris and Catherine Lacey as the Scott-Fowlers.

As rehearsals progressed it became clear that the actor playing one of the other major parts had a drink problem. Macowan decided he would have to be fired. However, the man had been a fine actor and Rattigan pleaded for him. Eventually Macowan told Rattigan that he must deliver an ultimatum to the actor, either he learned his lines in the next three days or he was out. On Monday, 12 June the play opened at the New Theatre, Oxford with the actor still in the cast, word perfect and giving a fine performance.

Rumour of an exciting and unexpected new play from the author of *French Without Tears* had got round theatrical circles by the time the play opened in London nine days later. When Rattigan arrived at the St James's with his mother and father on that Wednesday evening, it was packed with celebrities; the expectant mood was in sharp contrast to that previous first night on a rain-sodden evening at the Criterion almost three years earlier. In her handbag Vera Rattigan carried the champagne cork from the tense dinner before that earlier first night as a good-luck token, along with another from the dinner they had just had together. Rattigan had again had his hair cut. These were to become the elements of a ritual they went through before the London first night of each new play.

The newspapers all agreed that this first night would be the theatrical event of the week. They asked, 'Can he do it again?' Those who attended the first night hoping to see a bright young author fall flat on his face – and there must have been quite a few – were quickly disappointed. The evening went well from the start and at the end the audience broke into cheers and called for the author. This time clear arrangements had been made about curtain speeches. Rattigan had categorically refused to speak and had given instructions that Robert Harris and Catherine Lacey should thank the audience on his behalf.

In the small hours of the next morning Rattigan anxiously rushed through the reviews. They were uniformly good. CAN HE DO IT AGAIN? was transformed to RATTIGAN DOES IT AGAIN. *The Times* said that Rattigan's 'method of allowing his people gradually to reveal themselves gives to his play a genuine distinction'. In the *News Chronicle* the final paragraph of Anthony Squires' glowing review read: 'It only remains to wish this play the long and prosperous run that it deserves, to congratulate its author on having justified so conclusively his departure from the realms of comedy and to look forward to a long series of his triumphs during the next forty or fifty years.'

On Sunday came perhaps the sweetest praise of all. In the *Sunday Times*, James Agate praised Rattigan for having the courage not to take the easy way out by continuing with a line of commercial but vacant comedies. While he did not totally surrender to the play, he found many things in it to praise. He concluded his long article by saying: 'Nevertheless... I suggest that this play is worthy of respect.'

Three weeks later Rattigan celebrated at Lord's with Tony Goldschmidt and other school friends during the annual Eton v. Harrow cricket match. It was a moment of supreme happiness. In bright sunshine Rattigan moved among the fashionable throng, at twenty-eight the best-known young dramatist in London, the acknowledged hope of the rising theatrical generation. At last he was acclaimed and respected. He was among friends, and to crown it all, Harrow won. The captain was carried shoulder high; it was the school's first victory since 1908. The enjoyment of the moment was the sharper for the sense of approaching catastrophe. An observer[11] looking back on those two days in July 1939 recalled Rattigan and his young, seemingly carefree friends, standing out like figures bathed in the last brilliant rays of the sun against the background of an approaching thunderstorm. Appeasement had failed and another war was imminent.

The collapse into war and the collapse of Rattigan's hopes went hand in hand. Despite the good notices and the fashionable crowds at early performances, attendances at *After the Dance* soon fell off and on 12 August, after sixty performances, it closed. Simultaneously negotiations between Russia and the Allies which might have staved off war collapsed. Ten days later, Russia and Germany concluded the Nazi-Soviet Pact, and on 1 September Hitler marched into Poland. Two days later, a few minutes after 11 a.m. on Sunday, 3 September, Rattigan listened to Chamberlain's wireless announcement that Britain was at war with Germany.

Unlike their left-wing friends who had actually joined the Communist Party, Rattigan and Tony Goldschmidt did not find their reaction to the outbreak of war complicated by the Nazi-Soviet Pact. Hitler was plainly an aggressor who had violated all the ideals that lay behind their admiration of the League of Nations. For all their pacifism, their immediate impulse was to enlist. But like thousands of others they were rebuffed.[13] The machinery did not yet exist for taking huge numbers into the forces and the government as yet seemed half-hearted about the war. As autumn progressed, Rattigan began to accept the growing popular feeling that it was just a phoney war, and returned to a country cottage he had taken at Frensham Ponds in Surrey to face his own unresolved problems.

Notes

1   Rattigan described himself at this time as having had 'a nervous breakdown' when talking to a reporter a few years later *(Daily Mail,* 20 May 1939).

2   Letter, dated 6 March 1939, in the Rattigan Papers in the British Library. In fact, Gerald Savory was the most charming character and Rattigan and he would have had no trouble in getting on fine together. Like Rattigan, Savory was, until *George and Margaret,* an unknown author. He too had considerable difficulty following up his first success and, unlike Rattigan, never really succeeded. Savory's *George and Margaret* transformed the fortunes of the struggling management which put it on – H. M. Tennent Ltd, later the backers of many of Rattigan's greatest successes and the most powerful theatrical management in Britain. After the war Savory became a much loved and very successful Head of Plays at BBC Television, where he showed great kindness to the present author.

3   Recounted by Rattigan to the author in 1939.

4   Another element in the composition of the play and its characters (particularly the characters of Peter and Helen) may be a relationship that Rattigan had during the latter part of its composition with an attractive, charismatic, if rather earnest, Oxford

undergraduate called David Rankin. Rankin, who seems to have been wracked with guilt and uncertainty over his emergent homosexual leanings, was drowned in the sea off Cornwall on 28 July 1938. Officially deemed a bathing accident, it seems probable that it was suicide. During the months leading up to his death Rankin had kept a journal which includes several references to Rattigan. Among the papers found by Rankin's mother after her son's death there was a short poem, dated 7 July 1938, which describes Rattigan as he appeared at that time to an awestruck young man:

> The man had grey-blue twinkling eyes,
> And gracefully walked and talked
> His way through life with an obscene jest,
> A drink, or a substitute wife.
> His riches raised from a few light lines
> Quoted from a London stage,
> And he did not mind, nay, was rather proud
> That there was not a profound page.
> His talk was easy, and clever, and bound
> By no other convention than this –
> That it should never discuss a man's soul
> Nor a subject for laughter miss.

5   More than thirty years later, Rattigan's friend the distinguished theatre critic T. C. Worsley would dedicate the book of his own reminiscences of the Spanish Civil War, *Fellow Travellers*, 'For Terence Rattigan, who also in his time chanted Arms for Spain, with admiration and affection'.

6   I am indebted to Peter Osborn himself for much of the information about his relationship with Rattigan and to the three volumes of his book *Exit Praying*, op. cit., and to an interview Peter Osborn gave to Geoffrey Wansell for his biography of Rattigan, op. cit.

7   *Daily Telegraph*, 1 June 1938, and *Daily Express*, 3 August 1938.

8   Arthur Marshall, *New Statesman*, 9 December 1977.

9   *French Without Tears* clocked up its 1,000th performance at the Piccadilly Theatre on 3 April 1939.

10   Just how serious the *affaire* with Morgan was at this stage is hard to gauge. Osborn's own recollections appear contradictory.

11   Rattigan to Kenneth Tynan, *Evening Standard*, 1 July 1953.

12   Tony Goldschmidt's sister.

13   There is some dispute about whether Rattigan actually tried to enlist in the services immediately after the outbreak of war. But when I talked to Tony Goldschmidt's sister Lady Kaldor in 1978, she was in no doubt that Rattigan and Goldschmidt both tried to join up in the first few days of the war but got a 'chilling reception' when they did so. But when virtually all fighting ceased after Hitler had completed the subjection of Poland, they decided, like thousands of others, that this was 'just a phoney war'.

6

Per Ardua

There was a young man called Terry Rattigan;
Had one hit and then fell flat again;
Sat right down and then begat again;
Tireless Terry Rattigan.

Whoever put that verse about in the theatre in 1939 did not know the truth about the struggle Rattigan went through ever to write a play again. The impetus that produced *After the Dance* had occurred more than two years earlier and he had wrestled with the actual writing of the play for a year. Previously writing his plays had taken only a matter of weeks. Calling in Tony Goldschmidt to help with *Follow My Leader* was another indicator of Rattigan's loss of self-belief. Asked by a journalist in March 1938 why he was working with a collaborator, Rattigan had replied: 'If I hadn't I should have gone stark, staring mad...I brooded over the plot for so long that I completely forgot how to hatch...'[1] Since then he had written nothing original at all. There had been work adapting the two foreign plays and collaboration on the screenplay of *French Without Tears*. During the summer of 1939 he gave the impression to Michael Macowan, who was meeting him for the first time during the production of *After the Dance*, that he rather regretted becoming a playwright at all and felt that perhaps he should have concentrated harder on becoming an historian when he had the chance at Oxford. He was obsessively concerned that he had nothing on the stocks and repeatedly turned over possible historical themes. He rejected them all. By the autumn of 1939 he had still not managed to settle on a new play.

Rattigan became so desperate about his 'block' that he sought advice from a psychiatrist, Dr Keith Newman of Oxford City and County Hospital. Newman was a strange figure, well known around Oxford during Rattigan's time there. From an Austrian background, he had settled in Oxford after the *Anschluss* in 1938, renting a house from Wadham College. With blue eyes and the remnants of fair-to-gingerish hair, he had always seemed to enjoy exercising his influence over the young men he met. Once someone had fallen under his mesmeric attention, the person could find it extremely difficult ever to get free. More than one person who suffered under Newman's spell suspects that, having discovered that Rattigan was frightened that he had writer's block, Newman encouraged his belief in the block so as to increase his own influence over him. Be that as it may, Newman advised Rattigan that the best way to cure his block was to get into the RAF and see some active service.

As Rattigan became involved with Newman, so did others around him – Peter Osborn, Tony Goldschmidt and Anthony Asquith. Osborn was especially vulnerable to Newman's Svengali-like influence. Already beset by feelings of guilt and 'unworthiness' as a result of his homosexuality, Osborn had found out about Rattigan's affair with Ken Morgan and was consumed with jealousy. He contemplated suicide and fantasized about murdering Rattigan and then killing himself. It is hard to tell why Goldschmidt should have submitted himself to sessions with Newman. However, Anthony Asquith, like Rattigan and Osborn, was a person full of unspoken and unresolved tensions. Asquith and Rattigan had met during the filming of *French Without Tears* and had become very close friends. Asquith was the youngest son of Herbert Asquith, the Prime Minister at the time of Rattigan's birth. By 1940 Asquith was one of the highest paid film directors in Britain. Initially, Rattigan had been very much in awe of him. They met for the first time at a dinner party, but by the end of the evening Asquith's boundless enthusiasm over *French Without Tears*, and his evident enthusiasm for Rattigan, had broken the ice. Rattigan recalled: 'Frankly at that moment I more or less fell for him – fell for his personality, fell for his charm, fell for his enthusiasm and for his eagerness, for his way of life.' Asquith was nine years older than Rattigan, but they found they had many things in common. Asquith had broken with family tradition to enter the film industry. Since his youth he had loved films with the same single-minded enthusiasm Rattigan had for the theatre. , His financial affairs were chaotic, out of carelessness rather than deliberate extravagance, and like Rattigan he had to have an accountant to keep them in order. In total contrast to Rattigan, he cared little about his appearance or his creature comforts. In 1939 Asquith had started to drink heavily. He feared that he, like others in his family, was an alcoholic.[2]

When Rattigan began work with Asquith on *French Without Tears*, he found his first impressions confirmed. 'Working with Puffin [Asquith's nickname] was an absolute joy because instantly we discovered we had a lot of private jokes...those weeks of my introduction into films were weeks of giggling and laughing, and at the same time weeks of rewriting a not very good film script, which however turned out to be a good one; mostly through Puffin's inspiration.'[3] The film was not completed until after the war had begun, by which time the government had ordered the closure of all the cinemas for fear of bombing. When Asquith heard about this he persuaded his mother, the widow of the former Liberal Prime Minister, to arrange a meeting for him with the relevant cabinet ministers and representatives of the film unions. The government decision was reversed. *French Without Tears* was released during the first months of the war and played to large audiences.

After the completion of the film Rattigan and Asquith continued to spend a lot of time together. Between September 1939 and the summer of 1940 it was his film work with Asquith that kept Rattigan financially and creatively alive. However, it was Asquith who was having all the ideas. Rattigan seemed to lack creative inspiration – a symptom of his 'block'. Towards the end of 1939 Asquith had suggested writing an original film script about a ballet company stranded by the outbreak of war – based on what had happened to the Sadler's Wells Company while playing in Rotterdam. Rattigan had poured cold water on the idea. Then in 1940 Asquith persuaded Rattigan to work with Anatole de Grunwald on the script of a film he was making of Esther McCracken's stage success, *Quiet Wedding*. The film was a chore to all three of them but they got through the work on giggles and private jokes. They worked together in a room with a shorthand typist who took down everything they said and typed it up for the producer, Paul Soskin. If they were not careful, pages such as this reached him: 'Dallas enters left. Sits down. Camera comes into closer shot... then into close-up. Oh God, why have we to do this bloody script for this man Soskin?'[4]

With the coming of the war, the Lord Chamberlain's objections to *Follow My Leader* were no longer valid. The play was tried out in Cardiff in the week before Christmas, with Reginald Beckwith as the plumber-dictator, Walter Hudd and Francis L. Sullivan as the political rivals who put him in power, and Marcus Brown as the British Ambassador. Rattigan had approached Harold French about directing it, but he had turned it down, telling him it was rubbish and warning that this was the wrong moment for this kind of skit. Rattigan took French's reaction badly, and something of a rift developed between them. One of the cast stepped in as director. Rattigan's co-author was billed on the posters and in the programme as Anthony Maurice, the appropriately English-sounding nom de plume adopted by Anthony Goldschmidt. Less noticed, except by those closest to Rattigan such as Peter Osborn, was the actor playing the minor part of Paul – Kenneth Morgan.

The production transferred to London immediately, opening on 16 January 1940 at the Apollo. It was a bitterly cold, snowy night. Although the audience laughed enthusiastically, there was no real spirit to the evening. The bite had gone out of the comedy. What might have seemed pointed at the time of Munich in 1938 now appeared obvious and too easy. It must have been galling for Rattigan to read the notice in *The Times* next morning which began, 'The very ease with which dictators may be ridiculed on a democratic stage constitutes a difficulty for the dramatist. How can he hope to fantasticate the fantastic?' The reviewer chose not to reflect on the fact that this 'comic strip' had not been allowed on London's democratic stage in 1938, when it might have had more point and even done some good. Even so, *The Times* critic did concede that the scene where the British Ambassador, after being blown up in his embassy, appears in clothes that are torn and dusty but still correct, to draw the Foreign Minister's attention to 'the irregularity', was brilliant farce. The *Manchester Guardian*, which had not thought much of Rattigan's previous plays, called *Follow My Leader* 'thrice as witty as the same author's *French Without Tears*'. But events had overtaken the play. *Follow My Leader* ran for only eleven days.

Something of Rattigan's bitterness over the fact that, even after the success of *French Without Tears*, none of his plays had been put into production immediately after he wrote them showed through in a talk he gave at about this time to a gathering of aspiring writers.

It would be as well, when submitting your plays to managers, to remember three things. First, that all managers have the strongest possible aversion to putting on any play of any sort at any time at any theatre. Secondly, that though most managers are able to read, they are not able to read very fast and have, I fancy, to spell out the longer words with their index fingers. This results in a delay of from three to six months between submission of manuscript and its rejection. Thirdly, that no manager can possibly be expected to finger his way past page three or four of your manuscript if you haven't already made it clear that your play has fulfilled the following necessary qualifications – to wit: a single set: a maximum of eight characters: a happy ending: and a part for one of London's more elderly comediennes.

(Sixty years on little has changed, except that today's playwright will remark at the generosity of the maximum number of permitted characters.)[5]

But Rattigan's personal problems were about to be overtaken

by outside events. On 9 April 1940, Hitler attacked Denmark and Norway. Rattigan, like everyone else, was stunned. He acted on Dr Newman's advice and applied to join the RAF. He had heard that the RAF needed officer air-gunners, but Hitler's attack in the west had produced a new rush of volunteers and again Rattigan nearly didn't get in. The interview was going badly until he mentioned that he had written *French Without Tears*. One of the interviewing officers had heard of it and the selection board decided to take a chance. They assured him that he could always write for camp concerts in his spare time.[6]

Rattigan packed up his flat and sent his valuable papers to his mother for safe keeping. With memories of what happened to the young men who had fought in the First World War and with this one going badly, Rattigan, in common with the thousands of other young men who rushed to the colours in April and May 1940, expected to die. Usually so discreet, over the coming months Rattigan's sexual life seemed to grow more abandoned. On 6 May, the eve of the House of Commons debate that would bring Chamberlain down and make Churchill Prime Minister, Rattigan called in at a smart rendezvous for homosexuals off the Haymarket, a club named Le Boeuf-sur-le-Toit. Among the throng that night were Ivor Novello and a small party celebrating the commission as a second lieutenant in the Royal Sussex Regiment of one of their young friends, John Montgomery. Montgomery recognized Rattigan and, on his own admission finding him attractive, chatted him up. He told Rattigan how much he had liked *First Episode*. That night Rattigan went back with Montgomery to the Mayfair Hotel where he was spending his leave. Next morning they had drinks at the Berkeley and lunch at the Café Royal. As so often with sexual encounters in wartime, Montgomery and Rattigan were not to meet again until the war was over.

During the interval between Rattigan's acceptance for the RAF and his call-up, *Grey Farm*, the play he had adapted with Hector Bolitho, opened in New York with a German refugee actor, Oscar Homolka, in the lead. The critics hated it, and it closed within days. Rattigan had one final gloomy meeting with

Hector Bolitho over lunch in a London restaurant, and paid the bill with their meagre royalties. It was June 1940.

As France fell and the Battle of Britain raged, Rattigan went through his basic training. It was a new world and there was a great deal to learn: basic theory and practice of radio, Morse, airmanship, gunnery. Rattigan was totally absorbed. Towards the end of his training he wrote to Dr Newman:

Since I last wrote to you I have sprouted a few tiny feathers on my uniformed wings...I have passed my tests 100 per cent which is not unprecedented, or anything like it...Such exercises aren't at all difficult. What is difficult is to do correctly all the hundred little things connected with the whole business – to forget none of them or, if one does (and one nearly always does) forget one, to be able to find the fault and not to panic. Which sounds like Kipling's 'If', I'm afraid, but to a person like myself, always prone to intense panic and by no means the cool-headed unimaginative type, it was a triumph to find I had managed to stumble through all the tests while other worthier people were coming down from the skies in tears of desperation... The concentration is so enormous that from the moment one fell into the plane till the moment one jumped out and leant nonchalantly against the plane in the hope that someone on the road would think one was a fighter pilot, one was utterly and completely oblivious of one's surroundings and conscious only of that infuriating medley of knobs and dials before one's face. However I become a bore on the subject and indeed think and talk of little else. Forgive me...[7]

Basic training, initial aircrew training and officer training kept Rattigan busy until the end of February 1941. Then he spent a month at the RAF's No.1 Signals School, logging up more than twenty flying hours mastering basic signals. The importance to Rattigan of his time in the RAF, particularly the first two years while he was most involved in his training and operational flying, can be gauged by the fact that he chose to preserve so many of his flying log-books and exercise notebooks from that time. The letter to Newman quoted above was written while he was on the basic signals course. He also wrote to his father, describing his sense of achievement and the fascination of being a wireless operator. In the letter to his father, he mentions that Soskin (the producer of *Quiet Wedding*) has asked for him to be released to work on a new film with Asquith, but doubts if the Air Ministry will agree. Once he had completed his signals course, passing seventh in a class of forty-one, he was posted on to Manby in Lincolnshire for three weeks, and another forty-four hours of air-gunnery exercises in Wellingtons and Battles. On 18 May 1941, Pilot Officer T. M. Rattigan qualified as an air-gunner. After a short period of leave, during which he worked with Asquith on a film script (producing suitably morale-boosting films was regarded by the authorities as an important contribution to the war effort),[8] Rattigan was posted to his first operational station at Invergordon, on the Cromarty Firth in north-east Scotland, as a member of the crew of a Catalina. It was July 1941, exactly two weeks after Hitler attacked Russia.

That summer the Battle of the Atlantic reached its first peak. There was an urgent need for trained crews to man the flying-boats of Coastal Command (an arm of the RAF which, to the chagrin of the men in the Air Ministry, had been placed under the operational command of the Navy). Britain was losing hundreds of thousands of tons of merchant ships each month to German U-boats and was in danger of being starved into defeat. Had Rattigan been posted to Bomber Command, as his superiors at the Air Ministry might have wished, his chances of surviving the war might have been no better than those of young infantry officers of his parents' generation, posted to the Western Front in the First World War. As a pilot officer air-gunner wireless-operator in Coastal Command, Rattigan's duties entailed long sorties of twelve to eighteen hours over the North Sea and the Atlantic searching for German submarines. It was not immediately dangerous in the way people imagine war in the air to be, but called for enormous stamina and concentration. For the duration of the flight the whole crew was called upon to maintain the highest level of observation. The smallest lapse of concentration meant not only the possibility of missing an enemy submarine or surface ship – indistinct grey blobs on a grey sea – it could bring about their own destruction. Marauding long-distance enemy planes patrolled much of the ocean, waiting to pounce on any unwary RAF aircraft. The danger was at its greatest when the crew were returning to base after a long mission and were tired and inattentive. Responsibility for the plane's communications and the level of the crew's awareness fell particularly on Rattigan's shoulders as an officer air-gunner.

His new companions were a tough and varied bunch, mostly very different from people he was used to. Most had never encountered a writer before and at first did not know quite what to make of him. They found Rattigan a friendly man who was every bit as tough as they were, and he soon became extremely popular. One officer he served with, unlike many of the others, had an interest in the theatre and was well aware of Rattigan's considerable reputation; he described the quality of Rattigan's relationships in the RAF:

He and I both liked the theatre, we both liked music. This seemed to bring us together and I felt that I had a very special relationship with him. He made one feel bigger and better, because of his friendship, and he had the same effect on the other people because of his friendship with them. When I first noticed that he was getting on well with other people I was a bit annoyed, I thought I was the only special one. But I was quite wrong. There were thirty-two of us all in the same boat, all loving Terry very much.

Later, when Rattigan was promoted to the rank of flight lieutenant, he became the gunnery officer with 422 Squadron. This meant that on top of flying normal missions, he was responsible for maintaining the efficiency of both the guns and the gunners. He had to devise training programmes and see that each gunner fired the necessary number of training rounds each month. He would take his place in each crew in turn and go out with them on a long patrol of perhaps twenty hours, putting them through exercises in gunnery and observation. This was a particularly tough squadron, made up of Canadians, South Africans and Rhodesians. The officer quoted earlier said of Rattigan at that time: 'He was as tough as anybody else, but he was both a gentleman and a gentle person. He never hurt anybody, never said anything at all damaging. He would criticize and people would improve their performances because of what he had said, but he never criticized anybody for the sake of criticism and never aimed to hurt.'[9]

But back to 1941. In November, now a qualified air-gunnery Leader, Rattigan was ordered to proceed to Calshot on the Solent to join No. 95 Squadron to serve in sturdy but slow four-engined Sunderland flying boats. Within days of arriving at Calshot, Rattigan met up again with Peter Osborn, who had just entered the Royal Navy as an ordinary seaman. To mark his joining up, Rattigan presented Osborn with a ring which he wanted him to wear throughout his war service. In defiance of King's Regulations they went for 'a run ashore' together into bomb-ravaged Southampton. With Osborn, Rattigan could allow himself to indulge a side of his personality which was firmly not on show with his RAF colleagues.

> Terry...suggested that we should look in on a particularly notorious public convenience in one of the parks there. This acrid-smelling, blacked-out loo was fairly pullulating with activity, which had the strongest sense of excitement and danger, and an acceptable anonymity. We were men, threatened with extinction, pulsing hard with life, and prepared to spend it willingly, libidinously and with glorious bravado.[10]

By November 1941 Dr Newman's prescription had worked. Both the impulse to write and the uninhibited flow of dialogue returned unimpaired. His total absorption in his new occupation had slackened. There were long intervals of boredom between missions; days or even weeks of sitting about in Nissen huts waiting for the weather, for engines to be fixed, for replacement aircraft to arrive. War for Rattigan, as for so many others, was indeed long periods of boredom and inactivity interspersed with brief intervals of fear. Rattigan found he wanted to write a play about the RAF and his companions, about the war and how it was affecting them and their loved ones.

Grounded for eight days at Calshot by bad weather while waiting to fly out to join a Sunderland crew in Freetown, West Africa, Rattigan got on with putting down the first draft of his new play in a hard-covered exercise book. By 23 November, when the weather improved enough for his Sunderland to take off for Gibraltar on the first leg of the journey to Freetown, he had completed most of the first act. Over the Bay of Biscay, Rattigan's Sunderland was pounced on by a German fighter.[11] Rattigan described what happened after he had spotted the enemy plane:

> ... with about 100 mph more speed than us, pooping off with its cannon from a fairly safe range (we only have machine guns) and only coming in range as it broke away after each of its attacks – five in all – we of course pooped off everything we'd got at it, but without apparent effect. I should love to tell you it disappeared with smoke pouring from its engines, but in fact it did nothing of the sort. Having evidently expended all its ammunition, it pissed off for home flying a perfectly straight course.

The damage inflicted on Rattigan's Sunderland amounted to nothing worse than four shots in the tail – 'rather near me incidentally' – and they reached Gibraltar safely. Repairs in Gibraltar delayed them a further three days and Rattigan pressed on with his play. By 6.30 p.m. on 26 November, when they took off for Freetown, Act One was complete.

It was a fifteen-hour trip, the extreme limit of the Sunderland's range. Eight hours out one of the plane's four engines spluttered and died, appearing to be in acute danger of blowing up. There was no turning back and it looked as if they would have to ditch in the sea off Spanish Morocco. That would mean being interned for the rest of the war. But the sea swell was too great for the flying boat to land '... so there was nothing for it but to go on on three engines, without enough petrol and apparently no chance of getting there'.

Calculating the amount of fuel the aircraft had left, the captain decided to fly on and try to ditch near enough to the Gambian coast to get picked up by Allied Forces there. The plane had to be lightened as much as possible. It was Rattigan's job to supervise this. He ordered that everyone's luggage and personal possessions were to be thrown overboard. Even the frames of photographs of the men's girlfriends had to go. All the loose equipment was wrenched off the aircraft and an axe was taken to the stubborn parts. Just as Rattigan's kitbag was poised to go over the side, he remembered the hard-backed exercise book with the first act of his play in it. He called for the kitbag to come back. Watched with great suspicion by the rest of the crew, he opened it and took out the exercise book. He ripped the covers off and put them back into the kitbag; then, showing the others what they were, he stuffed the loose pages into his pocket. The plane flew on uneasily. 'Unexpectedly a beautiful godsend 30 mph tailwind suddenly sprang up and blew us into Bathurst, Gambia, 8 hours later, with enough petrol for 10 minutes more flying.'

Rattigan and the crew were eight days in Bathurst, waiting for a replacement engine, repairs and air testing. Rattigan pressed on with the second act of his play. During that second act the young pilot at the centre of the story, Teddy, describes the reactions of the crew and his own feeling of fear after a Messerschmitt has put a canon shell in the tail of their plane:

'You don't know what it's like to feel frightened. You get a beastly, bitter taste in the mouth, and your tongue goes dry and you feel sick, and all the time you're saying: This isn't happening – I'll wake up. But you know you won't wake up. You know it is happening, and the sea's below you, and you're responsible for the lives of six people. And you have to pretend you're not afraid, that's what's so awful. Oh, God, I was afraid tonight. When we took off and saw that kite on fire, I didn't think: There are friends of mine in that. I thought [slowly]: That might happen to us. Not very – pretty, is it?[12]

Finally, on 5 December they flew the last, uneventful, leg of their journey to Freetown. On arrival Rattigan was assigned to a crew as a wireless-operator air-gunner and began a gruelling schedule of anti-submarine patrols and convoy-escort duties – 'not quite as cissy as Sunderland trips are popularly supposed to be'. He was now desperate to finish his new play. In the humidity of Freetown this was no easy task. There was nowhere to work in private. Since the officers were crowded four to a bedroom, he sat out on the veranda of the officers' mess and wrote there. This was open to everybody and he felt he was making rather an exhibition of himself, but there seemed no alternative. 'It was a veranda of a former school with monkeys clambering about and everybody drinking gins and tonics going spectacularly to pieces in the White Man's Grave – all of them looking over my shoulder while I wrote the thing,' he recalled. The members of Rattigan's new Sunderland crew realized who he was when a group of local nurses attached to the base began rehearsing a very amateur production of *French Without Tears*. But that was no inhibition to other officers in the mess who looked over his shoulder as he wrote his new play. ' "I say, Rattigan, that's not a very good line, is it?" – "Well, I think it's all right, sir." – "Well, if you think it's all right, Rattigan, keep it, by all means." – "No, sir, I'll take it out if you think..." ' [13]

On Christmas Eve he was able to write to his parents enclosing two copies of the play and asking them to 'stick pins' in his agent's behind at frequent intervals about getting it put on as soon as possible. 'The play's appeal, if any, is immediate.' He had also sent a copy of the play back to his agent with another officer who was flying home on leave. But as he could not risk parting with his only copy, and since he could not get the use of a typewriter, he had had to copy the fractured manuscript in longhand into new exercise books.

Back in London, two managements and a film company turned it down – saying the public did not want to see war plays – before H. M. Tennent Ltd, the company that had staged *George and Margaret*, agreed to produce it. After some discussion Rattigan gave his play the title *Flare Path*, the name given to the lines of flares which lit the runway at night for returning aircraft. When the play was published he dedicated it to Keith Newman. [14]

In the summer of 1942 Rattigan, now promoted to Flying Officer, was posted back to Britain and the Air Ministry made it fairly easy for him to be in London between flying duties to attend casting sessions and rehearsals; they hoped the play would be a good piece of public relations for them. Anthony Asquith, who had not previously directed in the theatre, was to direct, and casting began in May 1942. A young actor was needed to play the hero, an RAF bomber pilot. Eric Portman suggested a nineteen-year-old actor who had not yet been called up, Jack Watling. He was a working-class lad, still green and quite unused to people from privileged backgrounds like Asquith and Rattigan. He was summoned to meet them one evening in the cocktail bar at the Savoy. They did not tell him that there would be a third member of the party scrutinizing him – the psychiatrist Dr Newman.

When the overawed Watling arrived at the Savoy, the bar was already fairly full. Rattigan and Asquith gave him a script and asked him to study it for a few moments. Then they asked him to read for them: 'Read quietly, old boy, there are other people about.' After he had read a page or two they said, 'OK, you've got the part. Dr Newman will be directing you.' It was not until rehearsals got under way that Watling discovered the meaning of this last remark. Asquith, of course, was directing the play, but Newman gave Watling special advice and took a close interest in him. Slowly the impressionable young actor fell under the domination of Newman until, after a year or two, he seemed to have almost no will of his own. Watling's was an extreme case, but Newman exerted a similar Svengali-like influence in varying degrees over Asquith, Rattigan and Tony Goldschmidt.

Flare Path was to tour for four weeks before coming in to the West End. Martin Walker, the actor whose career Rattigan had intervened to save during *After the Dance*, had been cast in one of the leading parts, that of Peter Kyle, a down-on-his-luck Hollywood film star who has avoided being called up to fight in the war. Phyllis Calvert played the married woman he is in love with. The production, by H. M. Tennent Ltd, was the first the company had staged since Hugh 'Binkie' Beaumont had become the firm's sole boss, so a lot was riding on its success. Before going out on tour the production was given a final run through at the Globe Theatre in London, the theatre where H. M. Tennent Ltd had its headquarters. Many of the office staff sneaked down into the theatre to watch. Among a small group of friends who had been invited to the run through by Beaumont was Noël Coward. Immediately the curtain fell on the run through Coward went over to Rattigan and berated him. He accused him of ruining his play by adding a sentimental ending in which a Polish pilot, missing on a bombing raid, is allowed 'to return from the dead to provide a happy ending'. Upset, Rattigan scuttled around the auditorium asking others what they thought. Kitty Black, then a mere office secretary (but later to become a successful literary agent and translator of plays), responded by asking Rattigan 'You've written a comedy, haven't you?' 'Of course.' 'Then you can't possibly kill off a leading character and turn it into a tragedy.'

Rattigan may have been reassured, but Beaumont remained concerned. After the dress rehearsal, held in Oxford where the play was to open its pre-London tour, Beaumont told Rattigan that he was unhappy with the happy ending. It was false and sentimental. Reminding him of what Coward had said, he added silkily, 'I have an instinct about these things, Terry dear, and it's seldom wrong. The public will always know if you're not truthful with them.' In fact, Rattigan had long had doubts about the ending himself. In his letter to his parents when he sent the original manuscript back to England he had admitted that the play might be regarded as sentimental. But, he had told them, 'not too much so for my taste'. Even if the ending was phoney, it should, he believed, be commercial. However, he kept his misgivings to himself. 'But happy endings do sometimes happen in real life,' he told Beaumont, 'and that's the sort of truth I'm after.'[15] Rattigan got his way. It was the start of a long, sometimes stormy, usually profitable but ultimately, at least as regards the enduring quality of Rattigan's work, questionable professional relationship.

Flare Path opened at the Apollo Theatre in London on 13 August 1942. Rattigan attended in uniform and hovered nervously at the back of the stalls with Anthony Asquith. It was a 'top brass' night as far as the RAF were concerned. Looking back on that evening, Rattigan remembered spending most of it 'standing rigidly to attention, while Air Marshal after Air Marshal approached the humble Flying Officer to tell him how his play should really have been written!' It was an emotional evening rather than a glamorous one. A number of people in the audience, especially the wives of airmen, were moved to tears which they did not try to conceal. Just two pages before the final curtain, Rattigan turned to Asquith and whispered, 'I think we've brought it off.' It was tempting fate. At that moment the curtain descended to halfway and stuck there. After a moment which seemed like an age, it slowly rose again and the audience broke into applause. The cast completed the play and the final curtain came down. It was the warmest reception Rattigan had received from a first-night audience since *French Without Tears*. Air Chief Marshal Sir Charles Portal, the Chief of the Air Staff, sent a message asking Flying Officer Rattigan to his box. He wished to be the first to congratulate him.

More important to Rattigan than the praise or blame of air marshals was the reaction of the critics. 'At long last I found myself commended, if not exactly as a professional playwright, at least as a promising apprentice who had definitely begun to learn the rudiments of his job.'[16] In the *Observer*, Ivor Brown claimed that Rattigan had made an able compromise between the routine war comedy and the grimmer reality of battlefield tragedies like *Journey's End*. He concluded: 'Altogether Mr Rattigan has scored his double: his play is guaranteed alternately to tickle all ribs and to raise a few lumps in the larynx.' James Agate, in a long article in which he quoted Byron and Milton and invoked Shakespeare, Schiller, Sherriff and Euripides, questioned whether it was morally permissible for a playwright to make capital out of the present storm and stress when there might be wives and sweethearts in the audience whose RAF menfolk were actually undergoing the tragedies depicted on stage. He concluded by saying that the play was better than simply good entertainment, but too sentimental to bear comparison with what Ibsen might have done with the same material. In an extremely perceptive review in the *New Statesman*, Roger Manvell said that 'the play was immensely effective alike in comedy and pathos', but accused Rattigan of not having the courage to give it the tragic ending that his story so clearly called for: 'This seems to me a wanton sacrifice to the wishes of the audience.' It was an accusation to be levelled at Rattigan with cumulatively deadly effect as one popular success succeeded another.

Flare Path differs from Rattigan's previous plays in that the plot is not built up organically out of an accumulation of small incidents and scenes between an ensemble of characters but depends on a central outside event – a night bomber raid on Germany. The action is confined to the residents' lounge of a hotel close to an RAF bomber base in Lincolnshire. It takes place over one night and the following morning as the womenfolk wait anxiously to see if their aircrew husbands will return safely from the bombing raid. One husband, a Polish count married to an English barmaid, Doris, seems to have been killed and is only restored to his stoical wife moments before the fall of the final curtain. News of his safe 'ditching' and rescue does not arrive until after Doris has had the contents of a letter left by him, to be opened 'only in the event of something happening' to him, read to her. It is only through this letter that she discovers the true extent of his feelings for her – love he has been unable to express because of the language barrier between them.

Once again, even in the guise of a war play, Rattigan is pursuing his familiar motifs. The main suspense of the play hinges as much on a central triangle situation, between a young bomber pilot, his actress wife and an ageing Hollywood star, as on the outcome of the off-stage bomber raid. The Hollywood star, Peter, has come to the hotel to try to reclaim the pilot's wife, Patricia, with whom he had an affair before she married. Peter now needs Patricia. His studio has decided to drop him. Since the war he has felt cut off. He can talk glibly about the fight for democracy, freedom and the rights of man, but they don't really mean anything to him. The rest of the world has turned its back on him and his pre-war world. Patricia has secretly continued to love Peter. Her boyish, extrovert, RAF-slang-talking husband Teddy treats her as a possession to show off, but is unable to satisfy her real emotional needs. At first it seems that she will return to Peter. However, during the course of the play Patricia discovers the extent of Teddy's vulnerability and need for her. After returning from the raid which, as one character says, has been 'a proper muck up from beginning to end', Teddy breaks down, revealing to his wife, the only person in the world he can tell, all his accumulated strain, fatigue and fear. As a result Patricia realizes that she cannot leave Teddy and she confronts Peter:

> ... I used to think that our private happiness was something far too important to be affected by outside things like war or marriage vows ... Peter, beside what's happening out there, it's just tiny and rather cheap – I'm afraid. I don't want to believe that, I'm an awful coward. It may be just my bad luck, but I've suddenly found that, I'm in that battle, and I can't –
> PETER Desert?
> PATRICIA Yes, desert.

Flare Path was the first play of Rattigan's of which almost all the critics remarked specifically on the excellence of his theatrical technique. His reputation as the country's leading theatrical craftsman was established. Although it is ostensibly a war play, *Flare Path* has Rattigan's trademarks stamped all over it. Doris and Patricia both have husbands who have been unable to find words to express their feelings. They only discover how much they are loved when it is almost too late, and in a sense by accident. The critics' major quarrel with the play was, as Beaumont and Coward had warned, the false happy ending which restored the count to his wife just in time for the final curtain. Rattigan can be accused of sacrificing a dramatically honest ending to the war effort, yet this ending is consistent with his other work. Patricia has chosen reason over instinct by sticking with Teddy, but she has by no means solved all her problems. James Agate told Rattigan that he had taken the easy way out by having Patricia opt for Teddy and duty, and had thereby avoided the need to examine the consequences of her decision. He suggested that Ibsen would have started his play two years after the fall of Rattigan's curtain and would have shown Patricia's struggle between the torture of physical hunger and spiritual thirst when the moral self-righteousness of her decision to do her duty had faded. Agate was not the only critic at the time to complain that the central love story did not carry conviction or live up to the theme of the interaction between the war and personal relationships. The play's major weakness lies in Rattigan's failure to explore Peter's character or Patricia's feelings about him. He gives enough to leave the audience in suspense but no more, thus ultimately undermining the play's credibility.

Another fault, to modern eyes, is the one-dimensional staginess of the working-class characters, particularly the sergeant air-gunner, Dusty Miller, and his wife Maudie. It was a weakness which Rattigan never overcame, and on the whole he avoided working-class characters, except for butlers and servants whom he had observed often enough to do well in a conventional way. The fact that this failure of characterization went unremarked at the time was partly due to the excellent performances of Kathleen Harrison and Leslie Dwyer, but more particularly to the fact that in such stagy characters Rattigan was only following the convention of the period which still depicted the working class on the stage as 'comic-cuts'.

The real achievement of *Flare Path*, however, was that it caught precisely the public mood of the moment. It is the major reason for Rattigan's amazing popular success, and arguably his chief claim to enduring reputation, that he managed to mirror and focus the public and private concerns of a vast British audience over a period of almost twenty years. This audience extended beyond middle-class theatregoers to millions of cinemagoers in every part of the English-speaking world and from every stratum of society. Rattigan gives Maudie a speech in Act Two about her husband in which he plucked a string which harmonized perfectly with public sentiment:

Mind you, I'm not saying I like him being a gunner; it's not good for him in those turret things. They're wickedly cold. He told me so himself – and he gets horrible backaches. He used to get them when he was working on the buses. Besides it's no good saying they always get back from these raids, because they don't – not all of them. Then I'm not saying I liked being bombed out and going to live in St Albans with Dave's Aunt Ella, who I've never got on with and never will – and working at the Snowflake – but what I say is, there's a war on and things have got to be a bit different, and we've just got to get used to it, that's all.

Reading that today, one cannot miss the patronizing flavour, but the speech worked perfectly in a London theatre where the air-raid siren was likely to go at any minute and the audience was made up of people who were either in the forces themselves or had menfolk who were.

Rattigan and Asquith reworked much of *Flare Path* about two years later in their film *The Way to the Stars*. They achieved an even greater degree of universal appeal and succeeded at the same time in making a memorable film. It was as though they had heeded the criticism levelled at *Flare Path*. The film was also set on the ground in and around an airfield and dealt with airmen and those who wait for their return. But this time, although there were love episodes, inequality of passion and emotion that went unspoken or was suppressed because of the exigencies of war, the unconvincing and inappropriate triangle story was avoided. The problem of matching a need for a characteristically British style of understatement with the need for dialogue which rose above the confines of naturalism was brilliantly solved by the introduction of John Pudney's poem, 'For Johnny'. When an officer breaks the news of a brother officer's death in action to his wife, he brings not a letter but a poem he has found among his dead comrade's personal effects.

It was a weakness in Rattigan as a dramatist that he was unable to write anything other than naturalistic dialogue, no matter how skilful. It was a failure that came to count against him more and more as the demand grew for something beyond vernacular speech to be heard in the theatre.

Flare Path was in every sense a turning point for Rattigan. It marked not only the end of his block as a writer, it was also the point at which he finally turned his back on any lingering temptation to be in any sense a writer of protest. His commitment to the socialist and pacifist views of his Oxford contemporaries was always more liberal than radical, but from now on his voice would become more and more the voice of acceptable dissent, raising only those questions that even those who dictated what was politically or artistically acceptable might raise.

None of this, however, should detract from the power and effectiveness of *Flare Path* in its day. A statement by an officer in the same squadron as Rattigan is eloquent testimony to its impact:

> I felt that it was too true. Something in me, something in all of us who had flown, was exposed. He knew us better than we knew ourselves and he perhaps expressed thoughts and words for us which we had just fumbled around. I felt, he's exposing us. He's come into our lives, he's taken our secrets and is now putting them out in public. He shouldn't do this. Then I realized that he was not exploiting us, he was talking about us, he was demonstrating us, our lives and the way we worked in war. He was quite right to do this. But at the time it was something of a shock to realize that he had seen so deeply into us.

Notes

1   *Sunday Referee,* 8 March 1938.
2   There is some dispute as to whether it was Rattigan who introduced Asquith to Newman or Asquith who introduced Rattigan. Rattigan certainly seems to have known Newman since his time at Oxford, where Newman was already a well known figure. However, Newman made a point of knowing as many of the leading personalities in society as possible, so it is probable that he had already met Asquith.
3   *Puffin Asquith: A Biography* by R. J. Minney, Leslie Frewin, London, 1973.
4   Ibid.
5   From an undated manuscript in the Rattigan Papers in the British Library titled *The Hazards of Playwriting.* Internal evidence in the text points to Rattigan writing it between the autumn of 1939 and summer of 1940. He may have given the talk in Oxford.
6   The selection board seem not to have heard of *Follow My Leader* or of Anthony Goldschmidt, as he did not get into the RAF and joined the army.

7   Quoted by K. O. Newman in *Mind, Sex and War – Blackouts, Fear of Air Raids and Propaganda*, Pelago, Oxford, 1941.

8   The film was called *Uncensored* and concerned a Belgian resistance group's heroic struggles to publish a clandestine newspaper. When it was eventually released, in 1942, it was a critical failure, but its redeeming feature was the performance of Peter Glenville, Rattigan's student-digs companion at Oxford, as a jealous lover who betrays the heroes to the Nazis. Rattigan also worked at about this time on another film, called *Day Will Dawn*, about Norwegian resistance fighters, with Harold French and Anatole de Grunwald. The fees from these films were a useful addition to Rattigan's meagre RAF pay. Among his expenses he now included supporting his parents in a large country house at Pepsal End outside Luton, which was a safe distance from the London Blitz. There were air-raids on London every night from September 1940 until late May 1941.

9   Roger Hunter interviewed by the author in 1977.

10 Peter Osborn, op. cit.

11 Rattigan recorded in his flying log-book that the German attacker was a Heinkel 115. However, other evidence in his log-book and descriptions he gave in the weeks immediately afterwards suggest that in fact the German fighter must have been a Heinkel 112V or a Focke-Wulf 190.

12 *Flare Path* in *The Collected Plays of Terence Rattigan*, Volume I, Hamish Hamilton, London, 1953.

13 Rattigan interviewed by Sheridan Morley for *Kaleidoscope*, BBC Radio 4, 4 July 1977. Rattigan described the incidents surrounding the writing of *Flare Path* a number of times over the years. In my account I have relied as far as possible on the descriptions Rattigan gave in the immediate aftermath of these incidents – his RAF log-book and a letter to his parents dated 24 December 1941.

14 Not only did Newman prove instrumental in guiding Rattigan on to sure ground as a writer, he also seems to have suggested the title Rattigan finally adopted for the play – *Flare Path*.

15 Recalled by Kitty Black in *Upper Circle: A Theatrical Chronicle*, Methuen, London, 1984 and in *Binkie Beaumont, Eminence Grise of the West End 1933–73* by Richard Huggett, Hodder & Stoughton, London, 1989.

16 Preface to *Collected Plays of Terence Rattigan*, Volume I, op. cit.

7

Ad Astra

Flare Path ran for 670 performances. For the first five months of the run Dr Keith Newman attended every single one. At the end of this marathon he published a book entitled *Two Hundred and Fifty Times I Saw a Play – or Authors, Actors and Audiences*.[1] It is a very strange book, which does not actually reveal which play it was that Newman had been watching. Newman's interest was in the creative process and the interaction between the play and the personalities of the author, actors and director, as well as the effect of different audiences on the play and its cast. Even though Newman expresses himself in language that sometimes appears to be deliberately obscure, he knew Rattigan very well by this time and what he says, as a trained psychiatrist, about the way in which his mind worked during the creation of *Flare Path* provides a key insight into Rattigan and into the relationship between his plays and events in his life. Newman tells us that through his own knowledge of Rattigan's personality he quickly became aware of a 'commissariat which provisions the characters and, different as they may be, makes them appear as belonging to one and the same family'.

Of Rattigan's play-making process he says:

Factual events and characters are, unconsciously, reduced to their elements and these particles, suspended in the air, create the very atmosphere the author must be susceptible to. Words and facts have disappeared and for a varying time his mind is filled with indefinite, yet strong, impressions and feelings. He has dissolved words and facts and has created a general atmosphere. The next step is the re-embodiment of both, still shapeless yet solid. They have become the author's personal property. Finally facts and characters are re-shaped into their original form and they emerge, though apparently unchanged, with a different quality. These three distinct processes I call dissolution, condensation and organisation.

Newman says that the author is then ready to produce a plot, and that from that point on, the conscious mind takes over the actual writing and application of stagecraft to the technical problems of making a theatrically effective play. He says also that the author seemed to have a skeleton audience within himself at the time of writing:

> The silent audience is not just the critical sense of the author, telling him what is technically right or wrong, or what is effective and what is not. The members of the silent audience represent the practical experience of the dramatist in life. They curb the idiosyncrasies which brought him into trouble before and they encourage those sides of his character from which he benefited in his social contacts.

He tells us that the author has to survive a conflict of high intelligence and a lowest common denominator of taste or reaction – a mass mind. The combination and conflict between these two produce drama and vitality. His common mind will produce rubbish, his intellect something lacking in life and excitement. Newman comments that Rattigan 'on the whole seems to enjoy himself most in occupations he does not excel in, while those of which he is a master find him rather bored'. The book is peppered with allusions to the dangers of success and the enjoyment of applause, which can turn the author from artist to hack businessman. He comments that too much looking at the box office during conception can cause the baby to be born with a squint. The book also gives some useful insights into the increasingly corrosive relationship between Rattigan and Newman.

Newman's sessions with Rattigan and Asquith continued through 1943. While Newman was closeted with one or the other, no one was allowed to disturb them, no matter who they were or how pressing their business. No one really knew what they were up to, and a great air of mystery surrounded their sessions. On Newman's death, the man who inherited his papers approached Rattigan and told him that he had found a number of pieces of paper in his handwriting. 'Oh, My God,' said Rattigan, 'destroy them. Whatever you do, don't let anyone see them!' By then Rattigan wished to forget the extent to which he had revealed his mind and working method to Newman. Rattigan was no different from other artists in not wanting to enquire too deeply into how his own creative process worked, or what triggered it off, for fear that self-consciousness might destroy it. Newman's interest in Rattigan and Asquith extended beyond the doctor–patient relationship and scientific enquiry into the creative process. He even persuaded them to form a canal company. (It never seems to have traded.)

In August 1942, immediately after *Flare Path* opened, Rattigan was posted to RAF Lough Erne in Northern Ireland. The war had reached a critical stage. The German advance in North Africa had at last been held but just one week after the opening night of *Flare Path* a British and Canadian force attempting a commando raid on the occupied French coast at Dieppe had been heavily defeated. The Russians, desperately trying to hold the Germans near Stalingrad, were pressing the British for more supplies of munitions and tanks. But German U-boats were still sinking dozens of British and American ships bringing supplies across the Atlantic and operating the convoys to Russia. Coastal Command's job of protecting the convoys and hunting U-boats was more vital than ever. Rattigan wrote to his parents telling them that the camp that he now found himself in was 'large, damp and Nissen-hutted. There is nowhere to go and nothing to do after working hours. To quote from a sergeant friend of mine, "We are fourteen miles from F– all."' Rattigan said he did not expect to get any leave for a long time and that he could tell his parents nothing about what he was doing as the censorship 'is even tighter than Freetown'. However, it is fair to surmise that he was again engaged on long-haul convoy escort and anti-U-boat patrols far out into the Atlantic and the North Sea. Even so he kept an eagle eye on the box-office returns for *Flare Path* back in London. As he excitedly told his parents they were 'better than *French Without Tears*'. He had already had offers for a production in New York and film offers – he had turned one for eight thousand pounds down and would 'discuss nothing under fifteen thousand pounds'. He had given his solicitors power of attorney to act for him.

In December, Rattigan sailed with his squadron for New York. They were going to pick up new aircraft – Catalina flying boats – from the Americans. At the start of the crossing, the entertainments officer on the troopship cornered Rattigan and said, 'I hear you write plays. Well, write me a short one for next Thursday would you? About twenty minutes?' Rattigan said no, he couldn't do that, and went to his squadron leader to complain. The squadron leader sympathized; nevertheless, Rattigan went away and wrote a frothy comedy thriller of exactly twenty minutes' duration, involving a house party and a butler who stole the silver, which was performed during the crossing by volunteers and was a tremendous success with the passengers.[2] During the crossing there was a storm and everyone was very sick – everyone except Rattigan. No matter what he may have felt like, he stalked about the ship, a picture of composed self-control. Finally, his squadron leader asked him, 'Terry, how do you manage to avoid this sea-sickness? Everybody else has got it.' Rattigan replied, 'Ah, I have a special arrangement with the management. They keep the ship still for me and someone else moves the scenery up and down.'

On arrival in New York, the squadron was billeted in a rather dowdy brown hotel until they moved on to pick up their new aircraft. But not Rattigan: *Flare Path* was about to be staged in New York, and as a Broadway author he was not going to stay in a cheap hotel. He moved himself into the Waldorf Astoria. From there he entertained his less fortunate RAF colleagues – at that time an RAF officer's pay compared with that of only an American rating. As well as standing them dinner in the evenings, he issued an invitation to them to watch him taking breakfast. For this he would put on a great act. Sitting in a silk dressing-gown, he would order an enormous tray of food to be wheeled in by uniformed waiters while he played the great man. When they had gone, everyone fell to and tucked in.

Flare Path opened in New York on 24 December 1942, with Alec Guinness making his first Broadway appearance as Teddy Graham. It was a flop. The *New York Times*, while praising the impeccable production, said the play seemed 'sentimental, slow and confused'. But Rattigan was not in New York for the first night. He had left the day before to fly in one of the new Catalinas back to Britain, via Bermuda to Prestwick. The leg from Bermuda to Prestwick, on Christmas Day 1942, turned out to be one of his worst experiences during the war. They passed through seven weather fronts and got hopelessly lost. Rattigan had lost his flying-boots in New York and was freezing cold and very frightened. After flying for more than twenty hours, they spotted the coast of northern Scotland in the first light of Boxing Day. They turned right and made their way down to Prestwick.

One of the first things Rattigan did when he finally got back to London was to check up on how *Flare Path* was doing at the Apollo. He sneaked up into the gallery to watch a performance. Unknown to him, Mrs Churchill had persuaded Winston to make one of his rare visits to the theatre that evening. Eleanor Roosevelt had seen the play on a visit to London a month or two earlier and had told Mrs Churchill that she must get her husband to see it. From his position at the back of the gallery, Rattigan could not see down into the stalls well enough to see who was in the audience and he was unaware of Churchill's presence. After the performance, Rattigan did not bother to go round and see the cast, and so when Churchill asked to be taken backstage to meet the actors, Rattigan was not among the people presented to him. Churchill told one of the actresses how moved he had been by the play. He said, 'It's a masterpiece of understatement,' adding with a smile, 'but we're rather good at that, aren't we?' The first

Rattigan heard of Churchill's visit was when a newspaper rang him for a reaction. He said, 'No one tells the author anything!'

More and more now, Rattigan was becoming a celebrity in battledress. The RAF had already given him leave to work on films such as *Uncensored* and in March 1943 he was seconded to work with a well-known American novelist and screenwriter, Richard Sherman, on a film dealing with an airfield during its transition from RAF to American Air Force use. The project had arisen out of Twentieth Century Fox's interest in *Flare Path* as a film. In January 1943, Fox had paid twenty thousand pounds for the rights and announced that Merle Oberon would play the leading female role. The Allied propaganda services (more correctly known as the Ministry of Information) also favoured the film. It was to be directed by William Wyler, who had made the tear-jerker *Mrs Miniver*, which had done a lot to promote support for Britain among American audiences in the days before the United States entered the war. As America started to step up its contribution to the war effort in Europe, and particularly to the bomber offensive against Germany, this new film was intended to promote harmonious relations between the British and the Americans. At the time there was considerable mutual resentment – Americans feeling that their boys had no business risking their lives in Britain in someone else's war, the British resenting the increasing number of American servicemen in Britain with money in their pockets to spend on local girls – a sentiment summed up in a popular joke of the time: *Question* What's the trouble with Americans? *Answer* They're over-paid, over-sexed and over here.

By 1943, Rattigan was spending so much time in London that he needed to re-establish a base there. Having moved his parents to a house in the country to escape the bombing, the flat in Stanhope Gardens was no longer available. Anyway Rattigan wanted something grander, more in keeping with his new-found status. For the moment he moved from place to place, three weeks in chambers borrowed from a friend in Albany, off Piccadilly, and a few weeks in a flat in Lower James Street. London itself was filling up not only with Americans, but with men in the uniforms of all the Allied countries – Australians, Canadians, South Africans, New Zealanders, Czechs, Poles and Frenchmen. While Rattigan was working on the grandiose Anglo-American film project, he had the idea for a stage comedy based on the petty national rivalries and broken hearts fostered by casual pick-ups made in London. The blackout, and the feeling of transience engendered in men on leave for a few days before returning to active service, led to an era of unprecedented sexual licence among both heterosexuals and homosexuals. In April 1943 Rattigan learned that his soul-mate and intellectual companion since Harrow (though emphatically not a lover) Tony Goldschmidt had been killed in action. The news hit Rattigan hard. As a result, a chance encounter a few months later must have had a particular poignancy. Rattigan picked up an army officer and they spent the weekend together at the Ritz. The army officer's name was Anthony Goldschmidt. Before the war he had been a friend of Kenneth Morgan. When the weekend was over Goldschmidt returned to his unit. Although never close friends the two men kept in touch for the rest of Rattigan's life.[3]

Ever since the success of *French Without Tears*, theatre managers and film producers had urged Rattigan to write a sequel, but Rattigan had shied away from the idea. To do so would represent a surrender to the label 'one-hit wonder'. But by 1943 Harold French had also suggested a wartime sequel to *French Without Tears*, and a film company had bought it. The idea centred round what would happen if an older, though not necessarily wiser, version of the man-hunting Diana from *French Without Tears* were now running English-language classes for Allied servicemen in wartime London. Rattigan and Anatole de Grunwald were drafted in to knock together a script. From Rattigan's point of view the only real attraction of such an idea was the fee.

Through the spring and summer of 1943, as work progressed on these film projects in the desultory way beloved of movie producers – spurts of urgent deadline chasing followed by periods of unexplained nothing – Rattigan had time to turn back to his own idea for a stage comedy set in wartime London. He had already made one false start and torn up the result in disgust (never a writer to waste his leftovers, he recycled discarded scraps from the aborted play into the film script). But sitting down again during a three-week break spent in borrowed rooms in Albany, he found the new comedy coming more easily than any play he had ever written. He set the play, called *While the Sun Shines*, in the Albany chambers where he was staying and dashed off the first draft in ten hectic days. He completed it a week later.[4]

He sent the draft to Hugh 'Binkie' Beaumont of H. M. Tennent. He was delighted. 'It's sheer Wodehouse mixed with Feydeau and Pinero and I love it. Your best yet, Terry dear.'[5] O'Brien, Linnit and Dunfee, who because they had invested in *Flare Path* had a contractual right to participate in producing the next Rattigan script, also loved it. So the two managements jointly accepted *While the Sun Shines* for immediate production. Although he had never directed a comedy before, 'Puffin' Asquith came in to direct and a brilliant veteran comedy actor, Ronald Squire, was hired for the older leading part. But where were they to find younger actors with enough experience and reputation to play the young Allied servicemen around whom Rattigan's plot revolved? Most of the obvious people were busy or away doing their bit in the war. The biggest problem of all was the main part – twenty-one year-old Bobby Harpenden. Rattigan had a bright idea, why not ask two of the stars who had been engaged to play in the film being made as a sequel to *French Without Tears* – Michael Wilding and Jane Baxter? She would be making her first West End comedy appearance since her success in *George and Margaret*, the play which had vied with *French Without Tears* as the comedy hit of the late 1930s. Jane Baxter liked the idea but Michael Wilding read the script and did not want to do it. He was too old. Rattigan phoned him and asked if they could meet for a drink. Half an hour later they met in the bar of the Ritz. Perhaps with more candour than tact, Rattigan told Wilding that he could not find anyone of the right age to play the part and with some misgivings Wilding allowed himself to be talked round.

An eighteen-year-old actress called Brenda Bruce was found to play the typist/tart-with-a-heart-of-gold part, Mabel Crum. She had just come to London from the Birmingham Repertory

Theatre, where she had played serious heroines. She was inexperienced at light comedy, and when the play opened on tour in October, Asquith and Binkie Beaumont were still very worried about her performance. Noël Coward, who had money in the production, attended a performance in Oxford and his opinion was sought about possible changes. The cast was lined up on the stage and Coward went down the line making ribald comments on each person's performance, imitating their mannerisms. Everyone else was laughing, but the young actress knew that the management were not very pleased with her, and dreaded what Coward might say. When he reached her, he said, 'And as for you, you're a very dim little actress.' Brenda Bruce burst into tears and through her sobs said, 'I know, I want to go back to Birmingham.' Binkie Beaumont said, 'Yes, well, I really think that if it hasn't improved at the end of the month that'll be it. It just doesn't work. It isn't right. You're much too sad.' Ronald Squire and Rattigan took pity on her, Squire coaching her every morning for the rest of the tour in his hotel room and Rattigan rewriting her scenes until they came right. When things went wrong Rattigan would say to her, 'It could be my fault, there must be a reason why you can't get it right.' Then he would go off and change a scene or the placing of a laugh line. Although he was an established author and she only a young actress in a subsidiary role, he never made her feel that she was putting him to any trouble. He devoted a lot of time to her, inventing word games to amuse her and break the tension when the company was on long train journeys, giggling, making jokes and generally helping to put her and everyone else at ease. When the month was up, Brenda Bruce was allowed to stay in the cast and when the play opened in London, she was one of the successes of the production. Understandably, Brenda Bruce fell for Rattigan, the kind, immensely successful and glamorous young man who always appeared in the theatre in immaculate flight lieutenant's uniform. 'He was quite fantastically good-looking. Really incredible.'[6] He took her out to dinner a number of times after the show and she hoped that a romance would develop. She was young and naïve; there was a feeling of constraint when they were alone together that she put down to her own inexperience. Both seemed shy, and slowly the meetings petered out. She never suspected that he was homosexual, and no one told her. Very few people, even in the theatre, knew.

Although the pre-London tour was drawing large and appreciative audiences – the production's costs were paid off in full even before the play reached the West End – as the London opening night approached more and more anxious midwives hovered around the production. Without Asquith being told, Harold French was asked to lend a discreet hand with the comedy to make up for Asquith's lack of experience. Keith Newman was also in regular attendance and it was he who came up with the perfect line to bring down the curtain with a big laugh on the first scene of Act Three after everyone else's ideas had been tried and failed.

While the Sun Shines opened in London on Christmas Eve 1943 at the Globe, next to the Apollo, where *Flare Path* was still playing to capacity houses. Since it was Christmas Eve, many theatres were closed and the first-night audience included many artists from other London shows. The anxieties of the pre-London tour were quickly forgotten as the evening turned into a tremendous success. It was Rattigan's most trouble-free first night to date. The reviews could hardly have been better. Although most said the play was an inconsequential piece of nonsense and some that the last scene was weak, all agreed that it was brilliantly funny. The *Manchester Guardian* began: 'There are at least nine reasons for justifying a visit to *While the Sun Shines*: the seven members of the cast who act with subtlety and polish; Mr Rattigan's light-hearted text, which has the inspired lucidity and economy of P. G. Wodehouse at his best; and Mr Anthony Asquith's production which has timing and authority.' Most astonishing was James Agate, in the *Sunday Times*, who began: 'About *An Ideal Husband* on its first production Mr Shaw wrote, "It is useless to describe a play which has no thesis: which is, in the purest integrity, a play and nothing less." And about its author: "In a certain sense, Mr Wilde is our only playwright. He plays with everything: with wit, with philosophy, with drama, with actors and audience, with the whole theatre." The same might be said today of Mr Rattigan, a playwright with the brains not to take himself seriously.' He continued: '. . . This piece is delightful, a little masterpiece of tingling impertinence.'

The play was to run for three years – 1,154 performances – making Rattigan the only author up to that time to have written two plays which ran for over 1,000 consecutive performances in the West End. He received more than twenty-one thousand pounds from the London run and a further thirty thousand pounds for the film rights, plus generous royalties from provincial and foreign productions.

The setting of *While the Sun Shines* is young Lord 'Bobby' Harpenden's chambers in Albany. It is the morning of the day before his wedding to Elizabeth, daughter of the Duke of Ayr and Stirling. Despite their aristocratic backgrounds, neither Bobby nor Elizabeth has been able to impress officer-selection boards sufficiently to get a commission, so both are doing their war service in the ranks. The play's plot revolves around two Allied officers – a Frenchman and an American – on leave in London, who try to make love to Elizabeth and to dissuade her from going through with her marriage to Bobby. Matters are complicated still further by the appearance of an extremely amenable ex-girlfriend of Bobby's called Mabel Crum – a lovely girl 'but not the kind you marry' – and the self-interested interference of Elizabeth's crusty old father, who is notorious for his delight in pretty girls and his unrelenting efforts to relieve his own shortage of cash by involving others in doomed business ventures and unsound investments.

The play consists of a steadily escalating series of hilarious misunderstandings and complications, but finally ends happily when Elizabeth decides to settle for 'ordinary quiet restful love' and marriage to Bobby in preference to the glamour of the American or 'the white hot burning passion of the heart' proffered by the Frenchman. Far from writing a sequel to *French Without Tears*, as so many people had urged him to, Rattigan had stood the basic idea behind it on its head – instead of centring on the pursuit of the various male characters by the man-hunting Diana the plot of *While the Sun Shines* is built around the attempts by the men in the story to pursue and win Elizabeth.

In spite of its many allusions to the war and the fact that many of the jokes depend on a knowledge of the prejudices and conditions of life in wartime London, *While the Sun Shines* survives, with *French Without Tears*, as Rattigan's best comedy. It is 'in the purest integrity, a play and nothing less'. The one area in which it fails to match Wilde is in memorable language. Although Rattigan's dialogue is extremely skilful throughout, there is nothing that raises the words above the simply naturalistic. Sharp though the exchanges are, the lines do not of themselves have the brilliance or sheer tingling pleasure characteristic of the very finest Wilde or Shaw. But if by the very highest standards Rattigan just fails in this one department – his Achilles' heel – he nevertheless succeeds triumphantly in every other.

The comic invention, and the way the hilarious lines and situations not only grow out of but top what has gone before, is masterly. This does not mean that the play is, in Rattigan's phrase, unaware of the time in which it was written – far from it – but everything in it is handled with a uniform and graceful lightness. This play is the reverse of *Flare Path*. Here we see, not the tragedy of war nor the ennobling determination to grin and bear it, but the petty stupidities and ludicrous muddle on the one hand and the opportunity for release in drink, parties and casual sexual encounters on the other. Here we see not so much the triumph of Allied cooperation as the confusion, rivalry and chaos. Talking about the play thirty years after it was written, Rattigan said that he saw the three central young men as pathetic figures because he assumed that all would perish in the war. This does not really come across in the play, except in the shared sense that the war pervaded everyone, both on stage and in the audience. Such awareness of impending doom as there is in the play relates almost exclusively to the sense of coming social change, and this is put to fine comic use. Colbert, the Frenchman, describes himself as '*socialiste*' and often refers to Bobby and his class as 'doomed'. Bobby himself jokes about 'swinging from a lamp-post' outside Albany and nasty Willie Gallacher (the British Communist leader) taking all his millions. The fact that he is not an officer he puts down to modern class prejudice – he went to a public school. In contrast, his butler's son is a lieutenant-commander.

The autobiographical elements in the play are both obvious and comparatively unimportant – such things as the selection of young servicemen casually picked up and taken to bed in blacked-out London are, as we have seen, clearly based on Rattigan's own experience and equally on that of his heterosexual friends. However, the drawing of one character in the play is worth noting: the duke (the part played by Ronald Squire) is Rattigan's first elderly figure and although many of his characteristics are taken from time-honoured comic stock, there are enough elements to confirm a suspicion that here we have the first in a long line of characters Rattigan would base on his own father. The enthusiasm, the gambling, the impecuniousness, the taste for suspect business ventures and unsound shares, the partiality to girls, are all echoes of Frank Rattigan. By 1943 he had lost none of his vigour or old-world zest. He was still much in evidence backstage, nudging the girls in the cast and inviting them to dinner.

From basking in the success of *While the Sun Shines* Rattigan now had to turn back rather less happily to his film work. Despite occasional more serious forays into the cinema, Rattigan would always regard his work on films as secondary to his real work which was writing for the theatre. To Rattigan writing film scripts was primarily an undemanding way of making money. The film suggested by Harold French as an appropriate morale-boosting wartime sequel to *French Without Tears*, which Rattigan had scripted with Anatole de Grunwald during the gestation of *While the Sun Shines*, was now well advanced in the production process. Predictably entitled *English Without Tears*, it was a comedy of manners about a titled lady who falls in love with her butler, Gilbey (the name plucked from the association which had outraged Rattigan's contemporaries at Harrow). The butler enlists and becomes an officer. There are endless misunderstandings of the ways of foreigners, who have come to Britain to fight in the Allied cause, before cooperation and mutual trust are achieved. Any similarity to discarded bits of *While the Sun Shines* must be regarded as far from accidental.

One of the disadvantages of being in uniform was that as the Air Ministry seemed to have decided that Flight Lieutenant Rattigan's talents were more effectively deployed for the war effort as a writer than as an air-gunner he could be posted to more or less any assignment they deemed necessary. There seemed rather less possibility of arguing with the Air Ministry than there had been with Warner Brothers as a studio contract writer. Early in 1944, he was seconded to the RAF Film Unit to work on a film about RAF Flying Training Command. Until this time all the RAF's propaganda efforts had been directed to showing how brave and effective were the operational Commands, such as Bomber, Fighter and Coastal. Now Flying Training Command wanted a look in as well. The director was another young wartime flight lieutenant – John Boulting. Boulting had already done months of research with another writer, including a tour of America where a lot of the aircrew training took place, and had amassed enough material for a three-hour script. What they needed now was someone to reduce this unmanageable material into a taut dramatic narrative. Boulting had gone to the head of the RAF Film Unit and said that he needed a first-class writer to dramatize his material and turn it into a story centred round a limited number of characters. Someone had read that the West End's hottest playwright, Terence Rattigan, was in the RAF and it was decided to try to get him. Lord Stansgate, who was head of public relations for the RAF, was approached and he promised to get Rattigan posted in. Boulting could not believe his luck – for his first feature film as a director he had landed the most talked-about playwright in London and it would not make an enormous hole in his budget.

When the two young flight lieutenants met at Pinewood Studios for the first time, Boulting was in considerable awe of Rattigan. In the event he found him charming and gentle, with a boyish giggle in spite of his obvious sophistication. 'Of course,' Rattigan said, referring to Boulting's bulky projected script, 'it's perfectly splendid.' Then he tactfully set about suggesting possible changes. Rattigan worked to create a 'humanized documentary', as both men liked to call it. The story that Rattigan eventually came up with, called *Journey Together*, served the purposes of Flying Training Command admirably, while at the same time providing him with the opportunity to explore further the way in which the war made people from different backgrounds mix and grow dependent on one another. This is the persistent theme of all Rattigan's wartime writing, and *Journey Together* was its most realistic expression. The film remains one of the most satisfying blends of documentary and fiction achieved in the cinema. When the film came to be shot, Boulting's luck had improved still further – RAF Sergeant Richard Attenborough and Aircraftman Jack Watling, both on service pay of a few shillings a day, had been seconded as his leading players.

During the months of their work together, Boulting found that Rattigan's mood never changed. He was continually calm and charming, even when his young director questioned his most carefully thought-out lines; he would patiently explain what he meant, how they should be played and, if Boulting was still unconvinced, would offer to change them. On only one occasion did Boulting see a change come over Rattigan and that was the result of deliberate provocation. He had begun to suspect that Rattigan was 'too good to be true', so he set out to needle him. One day, walking round the grounds at Pinewood, Boulting brought up the subject of Shakespeare: 'I think *Hamlet*'s greatness is highly questionable.' Boulting watched Rattigan shudder. Then with a visible effort at self-control he asked in his usual even tone, 'What do you mean, John?' Boulting expanded on his obviously blasphemous theme: 'Well, would you solve the climax of that play by a stage strewn with bodies and, "Goodnight, sweet prince..."?' As their gentle stroll continued, Rattigan launched into a thirty-minute model lecture on the play, its characters and its resolution.

The conversation about *Hamlet* seems to have had a bearing on the play on which Rattigan was working in breaks between wrestling with the film script for Boulting. Following on from the references and jokes in *While the Sun Shines* about the widely felt sense of impending social and political change brought about by the war, Rattigan was writing a much more considered comedy about the possible effects of these changes on family and personal

173

relationships. Calling the play *Less Than Kind*, he consciously modelled its plot on *Hamlet*. Interestingly, however, he chose not to resolve it with a stage strewn with bodies and, 'Goodnight, sweet prince...' *Less Than Kind* (the title itself a quote from Hamlet's aside: 'A little more than kin, and less than kind', after Claudius has addressed him: 'But now, my cousin Hamlet, and my son − ')[7] is a comedy. The play concerns an eighteen-year-old boy, Michael Brown, who, returning from five years' evacuation in Canada, is horrified to find his widowed mother living with a wealthy industrialist, Sir John Fletcher, a Tory member of the war cabinet. Michael has returned home fired with the spirit of 'fair shares for all', a government catchphrase which had exerted a profound influence on people in wartime Britain. Michael now looks forward to a fairer post-war society, in which there would be no place for reactionaries like Sir John. Michael accuses Sir John of having made his money by selling armaments to both sides during the 1930s, and of being a man whose idea of 'the liberty of the individual' remains the liberty to continue exploiting other people for private profit. A fertile subject for Rattigan, the play centred on the relationship between mother and son, and on the conflict which the mother, Olivia, feels between the love she feels for her lover, Sir John, and her maternal love for her son, Michael. The parallel with the underlying situation in *Hamlet* is clear, but because this is a comedy Rattigan points up the parallels to comic effect. Michael broods − his 'antic disposition'; takes to wearing a black tie − his 'inky cloak'; studies a book on poisoning; invites Sir John and his mother to a play called *Murder in the Family* and confronts his mother − in Rattigan's equivalent of the 'closet scene' − with her treachery to his father's memory, forcing her to choose between her lover and himself.

Early in 1944, when the play was still little more than an idea in Rattigan's head, Binkie Beaumont had taken the great star Gertrude Lawrence, Noël Coward's most famous leading lady during the 1920s and 1930s and still the embodiment of theatrical glamour, to see *While the Sun Shines*. He invited Rattigan to join them for dinner after the show. Gertrude Lawrence was probably doing no more than making polite conversation when she asked

Rattigan if he had got a play for her. 'No,' he replied, 'but I've got a good idea for one.' Rattigan, although himself now the toast of London, was still painfully insecure. None of his three successes had involved an established major West End star, so to get Gertrude Lawrence for his next play would be a great coup. Throughout his life Rattigan would remain almost pathetically prone to read too much into even the most casual encouragement from those he admired, and he idolized Gertrude Lawrence. He promised to send her his new play as soon as it was complete.

Rattigan got down to work immediately, using every spare moment he could find from his film commitments. The prospect of Gertrude Lawrence playing Olivia meant that he could strengthen the defence of romance and glamour inherent in the character, setting her glamour against the stultifying puritan tendencies of the more earnest socialists represented in the character of the son Michael. But by April 1944 the demands made on Rattigan by his work on patriotic movies had grown to such an extent that he seemed in danger of not being able actually to fit in getting the play down on paper. In addition to scripting the Flying Training Command film for Boulting, Rattigan's idea of a film promoting Anglo-American cooperation, developed from *Flare Path*, had resurfaced in another guise. After many consultations and changes of plan, Rattigan's idea of building the story round the changing role of a British airfield handed over to the Americans had been dropped, and Major William Wyler had returned to America, leaving Rattigan with his material. But Anatole de Grunwald believed in Rattigan's basic concept enough to take it to another producer, Filippo del Giudice (who had produced the film version of *French Without Tears*), and got him to set it up for Puffin Asquith to direct. So now a script was needed for this as well. In order to be able to write undisturbed, Rattigan took himself off to a hotel by the Thames much favoured by honeymooners before the war, the White Hart at Sonning. As he told his publisher in a letter written shortly after his arrival, he did not intend to leave until 'I have finished my two film scripts (official) and a play (unofficial)'. 'Unofficial' or not, there was no doubt which project was uppermost in Rattigan's mind. Only a few weeks later the play was finished. This he dispatched to Binkie Beaumont to send on to Gertrude Lawrence. He then returned to his chambers in Albany to continue work on the film projects.

By the summer of 1944 people in London had decided that the war was as good as over. On 6 June, the Allies had landed successfully in France, but just one week later the Germans launched the first doodlebugs against London. Soon dozens of these unnerving little pilotless jet planes, crammed with high explosives (V1s), were raining down and a new evacuation of schoolchildren was ordered. But Rattigan, de Grunwald and Asquith worked on in Rattigan's Albany chambers on the film script developed from *Flare Path*. In contrast to Rattigan, who was always immaculate in uniform, Puffin Asquith wore his so that he looked like a tramp. He had joined the Home Guard, although neither Rattigan nor de Grunwald could discover what, if anything, he ever did in it. He always wore his khaki battledress and heavy boots – in which he clattered up and down Albany's echoing stone steps. One evening Rattigan was waiting for him to arrive for a script conference when the liveried porter telephoned: 'Excuse me, sir, there's a person down here who says he's Anthony Asquith, but I can see that he's not, so I've sent him about his business.' Rattigan was horrified, but he couldn't help being amused. A few minutes later, the phone rang again and this time it was Asquith from a call box: 'I don't understand what they're doing – they've turned me out,' he said furiously. Trying not to giggle, Rattigan told him, 'Puffin, you see, the point is there are a lot of deserters about – in fact, there are quite a number trying to hide in odd corners round Albany.' Far from laughing, Asquith protested: 'I don't look like a deserter.' 'To him,' Rattigan replied, now forced to keep his joke going, 'you must have looked like one. I'm awfully sorry, Puff. Do come along. I'll talk to the porter and see that it is put right.'

Their script conferences went on at all hours of the day and night, regardless of the doodlebugs. Rattigan and de Grunwald listened for them with half an ear while talking. They had decided that when they heard the engine cut out they would dash out into the passage, which was the only place in the old building that might afford some shelter, and throw themselves on the floor.

Puffin kept walking up and down the room, talking rapidly as always and incessantly. We heard the buzz-bomb but he obviously was quite unconscious that there was any sound other than his own voice. The bomb came closer and closer and then suddenly we heard the cut-off. Tolly de Grunwald and I dashed into the passage, knowing that within seconds the bomb would drop and explode. I quickly threw myself on the floor and Tolly fell on top of me – or perhaps it was the other way round. After the explosion – the bomb fortunately missed our building – we came back. Puffin was still walking up and down the room. On seeing us come through the door he realized that we hadn't been listening to what he had been saying. 'This is no time for games,' he said, 'we're supposed to be getting on with the script ...'[8]

The film, now called *Rendezvous*, from Roosevelt's exhortation, 'Our generation has a rendezvous with destiny,' eventually began shooting in September 1944, but by the time the shooting was complete it was clear that the war would be over before the film could be edited and released. Accordingly, a new beginning and ending were devised which showed a disused and overgrown airfield, from which the film flashed back to tell the story of the successive groups of airmen, British and American, and their wives and girlfriends, who had flown from it during the war. When it was released the film was hailed as a patriotic masterpiece – a reputation which has endured. It was popular with the public on both sides of the Atlantic, and won the *Daily Mail* National Film Award. Rattigan, de Grunwald and Asquith had confined the story of their film, which was finally called *The Way to the Stars*, to the airfield and a hotel in a nearby town. Although it was a war film, there were only a few flying sequences and no scenes of combat.

While the Sun Shines continued to play to packed houses in spite of the doodlebug raids. Audiences' sense of shared experience with the characters in the play was heightened, and their enjoyment was, if anything, increased. When the air-raid sirens sounded, hardly anyone left the theatre to take shelter. The cast continued with the play, but with an ear cocked for explosions. Once, towards the end of the third act, there was a deafening roar and the Globe shook to its foundations. The theatre next door, the Queens, had received a direct hit and was flattened; luckily, it was empty at the time. The audience for *While the Sun Shines* remained in their seats and the cast finished the third act and took their curtain calls in the normal way.

On the night of 12 July, a doodlebug hit the Aldwych where the Lunts (Alfred Lunt and his wife Lynn Fontanne, more or less the royal family of sophisticated commercial theatre on both sides of the Atlantic) were playing Robert Sherwood's propagandist drama *There Shall Be No Night*. Although the performance was over and there was no one in the theatre, the damage to the building closed the production. The Lunts decided to look for a new vehicle. They wanted a representative British play to suit their combined talents, which they could open in London and then take back to Broadway. Alfred Lunt, who normally directed the productions in which they appeared, was an American, and at that time just over fifty. Lynn Fontanne, his British-born wife, was six years his senior. What they sought was a sophisticated vehicle in which they could play opposite each other – he preferably in the character of an American and she as an elegant Englishwoman.

As chance would have it, at just about the same moment Binkie Beaumont received a reply from Gertrude Lawrence about Rattigan's new play. She said that she did not recollect giving him any encouragement to write a play for her and that she did not like the play anyway. Rattigan was desolate, he had built his play round the idea of her playing the beautiful woman at its centre. But, as Binkie Beaumont pointed out to Rattigan over lunch at The Ivy, the doodlebug on the Aldwych, the Lunts' sudden need of a new play and Gertrude Lawrence's rejection added up to a potential godsend. Who better to play a woman fashioned as a defence of glamour in an age of austerity, of charm in an age of utility, than Lynn Fontanne, especially if her husband Alfred Lunt could play her lover?

But, as Rattigan diffidently explained to Alfred Lunt, at a meeting arranged with the help of Ivor Novello, the part of the woman's lover had been created as a supporting rather than a starring role. Lunt reassured Rattigan that the relative sizes of his and his wife's roles did not matter: 'Sometimes Lynn has the play and sometimes it's my play. Mr Rattigan, if your play is good, I'll be satisfied to hold a tray and let it be Lynn's play. The play is what matters.' Two days later the Lunts told Rattigan that the play, needed a few adjustments here and there, but fundamentally it was splendid and they would both be happy to appear in it, with Lunt himself directing. They wanted to start rehearsals right away.

By 12 August Rattigan had completed a revised script, in which Olivia's Tory-cabinet-minister lover, Sir John, is a Canadian (loosely modelled on Churchill's Minister of Aircraft Production, Lord Beaverbrook), thus making it possible for Alfred Lunt to play the part. Beaumont sent the play off to the Lord Chamberlain for a licence and casting began. But what happened next, and in particular Rattigan's attitude to it, is open to dispute. In the years that followed Rattigan himself would give completely opposing accounts.

The Lunts had told Rattigan that his play needed 'a few adjustments', but by the time the play opened in London in December these had amounted to a virtual rewrite.

He [Lunt] was so subtle about it that I didn't realize he was making me write a new play... Sir John Fletcher, the minister, that was Alfred's role, well wasn't he a little too brutal here? And my, but he was a dreadful reactionary, and in this passage here he was such a disagreeable Tory and 'they won't like it, you know'. And he'd lose the audience in this scene here. As I'd written it, Olivia's son was constantly scoring off Sir John. Gradually, so gradually I didn't know it myself, the minister began scoring off Michael, the son. In fact, Michael became a snotty character, while Sir John changed into a fine fellow, good hearted, a worldly chap doing his best for God, for England, and for Lynn Fontanne, and having to put up with this beastly little bugger of a left-wing socialist.[9]

Unfortunately Rattigan did not say any of this until twenty years later, by which time he was preoccupied with defending himself from a new generation of playwrights and critics who had accused him of being an old reactionary. At the time of the original production, both in public and in private, and a few years later when the play was published, Rattigan praised what the Lunts had done, claiming that they had improved his play. But one copy of the play he originally wrote survives among the Lord Chamberlain's papers – the copy which Binkie Beaumont submitted for a licence in August 1944. This confirms the extent of the changes made by the Lunts and by Rattigan at the Lunts' instigation. Quite a lot of the changes are no more than the kind of adjustments made during the rehearsals and pre-West End tour of any new comedy, sharpening up the jokes and adding new comedy business. But other changes do indeed fundamentally alter the values of the play, in effect turning them upside down. As explained earlier, parts of the play are consciously modelled on *Hamlet*; the effect of the changes made to *Less Than Kind* between Rattigan's original text and the play as it eventually appeared are roughly the same as if Claudius had been transformed into the hero and Hamlet had become the villain. So in the first act, when Sir John and Michael clash over politics, in the original version Michael is allowed to produce arguments that reduce Sir John to losing his temper, whereas in the final version Michael is made to look merely rude, stupid, adolescent and a bore. Rather than describing himself as 'an anti-fascist', in the original Michael describes himself as 'a Progressive' and when Sir John claims that, 'We're all Progressives these days,' Michael reminds Sir John of a recent speech of his that was anything but progressive, in which he attacked the idea of post-war planning and reconstruction. Michael goes on to point out that the emergency after the war will be just as big as it is now – 'If you can organize for war, why can't you bally well organize for peace?'

SIR JOHN My dear child, there is such a thing as the liberty of the individual.
MICHAEL Liberty of the individual, my fanny! You

reactionaries always shout a lot about individual liberty when all you mean is liberty for yourselves to go on exploiting other people for your own private profit. Liberty to you personally means a big, fat dividend for Fletcher-Pratt Preferred.

SIR JOHN (hotly) On the contrary, liberty to me personally means freedom from the tyrannical control of a soulless oligarchy. It is freedom in the highest, Periclean sense: freedom for private enterprise to flourish healthily for the good of all, unhampered by petty, stifling restrictions. Freedom for every individual to carve out his own career.

MICHAEL The way you carved yours out by selling steel to Japan in '31?

In the original Michael wins the argument hands down, whereas in the revised version he merely seems to regurgitate a lot of unsubstantiated rumours that he has picked up from others. In the original when Sir John is sent the wrong report by his office he explodes in bullying rage, whereas in the Lunts' version, which is certainly funnier, he is sweet reason and calm itself, making him an altogether more attractive and lovable character. In the original when Michael discovers that the house that Olivia is living in, and everything in it, is Sir John's he confronts Sir John on his own, not only making Michael a stronger character but creating a much greater air of tension. But when the play was eventually performed, Olivia was made to be present during the scene, making it more amusing but at the same time making Michael appear more stupid. Over and over again Michael is made to appear more unreasonable, more stupid, less considerate and generally a silly little boy and a caricature of the worst kind of puritanical Red. By contrast, Sir John is made progressively more lovable, tolerant, worldly and forbearing. In the end the point is reached where Sir John is credibly presented as the real upholder of the individual's rights and the bastion against a new order which will do away with charm and beauty in the name of drab uniformity. The third act is basically a completely different play from the one Beaumont submitted to the Lord Chamberlain's office in August 1944. Rattigan later claimed that he intended Michael to be the sympathetic character, a confused and vulnerable adolescent. And in the original text Rattigan does indeed show Michael's distress as he struggles with his ideals as they come into conflict with the attractions of money and gracious living. He can be seen as a portrait of the young Rattigan himself, while Olivia can be seen as an affectionate portrait of his mother, Vera. But in the play as finally performed by the Lunts in London in December 1944, Michael, Rattigan's Hamlet, is a prig who comes to see inconsistency and error in all his noble ideals, and in the last act abandons them because Sir John's wealth and position will help him to impress a reluctant girlfriend. The idealist and socialist accepts Sir John's mellow affluence as good taste and his use of privilege as realism – living in the world as it really is. Michael – and, if it is a self-portrait, by implication Rattigan – finally repudiates all that he has believed in. Gertrude (Olivia) is reunited with Claudius (Sir John) and they all live happily ever after. The parallels with *Hamlet*, which are already rather irritating in the earlier version of the play, ultimately only serve to underline the extreme cynicism of the finished version.

So what exactly did happen between August and December 1944? Did Rattigan acquiesce in the total reversal of the values of his play, or was he appalled, as he later claimed, only realizing the true nature of what was happening when it was already too late? As suggested earlier, there are reasons to doubt some of what he said later. Even in the course of the interview in which he made his accusations against Alfred Lunt, Rattigan added, 'In the end he was right. I wrote a far better play because of his suggestions.'[10] If he did not like what was going on – and he must have realized what was happening, at the latest during the provincial tour preceding the London opening, if not during the rehearsals – he was in a position to cry halt. By 1944 Rattigan was a powerful writer. He was the most commercially successful playwright in Britain, with a new-found critical reputation which he wanted to enhance; and as the play's author he had the ultimate sanction. Nor was he short of money. If he disapproved so much of what the Lunts were doing, why did he not stop them? Either they did not alter the play in ways of which he fundamentally disapproved, or he was short on moral courage.

A letter written by Rattigan to his parents describes the Lunts' rehearsals. 'The atmosphere of rehearsals in which we are all living is apparently the only atmosphere in which they can work happily. It is, however, reminiscent of John [Gielgud] with *A Tale of Two Cities*, only worse, because there are two of them.' Rattigan is very positive about Lynn Fontanne: 'She is going to be at least three times as good as Gertrude Lawrence would have been and about twice as good as I thought anyone could ever be in the part. She brings out all the comedy and at the same time is very touching at moments.' When he turns to Alfred Lunt there is no real hint that he thinks he is perverting the fundamental values of his play: 'All the rewriting at the moment is concerned with his part and practically everything that has been done is a big improvement, though of course it is nearly all at the expense of the boy, of whose part they are both a little jealous... The boy, poor little brat, is having a terrible time... Alfred's way of rehearsing him is to take him over three lines for three hours, finally reducing him to tears and hysteria.'[11] Throughout his life Rattigan was at pains to reassure his mother in his letters about the progress of productions of his plays, but even so one feels that had he been seriously worried about what Lunt was doing to his play there would have been greater evidence for this in this letter, which was written immediately before the play opened on its pre-London tour. All he says is that the boy's part has been reduced and he prepares his mother for the fact that some of her favourite lines have been cut.

By the time the play, now re-titled *Love in Idleness*, was ready to open on its pre-West End tour at the end of November, the changes to it had been so extensive that Beaumont found it necessary to resubmit it to the Lord Chamberlain's office for a new licence. Even after the tour had begun, the relentless process of changes continued. Alfred Lunt's technique with Rattigan was rather similar to his system for rehearsing the boy. No sooner had he approved Rattigan's changes to Act One than he would ask for more changes to Act Two; then he would move on to Act Three. Once these had been made he would turn to back to Act One;

and so on. The effect of the changes was to move the love affair between Sir John and Olivia ever more centre stage – a change acknowledged in the play's new title[12] – and reduce the once central role of Michael to a cipher, a villain who comes between true lovers.

When the play opened in Liverpool the notices were not good, although the reviewers went out of their way to praise the artistry of the Lunts. Noël Coward, who again had money in the production, came to an early performance. Although it has been suggested that his attitude towards the production may have been partly motivated by jealousy of Rattigan (previously the only English play the Lunts had starred in was one of Coward's), he did not want to lose his investment. However, he immediately detected that in turning *Love in Idleness* into a suitable commercial vehicle for their combined talents the Lunts had fundamentally damaged the play. He advised them to abandon the production immediately without incurring the additional costs of a London opening. Rattigan and Alfred Lunt sat in a dressing-room gloomily polishing off a bottle of whisky, while in the next room Coward made devastating comments about the play to Lynn Fontanne. Back in the Lunts' hotel room, as Coward continued to analyse the play and Rattigan tried in vain to get drunk, Lynn Fontanne motioned Rattigan to follow her into the bedroom. 'Look,' she whispered, 'nothing that Noël has said, or will say, can affect me. This is an enchanting play and we're going to do it in London. I know Alfred will want to close it. But don't worry. I shall talk Alfred round. I have faith in the play.' An hour later, Lunt beckoned Rattigan into the bedroom. 'My boy,' he murmured, 'as you can see, Lynn is disheartened by Noël's reaction. She's going to want to close the play. But no matter what Lynn says, we shall do it. It's a good play. Now don't say anything. Leave it to me to talk Lynn round to my way of thinking. I have such confidence in your play that I'm going to buy Noël's share in it.'

So why had Rattigan allowed the play's intrinsic strengths to be undermined and at the same time helped in the process of turning its intentions more or less on their heads? Rattigan had a pathological dislike of unpleasantness – later in his life we shall see him going to inordinate lengths to avoid scenes, allowing himself to be robbed by his servants to avoid having to confront them. On top of this there is no doubt that Rattigan was in awe of the Lunts and desperate to have them star in one of his plays. Although the play had serious intentions – it mattered to Rattigan that the characters should move the audience as well as make them laugh – it was a comedy. The Lunts were acknowledged masters in how to get sophisticated laughter from even the flimsiest material (during their careers they were criticized more than once for doing material that was not worthy of their talents). Rattigan, who was, as we have seen, one of the most accommodating of writers to the needs of actors, was therefore all too ready to bow to their superior experience and reputation. Lynn Fontanne said in an interview thirty years later that she, far from being worried that Sir John was too unsympathetic a character, was concerned from the start because Michael was too unpleasant and so killed the comedy: 'He spoiled the play every time he came on. Everybody hated him and he was a lot of the play.'[13] Another element in Rattigan not standing up for his original intentions was the impresario Binkie Beaumont. Although Beaumont cultivated a reputation for his company, H. M. Tennent, that everything must be of the highest standard, and although Binkie Beaumont himself acquired a reputation for ruthlessness, Beaumont's overriding goal was commercial success. And this meant stars. So H. M. Tennent's shows featured the greatest stars, often in the work of fine writers, always beautifully mounted and gowned. As time went on Tennent's productions took on something of the quality of a Fabergé egg – expensive, highly polished and intricate to behold, clearly the product of hours of detailed work by craftsmen, but lifeless. So what mattered to Binkie was to please the Lunts, even if, in the final analysis, it had to be at the expense of Rattigan's play. Beaumont was not the manager to stand up for the intrinsic quality of his writer's work against the wishes of his stars. Ultimately Rattigan's long association with H. M. Tennent, and Binkie Beaumont, although he gained so much from it, would damage the enduring quality of his work.

But there was one final factor in Rattigan's apparent failure to defend the intentions which had underpinned his play when he first embarked on writing it, probably the one that tipped the balance: Sir Henry 'Chips' Channon. This is how Chips recorded their first meeting, on 29 September 1944, shortly after Rattigan had started intensive work with the Lunts: 'I dined with Juliet Duff in her little flat stuffed with French furniture and bibelots – also there, Sibyl Colefax and Master Terence Rattigan, and we sparkled over the burgundy. I like Rattigan enormously, and feel a new friendship has begun. He has a flat in Albany.'[14]

In his book *Ruling Passions*, Tom Driberg, who knew Channon well, described him at this time: '"Chips", of American origin, was a social figure at least as glittering as Lady Cunard. He had a large house and a lot of money – the latter, I suppose, largely through his marriage...' Driberg continued:

> For Chips was one of the better known homosexuals in London, and he was rich enough to rent almost any young man he fancied – a handsome German princeling, a celebrated English playwright. His seduction of the playwright was almost like the wooing of Danae by Zeus: every day, the playwright found, delivered to his door, a splendid present – a case of champagne, a huge pot of caviare, a Cartier cigarette box in two kinds of gold...In the end, of course, he gave in, saying apologetically to his friends, 'How can one *not*?'[15]

Rattigan, of course, was the 'celebrated English playwright'.

Chips Channon was the forty-eight-year-old Conservative MP for Southend. He entertained the high and the mighty – cabinet ministers and royalty – at his house in Eaton Square. He counted among his intimates the Duchess of Kent, the Duff Coopers, the Wavells (then Viceroy and Vicereine of India) and members of Churchill's cabinet. He knew about the courtship of Philip Mountbatten and Princess Elizabeth long before it was public knowledge, and was approached by Buckingham Palace to loan them his house as a first home after their marriage. He was married to, but about to be divorced from, Lady Honor Guinness, the eldest daughter of the second Earl of Iveagh.

However, the seduction did not go easily. Rattigan resisted for some time. Here is how one of Rattigan's closest friends remembered it: 'It was pathetic really. Channon used to buy him these presents, which Terry could have bought six times over, but he was flattered by the social side, Princess Marina [the Duchess of Kent] and all that stuff. The trouble was he didn't want to pay the price. He would bring him here and he would say, "Oh, for God's sake get him drunk so that I don't have to go to bed with him."' When *Love in Idleness* was published it was dedicated 'to Henry Channon', a fitting acknowledgement of his capitulation; Rattigan had surrendered more than his body. The social world, the glamour which Rattigan described and finally sought to defend in his play, was the social world of Chips and his friends.

In fact the shift in Rattigan's position by the time *Love in Idleness* reached London represents a development of the position he seems to have reached in *After the Dance*. In the earlier play he proclaims the need and right of everyone to be true to themselves. This theme is restated in the first version of *Love in Idleness*, but by the time the play opened in London the only defender of this right is the reactionary Sir John. Individuality is a house in Westminster, dinner at the Savoy and entertaining the fashionable social élite to smart little dinner parties. In *After the Dance*, the young idealists are well intentioned, even though in practice their ideals lead to disaster. By the time Rattigan and the Lunts had finished rewriting *Love in Idleness*, Michael is seen merely to recite other people's ideas and is himself revealed to be a self-interested hypocrite.

Less Than Kind had reflected the upsurge of socialist ideas during the war, which would put Labour into power in 1945. Rattigan set out to confront the political and emotional implications of this in the relationship between Michael, his mother and Sir John. But in *Love in Idleness* he merely scoffed at the idealists – among whose ranks he had so recently counted himself. Despite the Beveridge Report (which he refers to in the play), the 1944 Education Act and a new forward-looking spirit, Rattigan, like most of the new circle of Conservative friends to whom he was becoming steadily more attached, did not really believe that this new mood was as widespread as the results of the

1945 election were to indicate. In the short term, *Love in Idleness* pandered to the prejudices of comfortably-off theatregoers. In the longer term, such a misreading of the public mood boded ill for Rattigan's lasting popularity.

Technically, also, *Love in Idleness* was a backward step. In the earlier draft, although it still needs work, the play is built up through the interaction of a number of fully realized characters of more or less equal weight. During previous productions of his plays Rattigan, with input from director and cast, had not only sharpened up sections of dialogue or business, he had developed and deepened the characters. During the rehearsals of *Love in Idleness* this did not happen. As a result the play was reduced to having only two complete characters – Sir John and Olivia, plus one two-dimensional character, Michael, who is little more than a caricature. There is no reason why a comedy should not carry weighty ideas, but simply on the level of provoking laughter *Love in Idleness* fails. There are far too few good comic situations, funny lines or shafts of wit.

The London opening night was Wednesday, 20 December 1944 at the Lyric Theatre, next door but one to the Globe where *While the Sun Shines* was still running. It was one of those 'big' first nights, when the ordinary playgoer, in the unlikely event of getting a seat at all, does not know whether to watch the performance in the stalls or on the stage. The Minister of Food was there, the Chancellor of the Exchequer was there, Air Chief Marshal Sir Sholto Douglas was there, the aristocracy was there, and Noël Coward, who thought it should not be opening at all, was there.

In the event, although nobody thought much of the play, the evening was a triumph and 'The Audience Went Wild With Delight', as one headline writer put it. Most of the critics thought the play thin stuff saved by the Lunts. James Agate deflated the image of Rattigan as a latter-day Wilde which he had promoted in his *Sunday Times* review of *While the Sun Shines*. Of this latest offering he concluded that Rattigan had failed to make a play out of any of the possibilities he had created for himself.

The play was billed as being limited to a three-month run

because the Lunts were committed to taking it back to America. The Lyric rapidly became 'the theatre you can't get into', and when the play was taken off, after the run had been extended to six months, it was still playing to capacity houses. In America, it became the Lunts' greatest success. They enjoyed 451 performances on Broadway, and played it altogether, in Europe, in New York and on tour, for almost four years.

Rattigan had started the war with a reputation based on one commercial success, which most people suspected was a fluke anyway, and two flops, which together had gained him only a small amount of grudging critical respect; he had been broke and suffering from a writer's block so severe as to need psychiatric help. Six years later, by the end of the war, a total transformation had been effected. He was, at thirty-four, the highest-earning playwright in Britain, reputed to be receiving over six hundred pounds a week in royalties – although he told journalists that the Inland Revenue only allowed him to keep twelve pounds of that. All three plays he had written during the war had been smash hits; he was the only playwright to have had two plays with runs of over a thousand consecutive West End performances; he had written four films, all of which had been well received and one of which, *The Way to the Stars*, was hailed as an undoubted masterpiece. Yet Rattigan nursed still greater ambition. He wanted to be a great playwright. This most publicly modest of men admitted to his most intimate friends that he wanted to be numbered with Shakespeare and Shaw. With the war over, he could devote his life to the realization of that ambition.

On the surface, Rattigan's life was a success story, yet there were dark clouds. In *After the Dance*, Rattigan had revealed a pessimistic side of himself in his picture of David Scott-Fowler, the writer who wastes his talent and destroys himself. Living above Rattigan in Hertford Street, Peter Osborn had witnessed the depressive side of Rattigan's make-up seen by few others. On bad days he would lie in bed with the curtains drawn, saying he had a migraine and refusing to go out. In *Flare Path*, Teddy, the brave pilot who fools around to show how little he cares when he is in truth scared almost to death, and Peter, the smoothly self-confident film star who is underneath a vulnerable child begging for mother love from his mistress, are both portraits in which Rattigan identified elements of himself. So, too, even in the first version of *Love in Idleness*, Michael is in part a cruel portrait of Rattigan past and present: the earnest young student who takes himself too seriously; the idealist prepared to compromise his beliefs for sex and money. Pacifism had not prevented war, and at least one of Rattigan's close friends, Tony Goldschmidt, had been killed in action. Now that he had money he found that, like Michael, he enjoyed it, not because it gave him the freedom to write what he liked, but because he could splash it about and impress others. In the staged version of *Love in Idleness*, the version Rattigan stood by and later published in his *Collected Plays*, Michael finally abandons all his principles and objections to Sir John Fletcher and what he represents. By 1945, Rattigan had found that he too enjoyed the flattering attention of those very Tories he had howled abuse at outside Downing Street and at Oxford; he could not resist dropping into conversations just how much he was earning, or offering a cigarette from his newest gold cigarette case to impress his friends; he enjoyed being seen in the most expensive restaurants, having chambers at one of London's most exclusive addresses, driving the newest Rolls-Royce. Rattigan drew characters with irreconcilable sides to their natures. But had he reconciled the conflicts in his own?

Notes

1   *Two Hundred and Fifty Times I Saw a Play – or Authors, Actors and Audiences,* by K.O. Newman, Pelago, Oxford 1944. Newman dedicated his book to Anthony Goldschmidt, killed in battle on Easter Day, 25 April 1943.

2   Anthony Creighton told John Osborne that while he was in Bomber Command during the war he had 'toured extensively' in an RAF drag show called something like *Boys in Blue* or *Things in Wings* directed by Rattigan, in which Rattigan, dressed in a tutu and carrying a wand, had sung a show-stopping number, 'I'm just about the oldest fairy in the business. I'm quite the oldest fairy that you've ever seen...' (*A Better Class of Person* by John Osborne, Faber & Faber, London, 1991). It seems likely that the actual extent of the tour was a few neighbouring air-force bases, which was quite common practice when one station had devised any sort of show or entertainment. It would be a mistake to read more into Rattigan's act as a fairy than into his earlier turn as Diana Coutigan at Oxford smokers.

3   After the war, Anthony Goldschmidt became a distinguished international civil servant, but he and Rattigan remained friends, although Goldschmidt remained virtually unknown to most of the other members of the small coterie that came to surround Rattigan. I only got to know of him when he contacted me after publication of the first edition of this book.

4   It was Rattigan who later told people that he had written *While the Sun Shines* in borrowed Albany chambers during one three-week leave. However, as he leased a set of chambers of his own in June 1943, Set K5, it is possible that he had moved in permanently by the time he wrote the play.

5   Richard Huggett, op. cit.

6   Brenda Bruce interviewed by the author in 1977

7   *Hamlet*, Act I, Scene ii.

8   R. J. Minney, op. cit.

9   *Stagestruck – Alfred Lunt and Lynn Fontanne* by Maurice Zolotow, Heinemann, London, 1965

10 Op. cit.

11 The Rattigan Papers, British Library. Letter to his parents, November 1944.

12 See *Taming of the Shrew*, Act I, Scene i, and *A Midsummer Night's Dream* Act II, Scene i.

13 Lynn Fontanne, in Anthony Curtis's BBC Radio 3 programme, *Rattigan's Theatre*, op. cit.

14 *Chips – The Diaries of Sir Henry Channon* edited by Robert Rhodes James, Weidenfeld & Nicolson, London, 1967.

15 *Ruling Passions* by Tom Driberg, Jonathan Cape, London, 1977.

8

The Winslow Boy

Henry 'Chips' Channon wrote in his diary for 10 August 1945:

> Terry came to lunch about 12.55. He said (he is a wireless
> addict), 'Turn on the news,' and we did, as we sipped our
> preprandial cocktails. The wireless announced that Japan had
> asked for peace, but insists on the rights of the Emperor. They
> want to save the Mikado. At long last the war is over, or ending.
> The streets were crowded with celebrating people singing and
> littered with torn paper...

Something of the quality of the time Chips and Rattigan spent
together can be gleaned from the entries in the expurgated
published version of Channon's diaries.

> *20th May 1945*   From Sturford Mead – where we are staying –
> I took Terence Rattigan over to Longleat... Henry Weymouth
> [the Marquess of Bath] took us all over the house and showed us
> the famous Shakespeare folios of which they have the first,
> second, third and fourth. Terry was fascinated and impressed and
> I saw his face light up as he took one down from the shelf and
> fingered it... In the evening we drove to Ashcombe to dine with
> Cecil Beaton, a long melancholy beautiful drive through isolated
> country. The house is romantic and amusingly arranged, and
> Cecil received us in Austrian clothes. Also there, an uninteresting
> couple, the Graham Sutherlands. He is a painter.[1]

By the late summer of 1945, Chips Channon, although he himself had retained his seat, was in a state of shock from the rout of Churchill and the Conservatives in the general election. To Channon, and most other Tories who had assumed that having won the war Churchill would win the election, defeat had come as a rude surprise. He and his friends feared what a Labour government, bent on socialism and with a powerful majority, might do to them and their privileged way of life. Rattigan, too, shared their surprise. Only a few years previously he would have been overjoyed at Attlee's victory; his feelings now were much more equivocal.

As we have seen, his political opinions, like much else, were in turmoil. With the exception of Puffin Asquith, who was by family tradition a Liberal, he had lost touch with the radical friends of his youth. Tony Goldschmidt had been killed. Many of his surviving radical friends had moved firmly into the Labour movement during the last years of the war, while Rattigan had drifted in the opposite direction. Despite sharing comradeship and danger with men from quite different backgrounds during his active service in the first years of the war, and getting so much out of it, Rattigan had found himself irresistibly attracted by the powerful and glamorous people with whom he came into contact as a 'war personality'. Unsurprisingly, most of these people were philosophically and politically conservative. The 1945 election had been the watershed. Rattigan almost certainly voted Liberal; but when the floodwaters of excitement subsided the Liberal Party, along with most of the middle ground in politics, seemed to have been washed away. Rattigan found himself uneasily alongside the Tories. It was perhaps inevitable, considering his family background, his education and his new wealth which he wished to protect from Labour, the traditional party of high taxation. But, in the words of Graham Greene:

The writer should always be ready to change sides at the drop of a hat. He stands for the victims and the victims change. Loyalty confines you to accepted opinions... but disloyalty encourages you to roam through any human mind; it gives the novelist an extra dimension of understanding... it is a genuine duty we owe to society, to be a piece of grit in the State machinery.[2]

On 19 August 1945, Chips Channon recorded in his diary: 'Terry read me out the first act of his new play about the Archer Shee case. I suggested the title of *Ronnie versus Rex*, and he has temporarily adopted it. So far, it is brilliant, dramatic and full of a sense of period.' The Archer-Shee case was the one that had so excited his parents' generation around the time of Rattigan's birth, in which a father had defied a reforming government by fighting for the rights of his son. When those who had taken up Archer-Shee's case succeeded in getting Parliament to suspend a debate on naval rearmament in order to discuss compensation for a thirteen-year-old naval cadet wrongfully dismissed for the theft of a postal order, they had hailed it as a vindication of democracy in the face of galloping dictatorship by state bureaucracy. An immediately suitable subject, then, as far as someone like Chips Channon was concerned, for 1945; or, as the virulently Conservative *Daily Mail* put it when the play eventually appeared, 'Mr Rattigan's tract for these particular times'. However, in Rattigan's hands it turned out to be something rather more complicated.

One of Rattigan's hobbies was famous trials and he maintained a whole shelf of books on famous cases, to which he added continually. He had read various accounts of the Archer-Shee case, the most recent published in 1943. Rattigan and Puffin Asquith used to play a party game with friends which consisted of thinking up the most ludicrous crimes and holding a mock trial in which each guest took on a role – as judge, defending counsel, prosecuting counsel, jury and so on. Rattigan's favourite role was prosecuting counsel. It was probably as a result of participating in one of these mock trials that Anatole de Grunwald suggested to Rattigan and Asquith that they should collaborate on a film about British justice – it was just before the end of the war and there was still pressure from the authorities for films which would promote traditional British democratic institutions. Rattigan suggested the Archer-Shee case and gave him the book.[3] De Grunwald rejected it as too dull. However, the idea had been growing on Rattigan: 'I got very angry and said that if he didn't want to do the bloody thing as a film I would do it as a play.' With the end of the war and Labour's victory in the general election, the appeal of the subject and its implications grew stronger for Rattigan. But Asquith warned that it would never work on the stage. It would have to be far too elaborate and expensive – as well as domestic scenes, there would have to be an enormous court scene. But Rattigan had got the bit between his teeth; he would do it without any court scene, he said. He would have one character, the defence barrister, who would represent all the legal side of the story. The two men argued enthusiastically and eventually laid a bet on whether Rattigan could bring it off. In his excitement Rattigan undertook to write it in the manner of a Granville Barker period piece.

When he sat down to do it he encountered an unexpected difficulty:

> For the first time I was faced with a ready-made plot; before I had worked out the setting in which to put it and the characters through whom to tell it. I had therefore to fashion characters who could, because they actually did, only behave in a certain way. I found it a dreadful task and, after hurling the play many times into my mental waste-paper basket, I decided that the only way that the impossible equation would work out was by dint of some judiciously concealed cheating... Once again, in fact, I found I could only write my play by allowing my characters to make their own story.[4]

Once Rattigan had made this discovery he found that 'the task, though not easy, proved on the whole a good deal less arduous than that of writing a light comedy.'[5] On 17 September 1945, Chips Channon could record:

> Terry returned to London, and we discussed his play, which he has now all but finished. It is being typed, and there are only a

few touches still to do. I advised against the title *The Hamilton Boy* [Rattigan had also tried *The Thompson Case*] and we decided on *The Winslow Boy*, which I suggested. Terry thinks only of his play, dreams and lives it, and it really is magnificent. What a genius he is.'He has completed it in six weeks.

Two days later Rattigan read Chips the completed typescript of the finished play. He dedicated it to Chips's son: 'For Master Paul Channon. In the hope that he will live to see a world in which this play will point no moral.'

The major problem that Rattigan had set himself by his determination to keep the court scene and other public events on which his plot ultimately hinged off-stage, was to find some way of describing those events in dramatic terms without resorting to having one character come on to the stage to give another information that he or she would in real life have already known. Rattigan avoided this trap by establishing the growing interest of the press in the story as a small man's fight for his 'ancient freedom' against 'the new despotism of Whitehall'. The latest editions of the newspapers are brought in, and choice chunks are read by one excited member of the Winslow household (as he had renamed the Archer-Shees) to another; an empty-headed woman reporter, who is more interested in the elegance of the curtains than in Arthur Winslow's explanation of the intricacies of the case, arrives with a photographer to do a 'human interest' story on Ronnie and his father's campaign. Through such devices we discover that after weeks of blank refusal Winslow's solicitor has at last got permission to view the evidence on which young Ronnie has been expelled from Osborne Naval College. Similarly we hear how public pressure, brought to bear through letters in the press and questions in the House of Commons, gets the case reopened. Even so, Rattigan had not overcome all the problems by the time rehearsals started. The most effective piece of reporting of off-stage events, when the eccentric maid Violet rushes in and delivers a long and excited description of the end of the trial, seems not to have been added until after the play had opened on its pre-London tour. The speech is a tour de force and, even today, after delivering it, actresses playing Violet frequently get a round of applause from the audience.

Throughout, Rattigan remains close to the essential facts of the Archer-Shee case. Apart from changing the names, he quotes verbatim (less one word) the actual letter sent by the Admiralty to Colonel Archer-Shee informing him of his son's expulsion from Osborne Naval College. The only question he ignores that might interest a present-day author dealing with the same material is how the campaign of public pressure was orchestrated. By changing the characters so as to exclude Archer-Shee's half-brother who was a Tory MP and therefore well placed to initiate such a campaign, Rattigan allows his audience to assume that the British press and MPs will respond vigorously enough to cause a national outcry whenever their suspicions of a case of injustice are aroused by an ordinary citizen who has sufficient belief in his cause to persist in it. Today that would seem a rather complacent assumption, and even in 1945 it reinforced the view of conservative-minded people that traditional British institutions were best left unquestioned.

As the play develops, Rattigan makes it increasingly clear that the real issue at stake is not Ronnie's guilt or innocence but his right as a citizen – although only a child, and accused of something as trivial as the theft of five shillings – to a full and fair trial with legal representation before a properly constituted and independent court. Against this human right Rattigan sets the opinion of those who believe that it is out of all proportion to create such a public storm over a five-shilling postal order, when the nation is faced by mounting crisis in Europe and the potential threat of the fast-growing German navy.[6] He poses too the question of the human priorities within the Winslow family. Arthur Winslow's health deteriorates under the strain. His elder son's career at Oxford is terminated because the cost of the case makes it impossible for his father to keep him there.

Perhaps the most famous scene in the play is the one that brings down the second-act curtain. On the advice of their solicitors, the family hopes to brief the country's most highly esteemed advocate, Sir Robert Morton. He is to interview

Ronnie, and on the outcome of that examination hangs his decision whether or not to take the case. He is a Conservative – 'for a large monopoly attacking a Trade Union or a Tory paper libelling a Labour leader, he is the best', the Winslows' campaigning suffragette daughter Catherine says, but not for a small case of this sort. He could not possibly have his heart in it. Sir Robert finally appears and Ronnie is brought in to face him. He subjects the boy to a fierce cross-examination, outlining the powerful evidence against him, making the boy contradict himself and finally reducing him to tears by venomously denouncing him as 'a forger, a liar and a thief!' While the family are still reeling under the shock, Sir Robert blithely sweeps out, announcing almost casually at the door: 'The boy is plainly innocent. I accept the brief.' The curtain rings down on a great Edwardian coup de théâtre, the audience left stunned and mystified for the interval by this sudden and totally unexplained reversal of what they had expected. Rattigan himself confessed that he had misgivings about that Act Two curtain – 'which when I wrote it made even me ashamed. I thought you can't have so theatrical a curtain as that these days, but then I thought, well, of course, in 1912 you could. So I left it in. Thank God, I did!' On the first night, that Act Two curtain was greeted with great cheers.[7]

Rattigan depicts Sir Robert as cold and supercilious, maintaining an almost unwavering professional detachment throughout, whereas Sir Edward Carson, who was the Archer-Shees' counsel in the original case, was emotional and hot-tempered about the issue from the outset. The reasons for Rattigan's characterization only become fully apparent at the end of the play. The case is not finally brought to proper trial in open court until Sir Robert has successfully brought a Petition of Right on the Winslows' behalf before Parliament. This was an ancient and complex procedure which taxed even Rattigan's mastery of stagecraft to explain convincingly in the theatre. Put simply, a Petition of Right proceeded from the medieval assumption that the king could do no wrong and that a subject could therefore only sue him, or his government, if he received royal assent for such an action. In practice this meant presenting a petition to

Parliament, which the Attorney General might sign on the king's behalf – the form of words then used being, 'Let Right be done.' Only after such endorsement could a case be brought to court. However, as endorsement of all such petitions was at the discretion of the government, the only way in which an unyielding government could be forced to endorse a petition was through a defeat in the House of Commons.

The Petition of Right system was not done away with until, after the publicity surrounding the success of Rattigan's play – when, ironically perhaps, it was a Labour government which abolished it as an anachronistic curb on the liberty of the subject and a survival from a less democratic past.[8]

While the parliamentary debate over the petition rages off-stage, Catherine sums up the democratic principle which is one of Rattigan's principal themes. She tells her doubting fiancé: 'If ever the time comes that the House of Commons has so much on its mind that it can't find time to discuss a Ronnie Winslow and his bally postal order, this country will be a far poorer place.'

News of the result of the court case comes early in the fourth and final act of the play. The Winslows have won; but each member of the family has sustained lasting damage as a result of their fight: the compensation paid is unlikely to cover the full financial outlay on the case; Arthur's health has been impaired; the elder son has no degree; Catherine has not made the marriage she wanted because, in an attempt to halt the Winslows' fight against the establishment, her fiancé's conventional family have withdrawn their consent. However, it is clear that the result of the case is not the play's main subject. Rattigan clears the stage for a final confrontation between Catherine, the progressive, and Sir Robert, the conservative, the two characters upon whom the play has increasingly focused. Each has betrayed an increasing interest in and respect for the other. Rattigan leaves his audience waiting to see if there will be a conventional happy ending.

Catherine starts the scene by apologizing for having misjudged Sir Robert. Then she asks why he is at such pains to prevent people knowing the truth about him; he replies that it is perhaps because he does not know the truth about himself. But why is he ashamed of his emotions, asks Catherine. 'Because as a lawyer I must necessarily distrust them.' We are right back in the heart of Rattigan country. Sir Robert goes on: 'Emotions muddy the issue. Cold, clear logic – and buckets of it – should be the lawyer's only equipment.' He wept at the verdict only because, 'Right had been done.' Rattigan does not dwell on the conflict between intellect and emotion but moves swiftly on to the final statement of the play's theme. 'Right had been done,' says Sir Robert. 'Not justice?' counters Catherine. 'No, not justice. Right. It is easy to do justice – very hard to do right.' Finally, Catherine asks him how he can reconcile his support for Winslow against the Crown with his political beliefs. 'Very easily,' Sir Robert replies, 'no one party has a monopoly of concern for individual liberty. On that issue all parties are united.' Catherine qualifies the sentiment: 'No, not all parties. Only some people from all parties.' Sir Robert accepts this – 'We can only hope, then, that those same people will always prove enough people.' And so they part, leaving Catherine, who only a little earlier had been despairing of the cause of women's suffrage, determined to continue the fight for women's rights. Not a conventional happy ending nor a rounding-off, but an ending characteristic of Rattigan; one where the audience can sense that the characters will continue their lives after the fall of the curtain, but with the courses on which they are set radically shifted by the events witnessed. Catherine accepts the loss of emotional happiness, embracing instead the opportunity for fulfilment in duty, a cause, an ideal for which to struggle.[9]

The Winslow Boy is a finely detailed statement of Rattigan's beliefs as a dramatist. While it may have started out as a reactionary tract, and in production may have given succour to reactionaries who did not wish to recognize its full implications, it emerges as a reworking of Rattigan's philosophical and emotional position in the light of the changed circumstances of the world at the end of the war.

Most of the play's faults stem from the circumstances of its conception and the limitations Rattigan imposed on himself while writing it in arguments with Anatole de Grunwald and Anthony Asquith. Rattigan brilliantly won his bet with Asquith by telling the story in the manner of an Edwardian play, without including a court scene. Indeed, he went one better, never moving his scene from the Winslow drawing-room. But while one cannot fail to admire the brilliance of Rattigan's technique, one is conscious of contrivance. The play remains too domestic to encompass the full implications of its theme. None of the characters, with the exception of Catherine, is quite rounded enough; and although all are given motives for their behaviour, their actions do not spring from revealed character. In other words, one senses the manipulative hand of the author.

In the autumn of 1945, Dr Keith Newman went finally insane and had to be permanently confined in a mental institution, a fate which relieved Rattigan of the last vestiges of the hold Newman had over him. At the same time it released the young actor Jack Watling from a hold so total that he was himself in imminent danger of mental collapse. Rattigan offered Watling shelter and a chance to relax in a house that he had acquired in Sonning on the Thames. While Watling was staying in Sonning, Rattigan read him *The Winslow Boy*. 'It was the best performance of the play I ever heard,' recalled Watling, who later played the elder son in the London production.

'It may sound cynical, but the war has been the making of me. Can't complain about a thing. Look at me and look at the Firm. And to think I owe it all to Hitler.'[10] If the war had improved Rattigan's fortunes it had dramatically transformed Binkie Beaumont's. Since the death during the war of the owner of H. M. Tennent Ltd, Harry Tennent, and Binkie Beaumont's first production as sole boss, *Flare Path*, Tennent's had grown into the wealthiest management and Binkie Beaumont into the most powerful man in the West End theatre. Of the thirty-six theatres open in May 1945, eight were playing H. M. Tennent productions. A year later the number had doubled. Three years older than Rattigan, like him Beaumont still looked incredibly young. He was quiet, immensely discreet, manipulative, always immaculately turned out – and he expected those around him to be the same. In time, his power would breed resentment. Beaumont had many things in common with Rattigan. Kitty

Black, who knew and worked with many of the brightest people of her generation, claimed that Beaumont was one of the most beautiful young men she ever saw and that he had the quickest brain she ever met. He had pale blue eyes and startlingly white skin. Although many people, even in the theatre, were unaware of it, Beaumont was a homosexual. Rattigan's friend from his early writing days with Gielgud, John Perry, had become Beaumont's lover and trouble-shooter in the company. In a sense Beaumont and Rattigan owed their success to each other.

Rattigan had told Beaumont about *The Winslow Boy* before it was finished. As soon as it was complete Rattigan's agent, A. D. Peters, sent it to him. Rattigan wanted Gielgud to play Sir Robert Morton, but he turned it down. Eric Portman was also approached, but he also turned it down – perhaps because he did not think the part was big enough. Finally Beaumont offered the part to Emlyn Williams and he accepted it.

The play opened on tour in late February 1946 and was a success even before it opened in London. The management received a letter from the surviving Archer-Shee daughter, on whom the character of Catherine was based, announcing that she was coming to see a performance when the production reached Bristol. It seems that she was a high-minded Tory and was annoyed to hear that Rattigan had made Catherine a liberal and a suffragette. Nervously, Rattigan travelled down to Bristol to meet her. He took her out for a champagne supper and charmed her into dropping her objections to the play.

The Winslow Boy opened in London on 23 May 1946 at the Lyric Theatre, previously the home of *Love in Idleness*. It was another huge success, Rattigan's fourth in a row, and did almost as well in America as in Britain. The play ran for 476 performances in London and 218 performances at the Empire Theatre, New York. It won for Rattigan the Ellen Terry Award – the first time the award was made – for the best play produced in London in 1946, and the New York Critics' Award for the Best Foreign Play of 1947. The reviews were the best he had ever had. As Rattigan himself wryly recalled a few years later, the play caused:

something of a critical sensation. It was generally felt to be very strange that a notoriously insincere *farceur* could so readily turn his hand to matters of fairly serious theatrical moment, and I found myself on the one hand warmly commended for my courage, and on the other sternly reprimanded for having hidden for so long my light under a bushel. I was myself conscious neither of the virtue nor of the vice, but for all that basked happily, if with a few pangs of conscience, in the sun of the critics' praise.[11]

Notes

1   Robert Rhodes James, op. cit.
2   Graham Greene, 'The Virtues of Disloyalty', his speech of acceptance of the Shakespeare Prize, Hamburg, 1969.
3   During the production of *Love in Idleness* the Lunts had also given Rattigan a copy of a newspaper article about the case.
4   *Strand Magazine*, February 1947.
5   Preface to *Collected Plays*, Volume I, op. cit.
6   Rattigan advanced the action to the eve of the 1914–18 war to heighten the gravity of outside events and of the German naval threat that confronted the Admiralty.
7   In fact, in winning his bet with Asquith and containing all the action in a single set, the Winslows' drawing-room, and at the same time having the defence barrister, Sir Robert Morton, represent the entire legal side of the story, Rattigan had to resort to some distortions of legal procedures and rules. Under what was known as 'the cab-rank system' a barrister was not allowed to accept or reject a brief on the basis of whether he believed the defendant guilty or innocent, as all defendants were supposed to be guaranteed an equal right to legal representation in court. In practice, which cases a busy barrister, such as Sir Robert, took would be determined by his clerk, who set the barrister's fees at such a level as to keep the number of briefs to a number that the barrister could handle. Also, no barrister would interview a potential client in the client's home in the way required by Rattigan in *The Winslow Boy*.
8   The Petition of Right system was done away with in 1947 under the terms of the Crown Proceedings Act as part of a major post-war reform of the law. I am indebted to the leading barrister and legal authority Mr Francis Bennion for this information and the material in the preceding note on legal practice at the time when the play is set.
9   When the play was produced in America, the Broadway producer tried to persuade Rattigan to give it a conventional happy ending by suggesting romance between Sir Robert and Catherine. Rattigan demurred.
10 Richard Huggett, op. cit.
11 Preface to *Collected Plays*, Volume I, op. cit.

9

Playbill

'Play-as-you-earn Rattigan' said a *Daily Express* headline in April 1946, over an article on his phenomenal earnings and tax liability. 'Mr Terence Rattigan, the playwright, has chambers in eighteenth-century Albany which are an example of the combination of selection, contrast and restraint in decoration and furnishing necessary to provide modern comfort without undue formality,' began a photographic feature in *Ideal Home* for April 1947. 'My ambition is static,' Rattigan responded to an *Auckland Weekly News* reporter in November 1946, when asked if his ambition had been affected by success. 'It always remains the same – not to be content with writing a play to please an audience today, but to write a play that will be remembered in fifty years' time.'

These three press stories give a fair impression of the public Rattigan in the period immediately following the production of *The Winslow Boy*. The article in *Ideal Home* illustrates the extent to which Rattigan was now regarded as one of the most fashionably elegant young men in London. Almost any article on the haunts or style of celebrities was likely to include a picture or comment from Terence (*French Without Tears*) Rattigan – in spite of his subsequent successes the label still stuck. For example, when the *Tatler* did an article on London's most famous 'showbusiness restaurant', The Ivy, there was a picture of Rattigan with a film producer, in perfectly cut double-breasted chalk-striped suit, beaming boyishly. He featured in the *Tailor and Cutter*'s selection of best-dressed men in London; his attendance at fashionable parties, discreet dinners with Greta Garbo and trips to New York aboard the *Queen Elizabeth* were all fodder for the gossip columnists. When the *Daily Sketch* did a feature on the famous, not to say superior, persons who inhabited Albany, it was inevitable that the first photograph in the spread was of Rattigan elegantly crossed-legged on a sofa, his left hand resting lightly on his white French poodle Tiffin. The fact of his residence in Albany was regularly slipped into news items covering his many activities. It was something of which he was proud – proof positive that he had 'arrived'. Of course not everyone who came into contact with Rattigan found the high gloss on his manner quite so seductive. In the autumn of 1946 he worked with Graham Greene on a screen adaptation of his novel *Brighton Rock*. Years later Greene told Michael Meyer that he had found 'talking to Terence Rattigan like walking on very slippery parquet flooring'.[1]

At the time when *The Winslow Boy* opened, a new vogue for what John Russell Taylor has called 'theatricalism' was already discernible in London. Verse plays by Christopher Fry and Ronald Duncan were receiving critical acclaim, if not commercial success. Poetic, colourful but ultimately vaporous, the work of Fry and Anouilh looked like a reaction to the war, Stafford Cripps's austerity budgets and continuing rationing. The new playwrights were the very opposite of Rattigan – their work was overstatement, where his was understatement. As far back as 1944, after *Love in Idleness*, Beverley Nichols had suggested to Rattigan in his column that he should write 'a play that will cause the sort of social uproar which it is one of the theatre's functions to create'. It would not have been surprising if Rattigan had now attempted a problem play in a contemporary setting or an epic, but his mind was working in a totally different direction. Among friends he had started to argue that the intervals between acts in the normal play disturbed the dramatic illusion – he had no time for alienation techniques. Although he later used long sequences of short impressionistic scenes, this was always to create illusion. Rattigan forecast the development of generally shorter plays in the theatre with running times of sixty to eighty minutes. He was frequently accused of being behind his time but here he was demonstrably ahead of it.

Voices had recently been raised criticizing the dearth of new plays by British dramatists. Rattigan's had been one. As guest critic of the *Sunday Chronicle,* he had lambasted an adaptation of a foreign play and called for original work in the British theatre. Among the older playwrights, James Bridie had also been vociferous, laying much of the blame on the commercial management of London theatres and the unhealthy policy which sought to increase the length of runs in order to maximize profits – thus reinforcing proven success and hampering experiment. Bridie was now writing largely for the Citizens' Theatre in Glasgow – a repertory theatre. Repertory and the notion of state subsidy seemed the best hope for the serious theatre. The wartime creation of CEMA, the Council for the Encouragement of Music and the Arts, later the Arts Council, had grown out of the belief that the arts should not be the prerogative of a cultured few, living in London and the big cities. Although this had resulted in worthy productions of Shakespeare and support for touring companies, it had, as yet, done little to encourage new writing. This was almost wholly left to daring amateur companies or professionals working for very little in a few small theatres and societies. But Rattigan's run of successes made him one of a select band of writers who could hope to get almost anything he wrote accepted for professional production.

Keith Newman had observed that Rattigan became bored repeating things he had mastered. Having succeeded with three-act plays and a throw-back to the Edwardian four-acter, he decided to try his hand at one-act plays. He announced that he was writing four one-act plays which would be produced by John Gielgud the following year. Gielgud seems to have given him some encouragement, telling him he was interested in the idea of playing four separate characters in the course of two evenings, if only because it broke up the monotony of a long run. Rattigan was notoriously inclined to take a polite expression of interest as encouragement to go ahead with a project, and he put it about that each play would be an hour and a quarter long and they would be put on two each night, turn and turn about. It was a dangerous scheme. The one-act play had fallen into almost total disfavour and it would be a brave management which put on a double bill, even with Rattigan's name behind it. For his first two one-acters, he chose subjects which touched on his deepest personal concerns. In both he drew on his past, making extensive raids on his 'writer's cupboard'. One was a deeply serious play, *The Browning Version*, which owed its origins to his time at Harrow. The second was little more than a skit on a theatrical family staging *Romeo and Juliet*, which owed a good deal to working with the Lunts and his experiences with Gielgud's Oxford production. Beneath the jokey surface, however, Rattigan's total addiction to his first love, the theatre, is clearly visible.

By late November 1946 *The Browning Version* was complete. It is about intellectual failure and the anguish resulting from emotional atrophy. Rattigan was enjoying greater critical and financial success than he had ever known, and at first sight it is surprising that he should choose this moment to write such a play. However, one has only to examine Rattigan himself and the events of his private life to see how such a theme seemed almost inevitable at this point in his career. Rattigan had enjoyed the critical praise of *The Winslow Boy*, but deep down he distrusted it. Although he freely admitted to reading critics avidly, to being lifted by their praise and cast down by their condemnation, he knew enough about their fickleness to rely on the inner conviction that the ultimate judge of success or failure was himself. When Agate had compared *While the Sun Shines* with Oscar Wilde, Rattigan reminded his public that the same critic had only a few years previously dismissed *French Without Tears*, on which the later play had been consciously modelled, as 'nothing'. 'No writer,' he remarked, 'can grow from nothing into Oscar Wilde between one light comedy and another.'[2] Rattigan's own assessment of his achievement so far was less favourable than that of some recent critics, but then he was measuring himself against the highest standards and not merely technical facility.

The intellectual disillusionment at the time of the production of *After the Dance*, which had made him ask whether he should have concentrated on history rather than becoming a playwright, had not been totally dispelled by his success. He still doubted whether he was fulfilling his intellectual potential. He had friends who criticized his work because it demonstrated no spiritual or philosophical quest. There was a growing suspicion that he was spending too much time surrounded by people who were not his intellectual equals. But the most important factor, the one that did most to precipitate the writing of *The Browning Version*, was undoubtedly emotional in origin.

Chips Channon was a glittering social figure – 'the iron butterfly', as Rattigan and his friends called him behind his back. For all his gaiety and social poise, Channon was at heart a failure. He had accepted gracefully the frustration of his political and creative ambitions and long ago decided on an observer's role. His distinction was to fill his butterfly role with such luxurious wit and elegance that he seemed to belong to Regency England rather than to the 1940s. His considerable creativity was poured into elaborate entertaining and his diaries, which he packed with outrageously frank observations on the foibles and follies of the important figures of his time – all of whom he went out of his way to meet. He intended his diaries to be a unique record that would, after their deaths, be published. But his marriage, which had done so much at the outset to buy him his social position, had just ended in amicable divorce. Now fifty, Channon had begun to feel himself a prematurely old man. His feelings for Rattigan were undoubtedly much stronger than for most of the young men he 'rented'; but they were not feelings Rattigan could reciprocate. He found Channon's demands increasingly difficult to meet. The consolation Channon might have found in Rattigan was not forthcoming.

After the completion of *The Winslow Boy*, but before finishing *The Browning Version*, Rattigan made up his mind to break off the relationship with Channon. He must have brooded on his decision for some time before telling Channon. The irony was that the feeling which he could not reciprocate for Channon, he had begun to feel for someone else. He would himself soon be racked by the very possessiveness he resented from Channon.

Kenneth Morgan, the young actor who in 1939 had played

Babe Lake in the film of *French Without Tears*, had largely dropped out of Rattigan's life while he was in the forces. But in 1944 Morgan had been invalided out of the navy and had contacted Rattigan, who put him in touch with his own fashionable doctor, William Buky. By 1946 Morgan had regained his health and re-entered Rattigan's life. However, his acting career was no longer quite fulfilling its pre-war promise. Since his discharge from the navy he had spent a year with a theatre company in Notting Hill Gate and the first six months of 1946 away from London in a tour. A great many other actors had been demobbed from the services by this time, and apart from a production at Hammersmith, work for Morgan had almost dried up. Now almost thirty, perhaps his stage personality had not matured to match his looks (a fate that befalls many juveniles who achieve success while they still look incredibly young). He was still wide-eyed, 'an elf', with an air of innocence, but not a colourful personality. Just how strongly Rattigan had been attracted to Morgan before the war is hard to gauge. Rattigan was now thirty-six and, although he was still casually promiscuous, the driving excitement and libidinous bravado associated with the kind of encounter he had experienced with Peter Osborn early in the war had abated. Osborn too had re-entered Rattigan's life, in spite of having stayed on in the navy as a regular officer. Their relationship however, although still warm, was now platonic. Whatever had or had not happened between Rattigan and Morgan before the war, Rattigan now found himself very strongly drawn to him. His role in the relationship with Chips Channon was now reversed: Rattigan became the pursuer, Morgan the pursued. And of course, relative to Ken Morgan, Rattigan was in the financial position of Chips Channon; he could now play Zeus to Morgan's Danae. Morgan moved in with Rattigan, who smothered him with gifts and affection. He started making Morgan payments, some under headings allowable for tax purposes such as 'For criticism of plays'. Rattigan had never felt so strongly about another person. But, like Rattigan with Channon, Morgan seems to have been unable fully to return his feelings. What Rattigan had observed in others he now began to experience in himself – the more desperately you try to make someone love you the less they do.

All this had, of course, to be concealed from the public. One of Rattigan's reasons for breaking with Channon had been the fear that their relationship was becoming too public. To be seen so much in his company might cause speculation. With the high-profile public positions they occupied, and faced with a press that was becoming less inhibited about prying into the private lives of public personalities, Rattigan had no option but to become ever more discreet about his sex life. The cruel repression engendered by the law, which still made those found guilty of homosexual acts, even between consenting adults in private, liable to severe prison sentences, is too easily overlooked today. Blackmail was not uncommon and criminal prosecution by no means unknown. It was understandable then that Rattigan, who was in any case naturally shy, was cripplingly reticent about his sexual relationships. It went deeper than his fear of offending convention or earning the disapproval of his parents. There were occasional lapses, but only among his friends or when he had been drinking – on one famous occasion he tried to pick up an actor at a party in front of the man's wife, and when the actor seemed reluctant, told him he was missing out on the best chance of his life. But normally he was extraordinarily discreet.

The degree of falsity and artificiality imposed on Rattigan by this necessary concealment can to some extent be gauged by the replies he gave to a reporter from *Woman* magazine in 1947:

He talked about the difficulty of writers – who are essentially creatures of mood – marrying. He believes friction is bound to arise if writer marries writer. Wouldn't want a wife to have anything to do with either the theatre or films, at least she should have to give up her work on marrying. Puts tact high on the list... she must have his interests completely at heart, be intensely loyal, alive to his professional faults, yet never mention them. He wants a good companion, someone with whom he could be silent for two hours and yet feel wonderfully entertained. He prefers someone of whom men will say, 'I don't understand what he sees in her.' He would want her to enjoy the things he likes, travel, tennis, golf, watching cricket. He thinks jealousy, justified or not, the most infuriating of emotions, hates dominating women, those who smother a man with devotion and drown him in glasses of milk.

The Browning Version, although based on an incident from his boyhood, is a reflection of Rattigan's enforced endurance of such concealment. Beautifully but unobtrusively shaped, it deals with emotional repression, falsity, failure and love in a densely packed yet completely satisfying hour and a quarter. The plot through which Rattigan opens up such large themes, while maintaining a completely convincing naturalism and a poignant, essentially English quality of understatement, is deceptively simple. The setting is that most British of institutions, a boys' public school. After eighteen years of increasing failure as a teacher, Andrew Crocker-Harris is being driven into premature retirement by heart trouble. During his time at the school he has progressed downwards; a brilliant and idealistic scholar when he started teaching, dedicated to communicating his own great love of classical Greek literature to the boys, he is now a desiccated pedant, held in contempt by his fellow teachers and feared by his pupils: 'the Himmler of the Lower Fifth'. He has been unable to satisfy the sexual needs of his wife, Millie, who with calculated destructiveness has turned to other men. She is carrying on an affair with a popular young master, Frank Hunter, which she has deliberately advertised to her husband. However, Frank is tiring of her, unable to reciprocate the feelings she has for him.

It is the penultimate day of term. The headmaster conveys to Crocker-Harris the school governors' decision not to grant him a badly needed pension, and asks him to forgo his right to speak last at the next day's prize-giving ceremony, in order that the speech of the master who coached the school cricket team to victory at Lord's may bring the proceedings to a popular climax. To all this, as to his wife's cruelty, Crocker-Harris placidly assents, registering no protest or show of feeling. He treats his situation as if it had no emotional meaning for him. 'You can't hurt Andrew,' his wife tells her lover. 'He's dead.'

Years of pent-up emotion are released by one small gesture: an act of kindness in which a boy, Taplow, who likes Crocker-Harris in spite of his forbidding exterior, gives him a leaving present – a second-hand copy of Browning's translation of his favourite play, the *Agamemnon* of Aeschylus. Crocker-Harris breaks down. This, for him, is the single success which 'can atone and more than atone for all the failures in the world'. With courage born of this one small show of gratitude, Crocker-Harris himself makes a small gesture of defiance and reclaims a shred of self-respect: he will, after all, exercise his right to speak last at the school prize-giving.

Rattigan said more than once that to a great extent the boy Taplow was himself while at Harrow, telling Gillian Hodson and me quite specifically that the central incident in the story – Taplow's gift to the retiring master – was based on his own school experience; and that the character of Crocker-Harris grew out of his speculation about how a human being reached the point, as his own Greek master Coke Norris had done, where he responded to an act of ordinary human kindness with unkindness. The *Agamemnon* had been Rattigan's favourite play at school, and he ascribed a large part of his determination to become a dramatist to having read it in translation in the Harrow school library after his discovery, despite Coke Norris's dry-as-dust teaching methods, that it was a living play and not a dead text.

But Rattigan's identification with the play and its characters goes much further than a few autobiographical details. One day while he was at work on it, his manservant came in to find tears streaming down his face. The character in whom people have seen most self-identification is obviously Crocker-Harris; but, as always with Rattigan, it extends in varying degrees to all the characters. It is most in evidence in the central trio – Crocker-Harris, Millie and Frank – both individually and in their relationship to each other.

Early in the play Frank Hunter, whom Rattigan describes in his stage directions as 'wrapped in all the self-confidence of the popular master', admits to Millie Crocker-Harris that after only three years as a schoolmaster he has slipped into an act with his pupils which he just can't get out of. 'My God, how easy it is to be popular,' he says, but goes on to explain that this is achieved at the expense of being oneself. The theme of deceit and falsity in relations between people pervades the play. Characters who hide their feelings, relationships which are not as they appear, bonhomie which hides pain, all have been much in evidence throughout Rattigan's writing. Yet in *The Browning Version* the full destructive force of these elements is revealed for the first time. He shows how deceit in personal relationships, the pursuit of popularity and emotional repression all lead to tragedy; not just to personal unhappiness but to a betrayal of integrity, the undermining of ideals and the destruction of the emotional security on which ultimately everyone depends.

The principal characters inhabit an emotional wasteland of unsatisfied longings, in which life has been almost extinguished by years of starvation from true human feeling or responsiveness, and this is heightened by the way in which the social relationships between even the minor characters are based on a polite dishonesty. The headmaster, whom Rattigan describes as being 'like a successful diplomat', is the most obviously socially correct, and therefore socially dishonest, of the minor characters. Throughout, Millie gives herself airs, making out that her father runs a large business, when in fact he has a clothing shop in the Bradford Arcade. The very first action of the play is a piece of deceit − before anyone else has appeared the boy Taplow surreptitiously takes two chocolates from a box on the table in the Crocker-Harrises' room, but, judging that he might not get away with the theft of two chocolates, he replaces one.

The play mirrors the complexity of Rattigan's own emotional world and inner conflicts at every turn. He no longer needs Keith Newman, here he is his own analyst. Central to Crocker-Harris's failure as a master has been his attempt to win popularity by encouraging the boys to laugh at him. By playing up to their delight in his mannerisms and tricks of speech, he has tried to compensate for his lack of natural ability to make himself liked. He rationalizes his behaviour by saying that more things can be taught by laughter than by earnestness, yet he knows in his heart, even though he is afraid to acknowledge it, that this has undermined his ability to communicate his true feelings for the great literature of the past. By being afraid to be himself he has betrayed both himself and the literature he loves. He knows that the origins of his failure go deeper than his illness: 'Not sickness of the body, but a sickness of the soul,' he says.

The same cankerous deceit and repression of true feelings that afflicts Crocker-Harris has entered the emotional relationships of each of the principal characters. All three central characters pretend to a concern for each other that they do not really feel; all become, with the possible exception of Millie, better off at the end of the play, after they have shed their pretences, by being themselves. Even the lovers are dishonest with each other. Frank has tired of Millie but has not told her, and has in any case never felt as strongly about her as he has allowed her to believe. Millie admits eventually to using Frank for emotional and sexual gratification. The ultimate irony is that Crocker-Harris knows about Millie's affair with Frank because she has told him, as she has told him about all her previous affairs. She tells Crocker-Harris the truth, but to her the truth is a weapon to be used specifically to hurt him. The use of the truth is Millie's greatest cruelty. Frank goes so far as to warn Crocker-Harris that she intends to kill him with it. It is Rattigan's central paradox: honesty is a prerequisite of emotional fulfilment, but at the same time it is the vehicle of deadly pain. Without honesty there may be no hope; with it there may be no comfort. It was a paradox which permeated Rattigan's own life.

In the film of *The Browning Version*, Rattigan added a scene in which a group of masters' wives discuss the Crocker-Harrises: 'Yes, a marriage of mind and body. It never has worked since the world began.' Here, as in so many film scripts based on his own plays, Rattigan makes a blunt statement of one of the work's major themes: inequality of emotion and mismatching of relationships. In both play and film, Crocker-Harris explains that he and his wife are equally to be pitied: 'Both of us needing from the other something that would make life supportable for us, and neither of us able to give it. Two kinds of love. Hers and mine. Worlds apart . . .'

Millie, unable to find what she requires in her husband, has turned elsewhere. She has become an embittered neurotic, not simply through lack of physical satisfaction, but through years of deprivation of emotional fulfilment and release which ought to come from the sexual expression of love – Rattigan is never interested, through his characters, in the damage caused by purely physical sexual deprivation.

The pain inflicted on those who love by the petty cruelties of their loved ones is beautifully observed. While Millie deliberately inflicts repeated petty humiliations on her husband, she in turn suffers from Frank's petty oversights. She has bought him a seat for a school cricket match at Lord's; he fails to turn up, and she asks if he has ever been in love with anyone: 'Do you realize what torture you inflict on someone who loves you when you do a thing like that?' When he confesses that he clean forgot, she begs for pity: 'Do you think it's any pleasanter for me to believe that you cut me because you forgot? Do you think that doesn't hurt either?' At another point, she notes triumphantly that Frank is still using a gold cigarette case she gave him – that he hasn't given it to another girlfriend. This sails very close to Rattigan's own experience: not only had Chips Channon been in the habit of showering him with similar presents, but Rattigan was also in the habit of giving his boyfriends gold cigarette cases, which had a habit of turning up in other hands.

But the love, and the failure of love, in *The Browning Version* is not cast in the mould of heroic tragedy or theatrical grand passion. It is more in keeping with its subject – the failure of a rather colourless schoolmaster. Devoid of human affection, such people become devoid of human dignity. One small gesture of human sympathy transforms the situation, and in the end Crocker-Harris's little act of defiance takes on great force as a symbol of the reassertion of human dignity. Crocker-Harris himself belittles his own situation, saying that it is not very unusual 'or nearly as tragic as you seem to imagine. Merely the problem of an unsatisfied wife and a henpecked husband...It is usually, I believe, a subject for farce!'

The denouement of the play caused Rattigan much trouble.

He recognized that a neat tragic ending – probably Crocker-Harris's death from his heart trouble – might win him praise from critics and audience alike. He was very tempted to send his audience home crying happily, and confessed that in his youth he would have contrived just such an ending. However, he felt that this was too easy – it was not only too pat, it evaded the issues he had raised. Later he was accused of having given *The Browning Version* a quasi-happy ending. This he disputed, but he did recognize that by giving the play an inconclusive ending he had upset the more conventional members of his audience. This was, of course, not the first time he had given one of his plays an ending which left the characters with problems to solve and lives to continue. Most of his endings are to a certain extent inconclusive. However, *The Browning Version* is perhaps the first occasion on which he took a calculated risk, deliberately leaving the play unresolved in the hope of making the audience continue to ponder the implications of what had been placed before them. Crocker-Harris's final act of defiance to the headmaster restores his dignity but does not solve any of his problems or wipe out his years of failure. He still has to live with the reality of his situation.

This is the message of many of Rattigan's mature plays: human beings cannot live unless they come to terms with the truth about themselves and their circumstances, no matter how painful that truth may be. Without self-knowledge there is no hope. However comforting self-delusion may be, it leads finally, like an addictive drug, to death. Rattigan sees men as ultimately the masters of their own fate, and says uncompromisingly that they may not opt out but must confront their lives for themselves. Love and friendship may help, but in the end each person is on his or her own. This is not a comforting view – despite the sneers of Rattigan's detractors – nor is it a bleak one. Rattigan's position is profoundly humanistic.

The mastery of the play is brought out by comparing it with the film, which is itself widely accepted as a classic of the British cinema and perhaps the finest of Anthony Asquith's films. In the theatre Rattigan manages to pack his wealth of feeling and implication into one set, in one scene lasting little over an hour, without strain or apparent contrivance. The film, although it conveys much of the same feeling, is both longer and more explicit, and therefore weaker. At the end of the film the Crock is seen making his prize-day speech to the school. He movingly confesses his failure, apologizing to the boys for having let them down. After a stunned silence the boys break into cheers. The audience is allowed to leave the cinema suffused in a glow of sentimentality, excused from thinking any further about the fundamental issues raised by the script. Its tragedy and challenge are undermined. The most remarkable feature of the film is the performance of Michael Redgrave in the central role. In his moving and perceptive book about his father, Corin Redgrave ascribes Michael Redgrave's extraordinarily powerful performance in part to his identification with the inner torment of Crocker-Harris and his own repressed bisexuality.[3]

The second play in the projected quartet of one-acters, provisionally called *Perdita*, was a sharp and deliberate contrast. Where *The Browning Version* had been a tragedy centred on emotional repression and an introverted character, *Perdita* was a farce about a theatrical family – the Gosports – who exhibit their changing feelings with the same extrovert panache as their theatrical costumes. Rattigan made no secret of the fact that his characterization of the Gosports – Edna Selby and Arthur Gosport – owed a lot to the Lunts. One character, a local newspaper reporter, enquires about the fact that the Gosports always act together and asks if they always play as husband and wife; he is told: 'No, usually as lover and mistress. The audience prefers that. It gives them such a cosy feeling to know they're really married after all.'

Perdita was set in a theatre in a Midlands town where the Gosports are dress-rehearsing their production of *Romeo and Juliet*, prior to opening on an CEMA tour. Edna is playing Juliet and her husband is directing as well as playing Romeo. The way in which they needle each other in rehearsal, and wheedle to get their own way, while keeping up a front of mutual admiration and adoration, is very reminiscent of descriptions by eye-witnesses of the Lunts' rehearsals. The fact that they are rehearsing *Romeo and*

Juliet leads one to expect references to Rattigan's own experiences in Gielgud's Oxford production, and one is not disappointed. The actor playing the one line, 'Faith, we may put up our pipes and be gone' (Rattigan's line at Oxford), leaves the production and a breathless, incompetent youngster is selected to replace him. He proudly tells his mother, whom he has sneaked into the back of the gallery, of his new found pre-eminence. He then sets about trying his one line with a series of different inflections, with the emphasis on a different word each time, to the increasing annoyance of the company.

Arthur Gosport's rehearsal methods and mannerisms owe something to Gielgud as well as to Alfred Lunt – particularly his absent-mindedness, caused by his total absorption in the production. His way of remembering the date of outside events by recalling which play he was appearing in at the time may be reminiscent of Gielgud, but the fact that he can only remember the date of the General Strike by recalling that 'it was the year Gladys Cooper opened in *The Sign of the Door*', caricatures many elderly actors. The habit of seeing important public events only in terms of their consequences for the theatre or the current production is a characteristic of almost the entire acting profession. Accordingly, Rattigan has Gosport's aunt, Dame Maud – a formidable old actress who is playing the Nurse – recall playing Juliet in 1914: 'I remember the date well, because the declaration of war damaged our business so terribly.'

The plot is extravagant, in the best traditions of farce. Amid the routine but hilarious chaos of their dress-rehearsal, the Gosports discover that they are bigamously married – Arthur having previously contracted marriage to a lady in a ceremony which he has absent-mindedly overlooked. In resolving this difficulty, Rattigan, unlike conventional farceurs, allowed his play to develop out of his characters. While he was working on the play, he wrote an article in *Strand Magazine* called 'How I Write My Plays'. In it he said that he had a formula for farce: 'a formula which, though extremely simple, has not, up to now, been generally followed. I believe in the farce of character – a contradiction in terms, most purist minded critics would say, but wrongly, as I think.' He argues that by creating believable characters and rooting the plot, however farcical, firmly in their behaviour, he encourages continuous audience laughter because he does not excite disbelief.

Rattigan himself later declined to defend the play as anything more than a soufflé designed to round off a meal of which *The Browning Version* was the main course. But, like all good chefs, he concocted a soufflé worthy of the rest of his meal which was, distinctively his own. Nothing concerned him more than the theatre, and here he expressed his attitude towards it more clearly than anywhere else in his writing. The Gosports, we are told, '*are* the theatre'. They are the theatre at its best and worst – 'They're true theatre, because they're entirely self-centred, entirely exhibitionist and entirely dotty, and because they make no compromise whatever with the outside world ... All through the ages, from Burbage downwards, the theatre – the true theatre – has consisted of blind, anti-social, self-sufficient, certifiable Gosports.'

Edna Gosport tries to explain the immense change that has come over the theatre in recent years – 'The theatre of today has at last acquired a social conscience, and a social purpose. Why else do you think we're opening at this rat-hole of a theatre instead of the Opera House, Manchester?' Dame Maud says she didn't know it was social purpose that had brought them there, she thought it was CEMA. Edna replies scathingly, 'CEMA is social purpose.' Later, the stage-manager explains that theatre with a social purpose is a contradiction in terms: 'Good citizenship and good theatre don't go together. They never have and they never will.' As far as the stage-manager is concerned, social purpose in the theatre seems to mean 'playing Shakespeare to audiences who'd rather go to the films; while audiences who'd rather go to Shakespeare are driven to the films because they haven't got Shakespeare to go to. It's all got something to do with the new Britain and apparently it's an absolutely splendid idea.' If that is a true reflection of Rattigan's theatrical beliefs – and there is every reason to believe it is – then it is hardly surprising that, apart from *Follow My Leader*, he never wrote a didactic play. There is also a sharp put down for the new vogue for high-flown, humourless verse drama.

For the third play in the quartet, *High Summer*, Rattigan reworked quite a lot of the ideas he had intended to tackle in *Love in Idleness*. Here again we have a son returning home to a widowed mother living in sin and comfort with a usurping father. Again the son is imbued with socialist ideals. But this time the son, who has become a painter after being disgraced and thrown out of the Diplomatic Service, is older and returns home because he is short of money. In *High Summer* the son is revealed as a phoney. It is made apparent even to him that his motives for returning home, to which he attempts to give a saving gloss of principle, are entirely self-centred – in addition to his need of money to support his self-indulgent lifestyle, he is animated by an unnatural and possessive love of his mother and by jealousy. He is a poseur, a facile technician with a limited gift rather than a true artist. He is incapable of real love for others. Those he might love he simply uses as objects for his own gratification. The only feeling he truly knows is self-love. Clearly then, a piece crowded with themes of potentially painful significance for Rattigan. Unfortunately, he fails to grapple with any of them effectively. The result is disastrous. Set in an Edwardian country house during a cricket match, the effect is merely flippant. In the words of the critic, and friend of Rattigan, B. A. Young, in his 1986 assessment of his work: 'It is a very poor piece that seems as if it might have been meant to be in the style of Oscar Wilde – not *The Importance*, but the more serious works – but has somehow slipped into the world of Dornford Yates.'[4]

But although Rattigan had once again jibbed at confronting his relationship with his parents head-on, in *High Summer* he does give an accurate indication of some of his other pressing concerns at the time when he was writing it. Despite the fact that in the preceding three years he had earned enough money to have settled himself comfortably for life, by early 1947 Rattigan was once more almost broke. His accountant told him that he would have to sell the house that he had recently bought in Sonning. He also told him that he would have to stop his lavish entertaining and extravagant holidays. After finishing his part of the work on *Brighton Rock* with Graham Greene he had put up at the Miramar Hotel in Cannes and lost a small fortune gambling in the casino. In two years he got through in excess of sixty thousand pounds (today the equivalent of substantially over a million).

Another concern was the living and financial arrangements of his parents. Early in the war he had moved them out of the bombing to a large country house called Pepsal End at Pepperstock, near Luton. There his father had adopted something of the style of the landed gentlemen among whom he had mixed in his heyday as a diplomat. He shot regularly in his grounds and kept a gamebook. After the war, tradesmen were encouraged to address their accounts to him as Colonel Rattigan. Of course it was Terence who was supporting him in this lifestyle. Since *Love in Idleness*, Rattigan had made settlements on his parents, ceding to them substantial percentages of the royalties or profits from his works. He also made them occasional payments for notional 'advice' on scripts. This was, of course, partly a matter of tax efficiency, but it was also a means of minimizing their sense of obligation while keeping them in comfort.

The fourth play in the quartet seems never to have been completed (at least no script or notes for it seem to survive, nor apparently are there any references to a completed fourth play in the correspondence). However, at the end of June 1947, a few months after completing the first three plays, Rattigan did give Anatole de Grunwald the script for an original film with the title *World Première*. This may contain the bits and pieces left over from the by then abandoned fourth play. It tells the story of a stage actor, Guy, and his silent-screen-star wife, Sonia. Guy's love for the theatre eclipses his love for his wife. However, when Sonia falls in love with a screen comic Guy discovers that he does love his wife. 'I am in the unhappy predicament of a man who falls in love with his wife after he's married her.' It is an uneasy mix of mistaken love, suicide, murder and farce. The script was never made into a film, but Rattigan stored away ideas from it for use years later.

Rattigan had told a journalist from a New Zealand newspaper in November 1946, shortly before he completed *The Browning*

Version, that he was working on four short plays. Early in January 1947, *The Browning Version* was sent off to Binkie Beaumont, with a note saying that it had been written for John Gielgud. *Perdita* and *High Summer* followed shortly afterwards. Gielgud read *The Browning Version* and told Beaumont that he 'was mad about it'. However Beaumont had not sent him either of the other two plays and when Gielgud enquired about them fobbed him off with a vague reply. At the end of January, before leaving for a trip to America aboard the *Queen Elizabeth*, Rattigan, buoyed up by this encouragement, however indefinite, told a *Daily Herald* reporter that his four new plays were to be produced, two each evening, in the autumn by Gielgud. While Rattigan was in New York, Beaumont even went so far as to write to his American agent confirming that he intended to stage *The Browning Version* that autumn with Gielgud. However, there was a snag. Beaumont was very far from convinced about the wisdom of staging pairs of one-act plays; the last new one-act plays to succeed in London had been Coward's *Tonight at 8.30* in 1937. Since then only Olivier, doubling in *The Critic* and *Oedipus* in 1945, had got away with such a thing. Disturbing London theatregoers spelt danger at the box office. Worse, *Perdita* sent up the Lunts. Even if Gielgud were prepared to do it there was no way that Binkie was going to risk offending two stars of the magnitude of Alfred Lunt and Lynn Fontanne. However, Gielgud was fully occupied with another production in New York and for the time being matters could be allowed to drift.

Back in England Rattigan had plenty to keep his mind off the fate that might befall his plays. Although a few months earlier he had confidently told a journalist that 'films are past their peak' and were losing their hold on the public, early in 1947 he and Anatole de Grunwald had set up their own film company called International Screenplays. Their first film was to be a compendium movie called *Bond Street*, a four-episode story concerned with the veil, wedding dress and pearls for a Mayfair bride, which all come from Bond Street. Apart from a young Kenneth Griffith, playing a spiv, no one came very well out of the film which was generally felt to be laboured. However, it paid some of Rattigan's bills. More important, but in the end little better, as then Rattigan had lost the enthusiasm which had originally fired him, was the adaptation of *The Winslow Boy*, which he and de Grunwald were working on for Alexander Korda.

Since the last years of the war, Asquith had been drinking heavily, and de Grunwald and Rattigan, though no mean drinker himself, had become increasingly anxious. Frequently they wondered whether he would be fit to direct at all when he went on to the studio floor. One day de Grunwald and Rattigan were asked to lunch at the Berkeley by Korda. That morning, de Grunwald phoned Rattigan and suggested they meet beforehand to decide what to do about Asquith's drinking, recalling that the last time they had lunched with Korda, Asquith had slumped into the soup. Luckily Korda, who was perhaps the single most powerful person in films in Britain at the time, had merely commented, 'Even that he does with so much grace.'

De Grunwald and Rattigan met at the Ritz, a short distance from the Berkeley. They ordered two dry Martinis, and de Grunwald suggested that as Rattigan was Asquith's best friend *he* must talk firmly to him. Rattigan thought de Grunwald should do it. As they talked, a waiter kept refilling their glasses. They had got no further than agreeing that one of them must say to Asquith that he *must* stop drinking because it was ruining his career, when they noticed that by now they should have been at the Berkeley for lunch. Now more than a little befuddled themselves, they dodged through the traffic and staggered unsteadily into the Berkeley, to be confronted by a stone-cold-sober Asquith, who demanded to know where they had been: 'Why are you late? Are you both drunk ?'⁵

By sheer willpower, Asquith managed to keep himself sober enough to complete at least a film a year during the six years between 1944 and 1950, at the end of which period he underwent a most rigorous cure and never drank again until his death in 1969. During the six years when he was fighting alcoholism, Rattigan tried to support him in his battle. While filming *The Way to the Stars*, Asquith had discovered a café used by long-distance lorry drivers on the Great North Road. It was run by an ex-regimental-sergeant-major and his wife. No alcoholic drinks were served and Asquith and Rattigan had formed a lasting friendship with the proprietor during the filming. Asquith found that by going up there when he was not working and living as the family did, rising at five in the morning and serving behind the counter, he could stop drinking altogether. It became a refuge for him. Rattigan seems to have accompanied him a number of times when he stayed there.

By the autumn of 1947 Gielgud had made Binkie Beaumont let him see the plays intended to go with *The Browning Version*. Beaumont sent him *Perdita*, telling him, 'I don't think you'll like it, it's a kind of take off of you and the Lunts.' Gielgud thought it 'mildly amusing, but not quite good enough to do with *The Browning Version*'.[6] But still neither Beaumont nor Gielgud made a decision. Finally in October, Rattigan sailed to New York for the Broadway opening of *The Winslow Boy*. The prospects for *The Browning Version*'s London production now seemed to hang on Gielgud. The two men met and strolled in Central Park, Rattigan waiting anxiously for Gielgud's decision. There was a long silence, suddenly broken by Gielgud. 'They've seen me in so much *first-rate* stuff,' he said, thinking aloud with more candour than tact. 'Do you think they will like me in second-class stuff?'[7] Gielgud had not intended to hurt Rattigan and Rattigan was far too well-bred to show his feelings. He replied mildly, 'Oh, I think they will, John.' Although Rattigan knew that Gielgud did not realize what he had asked him, it was nevertheless a shattering blow. Gielgud had now turned down two successive roles which Rattigan had written for him – Sir Robert Morton in *The Winslow Boy* and Crocker-Harris in *The Browning Version*. Five years later, Kenneth Tynan found that Rattigan still could not speak of that moment in Central Park when Gielgud made it clear he would not do *The Browning Version*.[8]

Once Gielgud had lanced the boil by telling Rattigan the truth, Binkie Beaumont no longer felt the need to disguise his real feelings about Rattigan's idea of an evening of one-act plays. Beaumont had actually told Rattigan that he liked *High Summer*, which he described as 'a period jewel'. If he was sincere it seems an inexplicable error of judgement, and it seems more likely that it was a 'political' assessment aimed at staving off losing the play that he did like, *The Browning Version*. In November, after returning from America, Rattigan gave *The Browning Version* and *Perdita* to Peter Osborn to read. Osborn was incensed that Tennent's was refusing to stage them and tackled Binkie Beaumont one day in the dress circle of one of his theatres. He told Beaumont that he thought that Crocker-Harris was the best character Rattigan had yet created: 'Binkie went white in the face, turned on his heel and walked away. I took the matter up with John Perry, and he was blunt: "It's no good, dear. If Binkie's made up his mind, that's that."'[9]

In the meantime Rattigan wrote to Laurence Olivier 'for advice'. Olivier had seen *Perdita* and said he would consider doing it. Rattigan obviously hoped that Olivier would now agree to do *The Browning Version* with his wife Vivien Leigh. But his hopes were soon dashed. The Oliviers did not think that *The Browning Version* was right for them. Rattigan and his agent now started to cast about frantically for someone else to do the plays. By early February a smaller but more adventurous management than H. M. Tennent had been found that was eager to present them – Stephen Mitchell. On 14 February 1948, Rattigan wrote a carefully worded and very courteous note to Beaumont (he did not want to jeopardize the chances of such a powerful manager presenting his plays in future), explaining his decision to offer his double bill to Mitchell. A few days later, Beaumont replied in a note couched in words that were equally honeyed, saying that he hoped this would 'make no change in our future plans together' (Rattigan was too valuable a commercial asset to lose to an upstart management).

Rattigan and Mitchell could now set about the task of finding a director, a cast and a theatre. It took the rest of the summer. Glen Byam Shaw, who had directed *The Winslow Boy*, turned down *Playbill*, the title decided upon for the double bill of plays. So Peter Glenville, Rattigan's companion from Canters House days at Oxford, was called in. In the last few years Glenville had branched out from an acting career to direct with the Old Vic

Company in Liverpool and subsequently, with increasing success, in London. This reunion was the beginning of a long professional association. When *The Browning Version* was published, it was dedicated 'To Peter Glenville in Gratitude'.

But casting continued to be a problem. Many of the actors approached to play Crocker-Harris were busy or turned the part down. But Eric Portman, one of those who had turned down the part of Sir Robert Morton in *The Winslow Boy*, after some persuasion, was saved from repeating his mistake. He accepted the roles of Crocker-Harris and Arthur Gosport. Mary Ellis played his wife in both plays, and Campbell Cotts, a redoubtable baronet and raconteur in private life before he had been induced to take to the stage, played the headmaster and the theatre manager.

After a short pre-London tour *Playbill* opened on 8 September 1948 at the Phoenix Theatre. It was an immediate success with audiences and critics alike. For the second year running Rattigan received the Ellen Terry Award for the best new play, and Eric Portman won the award for best actor. The critics thought both plays perfectly judged. The *Daily Mail*'s reviewer said that in both plays Rattigan's acute perceptive talent pierced to the very essence of his characters: 'one is looking at the workings of real human souls.' J. C. Trewin placed *Harlequinade*, as *Perdita* was renamed, among the classic plays about the theatre, comparing it favourably with *The Rehearsal, The Critic* and *Trelawny of the Wells*.

As so often before, Rattigan found that work which the critics and public had hailed in England was damned in America. *Playbill* ran for 245 performances in London but for only 62 when it opened a year later in New York. Although one American critic called *The Browning Version* a masterpiece, the majority were at best dismissive, at worst downright rude ('As playwriting, it is not too far from double bilge,' said *Time Magazine*).

In the *New York Times*, where Brooks Atkinson had dismissed *The Browning Version* as 'superior hackwork', Rattigan wrote a thoughtful article entitled 'Sea-Change Problem', on the differing receptions his plays had in Britain and America. He wondered whether plays of character, such as his, faced greater hazards when exported from their native countries than plays of ideas: 'Plays of

226

character, be they Russian, American, English or French, really demand a contribution from an audience which, when that audience is foreign and unversed in the customs, idiom and idiosyncrasies of the dramatist's native country, cannot readily be given. The portrait, however meticulously drawn, becomes blurred and coarsened and emerges often merely as a type.' However, the 'sea-change problem' did not beset *The Browning Version* everywhere it went. While Brooks Atkinson was condemning it as 'sentimental' in New York, a Danish critic, reviewing a production in Copenhagen, called it 'a modern version of *The Dance of Death*'.[10]

Rattigan himself said later that if he had one day to justify his choice of career before a heavenly jury, then *The Browning Version* would be the play he would want to represent him. Writing about the play at the time of its original production, Harold Hobson, who had now replaced James Agate as drama critic at the *Sunday Times*, said in the course of an extremely perceptive appreciation of Rattigan's distinctive qualities:

> As one listens wearily night after night to the banal, clipped, naturalistic dialogue of the modern drama, one's heart cries out for writing of courage and colour, for the evocative word and the mannered phrase. But Mr Rattigan makes one doubt the necessity of that cry. In *The Browning Version* there is not a single sentence that in itself would raise the emotional level of a railway timetable. There is hardly a word that would be out of place in giving an order for a pound of vegetables.

Yet, Hobson pointed out, the audience is moved to tears. And when Crocker-Harris makes his act of defiance at the end of the play, the heart responds 'as to the sound of a trumpet. It is not, Mr Rattigan reminds us, the intrinsic quality of the words that matter, but the amount and nature of the emotion they can be made to convey.'

Notes

1   Michael Meyer, *Not Prince Hamlet: A Life in Theatrical and Literary London*, Martin Secker & Warburg, London, 1989

2   Preface to *Collected Plays*, Volume I, op. cit.
3   Corin Redgrave, *Michael Redgrave, My Father*, Richard Cohen Books, 1995.
4   B. A. Young, op. cit.
5   From R. J. Minney, op. cit. and an interview by the author with Anatole de Grunwald.
6   Sir John Gielgud interviewed by the author in 1977.
7   This is Rattigan's version of what was said. Gielgud's biographer, Ronald Hayman, reports Gielgud's words as, 'I have to be very careful what I play now.' Either way, Gielgud's motives for turning down Rattigan's double bill of plays are clear. It is unclear whether Gielgud also saw *High Summer*, but either way it would have made little difference to his judgement.
8   Gielgud eventually played Crocker-Harris in both a BBC radio production in 1957, which Rattigan himself introduced on the air with a eulogy on Gielgud's talent and a paean of gratitude for his kindness to him as a young man, and on television in America in 1959. This latter version was directed by John Frankenheimer and marked Gielgud's American TV début. It was a triumph and Gielgud received glowing notices.
9   Peter Osborn, op. cit.
10 G. O. Harris, *Berlingske Tidende*, 12 October 1949.

10

Adventure Story

By the time *The Browning Version* and *Harlequinade* opened in London, Rattigan already had another play heading for production. This play, *Adventure Story*, was to open up not only the question of Rattigan's distinctive use of language, but the very nature of his claim to be considered a great playwright. People had long speculated about whether Rattigan, with what for most people would have been enough money to last him for life and an established reputation as a master craftsman, would now change his style and write to please himself. They could not accept that he might have been pleasing himself all along. To them, the fact that his plays had been commercially successful suggested that he must have been writing down to his audience. They made the illogical assumption that the best, most personal and most deeply felt work was incompatible with commercial success. They ignored the examples of Shakespeare, Marlowe, Congreve, Wilde and even Shaw, who were popular successes in their own day, as was Dickens, with whom Rattigan shared an uncanny ability to appeal to popular audiences.

Although Rattigan professed that he chose to tell the epic story of Alexander the Great in *Adventure Story* with no loftier intention than the one that had motivated him in writing all his plays, namely that he believed 'the chosen subject would make a good play', he admitted later that there was also an element of deliberately measuring himself against the demands of the commonly held view of the great play: an epic story, a central figure of heroic stature and a great, universal theme; in this case, the story of Alexander's twelve years of conquest in Asia which turned him from plain Alexander of Macedon into Alexander the Great, the subject of legend. Rattigan's aim was to explore the character of his hero in relation to the paradox of his unsurpassed material success and ultimate spiritual defeat.

There was a third motive which, if not immediately obvious from his choice of subject, would become apparent from his treatment of it. Having twice set out to confront through his writing the nature of his relationship with his parents, and twice shied away, an epic subject, grounded in historical fact, would offer a more clinical way into the subject and be less likely to hurt his parents: 'Cold, clear logic, and buckets of it'? Perhaps.

The story of Alexander (which his grandfather had touched on in his history of India) had appealed to him since he was a boy. Having made up his mind to write the play, he read all the available books. But he found that, while they more or less agreed about Alexander's achievements, they failed to agree about his character. Rattigan preferred the story as told by Plutarch and decided to rely on it for his outline. As he believed that 'action should arise out of character, not character out of action', and very little was commonly accepted by historians about Alexander the man, he was free to interpret the character of his hero in the way he felt was most likely to have given rise to his deeds.

I tried to discover what was in Alexander's heart that drove him on in his tempestuous, ruthless, invincible march... 'Absolute power corrupts absolutely,' said Lord Acton, and the story of Alexander does not belie this universally held belief. Yet the corruption of power is not the theme of *Adventure Story*. For even absolute power can only corrupt the corruptible and Alexander's tragedy was that he set out to conquer the world before he had succeeded in conquering himself.'For what shall it profit a man if he gain the whole world and lose his own soul?'

Rattigan pointed out that, measured by what he did, Alexander might well have been the greatest man who ever lived. 'But is it right to measure man's greatness simply by his deeds – isn't what you are more important than what you do?'[1]

At the beginning of the play, in a prologue in which he is seen on his deathbed, Alexander asks despairingly, 'Where did it first go wrong?' Eleven scenes follow, spanning Alexander's life from the age of twenty, when he embarked on his conquests, to his death at the age of thirty-two. Each scene attempts to supply part of the answer to that initial question, which is addressed by Rattigan in terms of his own life and inner experience; large elements of his portrait of Alexander are yet another projection of aspects of himself. The most striking merit of the play is the economy with which Rattigan manages to encompass his epic story. The play's recurring theme is stated at the outset when the Pythia at Delphi warns Alexander that there is one conquest he must make before any others – himself. 'Know yourself, Alexander,' she admonishes him. So the play's recurring theme, the importance of self-knowledge (the lack of which is the cause of Alexander's eventual spiritual downfall), is stated at the outset. Up to now, Rattigan's plays had hinted at the dangers inherent in the failure to express feelings, but *Adventure Story* was the first of a series of plays in which he explored both the importance and the devastating effects of self-knowledge. Alexander's progress as a man of action is underlined by his solution to the problem of the Gordian Knot. According to legend, whoever unties the knot will rule the world. Coming upon it early in his career he does not solve the problem, but simply severs it with his sword. So too with the central problem of his life – self-knowledge – he cuts through the problem, but leaves it unsolved.

Rattigan's Alexander, like Rattigan himself, must conquer to impress his father. After his first great victory over Darius and the Persian Empire, he asks the gods to ensure that his father knows what he has achieved: 'Let him see me now – in Darius's tent, wearing Darius's mantle – and let his eyes burn with the sight.' Later, on the eve of his decisive battle against Darius, after which he will either be 'Master of the World' or dead, Alexander prays: 'Father! Father! Philip! I invoke you, then. Look down at me now and sneer. Say – "See what a weak, effeminate coward I have for a son!" Say that, Father! You used to say it often enough in your lifetime. Say it now, and help me, for only anger can conquer fear!' (Rattigan, the leader of the Harrow OTC revolt and the pacifist who had voted against fighting for 'King and Country' at Oxford, had to some degree always been concerned to justify himself.) In contrast to his relationship with his dead father, Alexander takes his greatest risks, even leaving himself open to being poisoned, to demonstrate his trust in and love for Darius's mother who becomes a surrogate for his own absent mother. Alexander's need, thwarted in childhood, to give and receive affection and approval, conditions all his adult relationships.

With success Alexander turns slowly into a despot and begins to adopt the finery and manners of a god. He has established his hold over the Persian Empire but continues to pursue conquest not for strategic advantage but for its own sake. Alexander's single-minded dedication to achieving his ambition of world conquest causes him to question his own sanity. Increasingly troubled by uprisings, he becomes steadily more ruthless, less tolerant of criticism and distrustful of his lieutenants and friends. He justifies his own retention of power: 'Despot I am, because I must be.' He tells Hephaestion, his closest friend, that his ideal – 'The world state ruled over by the man-god, whose word is law, and who has dedicated his whole life and being to the welfare of all his many million subjects. No more war...' – justifies everything. These, of course, are the words and excuses of every despot. The obvious parallel is Napoleon; but Hitler, Mussolini and Stalin were more immediate parallels for Rattigan's intended audience. Also, though many of them would not have chosen to recognize it, they were the sentiments of those who were at that time opposing the dismemberment of the British Empire. India had won its independence in 1947 at the time of the play's gestation; Sri Lanka (Ceylon) and others followed while Rattigan was writing in 1948.

After the death of her son, Darius's mother vows never to speak to Alexander again, but at the end of the play she goes back on her word. Alexander calls their reconciliation his greatest victory. Yet he is driven by his devil to continue with conquest until the bitter end – bitter because as the Queen Mother warns him, his devil must therefore conquer him. Alexander asks whether it matters if he loses his soul, after conquering the world: 'I shall be remembered not for what I am but for what I do.'

Noble though Rattigan's intentions were in trying to grapple with great issues and to make understandable, and human, a legendary figure, and skilfully as he condensed his mass of material into a free-flowing narrative, *Adventure Story* did not really work, even on Rattigan's own terms. Towards the end of his life, in an interview with Holly Hill, Rattigan admitted that he had funked issues raised in the play. As we have seen, Alexander defended his actions in the play by the time-honoured formula of the end justifying the means, but the inherent evil of Alexander's vision is not spelled out in the play. Holly Hill asked whether Rattigan himself had recognized that evil:

'Of course, I didn't think it was a noble ideal,' Rattigan replied. 'But I think I was worried that it was very close to '45, wasn't it? It was '49 and with the memories of the Bunker in everybody's minds I didn't want to go on very much about it . . . I was afraid of the obvious cliché, you know – all conquerors are necessarily dictators, which I don't think is necessarily true, but it seems to have proved true up to now, hasn't it? I suppose I was trying to say that it depends on who has the ideal. I think what I meant is that if Alexander failed then everyone would. It would seem to me to make the most sense, because Alexander was a very special person. A world ruled by force of arms, and by one man – that is where the ideal must crash. Although he was taught by Aristotle and worshipped Athenian democracy, the fact remains that he still had to be the Persian tyrant, didn't he?'[2]

So the play fails on this important philosophical level, but it fails also as a study of character. Alexander does not carry conviction. What we are shown is a charming, idealistic, adventurous young man with a single-minded and eventually soulless ambition, whose character changes for the worse. In trying to humanize a larger-than-life figure, Rattigan trivializes him.

The play's major interest today is for what it tells us about Rattigan – a man who made no secret to his friends of his ambition to conquer his own chosen world, here writing about a legendary figure who succeeded in conquering his. In this play he put a mother-figure on the stage and showed his love of her; at the same time blaming a father-figure for making of him the failure as a man which he felt himself to be.

Rattigan wrote most of *Adventure Story* in February and March 1948 at a pub, the Stag and Hounds, at Binfield in Berkshire. Having sold his Sonning house he needed a new bolt-hole. It was a small unpretentious place with a green in front of it where the local hunt met and conveniently near his favourite golf clubs at Sonning and Sunningdale. He was now playing to a handicap of fourteen and told a reporter, 'I read every book that is published on golf and study the game terribly seriously, and the more I study the worse I play.' The Stag and Hounds was run by Mr and Mrs Newport, who kept a small upstairs room for him – this later became a small bedroom, a sitting-room and a bathroom which he retained for a number of years for about five pounds a week. The rooms were not very warm, but Mrs Newport guarded Rattigan's privacy fiercely and he was able to hide away and write undisturbed. Mrs Newport was one of a line of warm-hearted but slightly fearsome women who protected and mothered Rattigan. She was a stickler for correct behaviour and was very shocked at the idea of men bringing their girlfriends to stay at the Stag and Hounds – not a problem with Rattigan, but it was later when he bequeathed the room to some of his golfing companions. Mrs Newport insisted on punctuality and was very put out if her guests were late for a meal. Rattigan would go out of his way not to hurt her. She served ample portions of home cooking and always tried to prepare things she knew Rattigan liked. If she did serve something he did not like he would be careful not to let her know; when she was out of the room he would scrape the food into a newspaper, which he disposed of later. He always presented her with a cleared plate. Later he dedicated *The Deep Blue Sea* to Mr and Mrs Newport in 'affection and gratitude'.

When Rattigan returned to London in the spring of 1948, he

offered the completed text of *Adventure Story* to Binkie Beaumont. This time there was no hesitation. With a cast of twenty-two and elaborate sets it would be expensive, but Beaumont calculated that with the right actors it ought to succeed. That summer, while Beaumont tried to assemble a cast for *Adventure Story*, Rattigan's mind was taken up with the problems of getting on *The Browning Version* with Stephen Mitchell.

But that summer things started to go seriously wrong between Rattigan and Kenneth Morgan. Having allowed himself to be successfully wooed by Rattigan, Morgan was finding the relationship suffocating. It cannot have been easy for a young man, a talented actor who had himself previously tasted some success, to live in the shadow of Rattigan's popularity. All day Rattigan was out at meetings or casting sessions and each night, immaculately dressed for dinner, he was to be seen in fashionable restaurants, moving from table to table, from friend to friend, basking, albeit modestly, in the easy social life of his own celebrity and the ready adulation that is part of theatrical success. But as Morgan told a friend at the time, he disliked being dominated by Rattigan, he wanted to be something more than a satellite and lover. He resented in particular the way in which he was dismissed as a minor player when other people were around. More than once he heard himself referred to as 'Terry's boy' or 'Terry's little boy' without even his name added. 'Terry always treated his young men as if he were a tutor, and many of them (those who were not on the make) found this unbearable. As Kenneth had been well educated and brought up, and was theatrically mature, he resented Terry's patronage, and particularly the attitude of Terry's friends.'[3] Restless and feeling increasingly out of place, Morgan started to threaten to leave.

But Rattigan's mind was exclusively concentrated on the productions of his plays. He knew that his reputation as a writer was more on the line with *The Browning Version* and *Adventure Story* than at any time in his career. Ultimately this mattered to him even more than his love affair with Morgan. In any case, he could not believe that Morgan would readily throw over his luxurious champagne lifestyle, which brought with it the opportunity of meeting important people who could help his career. No sooner had *The Browning Version* opened in London in September 1948 than Rattigan was into the thick of preparations and casting for *Adventure Story*. Peter Glenville 'was to direct, George Wahkevitch was designing sets and costumes and music was to be specially composed by Benjamin Frankel. The whole production was going to cost three times as much as his earlier plays. He had agreed to put up three thousand pounds towards the costs and to pay for the music himself. To help in raising the money Rattigan turned to his parents for a financial guarantee. But by November, shortly after *Playbill* had opened and when rehearsals for *Adventure Story* were about to start, his father had become seriously worried about this. He raised doubts about the security of Vera Rattigan's guarantee. Rattigan wrote a letter to his father, enclosing a copy of a letter he had sent to his bank (Coutts), spelling out the position and trying to reassure him. He pointed out that Vera was 'in effect the owner of Rattigan Productions which has at the moment a balance of £6,000 and is, through *Playbill*, earning roughly £400 a week'. She is also to own twenty-five per cent of the management of *Adventure Story*, but only 'if after it opens it looks like making money'. He told his father that the proceeds of 'the sale of the other two cars' would go into an account that will be controlled for him by Bill Forsyth, his accountant, and that he was paying off his overdraft at a rate of seven hundred and fifty pounds a year. He also told him he was making regular payments to meet his income tax arrears and that he was 'not always quite as impoverished as I look'. He ended by saying, 'Last year I saved (Mary [his secretary] says Forsyth saved, but I repeat *I* saved) no less than £24,000; what I spent is I admit another matter.'4

As rehearsals began, in late November, Rattigan became increasingly tense. Even Shakespeare had balked at telling the story of Alexander! The cast was headed by a twenty-six-year-old actor playing his first starring West End role, Paul Scofield. Gwen Ffrangcon-Davies was playing the Queen Mother and at least two stalwarts from Rattigan's youth had important parts – Robert Flemyng (Kit Neilan in the original production of *French Without*

Tears) was Philotas and William Devlin (who had been in the OUDS *Romeo and Juliet*) was Bessus. Listed among the Greek soldiers was a young actor called Stanley Baker. In the important part of Alexander's closest companion Hephaestion was a virtually untried young Welsh actor whom Binkie Beaumont had got under contract on a ten-pounds-per-week standard one-year Tennent's contract, Richard Burton. Glenville had had high hopes of him at the audition, but three days into rehearsal it was clear that Burton would not do. So he was fired. Glenville told him it was because he was too tall beside Scofield. Rattigan wrote to him shouldering the blame himself. Burton later claimed that he was told that the producers were frightened that the audience would read a homosexual relationship into the friendship behind Hephaestion and Alexander. This was particularly ironic in view of the fact that there almost certainly had been a homosexual relationship been the real Alexander and the real Hephaestion. Alexander's extravagant grief over the death of Hephaestion is legendary and their relationship has frequently been compared to the relationship between the biblical David and Jonathan. But with the Lord Chamberlain, the commercial theatregoing audience and his own reputation firmly in mind, Rattigan had deliberately diminished that element of their relationship to a point where it had vanished. More significant, perhaps, was that Rattigan had made a drunken fumbling pass at Burton and been rejected. A new actor, Julian Dallas, had to be hired in Burton's place.

On 11 January 1949, Chips Channon drove down with his son Paul and the Duchess of Westminster for the first night of the tour of *Adventure Story* in Brighton. Before the show he met Rattigan in his room at the Grand Hotel. Channon recorded that he found Rattigan 'half-dressed, rather tight and maudlin, but loveable, as he always is before a First Night. I gave him, for luck, a coin minted in the reign of Alexander.'[5] The Brighton opening was attended by a galaxy of celebrities. Everyone wanted to see the show ahead of its London production because of the intense anticipation aroused by rumours of a completely new departure by the country's most successful playwright. That night Channon recorded in his diary his own impression of the first performance:

The play is an ambitious drama, or rather a series of episodes strung together on the theme of the general decay of Alexander's character. Though it is magnificently produced, Paul Scofield as Alexander did not particularly impress any of us. As the rich drama unfolded there were some of the usual mishaps which can occur in the provinces. The Brighton audience was puzzled by the play...We refused Terry's invitation to supper, and drove back to London.

After opening in Brighton the try-out tour was intended to move fairly swiftly to the Lyric Theatre, Hammersmith and then on into the West End. But the plan went wrong. There was no suitable theatre available and the tour had to be extended. While Rattigan was away from London tragedy struck. Kenneth Morgan met a young actor called Alec Ross and fell for him. Without warning, he left Rattigan and went to live in a bed-sit in a narrow Victorian terrace house in Manchester Street, a rather seedy area of Marylebone in the confusion of little streets just south of Madame Tussaud's.[6] Rattigan was shattered and for a while could not even discover where Morgan had gone. But he told himself that Morgan's new liaison would not last. He was sure he would miss the glamour and luxury of his life with him and return. He decided to play it cool. But as the weeks passed Morgan showed no inclination to do so.

John Montgomery, the young officer Rattigan had picked up in a club in May 1940, who was now working for Rattigan's London agent A. D. Peters, got to know Kenneth Morgan and Alec Ross very well during those weeks. He, his own partner, Alec Ross and Kenneth Morgan met regularly in a pub off Edgware Road and went around as a foursome.

Alec Ross was a very good-looking, thin, charming young man with beautiful manners and great kindness. He was an unpretentious and delightful person to be with. Kenneth realized this at once and left Terry high and dry, refusing to answer letters or return to the life in which he felt slightly out of place. With Alec he could express himself. He was, if anything, the dominant partner. Out together, Alec and Kenneth were a charming couple; Kenneth doing most of the talking, expressing himself as he never could with Terry, and enjoying a more simple, much poorer standard of life.

The final week of the tour of *Adventure Story* was in Liverpool, starting on 28 February. Rattigan was by now visibly edgy. Kenneth Morgan had still not so much as been in touch with him. Peter Glenville, the director of the play, knew of Rattigan's anxiety. On the Wednesday afternoon of the play's week in Liverpool the two men were sitting in Rattigan's hotel suite drinking tea and discussing the play when a porter appeared and delivered Rattigan a note. Rattigan read it, obviously very shaken. Then he handed it to Glenville, telling him to burn it, when he had read it, before the police arrived. The note told Rattigan that Kenneth Morgan had committed suicide.

Morgan's relationship with Alec Ross had been doomed from the start. John Montgomery, who met Morgan and Ross on three or four evenings a week during the last month of Morgan's life, had watched but been powerless to help: 'Alec was not really homosexual. He was not bisexual. He was simply heterosexual, but overwhelmed enough by the bright lights and stage and radio world, to accept whatever came along.' (Alec Ross had been a sound engineer at the BBC where he had been spotted by the famous cinema-newsreel narrator Lionel Gamlin, who helped him to get a start as an actor.) John Montgomery was in no doubt that it was Kenneth Morgan who persuaded Alec Ross to go to bed with him. Although Ross was not homosexual 'he liked gay company, which he found amusing. He was always laughing and cheerful and generous . . . and no doubt he tried his best with Kenneth. They were always together, and they were excellent company.' But Ross left Morgan in no doubt about his real sexual preferences. 'Alec always told him that if he liked anyone or anything it was women. More than once Alec told me: "Kenneth expects too much of me, and I can't return it. I don't care for him like that. I'm not really queer at all." He obviously made this clear to Kenneth, because it was this rejection which made him kill himself.'

On Tuesday, 1 March, Alec Ross and Kenneth Morgan had gone out for an evening in the West End. Returning home to their adjoining ground–floor rooms in Manchester Street the two men had an argument. Morgan, probably the worse for drink, had been noisy and Ross had tried to quieten him down – they had been in trouble with the other occupants of the house for being noisy at night before. Morgan marched out of the house and Alec Ross went to bed in his own room: 'I thought he would just walk round the block.' But by the time Morgan returned Ross was asleep. Overwhelmed by his unhappiness, Morgan wrote two suicide notes (one of them to Alec Ross), detached the rubber tube from the small gas cooker ring in his room, lay down by the fireplace, pulled the tube up to his face and proceeded to gas himself. That is how Alec Ross found him when he went into his room early the next morning – lying in front of the fire, with the tubing from the gas main lying loosely across his shoulder. Ross immediately raised the alarm, summoning the landlady. Morgan was still just alive. One of the other tenants called the ambulance and someone called Morgan's doctor – William Buky (also Rattigan's doctor and probably the person who got the message to Rattigan in Liverpool later that day). Morgan was rushed to St Mary's Hospital, Paddington, but died in the ambulance on the way. An inquest was held two days later at the Westminster Coroner's Court. It returned a verdict of suicide, by carbon monoxide poisoning, while the balance of his mind was disturbed.

Morgan's suicide note to Alec Ross told him why he had done it. 'The suicide note made it quite clear to Alec why it had happened . . . and told him this was the only way out, because Alec was not fully returning his love.' They weren't, as Kenneth discovered, very good in bed together '. . . It wasn't Terry's fault, or Alec's, that Kenneth killed himself. Like so many suicides, he did it as a gesture, hoping no doubt that Alec would rush in to rescue him. Alec Ross never recovered from the shock, any more than Terry did.'[7] Rattigan was heart-broken. He felt that in some way he was personally responsible for the tragedy. Its effects lasted for the rest of his life, influencing all his subsequent relationships.

Later that evening, as Peter Glenville and he went down together in the hotel lift, Rattigan seemed to have regained his composure. Apparently lost in thought, Rattigan suddenly said to Glenville, 'The play will open with the body discovered dead in front of the gas fire.' Later, when *The Deep Blue Sea* appeared, Glenville was convinced that the seed of the play had been planted within hours of Rattigan receiving the message about Kenneth Morgan's death. Rattigan's way of coming to terms with his deepest feelings and fears had always been through his writing and it was through his plays that he would eventually come to face his own feelings about Kenneth Morgan's death. Some time later, at Morgan's funeral, Morgan's mother asked Rattigan what he was engaged in writing at that moment. Again Rattigan started to outline the plot of a play that bore a distinct resemblance to the play that became *The Deep Blue Sea*. However, realizing who he was talking to, Rattigan quickly checked himself and did not go on.

In the days immediately following the suicide Rattigan feared that there would be a scandal in which he would be implicated. Suicide was still a crime and there would have to be an inquest and perhaps a police investigation. But luckily as the days went by and the inquest passed, none of the national newspapers picked up the story from the local Paddington newspapers and no one made the connection between an unknown actor called Kenneth Ball (Morgan's real name) and the famous playwright Terence Rattigan.

Rattigan's emotional fulfilment had always been dependent on the theatre and his success in it. Following the death of Kenneth Morgan, that dependence became, if possible, greater than ever. In the two weeks that remained before the London opening of *Adventure Story* there was no opportunity for grief. Rattigan threw himself into the task of promoting the play, granting even more personal interviews to journalists than usual; giving his views about the theatre, allowing them to photograph him in his Albany chambers; answering the inevitable questions about his bachelor status and his ideas about an eventual marriage. He told one reporter that, like Arnold Bennett, he would have time enough to consider marriage when he was forty. 'I have three years to go,' he said, touching a gold signet ring on his little finger. 'I wouldn't say I'm a confirmed bachelor, but I will say that I don't think writers make the best husbands.'

The London opening of *Adventure Story* was on 17 March. Rattigan went through his usual first-night routine. During the day, a Thursday, he had a haircut in the morning and a champagne dinner with his mother and father before the show. Chips Channon accompanied Rattigan's parents to the theatre and sat with them in a box. The theatre was packed with celebrities: Sir Alexander Korda was prominent in the front row of the stalls; near by were Lord Kinross, Cecil Beaton and Lady Juliet Duff. Everybody seemed to think that this evening would mark either the acceptance of Rattigan as a playwright of real stature or his final relegation to the ranks of the nearly great. Rattigan hovered nervously at the back of the dress circle. The tension in the theatre was unusual even for a first night. It lasted for the whole performance.

When the final curtain fell, the stalls celebrities started a chorus of cries for the author, while the circle cheered for Scofield. The curtain calls were still continuing – there were eight in all – as Rattigan slipped unobtrusively from the theatre. In the small hours of the morning, at a party in Binkie Beaumont's Lord North Street house, he read the reviews in the early editions of the papers. As he feared, he had not quite made it. Most of the critics commended him for his bravery in attempting a play about Alexander – a subject avoided by both Shakespeare and Shaw – but felt that Rattigan had overreached himself. 'A gallant failure worth a dozen so-called successes' (Ted Willis in the *Daily Worker*) was a fair summing-up of the views of critics of all political complexions that morning. The evening papers were less kind: 'The Rattigan Tragedy' was the *Evening News* banner heading to a review which began: 'Whenever a man finds he can do something supremely well, he itches to do something else that he can do only moderately well.'

In *Harlequinade* Rattigan had mocked the vacuous poetic word-making of some of the new dramatists, now the critics took him to task for the aridity of his own. His language, as an Oxford undergraduate critic called Kenneth Tynan pointed out, failed to rise to the occasion: 'His pagan legionaries move like gods and talk like prefects.'[8] A dozen years later John Arden, Robert Bolt and John Osborne would all solve the problem of writing vigorous modern language to depict epic happenings and outsize characters, without resorting to the airy nothings of the Ronald Duncan and Christopher Fry school.

Rattigan knew that he had failed in his own private struggle to stand alongside the great dramatists. A few years later he publicly summed up his feelings in a typically self-deprecating comment. It had, he said, taught him to know his own limitations. Yet to the end of his life he would recall *Adventure Story* with sorrow. It remained his favourite play: – 'no doubt for no more reason than that, like all parents, I nurture a special fondness for the child that dies in infancy'.[9]

Notes

1   *Radio Times*, 29 April 1949.
2   Holly Hill, op. cit.
3   John Montgomery to the author, March 1980. Kenneth Morgan was a stage name; his real name was Ball. He had adopted the name Morgan from the name on the shop-front of a shirtmakers – Morgan & Ball.
4   Letter to Frank Rattigan, dated 23 November 1948, the Rattigan Papers, British Library.
5   Robert Rhodes James, op. cit.
6   Exactly when Morgan left Rattigan and went to live with Alec Ross is unclear. John Montgomery thought that Alec Ross and Kenneth Morgan had been together for some months by the time the tour of *Adventure Story* began. But others who were with Rattigan during the tour believe it happened during the tour. It seems likely that it was shortly after the tour started.
7   Details of Kenneth Morgan's relationship with Alec Ross and of his suicide are taken from interviews by the author with a number of close friends of Rattigan's, but particularly from Peter Glenville, a long letter from John Montgomery to the author in 1980, the coroner's report, death certificate and reports in the Paddington newspapers of the time.
8   Quoted in a collection of Kenneth Tynan's criticism, *Curtains*, Longmans, London, 1961.
9   Preface to *Collected Plays*, Volume II, op. cit.

11

The 'Play of Ideas' Debate

As soon as he could get away from London and his involvement with launching *Adventure Story*, Rattigan returned to the privacy of the Stag and Hounds at Binfield. Despite the lukewarm critical reception, it still looked as if *Adventure Story* might run. So great had been the enthusiasm and the interest generated on the first night that, next morning, the management had clinched a record ticket-agency deal. Rattigan meanwhile seemed intent on overcoming his grief at the death of Ken Morgan and his disappointment over the critical reception of *Adventure Story* by throwing himself into his work.

The germ of the play that had started to form in his mind as soon as he heard about the death of Kenneth Morgan was still a long way from being a concrete idea. Time was needed for the immediate, sharp confusion of his emotions to recede. Time not only for private mourning but to confront his feelings of guilt. In the first weeks he had feared he might be implicated. He had told Peter Glenville to burn the note informing him of Morgan's suicide as soon as he had read it – 'before the police arrive'. So Rattigan turned to a play he had already been working on about his father, his affaires and his treatment of Rattigan's mother. He intended it to be a serious comedy. 'I knew I was going to touch on some very sore places,' he said later. But the play refused to take shape. In his present mood it looked as if it might well turn into a full-blown tragedy. But he was unable to concentrate. Normally it took him two months to complete the draft of a play, but after only three weeks he was back in London. Instead of writing a play he threw himself into a defence of *Adventure Story*, which was already showing signs of failing at the box office. In a series of articles and interviews he defended the play and his writing method by saying that 'plays should be about people rather than ideas'; the theatre was escapism from the difficult, austere times through which people were living – 'I have always believed that most people go there for amusement and relaxation, which, of course, includes mental stimulus, but always in terms of characters.'[1] It was a theme he was to nag at repeatedly over the ensuing months.

As the summer progressed, he accepted a commission from the BBC to write a television play for the 1951 Festival of Britain, and he toyed with at least two abortive film scripts. *World Première*, the script about the silent-screen star he had written for de Grunwald, was dusted down. In March Rattigan had announced that it was to star Marlene Dietrich. By August he was telling everyone that Puffin Asquith was to direct it and the Austrian actress Luise Rainer was to star. Still nothing came of it. At the same time he accepted another commission from de Grunwald to adapt *Love in Idleness*. Nothing came of this either. But simultaneously he went out of his way to comment on how much he hated adapting his own work for the cinema: 'I detest writing film scripts, the material is dead to me as soon as I have written it up for the stage, but neither will I let anyone else do it as then the whole spirit of the play is lost.' The general disenchantment of these months did bear fruit in a witty contribution to an anthology compiled by John Sutro called *Diversion*.[2] Rattigan's essay, entitled 'A Magnificent Pity for Camels', might perhaps be even more profitably taken to heart in certain quarters today than in 1949. Rattigan guyed the exaggerated credit accorded to film directors as the only creative begetters of films. Encapsulating a bitterness at the way writers were treated by the cinema which went right back to his experiences as a screenwriter at Teddington, Rattigan said: 'I believe the camera to be the enemy of the screenwriter's art... drama is inference and inference is drama.' He pointed out that that nonentity, the writer, provided not only the words for the actors and actresses to speak, but often the story around which the director arranged his fancy camera angles as well. He ended his light-hearted essay with this exhortation: 'So let the screenwriter throw off the shackles of the director (and the camera) and remember that the screenplay is the child not only of its mother, the silent film, but also of its father, the Drama; that it has affinities not only with Griffith, De Mille and Ingram, but also with Sophocles, Shakespeare and Ibsen.'

'The Babylon of Alexander has fallen; but here again is the babel of Maingot's', began the *Daily Sketch*'s Theatre Notes on 6 July 1949. *Adventure Story* had closed after only 107 performances and a new production of *French Without Tears* was being mounted. Robert Flemyng from the cast of *Adventure Story*, and a survivor from the original production of *French Without Tears*, was to star as Alan and to direct.

Suddenly Frank Rattigan was struck down by a stroke and for a few anxious weeks Rattigan was occupied with supporting his mother and making sure his father received the best treatment. By the end of July his father was out of immediate danger and Rattigan could again give his mind to his work. But he continued to be restless. At the beginning of August, after receiving the Ellen Terry Award for *The Browning Version* at the Savoy,[3] he set out in his new Rolls-Royce, accompanied by his chauffeur and his secretary, to drive to Copenhagen. He passed through war-shattered Germany, where he felt the people were hostile to him because they recognized from his Rolls-Royce that he was an Englishman. But he was overjoyed by the warmth of his reception in Denmark. Everywhere he went he was treated with the deference accorded to a great writer. He put up in Copenhagen's grandest hotel, the Angleterre, and luxuriated in comparing this visit with his first impecunious visit to the city in 1935. Then, he had sat in cheap bars eking out his Pilsner and struggling with his doomed play *Black Forest*. Now, he was conducted round the plushiest tourist spots by eager hosts; had some leisurely discussions with the Danish theatre company which was shortly to present *The Browning Version*, and held court, sitting up in bed in a silk dressing-gown, to journalists who queued to see him while he ate his way through substantial English breakfasts.

A few days later, his morale temporarily boosted, he made his leisurely way back to England. But again he did not settle to a prolonged spell of writing. By September, he was preparing to leave again – this time for New York and the Broadway production of *The Browning Version* and *Harlequinade*. He was away six weeks, but the New York production was another disappointment and the plays were not well received.

The loss of Kenneth Morgan, coupled inevitably in his mind with the rejection of *Adventure Story*, continued to obsess him. John Montgomery, who was now handling quite a lot of Rattigan's radio and film contract work in the A. D. Peters office, in an ill-considered moment had mentioned to Rattigan's secretary Mary Herring that he had known Morgan.

I was immediately asked to lunch (an unusual event because Terry seldom came to the office)...When I'd been given a couple of large gins I was gently quizzed about Kenneth. Having nothing to hide, I told him I had known Kenneth and Alec – and still knew and saw Alec...Although I told the story very carefully, not to hurt him or open up old wounds, he never really forgave me – not for anything I said, but simply because I had been there, and been out with Alec and Kenneth together when they were happy. Worse, I was still a friend of *Alec's*. This amounted to high treason.[4]

Not long after this Rattigan moved to another agent. Montgomery was convinced the cooling of relations between Rattigan and A. D. Peters dated from the conversation about Morgan.

While Rattigan was in New York he had written more articles defending his dramatic methods. When he returned home in November, the subject of his ideals as a writer was still very much on his mind, and he started to collect his thoughts for a major statement of his theatrical credo. He intended to challenge what he saw as the dominating dramatic doctrine of the day – a doctrine by which he felt he had been unfairly judged and found wanting. In the statement, he brought together thoughts that had nagged him during the months since the critical rejection of

Adventure Story and the hostile reception of *The Browning Version* on Broadway; they were ideas that had gathered throughout his struggle to get himself taken seriously, and went back to the reception of the original production of *French Without Tears* and his resentment at being tagged too popular to be really good.

At the end of November, Mary Herring sent the finished article, called 'Concerning the Play of Ideas', to Vera Rattigan. It was intended for a small publication called the *Theatre News Letter*, but the A. D. Peters agency was trying to place it somewhere more prestigious, possibly the *Evening Standard*. A friend of Rattigan's, T. C. (Cuthbert) Worsley, the drama critic of the *New Statesman*, heard about it and asked if he could have it. In allowing his article to be published in the left-wing *New Statesman*, Rattigan was in effect taking the battle to the enemy. He fully realized that he could expect a hostile reaction. His article opened: 'I believe that the best plays are about people and not about things.'[5] He amplified this by saying that he believed that the intellectual avant-garde of the British and American theatre 'are, in their insistence on the superiority of the play of ideas over the play of character and situation, not only misguided but old fashioned'. He blamed Bernard Shaw for driving the theatre off course by his campaign, begun in the 1890s, in support of Ibsenite theatre – the theatre which Shaw described as 'theatre as a factory of thought, a prompter of conscience, and an elucidator of social conduct'. He argued that after fifty years of domination by Shavian ideas the time had come for a change of critical values:

> ...the history of artistic endeavour is surely the history of change, and our painters are not still urged to paint like Burne-Jones, nor our poets to compose like Swinburne. Why then should our dramatists still be encouraged to write like late Ibsen or early Shaw?

So complete had been the Shavian–Ibsenite victory, he claimed:

> that in 1950 any defence of the theatre they defeated is considered to be no more than a naughty heretical joke. Daily,

we playwrights are exhorted to adopt themes of urgent topicality, and not a voice is raised in our defence if we refuse. That refusal is universally and blandly taken to indicate that our minds are empty of ideas, and being so, are despicable... Where are we then, those of us who hold, as I do, that the whole cult of the play of ideas is itself a heresy and is founded on a misconception and a misreading? In the intellectual and critical soup, without a doubt, so shunned and scorned and abhorred that no one is ever likely to take us seriously enough even to enquire what we mean.

He went on to explain that the misconception upon which the play of ideas was founded was that 'ideology equals intellect. It doesn't. The misreading is of Ibsen, who was considerably less interested in his own ideas than were his followers, and considerably more interested in his own characters than were his critics.'

Rattigan concluded with a defence of his own theatre:

From Aeschylus to Tennessee Williams the only theatre that has ever mattered is the theatre of character and narrative... I don't think that ideas, *per se*, social, political or moral, have a very important place in the theatre. They definitely take third place to character and narrative anyway. You see, if the ideas are of contemporary significance they tend to divide the audience, and if they are not they tend to confuse it... The trouble with the theatre today is not that so few writers refuse to look the facts of the present world in the face but that so many refuse to look at anything else.

When the article appeared, the editor announced that James Bridie would contribute an article the following week taking up the challenge Rattigan had thrown down, and invited others to join in. No one expected the storm of controversy that broke out. The argument raged for the next two months and spread beyond the *New Statesman* to the columns of the national press. It was reported around the world. Bridie argued that Rattigan had completely misunderstood Shaw: 'It is difficult to believe that he has ever read or seen a play by Shaw. Dear Terence, *are* these plays sociological tracts? *Are* their characters emotionally sterile gramophone records, or have you only been told that they are? Do tracts make us laugh? Do automata make us weep?' Bridie then turned to Rattigan's own plays, asking 'is there no sociological content in *Adventure Story*? Is *The Browning Version* barren of ideas?' Other correspondents rapidly supplied an answer. They implied that the reason Rattigan attacked the play of ideas was that, when he tackled such big themes, his ideas, his intellect and his means of expressing them were all found to be deficient. Even Peter Ustinov, who on the whole sided with Rattigan, pointed out that the thoughts of a creative artist about his medium are usually a blend of pride and prejudice and therefore suspect. A number of correspondents pointed out that vital and living drama was dependent on blending both people and ideas and that the two could not be separated – a fact so obvious, Rattigan said in his reply to the correspondence, that he had not seen fit to make it. Christopher Fry said that all this labelling was dangerous; a point which Sean O'Casey took much further by saying that 'we'd have to get ideas out of life before we could remove them from drama'. He went on to point out that Ibsen and Shaw, far from killing drama, had brought a dead drama back to a serious and singing life. He reminded Rattigan that throughout history writers, poets and dramatists had commented on, and often condemned, the activities and manners of their time. It was part of their glory: 'The thinker, the playwright and poet have shared in the struggle for the rights of man – and, if they didn't wield a sword, at least they carried a banner. They have helped to immortalize man's fight against intolerance, cod custom, ignorance and fear.'

Finally, Shaw himself joined the debate, pointing out that Rattigan was vulnerable as a reasoner, 'but he is not a reasoner, nor does he profess to be one...Mr Rattigan does not like my plays because they are not exactly like his own, and no doubt bore him; so he instantly declares that plays that have any ideas in them are bad plays, and indeed not plays at all...' (Rattigan was later to admit that his antipathy to Shaw's views stemmed in part from the fact that he had never found himself moved by any of his plays.)

Rattigan replied to the debate by characterizing himself as a fourth-former who had been caned by the senior boys for his cheek; nevertheless he was flattered to have been found worthy of the honour of a birching from the head boy himself. But, he said, he was unrepentant. He suspected that what he had said must have made some, perhaps dangerous, sense to have aroused such thunderous indignation. He clarified what he had said in the original article; he had not meant that no good plays contained ideas, nor that all plays of character were necessarily good plays. All he meant was that 'the successful creation of living characters upon the stage... has always been, is now and will remain a higher achievement for the dramatist than the successful assertion of an idea, or series of ideas...' Unrepentant though he claimed he was, this was a considerably less dogmatic statement than the one he had opened with.

Peter Ustinov had suggested that Rattigan's original article was in part the result of hurt pride. Looked at from the vantage point of today, it seems a truly amazing piece of over-emphasis to claim that the trouble with the theatre of 1950 was 'not that so few writers refuse to look the facts of the present world in the face but that so many refuse to look at anything else'. In 1950 there was no English Stage Company, no network of subsidized theatres; Kenneth Tynan was still an undergraduate, and John Osborne a struggling actor. In a country still in the grip of rationing, with the centres of its cities still scarred with bomb damage, aware that it was living under the threat of atomic weapons and struggling towards national recovery after being bankrupted by the war, the theatre seemed enslaved not so much by ideas as by wilful empty-headedness. True, the critics may have been guilty of over-praising the few half-good new plays that came their way, but for five years Rattigan had presided over the London theatre as its leading practising playwright. Even his detractors readily admitted that any new play by him was a major event.

Rattigan's creation of the Play of Ideas controversy was to have a profoundly damaging effect on his reputation and career. By his article he placed himself, in the minds of a new, though as yet uninfluential set of young writers and critics, irretrievably among the ranks of a reactionary theatrical establishment. The shape of things to come was discernible among the responses to Rattigan's original article. Ted Willis weighed in with a piece in which he looked forward to the day when the British theatre would find a new generation of dramatists uninhibited by present standards or examples, who would deal in 'ideas instead of trivialities'.[6] Most, significant of all perhaps was an article by a young writer, Robert Muller, in *Theatre News Letter* on 25 March 1950. Muller said that only haste could excuse, or persecution mania justify, Rattigan's article; what Rattigan had written was violently political: 'It makes a nonsense of the old adage that plays like *While the Sun Shines* and *French Without Tears* are non-political. The article proves them to be otherwise.' Muller, who knew that the article was no whim and had been a long time in preparation, went on to ask:

Who are these Playwrights of Ideas that make Mr Rattigan foam at the mouth, these spoilers of the drama who splutter ideas only because they cannot create character? Mr R. mentions Shaw and Ibsen in his lines, and between them we read the names of every other writer for the theatre who possessed that dangerous thing – a social conscience. It is all very transparent. Mr Rattigan condemns the writer of ideas whose ideas are not identical to his own. He does not condemn Mr Noël Coward's adventure into ideas, *This Happy Breed*, because it drew no bothersome conclusions. Only the Shavian penslavers who dare to plumb the lower depths and come up with an idea are the ones that rouse his fury and get his goat... Equate Character with Right Thinking and Idea with Subversive Thinking, and you begin to appreciate what Mr Rattigan is trying to say.

In hitting out at Rattigan, Muller and Willis were hitting out at the theatrical establishment. In the West End of London by 1950 this meant H. M. Tennent and the companies controlled by Binkie Beaumont. A brilliant entrepreneur, Beaumont had by 1950 established such a strong personal influence over the London theatre that people were frightened to oppose him. Matters had reached such a point that a Labour MP, Woodrow Wyatt, was secretly gathering information aimed at curbing his power. The objection to Beaumont was that, although he staged many brilliant productions, the domination of his taste to the growing exclusion of all others was unhealthy. Scores of actors, actresses, designers, authors, stage-managers, even members of the Society of West End Theatre Managers, provided Wyatt with evidence of how, because they were not members of Binkie's inner circle or had offended him in some way, they could not get work, get their plays performed or rent theatres in either London or the provinces for their productions. Beaumont was suave, homosexual and charming; the smile was said never to leave his face, even at his most ruthless. At Rattigan's instigation Beaumont seems to have taken steps to block the progress of Alec Ross's acting career and the record shows a marked decline in the quality and frequency of Ross's theatre engagements in the years after Morgan left Rattigan to live with Ross. The director Tyrone Guthrie, one of the few people with both the reputation and the courage to risk offending Binkie Beaumont, talked openly about Beaumont's disproportionate accumulation of power. He confirmed that more than any other single individual Beaumont could make or break the career of anyone in the theatre, adding that 'the iron fist was wrapped in fifteen pastel-shaded velvet gloves, but no one who has known Binkie can for a moment fail to realize that there is an iron fist'.

It is hardly surprising that many of the young people entering the theatre at this time, increasingly from working-class backgrounds, found the Beaumont style objectionable. His taste extended beyond what was seen on the stage into the private lives of those who worked for him. His preference for working with fellow homosexuals became notorious, especially among those who were not homosexual and often felt they were excluded for this reason alone. These charges were doubtless exaggerated but they were not groundless. It was not only young men who had cause to worry on account of Binkie Beaumont. The experience of Bryan Forbes, a young actor appearing in an H. M. Tennent production in the West End, was not untypical. Summoned without explanation to Beaumont's office high above the Globe Theatre he felt distinctly uneasy: 'Had my performance slipped, was I about to be fired, had I made some unguarded remark about my employer that had been reported back to him?' On being shown into the office he was very relieved to be told that they were very pleased with him. Beaumont moved swiftly on with a hint of menace in his silky, quiet voice, '"But we've got a little problem." Pause. Again the smile that implied anticipated complicity, "We're very b–o–r–e–d with Claire Bloom's virginity and we thought you could do something about it." "B–o–r–e–d" was given a special emphasis.'[7] (Claire Bloom was appearing in another H. M. Tennent production in the West End. It seems that there was some conflict between Beaumont and Claire Bloom's mother.) To his admitted shame, Forbes attempted to do Beaumont's bidding. He failed and, coincidence or not, never worked for Beaumont again.

Rattigan, of course, fitted naturally into the Beaumont stereotype – well spoken, homosexual, immaculately turned out and with a public-school background. But unlike Beaumont, Rattigan respected the sexual preferences of the many young men he helped and although he occasionally misjudged when he could make a pass at a young man without causing offence, as in the case of Richard Burton, he did not expect sexual favours in return. By 1950 he had enough of a reputation to stand on his own, as he had demonstrated by taking *The Browning Version* to Stephen Mitchell after Beaumont had turned it down. However, it would have been dangerous for even Rattigan to defy Beaumont. As it happened, he did not want to.

Unfortunately, as his most influential manager, Beaumont was not the sound creative adviser that Rattigan needed. One of Rattigan's problems was that he was becoming increasingly cut off from sound advice. Since the war, and particularly since the death of Tony Goldschmidt, Rattigan had become detached from the intellectual stimulus of his Oxford friends. Although he still worked with many of the most talented people in the theatre and

Vera Rattigan

Frank Rattigan

Rattigan (left) with Dorian Williams as Calpurnia in Harrow School's production of *Julius Caesar*   (*Keystone Press*)

Rattigan's father and mother at a first night

Flying Officer Terence Rattigan 1942 (*Paul Tanqueray*)

Rattigan aged thirty-seven in his Albany chambers

Rattigan in 1950   (*Angus McBean, Harvard Theatre Collection*)

Rattigan playing golf at Sunningdale in 1949. He was a passionate golfer
and claimed to read every book about the game

(*Rattigan Papers, British Library*)

Rattigan with Vivien Leigh with whom he became good friends after
the end of her marriage to Sir Laurence Olivier   (*Keystone Press*)

Rattigan on stage at the Theatre Royal, Haymarket, with some of the stars of his plays during a celebration of his 60th birthday – the first time he had agreed to appear on stage since *French Without Tears* (*Evening Standard*)

Rattigan with Jean Dawnay, a famous model and who was Rattigan's hostess at his most glamorous parties. Rattigan's mother hoped they would marry

Kenneth Morgan, who comitted suicide shortly after their affair ended. Rattigan was tormented by guilt (*Paramount/UIP*)

Adrian Brown who met Rattigan while he was scripting the film of *The Deep Blue Sea*

Michael Franklin, with whom Rattigan had a relationship from 1950 until his death   (*Angus McBean, Harvard Theatre Collection*)

Peter Osborn (centre), who as Rattigan said, 'probably is Sylvia', the recurring love of a man's life   (*Osborn Estate*)

Rattigan with Sir Noël Coward   (*Evening Standard*)

Rattigan aged fifty and his mother on the *Queen Mary*   (*Cunard Lines*)

Rattigan at the time of the making of *The Yellow Rolls-Royce*. His Rolls-Royce with personalized number plate, TR 100, was regarded by his friends as a 'great vulgarity' (*British Library, Rattigan Papers*)

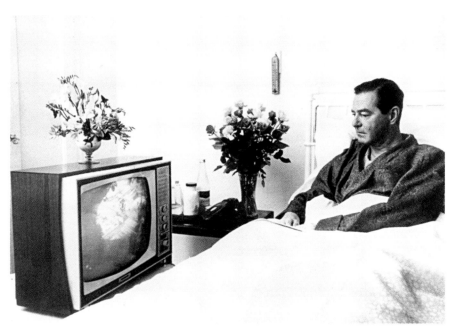

Rattigan in the London Clinic at the time of the BBC television
transmission of *Heart to Heart*, December 1962
(*Express Newspapers/British Library Rattigan Papers*)

Rattigan in a wheelchair, entering Her Majesty's Theatre,
London for the first night of *Cause Célebre* on 4th July 1977.
His last first night.   (*Hulton Deutsch*)

Rattigan at sixty   (*Anthony Crickmay*)

the cinema, in his private life Rattigan increasingly surrounded himself with people who were no match for him intellectually, often actors and designers who behaved in a subservient way to him. With the exception of Anthony Asquith, the people who surrounded him were no longer people who could challenge him creatively or intellectually.

Because of his very success, it was inevitable that Rattigan would be identified with Beaumont and the theatrical establishment, but with the 'Play of Ideas' controversy he branded himself as their leading apologist. He never lived it down.

Notes

1   The *Daily Herald*, 29 April 1949. Rattigan had first defended his methods in broadly these terms as long ago as 1937, at the time of the New York production of *French Without Tears*. It seems to have been a defensive posture he took up whenever he felt threatened by critical attacks on him for failing to be sufficiently serious.
2   Max Parrish, London, 1950.
3   The annual awards for 'Best New Play', etc., were instituted in 1947 when Rattigan received the award for *The Winslow Boy*.
4   John Montgomery, letter to the author, March 1980.
5   *New Statesman*, 14 March 1950.
6   *New Statesman*, 15 April 1950.
7   *A Divided Life – Memoirs* by Bryan Forbes, Heinemann, 1992.

12

Plays for Father

As soon as he had handed over his 'Play of Ideas' article to his agent, Rattigan turned back to the play which he had wrestled with without success in the weeks after the opening of *Adventure Story*. Having completed two plays in which he had put a mother figure on the stage and expressed a son's love of her ('shadowed o'er with the pale cast of Freud,' as Ivor Brown had said of Alexander in his review in the *Observer*, 'and always aching to lay his head on his mother's knee'), Rattigan now intended to put his father on the stage and damn him. One of the strongest impressions made on Michael Macowan by Rattigan in 1939 during the production of *After the Dance* was how often Rattigan would return in conversation to the subject of his father, castigating him as a reprobate. Years earlier he had outlined to Peter Osborn the play he would one day write about 'the Major', his father. Rattigan continued to blame his father for the pain he had inflicted on his mother by his succession of mistresses. He even attributed his own homosexuality, still a source of shame and regret, and his lack of feeling to his father. (Today geneticists and psychoanalysts may dispute which are the dominant factors in determining sexual orientation. However, in the 1940s and 1950s it was widely believed that male homosexuality was 'caused' by a deficient relationship between a child and its father; that that deficiency was itself caused by there being something wrong in the relationship between father and mother, resulting in an abnormally intense relationship between the child and its mother.)

So in the weeks leading up to Christmas 1949 Rattigan sat down to write the serious play about his father which he had so long intended; about 'the Major's' succession of affaires and their effect on his mother. But how? Frank Rattigan was now seventy years old and in failing health. How could he hold him up to public obloquy or even ridicule? If he did, his mother, who had stuck to him in spite of everything, would be almost as hurt as Frank himself. From these conflicting intentions, the essential weaknesses of *Who Is Sylvia?* grew.[1] By Christmas he had become dissatisfied and torn up what he had written. In the New Year he started again from the beginning. This time the play flowed and he wrote quickly. Although it was a subject of such intense seriousness to him, Rattigan now knew that he would have to keep it light.

'It was, if you like,' he told a journalist later, 'the play that led me to break with my previous dramatic writing. For it is based on the lives of two real people. A married couple...very good friends of mine.'[2] As soon as possible after he had finished *Who Is Sylvia?* he read it to his parents. 'They laughed until the tears ran down their faces and they gave me their blessing to use the material in this way.' Reading his plays to his parents after they were finished, but before they went into production, was a ritual that had begun during the two-year trial period when he had lived at home on an allowance. Although his father was no longer able to keep up his pretence of interest and nodded off during the reading, Vera Rattigan listened intently to every word, as ever, and was forthright in her opinions. Rattigan still valued her reactions and often made changes as a result of them. Had *Who Is Sylvia?* remained 'the serious comedy' he had first intended, ending with the central character, a philanderer identified with his father, being made to look both cruel and ridiculous, the customary domestic reading would have been a very painful occasion. In the event, both parents were able to laugh uproariously at *Who Is Sylvia?* as a gentle comedy on human folly – close enough to themselves for them to enjoy some sharpness in the humour, but not so close as to really hurt them.

Who Is Sylvia? covers three phases in the life of an amorist – a

Peter Pan figure who, even after he has reached his sixties and is no longer capable of turning desire into action, pursues a series of physically identical girls in the hope of attaining his 'Sylvia', a girl he met and kissed just once at a garden party when he was seventeen, but with whom he lost touch when she returned to South Africa and married someone else.

In each of the three acts, set in 1917, 1929 and 1950 respectively, Mark is in effect foiled in the act of trying to keep an assignation or further his relationship with each of the three successive Sylvias (each played by the same actress). Although Mark was clearly intended by Rattigan as a fairly forgiving portrait of his father, it also combines significant elements of self-projection. Rattigan had pursued (and would continue to pursue) a series of increasingly unsuitable and physically very similar younger men. When, in the first act, Mark's friend, accomplice and comrade in amorous escapades, an army officer called Oscar, accuses him of being 'an emotional Peter Pan' because of his obsession with Sylvia, Mark replies that he prefers to keep his emotions adolescent – 'they're far more enjoyable than adult ones'. Rattigan takes the sting out of any implied criticism of his father by suggesting that his affaires have been essentially inno-cent. But at the same time it seems to mirror the way Rattigan felt. The tragedy and pain of his affaire with Kenneth Morgan only served to highlight the virtues of the succession of transient affaires he had had until then, starting at Harrow, where his feelings were not so heavily engaged. For Rattigan himself 'Sylvia' (his 'unattainable ideal of womanhood') was perhaps Peter Osborn, to whom he gave a signed copy of the play when it was published, dedicated to 'Peter, who probably is Sylvia'. It seems more likely though that it was Penrose, the boy on whom he had a 'crush' at Harrow, or Philip Heimann, his undergraduate co-author of *First Episode*, who did indeed, like Sylvia, return to South Africa and get married.

In Act Two Mark's son Denis says to his father that he imagines a lot of people go through life in love with the same face, and that it is a form of narcissism: 'What you're really in love with is your vanished youth . . . You see, it's really yourself at seventeen that you love...Arrested development is awfully common, really. Practically everyone has it, in one form or another.' It is worth noting that almost twenty years later Rattigan gave an almost identically worded piece of dialogue to a character in an unproduced script called *Pas de Deux* to explain that character's own homosexuality, adding only (in line with a well-publicized theory of Freud) that it was a form of 'retarded emotional development'.

By the third act, set in 1950, Mark has risen to being an ambassador in Paris and Oscar is a general. By now in his sixties, Mark's amorousness goes no further than polite pretence. From the start he has tried to keep his affaires a secret from his wife, but now his wife reveals that she has known all along about her husband's 'Sylvias'. The only person who has been deceived is Mark himself. She explains that as she wanted to remain his wife more than anything else in the world she had to accept that, if there were things he needed which she couldn't give him, she would just have to accept his going elsewhere for them.

Specific references in the text, which would have been immediately understood by Rattigan's friends and his parents, direct us to identify Mark with Frank Rattigan. His son Denis is sent to a crammer in France but flies home at a moment's notice because he has fallen in love with an actress and intends, against his father's wishes, to go into the theatre. But Rattigan turns the actual relationship between himself and his father gloriously on its head when, in Act Two, Denis discovers that his father intends to leave the Diplomatic Service for one of his girlfriends. Denis says to Mark reproachfully: 'Oh, father! You're not giving up the Diplomatic, are you?...I know exactly how you feel and I do sympathize with you – really I do. But you've had such a brilliant career up to now, haven't you? I do think it would be an awful waste to throw it all away now.'

But no matter how skilfully he drew his parents to identify the character of the essentially harmless Mark with Frank Rattigan, it is possible to discern Rattigan's original, harsher intentions. Although Oscar has none of the external trappings of Rattigan's father, except significantly the nom de guerre ('the Major') by

259

which he likes to be known during his amorous adventures, Oscar is a much better-written part than Mark. As Peter Osborn immediately recognized when he saw the play, Oscar comes much closer to being a portrait of Rattigan's father than Mark. More callous and calculating, in the last act Oscar is shown up as the ridiculous figure he has been all along. Fat, breathless and loveless, in old age he clings to the idea of himself as a gay dog, oblivious of the fact that in doing so he only succeeds in making a fool of himself. Although for most of its length *Who Is Sylvia?* is a pleasant enough little romantic fantasy, there is an unevenness of tone and a sense of something darker lurking beneath the surface. Although later this would worry the critics, when Rattigan read the play to his parents they did not notice it, or chose not to see it. Eventually when *Who Is Sylvia?* was published it was dedicated: 'To my father, with love, with gratitude and in apology.'

In late January 1950, as well as reading *Who Is Sylvia?* to his parents, Rattigan had sent off copies to both his American agent Harold Freedman, his London agent A. D. Peters and to Rex Harrison, in the hope that he would play Mark. The first to respond was Peters, who told Rattigan candidly that he found the play unfunny and slightly embarrassing. Rattigan was furious and decided to 'walk out' on the Peters office. As we have seen, this may have been an excuse to cover his real reason, following his conversation with John Montgomery about Kenneth Morgan, but it is noticeable that Rattigan was finding it harder to take criticism, even from those who were his allies and advisers. This was partly the result of his run of success and the recent critical failure of his most cherished project *Adventure Story*, but it was also due to the fact that he was now increasingly surrounded by sycophants and people who were not his intellectual or creative equals. When *Adventure Story* did not work as he had hoped, he had blamed the actors, the director, everyone but himself. Earlier in his career when things had gone wrong he had taken the blame on himself, rewritten things and been open to other people's ideas. Even when the Lunts were subverting his intentions during the rehearsals for *Love in Idleness* he had been ready to concede that the result was a great improvement.

Peters remonstrated with Rattigan, saying that if his attitude were to prevail between writers and agents, the role of agents would be reduced to that of 'little more than "Yes-men"', and that in suggesting improvements which were intended to be helpful he was not implying that he had no confidence in the play – 'The essence of friendship is a desire to be helpful.' But Rattigan was unmoved. The years of friendship and support, especially when he was starting out, were forgotten.

Worse was to come. Rex Harrison turned down the part he had been offered. He did not think it was big enough and seems to have detected that although Mark was the lead, Oscar was the better part. On 9 February Harold Freedman wrote to Rattigan from New York with his assessment of the play. Although he was more tactful than Peters had been, he also thought the play needed serious work. Perhaps, he said, 'in getting away from the heavy treatment you told me you had started the play out with, you have finally landed on too light a treatment for it'. Rattigan replied that he would 'ponder deeply', but in practice did little to change the play. Instead he attacked Peters, accusing him of being 'quite happy to sit there with his arms folded waiting to say "I told you so" when the play fails or to cash in if it succeeds'.[3]

The person who was in the best position to persuade Rattigan to look again at the play, and who must have had his own interests at heart even if he did not have Rattigan's, was Binkie Beaumont, as he was due to present the play. But he seemed content to try to get a commercially viable cast and leave it at that. He approached Michael Wilding, but he was not available. David Niven and John Mills both turned it down. Eventually Beaumont and Rattigan decided to offer the part to Robert Flemyng. He too had doubts, but accepted it.

Rattigan had hoped that the enchanting Glynis Johns would play the succession of 'Sylvias', but her film commitments prevented her and the parts went to Diane Hart. Roland Culver, who with Robert Flemyng had been in *French Without Tears*, was cast as Oscar. So when eventually *Who Is Sylvia?* did open on 24 October 1950 at the Criterion everyone involved was very aware of the comparisons that were likely to be drawn between the previous first night of a Rattigan play at this theatre and the present one. In the event, although the first night audience were appreciative enough, the contrast could hardly have been clearer: 'This Will Not Do, Mr Rattigan' thundered the headline above Beverley Baxter's review in the *Evening Standard* next day. Rattigan made little secret of his disappointment with the actors; in fact, he was angry about the whole production. However, the press found little to fault in the playing, but were almost unanimous in detecting a more serious play lurking underneath. They regretted that Rattigan had not chosen to write it. They blamed him for wasting an interesting idea on a frivolity.

During the protracted business of getting a cast for *Who Is Sylvia?*, Rattigan had had time to turn his mind to other things. The previous December he had joined the board of the Renaissance Theatre Guild, an impecunious new venture led by Patrick Waddington, the actor who had played David in the original production of *First Episode*. This group of enthusiasts aimed to stage new works. Although Rattigan was not often able to attend their meetings he did continue to give them vital financial support. He knew at first hand the desperate need of young writers for encouragement and was generous with his time and advice whenever young writers approached him. A new playwright would be urged to get his or her work performed if at all possible, even if it was only in a church hall or by a school dramatic society. Hearing your dialogue spoken, however ineptly, was the only way to find out what would work on the stage and in the mouths of actors.

When Michael Meyer sent him his early, rather esoteric play, *The Ortolan*, Rattigan (who had previously read a tyro novel) wrote back with the encouraging news that he liked 'the characters, motivation and dialogue, and found it all convincing'. However, he told Meyer that it needed cutting and invited him to lunch at an expensive restaurant. While filling him with an excellent free meal, Rattigan explained to Meyer, 'Never forget that the spoken word is not twice nor three times, but five times as potent as the written word, so that what would occupy a page in a novel should take up only five lines in a play.' Rattigan recommended Meyer's play to a couple of directors, including Peter Glenville, but no one took it up.[4]

The English Playwrights Group was a rather different venture of this time. It was a group of British writers – Priestley, Bridie, Benn Levy, Peter Ustinov and Rattigan – brought together in emulation of the celebrated American playwrights' producing organization established by Maxwell Anderson, Elmer Rice and Robert Sherwood. They aimed to put on their own productions, eliminating the middleman-role of the impresario. In order to make it viable it was agreed that they needed rules on financial contributions and eligibility. At their first meeting, chaired by Benn Levy and held in Priestley's chambers in Albany (Rattigan had by then moved to Chester Square), Levy asked Rattigan, as the writer present with the most obvious claim to commercial success, to advise them in confidence on how to determine the level of financial success they should look for in writers qualified to join them. But Rattigan never got a chance to answer; Priestley, his hackles rising, interrupted. 'I think I ought to remind you, gentlemen, that I too have had my share of success...'

The group came to a premature end when, at their second meeting, Priestley said, 'I hope it is understood that as a result of this free association of dramatists, we all from now on write plays expressing the right ideas.' It was Bridie, rather than Rattigan, who responded first. 'I owe what little success I have known to expressing the wrong ideas, Mr Priestley, and I think it is really too late in life for me to change now – for any reason, however specious.'[5]

During the summer of 1950 Rattigan was making regular trips to Pinewood Studios to work with Puffin Asquith on the script for *The Browning Version*, for which he was receiving a total of thirty thousand pounds. In addition, the rights to *Love in Idleness* had at last been sold to RKO Pictures of America for a hundred and twenty-five thousand dollars as a starring vehicle for Cary Grant. In the event this would turn out to be another Rattigan picture that was never made, but he still received the fee.

He could now afford also to turn his mind, despite the fee being a fraction of what he would receive were it a film, to the commission he had accepted from the BBC for a Festival of Britain television play.[6] If *Who Is Sylvia?* risked offending his father, this play should more than make up for it. As the first television play by Britain's most successful playwright, the BBC intended it to be a television landmark. Rattigan had never written for television before, and had only a hazy idea of television technique. But he had become a keen, though sometimes critical, viewer; and he decided that something other than either a watered-down film script or a rather more mobile stage play was needed. He saw the potential strengths of television drama as its flexibility, its immediacy and its intimacy. The medium was best at bringing events into the home as they happened. Early on Rattigan decided he would build his play around one 'topical feature'.

For months he had been unable to decide what this 'topical feature' should be, but by the summer of 1950 had opted for a test match between England and Australia. Cricket was still Rattigan's favourite sport; although he no longer played very often, he still spent hours watching it. He confessed to a secret Walter Mitty dream in which he was a professional cricketer, dropped from the England team. After a disastrous second test in Australia, a cable arrives imploring him to fly out at once. He dashes for a plane and arrives just in time to help England win by the narrowest of margins. In 1950, cricket was a sport which television brought most effectively into the home, not only allowing many more people to see important matches, but allowing them to see what was happening at the wicket much more clearly than they could by going to the ground.

Rattigan determined to mix drama and reality in a novel way. His story would concern Sam Palmer, a much-loved England batsman playing in his last test, and the clash between his values and those of his son, an aspiring poet. The test match shown would be a real one; Sam Palmer, his son Reggie and the other principal characters would be played by actors, but members of the England team would appear as themselves. In 1950, before the arrival of drama-documentary or the docu-soap, it was a challenging idea. The action cut between the Palmers' house, the home of a successful poet, a pub near the ground, and the Oval – showing scenes from the match itself, the pavilion, the dressing-rooms and the players' balcony.

The son, although expected to be a good cricketer because of his father, is not really interested in the game. Reggie struggles to complete a poem rather than go to watch his father play in his last test match. On the day of his father's last innings for England, Reggie arranges to go and see a famous verse playwright who has shown an interest in his work. Sam, deeply hurt by this, nevertheless tries to show an interest in Reggie's work, though he doesn't understand it. He even gives him the money for his fare to visit the poet. Sam prepares to bat, with the match in a critical position, and an added weight of personal disappointment heavy on his shoulders.

When Reggie meets the playwright, he finds he is a cricket enthusiast and cannot understand why Reggie is not at the match. Together, they race by car to the Oval. But on the third ball Sam is out for a duck. Nevertheless, the crowd rises to him as he returns to the pavilion, cheering and clapping in appreciation of a great career – a turn of events inspired by the last innings in England of the great Australian batsman Don Bradman in 1948. The play ends with the playwright having dinner at the Palmers' house, both men comically in awe of each other, and Rattigan is able to work in some sincerely meant statements on the fallacy of the creative artist's work being superior to that of the performer or the sportsman.

The play is of course replete with autobiographical detail, personally significant nuances and private jokes. It is, however, patchy. The disappointment is the sharper because its central idea reveals that Rattigan had thought about the new medium and come up with a form that suited its special character at a time when most writers and producers still thought of television only as a medium for relaying stage plays.

Notes

1   After *Who Is Sylvia?* was completed Rattigan repeated more than once in letters and in interviews with journalists that he had set out to write a serious play but, realizing that it would 'touch some very sore places indeed', had eventually converted it to a comedy.

2   *Politiken*, Copenhagen, 20 December 1959.

3   The Rattigan Papers, British Library, letters dated 9 and 19 February 1950.

4   Michael Meyer, op. cit. Meyer became the leading British translator and biographer of, and authority on, Ibsen and Strindberg. He never ceased to be grateful to Rattigan for his encouragement at an arid time and continued to heed his advice in his own work.

5   *Dear Me* by Peter Ustinov, William Heinemann, London, 1977.

6   The year after *The Final Test* was transmitted, Rattigan agreed to let Anthony Asquith direct it as a film to be made by ACT, a company started by the union of film technicians of which Asquith was president, to provide their unemployed members with work. Both Rattigan and Asquith waived their fees, but were later persuaded to accept minimum fees when the union members argued that 'the labourer is worthy of his hire'.

13

The Deep Blue Sea

There seem to have been at least three versions of the play triggered by the suicide of Kenneth Morgan before the one which was accepted by Binkie Beaumont for production. The process of unconscious dissolution of real events and characters into their elements and their re-embodiment and reorganization into a play, described by Keith Newman at the time when Rattigan was writing *Flare Path*, proved exceptionally difficult on this occasion. Not only were the events that Rattigan was dealing with extremely painful, he would have to be extra careful to disguise from all but his closest friends the real-life origins of the story. In addition to these unavoidable difficulties Rattigan kept being called away to do other more pressing or immediately lucrative work.

Late in the summer of 1950, while Binkie Beaumont was still trying to get together a cast for *Who Is Sylvia?* and Rattigan was still working on the script for the film of *The Browning Version*, and before he had even completed a proper outline for his BBC Televison commission, Alexander Korda approached him about writing an original screenplay for David Lean about the new generation of jet aircraft and the breaking of the sound barrier. Lean had been impressed by a visit to the Farnborough Air Display the previous year and believed that the testing of a new high-speed jet would make a better basis for a film than the science-fiction stories which were being made about the possibility of flying to the moon. He had spent a year touring aircraft factories, talking to test pilots and designers and had amassed three hundred pages of background notes. But he still had no actual plot. To Rattigan, it sounded dangerously like a film of ideas rather than of character. He turned it down; he knew nothing about jets. But Korda and Lean were not to be put off so easily. A few days later, they approached Rattigan again; would he at least spend a day at Farnborough with them? Rattigan agreed. 'It was a wet day. One of these very fast aircraft – a Canberra, I think it was – flew in low.' His interest was aroused. 'Then, meeting the characters involved – test pilots, quiet young men absolutely unlike the types I had known during the war – suggested new writing possibilities.'[1]

Out of this unpromising beginning was born one of Rattigan's most philosophical and wide-ranging pieces of screen-writing. The central question posed, as relevant today as it was then, is about the justification for pressing on with experiments into the unknown, at great expense in money, skill and men's lives, for uncertain scientific and social results. Again Rattigan interpolated real people and real events into his fictional story. Thus the real life de Havilland Comet's test pilot, John Cunningham, is the pilot who gives the film's hero a lift during the test-flight programme, and the actual death of Geoffrey de Havilland when testing a prototype supersonic fighter becomes a turning point in the development of Rattigan's fictional story.

The plot of *The Sound Barrier* centres on Sir John Ridgefield, the self-made owner of an aircraft manufacturing company, and his determination to build an aircraft that will fly faster than sound. Ridgefield is a domineering father who is finally revealed as a man frightened of being alone, craving human love but unable to show his feelings. His son, determined to prove to his father that he doesn't lack guts, is killed undertaking his first solo flight when he has no real aptitude for flying. The male characters in the film attach shame to being weak or womanly, but it is the women who are more far-sighted and have a proper sense of proportion and real values.

At the end of the film, with the sound barrier successfully broken, but at the cost of the test-pilot hero's life, Ridgefield's daughter remarks that she sees the world as a pretty hostile place. Her father replies that we live in a hostile universe and that is why mankind has been given so many weapons with which to fight it: brains and imagination, which together equal vision. By allying courage to this vision, man can achieve success. In this scene, Rattigan makes one of the clearest statements of his own humanist beliefs. Today *The Sound Barrier* looks somewhat stagy, pieces of 'the play of ideas' protruding uneasily through 'the play of character and narrative'. Nevertheless it raised issues of ecology, pollution and 'science for science's sake' long before such debates were widespread. The film broke British box-office records and Rattigan was nominated for an Oscar for his screenplay.

During August 1950, Rattigan had gone away to the Stag and Hounds at Binfield to work on the Kenneth Morgan play. This was his second shot at it, but it was still not right and he knew it. He sent what he had written to Binkie Beaumont for an opinion. Beaumont agreed that it was not yet right and John Perry sent Rattigan a set of notes, telling him that the play needed more 'depth'.

In late September, less than two weeks into rehearsals for *Who Is Sylvia?*, Frank Rattigan went back into Luton hospital. This time he had a broken femur. With his father going downhill and his concerns over his mother, growing anxiety about the production of *Who Is Sylvia?* and his work on *The Sound Barrier*, the Kenneth Morgan play was once more put aside.

That autumn, just as the fictional *Sylvia* was about to take the stage, a new 'Sylvia' had entered Rattigan's life. He had begun a relationship with another pretty young man. Michael Franklin was almost twenty years younger than Rattigan. Small, straight-backed with an alert, almost watchful manner, neat features and a near retroussé nose, he bore a striking resemblance to each of the other young men with whom Rattigan had had sustained relationships. Franklin had more than a hint of an American accent and had been largely brought up in the United States, but was half British. He quickly came to be regarded by Rattigan's friends as little better than a prostitute. Too young to have achieved much, he claimed he wanted to make his way as a designer, but made no secret of the fact that above all he wanted to be looked after, preferably by some glamorous figure in the arts. He had recently tried inveigling himself into the favours of Benjamin Britten by offering his services as an opera designer but had got nowhere. B. A. Young, the critic, described Franklin's role in Rattigan's life at that time as 'the ideal companion of the moment... young, cheerful and good looking... [someone] who would always come to him, like a child to his mother, when there was something he wanted.'[2] Pointedly, Rattigan gave one of the aircraft engineers in the script he was writing for *The Sound Barrier* the name Franklin and his boss the line, 'Mr Franklin is very anxious to keep his job.' (In-joke or barbed comment, it would have been well understood by Rattigan's close circle.) After his experience with Kenneth Morgan, Rattigan took the precaution of not asking Michael Franklin to move in with him.

After less than a month the box-office returns made it look ominously as if *Who Is Sylvia?* was going to be Rattigan's second West End flop in a row. His pride was now more than doubly on the line and he immediately agreed to Binkie Beaumont's request to forgo his royalties in an effort to keep the production going. In the publicity surrounding the show, *The People* ran an article on 'Britain's Three Most Eligible Bachelors'. The three bachelors featured were Rattigan, Ivor Novello and Norman Hartnell (the royal dress designer). The article asked 'Why can't they find the right girl?' It is hard to believe that the editor of a Sunday paper which vied with the *News of The World* for circulation really had no inkling. It only served to underline the continued need for caution in Rattigan's private life. The need for concealment in England made it all the more understandable when he cut loose as soon as he got abroad. Someone who took over a rented apartment in Copenhagen a week after Rattigan had been there for a few days on a business trip, found that the doorbell of the apartment rang repeatedly. 'Half the young men of Copenhagen, blond and slim, were on the doorstep, asking for Mr Rattigan, including several trainee sailors.' Similar stories abound.

In the final weeks of 1950 Rattigan once more was able to turn to his Kenneth Morgan play and on 19 December a copy of *The*

Deep Blue Sea, Version No. 2 was handed to Binkie Beaumont. The play had occupied him on and off for almost two years. In an early version, probably the first and possibly incomplete, written within a year of Morgan's death, it had been the story of a disastrous homosexual love affair. But the copy given to Beaumont (headed *Version No. 2* but in fact at least version number three) was a complete reworking. This fairly closely resembled the play that was eventually put into production. However, Rattigan was still not satisfied with it and in January 1951 he returned to the Stag and Hounds in Binfield to go through all three acts again. By 7 February 1951 he had a 'third' version. But even after this there were more changes, albeit it minor, continuing even after the play had gone into rehearsal.

Rattigan was keen that either Margaret Leighton or Celia Johnson should play the lead, but Frith Banbury, who had been hired to direct, suggested Peggy Ashcroft. Rattigan, although a little apprehensive, jumped at the idea and agreed to talk to her about it himself. Fortunately for him, perhaps, she had forgotten all about the previous time they had worked together – in Gielgud's Oxford *Romeo and Juliet*. When Rattigan invited her to lunch, Ashcroft imagined that he wanted her for a comedy and was rather pleased at the thought. Looking forward to hearing about a role that would contrast with the heavy parts she had been playing for so long in the West End, she dressed accordingly. Her heart sank when Rattigan explained that the play opened with the woman he wanted her to play, Hester Collyer, apparently dead in front of a gas fire after a suicide attempt. By the end of the lunch she was less than enthusiastic, but agreed to take the play home to read. Although she found the play absorbing, by the time she had finished reading it she was convinced she did not want to do it. She found the woman she was to play selfish and unsympathetic. If she didn't sympathize with Hester, neither would the audience, and the play would fail. She turned it down. But Binkie Beaumont would not take no for an answer. He called her in for discussions and tried to persuade her that her judgement was wrong. After much heart-searching, she reluctantly agreed to take the part.[3]

Roland Culver was engaged to play Hester's husband. The major casting problem now was to find a young actor to play Freddie Page, an ex-Battle-of-Britain pilot for whom Hester has left her husband. Frith Banbury favoured a tall, fair-haired ex-commando called Jimmy Hanley. But playing golf one day with a rising, little-known actor called Kenneth More, Roland Culver suddenly had the idea that he might fit the bill. He suggested him to Rattigan, who remembered seeing him a year earlier giving a promising performance in a Lonsdale play, *The Way Things Go*, in Brighton. Rattigan suggested him to Binkie Beaumont, who in turn agreed to audition him. The audition was held at the Globe Theatre. The only people in the darkened auditorium were Beaumont, Peggy Ashcroft, Roland Culver and Rattigan. As Kenneth More walked on to the stage, Frith Banbury handed him a script and said, 'Here you are. You're Freddie Page. He's a sexy young man. This woman is mad about him, not because of his looks or his background, but because of his sex. Now go ahead: read.'[4]

More began at Freddie's first entrance, when he returns to the north-west London flat he is sharing with Hester after a golfing weekend at Sunningdale, cheerfully oblivious of the fact that he has forgotten Hester's birthday and thereby pushed her into attempted suicide. Nervous and in the dark about the plot, More's reading lacked the breezy self-confidence of the character. After a few lines Beaumont interrupted and called up to More, 'Can't you make it gayer?' Banbury also asked him to make it lighter. More's nerves were now thoroughly on edge, and he only succeeded in making his reading heavier. 'Thank you, Mr More. We'll write,' said Banbury. He was still convinced Jimmy Hanley was the actor for the part. However, Rattigan was now certain that, in spite of his clumsy reading, More had the right personality for the part. Beaumont was inclined to agree with him. A fortnight later, a second reading was held to decide the issue. It took place in the more relaxed surroundings of Rattigan's home.[5] Although More had now had a chance to read the script, Rattigan knew he would still be nervous, so when he arrived he took him on one side, asked him if he would like a drink, and poured him a stiff whisky. He watched him gulp it down, then said, 'And another?' More accepted with alacrity. This time, More read with much more confidence. At the end he turned to Rattigan with triumph written all over his face and asked: 'Howzat?' There was no need to reply; the part fitted him like a glove.

From the start rehearsals went well and Peggy Ashcroft was surprised at Rattigan's relaxed attitude. He made it clear immediately that he did not regard the text as sacrosanct: if the cast wanted to change the odd word here or there he would not mind in the least. If they needed help he would be on hand when required. Apart from that, he said, he didn't think it was the author's place to interfere: 'Once I've made any corrections to the script that I think are right and are agreed on, I wash my hands of the play. It's in the hands of the director and the actors.' No one was entirely happy with the third act and he had to do quite a lot of rewriting. He calculated that by the time the play opened he had rewritten that act seven times since the first draft.[6] Even after the play opened, Act Three remained a bone of contention.

The Deep Blue Sea had a brief pre-West End try-out at Brighton in February 1952, and opened in London at the Duchess Theatre on Thursday 6 March. The audience in the small theatre were held in hushed silence from the beginning. From his own intense feelings over the tragedy of Kenneth Morgan, Rattigan had developed a play of extraordinary tension as well as of deep feeling. He had drawn material from other experiences. The characters of both Hester and Freddie owed things to people he had met playing golf at Sunningdale and acquaintances from his RAF days. Although the play had its roots in a homosexual relationship, Rattigan's long creative process of assimilation and distillation had recreated this emotional experience into a play with a life and characters of its own.

The original homosexual first draft of the play, 'a long one-acter' was Rattigan's description, seems to have disappeared sometime between 1963 and 1974, so it is difficult to be sure about what was in it. Indeed, some people have doubted whether it ever existed at all outside Rattigan's head. Frith Banbury, the director of *The Deep Blue Sea*, talked to Rattigan a lot during the production and says that although Rattigan mentioned Kenneth Morgan a lot during their conversations he never once told him that there had been a homosexual version of the play. He adds that, as Rattigan was such a commercially minded writer he would never have written a homosexual play *per se* as he would have been all too aware of the fact that in the theatre of the 1950s it could never have received a commercial production.[7] However there are enough people who claim to have read the homosexual version, or to whom Rattigan talked in detail about it at the time, to make it seem probable that Rattigan did write at least the first draft of such a play and to provide some insight into what it may have contained. Bryan Forbes, a young actor whom Rattigan admired at the time when he was working on *The Deep Blue Sea*, has written twice about the homosexual first draft of the play that Rattigan gave him to read in the hope that he would be able to audition to play the part of a young man based on Kenneth Morgan.[8] The 'whole plot' of the play that Forbes read was 'built around a burnt-out homosexual relationship' and was 'concerned with aspects of love rather than aspects of salacious scandal' and was 'a brave attempt to put across a homosexual love affair without sensationalizing it'. However when Rattigan showed this version of the play to Binkie Beaumont he was, as Rattigan told both Bryan Forbes and Peter Osborn shortly afterwards, outraged. He was terrified and told Rattigan that it would ruin everyone connected with it. However Rattigan gave Forbes the impression during their conversations at the time that he was seriously contemplating sticking to his guns – there were other managements who might take the risk of producing it. Forbes believes that there was a masochistic streak in Rattigan's nature that quite relished the thought of the public vilification that this would risk. But Rattigan came under sustained pressure from all sides and finally caved in, accepting Beaumont's advice to rewrite it. Even then he did not entirely suppress his original homosexual version as he showed it to the director Alvin Rakoff in 1964. But in 1974, when Holly Hill talked to Rattigan in connection with a postgraduate degree thesis she was writing for an American university, he did not mention a homosexual version and she came across no references among his papers to there having been such a version.

Over the years since *The Deep Blue Sea* appeared a steady trickle of commentators have suggested that in the character of Hester in particular the play betrays its homosexual origins.⁹ This, surely, is a case of hindsight. At the time of the play's first appearance none of ·the critics detected a homosexual connotation. Peggy Ashcroft never thought of Hester as anything other than a convincing woman. Her initial antipathy to Hester did not result from any doubt about the authenticity of the character but from a lack of sympathy for the attitudes of a woman who was all too recognizable. Once she had started working on the role, Dame Peggy's antipathy turned to strong sympathy and she defended Hester's actions fiercely against all who criticized her. In this connection it is worth taking to heart Edward Albee's damning dismissal of similar suggestions about some of his plays: 'I do know the difference between a man and a woman', and his rejection of all proposals to restage some of his plays with the heterosexual relationships played as homosexual ones.

Rather than looking for the homosexual residue in Rattigan's characterization of Hester Collyer, it is more to the point to see in Rattigan's creation both a remarkable insight into women and an ability, rare among his contemporaries, to create credible female characters. As Professor Susan Rusinko has pointed out, it is not so much the specific nature of the sexual relationship as the deeply emotional implications of that relationship which concerned Rattigan and which are the core of the play.¹⁰ Hester Collyer is that rarity in post-war drama – a cracking good female lead. In *The Deep Blue Sea*, and through the character of Hester Collyer, Rattigan can be seen, far ahead of his time, exploring the dilemmas of women who feel that they have lost or never found themselves as individuals because they have been conditioned to shape their whole lives through their menfolk, their marriages and their love affairs. Rattigan was in a sense echoing Ibsen in *A Doll's House*, whose heroine also discovered that she could not live through the men in her life. *The Deep Blue Sea* was culturally prophetic. It appeared more than a decade before the general awakening to the specific issues confronting women and the emergence of the Women's Liberation Movement.[11]

The plot of *The Deep Blue Sea* is fairly simple. Its skill lies in the way in which tension is maintained, its value in the creation and exploration of the emotional relationships. The play is set in a dingy furnished flat in north-west London, where Hester has been living with Freddie Page for about a year since leaving her husband, Sir William Collyer, a judge. The action all takes place in one day, starting in the morning when Hester is discovered by other residents of the house in front of the gas fire after a suicide attempt (unsuccessful because not enough coins had been put in the gas meter), and ending late that evening when, now firmly separated from her lover, Hester again turns on the gas fire, but this time lights it, having apparently made up her mind to try to face the reality of life on her own. Rattigan called the play 'a study of obsession and of the shame that a sensitive, clear-minded and strong-willed woman must feel when she discovers she has inside her a compulsion that seems too strong for her to resist'.[12]

Slowly the reasons for Hester's attempted suicide, her feelings for Freddie and for her husband, are revealed. Questioned by the landlady about why she did such a wicked thing, she says only that she supposes it was the devil: 'When you're between any kind of devil and the deep blue sea, the deep blue sea sometimes looks very inviting.' Cross-examined by her husband, an amiable man who still loves her despite all that has happened, and wants her to come back to their comfortable life together, she explains further: 'Anger, hatred and shame, in about equal parts I think.' Anger at Freddie, hatred of herself and shame at being alive. Freddie still loves her as much as he did at the outset, she says, but his love compared to hers has always been zero. Nevertheless, he can still sometimes give her something that her husband cannot give her – himself.

Each of the characters is, as in other Rattigan plays, to some extent a projection of Rattigan himself. In surviving earlier versions of the play, where the author's process of assimilation and recreation is less complete, this is even clearer than in the finished version. So in earlier versions Collyer still betrays his feelings of hurt and bitterness about the loss of Hester to another man in a way that is much more raw and uncomfortable than in the version that was staged. When he tells Hester that it is only now that he has lost her that he realizes the true depth of his love for her, she replies: 'Bill, an emotion that comes solely from loss or frustration can't be a very solid one.' This sounds suspiciously like Rattigan's own position over the loss of Kenneth Morgan to Alec Ross. The parallel is even closer when, in the *No. 2* version, Collyer tells her, 'You know, Hester, I don't think I'd have minded nearly so much if it had been a well-known author or composer. Lord knows it could have been. You met enough of them with me. Even another lawyer. Of course I'd have felt losing you just as keenly but if I could only have had some respect for the man who beat me – '

Freddie, who has been unable to adjust to life since the war, complains about the unfairness of what Hester has done – if she had managed to kill herself it would be him who would have been blamed, first for breaking up a marriage and then for driving her to suicide. He complains that he is out of his depth. All his life he has tried to avoid getting tangled up in people's emotions, yet it always seems to be happening to him: 'Too many emotions. Far too ruddy many. I loathe 'em... She says I've got no feelings and perhaps she's right, but anyway I've got something inside that can get hurt – the way it's hurt now. I don't enjoy causing other people misery. I'm not a ruddy sadist. My sort never gets a hearing. We're called a lot of rude names, and nobody ever thinks we have a case...' Later, Hester tries again to explain to her uncomprehending husband the quality of her feelings for Freddie: 'Neither you nor anyone else can explain what I feel for Freddie. It's all far too big and confusing to be tied up in such a neat little parcel and labelled lust. Lust isn't the whole of life – and Freddie is, you see, to me. The whole of life – and of death too, it seems...' When Freddie makes up his mind to leave Hester, he tells her it is the only chance for either of them. They are literally death to each other.

It is another lodger, Miller, a doctor who has himself faced despair, who reminds Hester that most people manage to face life. When she asks how anyone can face life without hope he replies that to face life without hope can mean to live without despair.

To get beyond hope is her only chance: beyond hope lies life. 'Listen to me,' Miller says. 'To see yourself as the world sees you may be very brave, but it can also be very foolish. Why should you accept the world's view of you as a weak-willed neurotic – better dead than alive?' (In earlier versions Miller adds a specific reference to being 'unable to control your lusts'.) 'What right have they to judge? To judge you they must have the capacity to feel as you feel. And who has? One in a thousand. You alone know how you have felt. And you alone know how unequal the battle has always been that your will has had to fight.'

The Deep Blue Sea is undoubtedly Rattigan's finest full-length serious play, an opinion the first-night audience showed that they shared by breaking into prolonged cheering after the final curtain. It turned Kenneth More into a star and re-established Rattigan as Britain's most important practising playwright. The reviews were virtually unanimous in their praise. The only serious matter of contention was the ending. A number of critics argued that Rattigan should have allowed Hester to kill herself. Kenneth Tynan, hailing the play as 'the most absorbing new English play for many seasons', recorded how he had gone out at the second interval exulting that 'I was seeing the most striking new play I could remember'. But, he continued:

> I shall never forgive Mr Rattigan for his last act. It is intolerable: his brilliance lays an ambush for itself, and walks straight into it. If his heroine kills herself, he will merely be repeating the pattern, so he decides to let her live. But he has stated the case for her death so pungently that he cannot argue her out of the impasse without forfeiting our respect . . . Dishonestly, he makes her insist that she does not *deserve* to live, thus hauling in all kinds of moral implications which are totally irrelevant, since her point was purely that she could not *bear* to live. When, finally, she chooses survival, it is for all the wrong reasons.[13]

Rattigan argued strenuously for the rest of his life against Tynan and all those who agreed with him over the ending: a suicide would have been too pat; it would have been the sentimental ending, the one the audience wanted, the one he would have been unable to resist as a schoolboy dramatist when his heroines still 'measured their lengths' at suitably dramatic moments. However, the whole conscious intent of his adult writing had been to show the necessity, difficulty and courage of facing oneself and one's life as it really is. Hester had to live, but to live in the knowledge that she was living for nothing.

The play's main weakness is in the subsidiary characters, who are unconvincing because they have to fulfil representative functions in Rattigan's conscious design. Least convincing of all is Miller, the outcast who argues Hester out of her death. In earlier versions Miller has been struck off the medical register because he is a homosexual. Although he still does voluntary work in a diphtheria clinic in his spare time, he will get no credit for research he has done into a more effective cure for the disease. (An early draft has Miller saying: 'Some people are born different to others and it's no good pretending that that makes them wicked and striking them off registers just because of it.') By the final version Miller's offence is unnamed and unexplored. A potentially interesting character has become a plot device. Because the nature of his offence is hidden and any real discussion of his feelings is expunged, what might have been an interesting relationship between him and Hester becomes impossible.

Some of the reactions to the play when it opened underlined the plea for tolerance that Rattigan had embodied in it. Ivor Brown, in the *Observer*, suggested that all Hester needed was a good slap and a chat to a marriage guidance counsellor. When the play was shown on television, journalists even wondered whether it was suitable for family entertainment, fearing that the public were bound to find such 'worthless characters' and such honest emotion distasteful.

However the play struck a deep chord with British audiences. Once again Rattigan had demonstrated his uncanny knack for being in touch with the feelings of his contemporaries. In Freddie Page, people found more than an understanding portrait of a familiar type of Englishman. He was also something of an allegorical figure for the time – a war hero, living in the past and unable to come to terms with the present; beginning to age, his talents no longer in demand, he finds it difficult to make a satisfactory life or to find a job; his good intentions rebound on him. He could have been a symbol for Britain itself in 1952.

The play's special potency for the post-war British audience was underlined by its abject failure in New York, where it was dismissed as cleverly crafted soap-opera. Remarking that 'a romantic play which is not a comedy is the hardest thing in the world to put over on a New York critic', Kenneth Tynan wrote a long article in *Harper's Bazaar* of November 1952 about Rattigan, trying to prepare the American public for *The Deep Blue Sea*. He started by saying how tired he was of the way in which Rattigan was put down by people because of his success. Such people would say:' "Good commercial stuff – good theatre too . . . but he's not really a dramatist." "Good theatre": the phrase smacks of condescension, of giving the poor fellow his due; there is an unspoken "but" – which must someday be demolished. It implies that there is something improper in writing deliberately for your chosen medium – not print, or pure sound, but an upturned host of faces in a darkened hall.' Tynan went on to explain why he too had once dismissed him: 'I remember exactly when I gave Rattigan up for lost: it was in the autumn of 1950, when I saw *Who Is Sylvia?* . . . We had, I concluded, a competent, but minor playwright.' But Tynan, in a dramatic about-face, immediately recants:'I was quite wrong, which is why I am writing this. I had missed a clue, a vital signpost: it occurs in *The Browning Version*, during the long speech in which the schoolmaster ... speaks of himself, with arid desperation, as a traditional henpecked husband. "It is usually, I believe, a subject for farce." Enlarging on his relationship with his wife, he uses the crucial phrase, "the love she required, and which I was unable to give her".' Tynan goes on to explain how this clue – 'the conflict of two quite incompatible kinds of passion' – has become the germ of *The Deep Blue Sea*, by far the best thing Rattigan has written. 'I do not say Rattigan has taken on gianthood as a dramatist. His characters still think in terms of "niceness" and "unpleasantness", not of "goodness" and "evil", but they are less evasive than they ever were. They are talking about realities, probing past appearances, and scarring each other.'

Repeating that *The Deep Blue Sea* was the most striking new English play of the decade, Tynan looked hopefully towards Rattigan's future: 'There, to date, stands Rattigan, partially fulfilled, tall and softly smiling, crisp of speech and wise of eye. What next? Not, I am sure, a novel. He is scared of the freedom it implies; those infinite spaces of time and place terify him; he prefers the limits of the stage, the specific actor and the deadline. He may now club us with a masterpiece. Or perhaps his so acute ear for dialogue will betray him with ditchwater fluency again...' But, Tynan concluded: 'One distinction will probably never be wrested from him: I support it with a completely unauthenticated story. It was told me by a friend who arrived at a Knightsbridge party and was ushered upstairs to doff hat and coat. Pausing on the cloakroom threshold and peering through the crack of the door, he saw someone talking to the mirror. Rattigan had stopped in the middle of combing his hair to muse, with a little groan, "If you're not very careful, Terry Rattigan, you won't be the prettiest playwright in London." '

The prettiest; the wittiest; now the best...

Notes

1   Interview with Charles Hamblett in *John Bull*, 6 December 1952.
2   Many people testified to Michael Franklin having made a play for Benjamin Britten, although when I checked with Britten's biographer, Humphrey Carpenter, he had no record of the story. B. A. Young mentions the Franklin/Britten story in *The Rattigan Version*, op. cit.
3   Based on interviews with Dame Peggy Ashcroft in 1978 by the author and by Michael Billington for his book *Peggy Ashcroft*, published by John Murray, London, 1988.
4   In describing the casting and production of *The Deep Blue Sea*, I have made considerable use of the autobiographies of Kenneth More (*Happy Go Lucky – My Life*, Robert Hale, London, 1959) and of Roland Culver (*Not Quite a Gentleman*, William Kimber, London, 1979).
5   Peggy Ashcroft seems to have suggested a second reading in more relaxed surroundings, but accounts differ as to whether it took place in Rattigan's home or Beaumont's house in Lord North Street.
6   Noël Coward came to see the play during its pre-London tour and told Rattigan that he had written a marvellous first act, a good second act, but that the third act was no good.

7   Frith Banbury interviewed by Geoffrey Wansell for his book, op. cit.

8   Bryan Forbes, *That Despicable Race*, Elm Tree Books, London, 1980, and *A Divided Life*, op. cit.

9   See, for instance, Anne Edwards's biography *Vivien Leigh*, W. H.Allen, London, 1977, and *Not in Front of the Audience: Homosexuality On The Stage* by Nicholas de Jongh, Routledge, London, 1992.

10   Susan Rusinko, op. cit.

11   Holly Hill was probably the first critic to point out that Rattigan was ahead of his time in his awareness of the specific problems confronting women, as she was in pointing to the importance of his indefinite, as opposed to happy endings. I remain indebted to her for many insights over the years.

12   *New York Herald Tribune*, 2 November 1952.

13   Kenneth Tynan, op. cit.

14

The Sleeping Prince

In 1952, when *The Deep Blue Sea* opened, a sense of change was in the air. A month before the opening King George VI had died and a new young queen had ascended the throne. It became popular to look forward optimistically to a 'New Elizabethan Age'. The post-war Labour government of Clement Attlee had given way to the Conservatives led by Churchill. The old wartime Allies were engaged in a Cold War. People were sick of shortages, of rationing (a leftover from the war), of 'fair shares' – of precious little – 'for all'. In the theatre the Attlee government had laid the foundations on which a new creative flowering might be built. It had created the Arts Council and passed legislation enabling local authorities to raise a special rate with which to subsidize local repertory theatres. 'Austerity Britain' could at last start to make way for 'You've Never Had It So Good'.

Rattigan was forty. The critical acclaim that greeted *The Deep Blue Sea* confirmed his position as Britain's most important practising playwright. But although he had plenty of work to keep him busy – film scripts, public appearances, press interviews and business meetings – for the first time for ten years he did not have a new play in his head that he was eager to write. For someone so fuelled by the drive to write, this was a potentially ominous sign, reminiscent of the situation after the opening of *French Without Tears*. For the moment however, there were other worries to keep him from brooding.

Since his stroke in August 1949 and a fall in which he broke his femur the following year, Frank Rattigan's health had been a continual concern. In order to escape the worst of the weather Frank spent much of the winter of 1951–2 at a seaside hotel in Exmouth, Devon. Vera Rattigan had gone to visit him, but had chosen to stay on alone in their country house near Luton, in spite of the fact that it was, as she said herself, 'the coldest house in Bedfordshire'. It was nearer to her sons. Although Rattigan could provide for his parents, their well-being was a growing worry. Vera was at the first night of *The Deep Blue Sea* as usual, but for the second time Frank was not (he had missed the first night of *Who Is Sylvia?* following his broken femur). That morning Vera had received a letter from Frank, starting as usual 'Darling Old Girl' and full of cheerful comments on the weather, but written in terribly shaky handwriting. Three days later, on 9 March 1952, Frank Rattigan had another stroke and died.

A week later, once the funeral was over, Rattigan busied himself again in his work. He might have nothing as substantial as a new play to occupy him, but work was a distraction. By the end of April he had drafted a possible film script, or with a little adaptation, it might perhaps be turned into a play. Called *Innocents Abroad*, it concerned a woman returning to a room in France where she had been with her husband in the summer of 1939. He had been the only man she had ever loved. 'I wasn't nearly as important to him as his work. But I *was* important to him, I think.' Her husband has been killed in the war – to the relief of her parents as it has left her free to marry someone more suitable. It contained the germ of an interesting idea of considerable potency for Rattigan. But it needed more working out and never went any further.

By May he was occupied, through his own production company, with staging Rodney Ackland's *The Pink Room*. When it opened on 18 June at the Lyric Theatre, Hammersmith, a West End 'try-out' theatre, it was badly received. By the time it closed three weeks later it had lost Rattigan and his production company more than three thousand five hundred pounds.

He was also in negotiation about the New York production of *The Deep Blue Sea*. Harold Freedman, his American agent, had sent it to Margaret Sullivan, an American star who had not appeared on Broadway for seven years and was looking for a vehicle in which to make a comeback. In July, Rattigan appeared on television with the popular comedian–violinist Vic Oliver. At the end of the month an offer came in for ten thousand pounds, plus a handsome slice of the producer's profits, for the film rights to *The Deep Blue Sea*. In addition there would be a further five thousand pounds if he could complete a full screenplay for it by February of the following year.

In August 1952, Rattigan's brother Brian, who was a government solicitor working for the Ministry of National Insurance,[1] was diagnosed as being terminally ill with cancer. Brian was only forty-five years old and the news came as a terrible shock to Rattigan. Although he had never been particularly close to Brian, Rattigan had always felt a strong sense of duty towards his family. On 19 August, immediately after the diagnosis had been confirmed, Rattigan wrote to his brother:

DEAR BRIAN,

It's rather late at night to write letters (2.15 a.m. but I can't go to bed without getting this effusion (not a literary one, I assure you) off my chest.

It's been my profession all my life to use words dishonestly and now I need them to record, rather than induce, an emotion most honestly and deeply felt, they seem to be taking their revenge on me. I can't really blame them, I suppose. They've been wickedly exploited – for the vilest of motives – mere cash.

So I think the best thing is just not to try and find the beastly things at all, but merely to tell you this simple truth – that if ever and whenever my time comes to receive news as grave as the news you have received, I can only hope and pray I receive it as well as you have – but I deeply doubt it... Don't use this against me when you get well. But at this moment of trouble and anxiety I thought you should know how much your courage, resignation and unselfishness have helped those who care for you.

Sorry to be embarrassing, but I couldn't avoid it. Some things have to be said.

My love and every possible wish.

TERRY

Brian had only discovered the true gravity of his illness when a radio-therapist absent-mindedly left her notes on his bed-table. He had contacted Rattigan and together they had decided that they must break the news to their mother. Brian replied to Rattigan's letter the next day, saying, 'It is rather odd to think that if all this had never happened you and I would almost certainly never have revealed that we have a considerable affection for each other!' He goes on to tell him that he must try and convince their mother that there is no cause for her to worry. He ends: 'I certainly won't hold your letter against you in the event of my recovering but I shall always value very highly its obvious sincerity.' One month later Brian Rattigan was dead.

After the deaths of her husband and her elder son, Vera did not want to live on alone in the rambling family house in Bedfordshire. She wanted to move back into London so that she could see more of her one surviving son. The top-floor flat in Kensington where the family had lived during Rattigan's childhood no longer existed. The house, together with about a dozen others in the terrace on the east side of the square, had been flattened during the war, and in their place stood a nondescript modern block. On the opposite side of the square, a number of old houses had been joined together to form a residential hotel, the Stanhope Court. Vera Rattigan moved in. The majority of the other residents were, like herself, elderly gentlefolk, mostly living alone in polite, slightly reduced circumstances. Although their lives were occasionally enlivened by casual guests, the atmosphere in the hotel was tranquil. Vera, although now in her sixties, was still a spirited and strikingly handsome woman. She affected the style of the grand lady, attending the theatre regularly and taking a great interest and pride in all Terence's doings. Her famous son was a frequent visitor at the Stanhope Court, calling to pick her up or return her from an outing to the theatre or a party, and dropping in for a quiet dinner or tea with his mother.

Shortly after his father's death Rattigan had moved out of his Chester Square home into a penthouse flat in Eaton Square. The sliding plate-glass windows of his sixty-foot lounge opened on to a balcony fronted with well-stocked window boxes and looking out on to the mature trees in the square. To enhance the impression of an open-air atmosphere, he had the largest uninterrupted expanse of wall in the lounge covered with a black and white photomural blown up from an old French engraving of a forest scene. The dining room had photomurals on all four walls, comprising a complete panorama of old London. Simultaneously, he took a country house backing on to his favourite golf course at the club where Hester and Freddie were supposed to have first met in *The Deep Blue Sea*, Sunningdale.

Rattigan now had quite an army of professional advisers, housekeepers and others attending him. The most prominent was his fiercely loyal secretary Mary Herring, another in the line of tough women in Rattigan's life who tried to protect him from the distractions and depredations of an ever increasing swarm of hangers-on. She normally worked from a small study in the Eaton Square flat. In addition to doing his letters, keeping his appointments book and organizing his life – which still needed a lot of organizing – she typed up his manuscripts. He still normally wrote everything in long-hand in exercise books. Over the years the background music had changed from jazz to Puccini and he now seldom wrote at a desk. Dressed in an immaculate silk dressing-gown, he usually wrote on a writing board purchased for him by his mother when he was a young man. This he rested on his knee while stretched out on a sofa. At Sunningdale he had a board specially made to rest on the arms of a comfortable armchair.

His normal writing routine had varied little with the years. Starting at about 10.30 in the morning, he would work until about 3.00 in the afternoon, barely stopping for a light lunch brought to him on a tray by a housekeeper. Then a walk for two hours, or a round of golf or a game of tennis. In London, the walk often consisted of exploring obscure back streets. He would be back at work by five, and continued until eight or nine. He seldom worked later, unless he was very behind schedule, since it prevented him from sleeping. He reckoned that once he had prepared himself and was ready to start writing, he could complete a play, including final polishing, in about eight weeks.

Film scripts were even quicker. However, as we have seen, he would sometimes run into difficulties, in which case he might drop a play for months at a time before returning to it. While he was engaged in the actual writing, he would not go to the theatre and avoided reading novels, for fear of absorbing any of their style of dialogue. Film producers in particular were appreciative, not only of the speed with which he could work, but of the dispassionate view he took of his finished scripts. He was always open to suggestions for the changes which are part and parcel of the film-making process. Apart from his secretary and his agent, the other main organizer of Rattigan's life was his accountant, Bill Forsyth. Rattigan had been earning thirty thousand pounds a year or more for a decade. The hole made in his finances by the gambling sprees and wild spending of earlier years had been repaired, but only by Rattigan subjecting himself to tough management by others. Left to himself, he still remained hopelessly extravagant, spending lavishly on Rolls-Royces, restaurants, furniture and Savile Row tailoring. Although he jokingly wondered if people would take him more seriously if he wore pyjamas and had tousled hair, he still featured in the *Tailor and Cutter's* First Eleven of Best Dressed Men.[2]

He was generous to a fault, entertaining without stint and distributing expensive gifts. Yet he could boast that he did not owe a penny in income tax. This was achieved by Bill Forsyth who had instituted two accounts for his income. Into one went all his earnings, which Rattigan was not allowed to touch without Forsyth's express permission; the demands of the Inland Revenue were met from this account. Forsyth arranged for the payment of just five thousand pounds a year into a second account. This was Rattigan's spending money. Forsyth found that Rattigan soon used this up, so he got him to agree to a further restriction: all cheques above ten pounds had to be countersigned by Forsyth. A journalist recorded going out to lunch with Rattigan and, finding him moody, asked what was wrong. 'Money,' Rattigan replied. The previous evening, a friend had come to him with a hard-luck story and, much though he wanted to help financially, he knew Forsyth would never sanction the expenditure. Rattigan was wondering, not for the first time, how he could get his hands on some of his own money behind his accountant's back. 'They treat me like a child,' he complained, adding, 'and quite right too!'[3] The truth was that, although reassured by the success that large sums of money represented, and by no means above a little discreet showing off (driving Noël Coward down to Brighton one day in his Rolls-Royce, he could not resist pointing out that his was a more expensive Rolls than the one owned by Coward), Rattigan did not really care about money. It was important to him as a symbol only – as a means of purchasing those outward tokens of success that bolstered his self-esteem or, perhaps, as a means of buying friendship – but not in itself.

Rattigan's lackadaisical attitude showed up in the trouble he was always having with servants. While his vagueness sometimes made it difficult for them – summoning his housekeeper to lay on the food for a party, he often seemed incapable of being precise about what he actually wanted prepared, asking only for the inclusion of 'some of those nice little savoury things you made the other day' without any further description that might give a clue as to what they actually were – it also laid him open to being cheated. Here an onus of responsibility was laid on Mary Herring and the later secretaries, particularly as Rattigan turned a wilfully blind eye to successive cases of petty pilfering. But Rattigan seemed not so much to tolerate as positively to enjoy the human frailties of the people who worked for him. His inclination was to note their oddities for future use, rather than to correct them. One of many such couples, a husband and wife, who acted as butler and cook at the house in Sunningdale, became quite famous among those in theatrical circles privileged enough to be invited there. Arthur Abeles, a film producer friend, was convinced that the woman was positively the worst cook in the world, while her husband was the most inept butler. The pair were over-chummy and surly by turns with guests. A famous actress, pausing to consider how many courgettes to scoop on to her plate from the proffered vegetable dish, was prompted to ''urry up, dear, I haven't got all day', while a well-known mannequin had a large dollop of unwanted mashed potato slapped brusquely on to her plate with, 'Munch it up, dear, you're all skin and bone.'⁴ The thieving of this couple became so blatant, and the amount of the housekeeping money they were spending on themselves so great, that some of Rattigan's friends decided they could no longer smile and ignore it. They remonstrated with him. 'Oh,' he said mildly when they pointed out the extent of the couple's depredations, 'I thought my housekeeping allowance wasn't going as far as it should.' It was clear that the couple would have to be dismissed, but Rattigan could not face the prospect of a scene with them. So he went off on holiday to the South of France and left one of his friends to deal with them.

This pathological desire to avoid unpleasant confrontations frequently landed Rattigan in awkward situations. Face to face with a supplicant, he would agree to lend his name to an enterprise, write something or contribute money, because he could not say no. Later, someone else would counsel against it and Rattigan would reverse his decision. The result was frequent changes of mind and someone being delegated to convey his final decision and clear up the mess – his secretary, agent, solicitor, accountant or a friend. In contrast, over things that affected his work he was decisive and often quite stony-hearted. No one was more loyal to the actors who appeared in his plays, but if one offended by giving a performance that disappointed him, then he would have to wait a long time before appearing in another Rattigan play. Robert Flemyng, who had almost reached the position of a one-man Rattigan industry by the time of his appearance in *Who Is Sylvia?*, never again appeared in a Rattigan première. As we have seen, an even more loyal ally, A. D. Peters, his agent, backer and champion since the days before his success, had been dismissed, ostensibly, at least, because he had criticized *Who Is Sylvia?* Yet even his closest friends never saw him angry, though they knew that often he must be seething inwardly. Forced into a corner, Rattigan remained scrupulously polite. On one occasion, a man who claimed to have evidence of Rattigan's homosexuality and threatened to reveal the real-life origins behind the plot of one of his plays attempted to blackmail him. Rattigan invited the man out to a good restaurant for lunch. During the meal he was the perfect host, polite and smiling, never alluding to the matter they were there to discuss. Then, after coffee and brandy had been served, he said, 'Oh, by the way, what an extraordinary letter you sent me. I hope you won't send me another one, because if you do I shall send it to my solicitor. Would you like some more brandy?' Rattigan was not bothered by the man again.

Although he was by no means tired of London, he loved the country. The reason for choosing a house at Sunningdale was almost entirely due to his enthusiasm for golf and his liking for that course in particular. He had been playing there regularly for a good many years before being able to get the house, which had a large garden with a gate leading directly on to the course. Rattigan had taken up golf during his first term at Oxford. After being dropped from the Harrow cricket eleven in his last term, he had realized that he was unlikely to get a cricket blue and had taken three perfunctory golf lessons, bought a few clubs and taken to playing by himself at the North Oxford course. In the last few years he had played with increasing dedication, steadily working his handicap down to nine, making him an averagely good golfer. His form was erratic; he had a good drive but putted badly. He found it an ideal game because it demanded such complete concentration on the actual shots that it effectively took his mind off his writing and allowed him to relax. His enthusiasm for the game became so well known that Stephen Potter, the humourist who invented 'Gamesmanship', published a 'Rattigan gambit' for achieving the upper hand over opponents who used a trolley for their clubs. It entailed progressively loading up your opponent's trolley with items such as discarded clothes and craftily lead-weighted golf balls until the opponent can scarcely drag the trolley around the course. Rattigan entered into the joke by outlining another gambit, relating to new rules of the game as issued in a small handbook. This, he claimed, was an all-embracing but exceedingly effective ploy:

> At a given moment, preferably when the opponent has chipped within a few feet of the pin, give a start of surprise, pull out from the hip pocket a copy of the new rules and, quickly flipping over the pages, study a passage at random with a grave and concentrated frown; after ten seconds raise the eyebrows; after a further ten, shake the head slowly from side to side; then replace the book in hip pocket with, if necessary, a short sharp laugh; finally gaze thoughtfully at the horizon with the eyebrows in the elevated position, while the opponent addresses himself to his putt – or more correctly to his putts.[5]

Rattigan's favourite golfing partners were Stephen Mitchell, the impresario who had put on the two one-act plays in *Playbill*, and a young film producer, Tony Darnborough. Other regular golfing friends were Arthur Abeles, also a film producer, and Harold French. They never put less than ten shillings each on a round and never more than ten pounds. Mary Herring appears to have regarded these friends with strong moral disapproval. According to Darnborough, if she picked up the phone when he was calling Rattigan she would say, 'I pray for you all the time.'

In the afternoons, after a round of golf, Rattigan and his friends would repair either to the bar or to his home for a drink. If he wanted to carry on writing on these occasions he would sit in the lounge window while his friends played the record player and talked. Putting his feet on a footstool, he scribbled in a notebook, apparently oblivious of the noise around him. If his friends volunteered to go away and leave him in peace he would say, 'Oh no, old boy, don't bother.' His style as a host remained very much that of the gallant head-boy. He drank a lot, but never seemed drunk. Since watching Puffin Asquith struggle with drink, he was cautious; after a string of hangovers he would conscientiously cut down his consumption. Under the charm, tinged with engaging, shy modesty, the cold detachment of a natural observer had never disappeared. 'The man is a fish, a hard cold-blooded, super-cilious...fish', Catherine had said of Sir Robert Morton in *The Winslow Boy*. Rattigan saw the same quality in himself, and thought it a fault as well as a necessary attribute of the playwright. Sometimes it did come dangerously near to seeming a fault to others, too. On one occasion some guests discovered he had recorded their conversation at dinner, when he played back a particularly foolish argument they had been having to reinforce his own assertion that they were being stupid. It was all taken as good fun, but at least one guest did wonder how many other times they had been recorded in order to supply raw material for a script.

Once Rattigan had got his Sunningdale house, he had no further need of his rooms at the Stag and Hounds, and so he bequeathed them to Arthur Abeles and Tony Darnborough as a venue in which to entertain girlfriends. It was an act which was consistent with Rattigan's concern to be a considerate host.[6] It spared his friends any embarrassment they might have felt over the changing assortment of young men he entertained together with other homosexual friends at his Sunningdale home, which was, in any case, not over-furnished with bedrooms. Although he made no secret of his homosexuality to his heterosexual friends in the 'Sunningdale set', he still liked, as far as possible, to maintain a strict segregation between that compartment of his life and the rest. In any case the 'gay' young men would hardly have mixed with his more conventional heterosexual companions. Inevitably they came into contact sometimes; then Darnborough and Abeles and company would shake their heads tolerantly at 'Terry's little weakness', mildly regretting that so many of the young men seemed 'pretty rough trade', and dismiss them as 'purely medicinal'.

The young man who meant most to Rattigan was still Michael Franklin. However the relationship was far from easy. Franklin was temperamental, frequently causing hysterical scenes, threatening to walk out for ever or to cut his wrists. Although the masochist in him seemed quite to enjoy these outbursts, with the suicide of Kenneth Morgan still fresh in his memory Rattigan found these scenes distressing. Yet because of his horror of confrontations he often left his friends or his professional advisers to sort things out. Franklin had made no secret of the fact that he wanted to be kept: Rattigan wanted sex and Franklin was there to provide it – 'He was a service as it were.'[7] He exacted a high price. B. A. Young recorded how, in the spring of 1953 when Rattigan was away in America, he received an unexpected telegram: 'Please see to Michael's requirements which do not include a Jaguar. Love Terry.'[8] As a way of providing him with an income Rattigan made Franklin responsible for the decoration of his homes. This was almost certainly a contributory factor in Rattigan's frequent changes of home in later years.

The segregation between the sexual 'compartment' of Rattigan's life and the rest had been one of its more striking features ever since he left Oxford, but it was probably never more marked than at this period. Unlike Mark in *Who Is Sylvia?*, who boasted just before his final unmasking that by dividing the illicit and romantic from the domestic and secure he had found the secret of successful living – 'to divide them into two worlds and then to have the best of both of them' – Rattigan feared their collision. This was largely due to the intolerant and narrow-minded legal and social strictures that still applied to male homosexuals. Yet his almost flamboyantly conventional, conservative lifestyle sometimes seemed not so much camouflage as over-compensation. He still felt regret, even self-disgust, over his homosexuality. During this period he confided to a number of close friends, people he had known for a long time such as John Perry and Peter Glenville, that, entering his forties and his looks starting to fade, he thought again about marriage and regretted not having children. He had come to enjoy the company of women at least as much, if not more, than that of men. He said he had made further sexual experiments with women after the abortive encounter with a prostitute in his youth, but never with any success or enjoyment. In such circumstances he was much too realistic seriously to contemplate marriage.

This division of Rattigan's life led to some pretty close shaves when the two worlds threatened to collide, circumstances which were not quite as funny in real life as they might have been on the stage. The young men who were his sexual partners did not like being bundled out through the back door when 'straight' guests were coming. They were resentful of the implication that they were not good enough to meet the celebrities with whom Rattigan consorted in his 'other world'. Rattigan seems to have gone to particular lengths to avoid them meeting his mother – not always an easy task, especially as she lived with him at Sunningdale for quite extended periods. Although her suspicions may have been aroused, Vera seems still not to have known of her son's homosexuality; or if she did, she refused to admit it. She continued to cherish hopes that he would marry. Stephen Mitchell was sitting beside Vera at a Rattigan party when she said quizzically, 'Why are there always so many young men and so few girls at Terence's parties?'

Two beautiful women were regular guests at Rattigan's parties – Jean Dawnay and Margaret Leighton. Jean Dawnay was one of Britain's top models. Whenever Rattigan threw a particularly grand party or entertained groups of celebrities as house guests at Little Court in Sunningdale, Dawnay acted as his hostess. On other occasions Rattigan's guests could be pretty outrageous. One man, a successful fashion designer, regularly turned up wearing very expensive women's clothes but at the 'respectable' parties where Dawnay acted as hostess, the man always turned up dressed in immaculate conventional attire. Dawnay had met Rattigan when she had been going out with Tony Darnborough. Rattigan had asked Darnborough if he would mind if he took her out to dinner. She and Rattigan hit it off immediately. As a beautiful and famous single woman she was very much in the public eye, under pressure from the press and feeling as if she was being forced to live in a goldfish bowl. By contrast, Rattigan was courteous and very correct, taking a protective and almost paternal interest in her. Behind Dawnay's worldliness Rattigan saw someone essentially innocent and vulnerable. To Dawnay, Rattigan was a refuge where there would be no question of sex after dinner or a night out. He even made a room in his Sunningdale house permanently available for her to use whenever she wanted it.

After one of Rattigan's parties, Vera Rattigan looked at her son, then over at Dawnay, and asked, 'When are you two getting married?' On another occasion Vivien Leigh asked Rattigan and Dawney straight out when they were planning to marry. Whether Vera really hoped that her son would marry Jean Dawnay is hard to tell. She said rather different things about her hopes to different people. But a few years later, when the actress Margaret Leighton had more or less taken over Dawnay's role in Rattigan's life, Vera told more than one person that she hoped that he would marry her. For her part, Margaret Leighton told friends that she would marry him tomorrow if he asked. He never did.

Some of Rattigan's parties at Sunningdale amounted almost to theatrical state occasions. Then there was no suggestion of there being too many young men present. One of the most famous of these occasions was for Coronation Royal Ascot Week in June 1953. Jean Dawnay was Rattigan's hostess for the week. The house-guests of honour were the ruling monarchs of the British Theatre, Sir Laurence Olivier and his wife, Vivien Leigh. They were due to appear in his new play, *The Sleeping Prince*. This was a very slight piece, which he called 'an occasional fairy tale' – the occasion being the Coronation. Rattigan claimed that on 1 January 1953 he had woken up with the customary blinding hangover and, later in the day, to the equally blinding thought that this was Coronation year and that he ought to do something about it, since everyone else seemed to be doing something for the occasion. But what? About a month later, he claimed, when he was about halfway through writing the play, the telephone rang in his Sunningdale study, a little after midnight. He did not suppose, he said, that a call from Olivier after midnight was going to be about the weather, and immediately suspected that 'something was afoot'.[9] 'After only the minimal exchange of "darling old boys" and "loveys", the voice changed into that quietly imperious register. "I hear you're writing a play for the Coronation that might suit Vivien and me."'

The real story behind the genesis of *The Sleeping Prince* was a good deal more complex. Rattigan was correct in saying that he felt he ought to be doing something that would mark the

Coronation as everyone else seemed to be doing something about it. William Walton was composing a Coronation march and Benjamin Britten a Coronation opera, *Gloriana*. However, the thought had occurred to Rattigan a long time before 1 January 1953. Ever since the death of George VI in early February 1952 people had been talking about ways to mark the Coronation. Alexander Korda had talked to him about a possible film about monarchy, which Rattigan had rejected. Somehow it was just taken for granted that Rattigan would write a play for the event. He and his mother were very aware that his father had had a minor official role at the last two coronations. So, as his friend B. A. Young expressed it, although no one commissioned him, and he was not in the position of Poet Laureate, Rattigan in effect commissioned himself.[10] He seems to have come to a firm decision to write the play, and to have decided on the nature of its subject matter, sometime during the autumn of 1952 while he was in America.

Immediately after his brother Brian's death in September 1952, Rattigan went to America to attend to the Broadway production of *The Deep Blue Sea*. He arrived to find the production in deep trouble. Margaret Sullivan, who had so much wanted to play Hester, was proving unequal to the role. As he reported to his mother: 'The simple truth is that she's not a good enough actress to play it.' He warned his mother to expect the play to fail when it opened in New York, advising her 'to be like me, and try to take things philosophically'. In fact, as with other recent productions of his plays that had seemed en route to failure, he took things anything but philosophically. The cast and director were already blaming each other for the fact that the production was not working and Rattigan joined in. He told his mother that the director, Frith Banbury, who had served the play so well in London, had 'entirely lost control of the situation and is now hanging on by his teeth, trying to avoid getting sacked'. Banbury blamed Margaret Sullivan and was disappointed by the actor playing Freddie Page, Jimmy Hanley, the actor Banbury had originally wanted in preference to More for the London production. (Kenneth More had been unable to be in the American production owing to film work.) Margaret Sullavan had become moody and seemed to blame everyone, although she and Rattigan still managed to get along all right together socially.

The play was duly slaughtered by the critics when it opened on Broadway in November 1952, although Margaret Sullavan's personal standing with the public earned it a run of 132 performances. By the time Rattigan left New York by sea, three weeks later, he had definitely decided on his Coronation play. He wrote to his mother that he planned to disembark in Cannes and spend the first week of December there working 'on the next play... a trifle about Kings and Queens for the Coronation... a plot of my own'. He would work on it in earnest, he told her, when he got back to England for Christmas. In the interests of maintaining the carefully crafted illusion he had created for his mother of having to fight off the advances of legions of predatory ladies, and to give additional cover for his decision to get off in Cannes, in the same letter Rattigan dwelt at length on the antics of a fellow passenger, 'a decorative lady with a six-year-old child', who had been pursuing him unsuccessfully. Rattigan almost certainly spent more of his time in Cannes at the gaming tables and chasing young men than he did working on his play. As a result, when he woke up on 1 January 1953 'with the customary blinding hangover' he probably did have little or no vestige of a Coronation play written down, but he certainly did have a very clear idea of the play that he intended to write.

It seems that largely as a result of conversations with his mother and remembering his father's involvement with past coronations, he had decided to set his play at a coronation, that of King George V and Queen Mary, the coronation which had coincided with his birth. He later claimed that as his birth had deprived his mother of the opportunity of being present at the ceremony, he was making it up to her through the play. The idea was also prompted by some memoirs of the period which he had been reading. The background was further filled out by details of his father's experiences as official host to the Grand Vizier, the most colourful of which had been diplomatically excluded from his book of autobiographical memories. More routine details came from some little books marked 'Strictly Confidential' proffered by his publisher and schoolfriend, Roger Machell. These, preserved by members of Machell's family, had been issued to visiting royalty and officials during the 1911 Coronation and contained notes on procedure, useful private addresses and telephone numbers, etc. For Ruritanian detail, there were the three volumes of Queen Marie of Romania's diaries and memoirs, in which the Rattigan family featured.

Rattigan knew that if he was to get the play on in time for the Coronation in June, he would have to work very fast, even by his standards. On one thing he was quite positive from the outset: his play was to be a very light comedy of the sort that he was supposed to have grown out of. He knew that in this he risked a panning from the critics, but he intended to offset their rage by making it clear that this was not meant to be a serious offering to follow *The Deep Blue Sea*, but simply a little nonsense for a great occasion. He planned to make his strictly limited intentions clear by having a small-scale production, with a short run of three months and a non-star cast.

His aim was to stand a familiar romantic cliché on its head and play the results for laughs. The setting was the Carpathian Legation in London on the eve of the Coronation. The Regent of Carpathia, deliberately depicted to be as far as possible from the romantic idea of the Ruritanian prince conjured up by his title (though remarkably close to the real picture painted of Romanian princes in memoirs of the time when the Rattigans had served there), treats love as 'purely medicinal', a favourite sport so long as it does not interrupt state routine and can be scheduled to fit into an hour at the end of a busy day. In his four-day visit to London he has only one such available hour. An American chorus girl, appearing in London, Mary Morgan (the name Morgan is undoubtedly deliberate), is hastily acquired. To the Regent's dismay she proves reluctant to be seduced. If she is going to succumb at all, it will only be to the accompaniment of tzigane music, high-flown speeches and the full paraphernalia of a traditional royal seduction, as in romantic fiction. Since there is no time to acquire a more compliant girl, the Regent reluctantly turns on the standard romantic accompaniment for a seduction, but with too much success. Mary takes the empty endearments seriously and by next morning has decided to stay with him for life.

The Sleeping Prince, the lightest soufflé, nevertheless clearly depends on familiar strands of the Rattigan leitmotif. Writing of The Deep Blue Sea, Kenneth Tynan had said that its keynote was 'the failure of two people to agree on a definition of love'. This, too, is the keynote of The Sleeping Prince, but with completely different consequences. In the same article, Tynan had reflected on Adventure Story and the way in which Alexander and Rattigan had both seemed to spend their whole careers repeatedly killing their fathers.[11] It is significant that in even such an inconsequential piece as The Sleeping Prince the principal sub-plot centres on the young heir apparent, who tries to start a revolution in defiance of the Regent, the father figure. The play abounds in biographical references. In the first scene, the Regent confers on the telephone about a crisis involving the entente powers and their ambitions in Morocco, an echo of one of Frank Rattigan's diplomatic involvements. Mary and the young heir apparent provoke an incident at a state ball when Mary, like Frank Rattigan, 'alters the tempo' of one of the rather staid dances. One character refers to 'dear, witty Mrs Asquith', and Mary reproaches two characters for talking as if they were George Bernard Shaw.

Once Rattigan had started work on it, the play had taken shape very quickly. By 23 January 1953 he had finished the first act and wrote eagerly to John Perry, Binkie Beaumont's partner, asking him to send out what he had written to actors with a view to getting them to agree to appear in it. It is hard to pinpoint the moment at which the Oliviers became interested in the idea of doing The Sleeping Prince. It may have been late in 1952, after Rattigan had had the initial idea (Olivier's memoirs are unclear on the date), but he had certainly talked to Laurence Olivier by 23 January 1953. Olivier had been looking for a suitable Coronation vehicle for Vivien Leigh and himself in the autumn of 1952, but when he had mentioned this to Rattigan he had not been forthcoming. As a result by January 1953 Olivier had decided on a revival of *The Admirable Crichton*, with Alfred Lunt directing. But in his letter to John Perry of 23 January, Rattigan told him that when Olivier had approached him earlier he had been 'non-committal', but now he urged him to approach the Oliviers again in the hope of persuading them to do his new play instead.

In theatrical circles it was common knowledge that Vivien Leigh had been unwell, on top of which rumours were rife that the Oliviers' marriage was on the rocks. Early in February Vivien Leigh left the Oliviers' home at Notley Abbey in Buckinghamshire for Ceylon to star opposite Peter Finch in a film called *Elephant Walk*. By the end of the month she and Finch were drinking heavily and had started the serious affair that would ultimately lead to the end of the Oliviers' marriage. Olivier's memory of how he and Vivien Leigh became involved in *The Sleeping Prince* was that a short time after his first approach to Rattigan he had bumped into him at a party and taken him to one side. Olivier asked him, 'If, by any chance, he might have something in the oven for Puss [his pet name for Vivien Leigh] and me for this very special year?' As tactfully as he could Rattigan asked if Vivien Leigh would really be up to the rigours of a West End run by the summer and Olivier assured him that she would. Olivier recorded that Rattigan then said that 'as a matter of fact, yes, he did have something that might suit us very well indeed'. Rattigan would later protest that he had said that the play he was writing would not suit the Oliviers, that their gigantic talents would overturn his plan for a slight frivolity intended to do no more than mark the occasion, and that, privately, he thought Vivien Leigh unsuitable casting. However his letters show that he was eager to get the Oliviers from the outset.

But John Perry and Binkie Beaumont were not so keen on the idea and Beaumont told Perry to tell Rattigan that H. M. Tennent could not commit on the basis of a draft of the first act alone. The real reason, however, was almost certainly that the involvement of Olivier would mean Tennent's losing total financial control of the production. On 29 January, Rattigan wrote furiously to Binkie Beaumont threatening to take the play to Stephen Mitchell if

Tennent's did not make an immediate decision to produce on the basis of the draft of Act One. It was unreasonable, even for a writer of Rattigan's standing, to demand a decision on the basis of the first draft of the first act alone and it would have been reasonable for Beaumont and Perry to delay their decision. But there was more to their delay than met the eye. To them, as to Rattigan, the important thing was getting the right stars. The Oliviers had their own production company, and their involvement would indeed mean that Tennent's would lose total financial control of the production. But Rattigan's threat seemed to work. By the end of February, by which time he had completed all three acts, Beaumont had agreed that H. M. Tennent Ltd would present *The Sleeping Prince* jointly with Laurence Olivier Productions, with the Oliviers starring and Alfred Lunt directing, for a West End opening in June to coincide with the Coronation. Rattigan now started to press his New York agent to try for a Broadway production starring Audrey Hepburn. Any idea of *The Sleeping Prince* being a slight *pièce d'occasion* with a non-star cast to attract little attention had been sacrificed on the altar of Rattigan's worship of stars, glamour and the big theatrical event. But he knew the risks. With *The Deep Blue Sea* still running he was being unbelievably naïve, or wilfully self-deluding, if he thought that any new play of his could now sneak past more or less unnoticed, let alone one starring the Oliviers. He had had the experience of *Who Is Sylvia?* to teach him about critical expectations.

But by the end of March, when the *Elephant Walk* film unit flew from Ceylon to Los Angeles to shoot studio scenes, Vivien Leigh was in the throes of a serious mental breakdown. She had to leave the production and return to hospital in London. By April production of *The Sleeping Prince* had been postponed, with the hope that it could go into rehearsal in July or August. The film company seemed likely to demand that the Oliviers repay her fifty-thousand-pound fee. With Vivien Leigh receiving ECT treatments, Olivier was determined that she should appear in *The Sleeping Prince*. He was convinced that this would be the best means of returning both his wife and their marriage to good health. In order to reduce the pressure on Vivien Leigh, Laurence Olivier decided that he should direct the play himself and Alfred Lunt stepped down. But when Binkie Beaumont suggested to Olivier that they should have Glynis Johns or Rosemary Harris standing by to step into Vivien Leigh's shoes if she should not be well enough to open, he would not hear of it, insisting that Vivien Leigh would be OK.

During the summer, as the Coronation passed and the production was put off again, Rattigan fretted. He passed most of his time at Sunningdale playing golf, playing in a charity cricket match, attending other people's premiéres and getting accumulated frustrations off his chest in at least three pieces of non-dramatic writing. He wrote prefaces to the first two volumes of his *Collected Plays*, which were due for publication that autumn, and an anonymous article entitled 'Drama v. Binkie'. This article reflected not only his own bitterness against Beaumont but the fact that the MP Woodrow Wyatt had now collected so much evidence that he was ready to lay a bill before Parliament aimed at curbing H. M. Tennent's monopoly power and Beaumont's ability to use tax exemption rules to inflate his profits. Rattigan's article was cast in the form of a judge's summing up in a case brought by 'Drama' against Binkie Beaumont, the managing director of H. M. Tennent Ltd, for 'the offence of causing grievous bodily harm to the British Drama'. Rattigan finds Binkie not guilty of having used his power solely to promote his favourite established actors, directors and designers, of operating a monopoly and of demanding sexual favours in return for work. But on the central charge of not taking risks by giving chances to new actors, actresses and dramatists, he finds him culpable. He concludes: 'Compared to the great impresarios of the past, such as Sir Charles Cochran or Diaghileff, Binkie is guilty. Binkie's talent is as a manager of genius but the theatre stands in urgent need not of a manager but of an impresario.' Disingenuously Rattigan then concludes that, nevertheless, 'Binkie is not guilty of the crime of causing grievous bodily harm to the British Drama.' Had Rattigan published this article under his own name and rather than the Prefaces, which he wrote at the same time, he might have done his reputation much less harm. Sadly his fear of confrontation and of offending London's most powerful manager prevented him.

By the time rehearsals for *The Sleeping Prince* began at the Haymarket Theatre on 31 August 1953, a quite unreasonable amount was riding on the play, not only the public and critical expectations aroused by any new work from Rattigan and starring Laurence Olivier and Vivien Leigh, but the future of the Oliviers' marriage. As long ago as 1951 Kenneth Tynan had written an article drawing attention to the fact that to Laurence Olivier acting was a form of lovemaking and that it was through his transforming power over Vivien Leigh's acting that he expressed his love. Tynan had accused Olivier of subduing his own 'blow-like ebullience to match her... levelling away his towering authority, he meets her halfway.'[12]

Taken purely at the level at which Rattigan had said he intended it, as a light fantasy with which to celebrate the Coronation, *The Sleeping Prince* was on the whole admirable. However, as a vehicle for the comeback of Sir Laurence Olivier and Vivien Leigh after a two-year absence from the London stage it was dangerously inadequate. Their last appearance together had been in a season in which they played opposite each other in *Antony and Cleopatra* and *Caesar and Cleopatra*.

Rattigan attended rehearsals more than was his wont, largely for the simple joy of watching Olivier work on the part, although he continued to think Vivien Leigh miscast – 'one of nature's grand-duchesses if ever I saw one', rather than 'a chorus girl thrilled to her Brooklynese death at the prospect of meeting a real grand-duke in the flesh'.[13] He was fascinated by the amount of trouble Olivier took, building up his performance from a mass of tiny details, discarding some, retaining others, continually experimenting. Sometimes proceedings would come to a halt because Vivien Leigh could not help giggling at some piece of business her husband had put in or the way he played a line. 'Is it as funny as that?' Olivier would ask anxiously. 'Terry, what do you think?' In paroxysms of laughter Rattigan would reply, 'Yes, marvellous.' Quite often Olivier would then say, 'No, I think it's too much. It's out.' Olivier was very faithful to Rattigan's text and even to the stage directions. Rattigan commented ruefully, 'Most directors don't even read them.' He had not expected Olivier to be such a perfect light comedian and was bowled over with admiration.

His last remaining fear about Olivier, that he would prove 'Prince Utterly Irresistible' rather than 'Prince Uncharming', was laid to rest at the dress rehearsal before the opening in Manchester. Going to Olivier's dressing-room just before the curtain rose, he was confronted by a monocled, dull-looking little man with an anaemic complexion, a thin, prissy, humourless mouth and centre-parted hair plastered repulsively down over his ears. Rattigan claimed that it was only when he noticed the Edwardian costume and the Order round his neck that he recognized him as Olivier – his own, true, living, breathing Sleeping Prince.[14]

The play opened in London at the Phoenix Theatre on 5 November 1953. People had by now had rather too much of the Coronation, and the play threatened to be a damp squib. Whatever Rattigan's private fears about the play's reception that evening, he kept up his usual self-confident appearance. In the afternoon, he played a round of golf with Tony Darnborough. He was in winning form. In desperation Darnborough tried a little gamesmanship. Each time Rattigan addressed the ball he would remind him of the approaching first night, saying something like, 'I think we're going to be late for the curtain.' Each time, Rattigan drove or putted with more confidence. At the first night itself he maintained the same self-confidence. Reactions to the first act were by no means clear-cut and when he went round to Olivier's dressing-room in the interval, Sir Laurence asked, 'How's it going out there?' 'Pretty good,' said Rattigan. 'But I must say I think you are a little down. Are you sure you're feeling all right?' 'Perfectly,' replied Olivier. 'Tell me, Terry, how are they liking Puss?' 'Very much indeed,' Rattigan replied. Olivier shook his head. 'I don't think so. I don't think so at all. I don't think she's going over as well as she should be.'

During the next act Rattigan noticed that Olivier had lowered his performance even more. The impression from the front was that Olivier was way below par. As the run continued, that impression was maintained, and both critics and public were disappointed. Although a number of critics conceded that a *pièce d'occasion* was not to be judged by the same standards as would apply to works written without any conditions attached, the prevailing view was summed up by Milton Shulman in the *Evening Standard:* 'It seems a pity that in these spare times so much talent should have gone into so little.'[15] Although Rattigan had anticipated such attacks, he was still very bitter when they materialized. But with such names the play could hardly fail to draw audiences and it ran for 274 performances, Vivien Leigh missing hardly a single one. The Oliviers' marriage seemed repaired, for a while at least. *The Sleeping Prince* would have run longer if the Oliviers' commitments had allowed.

Three years later, Rattigan consented to allow the play to be done on Broadway, where it could in no sense be expected to be taken as a *pièce d'occasion*. With Michael Redgrave and Barbara Bel Geddes starring, it ran for only 52 performances. Rattigan had only himself to blame when the critics slaughtered it. *The Sleeping Prince* was a sleeping pill: 'Playwright Rattigan here blindly scattereth poppyseed while contriving poppycock,' said *Time* magazine.[16]

Notes

1   Today part of the Department of Works and Pensions.
2   *Tailor and Cutter*, 15 February 1952.
3   *Picture Post*, 5 April 1952.
4   The story was recalled by Arthur Marshall in the *New Statesman*, 9 December 1977.
5   Stephen Potter, 'R & A-manship', *Sunday Times*, 18 June 1950, and Terence Rattigan, *Sunday Times*, 25 June 1950.
6   Mrs Newport's moral attitudes seem to have had something in common with Mary Herring's. As a result the plan did not bear fruit.
7   Frith Banbury interviewed by Geoffrey Wansell, op. cit.
8   B. A. Young, op. cit.
9   Rattigan's contribution to *Olivier*, edited by Logan Gourlay, Weidenfeld & Nicolson, London, 1973.
10   B. A. Young, op. cit.
11   *Harper's Bazaar*, November 1952.
12   Quoted in *Darlings of the Gods* by Gary O'Connor, Hodder & Stoughton, London, 1984.
13   *Olivia*, edited by Logan Gourlay, op. cit.
14   Ibid.
15   *Evening Standard*, 6 November 1953.
16   *Time*, 12 November 1956.

15

Aunt Edna

In the week that *The Sleeping Prince* opened, Hamish Hamilton published Rattigan's *Collected Plays* in two volumes, each with a preface by the author. They contained all the produced plays which Rattigan had written on his own, except one – *After the Dance*. The decision to exclude *After the Dance* was not difficult as it was much the least well known. In addition, to include it would undermine the argument which Rattigan wanted to pursue in his Prefaces. Written in the summer, while *The Deep Blue Sea* was in the second year of its successful West End run, Rattigan intended to use the prefaces to press the claim that the popularity of his plays was no disqualification for taking them or their author seriously.

He began his first Preface by saying he found himself at something of a disadvantage when it came to being presented to the discriminating public as a serious dramatist because all the plays in the first volume had been successes; he could not therefore commend them on the grounds that undiscriminating audiences had rejected them. He intended to argue, therefore, that the fact that they had been uniquely successful with West End audiences might imply positive virtues. That this begged the question as to whether *After the Dance* was, therefore, a bad play was immaterial as no one was likely to remember it. Even so, this was a difficult, even a dangerous, argument for Rattigan to pursue. But, as we have seen, it was a matter of intense importance to him. He covered himself by adopting a characteristically mock-modest, banteringly apologetic, schoolboy tone. Unfortunately, it was a line of argument which was inimical to the public-schoolboy ethos and gentlemanly self-effacement. The result was simultaneously to weaken his case and hand a lot of ammunition to his critical enemies. In the Preface to Volume I, having cited the repertory manager who told him: 'What's so nice about doing your plays in my theatre is that their profits pay for the good ones' – and called in aid Lady Bracknell's reproof to her nephew: 'Never speak disrespectfully of society, Algernon. Only people who can't get into it do that' – to deal with highbrow playwrights who sneered at his lowbrow success, Rattigan went on to suggest that down the ages popular taste had not been so bad as snobs have supposed. That the plays in the volume scored five successes out of five must indicate not just luck but a common denominator that made them appeal to audiences. This Rattigan described as a 'sense of theatre', a vague concept allied to the ability to thrill an audience through the power of suggestion; to move it to tears or laughter through the implicit rather than the explicit. A 'sense of theatre' was, Rattigan claimed, an instinct, a creative gift rather than a craft to be learned. It entailed being able to act simultaneously as one's own audience while in the actual process of writing a play. This gift manifested itself in the negative virtue of knowing what not to have your actors say rather than in anything more recognizably positive. While it was not a quality which would on its own ensure great drama, it was a quality shared by all great dramatists. It was the quality which Rattigan knew he possessed, and without which he knew he would have had no hope of achieving his one great ambition: 'to write, before I die, one great play'.

To press this bold argument further, in the Preface to Volume II Rattigan sought shelter behind the creation of a comic figure to personify his idea of the audience which down the ages had not been bamboozled by changing fashions or pretensions, who ultimately sifted the dramatic wheat from the theatrical chaff. This was Aunt Edna. She bore a striking resemblance to Vera Rattigan.

She is, we are told, a nice, respectable, middle-class, middle-aged, maiden lady, with time on her hands and money to help her pass it, who resides in a West Kensington hotel. There she dispenses opinions on the arts over the teacups with her cronies. She enjoys pictures, books, music and the theatre, and although she does not bring much discernment to any of them she 'does know what she likes'. Rattigan tells us she does not appreciate Kafka: 'so obscure, my dear, and why always look on the dark side of things?' She is upset by Picasso: 'those dreadful reds, my dear, and why three noses?', and she is against Walton: 'such appalling discords, my dear, and no melody at all'. She is, in short, 'a hopeless lowbrow'. But no playwright dare ignore her or his play will fail. She will broadcast her disapproval of a play that has displeased her at a matinée to the other potential members of the audience in her hotel and beyond that same evening: 'Oh, it was so dull, my dears, don't think of going to it. So much talk, so little action, so difficult to see the actors' faces, and even the tea was cold.' She is immortal and international, her voice as powerful in Moscow as in London; she sat on the hard stone seats of the theatre in Athens, clutching her neighbour's arm and whispering: 'My dear, do look at that blood on the actor's mask. He's supposed to have blinded himself. I'm so glad it didn't happen on stage, though. I always say you can rely on Sophocles.' She was shocked and intrigued by Euripides and dissolved into laughter at Aristophanes. At the Elizabethan Globe she took on the aspect of Queen Elizabeth and held sway over Shakespeare and his contemporaries. In Restoration times she assumed the attributes of one of Charles II's naughtier mistresses, and in the Victorian era took on the image of the queen herself. Although Aunt Edna may sometimes enjoy the trivial she will always appreciate the best. What Aunt Edna does not like, no one will ever like. While she enjoys a little teasing and even some bullying, a dramatist must never go so far as to incur her displeasure. Rattigan said that in his attempts to grow from a playwright into a dramatist he tried to distance himself from Aunt Edna just enough to overcome his tendency too consciously to please the audience, but at the same time he tried not to go too far for Aunt Edna. He said: 'A play does not fail because it is too good: it fails because it is not good enough,' and applied the same harsh logic to his own isolated failure, *Adventure*

Story. (A veil was drawn over the fact that *Who Is Sylvia?* had had to be kept going with financial assistance from Rattigan and others.)

Rattigan had written this Preface in the disconsolate summer of 1953. At the time he and his editor at Hamish Hamilton, Roger Machell, were blissfully unaware of the harm the second Preface would do Rattigan. Machell later recalled that he and his colleagues had found Aunt Edna 'awfully amusing, written slightly tongue-in-cheek. I couldn't imagine anyone taking it completely seriously. I never thought for a moment that it would be used as a stick to beat him with.'[1]

The conflict between popularity and quality had dogged Rattigan in his dealings with the critics ever since James Agate attacked *French Without Tears.* With his Prefaces Rattigan had laid himself wide open and the attacks began the moment the books were published. In the *Daily Express,* John Barber told him in no uncertain terms to 'come off it, Mr Rattigan'. He said he knew why Rattigan was cross – it was because the critics had not liked his later comedies and had stopped praising him: 'That is what hurts.' But he warned that he would go on nagging him to write his best: 'You say you do not want to pander to Aunt Edna in the stalls. Then don't . . . Sad isn't it? To be so prosperous, so gifted – and so spoiled. For that is what it comes to – to be so avid for more success and more success that it gets harder every morning to sit down in humble obedience to your own finest instincts.'

Still more significant for what it portended for the future was an article by Kenneth Tynan, newly installed as drama critic of the *Observer.* Tynan still regarded Rattigan as the most promising British dramatist, but the conjunction of the Prefaces with the production of *The Sleeping Prince* confirmed his worst suspicions. He pointed out that Rattigan was wrong to say that plays which failed did so because they were not good enough for Aunt Edna – they failed because they were not bad enough for her. Rattigan was blind to her failings; she went to *Hamlet,* for instance, not because she recognized its quality but because generations of highbrows had told her to. She follows, never leads, intelligent taste. Rattigan's output was marked by the negative virtues associated with pleasing her: 'that marketable quality known to cynics as ingratiation and to romantics as charm...tact, understatement, avoidance of cliché – the hallmarks, in fact, of the "gentleman code" which holds so much of West End playwriting in curious thrall'.

By November 1953, when the *Collected Plays* were published, Rattigan was already thinking about his next play, or more correctly, pair of one-act plays, *Separate Tables*. In these, too, the residence of Vera Rattigan in the Stanhope Court Hotel was an important element of the inspiration. Rattigan in fact dedicated them to his mother.

The inspiration there was that my mother was in a hotel for old people in Kensington and I used to go and have dinner with her, and I used to observe the people sitting at these tables all around, occasionally visited by their sons, and their nephews and their grandsons, and I wondered about them. I wasn't told much about them, I just tried to imagine what they would be like, what their lives would be like. I stuck it in Bournemouth just in case I was sued by the hoteliers.[2]

The distance the characters in the plays travelled from their real-life origins in the course of the working of Rattigan's creative mind is even greater than the distance between Kensington and Bournemouth. Nevertheless, those origins can still be detected in the finished plays. There is ample evidence in the way Rattigan's creative mind worked throughout his career for seeing in the relationship between the domineering Mrs Railton-Bell and her sexually repressed daughter Sibyl an extreme reshaping of Rattigan's relationship with his own mother. The very fact that the bogus major calls himself 'the Major' is a signpost directing us to look to Rattigan's own family background for clues to the character's genesis. In the first play the quality of the lovers' quarrels, indeed of their relationship in general, draws directly on Rattigan's experience with his own lovers.

The origins of both plays in *Separate Tables* lay in events in the lives of two people who mattered a great deal to Rattigan. Jean

Dawnay, his fashion model hostess at the house party at which the Oliviers were guests of honour during Royal Ascot Week in 1953, was more than simply a beautiful woman. Brought up without a mother, she had during the war worked in a parachute factory and been the youngest WAAF. By late 1947 she had graduated via jobs in the cypher and codes section of SOE and as PA to a senior officer with the British Forces occupying Germany to being an air-hostess with a rather grand private charter airline. Despite a difficult start in life she was ambitious. But the opportunities open to a girl at that time were strictly limited. Her looks were likely to be her most marketable asset, so she had her teeth fixed on an instalment plan and set about learning to be a fashion model. Within three years she was, with Barbara Goalen, perhaps Britain's best-known model. She worked for Dior, Beaton and Armstrong-Jones; had 'shown' before the Queen; and was, as the gossip columns never ceased to remind their readers, the friend of Aly Khan and a string of socialites and playboys.

What intrigued Rattigan was the vulnerable, inexperienced girl behind the confident worldly exterior. She had catapulted herself so far and so fast that she had arrived quite unprepared in an alien social world, which was often as frightening as it was exciting. Jean Dawnay was refreshingly direct. When she met Rattigan, about 1950, she was unaware who he was; she knew nothing about the theatre or his reputation as 'the great playwright'. She was totally unimpressed by the sycophants and hangers-on who surrounded him. She had found Rattigan's homosexuality a relief, because it took the sexual pressure off her. As a result she and Rattigan had developed a mutually confessional relationship, in which there was affection without sex. She talked candidly about her problems and love affairs; Rattigan talked candidly about his. What she could not understand about Rattigan and his friends was that none of them had any comprehension of permanent relationships.

Jean Dawnay was at this time continually falling in and out of love, but she knew that none of the men was really 'right'. One story she told Rattigan seemed to affect him particularly and he asked her to repeat it. She had been attacked by a boyfriend, badly enough for her screams to have led to the police being called. She had told the man that their relationship would have to be broken off. What appeared to have particularly annoyed the man was the calm way in which she broke the news to him and continued to appear unruffled when he argued with her.

By January 1954 Rattigan had got far enough in his mental preparation of his new plays to be able to write to his New York agent saying that he had 'a rather exciting idea for two short plays' which might be right for Eric Portman, the actor who had starred in *Playbill*. He had even made some preliminary outline notes. In these notes the plays are already set in a residential hotel, like the Stanhope Court. The first concerns a couple whose relationship draws both on the story told to him by Jean Dawnay and on his own current emotional and sexual preoccupations. Headed 'Table by the Door – Reverse of DBS' (initials for *The Deep Blue Sea*), the notes outline the core characters and themes:

Better for evil affinity to continue to torture each other, than to be tortured alone.

Great beauty in decline. No love in her life. Cold. Friendless too. Therefore alone. He alone because of scandal, drink, prison? Not liked by fellow guests as it is known he is famous. [The word 'famous' is not clear in the notes and could be 'Janus', which would raise other interesting, and relevant, possibilities for the resulting play.]

Her need for him and his need for her incompatible.

Rattigan's plays had often developed as much from a few key passages of dialogue as from an idea or theme. The notes that he had scribbled for himself by early 1954 included a number of such key dialogue passages. Some of them eventually made it, with very little alteration, into the text finally staged almost a year later:

JOHN   Tell her to go away and leave me in peace.
MISS C (Quietly)   Is it peace, John?
JOHN   A kind of peace, yes.

MISS C   It's not even really living, is it? Be honest, now, is it? I know there's the outlook and your pals at the Feathers and – well – me. But is it living?

JOHN   That's very sad, but unhappily not even Anne can change that law of the universe that says that time must pass and even models must grow old.

MISS C   Oh, yes. She has to face what's coming to her, I know. It's the thought of living alone that's driven her to drugs.

JOHN   She doesn't have to face it alone. There must be lots of men –

MISS C   Apparently there's only one she needs.

JOHN   Why? What has he ever had to offer her except the sort of life that bores her and the sort of love she can't accept?

MISS C   I can't tell you why, dear. Why do you need *her*, if it comes to that?

JOHN   I don't.

MISS C   You do. You both need each other, and only each other, and that's what's so sad. Because it seems to me that the two needs are so opposite that when you bring them together they must explode and blow you both up.

MISS C (to John)   I had hoped to bring you alive, but I didn't. *She can.* She can kill you. She can make you live. That's *better* than the slow death of loneliness.

JOHN   I don't think people were really meant to live together, you see. Make love, of course, like animals, but not live together.

The play that eventually grew from these notes, the first play in *Separate Tables* – renamed *Table by the Window* – centres on a fashion model, Anne Shankland, and her stormy relationship with her ex-husband John, a former Labour politician turned journalist. When the play opens she is forty and her looks are fading. Her inability or unwillingness to gratify his overpowering sexual needs during their marriage resulted in his attacking her, his imprisonment and disgrace for attempted murder, and their divorce. Lonely and frightened for her future, divorced from a second husband, also on grounds of cruelty, Anne has sought John out in the quiet hotel where he has secluded himself since his release from prison. She hopes to effect a reconciliation. Again, Rattigan is delving into the conflicts between different kinds of need and the clash between incompatible types of love. 'Girls,' John asks rhetorically, 'which husband would you choose? One who loves you too little or one who loves you too much?'[3]

John married Anne because his love, his craving for her, was so violent he could refuse her nothing – not even a marriage he knew was bound to be disastrous because of the gulf between his rough working-class background and her Kensington upbringing. She, he claims, married him rather than any of her other, wealthier suitors because she wanted the enjoyment of enslaving someone as wild and brutal as himself. She now needs him as the only person she has ever been fond of. She is losing the art of making people fall in love with her and fears loneliness – the hotel, full of lonely old people, she says, gives her the creeps. John needs her in the same way as he always did, and against reason. He has started a nice, sensible little affair with the hotel manageress which had seemed to be leading to marriage, but seeing Anne again confirms for him that he can only really love one type of person – the prototype – Anne. The element of autobiographical projection here, in Rattigan's string of relationships with nearly identical young men, and his current tempestuous (and in the eyes of his friends unsuitable) relationship with Michael Franklin, is obvious.

Realizing that Anne has staged the whole meeting, that it wasn't the hand of fate which brought them together again, John becomes very angry and is on the point of trying to strangle her again. Eventually, with help from Miss Cooper, the hotel manageress, who renounces her own claims on John, they are reconciled. They have little hope together, but none apart. In this play, like *The Deep Blue Sea*, love is seen as a disaster. The principal characters are like addicts; once they have tasted each other they cannot overcome their dependence, even though they know that they will destroy each other.

When Rattigan showed the play to Jean Dawnay she was horrified, not simply because some of the details made it seem likely that people in the story might recognize themselves

(Rattigan readily agreed to make changes which protected their anonymity) but because the model appeared such a hard bitchy character. Jean overlooked the vulnerability of Anne and the skill with which Rattigan had projected her into an imaginary future; a future which he was beginning to understand and fear for himself, in which his saving vitality had been exhausted, leaving only a creaking husk. (In fact, Jean Dawnay escaped the fate that Rattigan had imagined for somebody blessed with her fatal attractiveness; not many years after the production of *Separate Tables* she began a long and successful marriage and is still today a lady of great beauty and vitality, leading a full, useful life. She has a daughter as gifted as herself.)

The second of the two interrelated plays, set in the same residential hotel, which make up *Separate Tables*, also focuses on Rattigan's immediate concerns. It was triggered by a very recent, traumatic event in the life of his long-time hero John Gielgud. In 1952, following the escape to Moscow of the British-born Soviet spies Burgess and MacLean, a crackdown on homosexuals had begun. Probably instigated by bigots in the American counter-intelligence services, it was eagerly prosecuted in Britain by the new Conservative Home Secretary Sir David Maxwell Fyfe and the police. Prosecutions for homosexual offences multiplied seven-fold on pre-war figures to more than two thousand five hundred a year by the mid-1950s. These included hundreds for acts between consenting adults in private, sometimes dating back as far as ten years. Thousands of otherwise innocent homosexual men were terrorized. Among those who committed suicide was Dr Alan Turing, who had cracked the Nazi Enigma code during the war. Even Noël Coward, a lifelong Conservative, was moved to record in his diary that, 'The police are empowered to frame individuals, to extort terrified and probably inaccurate confessions and betrayals from scared young men.'[4] The attitudes associating homosexuality with Communism which had characterized European fascist parties in the 1930s now ruled among the governing élites in Britain and America. Its clearest expression in America could be seen in the proceedings of Senator Joe McCarthy in the House Un-American Activities Committee. In Britain it found expression in the utterances of senior cabinet ministers like Lord Hailsham, who pronounced homosexual practices 'as much a social and moral issue as heroin addiction'. Maxwell Fyfe told magistrates he wanted 'a drive against male vice' and Scotland Yard officers started visits to prominent homosexuals in the arts world. Cecil Beaton and Benjamin Britten both received such calls. By 1953, a wave of high-profile arrests had begun. In August Lord Montagu of Beaulieu was prosecuted for an alleged indecent assault on two boy scouts. When he and his fellow co-defendants were acquitted he, with two other friends, was rearrested for an offence committed with consenting adults two years earlier. It was made abundantly clear that whatever they did, Montagu and his co-defendants would not be acquitted a second time; evidence was doctored, witnesses pressured.

In 1953, less than two weeks before the London opening night of *The Sleeping Prince*, Gielgud was arrested and charged with a homosexual offence. He was fined ten pounds and told by the magistrate to see a doctor. What should have been a matter of little consequence was picked up by the *Sunday Express* and plastered, together with a photograph of Gielgud, across their pages. The news broke a day or two before Gielgud was due to open in N.C. Hunter's *A Day by the Sea* in Liverpool. The manager of the theatre started to receive ominous telephone calls, and it began to seem that if Gielgud appeared on stage there would be some sort of demonstration against him. But Gielgud, with moral support from Binkie Beaumont, John Perry and his co-star in the play, Sybil Thorndike, was not to be intimidated. When the opening night arrived, the back-stage atmosphere was understandably tense, but as Gielgud made his entrance there was no demonstration; the audience in the packed house seemed somehow just to sigh and the performance continued as if nothing untoward had happened. Rattigan was very moved: 'He had enough courage to go on and the audience had enough grace and sympathy to accept him purely as an actor. Everyone reacted with dignity rather than hysteria, as might have been expected. The acceptance by these very ordinary people of something about which they had little understanding was very moving. In these people there was a strong feeling of humanity.'[5]

When the news of Gielgud's arrest broke, Rattigan said to his friends, only half-jokingly, 'There'll be no Sir Terry now.' He, like many another homosexual, was by now genuinely alarmed. The humanity he applauded in that Liverpool audience was far from universal. The popular press were indulging in one of their orgiastic outbursts of circulation-inducing moralistic fervour, complete with leaders on evil men in high places. When one of the defendants in the Montagu case sought refuge from the hounding of the press in Rattigan's London flat, Rattigan turned him away. He dared not risk becoming publicly associated with anyone in the case or with homosexuality. Above all, he told the man, he was frightened of doing anything that might lead to his mother finding out he was himself homosexual.

But Rattigan was very moved by these happenings and by the events in the Gielgud case in particular. And it was these that inspired the second play in *Separate Tables*. However, even if Rattigan had wanted to make its principal character – the Major – a homosexual, the Lord Chamberlain's office would almost certainly have banned it. This would have condemned the play to a limited run in a club theatre. To consign this, or any of his plays, to a minority audience would have been unthinkable to Rattigan. So he made the Major's offence the 'lesser' one of touching up women in a cinema. This had important compensatory virtues: 'If I had written the man as a homosexual, the play might have been construed as a thesis drama begging for tolerance specifically of the homosexual. Instead it is a plea for the understanding of everyone.'[6]

The second play in *Separate Tables* makes a perfect contrast to the first and gains considerably thereby. Its effectiveness is heightened by Rattigan's idea of having the two leading parts played by the same two stars. So the glamorous fading ex-model becomes a dowdy young spinster, Sibyl, suffering extreme emotional repression at the hands of a selfish and domineering battleaxe mother, Mrs Railton-Bell. John, the rough, working-class ex-politician, becomes the bogus 'Major' Pollock, affecting a public-school background, a pukka accent, a distinguished career and perfect social conformity. The only grounds for suspicion of him are, as Rattigan directs, that he seems almost too exact a replica of the traditional retired Major figure to be entirely true.

When the play opens, the Major appears to have got away with his offence, until Mrs Railton-Bell finds 'the story' – his minor sexual misdemeanour – tucked away on an inside page of a local newspaper. The element of self-projection, as well as of a portrait of his father, in the Major's character is both heightened and signposted for those in Rattigan's intimate circle who were 'in the know' by an in-joke. The names he chose to give to the people quoted in the local newspaper as giving evidence to the court about the Major's crime are Mrs Osborn and Inspector Franklin, while the Major's address is given as Morgan Crescent. Mrs Railton-Bell calls a meeting of the other residents with the intention of getting them to allow her to go to the manageress on their behalf and ask for the Major to be expelled from the hotel. The Major is, in effect, tried in his absence by his fellow guests, each of whom strikes a different moral attitude. The only person to side with the Major, a young doctor, accuses Mrs Railton-Bell of conducting the meeting in a manner worthy of Senator McCarthy. His defence of the Major is the rational one: 'The Major presumably understands my form of lovemaking. I *should* therefore understand his. But I don't. So I am plainly in a state of prejudice against him.' He asks what actual harm the Major has done from the standpoint of Christian ethics and concludes: '... apart from possibly slightly bruising the arm of a certain lady and telling a few rather pathetic lies about himself, which most of us do anyway, he has done nothing to justify throwing him out of the hotel'.

Another guest, a retired schoolmaster, cites the wave of vice and sexual excess which has swept the country since the war as evidence of the adage that tolerance of evil may itself be an evil. He is, however, unhappy about siding with someone whose motives are as doubtful as Mrs Railton-Bell's. He says, in a comment all too reminiscent of the situation Rattigan had found himself in during the previous ten years: 'The trouble about being on the side of right, as one sees it, is that one sometimes finds oneself in the company of such very questionable allies.' When Mrs Railton-Bell's deeply repressed daughter is asked to express her opinion, the girl becomes hysterical and the meeting breaks up. The young doctor comments that if she could only once publicly stand up to her mother it might save her soul.

In the play's most touching scene, which is written with such mastery as to banish the basic implausibility of the situation, Sibyl encounters the Major and asks him why he did it. 'Why does anyone do anything they shouldn't – like drink or smoke?' he asks. Since the newspaper report has exposed his pretensions to being an ex-war hero, and revealed that he was nothing more than a lieutenant in charge of a small supply depot, the Major drops his façade, and in a moving confession, which Rattigan clearly invested with many of his own deepest feelings, tries to explain how he reached his pathetic state:

> You wouldn't guess, I know, but ever since school I've always been scared to death of women. Of everyone, in a way, I suppose, but mostly of women. I had a bad time at school – which wasn't Wellington, of course – just a council school. Boys hate other boys to be timid and shy, and they gave it to me good and proper. My father despised me, too. He was a sergeant-major in the Black Watch. He made me join the Army, but I was always a bitter disappointment to him... [Getting his commission during the war was the one success of his life.] It meant everything to me... Being saluted, being called sir – I thought I'm someone now, a real person. Perhaps some woman might even – [He stops.] But it didn't work. It never has worked. I'm made in a certain way, and I can't change it...

Sibyl is the first person he has ever talked to in this way. He supposes they have drifted together in the hotel because they are fundamentally alike: '... We're both of us frightened of people, and yet we've somehow managed to forget our fright when we've been in each other's company.' He has told lies about himself because he doesn't like himself as he is and so has had to invent a new person.

The Major is eventually encouraged to overcome his fear, risk the hostility of his fellow guests and stay on in the hotel. His possible salvation lies in the fact that his façade is now exposed and he will have to live among his fellow guests as himself. Finally the Major takes his place in the dining-room with the other residents at dinner. His entrance is greeted with a shocked silence. Slowly, one by one, each guest acknowledges him. Finally, Mrs Railton-Bell, who has been glorying in her 'victory', is isolated. Standing up, she orders her daughter to leave the dining-room with her, but Sibyl also acknowledges the Major and refuses to leave.[7] This tiny public gesture of defiance brings the curtain down on a note of triumph for humanity over repression and prejudice.

Rattigan's work on *Separate Tables* was interrupted when it seemed that he had succeeded in persuading the film star Tyrone Power to play Alexander in a revival of *Adventure Story*. During March 1954 Rattigan redrafted sections of the play, trying to strengthen and clarify its beginning and end in particular. However, his changes did not alter the fundamental problems with the play and his hopes faded. Of all his plays *Adventure Story* would continue to be the one which for years to come he fought hardest to see revived and wished above all to see win critical acceptance.

Rattigan did not finish writing *Separate Tables* until June 1954. One of the first people to receive a copy was Laurence Olivier. He loved it and expressed a strong interest in doing it with Vivien Leigh. However, as he would not be free of his other commitments for a further eighteen months Rattigan wisely looked elsewhere. In the homophobic atmosphere gripping the country that summer and with the feeling aroused against Binkie Beaumont in particular (Woodrow Wyatt's Theatrical Monopolies Bill had finally been debated in Parliament that March and although it had got nowhere had led to the airing of many grievances, supposed and real) H. M. Tennent Ltd might not be the safest management to present a pair of plays pleading for sexual tolerance. In any case, Rattigan was still smarting from the treatment he had received from Beaumont before *The Sleeping Prince* and had previously promised Stephen Mitchell, who had presented *Playbill*, that if he ever wrote another pair of one-acters he would offer him first refusal. Mitchell read and accepted them with alacrity.

After a short provincial tour, *Separate Tables* opened at the St James's Theatre on 22 September 1954. Like *Playbill*, *Separate Tables* was directed by Peter Glenville and starred Eric Portman, with Margaret Leighton playing Anne and Sibyl. After the first night, Rattigan took Jean Dawnay backstage and introduced her to Margaret Leighton by saying that she was the original for the character of Anne Shankland. Leighton seemed resentful when given this information, but as Jean Dawnay came to play a less important role in Rattigan's life over the next few years, it was Leighton who took Dawnay's place.

Separate Tables was an enormous success. It ran for 726 performances in London and was a huge critical success. The reviews were liberally sprinkled with words like 'dazzling', 'masterly' and 'triumph'. But even now the damage done to Rattigan's reputation by his creation of Aunt Edna was apparent as she was called forth to chastise him. The critic of *The Times* blamed his subservience to her for the 'faint streak of falsity' he found, particularly in the play's ending. Kenneth Tynan wrote his review in the *Observer* as an imaginary conversation between Aunt Edna and a Young Perfectionist. After the Young Perfectionist has explained the plots, Aunt Edna comments: 'I knew I was wrong when I applauded *The Deep Blue Sea*. And what conclusion does Mr Rattigan draw from these squalid anecdotes?'

> YOUNG PERFECTIONIST   From the first that love unbridled is a destroyer. From the second that love bridled is a destroyer. You will enjoy yourself.
>
> AUNT EDNA   But I go to the theatre to be taken out of myself!

Aunt Edna suspects that the Young Perfectionist is a bit 'peeky' and asks what is biting him:

> Y.P.   Since you ask, I regretted the Major's crime was not something more cathartic than a mere cinema flirtation. Yet I suppose the play is as good a handling of sexual abnormality as English playgoers will tolerate.

A.E.   For my part, I am glad it is no better.

Y.P.   I guessed you would be; and so did Mr Rattigan. Will you
accompany me on a second visit tomorrow –

A.E.   With great pleasure. Clearly, there is something here for
both of us.

Y.P.   Yes. But not quite enough for either of us.

Two years later, when *Separate Tables* was presented in New
York, Rattigan told the producer that he would like 'the Major's'
offence in the second play to be the one that he originally had in
mind when he first conceived the play, a homosexual offence. This
would make him 'self-confessedly an altogether different being
from the others and his behaviour quite outside their normal
experience'. Their final acceptance of him would, therefore be of
him as a being 'different' from themselves, 'an outsider', and as a
result all the more powerful. Rattigan actually wrote a version in
which 'the Major's' offence is importuning for a homosexual
purpose. He did this without changing a single line of 'the
Major's', but by simply changing the description of his offence
and some of the lines of the other characters when talking about
it. Although a number of the people that Rattigan consulted were
in favour of the change, the American impresario, Bob
Whitehead, was firmly against it. However, Rattigan continued to
push for it and it was not until he arrived in New York for
rehearsals that he was finally talked out of it. Eric Portman, himself
a homosexual, had absolutely no desire to play Pollock as a
homosexual. He regarded his sexuality as an entirely private
matter between himself and those closest to him. He had no wish
to suffer the kind of attentions from the police and blackmailers
recently suffered by others. That clinched the matter. But not
before Whitehead had told Rattigan that there had been so many
plays about homosexuality on Broadway recently that they had
become something of a cliché. His proposed changes had the
effect, Whitehead told him, of making his play smaller. By making
it a play about homosexuality, he diminished the universality of its
message about man's inhumanity to man.

When *Separate Tables* opened on Broadway the reviews were for once as good as they had been in London. The production ran for 322 performances. The director, Peter Glenville, later claimed that he had never even been shown the homosexual version and Rattigan said that when it came down to it his rewrite did not work: 'the reconception had become so real that it could not be bent back'.[8]

Reading the homosexual version today the clear benefit of making 'the Major's' offence more appropriate and relevant seems outweighed by the loss to the relationship between Pollock and the repressed Sibyl. While Pollock's offence is touching up women there is an element of danger in Sibyl's friendship with the Major. Her act of courage when she defies her mother is all the greater as a result. Her gesture remains liberal and open-minded, but her acceptance of his 'otherness' contains an additional element which seems even more admirable and relevant in the circumstances of today.

Notes

1 Roger Machell in interview with Holly Hill, August 1975.
2 Rattigan in a BBC Radio 4 interview with Derek Hart, recorded on 26 November 1969.
3 It is interesting that Jimmy Porter in John Osborne's *Look Back in Anger* asks almost the same rhetorical question.
4 *The Noël Coward Diaries*, edited by Graham Payn and Sheridan Morley, Weidenfeld & Nicolson, London, 1982; entry for 10 November 1955.
5 Interview with Arthur Gelb, *New York Times*, 21 October 1956.
6 Ibid.
7 Rattigan's choice of the name Sibyl, despite the spelling, was almost certainly intended as a compliment to Dame Sybil Thorndike for her role in the incident which originally inspired the play. Accounts of the events which inspired the play can be found in *Heterosexual Dictatorship* by Patrick Higgins, Fourth Estate, London 1986 and *Peers, Queers and Commons* by Stephen Jeffery, Routledge, London 1991.
8 'Rattigan talks to John Simon', *Theatre Arts*, April 1962.

16

Variation on a Theme

Writing of the dangers of early success a few months after the opening of *Separate Tables*, Harold Hobson in the *Sunday Times* said that only in exceptional cases was it not damaging. 'One of them, the most illustrious, is Mr Rattigan. Mr Rattigan began with a huge popular success. This success made my predecessor [James Agate] gravely uneasy. It need not have done. Mr Rattigan could hardly have developed finer qualities if, in his early days, he had been as viciously attacked as Ibsen.'[1] Perhaps Hobson spoke too soon. Nineteen years were to elapse between the production of *Separate Tables* and the London presentation of a new Rattigan play of comparable quality.

The reasons for this are complex – partly the result of the position Rattigan had worked himself into personally and professionally by the mid-1950s, and partly the result of changes which were going on in the outside world and the theatre alike. What happened in the theatre between 1955 and 1958 was in one sense a reaction to Rattigan's run of uninterrupted success. Starting with *Flare Path* in 1942, Rattigan had had ten new plays produced in twelve years. All but two of these had been big commercial successes, and six of them had been greeted with reviews that ranged from favourable to ecstatic. A reaction was inevitable. But Rattigan, whose fulfilment was so dependent on theatrical success that he was one of the writers least able to withstand critical disapproval, was almost totally unprepared for a critical onslaught. Worse, he had armed his future attackers, and aligned himself with their enemies, by his articles on the 'Play of Ideas' and by the creation of Aunt Edna. Worst of all, the creative and personal consequences of his years of crisis had led him to court fashionable society and surround himself with sexually congenial but intellectually inferior sycophants, and in the process he had cut himself off from intellectually rigorous companionship and the vital forces at work in the arts. Rattigan had once been a radical; he was still a liberal humanist, but very soon no one under forty would believe it. In 1955, in 'The Lost Art of Bad Drama', Kenneth Tynan wrote that 'Mr Rattigan is the Formosa of the contemporary theatre, occupied by the old guard, but geo-graphically inclined towards the progressives.' Like Formosa, he was about to become completely isolated; an embarrassing reminder of an old regime whose previous services were forgotten or derided in a world of changed alliances.

In 1955 the straws were already in the wind. The verse revival had started to wilt as quickly as it had bloomed. T. S. Eliot and John Whiting were seen as at best minority playwrights, and the view that verse drama was nothing more than a new way of disguising old trivialities had gained ground; 'the era of Fry' was short-lived. Coward seemed finished. Increasingly, the tastes and concerns of a new, younger generation of theatregoers would come to determine the success or failure of any new play. To these people, who would become the 'meritocracy' of the Wilson era, largely state educated and often from poorer homes than the people who had made up the theatre audiences of the 1930s, the theatre seemed dominated by people who had made their reputations before the war. To them the theatre no longer seemed to tackle contemporary issues. One of Rattigan's own Oxford contemporaries was to become a key figure in the wave of change that by 1954 was gathering strength unseen: George Devine. In setting out the aims of the new theatre he wanted to found he wrote: 'The theatre in England seems to exist in a world of its own and not to be in touch with contemporary attitudes, with the contemporary search for new values or, in any way with other branches of the arts.'[2] Of the younger playwrights, Ustinov was clever but so far little more; Dennis Cannan looked interesting rather than revolutionary, and had in any case not produced enough work for any conclusions to be drawn; in meagre times N.C. Hunter was over-encouraged on the evidence of some subfusc Chekhovian imitation. Alan Melville, Wynyard Browne and Warren Chetham Strode were workmanlike but no more. Hope for the serious theatre rested squarely with Rattigan. Looking back three years later, Kenneth Tynan recalled: 'The climate on the whole was listless. We quarrelled among ourselves over Brecht and the future of poetic drama; in debate with foreign visitors we crossed our fingers, swallowed hard and talked of Terence Rattigan; but if we were critics, we must quite often have felt that we were practising our art in a vacuum.'³ Tynan was not alone in crossing his fingers over Rattigan. Increasingly, commentators on the theatre asked what he would do next. They noted that he was now in his forties; it was the next decade that would decide whether he was more than a supremely competent craftsman.

There had been potentially ominous signs that Rattigan might need a mental breather after *The Deep Blue Sea*. Since then immediate events had inspired *The Sleeping Prince* and *Separate Tables*. Now, not only was he creatively exhausted, there was a backlog of creatively undemanding but very well-paid film work that demanded his attention. With this he could happily recharge his batteries while keeping himself and his increasingly extravagant entourage in the style to which they had become accustomed.

Despite his long run of successes Rattigan was still pathetically insecure. He told friends of an elaborate fantasy of his in which he is dying in poverty in a single London room. Summoned to the home in Brighton of Sir Jeremy Spenser, the director of the National Theatre (Jeremy Spenser was the young actor who played the boy-king in *The Sleeping Prince*) to discuss the possible revival of one of his plays, Rattigan spends his last few shillings on the rail fare to Brighton. He arrives at Sir Jeremy's house only to discover that Sir Jeremy has forgotten all about their meeting. Rattigan is left destitute in the streets of Brighton, not having even the money to get himself back to his London attic.

Ever since *The Deep Blue Sea* opened in London there had

been proposals for a film version. A succession of stars and producers had come and gone. While he was in New York in July 1954 Rattigan had actually had lunch with Deborah Kerr to discuss her playing Hester, but in the end her other commitments had got in the way. Finally, by August, Alexander Korda had bought the rights and Vivien Leigh had agreed to star, with Kenneth More again playing Freddie. Vivien Leigh was understandably nervous about comparisons with Peggy Ashcroft and vetoed Anthony Asquith, who Korda and Rattigan hoped would direct. After yet more toing and froing, Korda sold on his rights, at a profit, to Twentieth Century Fox. They saw the story as a popular drama and put in the director of a successful shocker called *The Snake Pit*, Anatole Litvak. Immediately after the London opening of *Separate Tables*, Rattigan went to Paris to work with Litvak on the script. Litvak was an intense, determined man and the working relationship was not at all like the relaxed days Rattigan spent with Puffin Asquith. Worse, the film was to be the first made in Britain in CinemaScope, a wholly unsuitable format for a claustrophobic drama played out in a dingy flat. And almost every change that Litvak wanted weakened the original play.

One evening, Rattigan was sitting alone drinking in the Boeuf-sur-le-Toit, off the Champs Elysées – a favoured meeting place of Paris intellectuals as well as a stylish rendezvous for homosexuals – when a fair-haired young Englishman approached him: 'You're Terence Rattigan, aren't you?' Lonely and dispirited, Rattigan was glad of someone to talk to and invited him to sit down. Although he didn't recognize him, Rattigan had met Adrian Brown two years previously when he had sat next to him at an Oxford 'smoker'; Brown had since joined the Marquis de Cuevas Ballet Company, which was appearing in Paris. Although Brown was a lot brighter than many of Rattigan's young men he conformed physically to the Rattigan type: small, neat, fair and bright-eyed. Rattigan told him he was very pretty and Brown replied that so was he. Rattigan asked Adrian Brown which of his plays he liked best. When Brown replied, '*Adventure Story*,' Rattigan was very pleased. In spite of the tie with Michael Franklin, a relationship now started which lasted on and off for some ten years.

Returning to London from 'being Litvak'd' in Paris, Rattigan faced a crisis on the film of *The Deep Blue Sea*. At a pre-shooting conference with Litvak, Vivien Leigh and other members of the crew and cast, Kenneth More blew up and said, 'Gentlemen, we can't start this film. The script is no good.' Litvak seemed astonished, but before anyone could intervene More pressed on, and with some justification. 'Frankly the trouble with the script is that there's too much Litvak in it and not enough Rattigan.'[4] Rattigan tried to calm him down, but More wasn't going to be silenced: 'I'd almost go so far as to say that all Rattigan has come out and all Litvak has gone in.' 'Oh, that's not true!' lied Rattigan loyally. 'Litvak and I spent months in Paris preparing this script. I was leaning over his shoulder the whole time.'

But this was not the only row now engulfing *The Deep Blue Sea*. In the role of Hester, Vivien Leigh was reliving emotions and experiences dangerously close to those she had so recently been through with Peter Finch and Laurence Olivier. Already nervous about comparisons with Peggy Ashcroft, she, too, began making difficulties about the script and the way Litvak wanted it played. On 10 November, Rattigan wrote to Korda:

DEAR ALEX,

If things should get really tough, I give you free permission to quote from a letter which I nearly (but happily not quite) wrote to Vivien this morning. It would have been this: Dear Vivien, You are a silly, hysterical stubborn bitch. I am a silly, hysterical stubborn bitch. If the two of us were not silly, hysterical stubborn bitches, you wouldn't act as well as you do, and I wouldn't write as well as (I think) I do. That being the case let us both simply press on to do the best we can for each other, for ourselves and for the film. Love,

TERRY

Shooting finally got under way in December, but the film remained a grotesque and unsubtle exaggeration of the original play. At the same time as he was battling over the film version of *The Deep Blue Sea* he also became caught up in a protracted series of manoeuvrings over a possible film of *The Sleeping Prince*. Rattigan, who had never regarded it very seriously as a stage play, thought that it would make an ideal basis for a film. But what mattered, as he knew perfectly well, was the star and who directed it. One tantalizing possibility was Marilyn Monroe, but Twentieth Century Fox, who had Monroe under contract, did not think it was a suitable vehicle. Rattigan wrote to the head of Fox, Darryl Zanuck, asking him to think again. But Zanuck was not to be moved, he did not think that the story had 'mass audience appeal'.

In March 1955, Rattigan flew off on a triumphal tour of Australia, giving interviews, attending packed gala performances of his plays and cheered by audiences calling 'Author'. Travelling with the designer Michael Weight, he flew on in mid-April for a few days recuperation in Singapore. Then he returned to London via the Middle East, where he announced he would do some background work for a film he wanted to script about Lawrence of Arabia. Rattigan's interest in T. E. Lawrence went back to his early childhood, the time his family spent in Cairo before the First World War and his father's stories about his friendship with Ronald Storrs. His interest was quickened by the publication that year of Lawrence's long-suppressed reminiscences of his life in the RAF called *The Mint*. This is a frank account of life among the other ranks during the time he spent trying to hide his identity as an ordinary aircraftman under the assumed name of Ross. They raised again the never satisfactorily resolved enigma of why Lawrence, having achieved legendary fame during his leadership of the Arab Revolt, should after the war have sought anonymity. It was a question that fascinated Rattigan. He and Puffin Asquith wanted to set up an epic film which would tell Lawrence's story and throw light on the mystery. As work moved slowly forward on the film script over the next two years the names of various stars to play Lawrence were bandied about in the casually optimistic way which is the stock-in-trade of agents and film producers. One of the names was Richard Burton, the young actor Rattigan had made a drunken pass at during the rehearsals of *Adventure Story* and who had then been fired. Six years later he was on the way to becoming a superstar. Such is the way of showbusiness.

At the beginning of August, while Rattigan himself still had no new play of his own on the stocks, a new play by Samuel Beckett opened at the Arts Theatre, directed by a young man recently down from Cambridge, Peter Hall. The play, *Waiting for Godot*, immediately became the subject of heated debate and two months later transferred to the Criterion, where Rattigan had enjoyed his own first success. Although directed in a style as close to conventional stage naturalism as Beckett's lines would allow (the London theatre was still some years away from being ready to accept the non-naturalism of some avant-garde European theatre), the play's evocation of cosmic disillusion was a revolutionary break with accepted West End theatre practice. Its stark allegorical quality, posing fundamental philosophical questions of meaning, life and death, pain and purpose, destiny and God, without any conventional plot, divided critical opinion. To many, especially the younger generation, it offered hope of a new, more adult theatre. Many of the old guard dismissed it as rubbish. One of these was Rattigan's friend John Gielgud, who said simply that he didn't understand it and therefore couldn't see that it was important. Rattigan himself hurried along to see it.

Shortly after its transfer to the Criterion, an article by Rattigan was published in the *New Statesman*, headed 'The Arts and Entertainment: Aunt Edna Waits for Godot'.[5] It took the form of a conversation between Aunt Edna and her nephew immediately after they have seen a performance of the play. Although the quality was essentially light (it is a good deal wittier than the original Preface in which he had introduced Aunt Edna), Rattigan took the opportunity to correct misapprehensions about Aunt Edna's tastes and to modify some of the more extreme views he had expressed in the Prefaces about the dominance of popular taste. He represented Aunt Edna as very cross because the critics had told her she wouldn't like the play. To her nephew's surprise she tells him she has enjoyed her evening very much – not the play, but:

> ...the evening. There's a big difference. How could I like the play, seeing that Mr Samuel Beckett plainly hates me so much

that he's refused point blank to give me a play at all? [But, she says, Mr Beckett is making a great mistake to hate her.] If he didn't he might have written a very good play indeed. I suppose he's a highbrow, but even a middlebrow like myself could have told him that a really good play had to be on two levels, an upper one, which I suppose you'd call symbolical, and a lower one, which is based on story and character. By writing on the upper level alone, all Mr Beckett has done is to produce one of those things that thirty years ago we used to call Experimental Drama – you wouldn't remember that, of course, and that's a movement which led absolutely nowhere...

By taking a superior attitude to Beckett, Rattigan was laying up trouble for himself in future. Not simply through his plays, but through the 'Play of Ideas' debate, the Prefaces and now this, he was identifying himself ever more firmly in the minds of the younger generation with a theatrical establishment which was hostile to new ideas and new voices.

One of the reasons that Rattigan had time enough to advise Samuel Beckett on how to write his plays but no time to get down to a new one of his own was that he had become embroiled in an extraordinary series of events surrounding the possible film of *The Sleeping Prince*. Since the suggestion about Marilyn Monroe starring as the girl had first been mooted earlier in the year Rattigan had remained tantalized. What a coup it would be! But his hopes seemed to have been dashed. So wanting *a* film, even if he could not get *the* film, and hoping for a New York stage production as well, he had informally offered the film rights to both Anatole de Grunwald and Binkie Beaumont. But for any film version of *The Sleeping Prince*, especially one with Marilyn Monroe, Rattigan knew that the crucial ingredient would be the director. Months elapsed while different names were tossed about for stars and directors for both film and Broadway stage productions. Then Rattigan's New York agent came up with the idea of William Wyler as director. Rattigan knew him from the aborted wartime film version of *Flare Path*. He jumped at the idea. It was agreed that he should go out to Hollywood for discussions.

Using the cover of attending the Ryder Cup Match about to be played in Palm Springs to avoid having to tell Beaumont and de Grunwald what he was up to, Rattigan flew out on the evening of 2 November.

Arriving in New York on the first leg of his journey, he was due a ten-hour wait at Idlewild Airport before flying on to Los Angeles. As he followed a stewardess into the International Transit Lounge, a man approached him. 'Are you Mr Rattigan, sir?' he asked. Rattigan acknowledged that he was. 'I have a message from Miss Marilyn Monroe. She'd be happy if you'd take cocktails with her in the Barberry Room at 4.30 this afternoon.' Rattigan recalled: 'I imagine that to most people that news would have been electrifying. I'm afraid it wasn't to me.' Unknown to Rattigan, Marilyn Monroe had been monitoring what was going on. She had recently set up her own production company and was looking for a suitably prestigious subject. After keeping him waiting for an hour in the Barberry Room, Monroe swept in, wearing dark glasses, followed by a posse of agents, lawyers and advisers. She bought him a stiff cocktail, his fourth, and after the formalities got down to business. This was made difficult by the fact that Monroe's quiet, shy manner meant he only understood about every third word she said, while she appeared to understand nothing at all that he said. However, he grasped the central points – if no definite offer materialized from Wyler's company she would buy the rights. The terms she was talking were in multiples of hundreds of thousands of dollars rather than tens of thousands. She was prepared to write out a contract on the bar table there and then. She had by now removed her dark glasses. She gazed straight into Rattigan's eyes and asked with that distinctive quality of knowing innocence: 'Do you think there's a chance that Sir Larry would do it with me?' Rattigan felt unable to say anything other than that he was sure he would. Indeed, he went so far as to assure her that he would leave no stone unturned to see that he did. Rattigan went on to Hollywood, saw Wyler and the Ryder Cup, then, returning, saw Wyler's producers and found there was still no definite offer forthcoming. On the way back through New York he phoned his agent and told him to tell Marilyn Monroe that the rights were hers.

For the next few months Rattigan boasted that he was employed by Marilyn Monroe. But such large sums of money, as Rattigan must by now have known, do not come without problems. Any new work had to be put off indefinitely. Olivier was fired up by the idea of directing and co-starring with Marilyn Monroe and barely a week after Rattigan's return from America the two men met at Rattigan's house in Sunningdale to discuss both the possible film and Broadway versions of *The Sleeping Prince*. However, while Rattigan's agent was negotiating a rights deal with Marilyn Monroe's film company, a row was developing with Anatole de Grunwald over the informal promises about rights that had been made to him. At the same time as Rattigan was in America talking to Monroe, de Grunwald had approached the veteran director John Huston about the project. Soon accusations of bad faith were flying back and forth, until, on Boxing Day 1955, Rattigan cabled his New York agent despairingly, 'Imbroglio getting beyond me.' Rattigan's unquenchable desire both to please everybody and never to pass up any opportunity that might lead to a lucrative deal, had landed him in scrapes before, but this one was bad even by his standards. Once again he threw up his hands in helpless horror and called on others to sort out the mess for him. Meanwhile he turned his attention back to the screenplay he was writing with Anthony Asquith about T. E. Lawrence.

By early February 1956, the contractual problems over *The Sleeping Prince* were sufficiently straightened out for Rattigan and Olivier to fly to New York for discussions with Monroe. Two days later, on 9 February, the discussions had progressed far enough for the film to be announced to the public. At the press conference Rattigan appeared on the platform to pose for the photographers with Olivier, Monroe and Milton Greene (Monroe's business partner). When Marilyn appeared she was wearing a very low-cut black sheath dress. She left no one in any doubt about who was the centre of attention. At a strategic moment one of the dress's shoulder straps obligingly broke and a journalist was called upon to supply a safety pin to save the dignity of the occasion. During the rest of the conference, Monroe made it clear who was the boss. Although Olivier was billed as the film's director, Monroe pointed out a number of times that she 'owned' the play.

Less than a week later Rattigan and Olivier were back in England working on the screenplay. But the work went badly. Rattigan expected, after preliminary discussions with Olivier, to be left alone to draft any new scenes on his own. But Olivier wanted to work alongside him throughout. By early March, Rattigan was privately threatening to walk out unless he was left to work in his own way. As with so many of Rattigan's private threats, it came to nothing and by April Olivier and Rattigan were working together at Gleneagles, which no doubt gave Rattigan a chance to work off his frustration on the golf course between the sessions with Olivier. Olivier seemed oblivious of Rattigan's rage, cabling his son Tarquin in late April that the work with Rattigan was going well and that their 'first full treatment should be through about the middle of the week. We shall have to give it a terrible combing over as it looks like getting on for 3 hours.'[6]

By mid-May they had a complete script and sent it over to Monroe in New York. Milton Greene cabled back, 'Wonderful... Couldn't be more delighted.' But this still was not the end of it. Over the months to come Rattigan would be repeatedly brought in to write scenes as required. By June, Olivier was assembling a crew and the rest of the cast, and Rattigan was arguing with him about the amount of music needed. Rattigan wanted as little as possible while Olivier wanted a big score by Richard Adinsell, composer of *The Warsaw Concerto*. Early in July the whole project was suddenly thrown into doubt when rumours reached the production office that Marilyn Monroe's new husband, the playwright Arthur Miller, was going to have his American passport removed. Monroe certainly would not come without him. Having refused to answer a question in front of the notorious Senator McCarthy's anti-Red Un-American Activities Committee, Miller was in danger of being thrown into jail.

But on 14 July, after much string-pulling and dozens of transatlantic phone calls, Marilyn Monroe arrived in England with Arthur Miller amid much hullabaloo. After what Olivier gleefully told Arthur Miller was 'the largest press conference in

British history', Monroe and her husband went to stay in supposedly quiet seclusion in a house only a few miles from Rattigan's at Sunningdale. A month later, on Saturday, 18 August, Rattigan threw perhaps the grandest of all his grand Sunningdale parties, with Jean Dawnay as his hostess, to welcome them. At the start everyone lined up to meet Marilyn, who was dressed in an Edwardian costume she had worn for the tests for the film. She and her husband more or less held court in an arbour in the garden while all the great names of the theatre waited patiently to be introduced. Through the evening the legendary American showbusiness columnist Louella Parsons moved among the guests, dressed in black like a witch except for the cross around her neck, hissing outrageous asides into famous ears. As the guests started to drift away in the small hours of Sunday morning, Rattigan and Marilyn were still waltzing exquisitely in the room which had been turned into a ballroom. It had been a party worthy of his great mentor, Chips Channon. This was the public image of Rattigan at the height of his wealth and fame, exquisitely turned out, host to the great and the beautiful, doing everything he attempted with seemingly effortless grace. But one observer that evening, a young third assistant director on the film, Colin Clark, was not convinced. He left early and went to a club. He wrote in his diary next day: 'The party just never gelled. I bet it would have been another matter if we were all queer. (Gaiety, everyone!)' Clark's was the authentic voice of the new generation that was, unrecognized by Rattigan, already sweeping him and his kind of theatre away.[7]

The filming of The Prince and the Showgirl, as the play was re-titled, dragged on through months of widely publicized disputes and acrimony. When it was released a year later it was less than a success, in spite of the column yards of publicity that it received around the world. But two months before Marilyn Monroe had even arrived in England, while Rattigan and Olivier had still been struggling with the screenplay, an event of more significance for Rattigan's future than The Prince and the Showgirl had occurred. On 8 May 1956 a new play had opened almost unheralded at the Royal Court Theatre, recently taken over by the English Stage

Company and run by George Devine, Mercutio in the Gielgud production of *Romeo and Juliet* at Oxford. Rattigan had been at the first night of *Look Back in Anger,* by a then unknown young actor, John Osborne. He had gone with Binkie Beaumont. In the first interval he bumped into his friend, the critic T. C. Worsley, in the bar. 'Marvellous, isn't it?' said Worsley. Rattigan and Beaumont clearly didn't think so; they were planning to leave. Worsley persuaded Rattigan to stay to the end, but Beaumont left. Afterwards Rattigan and Worsley had a violent row about the merits of the play, Worsley arguing that this play would be seen as one of the great events of the period, Rattigan conceding only that it was quite well written; it was badly constructed and he couldn't see what there was for Jimmy Porter to look back in anger about. In his review for the *New Statesman* a day or two later Worsley wrote: 'His [Jimmy Porter's] is genuinely the modern accent – one can hear it no doubt in every other expresso bar, witty, relentless, pitiless and utterly without belief... don't miss this play. If you are young, it will speak to you. If you are middle-aged, it will tell you what the young are feeling.' Unfortunately Rattigan did not, or could not, heed Worsley's point.

At the end of the performance a *Daily Express* reporter had asked him what he thought of the play, and Rattigan had said that this young man, Osborne, was simply sitting there saying, 'Look, ma, I'm not Terence Rattigan.' This remark was duly reported and, as interest in the play mounted, the press started to create a largely false, but very damaging, contrast, first between Rattigan and Osborne and then between Rattigan and all the 'New Wave' playwrights who followed in Osborne's wake. Although he later corrected his hasty first-night statement, Rattigan's remark did betray a theatrical arrogance. As his friend B. A. Young pointed out twenty years later in his preface to the fourth volume of Rattigan's *Collected Plays,* Rattigan simply could not believe that there was an audience for the social outcry of the new generation of the underprivileged. Even though, in his own more oblique way, Rattigan had attacked many of the things that Osborne was attacking, Jimmy Porter's raw polemics and the play's emotional violence was an affront to Rattigan's theatrical method. At that moment Rattigan no more understood Osborne than his parents' generation had understood him when he attacked OTC parades at Harrow or voted against fighting for King and Country at Oxford.

As for Osborne, Rattigan was never a specific target. He represented what Osborne called 'the pale side of the establishment'; if they were going to sweep the establishment away, then Rattigan would be one of the casualties. Osborne and his friends resented much more someone like Noël Coward, whom they saw as a decadent showbusiness butterfly, the epitome of the vulgarity and conservative narrow-mindedness they associated with Binkie Beaumont and the West End.[8] But by his 'Play of Ideas' articles, the Prefaces and in his condescension towards Samuel Beckett, Rattigan had made it seem that he was the mouthpiece of that establishment which Osborne and his contemporaries were attacking.

The important point about *Look Back in Anger* was that, as Kenneth Tynan said, it lanced a boil which had been coming to a head for some years. The post-war generation had at last burst triumphantly on to the stage, and, through Jimmy Porter, John Osborne articulated their long pent-up attitudes. Significantly, the day after their arrival in England, Laurence Olivier asked Marilyn Monroe and Arthur Miller which of the plays running in London they would like to see. Arthur Miller said *Look Back in Anger*. Olivier was appalled, telling him that it was just 'a travesty on England'. But Miller persisted and Olivier accompanied him the next evening. After the performance they were introduced to Osborne and Miller was astonished to hear Olivier ask in his most beguiling tones: 'Do you suppose you could write something for me.' The result was *The Entertainer* and a change of direction in Olivier's career.

However, the revolution did not come about all at once. It took time to gather momentum, and four months later Rattigan was apparently still completely unaware of the threat to him. That autumn he wrote an appreciation of Noël Coward, making ample amends for his dismissive undergraduate criticism of *Cavalcade*. Hitherto he had been careful to dissociate himself from Coward, pointing to the differences in their style and subject matter, and reminding people that Coward belonged to the generation before his. Rattigan's foreword to *The Theatrical Companion to Noël Coward* helped prompt the indiscriminate coupling of their names in the attacks of the ensuing years. That autumn also, in an article in the *New York Times*, Rattigan again attacked Shaw, adding the name of Brecht, whose work had just been presented in London for the first time by the Berliner Ensemble.[9]

That autumn, which split Britain over the Suez Crisis and offered a sight he would once have welcomed, that of crowds demonstrating in their thousands against a British government's use of armed force, Rattigan was in America. Late in August, with filming for *The Prince and the Showgirl* at last underway, he had escaped. *Separate Tables* and *The Sleeping Prince* were due to open almost simultaneously on Broadway at the end of October. He took his secretary, Mary Herring, with him to help deal with the flood of offers, press interviews and complex hotel and travel arrangements involved in trying to keep track of two productions which were 'on the road' to Broadway at the same time. Basing himself and his mother, whom he showed off proudly to American journalists, in a plush suite at the Ambassador in New York, he shuttled back and forth between Philadelphia, Princeton, Boston and New York, often uncertain which town he was supposed to be in, when, or for which play. He explained to Emory Lewis of *Cue* magazine: 'I'm never quite sure which I'm working on. I think I've changed the second act of one of them in Boston and it turns out to be the other play. I ask my faithful secretary, Miss Herring, where we are to go each morning – north or south. I'll never open with two efforts again. We had to bring over *The Sleeping Prince* now, because of contractual arrangements with Miss Marilyn Monroe...'[10] When *Separate Tables* opened at the Music Box Theatre in New York on 25 October, despite all Rattigan's fruitless agonizing about whether the Major's offence in the second play should be changed from touching up women to soliciting men outside a toilet, it was hailed by the critics as 'Absorbing' and 'Superb'. The *New York Morning Telegraph* told its readers: 'Here is an evening in which a literate and forgiving writer takes careful study of his fellow man, and for every sin in the book finds a way to forgive. [It is] a deeply serious and studious demonstration that to be tolerant is to be wise.' However, the Broadway first night of *The Sleeping Prince* a week later, starring Michael Redgrave and Barbara Bel Geddes, turned out to be a truly grisly occasion. Rattigan's lack of contact with events outside his own immediate world had even led him to insist that, despite the growing crisis over Suez and the Hungarian Uprising, jokes about 'British imperialism and French greed' and a hapless off-stage Hungarian violinist stayed in despite their obvious insensitivity in the circumstances of the moment. The first-night audience's reaction to both, as Michael Redgrave had warned Rattigan, was hostile. Without either the Oliviers or the sustaining glamour of Marilyn Monroe, the Broadway production was ripe for slaughter. *The Sleeping Prince* opened on Broadway just two days after the British- and French-inspired Israeli attack on Egypt. It could not have opened at a worse moment and duly got its just desserts. Noël Coward attended the first night. He wrote in his diary: 'On Tuesday night I attended the opening of *The Sleeping Prince* and it was completely disastrous. The audience, typical Gilbert Miller–Park Avenue morons, were vile. The play was monumentally miscast. The wit of Larry's performance in London, where nobody really appreciated it, gave the play the lift it needed. This turgid misrepresentation was quite unbearable.'[11]

After returning briefly to London and spending Christmas in Cannes, giving interviews to British newspapers about his tax affairs and his Broadway experiences set against the background of the Suez and Hungarian crises, Rattigan flew out again to Hollywood to write scripts for *Separate Tables* and a long-projected screen version of *Love in Idleness*. On the way he stopped off to spend ten days with Noël Coward who had recently moved to Jamaica. Coward recorded his impressions of Rattigan at this time:

Terry is a most curious mixture . . . He is light, sweet, ready to giggle, incredibly silly over his emotional life, weak and stubborn at the same time – they usually go together – and yet he is capable of writing *The Deep Blue Sea*, *Separate Tables*, *The Browning Version*, etc., plays so richly impregnated with human

340

understanding and compassion. He is drinking too much and allowing himself to become podgy; on this I lectured him mildly...[12]

Flying on to Beverly Hills at the end of January, he shared a house with Rex Harrison. Shortly before Rattigan arrived Rex Harrison had learned that Kay Kendall had terminal leukaemia, but he was still desperately trying to conceal from her the seriousness of her condition. Rattigan gave Harrison a lot of sympathetic support over the ensuing months as Kay Kendall grew progressively weaker.[13]

This was Rattigan's first sustained dose of Hollywood and he hated what he called 'the swimming-pool and star-value protocol general hysteria' – the way in which people were valued by the size, shape and depth of their swimming pool, the size of their contract and whether they were judged to be going up or down. The continuous parties, not something he normally objected to, irritated him too, because the guest lists were always drawn up on the basis of the same star protocol. 'They started at 7.30 but there was never any food before 10 – ' by which time, he objected, everyone was 'fried' with highballs. Domestic arrangements were another problem. Harrison hired them a temporary cook. Before she arrived, she phoned to say that she had just bought a Cadillac and was worried about driving it up the steep hill to their house, so could they send their chauffeur to drive it up for her. Harrison went down and drove it up himself – he had no chauffeur. Next day the girl gave up the job. Finally, they found two other servants: a cook called Hester and a housemaid called Patsy. But what upset Rattigan most was the way in which he was expected to work. The interminable story conferences and general hysteria depressed him, he told a reporter when he arrived back in Europe, 'The first thing they always do is hand out tranquillisers – little pills that keep you working and keep your temper. The desks are piled with them – all colours, sizes, shapes. The consumption is fantastic.'[14]

In six weeks he had written only forty-five pages. In spite of offers to stay in Hollywood, totalling more than two hundred thousand pounds for four scripts over seven years, he sailed home on the *Queen Mary* in disgust. He was not going to do hack work in front of a heated swimming pool, even at that price. In future he would work from the calm of his own home. Nor was he going to move out of England to a tax haven, as Noël Coward and some British film stars had done. He announced repeatedly that living in England mattered to him and if the privilege of doing so was expensive, so be it.

By now Rattigan had developed a self-important willingness to pontificate to the press on even the flimsiest of pretexts. So while he was passing through New York on his way back from Hollywood he had rushed off a letter to the editor of the *Observer* taking Kenneth Tynan to task for saying in an article that in the eyes of American and European observers the British theatre was currently 'no more than an elaborate joke'. Rattigan accused him of trying to cut his way into the theatre with the point of his pen, as Shaw had done. Delighted, the editor of the *Observer* gleefully headed Rattigan's letter and Tynan's reply 'Rattigan versus Tynan', so sharpening still further the public impression that Rattigan was at war with not only Tynan, but with the whole new Royal Court generation of dramatists.

After his return to England work on the screenplay for *Separate Tables* kept Rattigan busy until June. As soon as he had dispatched this he turned back to his script about T. E. Lawrence. He had completed a first draft back in January, but knew it was much too long. Now the Rank Organization had said they would consider financing the film provided he did a new draft. Rattigan's tax return for the year to 5 April 1957 showed that he had earned taxable income of thirty-one thousand nine hundred and sixty-two pounds, suggesting that the gross amount he had received in fees both in Britain and abroad must have been considerably higher. Most of this he had received from his work on films. But he told his friends that he hated the cinema and intended to do no more for at least three years. By July he had started work on a play. He toyed with a story based on issues raised by the Christie murder case tentatively called *Man and Boy* (an impressionable young man, Timothy Evans, had been hanged for murders committed by his landlord, John Christie). But he dropped it and opted for a modern reworking of Dumas' *La Dame aux Camelias* – *Variation on a Theme*. It was written with (and later dedicated to) Margaret Leighton in mind as its star. In fact, the play came very close in places to paralleling events in Margaret Leighton's own recent life. Rattigan and she had become very close during the London production of *Separate Tables*. By 1957 she had replaced Jean Dawnay as his Sunningdale hostess and Rattigan was to remain devoted to her for the rest of her life. But as so often with Rattigan, the play dwelt above all on events and powerful emotions in his own life. In mid-July, shortly after starting work on the play, he told a journalist that people were likely to be shocked by the 'frankness of its theme'. He told another that in this play he intended 'to blow up the Establishment'.

In *Variation on a Theme*, Rattigan's Marguerite Gautier is Rose Fish, who, unlike Marguerite, has married her men rather than merely being kept by them. Already wealthy as a result of three good marriages, she is about to marry a rich German banker, but falls for Ron, a young ballet dancer even more unscrupulous than herself. Ron bends his sexual tastes to suit his needs. When Rose meets him he is living with a homosexual choreographer, who is keeping him; seeing the prospect of an easier and even more luxurious life as Rose's lover, he makes a successful pass at her. Problems arise when they realize that they have really fallen for each other and cannot bear to live apart, no matter what it may cost them in wealth, health or even happiness. Like so many Rattigan lovers, they are a bad match, quarrelling and hurting each other despite being drawn irrevocably together. By leaving the choreographer for Rose, Ron forfeits advancement in his career. By taking Ron as her lover, Rose loses both her German banker and eventually her life, since she is, like Marguerite Gautier, a consumptive and has been told by her doctors that she must live in an expensive Swiss sanatorium.

In August 1957, shortly after Rattigan had started to work on *Variation on a Theme*, Margaret Leighton had married the rising young actor Laurence Harvey, a Lithuanian who had been brought up in South Africa. Leighton, who was considerably older than Harvey, had met him in 1952 when she was starring at Stratford-upon-Avon and he was a promising younger member of the company. At the time she was married to the successful publisher Max Reinhardt, while Harvey was being kept by a wealthy film producer, who was making it his mission to turn Harvey into a film star. The novelist John Braine who met both men at this time observed that the film producer fussed around Harvey 'like a mother hen'. Harvey gave Braine the impression of someone clearly on the make, using sex in an absolutely calculated way to advance his career. Margaret Leighton fell for Laurence Harvey and, early in 1955, with Harvey cited as co-respondent, was divorced by Max Reinhardt. In *Variation on a Theme*, the cheeky, calculating way in which Ron thrusts himself on the attention of Rose, is very reminiscent of the way in which Harvey had conducted his courtship of Margaret Leighton at Stratford, where she was already an established star.[15] Ron, having fallen in love with Rose in spite of himself, hesitates before leaving the choreographer for her. Harvey hesitated before leaving the protection of the film producer and marrying Margaret Leighton. When they did marry, it was a short-lived disaster, as Rattigan and many other friends had predicted. Rattigan came to hate Harvey for the way he treated Margaret Leighton, although he probably also pitied him for the weaknesses that led to his vanity and posturing. Although initially he was eager to have Harvey to star in various of his projects (partly to please his adored Margaret Leighton and partly because of the box-office benefits of his name) he soon came to think little of Harvey's abilities as an actor. Ron is depicted as self-centred and worthless, confusing money with talent, a second-rank dancer whose success was not due to ability or real love of ballet, but to being kept at it by the hard-working and devoted choreographer who had promoted him. Like Laurence Harvey, Ron Vale has changed his name (he dances as Anton Valov) and romanticized his origins.

Much though the plot and characters owe to Dumas and the Harvey-Leighton affair, *Variation on a Theme* owes still more to Rattigan's own experience. In September 1957, the Wolfenden Committee made its eagerly awaited report, advocating reform of the law relating to homosexuals and the abolition of penalties for sexual acts in private between consenting adult males. The report is actually alluded to in the text and it seems probable that Rattigan hoped, in keeping with the mood of liberal optimism which briefly prevailed, that he might be able to write a frankly homosexual play which would perform some of the functions of a confession. In the event, neither the public climate nor the cast of his own creative mind permitted such a thing.

Adrian Brown who, it will be remembered, had begun a relationship with Rattigan late in 1954, is in no doubt that Rose Fish is to be taken as a self-portrait of Rattigan and that Ron Vale is an amalgam of himself and others. Kurt Mast, the German banker, can be taken both as representative of the wealthy protectors in Rattigan's own past, particularly Chips Channon, and of the wealthy employers, particularly in the film industry, for whose ample cheques Rattigan often felt he prostituted his talent. When Rose finally deserts Kurt for a life of poverty and discomfort with Ron – significantly they will have to live off his comparatively meagre earnings from the theatre – one senses that Rattigan is not only following the dictates of Dumas' story, but symbolizing his own, repeatedly deferred, desire to turn his back on Hollywood and devote himself to the theatre. Work on the play was interrupted a number of times by Rattigan's obligations to film companies requiring him to undertake rewrites to various film projects, including the Lawrence film and *Separate Tables*. During his work on *Separate Tables* he was paid at a rate of a thousand dollars a day, and acquiesced in making changes to the end of the final scene between Sibyl and 'the Major' which implied the possibility of a future romantic attachment between them.

Rattigan's choice of names for characters is often significant, but nowhere more so than in *Variation on a Theme*. There is actually a minor character called Adrian, a gigolo whose wealthy lady patron is pointedly called Mona. Rattigan's friends would undoubtedly have enjoyed the joke. They would also have recognized his self-projection in Rose Fish. 'Fish' has allusive undertones in Rattigan.[16] Sir Robert Morton, the defence lawyer in *The Winslow Boy*, who seemed incapable of the personal feeling that Rattigan identified with himself, was described as 'a fish' and as 'fishy hearted'. Rose too seems unfeeling, keeping herself above emotional involvement in single-minded pursuit of the main chance. When she meets Ron, it is only slowly revealed that what she really craves is genuine love. Much of the play charts her struggle with her desire to abandon herself to her feelings. Adrian Brown had found Rattigan like Rose, in that he had a strong desire to be loved, both emotionally and physically, but found difficulty in reciprocating. The idea of himself romanticized into a latter-day Marguerite Gautier was both appropriate and pathetic: appropriate because of his increasingly pity-seeking hypochondria, which made him prone to striking attitudes in private which were in keeping with the nineteenth-century dying heroine; pathetic because of the implied self-disgust. Like Rose, Rattigan was drawn to, though not of course exclusively, 'the bad boys' – the ones he knew were worthless, who he knew would use him, were likely to behave embarrassingly, make scenes and demand money. Above all Rattigan needed to be needed. In the play, when Ron falls and breaks his ankle, Rose rushes to him, breaking a date with her wealthy protector Kurt: 'I'm needed by Ron.' B. A. Young recounts how important this line was to Rattigan. Being needed was the feeling which, Young says, 'was the nearest Terry came to love'.[17]

When Adrian Brown (not one of Rattigan's 'bad boys') first met Rattigan he was a minor ballet dancer who had directed while at Oxford and had ambitions to get back into the legitimate theatre as a director. Subsequently, Rattigan made him an allowance to go back to London and start making his way as a director. Within a few years he was directing plays in the West End, and went on to become a respected television and opera director, winning an international Emmy Award for *The Belle of Amherst* starring Claire Bloom. Brown had been dazzled by the circle he suddenly entered – dinner with Gielgud, lunch with Robert Graves, figures he had hitherto only admired from afar. In such superficial respects – being a ballet dancer and his obvious wonder at Rose's life and friends – Ron Vale is very like Adrian

346

Brown. Also, known to Rattigan but almost no one else, Adrian Brown's actual first name was Ron. However, in other respects Ron Vale and Adrian Brown are different. The feeling between Adrian Brown and Rattigan was never very intense; there were not the scenes and recriminations of the play. Here Rattigan is drawing on other relationships, those with Kenneth Morgan and others. At one point Ron Vale threatens to go off with another, wealthier woman in order to make Rose jealous. One of Rattigan's young men had calculatingly played him off against Ivor Novello by moving back and forth between the two. Kenneth Morgan had led Rattigan a painful dance with his infidelities.

Michael Franklin, by this time known disparagingly as 'the Midget' by people around Rattigan, had become almost universally disliked among those friends because of the way he, as they saw it, repaid generosity and affection with ingratitude. Yet Rattigan persisted in the relationship. Franklin had told friends that he thought in having the model Anne Shankland go back to her 'unsuitable', violent politician husband in the first play in *Separate Tables*, Rattigan was in effect depicting his own return to his unsuitable lover Franklin. Franklin jeered at the disappointment of Rattigan's friends. But *Variation on a Theme* provides a much clearer insight into Rattigan's feelings about his relationship with Franklin. Rattigan probably made much greater allowances than his friends for the jealousy Franklin must have felt at Adrian Brown's arrival on the scene. So when Franklin turned up on numerous occasions to throw tantrums, not only in front of people like Adrian Brown of whom he might have had some reason to be jealous, but in front of people such as Stephen Mitchell who were important to him professionally, Rattigan understood and even accepted his motivation. On one such occasion, in the Hotel Martinez in Cannes, Franklin physically attacked Rattigan and on another threw money back in his face. Both scenes are alluded to in *Variation on a Theme*. In Ron Vale, Rattigan fashioned a character who was an amalgam of many people he had known, and who perhaps even owed something to his own treatment of Chips Channon. In the play, the worse Ron behaves, the more Rose feels for him. However much he may hurt or embarrass her, she recognizes in his jealousy the love that she so desperately craves. In his own relationships Rattigan had felt the same. His relationship with Michael Franklin, despite the massive and vocal disapproval of his friends, lasted for the rest of his life. Rattigan himself was disparaging about Franklin but, although he often didn't see him for long intervals, he never deserted him. His overpowering need to be needed and Kenneth Morgan's suicide had bitten deep.

Rattigan also created two people who loved Ron – Rose, and Sam Duveen, his homosexual choreographer patron, who before he leaves him describes what it has been like loving someone who needs people but is himself incapable of real love: 'You don't seem to understand that the Rons of this world always end by hating the people they need. They can't help it. It's compulsive.' Each of Ron's many tantrums in the play seems to have had its counterpart in real life. Sam describes Ron's reaction to the promotion of a rival dancer: 'When Ron heard the news he did his best to carve up the new boy, then came home and staged a phoney suicide scene with me, and when that didn't work got into his car [given to him by Sam] and roared off into the night...I didn't follow as I used to, because I'd had it...' That sounds very close to Rattigan's reaction to Kenneth Morgan after he moved out to live with Alec Ross. Something similar happened later with Michael Franklin who, having failed in an attempt to provoke Rattigan by flirting very ostentatiously with a local boy when they were on holiday in the Mediterranean, jumped into his sports car (given to him by Rattigan) and roared off. On that occasion Rattigan did not follow himself, but sent a friend after him in his Bentley. On another occasion, soon after Rattigan had started working on the play, Franklin had threatened to throw himself off a balcony of the Hotel Martinez where they were on holiday. As one of his other lovers commented shrewdly, Franklin's tantrums made Rattigan like him all the more: 'Terry liked the Midget *because* he cared enough to make scenes.' In the play Sam learns from his experience with Ron not to make too heavy an emotional investment in one person, as Rattigan had with Kenneth Morgan.

In his turn Ron spits out his resentment at the way Rose keeps him in a separate compartment, divided off from the rest of her life and her high-society friends, just as Rattigan tried to keep his boys away from his 'straight' friends: 'I wonder. Have you ever thought what it's been like for me, asked over here a couple of odd evenings a week whenever there's no important people around – because common Ron mustn't meet important people – oh, dear no, that'd never do...' However unscrupulous, ungrateful or difficult his boyfriends, Rattigan could still feel sympathy for them – a fact his straight friends found incomprehensible. Ron says: 'You all think I'm a proper bastard, I know, and just out for what I can get, and I dare say you may be right. But that's how I was told when I was a kid – in this world, Ron boy, they said, you got to work it so it's "F.U., Jack, I'm all right", or you go under – and Christ, Rose, that's true. Look at the people who do go under – even in this bloody welfare world. What's so wrong in looking after yourself? You've done it all your life, haven't you?...'

Because of the competing calls of his film work, Rattigan did not complete *Variation on a Theme* until December 1957. As soon as he had done so he dispatched copies to Margaret Leighton (then playing in *Separate Tables* in New York), who he hoped would star as Rose, and to John Gielgud, who he hoped would direct. Then he set off for a brief holiday with Rex Harrison and Kay Kendall in Switzerland. By February 1958 both Gielgud and Leighton had said yes and Binkie Beaumont had agreed that Tennent's would put it into production immediately. Rattigan had even suggested, albeit rather tentatively, that Laurence Harvey should play Ron. Harvey turned it down, probably recognizing, and fearing others would recognize, the facets of his own behaviour which had gone into the creation of Ron; perhaps recognizing, too, the weaknesses of the play and the way in which theatrical times had changed in the two years since the opening of *Look Back in Anger*.

That both Gielgud and Beaumont should have agreed to do the play with such unquestioning alacrity was a measure not only of the extent to which Rattigan had lost touch with the feelings and taste of his audience, but of the extent to which other leaders of the theatrical profession had become isolated behind the walls of theatrical success. Rehearsals began in March 1958, but things soon started to go wrong. The boy playing Ron, Tim Seeley, who had been engaged on the strength of one West End starring role in *Tea and Sympathy*, had to be replaced after one provincial critic had suggested that, because Seeley looks so young and handsome, the play was simply about Margaret Leighton's cradle-snatching. Jeremy Brett took over, to Margaret Leighton's private dismay. Rattigan, as on previous occasions when things started to go wrong, blamed the director and cast. He complained to friends that as all Gielgud did as the director was '. . . turn his back on the players and correct their intonations, it doesn't have very much effect'.[18]

The play opened at the Globe Theatre on 8 May to generally disastrous notices. It was not helped by what the critics agreed was a downright bad production. Far from being an iconoclastic demolition of the Establishment, as Rattigan had promised, *Variation on a Theme* seemed a pallid star-vehicle. On this occasion, his usual mastery of understatement and the oblique approach had betrayed him into downright evasion. In the new climate of forthright committed theatre, the play received an even harsher handling than it merited. It seemed to epitomize the worst of the old vices. For Rattigan's reputation as a serious playwright, the timing of its appearance could not have been worse.

Tynan accused Rattigan of clumsily disguising a blatantly homosexual theme in an attempt to please both the Lord Chamberlain and Aunt Edna. Harold Hobson, who slaughtered both play and production under a headline which asked 'Are Things What They Seem?'[19] had felt he was watching a play which was really about something which was not its ostensible subject. The *Manchester Guardian* said that the play was about a concealed homosexual liaison, while in *The Spectator* Alan Brien asked why, in spite of the play's other deficiencies, sizeable stretches of it gripped and shocked as a real play should – answering, 'Because the subject should be a homosexual relationship between a bored and ageing *rentier* and a sharp, oily male tart.' Only T.C. Worsley carried on a spirited defence of the play, in the *New Statesman* and the *London Magazine*. He seems on this occasion, however, to have slipped below his normally high standards as a disinterested critic.

Claiming to know the lady upon whom the story was based, he accused the critics who had said it had a covert homosexual theme of 'a seamy line of personal smear'. Worsley, a close personal friend of Rattigan's who frequently travelled with him and benefited from his hospitality, certainly did know that the 'case' the play was based on was that of Margaret Leighton, although he tactfully did not reveal her name. Nor, however, did he admit to his own equally good knowledge of other elements of the play's background. By attacking his fellow critics in this way, while not declaring his own hand, he brought his critical reputation and, by association, Rattigan's into unnecessary disrepute.

Notes

1 *Sunday Times*, 2 January 1955.
2 George Devine in 'The Royal Court Theatre', *International Theatre Annual*, No. 2, ed. Harold Hobson, John Calder, London, 1957.
3 *Curtains* by Kenneth Tynan, op. cit.
4 *Happy Go Lucky* by Kenneth More, op. cit. and *More or Less* by Kenneth More, Hodder & Stoughton, London, 1978.
5 *New Statesman*, 15 October 1955.
6 *My Father Laurence Olivier* by Tarquin Olivier, Headline Book Publishing, London, 1992.
7 Colin Clark's diaries, *The Prince, The Showgirl and Me* (HarperCollins, London, 1995), provide a uniquely candid and engaging blow-by-blow account of the making of *The Prince And the Showgirl*. In describing events associated with it, I have also drawn on an interview I did with Sir John Gielgud in 1977 and *Laurence Olivier* by Donald Spoto, (HarperCollins, London, 1991), *Timebends: A Life* by Arthur Miller (Methuen, London, 1987), *My Father Laurence Olivier* by Tarquin Olivier (op. cit.) and *Confessions of an Actor* by Laurence Olivier, Weidenfeld & Nicolson, London, 1982.
8 Based on an interview by the author with John Osborne in 1977.
9 *New York Times*, 23 September 1956.
10 *Cue* magazine, New York, 25 October 1956.
11 *The Noël Coward Diaries*, op. cit.
12 Ibid.
13 *Rex – An Autobiography* by Rex Harrison, Macmillan, London, 1974.
14 *Daily Express*, 3 April 1957.
15 Rose in the play has been brought up in Edgbaston, Birmingham. Margaret Leighton had spent much of her childhood in Edgbaston.
16 Rattigan also said later that he may have chosen the name Fish out of some subconscious association with Mary Herring. Rose Fish in the play started her career as a very efficient secretary.

17   B.A.Young, op. cit.
18   Ibid.
19   *Sunday Times*, 11 May 1958.

17

Ross

Immediately after the opening of *Variation on a Theme*, Rattigan retired to Cannes to nurse his wounds among the gambling set that he had so recently said he despised. 'I don't mind the criticisms,' he said, 'but I do wish somebody had given me credit for kicking Aunt Edna down the stairs. It would have been so easy for me to make it an Aunt Edna play, to have given the woman a heart of gold. But I purposely took the most Aunt Edna play of all time, *La Dame aux Camélias*, and showed up the characters for what they really are.'[1]

Meanwhile, back at home, even more damage was being done to his reputation by a story spread around about a schoolgirl playwright called Shelagh Delaney. It seemed that she had attended *Variation on a Theme* during the first week of its try-out in Manchester, and was so maddened by seeing her favourite actress Margaret Leighton wasting her time traipsing about in rubbish that she had gone home and written a play in a fortnight. This, *A Taste of Honey*, she sent to Joan Littlewood at the Theatre Workshop, a radical theatre group in London's East End which was just gaining overdue recognition. It had gone into immediate production and opened only two weeks after *Variation on a Theme*. Rattigan's detractors could claim, with some justification, that the schoolgirl's play had the virtues that his lacked: it had honesty in place of evasion and vigour in place of tired technique. *A Taste of Honey* was a huge success and transferred to the scene of Rattigan's first triumph, the Criterion.

Rattigan was awarded the CBE in the Birthday Honours List in June, and subsequently invited to a private lunch with the Queen. But among the younger generation he was by now an object of scorn. In July, when Arnold Wesker's *Chicken Soup with Barley* opened at the Royal Court, Rattigan wrote to its young author congratulating him on a fine play. Wesker's reply was contemptuous, implying Rattigan would be better employed writing better plays himself. Although disappointed, Rattigan's reaction was open hearted rather than bitter. That summer he took the chance to make amends for a similar slap-down he had administered to a struggling dramatist when he himself was a young man. Lionel Hale, the luckless playwright whom he had advised 'to learn the bitter lesson of his own limitations' in his review for *Cherwell* of *Passing Through Lorraine*, approached him with an offer to back a new play he had written. Rattigan invested six thousand pounds.

But in the meantime another blow had fallen. Filming of the script about T. E. Lawrence had at last been about to start, after many delays. Against Rattigan's wishes, Asquith had cast Dirk Bogarde as Lawrence; Rattigan conceded that he was a good actor, but hardly right for Lawrence. In spite of repeated remarks about hating the cinema, Rattigan had always excepted his work with Asquith and he had invested a lot of effort in the script. Returning from Iraq, where they had been hunting for locations, Asquith and Anatole de Grunwald were passing through Immigration Control at London Airport when they were given a message from Rank, the production company, that the film had been abandoned. Another crisis had hit the British film industry and the seven-hundred-thousand-pound budget for the film was simply too much. Three years' work, albeit intermittent, was to be thrown away. Asquith, Bogarde and Rattigan were desolate over the death of their project.

However, since the critical rejection of *Variation on a Theme*, there seemed to be a new resolution about Rattigan. He set about reversing a process that he had employed so often with his rejected or abandoned stage plays, he settled down to turn his T. E. Lawrence screenplay into a free-wheeling stage play. Like

Adventure Story, it was an epic, covering the rise and fall of a legendary hero in a series of short scenes, but the flow was more supple and the style more appropriate to its subject. The play, *Ross*, was almost certainly better for having started life as a film.

While Rattigan worked, the theatrical world beyond his study in Eaton Square continued to change. He had told people that he wanted to write plays that were bolder in both their sweep and the candour of the emotions that they explored. The advances in theatrical technique and public taste now being ushered in seemed set to provide him with a greater opportunity than ever before. Woodrow Wyatt's Theatrical Companies Bill, which had been debated in the House of Commons in June 1954, had had its desired effect. Although the bill had been defeated, the Treasury had amended the entertainment tax rules so as to curb Binkie Beaumont, or any other theatrical impresario who might be tempted to try the same thing. He was prevented from operating his profit- and non-profit making companies, H. M. Tennent Ltd and Tennent Productions Ltd, in such a way as to manipulate the tax exemption rules to maximize his profits and strengthen his stranglehold on the West End theatre. By the late 1950s Beaumont's grip was being prised loose and other younger, more adventurous managements were able to mount successful productions in London. In addition, government subsidy of the arts through the Arts Council had resulted in the creation of a chain of provincial repertory theatres which were willing to present challenging new plays. The first visit to London of the Berliner Ensemble, presenting the works of Brecht, in the autumn of 1956, together with the influence of French directors such as Roger Planchon, was inspiring a new breed of theatre directors and designers – people like Joan Littlewood, Peter Coe and Sean Kenny – creating new, more free-wheeling and fast moving styles of production. Together with the new writers, they had removed many of the theatrical restraints with which Rattigan had had to contend as a young writer. Laurence Olivier's invitation to John Osborne (after his visit to *Look Back in Anger* in the company of Arthur Miller) had resulted in 1957 in *The Entertainer*. Shelagh Delaney's *A Taste of Honey* had not only put a homosexual on the stage in the character Geoff, but had shown him and his sexual orientation in a positive light.

In November 1958, the House of Commons at last got round to debating the Wolfenden Report. The Home Secretary, Rab Butler, indicated that the government was not yet ready to legislate to change the law to permit homosexual acts between consenting adults in private as he did not believe he could yet carry public opinion with him if he did so. However, he did acknowledge the suffering caused by the law as it stood. As though to underline the need to push the government forward, six days before the debate a junior Foreign Office minister was charged with an act of gross indecency in St James's Park and had to leave the government. In deciding at this moment to tell the epic story of T. E. Lawrence on the stage and to attempt an explanation of his decision to leave public life at the height of his fame and seek anonymity under the name Ross in the ranks of the RAF, Rattigan had set himself perhaps the greatest challenge of his career. He had also created his greatest opportunity.

Rattigan shut himself away to concentrate on his play, turning away all offers of other work. He took a short break at Christmas, entertaining a large party of house-guests at Sunningdale, which included his mother and Peter Osborn. Osborn, now a regular Lieutenant Commander in the navy, was stationed at the Royal Naval College, Greenwich, as an instructor. A convinced Christian, struggling between guilt over his homosexuality and a growing desire to be ordained in the Church of England, he accompanied Vera to Eucharist on Christmas Day, more or less forcing Rattigan to attend as well.

With Christmas over, Rattigan returned to T. E. Lawrence. He completed *Ross* at 6 a.m. on 13 February 1959, the morning of the British première of the much messed-around Hollywood film of *Separate Tables*. In contrast to its reception in America, which had been ecstatic, earning Rattigan and his co-screenwriter John Gay, an Oscar nomination, the British critics were generally unimpressed. They found it a bore. Immediately afterwards Rattigan left on a three-month world tour through the Far East, Australia and New Zealand, combining work and relaxation.[2] On his way home through Hollywood, he turned down a lucrative offer to script a film from Nabokov's novel *Lolita*. He was sticking to his resolution to reject easy film money and honour his vocation for the theatre. In late April he saw the CBS television broadcast of *The Browning Version* directed by John Frankenheimer, in which Gielgud at last played the part written for him and for which he received glowing notices. In May he returned home aboard the *Queen Elizabeth* with Margaret Leighton, whose marriage to Laurence Harvey was by then in trouble.

Ross called for a big cast and a kaleidoscope of fast changing sets. Before setting out on his world tour Rattigan had sent the script, not to one of the new impresarios, but to Binkie Beaumont. On Rattigan's return he found Beaumont eager to put it into production as soon as possible. Beaumont accepted that this would be an expensive production but, famous for his parsimony, he wanted a number of cuts and economies. Extravagant scenes left in from the film version, such as one which involved Ronald Storrs and twenty airmen in a billet with twenty beds, singing at a piano, were to be cut. Rattigan, for his part, regarding this as perhaps his most important play, also wanted to make a number of changes and improvements. He threw himself into revising and preparing *Ross* for production. Alec Guinness was to star as Lawrence and Glen Byam Shaw, who had done *The Winslow Boy*, was to direct.

The production ran into trouble almost immediately. As a result Rattigan had to divert his energies away from making the improvements to the play and the changes required by Binkie Beaumont. Instead he had to win the approval of the Lord Chamberlain's office to granting the play a performance licence. One of the more arcane considerations taken into account by the Lord Chamberlain before granting a licence was the possibility of members of the family of any deceased person depicted in a play being caused offence. When Rattigan and Beaumont had approached the Lord Chamberlain's office with *Ross* he had advised making every effort to get the prior consent of any surviving close members of the Lawrence family. This was complicated by the fact that, since the dropping of the Asquith film, the powerful American producer Sam Spiegel had announced his own epic Lawrence film. Spiegel seemed set on preventing production of the Rattigan play, lest it steal some of his thunder. Worse, Lawrence's brother had sold the film rights to T. E. Lawrence's own account of his story, *Seven Pillars of Wisdom*, to Spiegel. So, with a heavy heart, in late June Rattigan wrote to Professor Lawrence, a distinguished archaeologist, outlining the history of the project and professing his deep admiration for T. E. Lawrence. Assuring him that 'whatever my shortcomings as a "dramatic biographer", my heart is in the right place', Rattigan summed up his intentions as being 'to do full justice to the character and memory of a very great man'. Before replying, Professor Lawrence discussed Rattigan's play with his mother and surviving brother. They were appalled. To them the play suggested that T. E. Lawrence was a weakling who made up for this deficiency by blood-lust and 'other uncontrolled neurotic impulses'. The result was that the Lord Chamberlain seemed almost certain to refuse *Ross* a licence. It now looked as if *Ross* would either have to be postponed indefinitely or put on in a club theatre, which would rule out a lavish, star-studded production.

Glen Byam Shaw proposed mounting a campaign in support of the play. He would send it to Siegfried Sassoon and suggested that Rattigan send it to Robert Graves, both of whom had known T. E. Lawrence well and, it could be argued, were as much authorities on T. E. Lawrence as Professor Lawrence. Sassoon wrote back promptly, saying that he found the play a sympathetic and effective portrait. Rattigan, who knew Graves, left Beaumont to write to him. That was, perhaps, a mistake. Graves replied saying that he would advise Professor Lawrence to ask Rattigan to make changes. One cannot libel the dead, he said, 'but on the other hand one can be prevented from misrepresenting the dead by the copyright laws'. What Graves did not mention was that he was also acting as a consultant to Sam Spiegel on his film. Now Rattigan did write to Graves, telling him that he was anxious to make such changes as he could to bring it nearer to the historical truth, '... without destroying the play's theatrical life...' In mid-October Graves responded, saying that he had consulted Professor

Lawrence and that, while he accepted that the play was good theatre, there seemed no good reason for hurting a lot of people and flouting history.

At this point Beaumont called in Peter Carter-Ruck, an expert on copyright and soon to become known as the doyen of libel lawyers. He also purchased the rights to Basil Liddell Hart's biography *T. E. Lawrence – In Arabia and After* as their 'source work'. Beaumont's aim was to ensure that if Tennents went ahead, there could be no basis in copyright for an injunction preventing production. In addition, Beaumont drew up a memorandum, setting out each of the steps that he and Rattigan had taken, without avail, to meet the Lawrence family and to counter any possible objections they might have. He attempted to show that under all the circumstances the family were withholding their consent without good reason. This he sent to the Lord Chamberlain, reminding him that it was always open to Rattigan or Tennents to have the play performed in a club theatre, in another country or to induce someone to produce it on television, over none of which he had jurisdiction. He also said that, if the play were licensed, they would be willing to put a notice in the programme, similar to the one used for the production of *The Winslow Boy*, explaining that, although the play was based on an historical figure, neither the events nor characters were necessarily factual.

At the end of October the Lord Chamberlain responded. Acknowledging that the policy of protecting 'the feelings of individuals whose near relations are the subject of a playwright's attentions' was very difficult to implement in practice, he explained that in the rare cases where he did exercise the powers of his office, it was usually in order to prevent the painful publicity which frequently followed the production of a play. However, it had been his experience over many years, that the banning of a play often created more publicity than allowing production to proceed. The banning of a play is news and editors make the most of it: 'matters that may have been touched upon lightly, or possibly not mentioned at all, are dragged into the light'. Acknowledging that his office only had control over what was performed in public theatres in the United Kingdom, and that much had already been said and written about T. E. Lawrence, who is '...an historic and controversial character...', and taking into consideration all the foregoing points, he had concluded that '...it would not be in the best interests of the relatives...' for him to refuse a licence. At the same time he was sure that Mr Rattigan would endeavour to meet the objections of Professor Lawrence to any particular passage.

Unfortunately by this time Alec Guinness was no longer immediately available, so rehearsals could not begin until late February. But in the meantime Rattigan wrote to Basil Liddell Hart, saying that the play was not a history, but 'a dramatic portrait' which was really about character rather than events. The play was not, he assured Liddell Hart, based on his book, it was '...entirely different...a complete reconception'. However, he told him, he did very much want to take up his offer (which had followed Beaumont's purchase of the rights in Liddell Hart's biography) of expert assistance. Rattigan went back to tinkering with his script. He was to continue making changes and adjustments right up to the play's London opening in May 1960.

While the drama over getting permission to stage *Ross* was being played out, other important events were also happening in Rattigan's life. At the end of May 1959 he had accepted an invitation from Peter Osborn to be his guest at a formal navy dinner in the great Painted Hall at the Royal Naval College, Greenwich. It was Osborn's farewell dinner, an event of considerable emotional significance for him. Perhaps fearing that emotion, Rattigan cried off at the last moment, getting his secretary Mary Herring to type Osborn a formal note saying that he was unable to attend. Hurt and disappointed, Osborn wrote back suggesting an alternative date. With his letter Osborn enclosed an acrostic sonnet he had composed called 'Come of Age'. It was exactly twenty-one years since he and Rattigan had become lovers at Sonning. The first letter of each line spells out the name TERRY M RATTIGAN. The poem recounts the bitter emptiness of his enduring, but inadequately returned, love for Rattigan. Rattigan replied at once in a brutal, three-line note. The sonnet was '. . . a piece of tactlessness so monumental in its insensitivity and boorishness that I find it hard to believe that it could have emanated from a friend . . .' He did not wish to dine with Osborn and resented his reproaches. On 7 July, Osborn responded: 'The reproaches are my own and have nothing to do with you. I am as I am, and I was trying to tell the only friend that I have in this world of my troubles. You may not understand or agree with my heart-searchings, but do I deserve such a stern and harsh rebuke?' He concluded a long letter by telling Rattigan that all his striving since the war to live in 'brave independence – a hard and bitter struggle, full of defeats, and every moment of it aware of my need of my dearest friend – is come to nothing. I wonder that you who understand the grief of loneliness should inflict such pain on me.'

Again Rattigan responded at once, this time at greater length and inviting a reply – 'Be honest when you answer. No balls about *your* guilt complex, self-hatred and loneliness. Other people can experience these things too, you know, besides Commanders RN.' Osborn replied two days later, on 13 July. He tried to get Rattigan to understand the agony he felt over his continued failure to conquer 'the sin' of his homosexuality. Rattigan might call this balls, but to him it was real. He told Rattigan that 'the happiest moment of my life was when I was able to accompany you and your mother to the little tin church at the bottom of the drive'. He ended by telling Rattigan how much he continued to admire him. Extending his continued and unconditional affection, he offered Rattigan sympathy in his own unhappiness: 'That you should be unhappy in your alliances fills me with deep sorrow, and my continual reproach is that I should have failed you with my inadequacy. I apologize for being as I am.'

Rattigan had decided to put his Sunningdale house on the market, cutting his roots and breaking free of his 'turmoils and complexities'. From now on he intended to live a more itinerant life, free of the emotional demands made on him by boyfriends and his mother. On 17 July an advert appeared in *The Times*, offering Little Court, Sunningdale for sale.

The house did not sell immediately and by September he was working on a musical version of *French Without Tears*. The idea seems to have emanated from Billy Chappell who was best known as a stage designer. Musicals and plays with music were enjoying a wave of popularity. *My Fair Lady* was packing in audiences at Drury Lane and *Fings Ain't Wot They Used To Be* and *The Hostage*, both from Joan Littlewood's Stratford E15 Theatre Workshop, were making hugely successful transfers to the West End. Binkie Beaumont wanted a Tennent's musical and was strongly in favour of what was already a dangerous idea. *French Without Tears*, whatever its virtues, hardly seemed the stuff of the political music-hall shows of the Theatre Workshop or of lavish Broadway spectaculars such as *My Fair Lady*. An already threadbare scheme was made worse when Robert Stolz, whose biggest hit had been *White Horse Inn* before the war, was brought in as composer. One has to ask why Rattigan should have let it go ahead. Perhaps he thought it a harmless bit of fun that might make him an additional bit of money. Also he was fond of Billy Chappell, and it would give him an additional break as a director. But there must also be the sneaking suspicion that he wanted to show himself the equal of Bernard Shaw, whose play *Pygmalion* was the basis of *My Fair Lady*. Adrian Brown and others who knew him intimately, have testified to the fact that Rattigan wanted to be seen in the direct line of succession from Shakespeare through Shaw. Unfortunately Stolz and Dehn (Paul Dehn, the lyricist) were no Lerner and Loewe.

By October Rattigan was talking openly about writing a play stemming from the death from leukaemia of Kay Kendall. He had seen a lot of Rex Harrison during the two years that Harrison had tried to keep her life as normal as possible so that she should not know she was dying. After living with Harrison in Hollywood, he had stayed with the couple in St Moritz during one of Kay's temporary rallies. After Kay died, Harrison had gone to stay with Rattigan at Sunningdale. There, with the assistance of Harold French and his wife Peggy, Rattigan tried to help Harrison recover from his grief and two years of intense physical and emotional strain. On 6 November the press got wind of the possibility that Rattigan was writing a play about Harrison and Kendall, and the London *Evening Standard* published a story by Thomas Wiseman. Harrison was furious and four days later

Rattigan put out a strongly worded denial, saying that he was not at the moment, nor would he be in the foreseeable future, engaged on such a project. The idea lingered, however, and a dozen years later did form part of the basis of one of his last plays.

By December 1959 he was telling journalists that he was working on a comedy, perhaps with music, *for* Rex Harrison. It was, he said, to help Harrison get out of his depression over the death of Kay Kendall. It would be both serious and satirical. But work on this was interrupted first by moving house and then by the run up to the production of *Ross*. Rattigan had one last Christmas at Sunningdale, with a house party of his closest friends. 'The Midget' (Michael Franklin) was there, Vera Rattigan, Margaret Leighton and Laurence Harvey, Harold and Pegs French, Billy Chappell, who, as at other Sunningdale Christmases, did the decorations, and, much to his surprise, Peter Osborn. Out of the blue, on 1 December, Osborn had received an invitation from Rattigan to join him for the Christmas holiday. He and Vera attended midnight mass and Rattigan presented him with an Italian pullover as a Christmas present. When they got a few moments together, Rattigan asked if he would be willing to bring his mother out to visit him in Ischia, where he was planning to go once the house was sold. They also talked about Rattigan's continuing difficulties with the Midget. Although relations had been easier in recent months, the Midget was still inclined to fly into jealous rages, create hysterical scenes and chase off after other men.

Rehearsals for *Ross* finally got underway at the YMCA off Tottenham Court Road on 22 February 1960. As the openings of both *Ross* and the musical adapted from *French Without Tears* (for which one of the original, discarded, titles had been resurrected, *Joie de Vivre*) approached, the press seemed on the point of making a fresh and more serious evaluation of Rattigan's accomplishments as a dramatist. Articles in the *Daily Express*, *Daily Mail*, *Evening Standard* and *Manchester Guardian* all conceded that he had been too readily dismissed, and saluted the way in which, while sticking courageously to his belief in the well-made play, he had deepened his art and extended his range. The *Manchester Guardian* likened him to Molière, as a dramatist who alternated between serious plays and 'occasional entertainments'. His generally left-of-centre sympathies were recognized, and it was suggested that the Royal Court would do well to respond to his stated desire to write something for them. No such invitation was forthcoming.

In an unusually frank interview with Robert Muller, one of his fiercest critics in the 'Play of Ideas' debate, he had said that although he had made a mess of his personal life he had done what he could with his talent. His aim was what it had always been – to write a masterpiece: 'The two greatest dangers to the middle-aged playwright are sentimentality and disenchantment.' He did not intend to succumb to either. He renewed his defence of the well-made play and attacked some of the new playwrights: 'I may be old-fashioned about some of these new playwrights, but they've just got to learn their job. It's not really a help to a writer to be called a genius with his first play.' Slipping into the theatre with a farcical comedy, he could now see, had been an advantage; no one had expected anything of him and he had had a chance to learn his craft. 'If I'd started off with an angry political play I might have been called a genius, and that could have finished me.' He recalled his own political anger and being charged by the police when protesting about the Spanish Civil War. 'In the late thirties we had things to be indignant about... Because I've always put character before ideas in my plays, people think I have no political views... People just never think of me in that sort of way. I suppose I wear the wrong kind of clothes.' But, he pointed out, a rich writer suffered the same frustrations as a poor one and the same compulsions: 'Every playwright is compelled to write the same play over and over again. He would be dishonest if he didn't.'[3]

Rattigan said a great deal, far more than was his custom, both before and after its production, about his intentions in *Ross*. Some of it was inevitably contradictory, but the most important elements are clear. His own notes to himself, written before he started to turn his abandoned film script into a stage play, confirm his main thrust at the outset. Just as he had set out in *Adventure Story* to answer the question 'Where did it first go wrong?' in respect of Alexander, so in

Ross he searches for the 'flaw' in Lawrence which caused him, at the height of his success, to feel driven to seek anonymity in the ranks of the RAF under the name of Ross. 'Oh, Ross, how did I become you?' Lawrence asks. In his notes to himself Rattigan had given the outline of his answer:

> Lawrence – whose original motive in going to the desert and escaping from 'muddy intellect' was to *find* himself, is *shown* himself by the General, and the shock is enough to make him a mental suicide and destroy his will and purpose... 'I should have left myself undiscovered – and grown into middle age a dull, frustrated, over-thinking archaeologist, who never, in all his life, would have done anyone any harm. Not even himself.'

Elsewhere Rattigan's notes on *Seven Pillars of Wisdom* include Lawrence saying: 'I long for people to look down on me and despise me... I'm too shy to take the filthy steps that would publicly shame me and put me into their contempt. I want to dirty myself outwardly, so that my person may properly reflect the dirt which it conceals.'

Opening his play after the war with Lawrence masquerading as Ross, Rattigan 'flashes back' to chart his victorious progress as leader of the Arab Revolt and discover the 'truth' that led his hero, who seemed so much to enjoy success, limelight and subtle showing-off, to hide himself away out of his own sense of self-disgust. The essence of Lawrence's inner life, Rattigan pointed out, was contained in *Seven Pillars of Wisdom* and consisted of persistent self-defeat throughout the crucial and outwardly victorious years. When Robert Muller interviewed him for the *Daily Mail*, Rattigan would not reveal what had happened to change the carefree young Rattigan into the sad, disenchanted middle-aged Mr Rattigan who, while having everything he could want materially, was clearly so desolate spiritually. 'I may be a success as a writer, but as a person I am not.' All he would say was that he had put more of himself into *Ross* than he had dared in any previous play.

Rattigan had settled on one incident in particular as the

turning point in Lawrence's life: his capture by the Turks at Deraa, where, according to Rattigan in *Ross*, but not to Lawrence in *Seven Pillars of Wisdom* (nor to Liddell Hart), he had found sexual gratification when being beaten and homosexually assaulted. Rattigan said that anyone reading *Seven Pillars of Wisdom* would see that the man was devastated by the revelation that he had homosexual and masochistic tendencies. 'This was before Freud, you remember,' he told Frances Herridge of the *New York Post* just after the Broadway opening. 'To him it was shattering to suspect what was in the back of his tremendous willpower. He couldn't live with himself. You might say he committed mind suicide, wanting to be a number in the Air Force.'[4] Rattigan's answer to the question he gives Lawrence at the beginning of the play, 'Oh, Ross, how did I become you?' is that he had worshipped the false God of his own will, which had been responsible for his triumphs, but he was destroyed psychologically by the discovery that what lay behind that willpower was not strength and integrity but inclinations which he could not face and which he despised in himself. The parallels with speculations about the psychological motivations of Hitler are obvious, and were fascinating to Rattigan as to many people who had lived through the rise of Nazism and the war years. But Rattigan also saw parallels between himself and Lawrence, the lack of feeling, the ruthlessness and the sexual guilt. The recent exchange of letters with Peter Osborn, and his intolerance of Osborn's self-examination and sense of unworthiness, betray Rattigan's own inner turmoil.

Peter Glenville, Rattigan's friend from their days together at Oxford and often his director, knew Rattigan almost as well as anyone. He argued that from his student days onwards Rattigan's major deficiency both as a playwright and as a man was a lack of a spiritual quest or desire to confront life's higher mysteries. Defenders of *Ross* may say that to avoid the 'mysteries' in dealing with T. E. Lawrence is to avoid the cant, but surely it is a deficiency in any play which claims to be based on either Liddell Hart's biography,[5] or *Seven Pillars of Wisdom*,[6] so completely to subdue the spiritual and wider philosophical questions posed by

Lawrence's career, character and writing. Liddell Hart, pointing out that what most astonished the public was Lawrence's disregard of the pleasures that ordinary men pursue, found no great mystery in his self-immolation in the RAF, which he likened to medieval man's choice of the monastic life. 'The drab mind instinctively seeks a colourful explanation of the simple,' he said. What to some people was Lawrence's greatest success – his rejection of worldly success and abnegation of the self – Rattigan interpreted as a symptom of inner failure.

After a short pre-West End tour the play opened at the Theatre Royal, Haymarket. This was a large theatre with over nine hundred seats, but the play enjoyed a longer run than any of Rattigan's serious plays.[7] The critics praised the play as more than a magnificent piece of story-telling and economic stagecraft. 'It is long since I remember a new play that has been more enthralling in the theatre, or that is likely to start more discussion outside,' wrote J. C. Trewin in *The Lady* of 26 May 1960. Kenneth Tynan did not catch up with the play until Alec Guinness had left the production and the part of Lawrence had been taken over by Michael Bryant. He then wrote a scathing review: 'For the second time in his career (*Adventure Story* was the first), Mr Rattigan shows us a conquering hero who is stopped dead in his tracks by a revelation of sexual abnormality somewhere east of Suez.' He continued: 'But my main objection to *Ross* is not that its view of history is petty and blinkered; so, it might be urged, is Shakespeare's in *Henry V*. What clinches my distaste is its verbal aridity, its flatness of phrase, and – above all – its pat reliance on the same antithetical device in moments of crisis.' Tynan went on to list examples. To take just two from Tynan's eight: ' "And is this only the beginning?" "It may be the ending too;" ' and: ' "There's nothing in the world worse than self-pity." "Oh, yes there is. Self-knowledge." '[8] While the first is certainly pat, it could be argued that the second is not only an effective reply but an economical way of developing the dialogue. It was a device that Rattigan had used from the start of his career, but over the years he had become too pleased with it and had started to over-use it, so that in *Ross* it seemed merely slick and consciously clever rather than enlightening.

In contrast to Tynan, Harold Hobson called Rattigan 'the brightest and wittiest of our dramatists', and said that by posing the central question of why Lawrence recoiled from his success, he had made him into '. . . the uneasy spectacular symbol of the conscience of the West in the twentieth century. After both the great wars of our time the victorious powers have been assailed by feelings of guilt . . .'[9]

Noël Coward was among the first-night audience. In his diary he noted that the play was 'beautifully constructed and movingly written', but he found there was something lacking. He put this down in part to Guinness's performance and to Binkie Beaumont's 'subtly decreasing interest in the theatre' which had allowed slack production management on the first night. But he also sensed some elusive missing ingredient in the play itself, a feeling of contrivance at its centre.[10] Coward's sense of ultimate disappointment was widely shared by audiences during the 762-performance London run.

Immediately before the West End opening of *Ross*, Rattigan had been ill. As rehearsals started he was recovering from flu but was determined to be available if required. He got up too soon and, by April, with both *Ross* and *Joie de Vivre* in rehearsal, was walking between the two rehearsals at the YMCA off Tottenham Court Road and the Theatre Royal, Drury Lane. He collapsed and spent the first two weeks of May in the London Clinic with viral pneumonia. His doctor ordered a complete rest and he went off to Brighton to recuperate. He fell for Brighton, and by the time *Joie de Vivre* was ready to open in London on 14 July he had taken a three-year lease on a seventh-floor flat in a block called Embassy Court. As a result of his illness he had seen little of the pre-West End tour. If he had, he might have done more to improve the play and the production. After all it was an expensive show to mount (twenty thousand pounds against the ten thousand for *Ross*, substantial percentages of which he had invested himself), with a cast of thirty, complicated settings, an orchestra and dancers. But it was not Rattigan's way to interfere in productions, even one as inept as this was turning out to be.

The reactions of provincial audiences and those at the London preview had been favourable. But the dress rehearsal had been as disastrous as the one before the opening of the original production of *French Without Tears*. The conductor had fallen off the podium, two of the singers developed laryngitis and the pianist had a nervous breakdown, claiming that he had had a vision in which he had been in touch with Napoleon and Jesus Christ and would reveal all on the first night. If Rattigan was worried at all he concealed it pretty well. On the morning of the first night, 14 July, the papers carried splash stories, asking if Rattigan could repeat the success of the original production of *French Without Tears* with this musical reincarnation. Rattigan himself, always nervous and superstitious before a first night, was understandably reluctant to say too much about the production, preferring instead to talk about the success of *Ross*.

The Queen's Theatre was packed with an expectant audience. Rattigan stood, outwardly relaxed and confident, looking surprisingly little aged by the twenty-four years that had elapsed since that first, seemingly much less auspicious, first night. Strategically placed in the upper circle was his secretary. The curtain went up on Monsieur Maingot's French crammer, set this time not in a small French west-coast town in 1936, but in a Mediterranean sunspot in 1960. Rattigan had told Robert Muller that he was trying to 'project the middle-aged me into the youthful me', but, as Harold Hobson pointed out to him in his review, in attempting to modernize his youthful success by dragging in mention of the H-bomb, swear words and references to the Royal Court playwrights 'as if they were a compulsory allusion in an examination paper', he only achieved 'a sort of political hypocrisy, a sad effort to appear up to date'.[11]

Nevertheless, at the interval it seemed to be going quite well. W. A. Darlington, the critic of the *Daily Telegraph* and a very experienced first-nighter, was preparing to write a tolerant review saying that, although nothing like as funny as the original, the show had kept its audience reasonably well entertained.[12] But before the interval ended Rattigan's secretary had made her way down from the upper circle and sought him out. 'Bad news,' she told him. 'I've heard a whisper that it's going to get the bird.' Rattigan didn't believe it. But as the show got under way again there was an indefinable, but tangible, air of tension in the theatre. Then it happened. The line, 'It isn't funny – it's a bloody tragedy,' was greeted with roars of agreement. The unkind laughs and the rhythmic rounds of applause mounted. The curtain calls were clearly going to be a disaster. Darlington, who had been to many disastrous first nights, was convinced that this wasn't a prearranged demonstration but a spontaneous reaction from the audience.[13] In the view of Harold Hobson, one of Rattigan's most consistent advocates, their disapproval was well merited – there was something both 'peculiarly revolting' and 'pathetic' about the show. Rattigan's first reaction was to feel terribly sorry. As the jeering continued, his surprise quickly turned to resignation. He looked at Billy Chappell beside him, and then walked out of the theatre and round to the stage door. Behind the set he called together the stage management and those members of the cast who were waiting for their cues and said firmly, 'They're going to give it to us, so no special calls. Bring the curtain down and keep it down.' The final curtain was almost on them. When it fell, there was a storm of booing. It did not rise again, and when the house lights went up the audience slowly picked their way out of the theatre in a disordered daze.

Next morning, Rattigan sat among the debris of the grim first-night party in his Eaton Square flat and faced a reporter from a London evening paper, who was eager to know how the man who had known nothing but success was taking failure. He was not believed when he said he had known worse moments. His main concern was for the cast: 'Poor darlings. I felt so sorry for them.'[14] That afternoon, putting a brave face on what had happened, he climbed into his Rolls-Royce and was driven to the races at Ascot. There, no one mentioned the play at all: 'It's odd,' he mused, 'they all behaved as though my mother had just died. Most peculiar.' That afternoon he backed more losers than winners.

On Saturday night, after four performances, *Joie de Vivre* closed. In his scathing notice next day, Harold Hobson nevertheless concluded by saying that though bruised in spirit and flushed with embarrassment, he was left:

brooding over the extraordinary talent of Mr Rattigan. Here is a man who has a greater sense of the theatre than any of his contemporaries except Jean Anouilh, a man who, lacking only the fertilizing flood of words, can be witty or touching, or, as in *Ross*, delicately and penetratingly perceptive in dangerous quarters of the human spirit. In the thirties several dramatists of promise appeared, Ronald Mackenzie, J. B. Priestley, W. H. Auden and Mr Rattigan himself. What has become of them? Mackenzie died. At some time in his career Mr Priestley became a politician and Auden a professor. Only Rattigan remains. . .[15]

Notes

1   *Evening Standard*, 17 May 1958.
2   Wesker denies that his letter was intended as contemptuous of either Rattigan or his plays. Nevertheless, Rattigan seems to have put that interpretation on it.
3   Michael Meyer records how, a few months later, when he and Graham Greene were spending a night in a hotel in Fiji, a young American, mistaking them for a homosexual couple, attempted to strike up an intimacy with the explanation that he was a friend of Terence Rattigan. Michael Meyer, op. cit.
4   *Daily Mail*, 23 September 1959.
5   Quoted in *Theatre Arts*, New York, April 1962. Interview given in December 1961. T. E. Lawrence told Herbert Wilcox that, far from finding sexual gratification in being beaten and sexually assaulted by the Turkish general at Deraa, he had 'fought *off*' the general with 'a knee kick which resulted in him being uninterested, in homo or any other kind of sexual activity for a week or two.
6   *T. E. Lawrence: In Arabia and After* by Liddell Hart, Jonathan Cape, London, 1948.
7   *Seven Pillars of Wisdom* by T. E. Lawrence, Jonathan Cape, 1935.
8   The possibility of a film based on *Ross* was again briefly mooted and Rattigan received £10,000 from the producer, Herbert Wilcox, as a down payment on the rights. But the plan soon evaporated, leaving Sam Spiegel alone in the field to make his Robert Bolt-scripted film *Lawrence of Arabia*.
9   *Observer*, 5 February 1961.
10 *Sunday Times*, 15 May 1960.
11 *The Noel Coward Diaries*, op. cit.
12 *Sunday Times*, 17 July 1960.
13 *Daily Telegraph*, 15 July 1960.
14 The story about Rattigan's secretary warning him in the interval that *Joie de Vivre* was going to 'get the bird' was told by Rattigan to a journalist the next morning. Twenty years later, Mary Herring, Rattigan's secretary, wrote to tell me that it was not true. Perhaps Rattigan made it up in the hope of bolstering the cast's shattered morale, or his own. Forty years on it is hard to know, but there were certainly others in the audience that night who did think that the booing and catcalls were prearranged.
15 *Evening News*, 15 July 1960.
16 *Sunday Times*, 17 July 1960.

18

Not for Fun

Rattigan was probably more hurt by the disaster that had befallen *Joie de Vivre* than he ever admitted. The rawness of his feelings burst out in a letter he dashed off to Kenneth Tynan in reaction to his scathing review of the first act, Tynan having admitted that at the first interval he had chosen to go out to dinner rather than sit through any more. Rattigan claimed to be writing as a well-wisher, warning him that Billy Chappell was determined to sue Tynan for the attack levelled at him in his review but that he would try to talk him out of it. This was such a piece of transparent nonsense as to make Rattigan look ridiculous (there was no way that Chappell could or would have brought an action on the basis of the remarks in Tynan's review). Rattigan went on to attack Tynan's championship of Brecht, whom, Rattigan claimed, audiences found '...a cracking, pedantic, didactic, ill-translated old Marxist bore...' A flurry of correspondence ensued, the net result of which can have done nothing to increase Tynan's respect for Rattigan.

Rattigan returned to the flat he had taken in Brighton and tried to take his mind off the failure of *Joie de Vivre* by concentrating on the comedy he had talked about writing for Rex Harrison. By October he had completed a three-act draft, tentatively called *Like Father*. It combines a number of Rattigan's immediate concerns with an enduring preoccupation – sons in revolt against fathers. It is set in the immediate present – 1960. The father is Bert Leavensworth, a successful painter, a left-wing lion of the 1930s. He has got 'sort of emotionally fixed' in the thirties, the time when 'he made his great decisive revolt' against his father, by coming down from Cambridge without a degree. Rattigan clearly intends that the audience shall recognize Bert as a Bohemian character based on Augustus John, while, less obviously, some of his unattractive characteristics owe something to Robert Graves, who Rattigan felt had let him down during the struggle with Professor Lawrence over *Ross*.

The other main protagonist is Bert's son Gussie who, having proved inadequate as a painter, has adopted the persona and style of a beatnik poet. Unknown to his father, while in Paris he has been studying economics and has become articled as an accountant to his father's firm of tax advisers. He has decided that democratic capitalism is a more effective way of achieving the aspirations of Marxism than Communism, which in order to operate requires dictatorship. At the start of the play Gussie returns home to introduce his fiancée, Margaret, to his father.

There are two other central characters: Bert's long-term girlfriend Suzy, an ex-stripper, who is his model, and Margaret's father, a general who, it is revealed, was a contemporary of Bert's at Eton and fought for Franco's side in the Spanish Civil War, while Bert fought for the socialist government side. Being a comedy, the antagonisms between the characters are eventually resolved and it becomes clear that the new generation, as represented by Gussie and Margaret, are just as determined to upset their parents as Bert or the general ever were – it is just that their form of revolt is to conform. Along the way there is a series of jokes about having to appear unkempt and ill-dressed in order to be recognized as part of the new, young generation and about taking part in political demonstrations and Ban the Bomb marches without knowing what they are about.

This is a very feeble effort and Rattigan seems to have known it. He made repeated changes and does not ever seem to have shown it to a management, nor even to Rex Harrison, its intended star. It was destined to go nowhere. But, as was his wont, Rattigan purloined ideas from it and reused them in other scripts.

'It's not for fun, it's for money,' a character in *The VIPs* says, explaining why she is going to America. Rattigan's resolution not to waste his time on films was weakening. Anatole de Grunwald, who had recently signed a contract to produce films for MGM, approached him and asked if he would submit an original script. Checking in at London Airport in October, on his way to America to discuss the Broadway production of *Ross* and the staging of a musical version of *The Sleeping Prince*, Rattigan was, as usual, shown into the lounge reserved for VIPs. As he sat idly wondering who the other passengers in the room with him might be – presuming them to be generals, civil servants and business magnates – a fog came down 'like the curtain at the Queen's Theatre', he commented ruefully later. As flights began to be delayed, the calm of the room was slowly broken, executives and government officials began to fume. Alternative travel arrangements were discussed, then cancelled, then reconsidered. The day wasted away in growing bad temper. The airport remained closed for forty-eight hours. With nothing else to do, Rattigan began to imagine the drama behind the anxious enquiries to flustered stewardesses and the furious explosions about cancelled meetings and lost contracts. By the time he arrived in New York he had an idea, which he thought might suit de Grunwald, for a 'compendium movie' set in a VIP lounge and revealing the dramas of an assortment of people trapped there by a sudden fog. His central story was based on an incident five years earlier, when Vivien Leigh had attempted to leave Laurence Olivier for Peter Finch. She and Finch had been thwarted when they were trapped in the VIP lounge at Heathrow by fog.[1] Flying on from New York to Hollywood, Rattigan sold the idea to de Grunwald for a fee close on forty thousand pounds.

Returning home in November, Rattigan told people that he had another idea for a play 'brewing'. It was to be about the effects of a scandal on a politician's family. But he seemed restless. Bouts of energy were followed by heavy drinking and listless moving from place to place. As Christmas approached he embarked on a hectic round of partying with a group of friends: Rex Harrison, who was trying to get over the death of Kay Kendall; Vivien Leigh, exchanging her marriage to Laurence Olivier for a relationship with an actor called John Merivale; Emlyn Williams and his wife, and Margaret Leighton, whose disastrous marriage to Laurence Harvey was about to end in divorce. Rattigan seemed to gain in strength by taking on a protective role to them all and at the same time to find·release from his own disappointments in trying to cheer up each of the others. But there was something desperate about their high spirits as each took it in turn to throw a party in their own home. As John Merivale put it, 'Here we are, a group of greats in the London theatre, behaving like children.' They even called themselves 'The Group' and Rattigan had a group tie designed for them by Turnbull and Asser, which was dark blue with a pink alligator. The tie was dropped after Rattigan and Margaret Leighton spotted someone they did not know wearing one in a restaurant.

Early in January 1961 Margaret Leighton's divorce was heard. In a theatrical gesture Rattigan secretly enjoyed, she entered the court supported on his arm, dressed from head to toe in black, as if in mourning. John Mortimer, the barrister playwright who was acting for her, later said it was one of the easiest 'undefendeds' of his career. Hermione Baddeley claimed that Leighton's marriage to Laurence Harvey had reduced her to 'a gibbering mass of nerves'.[2] She had become frightened of him and he was violent when drunk. Rattigan's own feelings towards Harvey were more complex. When the American impresario David Merrick invited Harvey to star as Lawrence in the Broadway production of *Ross*, a role for which he might have been very suitable, Rattigan, who had right of veto on casting, quietly but firmly blocked it. He thus denied Harvey an important opportunity of gaining recognition as a serious stage actor in addition to his fame as a film star. However, a few years later, Rattigan was one of the few mourners at Harvey's sparsely attended funeral. He had a sympathy for anyone as unloved because of his emotional failings as Harvey soon became. But he continued to have a deep affection for Leighton as well. In February, Rattigan turned over his flat in Embassy Court in Brighton to Michael Franklin. In its place he bought a house in Brighton. Called Bedford House, a Regency building with a view of the sea, one of its features was to be a

Margaret Leighton bedroom, kept exclusively for her use whenever she wanted it.

By April he was off to stay in a villa in Ischia rented from Sir William Walton. There he intended to work on the two plays he had said he was writing for Rex Harrison. The first, now provisionally called *Like Father*, was more or less finished. The second, *Like Son*, was to be the serious play about a scandal or a resignation in a politician's family. Inspired by recent rows and resignations in both Macmillan's Conservative government and in the Labour Party, it was to contain a part for Rachel Roberts, with whom Rex Harrison had by then started a much publicized affaire.

In May, Rattigan turned up at the Cannes Film Festival, where the press stage-managed a meeting between him and some marijuana-smoking 'beat' poets, headed by Allen Ginsberg. Rattigan announced that he had gone to Cannes in order to write a preface to the third volume of his *Collected Plays*, in which he intended to kill off Aunt Edna. The book did not in fact appear for another three years, and then he only tried to modify the image of Aunt Edna by writing his preface as a mock trial in which Rattigan is being sued for libel by Aunt Edna for trumpeting abroad a distorted and perverted image of her. He knew he could not kill off Aunt Edna without it seeming an insincere gesture and without being accused, once again, of bending to popular demand. Like it or not, she was his most famous character and he was stuck with her. In any case, he had long said that by Aunt Edna he meant 'the great audience', not merely prurient, matinée-going old ladies. He still held the view that for a dramatist to deride or dismiss the audience was suicide, sacrilege to the god of drama, and that it was audiences rather than critics who, sooner or later, established what was or was not a masterpiece. The fact that since 1956 audiences had worn jeans rather than dinner jackets was to be welcomed, he said, but did not alter his thesis about the dramatist's relationship with the public or the primacy of character and plot over ideological content. The only development that had surprised him was the continuing popularity of Samuel Beckett, Ionesco and the 'anti-dramatists', but he remained confident that the public would soon see them for what they were and dismiss them.

It was hardly surprising that Rattigan did not complete the preface to the third volume of his *Collected Plays* in 1962. By the summer he was deeply involved with two new plays. One the play about a political scandal he had said he was writing for Rex Harrison, the second inspired by a disgraced financier at the height of the Great Depression, Ivar Kreuger, a new biography of whom had appeared a few weeks earlier.[3] By June, the play for Rex Harrison had been lost to the stage for ever. It was being transformed into a television script. This was the result of an approach by the BBC who, with thirteen other European television networks, were trying to attract the best writers in each country to write for the medium. At that time television could only pay seven hundred and fifty to a thousand pounds for a play, and many highly paid dramatists refused commissions. To overcome this, each of the television networks in the scheme undertook to commission a play from a leading author and guaranteed to produce all the plays commissioned. This would guarantee the authors fees of up to thirty-five thousand pounds each and an audience of up to eighty million. It was an offer bearing prestige and a fee not far short of what he might receive in Hollywood, and contrasted with the fee of three hundred pounds and two showings he had received for his earlier television play, *The Final Test*. Rattigan had been brooding for more than six months on his idea about a scandal inside a Tory cabinet, and this seemed to offer a way of doing it. Two other recent happenings were also on his mind. One was the use of television in American politics, particularly the confrontations between Kennedy and Nixon during the 1960 presidential election, which Rattigan had seen during his visit to America the previous autumn. It was Nixon who fascinated him. Although shown up by Kennedy in their confrontations, Rattigan remembered how some years earlier Nixon had pulled himself back from political extinction in California, after being accused of accepting bribes, by an emotional television appeal. Then Nixon had appeared, complete with his wife and the family dog, and tearfully told the electors that all he had done was to allow someone to pay for a family holiday which they all, particularly his wife, needed after the years of struggle in politics – from which they had never made money. He had not done anything that any other ordinary man who cared for his family would not have done under similar circumstances. It was powerful emotional stuff and banished the 'Dirty Dicky' image for long enough for him to become Eisenhower's vice president.

The other happening which affected Rattigan's choice of format was the series of interviews done on British television by John Freeman (himself a former junior Labour minister and editor of the *New Statesman*) with leading public figures, called *Face to Face*. These had represented a breakthrough because Freeman had probed into the private lives behind the public faces, a thing previously unheard of on television, which until then had treated public figures more as idols to be worshipped than as people to be examined. In one interview, Gilbert Harding, a radio and television personality noted for his gruff manner, had actually broken down in front of the cameras and wept. Harding could have been a Rattigan character, he was such a typical victim of a peculiarly English type of emotional repression. Rattigan must have identified very closely with Harding during the passage in the interview with Freeman that caused him to break down:

FREEMAN   Is there any truth in the notion I have at the back of my mind that it is this particularly deep relationship that you obviously had with your mother which has made it impossible for you to marry?

HARDING   Yes, I think so. You see, my sister didn't marry and I didn't marry and my mother was a widow when she was thirty and so when we came to live together we put up a sort of cloud of sexual frustration that was enough to block out the sun, and I've never been particularly affectionate; one of my troubles is that I don't attract affection very much and when I do I tend to repel it. I'm not an intimate or cosy person. I don't really like living in close contact with anybody. I think I'm pretty difficult to live with.

FREEMAN   Are you lonely as a result of this?

HARDING   Profoundly lonely, yes.[4]

Once again Rattigan found a way to write a television play that exploited the distinctive qualities and strengths of the medium. His plot centred on a television interviewer, David Mann, whose vastly popular series of *Face to Face*-type interviews is dedicated to bringing to the public 'the truths of the heart'. He is preparing an interview with Sir Stanley Johnson, a cabinet minister whose carefully fostered 'I'm an ordinary no-nonsense bloke like you' public image has put him in line of succession as a possible prime minister. During the course of his preparation for the interview, information comes into Mann's possession that Johnson accepted payments amounting to bribes while a junior minister and that he has a mistress and is not the beer-drinking family man of the people he has made himself out to be. The play traces the various personal and professional pressures which are put on Mann not to use this information during the interview. Johnson, who seeks the advantages to his career that an appearance on a popular television programme will bring, uses his contacts in the Establishment in an attempt to tame David Mann and turn the interview from an inquisition into a showcase.

Rattigan's demonstration of the various ways in which pressures are brought by powerful people to bear on supposedly impartial television organizations remains as relevant today as when he wrote it. Finally Johnson is panicked into making a direct appeal to the public on the air, emotionally confessing to accepting one small payment. He offers to resign, but asks the viewers if he has really done anything that each of them would not have done. Like Nixon, he claims that all he did was to accept a little help so that his poor wife could have a much-needed holiday. He even manages to bring in the family cat, which we already know he secretly hates. At the end of the interview, viewers' telephone calls start to come in. The overwhelming majority support Johnson and say he must not leave public life. But, suggests Rattigan, the few dissenters may one day swell into a large enough chorus to chase him from office. Prophetic, indeed.

The play, *Heart to Heart*, was finished late in 1961 at Noël Coward's home in Jamaica and the BBC started work on the production in the early spring of 1962. Rattigan was staying at the Hotel Martinez in Cannes, and Alvin Rakoff, the man selected by the BBC to direct it, was despatched with a producer to meet him. On the night they arrived, Rattigan took them to dinner in the best restaurant in Cannes and then on to a nightclub. The main feature of the club was a troupe of exceedingly beautiful girls who finished their act by stripping down to G-strings. The two BBC men were carried away by the exotic life Rattigan had introduced them to, and the producer seemed to want to sleep with one of the strippers. Rattigan, ever hospitable, approached the girl and offered a generous sum of money. When this was refused he approached the owner of the club with a still bigger sum. Even when it reached five hundred pounds for one girl for one night, the owner and girls still resolutely refused.

The next day the producer had to return to London, but Rattigan and Rakoff again visited the club. Still mystified by their unyielding rejection, Rattigan invited the owner, an American lady, to have a drink with them. After some time, because, she said, she could see they were 'men of the world' and she was in any case a fan of Rattigan's, she confided in them. Her strippers were in fact men who had had elaborate hormone treatment. She made it an absolute rule not to let her 'girls' meet British men as they became not just abusive, but violent, when they found out the truth. However, as she realized that Rattigan and Rakoff were 'not like the Englishmen who usually frequented the club' she offered them a 'girl' each for the night. It was now their turn to refuse. Rattigan said: 'I like men, not men dressed as women,' while Rakoff said that he liked women.

Rakoff found Rattigan a strange mixture of confidence and diffidence. Flitting between the fleshpots of Europe, dashing off Hollywood scripts for *The VIPs* and *The Yellow Rolls-Royce*, he nevertheless asked Rakoff more than once whether he wouldn't rather be working with Wesker or one of the new playwrights. He confided in Rakoff and his wife about his homosexuality, subscribing to the view expressed in a new book on the subject that its root was not overpowering mother-love but a failed relationship with his father. He asked anxiously about the Rakoffs' relationship, not its sexual but its emotional aspects. He was eager to hear about any other liaisons they might have. He was now turned fifty, but his mischievous energy was undiminished. His relish for gossip was unabated and he could still not resist setting up disputes between people and then sitting back to see the results. He loved making indiscreet remarks to journalists about celebrities he knew, but then swearing them to secrecy, tantalizing them with information they could not use and watching them squirm. A regular companion at this time was Robin Maugham (Somerset Maugham's nephew and also a writer) who, like him, had a house in Brighton. Maugham was a frequent visitor to Ischia, where Rattigan now had two villas managed and let for him by the stage designer Michael Weight. A procession of the great and famous came to stay – Elizabeth Taylor, Richard Burton, Roddy McDowell. Rattigan's stays there were often what he termed 'very debauched'. On one holiday he and Robin Maugham sat up together with a bottle fourteen nights in a row until sunrise. One evening Rattigan appeared in a very distraught state: he had lost the only script of *The Yellow Rolls-Royce*. There was a frantic search of the villas, before Maugham eventually found it on top of a ladder propped up against the side of his house.

The least popular person in the 'Rattigan set' at this time was still Michael Franklin. Rattigan's other friends still thought he treated Rattigan badly. In *Variation on a Theme*, one of the characters had been given the line: 'Adrian . . . He's hell, that one. He'll have to go . . .' And sure enough, shortly after the production of that play, Adrian Brown had gone, leaving the field clear for Franklin.[5] Almost everyone who got to know Rattigan in the early 1960s was struck by how 'besotted' he seemed with Franklin, noticing his extraordinary generosity to him. A scene typical of the kind that so distressed the people who cared for Rattigan was witnessed one day by Robin Maugham and a group of Rattigan's friends while they were sitting drinking by the harbour in Ischia. After 'making eyes' at a local boy, Franklin left to go off with him. When he returned some time later, Rattigan, not wishing to make a scene, passed him a note saying, 'Don't you ever do that again in my presence.' Franklin then ran off, jumped into a little sports car (a gift from Rattigan) and roared away. What so distressed Maugham was that Rattigan, instead of ignoring Franklin, asked Maugham to accompany him in the Bentley so that he could follow Franklin and make it up with him. This was by no means the first time that something similar had occurred.

Another regular visitor to Ischia was Vera Rattigan, still sprightly, even in her seventies. Adrian Brown had found only two or three years previously that Rattigan had got very anxious if he discovered that his mother had called him on the telephone while he was out and Brown had answered. But now Rattigan had given up careful concealment of his homosexuality even in his mother's presence. She never made any comment, except occasionally to tick him off for his bad language. Peter Osborn acted as Vera's courier-escort on her journeys to and from England, and if he was around she would make some mildly disapproving remark, while playing up to him in a kittenish way: 'Terence, dear, you really must not say that – particularly in front of the clergy' (by this time Osborn was preparing for ordination in the Church of England).

Although the law on homosexuality had still not been reformed, there had been another debate in the House of Commons about liberalizing the law (a new young Conservative MP called Margaret Thatcher was one of those who voted in favour of the motion). There had also been two comparatively explicit films, one about Oscar Wilde, the other the ground-breaking *Victim*, starring Dirk Bogarde, about the blackmail of a homosexual. Rattigan was now more relaxed about preventing any hint reaching the public. As late as 1959, he had briskly put down a Danish reporter who asked too bold a question about his bachelor status. He still played the game for journalists, especially when they asked questions about him and Margaret Leighton. But his plays themselves, and particularly his statements about *Ross*, left no one in any real doubt about where he stood. Rattigan was instrumental in persuading Robin Maugham to publish a novel called *The Wrong People*, which had a homosexual theme. It appeared in America under a pseudonym and flopped, but Rattigan pressed him to publish under his own name in England. The result was a bestseller. Maugham was very touched to receive a telegram from Rattigan on his sixtieth birthday: 'Dearest Robin, your uncle thought you would never make a writer and I thought you would never make sixty. I am delighted we have both been proved so triumphantly wrong. Great love, Terry.' It was, however, typical of Rattigan that at about the same time he said to another friend: 'Maugham! He couldn't write bum on a wall; and if he could, he'd spell it Baugham.'

While they were working on *Heart to Heart*, Rattigan took Alvin Rakoff to meet Elizabeth Taylor and Richard Burton, who were in Rome making *Cleopatra*. Despite his first unfortunate encounter with Burton, when he had made a drunken pass at him and then agreed to him being fired from the cast of *Adventure Story*, Rattigan hoped to persuade Burton to play David Mann in *Heart to Heart*. After making a series of lunch dates with Elizabeth Taylor, each of which was cancelled, Rattigan and Rakoff were finally invited to meet her at the studios. They were shown into a very long room where Miss Taylor was sitting at the far end. As they approached, Rattigan muttered to Rakoff, 'Nobody could live up to this entrance!' After the meeting with Taylor and Burton, Rattigan returned triumphantly to England brandishing Richard Burton's signature on an agreement to play David Mann in *Heart to Heart,* opposite Ralph Richardson as Sir Stanley Johnson. Elizabeth Taylor and Richard Burton were not yet married, but Rattigan became one of the great champions of their relationship. If they really loved each other, he kept telling them, then they must allow nothing and nobody to stand between them. He told Rakoff one day that he would probably write a Burton-Taylor story. Appropriately they did later play the tempestuous lovers in *The VIPs*, based on Vivien Leigh's fog-thwarted flight with Peter Finch.

But filming on *Cleopatra* dragged on far beyond the schedule, with the result that Burton was unable to play David Mann in *Heart to Heart*. The recording was made at the BBC Television

Centre in November 1962, with Kenneth More in the part. Press reactions were very favourable. In the *Daily Express*, Herbert Kretzmer said that *Heart to Heart* was a savage exercise in Establishment-debunking which brought Rattigan into common alliance with Osborne and Wesker.[6] The only notable person who seemed not to like it was John Freeman. Television drama was just entering the decade of its greatest strength and had Rattigan been prepared to concentrate on writing for television rather than films in the next few years his reputation during the last fifteen years of his life might have been very different. Rattigan's greatest strengths as a writer, his emotional probing of the deepest and most personal feelings of his characters, were ideally suited to the intimacy and intensity achieved in the best television studio drama of the 1960s and early 1970s.

As the week of previews and press conferences leading up to the transmission drew on, Rattigan went down yet again with a virus infection. The day before the transmission date, Thursday, 6 December, he was in the London Clinic with jaundice. He watched the play from his hospital bed. A few weeks later, although still not fully recovered, he was strong enough to embark on a ship bound for Hong Kong at the start of a voyage round the world. There were by now serious fears about the state of his health, but it was hoped that the cruise would give him the relaxation he needed for a full recovery. He tried to avoid the other passengers, but inevitably it became known that the famous playwright was on board. His fellow passengers became inquisitive and wanted to know what he was doing. 'Oh,' he assured them, 'I'm travelling with my secretary and writing a play.' So that explained it, the passengers told one another, and it accounted for the little old lady they had noticed going into his cabin every morning: an embellishment that so delighted Rattigan that he gleefully passed the story round among his friends in Ischia on his return. The person the passengers had mistaken for an old lady was Michael Weight, whose nickname among Rattigan's intimate circle was, appropriately, 'Mother Weight'.

By March, when he reached New York on his way home,

Rattigan seemed completely recovered and he threw himself into arrangements for the production of *Man and Boy*, the play about the disgraced financier Ivar Kreuger, which he had embarked on at the same time as *Heart to Heart* in the spring of 1961.[7] By early June 1961, Rattigan had been about halfway through a first draft, and felt confident enough about the way it was turning out to write to Binkie Beaumont about it. Although Rattigan had got the idea from Robert Shaplen's newly published biography, the spark that had fired Rattigan's imagination was his discovery that Krueger had had an illegitimate son. The issue of public façades covering private corruption was much in his mind during 1961, and Rattigan wondered how Krueger's son would have reacted to the public unmasking of his father as an arch-criminal. *Man and Boy* is the first of a sequence of plays, continuing until Rattigan's death, which feature boys who have their illusions about their father-figures shattered. In this sequence of plays it is possible to detect Rattigan undertaking a gradual reassessment of his relationship with his own father and of his father's importance in his own development. In the play, the financial wizard (whom Rattigan significantly gave a Romanian rather than a Swedish background and renamed Gregor Antonescu) is presented as a heartless villain who has built his empire on fraud. The man without feelings is an emotive figure for Rattigan, while Antonescu's illegitimate son, Basil, is by contrast weak: a musician who has run away from his father and believes he hates him, but who discovers he really admires him. The boy is a socialist who believes that the collapse of capitalism must usher in a better alternative.

Rattigan had decided to centre his plot around Antonescu's attempt to lure the chairman of a powerful business corporation into a deal which would give him one last chance to save his own business empire from collapse and himself from exposure and ruin. Knowing the man, Herries, to be a homosexual, Antonescu pretends to be one himself. He arranges to meet Herries in the flat of his estranged son, Basil. His intention is to imply that Basil is a young lover whom he would be willing to make available to Herries in return for his agreement to a merger between their two companies. Writing to Binkie Beaumont about the play on 7 June 1961, before he had completed a first draft and while he was still undecided as to whether *Man and Boy* would be a full-length play or one of two one-acters, Rattigan said,

> ...moneywise I don't need to work for (five) years, so why should I? For one reason only, dear Binkie, and you know it... in the hope of increasing my reputation. Rex Harrison, the Haymarket, and H. M. Tennent productions are all nice things to have, and God knows I don't scorn them, but, for me, they don't, any of them, come near the point – which is terribly simple – namely, will this new play(s), be good or bad? Nothing else matters. Nothing at all...

He goes on to say that if no management will do it, it will not matter as it will be published and '...possibly be read by some historian of the theatre in fifty years time and pronounced as "the best work of a fashionable contemporary dramatist: ironically never performed in his lifetime"'.

By the end of June, Rattigan had finished his draft. It had turned into a full three-act play. He had it typed and taken to London for delivery to Binkie Beaumont. As Rattigan noted to himself, the essential shape of his play was: 'Act One: revelation to the audience that Boy, despite protestations to the contrary, loves Man. Act Two: revelation to the audience that Man, despite his brutal treatment of his son, loves Boy... Act Three: final and irrevocable rejection by Man of Boy, without letting Boy know of his own need and his own love...'

Beaumont was enthusiastic, but cautious. In mid-August Glen Byam Shaw, who had directed *Ross*, flew out to Ischia for a week of discussions about *Man and Boy*. Rattigan quickly became worried by Byam Shaw's reaction. Central to Rattigan's concept for the play was Antonescu's essential inhumanity. He should be 'as evil as Iago', but Byam Shaw resisted this idea, suggesting to Rattigan that he, and Rex Harrison as well, would want to soften the character into someone Rattigan described as merely 'naughty and charming as Raffles'. Before Byam Shaw left he swore

Rattigan to absolute secrecy about what had been said. But as soon as he had gone Rattigan wrote again to Beaumont. He started by dismissing Byam Shaw's reaction as being due to conflicts within his own psychological make up: 'Both of us know the real truth that lies behind Glen's one-hundred-and-fifty-percent masculinity, and neither of us are anything but hugely sympathetic to it. But both of us occasionally need reminding of it.' As worrying as Byam Shaw's own reaction were the reported comments he had passed on to Rattigan from Rex Harrison, the play's intended star. Rattigan told Beaumont that Byam Shaw and Harrison wanted to weaken 'the essence of the play', which, Rattigan said, was '. . . the conflict between inhumanity (the Man) and humanity (the Boy) . . . Effeminacy = homosexuality on the stage is usually embarrassing. But effeminacy = weakness = softness = contrast to virile father, and *minus* abnormality happens to be the play, and that's that ... Rex doesn't want (Glen says) to pretend to be member of the "*brotherhood of buggers*" – exact quotation.'[8]

Realizing that Beaumont would be very worried by the prospect of losing *Man and Boy*'s intended star, three days later, on 25 August 1961, Rattigan wrote to Beaumont again. After restating his doubts about Byam Shaw as the director, he says he will tell Harrison that '. . . there is all the difference in the world between acting a thing, and acting *pretending to be* a thing. I shouldn't have to tell any actor this, but plainly I have to tell him. The second thing I'll tell him is that only a cunt wouldn't relish playing a shit.' Lest Beaumont should be in any doubt, Rattigan told him that he would rather withdraw his play than have its centre altered.

By September it was clear that no meeting of minds was possible: neither Harrison nor Byam Shaw would change their views about how the play should be done, and Rattigan would not rewrite it to meet their objections. However, Peter Glenville had now also read it and he immediately grasped the point. Rattigan was delighted, but the damage had been done. Beaumont was now seriously alarmed and started to prevaricate. In October there was a further setback. Peter Glenville had to pull out for tax reasons. Writing to Rattigan he said how sorry he was to have to let him down, but how proud he was that Rattigan should '... deliver such a strong bodyblow [which would] surpass the formless shock tactics of the new-wave writers...'

Rattigan was now seriously worried about the fate of his play, to which he attached so much personal importance. On receiving Glenville's letter he wrote to Laurence Olivier, begging him to do *Man and Boy*, 'There is no other actor,' he told him, confessing that he has been surprised at himself about how tough a line he has been taking over the play. Sacking people, he told Olivier, was not his usual line: 'That sort of moral courage is hardly my strongest suit. "Oh yes, dear Binkie, I do so agree," is more my line of dialogue.' But it was in vain. In November, Olivier phoned Mary Herring to say that he could not do *Man and Boy* because of his commitments as the director of the newly launched Chichester Festival Theatre. In a letter Olivier amplified his reasons for rejecting *Man and Boy*: '... I am not sure how much I want to shock them in a modern play. I mean passing off your own son as a queer and all that! I mean it's simply no good if they are simply not going to understand what the hell is going on – it's *not* that I'm frightened of *shocking* them.' But all was not lost. A few days later Rattigan received a letter from Binkie Beaumont suggesting other directors. For the moment, however, there were other commitments to which Rattigan now had to turn his attention. There were preparations for the BBC production of *Heart to Heart*, now almost complete, and the Broadway production of *Ross*, which was to star John Mills.

Dashing over to New York for *Ross*, he took the draft scripts of *Heart to Heart* and *Man and Boy* with him. As part of the build-up to the Broadway production of *Ross*, Rattigan gave an interview to the magazine *Theatre Arts*. He told his interviewer that although he had not realized it at the time, *Man and Boy* was a sequel to *Ross*: '*Ross* is about a man who tries to be God and this is about a man who tries to be the Devil. It's a different setting and period, but similar in theme. It's about one of those financial wizards who live without human emotion of any kind.' He also suggested, although he knew by this time that it was not true, that

Rex Harrison would be playing the lead.[9] At a party a few days later someone put the manuscript on a stand together with a score by William Walton and, as a joke, surrounded them with laurels and stood a candle in front of them. A quiet, greying man in his fifties, whom Rattigan did not recognize, picked up the manuscript and asked if he could take it downstairs to read. When he returned he expressed an interest in doing it. While he had been out of the room, Rattigan had found out who he was: he was the veteran film star, Charles Boyer.

When *Ross* opened on Broadway on 16 December 1961, it got a critical mauling. With typical *New Yorker* brio, the magazine dismissed it in a play on the words of the title: '*Ross*, A Portrait without Depth'. Deeply discouraged, Rattigan returned to Europe, breaking his journey to stay with Noël Coward in Jamaica and complete work on *Heart to Heart*. He continued to worry about who should star in *Man and Boy*, but thought no more about Boyer's expression of interest. But Boyer did not forget. In late May 1962, Beaumont phoned Rattigan to tell him that Boyer had been in touch with him and would be happy to play Antonescu in both London and New York. Eager as always to have a star, Beaumont told Rattigan that he believed Boyer would be ideal. Ever since he had started work two years previously on *Heart to Heart* and *Man and Boy* simultaneously, Rattigan had been switching concentration between the two plays in quick succession. So, in early June 1962, as soon as Alvin Rakoff returned to London to start work on the production of *Heart to Heart,* he was replaced as Rattigan's guest by Charles Boyer. Their discussions about *Man and Boy* did not really reassure Rattigan. Boyer had been a screen charmer, could he really convince an audience that he was the truly evil man whose coldness Rattigan had repeatedly said was the essential heart of the play? Also to engage Boyer would mean delaying production for a further year, with only a short run in London before a transfer to Broadway, as Boyer was reluctant to be out of America for too long. But Beaumont was insistent and Rattigan capitulated – the 'moral courage' he had boasted of to Olivier the previous November had evaporated.

The stress of more than a year of working on two plays at once, plus sudden script conferences and requests for additional sections of dialogue for the film of *The VIPs*, together with continuous heavy drinking and the fact he continued to feel that he, and more important to him, his work, had been rejected, were beginning to take their toll on Rattigan. Returning to England to take up residence in the house he had acquired in Brighton, he was not a happy man. The house, which he had bought largely at Michael Franklin's suggestion – in part so that he could pay him a substantial fee to design and redecorate the interior – was a disaster. Walking along the seafront on his way to a party given by his friend T. C. Worsley, Rattigan bumped into B. A. Young. 'I've just moved into my new house after waiting eighteen months,' Rattigan told him mournfully, 'and it's uninhabitable. There isn't a single room I can bear to sit in.' Shortly afterwards he took off to Scotland to play golf. But he continued to be restless. In October he was in America, for advance discussions about the New York production of *Man and Boy*. While he was there he sold Anatole de Grunwald another pot-boiling compendium-movie idea – *The Yellow Rolls Royce* – tracing the career of an elderly Rolls from grace to disfavour. The idea had come to him as he sat in his own Rolls in a London traffic jam, speculating on the looks of hatred, compounded with envy, he received from the occupants of other cars in the jam. His Rolls boasted a personalized number plate – TR100 – 'a vulgarity that attracted endless mockery from us all', according to B. A. Young.[10] He remembered also the old Rolls-Royce found by Puffin Asquith and Anatole de Grunwald while looking for locations in Iraq for the abortive Lawrence film; the car was said to have been used by General Allenby when he was in command of armies in the Middle East during the First World War. Rattigan's agent managed to get MGM to pay him a hundred and twenty-five thousand dollars for the outline and script, but the film has not stood the test of time and looks anaemic.

By December, as we have seen, he was suffering from jaundice. But by the time he reached New York, in the early spring of 1963, on his round-the-world trip with Michael Weight, he seemed completely recovered. While he was in America he completed arrangements for the Broadway production of *Man and Boy*, conferred with his agent Harold Freedman about the sale of film rights to *Heart to Heart* (for a fee of forty thousand dollars) and accepted a commission from the producer Ray Stark for an original scenario for a film musical about a ballet company, to be directed and choreographed by Herbert Ross with a score by Michel Legrand. In devising an original story, he planned to draw on the experiences of Adrian Brown, on his long-standing acquaintance with Frederick Ashton and on the story of Diaghilev and Nijinsky. In April, he sailed back to England aboard the *Queen Mary* and then went on to Ischia. There he complained to his early summer guests, who included Robin Maugham, of headaches and a sore throat. Every night his temperature shot up, but no one suspected there was anything seriously wrong with him. Because he had always been something of a hypochondriac, they tended to dismiss his illness: it was just 'Terry being unwell again and drawing attention to himself'. Some suspected that the jaundice that winter had really been incipient cirrhosis of the liver from the years of hard drinking. However, the tally of mysterious viral infections since his illness three years earlier, just before the opening of *Ross*, was mounting. The up-and-down pattern of his health was in itself a cause for concern, and a specialist had been called in. That spring, the specialist made a firm diagnosis: leukaemia. Ever since Kay Kendall's death, Rattigan had had a particular dread of leukaemia.

'At first I had to get over the alarming discovery that I am mortal. That not only would I die, but I was likely to do so in a short while.'[11] While still getting over the initial shock, he had to take steps to stop the news being trumpeted in all the papers. Above all, he didn't want his mother, who was due to come out to Ischia for an early summer holiday, to find out. He wrote to Robin Maugham, who had returned to England a few days earlier, telling him about the leukaemia but swearing him to secrecy. He wanted no one else to know. When his mother arrived, he got up from his bed and put on a brave show. He got through the holiday without her discovering the truth, although she must have suspected something, if only because he was now visibly losing weight. Having watched Rex Harrison nurse Kay Kendall, Rattigan had no illusions about the course it would take. Despite periods of remission, he would dwindle to an inevitable end. This, he was told, would be in about six months. He ordered his Brighton house to be put on the market and himself prepared to stay in Ischia, concentrating the rest of his time on the thing that mattered most to him: his writing. Rather than trying to complete one last 'great work', he got on with the commissions already in hand, the filmscript of *The Yellow Rolls Royce*, the outline for a new film idea he had had in which Rex Harrison would play Edward VII, and some final corrections to *Man and Boy*. In his condition, the heat of the southern Italian summer was debilitating, and he was relieved when a message arrived from Binkie Beaumont summoning him back to London for urgent consultations about the play. In view of his determination not to let anyone know how ill he was, he could not in any case refuse to go.

In fact, the summons to return was not what it seemed. Robin Maugham, who knew enough about leukaemia to know that the heat of an Italian summer would be bad for Rattigan, had let Binkie Beaumont into the secret and together they had concocted the excuse to get him back to England. Once back in London there would be medical rather than theatrical consultations. Rattigan returned, and by midsummer he was undergoing another round of tests and blood counts. Inevitably the news of his illness did leak out and before long a newspaper approached him with an offer to buy his story. He refused. But the whisper grew in theatrical circles. Binkie Beaumont had confided in Noël Coward, telling him that Rattigan had cancer – 'of the liver, presumably' – and when Rattigan wrote to Coward admitting that he had been unwell, Coward wrote to Binkie telling him that Rattigan was being terribly brave, but that '...reading between the lines, this optimism is false...' Then at a party an actor came up to him and said he was terribly sorry to hear that he was going to die. This brought matters to a head. Rattigan told his doctor he must go back to the specialist –'my executioner'– and force him to give an estimate of how long he had got. Rattigan claimed, unlikely though it may seem, that he was eventually given an exact date in September by which he would be dead. It was just after *Man and Boy* was due to open in London.

'A crash course in how to live' was what Rattigan later called those weeks. 'My priorities changed; time became the most precious commodity in the world. The most commonplace event was an occasion.'[12] He pared down his friendships, spent time only with those people he really liked and worked harder than ever before. He completed his film scripts and started to map out a serious play he had been intending to write about the law and insanity. He contributed an article about Aunt Edna to a new debate raging in the *Daily Telegraph*, and started to give confident interviews to journalists about *Man and Boy* and his film *The VIPs*, which were due to open almost simultaneously. In an interview he gave to Peter Evans of the *Daily Express* in early July, he said that he wished the critics would take him more seriously, pointing out that he was once an angry young man, but that anger does not sit well with middle age and that he had not been really angry since the Spanish Civil War, when his generation had really had something to be angry about.

He still attended cricket matches at Lord's, and the boyish, irreverent humour was largely undimmed. In June, a new Pope had been elected, and shortly afterwards he was watching a cricket match in the members' area at Lords when he spotted the famous cricket commentator, E. W. Swanton, considered by a number of fellow members to be a pontificating bore. Rattigan went over to him, and with a straight face and in a voice loud enough for the other members to hear, said to him, 'I so want to commiserate with you about not being elected Pope.'[13] Although he was cutting out dinner dates with insistent, but boring, London hostesses, and avoiding dull nightclubs, Rattigan still continued to go to parties. When he heard the smug, pretentious conversations of his friends he was apt to crash in with remarks like, 'You people are all fools. Don't you know you won't live for ever.' When his friends objected that his conversation was hardly calculated to brighten up a party, he would reply that if a man couldn't live to enjoy his own death what could he do?[14]

The appointed day was less than two months away when Stephen Mitchell prevailed upon him to seek yet another medical opinion, this time from the specialist, Sir Horace Evans. After more tests showing that the red corpuscle counts were not as low as expected, Evans told him he had not got leukaemia; he had had a series of virus infections which together made up a pattern that looked suspiciously like leukaemia. Evans is reported to have concluded by telling him, 'We haven't met before, but in view of the life I understand you have led you are a remarkable specimen.'[15]

When *Man and Boy* opened in Brighton for two weeks on Monday, 19 August 1963, prior to going on to London, Rattigan triumphantly announced to local journalists that he was taking his house in Brighton off the market. He confessed that he had not been too well since the winter, but that he had really started to feel better since he returned to Brighton a few weeks ago: '...the view might not be as good as Ischia, but the air is a damn sight better. Now I am taking walks along the seafront every day and I am taking up golf again.' In fact, blood tests were still being made regularly and he had only Sir Horace Evans' opinion to set against the diagnosis of the earlier specialist. He was by no means absolutely certain in his own mind that he was out of danger or that he would survive beyond the 'appointed day'.

Man and Boy opened in London on 4 September at the Queen's Theatre, the scene of the calamitous first night of *Joie de Vivre*. Rattigan, still half believing that this might be his last first night, waited anxiously to see how the show would be received. He had fussed during rehearsals, giving endless notes to the luckless director, Michael Benthall (approached after a long line of others had turned it down), and to the actors.

Although the programme credited Robert Shaplen's recent biography of the Swedish swindler/financier Kreuger for 'suggestions', the plot of the play was largely invention. Antonescu, as Rattigan had renamed Kreuger, is presented as an unfeeling monster. The tension hangs on whether the corporation chairman, who could save Antonescu's fortunes, will swallow the bait and believe that Antonescu's son, Basil, is sexually available in return for his cooperation in Antonescu's refinancing merger scheme. Regrettably Rattigan does not adequately explain the background to Antonescu's rejection of emotion and the underlying causes of his unscrupulous pursuit of power. At the very end of the play the voice of a radio announcer pronounces that 'to be absolutely powerful a man must first corrupt *himself* absolutely', making *Man and Boy* the third, with *Adventure Story* and *Ross,* in Rattigan's trio of plays about the corrupting qualities of power. It shares many of the other plays' essential weaknesses. Despite characteristic understatement, Antonescu remains essentially the villain of melodrama rather than a rounded human being. The other characters are either too unpleasant or not sufficiently developed fully to engage the audience's interest or sympathy. Set in Basil's flat in Greenwich Village in 1934, the play contains many allusions and plot details, some of which would have been recognizable to his friends some not, which reflect Rattigan's own concerns and relationships. Antonescu, a Romanian, speaks in diplomatic French to his son at moments of potential embarrassment, while his son develops a stutter whenever he has to reply in French. Antonescu, operating by methods that are reminiscent of Binkie Beaumont, employs people to maintain an 'intelligence system', filing away important, and potentially embarrassing, pieces of private information on the people he comes into contact with. When Antonescu turns up unannounced in the flat where Basil is living with a girlfriend, it recalls the way in which Frank Rattigan used to turn up unannounced when Rattigan was living in a flat in Hertford Street with Peter Osborn before the war. The fact that, at the start of the play, Basil has disowned his father because of his deceptions, and that his father regards him as a sissy, reflects Rattigan's relationship with his own father, as does the fact that by the end of the play Basil comes to recognize that he secretly admires his father. Basil's 1930s' socialism reflects Rattigan's own beliefs as a young man, while his realization during the play that his political beliefs are founded on falsehoods acknowledges Rattigan's own move away from the uncomplicated idealism of his youth. At the same time one can see in Basil an attempt to create a young man with some of the laudable qualities which the Lunts had removed from the young idealist Michael in *Love in Idleness*. Both Antonescu and Herries, the homosexual financier whom Antonescu hopes to ensnare, have clear affinities with Rattigan himself. Herries has even had a previous boyfriend who died of an overdose. The play's major failure is that Antonescu's final downfall is not brought about as a result of any interaction of the characters or confrontation seen on the stage, but through the discovery of further frauds, which we learn about from a radio announcement at the beginning of the third act. The play ends with Antonescu facing a lonely death; suicide is his only way out. The final speech of the play, by a radio announcer speculating on Antonescu's whereabouts, was remarkably appropriate to Rattigan's own situation on the first night as he waited unrecognized at the back of the theatre for the audience's reaction: 'Wherever he may be tonight...it is certain that this suave, cool, elegant and utterly charming personality is showing the same unruffled front that he has always shown to the world, through every crisis that has beset him...' Sadly, this portrait of Rattigan was no longer true. The stiff upper lip and public-schoolboy code were crumpling into a new kind of desperation. The instinctive writing of his youth had for the moment been replaced by a self-conscious striving after effect.

The reactions when they came were more contradictory than for any play he had written. In the *Daily Mail*, while admitting that Rattigan might not have explained the psychology of great men who turn to crime, Bernard Levin spoke of his 'unfailing dramatic cunning; his narrative power, faultless in its patient unwinding; above all, his restless imaginative curiosity about the springs of human activity; these fuse, hot and glowing, into his finest work and a play that outdistances all but a handful of authors writing in England today.'[16] In contrast, David Nathan in the *Daily Herald* started his review: 'The next time "disgusted" writes to complain that our young playwrights are obsessed with squalor and homosexuality and cites Terence Rattigan as the preserver of all the traditional values, I will recount the plot of *Man and Boy*.' He concludes: 'The whole play, in fact, seems false and hollow with much profundity intended and none achieved... The play is here for only eight and a half weeks before going to New York. New York is very welcome to it.'[17]

Rattigan again turned to blaming others for his failure. A week after the opening he wrote to Binkie Beaumont accusing the director, Michael Benthall, of 'staging rather than directing' *Man and Boy* and told him that he should accept Benthall's offer of resignation before the transfer to Broadway. Regrettably for Rattigan, although he cut and tightened, when it opened in New York in November 1963, *Man and Boy* (still directed by Benthall) received even less of a welcome than it had in London. American critics found it dull. The *New York Times* said that it appeared to be about 'an important and arresting theme', but it is hard to believe that, in its portrayal of Antonescu, 'it could avoid so thoroughly the meaning of such a life in its relation to society'. Noël Coward, who saw the play in New York, concluded that Boyer was very good but 'the play really won't do'. It ran for only 54 performances. In the same week as *Man and Boy* opened at the Queen's Theatre, Rattigan's film *The VIPs* opened in London. This also received a critical drubbing. Rattigan was so incensed that he did something his pride would never have allowed him to do earlier in his career, but which he now seemed to do with self-demeaning frequency. He wrote a twenty-five-page letter to his most outspoken critic, Alexander Walker. Walker sought an interview with Rattigan. When they met, Rattigan confessed how much the critics had hurt him; how he now dreaded even the word 'craftsmanship' when applied to him, as it was usually intended as 'a term of abuse meaning insincere'; how he hated the insistence that he was 'glib', 'slick', that his work was 'unfelt'; how painful it was to be told he had 'a cliché-ridden mind'.[18]

Notes

1 See *Vivien* by Alexander Walker, Weidenfeld & Nicolson, London, 1987.
2 Hermione Baddeley quoted by Des Hickey and Gus Smith in *The Prince – The Public and Private Life of Laurence Harvey*, Leslie Frewin, London, 1975.
3 *Kreuger, Genius and Swindler* by Robert Shaplen, André Deutsch, London, 1961.
4 *Face to Face with John Freeman*, BBC Books, London, 1989.

5   Adrian Brown did come back into Rattigan's life briefly a few years later.

6   *Daily Express*, 1 December 1962.

7   Rattigan had also used the title *Man and Boy* for his earlier unrealized play about Evans and Christie.

8   The Rattigan Papers, op. cit. In Nicholas de Jongh, op. cit. Anthony Page has recalled the difficulty experienced in recruiting a male star willing to play the homosexual lead, Redl, when the Royal Court produced John Osborne's *A Patriot for Me* a couple of years earlier.

9   The interview was not published until April 1962.

10 B. A. Young, op. cit.

11 To Sheila Duncan, *Daily Mirror*, 13 May 1964.

12 To Clive Hirschorn, *Sunday Express*, 20 September 1970.

13 Recalled by the writer Michael Meyer.

14 Interview with Sheila Duncan, *Daily Mirror*, 12 May 1964.

15 Some years later, when the specialist who had predicted his death was appointed as one of the Queen's physicians, Rattigan sent him a note saying that if he ever saw a medical bulletin posted on the gates of Buckingham Palace announcing the death of a Certain Person, he would send Her a note saying, 'Get a second opinion.'

16 *Daily Mail*, 5 September 1963.

17 *Daily Herald*, 5 September 1963.

18 *Evening Standard*, 25 October 1963.

19

Lost to Permissiveness?

Beset though Rattigan now felt, his health continued to improve.
The predicted date of his death had passed, and he stayed on in
New York after the première of *Man and Boy* to work with Noël
Coward on a birthday tribute to Sir Winston Churchill – *Ninety
Years On* – which BBC Television had commissioned for
transmission late the following year. He was still in New York for
the opening in December of a musical adapted from *The Sleeping
Prince, The Girl Who Came to Supper* (with lyrics by Noël Coward).
This was much better received than *Man and Boy* had been,
although a number of critics went out of their way to say how
much Harry Kurnitz had improved on Rattigan's original script.
So, with his film work, the money continued to roll in.

Early in 1964, Rattigan was back in England, commuting
between the Brighton house and his Eaton Square flat. The old
high-life had resumed and he seemed surrounded by friends. Yet
the inner loneliness which he had quietly endured all his life was
now greater than ever. Bereft of the success which had been such
an important element in his fulfilment, Rattigan needed friends,
but by now many were dead or had grown apart from him. Too
many of those who now surrounded him were sycophants rather
than friends. The brunt of his loneliness and uncertainty fell
increasingly on his staff – a long-suffering housekeeper and a
secretary. Mary Herring had threatened to leave him once too
often, and on the last occasion Rattigan took her at her word and
did not ask her to return. When a new secretary proved

inadequate, he consulted Binkie Beaumont, who suggested Sheila Dyatt; she had previously worked in Beaumont's office and, like Rattigan, lived in Brighton and also had a flat in London. She quickly found that Rattigan was not an easy person to work for. The disciplined hours of writing were now a thing of the past. He rose late, worked for perhaps an hour before lunch and then again for an hour later in the afternoon. He now often wrote at night and even when he finally went to bed took a notebook with him. Everything was still written in long hand in exercise books, but he was continually running in and out of his secretary's room, changing a word here or a detail there. If she stayed on typing late in the evening, he would tell her he didn't pay her to stay until all hours, but if she didn't stay he complained that she wasn't interested.

One of the things which most shocked Sheila Dyatt was the number of people who simply sponged off him, especially when Rattigan was in Brighton. There was always a gang of people in the house, eating his food and downing his drink, who never seemed to reciprocate his hospitality. One Easter, when Sheila Dyatt had been with him only a short time, Rattigan collapsed with a fever in the Eaton Square flat. There was no one else to look after him, so Sheila Dyatt stayed and nursed him through the Bank Holiday. His mother telephoned him, but no one else came near him. It was then that she first realized the full extent of his loneliness. Here was this great and successful man, with 'lots of people who liked him, but no one who really cared for him', left alone in his sumptuous London flat to fight his illness, the only person with him a secretary he hardly knew. Yet there remained an oddly aloof quality about his attitude towards her. A few months afterwards he suddenly said out of the blue, 'I don't think you're really interested in the work. I'm sure you'd make a very good secretary to a businessman or something, but you're not right for me. I think you'd better go by Christmas.' She replied that if she was going she'd go quicker than that. Next day, when she told Binkie Beaumont that she had been fired, he was very surprised; Rattigan had been singing her praises to him only a day or two before, and he advised her to ignore it. Rattigan, who had always rung people at all hours of the day and night, then telephoned Beaumont. As always with anything that might be remotely tricky or could lead to some sort of confrontation, he circled round the point before making it clear that he wanted Beaumont to patch things up for him with Sheila Dyatt. Beaumont, having already spoken to her, said nothing more. The only time Rattigan referred to the incident again was some time later when he told her he was glad she had not left.

One of those who availed themselves of Rattigan's generous hospitality in Brighton was T. C. Worsley. Unlike others, he did at least repay him with his pen. We have already noted his defence of *Variation on a Theme*; but when J.W. Lambert in the *Sunday Times* and Penelope Gilliat in the *Observer* raised doubts about the real subject of *Man and Boy*, suggesting it was about an older man and his boy lover thinly disguised to look like father and son, Worsley again raced to Rattigan's defence. In an article in the *London Magazine* he said: 'This seamy line of personal smear is not criticism; it is gossip journalism.'[1]

Shortly afterwards, Worsley devoted a full-length article to a critical reappraisal of Rattigan's work.[2] He pointed to the recurrent themes of humiliation and obsession, saying that, although their range may be narrow and their scale small, they are true and exact, persuading us to experience and sympathize with a corner of human weakness. Although, as early as 1957, the novelist C. P. Snow had raised objections to the way the critics underrated Rattigan, Worsley's defence was long overdue. But it failed to provoke any further reappraisals. For Rattigan himself Worsley's efforts, though gratefully received, made little real difference. He was too honest with himself to be able to overlook the fact that Worsley was beholden to him. He remained more discouraged than he had ever been in his life. It says much for Rattigan that even at this low ebb he backed others in whom he saw ability. In May 1964, Rattigan went with Vivien Leigh to see a try-out at the Arts Theatre of a new play called *Entertaining Mr Sloane* by a young, first-time author called Joe Orton. He immediately spotted that here was a new talent – 'What Orton had to say about England and society had never been said before.'

He detected the authentic voice of the 1960s and he admired its construction: '... Orton understood that a play, if it's any good, has to have its basis in structure. What was going to happen to Mr Sloane? It's no more than telling a story. And there's no theatre without story and never has been.' Vivien Leigh saw the play as funny and rather camp, but Rattigan told her it was much more than that. 'I saw style – a style that could be compared with the Restoration comedies. I saw Congreve in it. I saw Wilde. To me, in some ways, it was better than Wilde because it had more bite.' Vivien Leigh told Rattigan that if he felt so strongly about it he should write to the author.

On 14 May, Rattigan wrote to Joe Orton:

DEAR JOE ORTON,
I don't think you've written a masterpiece – and you wouldn't want me to say you had – but I do think you have written the most exciting and stimulating first play (is it?) that I've seen in thirty (odd) years' playgoing.

He went on to tell Orton that he was convinced that before the decade was out he would write a masterpiece, '... provided, always, that you don't try to...'

Orton was delighted to get a fan letter from Rattigan, and Rattigan invited him to lunch at The Ivy. To the horror of the waiters, Orton turned up dressed in black leather and without the obligatory tie. Rattigan liked Orton immediately and they ended up being photographed with Rattigan's orange and yellow tie draped around Orton's neck. Rattigan approached the impresario Donald Albery, offering to invest three thousand pounds in a full West End transfer for Orton's play. In June, *Entertaining Mr Sloane* opened at Wyndhams and became a critical hit. In July, Rattigan asked Orton and his boyfriend Kenneth Halliwell to spend a weekend with him in Brighton. Halliwell turned out to be a major embarrassment. Wildly jealous of Orton, he arrived wearing make-up and determined that Orton would never get a chance to speak at all. He talked on and on, suggesting that it was really he who had written Orton's play. Rattigan was unconvinced and by the second day of the visit very bored. He called on his neighbours, Laurence Olivier and Joan Plowright, to come over and help relieve the pressure. Halliwell then proceeded, in Rattigan's words, to bore the royal pants off them as well. In November, Rattigan invited Orton to be his companion on a trip to Hong Kong, provided that he left Halliwell behind. Orton refused and the friendship between Rattigan and Orton lapsed.[3]

One person who made some return, beyond the obvious, for Rattigan's hospitality was the Midget, Michael Franklin. He now arranged all the decor of Rattigan's homes. As well as the flat in London and the house in Brighton, Rattigan had bought a mansion in Scotland which he had little use for, but in which Franklin often lived when Rattigan was abroad. Unfortunately Franklin's ideas about interior design were another frequent source of dismay to his friends, and sometimes to Rattigan himself. His Brighton bedroom, which faced the sea, had heavy curtaining, and Rattigan regularly complained to Sheila Dyatt that there wasn't enough light. As he never did anything about it himself but continued to complain, she volunteered to replace the curtains with some light net. This she duly did and Rattigan thanked her. But when she came in the next day the net curtains had gone and the heavy ones were back. Rattigan looked a bit sheepish but made no comment. On an earlier occasion Vivien Leigh had come to visit the house. She was horrified to see what had been done to a perfect Regency façade and an impeccable interior. The outside had been flattened so that it looked as if it belonged in Belgravia rather than Brighton; the inside had been stripped completely and the staircase replaced by one from a Chelsea antique shop. Despite frantic signs from Rattigan, Vivien Leigh went on at length about what an awful shame it was to have spoiled such a beautiful house. Franklin was out of sight in a lavatory, but overheard everything she said. Robin Maugham, who was there, and other friends among whom the story quickly spread, were delighted at the Midget's discomfiture.

The problem of loving someone who is widely disliked by one's friends, and continuing to love them despite being able to see their faults, was at the root of Rattigan's next play. In the spring of 1964, he concluded a deal with Associated Television. They were to transmit two or possibly three of his stage plays – *Variation on a Theme* and *The Browning Version* were the ones finally agreed on – and he was to write a new play specifically for television. 'The most important drama shows ever produced for television,' announced Lew Grade, boss of ATV, with characteristic ebullience. The new play was to be introduced by the Duke of Edinburgh, and some of the proceeds were to go to his Award Scheme and a fund with which he was associated to save the sailing clipper, the *Cutty Sark*. An appropriate subject was needed and Rattigan voiced a long-nurtured idea of a play about Nelson. Discussions were held at Buckingham Palace. Rattigan told the Duke of Edinburgh that after some consideration he didn't think he could do it. Nelson was too much of a success story. A further meeting was arranged but Rattigan still said he hadn't found a way into the subject: 'The man was too bloody successful. I can't be sorry for him, and I can't write about anybody for whom I can't feel compassion. I prefer failures.' (Sam Duveen, Ron's choreographer patron in *Variation on a Theme*, was also unable to like people unless he first felt sorry for them.) It was Prince Philip who got over Rattigan's block. He reminded him that Nelson did suffer one great defeat – he was unable to get the nation to accept his mistress, Emma Hamilton.

That fired Rattigan's imagination. Why had the nation, which honoured Nelson's wishes over so much else, refused to accept his bequest of Emma Hamilton? 'It wasn't meanness – they gave a lot of money to his brother. It wasn't snobbery – she was the wife of the British Ambassador to Naples and was perfectly acceptable as Lady Hamilton. And it wasn't prudishness – that age was as permissive as our own. Then, I thought, isn't it just possible that no one liked her? That she was an absolute cow?'[4] That was the breakthrough. Researching into the history of the romance with Lady Hamilton, Rattigan came to the conclusion that it was probably Nelson's first real love affair. 'He was probably forty when he met her. His wife was a cold woman. And though he'd probably spent a lot of time in brothels, this was the first time he'd done it with an expert.'

The script which Rattigan finally came up with was for a play to be called *Nelson – A Portrait in Miniature*, set during Nelson's last brief visit to England just before the Battle of Trafalgar. Nelson, already a national hero, is cheered in the streets. The only blemish on his image is Lady Hamilton, who is no longer the beauty of Romney's portrait, but an overblown, thick-trunked, coarse, hard-drinking forty-year-old. When she appears at his side, the cheering wavers and some people actually laugh or jeer. The conflict between Nelson's public and private life is exposed through a hero-worshipping teenage nephew, George Matcham. George cannot understand why Nelson, a compassionate man loved by both his family and his men, has treated his estranged wife with such cold cruelty. He is unable to believe any evil of Nelson and assumes that Lady Nelson must have done him some awful wrong. During the play he is steadily disillusioned about his hero (who is, of course, a father figure). He is shocked by Lady Hamilton's vulgarity, which so ill befits the woman beloved by his hero. Nelson confesses that he can see Lady Hamilton as the world sees her and dies 'a thousand deaths' each day he is with her. Yet he cannot bear to be apart from her. 'How can a love be so deep that begins and ends in the bed?' he asks rhetorically, answering that although a love which can overcome his disgust isn't perhaps the love most suited to a hero '. . . it is the one most suited to me'. Therefore, it is 'the greatest, the most enduring and the deepest of all.'[5] By contrast, in *Man and Boy*, Antonescu, the man with lots of sexual partners, but none he loved, had said, 'I don't think you can measure loneliness by the dimensions of a bed.' *Bequest to the Nation*, as the Nelson play was called when it was later adapted for the stage and published, was dedicated to the person whose love had been the underlying subject of its conception – 'For M.J.F.' – the initials of Michael Franklin.

Shortly after the television transmission of *Nelson – A Portrait in Miniature*, Rattigan announced that he was selling up his homes in England and going to live abroad. 'Everything,' he explained, 'has happened together. This winter I've had three virus infections and, as I said to a member of the Test team, "Unlike some of you, I catch everything that's going."'[6] His doctor had been pressing him for some time to live somewhere warmer in the winter. It was a decision he had resisted for years, and even now he didn't intend to leave Britain for good. However, he had signed contracts to write two Hollywood film scripts and more offers were coming in all the time. The tax advantages of staying out of the country for at least a year were enormous. On top of that his landlords in Eaton Square had just announced that they were going to double his rent. It seemed a good moment to go.

Inevitably, there were deeper reasons underlying his decision. As he told a BBC Radio interviewer only a few weeks before his death, he had kept his vow not to yield to the financial temptations of Hollywood until he discovered that any and every play he wrote was going to get 'smashed' by the critics. 'I had no chance with anything. They didn't give me reasons for it, they just said, "It must be bad; it's just the old effete theatre. It has nothing to do with the ongoing movement of the time." I thought the time has come. I'm not getting any younger and I haven't saved any money.'[7] Hollywood was still making him handsome offers of up to a hundred and fifty thousand dollars per film and he decided he had better cash in while he still could. Even if it was not work he liked, it was easy.

He did not return to England for a year. Even when his mother fell ill the following Christmas he did not enter the country, although he flew back across the Atlantic to be near her. He got as close as Paris and, from an apartment he had taken there a few years previously, telephoned her twice a day in the London Clinic where she was suffering from eye trouble. It had been pointed out to him that in previous cases people who had set foot in the country for whatever reason without completing a full year of non-residence had been made to pay tax in both Britain and their chosen country of residence. For almost a year Rattigan shuttled restlessly about the world like some latter-day Flying Dutchman, moving uneasily between Hollywood, his villa in Ischia and his Paris apartment. In February 1967, he rented a house, somewhat unfortunately named 'Sitting Pretty', in Bermuda. As this was one of the few places in the world where there was no income tax, where the climate was suitable and which was still under British rule, he decided to look for a permanent home there.

By May 1967, he had established his non-residency in the United Kingdom for tax purposes and was able to return for brief periods. His first priority was to visit his mother, who was now eighty-three. She still had the house at Pepsal End that Rattigan had bought for her and Frank during the war. In June he was back for Ascot and in August he returned again to attend a thanksgiving service at St Martin-in-the-Fields for the life of Vivien Leigh. Between visits aimed at getting his financial and domestic affairs into good order he still kept up with his friends and the London theatre. The Brighton house and some of the furniture had gone, bringing in over thirty thousand pounds, and the Eaton Square flat was no longer his. He had bought a house overlooking the Atlantic in Bermuda and was redistributing his remaining furniture and valuables between this house, Ischia and storage depots. Sheila Dyatt was kept on a retainer, but increasingly Peggy French, with her husband Harold, the director of the original production of *French Without Tears*, was taking over the administration of his daily routine. Michael Franklin continued to look after his possessions in Britain, and his agent, solicitor and other advisers took charge of documents, manuscripts and other matters. Rattigan, such a dedicated patriot, was a tax exile. It was a role he hated.

In 1967 the Homosexual Offences Act had at last decriminalized homosexual acts in private between consenting males over the age of twenty-one. Rattigan's friend Cecil Beaton recorded in his diary:

Of recent years the tolerance towards the subject has made a nonsense of many prejudices from which I myself suffered acutely as a young man. Even now I can vaguely realize that it was only comparatively late in life that I would go into a room full of people without a feeling of guilt...But when one realizes what damage, what tragedy has been brought on by this lack of sympathy to a very delicate and difficult subject, this should be a great time of celebration...For myself I am grateful. Selfishly I wish that this marvellous step forward could have been taken at an earlier age. It is not that I would have wished to avail myself of further licence, but to feel that one was not a felon and an outcast could have helped enormously during the difficult young years.[8]

Despite the more liberal attitude in Britain, Rattigan remained guarded about his sexual preferences. As in his youth, it was only while abroad that he felt able to let his hair down sexually. When he was staying in his flat in Paris he would frequently pick up young men in local bars and take them back with him for the night. Pegs French had taken a flat below his and as a result found herself called upon to provide services that someone less broad-minded might have regarded as beyond the call of duty. Whenever a young pick-up proved troublesome, as happened not infrequently, Pegs French would receive a phone call, asking her to come up to Rattigan's flat immediately to help him to get rid of the young man.

The late 1960s remained an arid time for Rattigan. The movie dollars still rolled in, but in the era of 'swinging Britain', anti-Vietnam demonstrations and the Rolling Stones, he seemed hopelessly out of date. As though to underline his irrelevance, someone revived *The Sleeping Prince* at the St Martin's Theatre. Reviewers recalled with astonishment that Laurence Olivier and Vivien Leigh had only fifteen years earlier wasted their talents in this flimsy bubble: 'Give it a whiff of flatulence and it shatters,' said the *Observer*.[9] The only faintly cheering event of that year, as far as Rattigan's survival as a serious playwright was concerned, was a fifteen-minute trifle written for Margaret Leighton to perform as a solo turn in a BBC2 Television slot called *All on Her Own*. In it she played a widow missing her booze-and-rugby-loving husband, addressing the empty sofa where his body was found, wrestling with her sense of guilt and trying to convince herself that his death was an accident. Although one might see it now as a pale forerunner, twenty years ahead of its time, of Alan Bennett's brilliant series of television monologues *Talking Heads*, by Rattigan's lights it amounted to a competent exercise, but little more.

By the time of its transmission in September 1968, Rattigan seemed once again to be on his deathbed. He had been in Pompeii for a musical remake of *Goodbye, Mr Chips*, starring Peter O'Toole and Petula Clark. This was the script he had left England to write in Hollywood two years earlier. He had done a workmanlike job, bringing elements of Crocker Harris to the character of Mr Chipping. Nevertheless, it was a sad waste of his talent to have to rework material from his masterpiece *The Browning Version* in this way. On location he was seized with a violent pain and rushed to a Naples hospital to be operated on for a burst appendix. For two weeks he lay in a state of delirium, thinking, as did all those around him, that he was on the point of death. He found he was no longer afraid of dying; he had crossed that bridge during the leukaemia scare. Sheila Dyatt rushed to Naples when she heard the news. Again Rattigan had given instructions that his illness must be kept out of the papers for fear of upsetting his mother. By the time Sheila Dyatt arrived the appendix had gone gangrenous. The hospital was dirty and Rattigan's soiled bedclothing was left unchanged. He was hot in the day, but cold at night as he was only covered with a sheet. He suffered agonies of dehydration, yet the Italian doctors refused to give him water. Fortunately, Rattigan's own doctor, Dr Buky, was holidaying in Italy and was found and called in. In the meantime, Sheila Dyatt had also informed the British Consul; she did not want to be accused by Rattigan's mother and friends of keeping the whole affair secret if he did die. At the climax of the infection, Sheila Dyatt and Dr Buky left the hospital for the night, convinced Rattigan would not survive till dawn. But when they returned the next morning they found him sitting up in bed. From then on he began to gain strength. Although the hospital was loath to lose such a famous patient, he was removed as soon as possible to Switzerland and then on to Baden-Baden. There he finally recovered. The crisis had lasted some six weeks.

Rattigan went back to making money from commissioned filmscripts. He had already completed *A Killing for Hawks*, a melodrama about First World War pilots, based on a novel by Frederick E. Smith. In Rattigan's hands it became an overwrought emotional drama about love, guilt and suppressed homosexuality. It was not made. In 1969 he interested John Boulting in a story about explorers in the Australian outback in the 1860s and completed a two-and-a-half-hour script, entitled *Burke and Wills*. John Boulting was not happy and it was never used.[10] The one script that did seem to interest him was that of a musical set in the ballet, an idea put to him by Ray Stark in 1963. Other things had repeatedly got in the way, but by December 1968 he had completed a full script. Entitled *Pas de Deux*, it consisted of fifteen scenes, seven songs and seven dances. As soon as it was finished he put it in a large envelope and wrote on the front 'Unrevised and uncorrected. In fact, unread.' Other commissions and concerns intervened and it seems he may never have got it out again. Nevertheless, the concept lingered. Five years later he incorporated many of the ideas he had explored in *Pas de Deux* into an even more startlingly interesting television script about Nijinsky, which had been commissioned by the BBC.

Pas de Deux, although raw and unfinished, bears some careful examination, partly because it reveals a sharp movement away from the conventional box-set style of theatre which had been his *métier* for most of his career – so much so that it is quite hard to see how, in practice, the script could be adequately staged in a conventional commercial theatre – and partly because of what it tells us about Rattigan himself. It calls for performers of even greater virtuosity than the original Broadway cast of *West Side Story*, a large orchestra and the use of the whole theatre. Sharpened up and polished considerably, with the right performers, it could be sensational. Yet its subject matter does not suggest that it would find a sufficiently large popular audience to sustain the high production costs.

Leon is an ambassador. Although married, he maintains a series of boys with 'slanting eyes'. His new boyfriend is David, a boy from the local ballet. David is '...an emotionally retarded narcissist looking for a father substitute...' He hates his stepfather and is scared of his mother. But David is also the boy in the ballet company whom all the girls fancy. David's main partner in the ballet is Amy. When they dance together they are technically perfect but cold. Brought together by a choreographer who makes them swap roles, clothes and genders, they start to dance with feeling and come together personally. With the ice between them broken, Amy can ask David why he likes having Leon around.

DAVID   For a whole lot of reasons.
AMY   One of them bed?
DAVID   Oh no. That's just the price I have to pay for having him around. It's a small price to pay, and worth it.

Amy tells David that she feels exactly the same way about men. Giving them sex is 'such a little thing to do to please people'.

Later Amy asks Leon what makes a man prefer boys to girls. Leon replies, 'Well, in three words – retarded emotional development.' To which Amy responds delightedly – 'But that's what David's psychiatrist says is the matter with *him*.' Later in the same scene Amy asks Leon:

AMY   What you mean is that in loving David you're just loving yourself when you were young, and David just loves you loving him. Right?
LEON   Right – with reservations. The use of the word 'loving' is a little inexact.

In another scene Leon's wife discovers that he has gone to bed with Amy. She is 'understanding' about him sleeping with boys, but this makes her furious. Sleeping with a girl is a threat to her.

Willy, the choreographer, plans a new ballet which he intends to call *Orgasm*. 'What is the only reality humanity knows? The sexual act. What for a few moments brings mankind close to the angels? The sexual act.'

Leon's one real virtue is complete honesty, complete self-knowledge. His pagan philosophy teaches him that there is no harm in anything, provided that it does not harm other people.

The extent of *Pas de Deux*'s alignment with Rattigan's own philosophy, with his own feelings and thoughts about himself, and about his relationships with Chips Channon, Kenneth Morgan,

Peter Osborn, Michael Franklin and a succession of other young men, is clear. Because this script has not been worked on and honed down, and because much of it was intended to be expressed in dance and music, it is much less encoded than anything else among the writings that survived his death. If suitable music could be composed for it, and sufficiently versatile performers found, it would be interesting to see the effect of even a small-scale experimental staging.

After the television transmission of *Nelson − A Portrait in Miniature* Binkie Beaumont had asked Rattigan to rewrite and expand it for the stage. He did not complete the task until 1970. Beaumont was delighted and accepted it immediately. Retitled *Bequest to the Nation* it would be the first new play by Rattigan to be seen in the theatre for seven years, even if it was only the rewrite of the already flawed television script. By the time of the opening in the West End in September 1970, there was an air of expectancy and a seeming willingness to welcome Rattigan's return. In turning television script into stage play, Rattigan had tried to heighten the contrast between Nelson's blameless public image and the vulgarity of his mistress. The result was not only to make her coarser but to make the whole fabric of the play cruder. He also dragged in uneasy parallels and allusions to *Antony and Cleopatra* which, if anything, showed up the play's shortcomings rather than pointing an effective ironic contrast.

At the heart of both the television and stage versions of the play lies Nelson's sexual obsession with Emma. In the stage version the nature of Nelson's sexual love emerged in a frank, even raw, confession to Hardy. In answering the question, 'How can any love be respected that begins and ends in the bed?' Nelson summed up the feelings that had obsessed Rattigan's writing since the early 1950s and whose roots went back still further:

...in the release of the bed there lies an ecstasy so strong and a satisfaction so profound that it seems that it is everything that life can offer a man, the very purpose of his existence on earth ... You must remember, you see, that even at that age, I was still the rector's son who, from the cradle, had been preached the abomination of carnal love, and the ineffable joys of holy wedlock. But when at last I surrendered to Emma, I found – why should I be ashamed to say it? – that carnal love concerns the soul quite as much as it concerns the body. For the body *is* still the soul and the soul *is* still the body. At least they are for me...

The conflict between carnal and spiritual love had always been a theme of Rattigan's writing, but starting with *Separate Tables* the two had become increasingly divorced. This can be traced both to events in his private life in the early 1950s – the growing sexual dependence on 'rough trade' deplored by his friends – and to the increasing freedom to write frankly about sex in the theatre which accompanied the more liberal atmosphere of the late 1950s.[11] Starting with *Separate Tables*, but particularly from *Variation on a Theme* onwards, sex had become something to be bartered, something to be ashamed of and finally an open obsession. Although a reflection of the experience of Rattigan the man, this did not help Rattigan the dramatist. A shy man, with a veneer of social ease but tortured by self-doubt, Rattigan made his art depend upon the oblique, the implicit, the struggle of frightened, damaged people to find self-expression and fulfilment in a society whose strict moral codes inhibited them. Once the moral codes had been relaxed in the theatre, Rattigan was not only out of fashion, he was stranded. Not only his technique as a writer but his background and lifetime's conditioning meant that however passionately he resented the old hypocrisies, he was not equipped to make do without them. The result was that when he tried to confront sex in his writing, however frankly and sincerely, in the permissive atmosphere of the post-Osborne theatre, he seemed evasive, insincere and sometimes actually embarrassing. In the nineteen years between the production of *Separate Tables* and the appearance of *In Praise of Love*, his best play was undoubtedly *Heart to Heart*. Perhaps because of the less permissive atmosphere of television, the play did not depend on sexual revelations; the drama was taut and controlled. It depended on implicit dishonesties, threats and conflicts in both the emotional and political relationships, culminating in a confrontation and a self-revelation whose power lay not in its frankness but in the realization of its full implications. Similarly, in the unperformed *Pas de Deux*, the requirements and restrictions imposed by the conventions of the musical produce something much more economic, creative and satisfying.

By the time he came to write *Bequest to the Nation*, the creative process of assimilation of experience and feelings described by Keith Newman at the time of *Flare Path*, had been replaced by a more direct translation of those feelings and experiences on to the page. The result was to undermine the essentials of Rattigan's art. He had long feared that critics and commentators on his achievements would make him self-conscious. Now their rejection had the same effect.

As though to provide an opportunity to rub salt into the wounds of Rattigan's rejection, a revival of *The Winslow Boy* opened six weeks after *Bequest to the Nation*. The prevailing theatrical atmosphere of 1970 highlighted the sometimes cumbersome craftsmanship of this exercise, while making suspect the ideals which had guaranteed its acceptance by the theatregoing audience of 1946. In *New Society*, Albert Hunt wrote a devastating denunciation of Rattigan headed 'Danger: craftsman at work'. Noting that the writer of the programme note had said that nostalgia was the 'in' thing that autumn, Hunt examined Rattigan's technique, concluding that the much-praised craftsmanship was overrated: 'It consists largely of setting up the obvious in a somewhat laborious way.' In dismissing *The Winslow Boy* he dismissed Rattigan's entire output: 'It's...facile knowingness that's at the heart of Rattigan's theatre. For if he sacrifices everything to plausibility it's not because of some dramatic theory, it's because that's the way he responds to his material. Every complexity can be explained away, every facet of human experience reduced to a simple matter of manipulation. What *The Winslow Boy* says in the end is that there may be wrongs, but that in our good old British democracy, with its right-thinking men of all parties, always ready to come together that right may triumph, we, the audience, live in a world in which everything can be solved by a little craftsmanship. It may be that smugness, not nostalgia, is really the "in" thing in the autumn of 1970.'[12]

In an article which asked the question which many critics had long given up posing, let alone trying to answer, Ronald Bryden used the revival to wonder why Rattigan had not turned into the playwright he promised to become twenty-five years earlier. In *The Winslow Boy*, he said, he saw 'the weaknesses in his later work: the easy, sentimental, mechanical plotting, the flattering reassurance of the middle-class audience'. But Bryden was also one of the first to detect, or rather to rediscover, some of the real underlying significance of what Rattigan had been up to. Comparing his position in the conventional British theatre of the 1940s to that of dramatists working behind the Iron Curtain, he pointed out that Rattigan had been forced into 'hiding the play he wanted to write behind the one his audience would accept'. Lurking beneath the self-congratulatory glow of *The Winslow Boy*'s main plot Bryden noted the way Rattigan had kept running the apparently unimportant sub-plot about the suffragette daughter's engagement to an army officer and the way in which he used this at the end of the play to explode the virtuous face of the Establishment. Here he showed the other face of traditional British 'decency', the one that is willing to ruin the girl's happiness in an attempt to stop the Winslows' 'anti-Establishment circus... the face which frowns on breaking ranks, rocking the boat, wearing long hair, showing emotion, which would exclude foreigners, jail homosexuals, birch louts who won't stand up for the Queen'. This was the same Establishment which prided itself on its tolerance. Bryden noted that the 'new wave' of dramatists were now themselves part of the Establishment, but he concluded: 'There hasn't been much tolerance in, for instance, the treatment of Rattigan and his recent work.'[13] The revival of *The Winslow Boy* ran for more than six months, almost twice as long as the new play, *Bequest to the Nation*.

The bitterness of the attacks on Rattigan were compounded of more than a reaction against his years of success; they owed a great deal to the disappointment of those who had hoped for so much from him and were disillusioned. Once the restrictions on what could be said in the theatre had been lifted, he had tried after 1956 to come out into the open, but he was not at ease there. He was the creature of his upbringing; his strength was implication, not rhetoric; he was better as a subversive in an occupied country than as a revolutionary at the barricades. Like many a resistance fighter he was not an effective leader after the liberation. However, by 1970 the liberators of the 'new wave' had themselves begun to look like a theatrical dictatorship. Perhaps Rattigan would find a new subversive role. Ronald Bryden had begun his article on *The Winslow Boy* with a statement: 'Against the gains our new theatrical freedoms have brought us should be set one major loss: Terence Rattigan.' He ended: 'The play stands up, a monument to the playwright we lost to permissiveness.'

Notes

1   *The London Magazine*, October 1963.
2   *The London Magazine*, September 1964.
3   The quotation from Rattigan and much of my description of Rattigan's involvement with Joe Orton is based on *Prick Up Your Ears* by John Lahr, Allen Lane, Penguin Books Ltd, 1978.
4   Rattigan to Howard Kissel in an interview in *Women's Wear Daily*, 17 April 1973.
5   ATV production script.
6   *Daily Mail*, March 1966.
7   Interviewed by Sheridan Morley, op. cit.
8   Hugo Vickers, op. cit.
9   *Observer*, 12 May 1968.
10 In the thirty years since Rattigan wrote it there have been a number of expressions of interest in filming *Burke and Wills*. A few years ago United Artists bought the rights and Rattigan's script could yet become a film.
11 The Lord Chamberlain's censorship had finally been done away with in 1968. Together with the repeal of laws against homosexual acts by consenting males in private, this was one of the long overdue reforms enacted by Harold Wilson's Labour government.
12 *New Society*, 6 November 1970. Today Albert Hunt's article seems even more stuck in its period than the Rattigan play he attacked.
13 *Observer*, 6 November 1970.

20

In Praise of Love

In June 1971, Rattigan was sixty. His best birthday present was undoubtedly the knighthood conferred on him in the Queen's Birthday Honours list. He was only the second playwright to be so honoured since the First World War – the first being Noël Coward. On the lawn of his Bermuda home the staff erected a homemade banner offering their congratulations to 'Sir Terrence'.

Whether it was the knighthood or the fact that he was missing England and had in any case now saved enough money from film scripts to be able to afford to live in England again, is uncertain; but a few days before the publication of the honours list the newspapers welcomed Rattigan's announcement that he had decided to resume living in England. When news of his knighthood broke, the *Sunday Express* commented: 'Many people must have been touched that in Mr Rattigan's case the sentimental pull of home was stronger than the appeal of tax relief. Then yesterday the rest of the world heard the news that Terence Rattigan must have known for many weeks: that he was being knighted in the Birthday Honours. Now, it may well be that the knighthood had no connection whatsoever with his return to Britain. But ought he not to have waited for the official announcement before giving us all that guff about the joys of friends, cricket and home?'[1] Rattigan objected strongly, and the paper published a retraction, saying that they had not meant in any way to impugn his motives for returning and accepted that his decision had been made months before he had received any indication that he was to be honoured.

The truth, as so often, probably lay somewhere between the two statements. The news of the honour may well have reinforced an already strong desire. His interest in returning cannot have been unconnected with his mother's worsening health. It is, however, curious that the actual announcement of his intention to return permanently did not occur until immediately after her death, at the age of eighty-six. In April she had insisted on moving, as was her habit, out of her small London residential hotel back into the family country house at Pepsal End for the summer, the house she had once described as 'the coldest house in Bedfordshire'. Shortly afterwards she went down with pneumonia. She died on 23 April 1971. In the last few years Vera had become a rather difficult and self-centred old lady. Although outwardly unchanged, relations between her and Rattigan had worsened. He had probably begun a reassessment of his attitude towards her before her death, but it only came to the surface in his work immediately before his own death, in his last completed play.

Plans to celebrate Rattigan's sixtieth birthday with revivals of his work suggested the possibility of the rehabilitation of his critical reputation. He moved into Claridges while he looked for a London flat and a country home near a golf course. He was to lecture at the National Film Theatre in connection with a season of his films. A London revival of *The Browning Version* was in preparation, which was to star John Mills, as well as numerous provincial productions. No less than four of his plays were to be produced on television. The most curious announcement was that Thames Television was to produce a Rattigan play which had been 'lost' for twenty-five years.

John Kershaw, the story editor of a series called *Armchair Theatre*, had written to all the agents of well-known playwrights asking for rejected or little-known plays. From Rattigan's agent, Dr Jan Van Loewen, he had received *High Summer*. This turned out to be none other than the third of the one-acters written for John Gielgud in 1947 to go with *Harlequinade* and *The Browning Version*. Unperformed and unlamented, *High Summer* is the play which B. A. Young dismisses as 'a very poor piece' belonging to the world of Dornford Yates, but which Binkie Beaumont had told Rattigan was 'a period jewel'. When Peter Duguid, the television director selected by Thames TV, read the script he became convinced that the management had finally 'gone mad'. However, he agreed to do it if Rattigan could be persuaded to make some alterations. Being used to 'the blood, sweat and tears' of Stratford, rather than the rarefied atmosphere of Binkie Beaumont's West End, which Rattigan personified, Duguid was extremely nervous before their meeting, which had been arranged in Rattigan's suite at Claridges. But Rattigan put him at his ease immediately when he said, after the introductions: 'I've been looking at this piece – it's awful, isn't it?' They parted with Rattigan promising that he would look at it again and do some rewriting.

Rattigan suggested Margaret Leighton for the principal role and she agreed to do it. But when the script came back from Rattigan and she read it, she said to Duguid: 'I don't know what he's doing letting this go on.' Duguid, still unhappy with the script himself, sent it back yet again to Rattigan, who by this time had returned to Bermuda. Duguid heard nothing for a month and was getting worried; at last it came back with a note from Rattigan agreeing that indeed the scene which most worried Duguid was bad and he had rewritten it, incorporating his suggestions. Duguid called a meeting with Margaret Leighton and Christopher Gable (playing the other lead) and together they decided there was enough to make it a reasonable production. Despite the strong cast, which also included Roland Culver, Thames gave it a cardboard production (it was finally transmitted on 12 September 1972) which did nothing to disguise its essential weaknesses. If Gielgud's original rejection of the *Playbill* idea as 'second-rate' stuff had been applied only to this play, it would have been fully justified.

Even after the birthday year was over, the honours and the revivals continued. In January 1972, there was a midnight matinée in Rattigan's honour at the Theatre Royal, Haymarket, at which he broke his rule of not appearing on stage for the first time since the opening of *French Without Tears* when he acknowledged the cheers at the end. At the beginning of May he spoke at a Gallery

First Nighters' Club dinner in his honour at the Criterion, attacking those modern playwrights who 'despise their audiences', and confessing that although he had tried to move with the times he recognized that now he really was 'an old square'.

Although he did not say it, when he addressed the Gallery First Nighters Rattigan already knew that he had only a limited amount of time left to him. A few days earlier he had been told by Dr Buky that he really did have leukaemia. His health had been suspect ever since his illness at the time of the television transmission of *Heart to Heart* in December 1962 and the leukaemia scare the following year. Despite periods of remission, he had had repeated bouts of illness ever since. In October 1971, he had been ill in Bermuda, but shrugged it off as flu. But this time, unlike 1963, there was no doubt about the diagnosis, although Dr Buky could not tell him how long he might have to live. As he had repeatedly told Binkie Beaumont and other close friends, all that really mattered to him was to write at least one great play before he died. The last few months or years would give him one last chance to achieve this.

Beyond his immediate circle of close friends, Rattigan was now being looked upon as if he were some old master whom people had suddenly discovered was still alive. The impression had been heightened perhaps by the fact that he had moved back into the Albany, taking over the double set of chambers H5 and H6 from Mrs Pat Frere (daughter of the novelist Edgar Wallace) and her husband. Arrangements for this had been made while he was in England the previous autumn and by the spring of 1972 he was comfortingly surrounded by pieces of his old furniture, the padded board on which he had written all his plays, and some additional antique furniture collected by his father and left him by his mother.

But before he could turn his attention to writing the 'one great play', he had to attend to the business of making money and fulfilling previously agreed contracts. First in line was the film script of *Bequest to the Nation*, which he had agreed to do for the autocratic Hollywood independent producer, Hal Wallis. For this he was to receive seventy thousand pounds (in today's money that would be over a million pounds). Rattigan had always had a cavalier attitude to Hollywood money, but now he regarded it simply as 'fairy-gold', and he hardly bothered to adapt the play at all. With just under three months to go before the filming was due to start, he received the film's director James Cellan-Jones in his Albany chambers. Cellan-Jones was apprehensive about meeting the 'great man', especially as he knew he was going to have to let Rattigan know that the script wouldn't do as it stood. Rattigan, who had not been well again, was sitting up in bed. Rattigan and Cellan-Jones's first meeting was conducted as though they were playing a stock scene themselves: 'naïve young director meets famous author' (Cellan-Jones was a distinguished television director, but this was his first feature film). Fortunately, Cellan-Jones is a modest man and was quite prepared to play his part. Unfortunately, some of the others involved in the production turned out to be not quite so unassuming.

In fact, Rattigan and Cellan-Jones soon became great allies. Rattigan nurse-maided Cellan-Jones and offered him moral support from then on, remaining calm and amenable in the face of Hal Wallis's dictatorial insistence on script changes and the unprovoked outbursts of some of the actors during the shooting. One actor who did not behave badly during the shooting was Rattigan's beloved Margaret Leighton, playing Lady Nelson. Now in poor health, she found the shooting a great strain. Rattigan also had to go back to hospital that summer, but he found the time and energy to go to Bath, where the film unit was doing location shooting, to comfort her and give her moral support.

Soon after the film was complete, the young American critic Holly Hill interviewed Rattigan as part of a postgraduate thesis. He left her in no doubt about what he thought of Wallis's interference. Wallis had removed the repetition towards the end of the script of the line about the soul being the body, and the body the soul, thus seriously damaging the central intention of the script. Rattigan complained to Holly Hill that Wallis did not understand the use of dramatic repetition. It had been said once, so it was out. 'It's very ABC with him.'[2] On its release the film was savaged by the critics. Although most of the attacks were levelled against Rattigan himself, he still found time to sympathize with Cellan-Jones. At the première, which was attended by Princess Alexandra and Lord Mountbatten, Rattigan and Cellan-Jones arrived without the paper invitations and were barred from the cinema by the commissionaire, who would not accept that they had anything to do with the film. Rattigan eventually managed to sneak into the back of the auditorium, but Cellan-Jones spent the entire performance in the manager's office.

Glenda Jackson, who starred in the film, was conspicuous by her absence at the royal première and in a television appearance made no secret of the fact that she thought she had given a poor performance in a part for which she had been badly miscast. Rattigan, who had so far maintained a dignified silence on the subject, now responded to the inevitable press questions. He did not think she had behaved very well, he said. Pressed further, he added gently that although he might be old-fashioned, in the old days 'one's leading lady didn't feel it necessary to say such things, even if they were true. A film is, after all, a team effort. Perhaps it is the new fashion to knock the film you're in. But she has not, so far as I know, returned her cheque.' Saying that he was trying hard not to damage the film's chances any more than Miss Jackson had already done, he claimed that she was very good, but added mischievously, 'In saying she's miscast I'm afraid she's right. It's a pity we didn't cast Liz Taylor, who would have loved to do it and would have done it for practically nothing.' (Miss Jackson was reputed to have received seventy thousand pounds for her efforts.) Finally Rattigan demolished her, proving he could be just as waspish, when he thought the occasion merited it, as any of the new generation had been about him: 'Of course Miss Jackson did leave rather a lot out – Emma Hamilton's love for Nelson, for one thing, which is quite important. She played her as a mean-spirited bitch, instead of a great-hearted whore, but I suppose that is her range. And she could not possibly look fat enough.'[3]

Revivals of Rattigan's early work increased rather than decreased in number after the end of his sixtieth birthday celebrations in 1971. His self-confidence had been so undermined by the critical hammering he had received in the years since 1956 that he was not at all sure how audiences might now receive even his past successes. When *The Winslow Boy* had been revived in 1970, he had told its director Frith Banbury that he ought to play the shortened Broadway text. But two revivals in the early 1970s were to prove particularly influential in helping a proper reappraisal of his achievement and had a great effect on Rattigan personally. The first, *While the Sun Shines*, opened at the Hampstead Theatre Club in December 1972.[4] When he heard about the revival, Rattigan nervously provided some rewrites for the director Alec McCowen, a distinguished actor directing his first play. Rattigan thought he might want to explain bits of the action and dialogue which would seem unintelligible or dated to a modern audience with no first-hand knowledge of the war. McCowen tactfully accepted but didn't use them. He recognized that *While the Sun Shines* was now a period piece and part of the interest in a revival lay in playing it as that.

When Rattigan arrived for the previews, having agreed to sit up on the stage after the performance and answer questions from the audience, he found the theatre had been adorned with pictures of Churchill, the youthful General de Gaulle, and old programmes which reminded their readers that 'tube trains don't run during air-raid alerts'. The foyer loudspeakers blared out Tommy Dorsey's 'I'll be Seeing You'. Although some of the parts were stupendously miscast, Rattigan was excited to find the predominantly young audience rocking in their seats with laughter. 'Oh, the whole thing is utterly reprehensible, and yet I thoroughly enjoyed it,' commented John Crosby in *Plays and Players*.[5] The same thing happened again six months later, when Frank Dunlop, in spite of opposition from the Arts Council (touched on in the Introduction to this book), staged *French Without Tears* at the Young Vic. The majority of the critics, although in some cases rather shocked or surprised at themselves, found that they too were laughing. 'So we were not wrong, those of us who remember *French Without Tears* as delicious, and somehow something more than a mere frolic,' began John Barber, a critic of the older generation and a contemporary of Rattigan's at Oxford, in his review in the *Daily Telegraph*.[6] His conclusion, that it was 'a beguiling classic of its kind', was echoed by the younger critics. 'The one great theme that runs through all our comedy and farce is the nervous fluster to which the average Englishman is reduced by sex, and Rattigan's play demonstrates this to perfection... Far from being a tenuous *divertissement* the play in fact mocks certain durable aspects of the English character with affectionate skill,' commented Michael Billington in the *Guardian*,[7] adding, 'and it's interesting to reflect that much of Rattigan's later, serious work... is likewise concerned with the paralysing emotional reticence of the English male.'

Rattigan was, in his own words, 'terribly encouraged'. Not least because as well as laughing new young audiences had found some substance in the comedy. They were more enthralled by the serious passage about the young man's pacifism in *French Without Tears* on the hard wooden benches at the Young Vic in the 1970s than they had been in the gilt and velvet of the Criterion in the 1930s. The boost to Rattigan's self-belief came at an important moment. At the time of the Hampstead revival of *While the Sun Shines* he had been working on a new pair of one-act plays and by the time of the Young Vic revival of *French Without Tears* he was waiting for this new double bill to go into production. Knowing as he worked that he was terminally ill, and believing that these two plays were likely to be his last, there would be every reason to suspect that whatever he turned out now might, in some sense at least, be Rattigan's theatrical testament. The text of the more substantial of the two plays, in particular, provides such abundant evidence for this suspicion as to leave the issue beyond serious doubt.

With the exception of *Heart to Heart*, written for television, all his plays since 1958 had been period pieces. In the more substantial of the two plays, *In Praise of Love* (ultimately the title given to the complete double bill), he returned to a modern setting and subject, while making no concessions to changes in theatrical taste since the 1950s. The genesis of *In Praise of Love* is complex, but the initial impulse and the necessary self-confidence seem to have grown from the spate of revivals and the renewed interest in Rattigan's work which began in 1971.

It will be recalled that in that year Stephen Mitchell had

announced a revival of *The Browning Version,* starring John Mills. To accompany this, a lighter piece had been needed to replace *Harlequinade,* which was now thought to be too dated. At first Rattigan thought of writing a play set before the opening of *The Browning Version,* showing Millie Crocker Harris before she married the classics master. This was quickly abandoned in favour of a lighter piece featuring an amateur company rehearsing *The Browning Version.* Rattigan had been very amused by the group of local nurses who had been rehearsing *French Without Tears* when he arrived in Freetown after the hair-raising wartime flight when he had nearly lost his manuscript of *Flare Path.* He had remembered that incident and other amateur productions, and decided to set his play among a group of present-day amateurs in a British colony, possibly Bermuda. A potentially disastrous notion, it was fortunately dropped. The important point that emerges from both ideas is the temptation to spoof the play which he had always regarded as his most accomplished work. 'If today I had to justify my choice of career before a heavenly jury, this is the play I would want to represent me,' he had said in 1957.[8]

The idea of doing a completely new double-bill of short plays seems to have grown out of the talk of reviving *The Browning Version.* He still had the comedy about a successful Marxist painter confronted by a conformist son, which he had completed for Rex Harrison in 1961. This had never been used, because the play with which it was to have been paired had been shaped into *Heart to Heart* in response to the BBC commission. Rattigan re-examined it. While keeping much of the surface form of a comedy, he decided to change and deepen it. In one of his most audacious dramatic strokes, he made comedy dialogue carry a deeply serious personal story. The painter was turned into a writer and the son into a Liberal, about to have his first play done on television. Most important of all, the wife and mother was dying of cancer, which the husband was trying to conceal from her. Rattigan also said that an ingredient in the final choice of subject had been Binkie Beaumont's suggestion that he should try a comedy about death.

From the time of Kay Kendall's death Rattigan had mulled over the idea of writing a play about her and the way Harrison had fought to preserve her happiness by keeping the truth about her illness from her until the end. There were, too, the obvious autobiographical elements from his own confrontation with the mistakenly diagnosed leukaemia in 1963, the time he had been given up for dead in the Naples hospital in 1968 and the recent definite diagnosis that he had leukaemia. Finally, and perhaps decisively in triggering off the completion of this long-contemplated project, the impresario who had been planning to present the revival of *The Browning Version*, his friend Stephen Mitchell, had recently gone through a similar ordeal, watching his wife die of leukaemia and trying to conceal the truth from her until the last possible moment. At a deeper level, the death of his own mother may have played a part in the play that finally emerged, especially in the discussion of how both son and husband will face the world without her.

The play is so packed with personal references and allusions as to make it unique in Rattigan's career. Perhaps because the play first began to take shape in his mind twelve or thirteen years earlier, and had never been long absent from his thoughts over the intervening years, his distinctive process of absorption and distillation had rarely worked more effectively. Inside a simple plot and a light texture is condensed a depth of feeling and a degree of perception equalled in its economy and richness only by *The Browning Version*. Rattigan had said, half-jokingly, to his publisher a couple of years previously that perhaps he ought to write his autobiography while his memory was still intact. The idea of doing some sort of autobiography seems never to have been far from his thoughts during these years. Inevitably, *In Praise of Love* operates on a number of different levels. But as a piece of elliptical, condensed autobiography, which would only have been understood at the time by a handful of people who knew him very well, and by them only incompletely, it is truly astonishing. Without dissecting almost every line, it is impossible to convey the concentrated richness of its autobiographical texture, but a brief outline of the plot and certain of the strands running through it may indicate some of its qualities.

The setting is the fourth-floor London flat of Sebastian and

Lydia Cruttwell. At the start, Sebastian is struggling to meet his deadline for an article about Shakespeare for the *New Statesman*. He is a Marxist who twenty-five years ago wrote a novel which was hailed as a minor masterpiece, but he gave up and became a critic ('joined the enemy') when the reviews of his second book were unfavourable: 'They all turned on you for not writing the original novel all over again.' He is, however, diffidently contemplating a new book. With the passing years his Marxism has become more rhetorical than real: 'He only spouts Marxist revolution as a spell to prevent its ever happening.' His son, Joey, a budding playwright, incenses his father by campaigning for the Liberal Party, portrayed by Rattigan as the new generation of idealists. Joey's mother, Lydia, is an Estonian refugee who married Sebastian after he found her in a Berlin brothel at the end of the war, where she had been working to save herself from death in a Nazi concentration camp. He married her to rescue her from the fate that would have befallen her at the hands of the Russians if she had been returned to her native country. She has incurable leukaemia, but is determined to keep the knowledge of it from Sebastian and to devote the rest of her time to finding someone to take her place as mother, wife and servant.[9]

The fourth character is Mark, their mutual friend and confidant. He is a best-selling popular novelist, whose books are snapped up by Hollywood for huge sums before they have even appeared. His work no longer gets reviews, the critics simply dismissing each new book as a carbon-copy of the last. Sebastian envies Mark, but sneers at his success and makes a show of boorish ingratitude for his lavish presents and hospitality. Mark's writing is not literature, he claims, but a sell-out, a calculated manipulation to maximize sales.

All four characters owe something to real-life models among Rattigan's acquaintances, yet are fully realized fictional people. Simultaneously, however, all four are facets of himself: Mark, the free-spending and publicly popular self; Joey, the youthful idealist clashing with his father and worshipping his mother, naïvely setting out to be a playwright; Sebastian, the literary idealist who, behind a bantering façade, hides both diffidence and strong emotions; Lydia, the refugee dying in the country of her choice, with so much love to give but no one with whom to share it, trying to face her own end without whimpering – as Rattigan himself was determined to do. Their clash is the clash within himself; and, in a more intense way than in any other play, the stage becomes the symbolic arena in which Rattigan works through the central conflicts of his own life. Yet there is no disguised striptease about this play. Nothing masquerades as what it is not; the charge that 'its real subject is something other than its ostensible subject' cannot be levelled at this play. Sex is subsumed to emotion; the conflicts centre on the revelation of feeling. It is a play about the nature and expression of love.

It takes the form of a psychological suspense story. The initial veneer of comedy is slowly peeled away as the audience is allowed to perceive the depth of emotion that each character hides behind jokes or boorish behaviour. By two-thirds of the way through, an almost unbearable tension has been created. The inevitable crisis is precipitated when Sebastian, who has that afternoon received final proof that his wife's condition is incurable, fails to come home in time for the transmission of his son's first television play. He has tried to keep the fact of his wife's illness from her and still believes he has succeeded, but knowledge of the certainty of her impending death has made him forget his son's play. When he returns, Lydia lashes out at him. Then, left alone with Mark, he breaks down and weeps. Cursing himself for his show of weakness, he questions whether, despite all their years of marriage, he has only really loved Lydia since he knew he was losing her:

Did I feel about her like this from the beginning? It's possible. And wouldn't allow myself to? Yes, possible. [*Angrily*] Do you know what *le vice Anglais* – the English vice – really is? Not flagellation, not pederasty – whatever the French believe it to be. It's our refusal to admit to our emotions. We think they demean us, I suppose. [*He covers his face*] Well, I'm being punished now, all right – for a lifetime of vice. Very moral ending to a Victorian novel. I'm becoming maudlin. But, oh Mark, life without Lydia will be such endless misery.

Yet, confronted with Lydia, Sebastian still cannot reveal his true feelings for her. So Mark allows her to find out that Sebastian knows the truth about her illness by revealing where he has hidden the papers with her monthly blood counts.

The audience now expects a tearful reconciliation and an open declaration of their true feelings. In a stroke of heart-breaking skill, which is symbolically and emotionally consistent, Rattigan denies them the sentimental ending. The pretence is maintained between the two, their love remains unspoken. Lydia, now aware that Sebastian's boorishness and unfeeling jokes are a cover for his feelings, has no immediate need to shatter his illusions. Now that she knows the truth it is easier for all three of them – husband, wife and son – to endure their situation so long as they continue to avoid too overt a confrontation of the pain which has been an integral part of the discovery of their love. For them, and for Rattigan, there is an eternal conflict between love and pain, between revelation and concealment. No element can be banished; all that can be hoped for is temporary equilibrium. The last ten minutes of the play are among the most perfectly crafted and economically effective passages anywhere in British drama.

The play is as fine a statement about the loss of illusions which had beset the 1970s as any written by younger and more obviously idealistic dramatists. It condemns both the easy permissiveness and the blind extremism to which disillusioned idealists have turned in desperation. It reminds them of the stern disciplines of rational moderation and true humanism. Joey attacks his mother for putting up with Sebastian's callousness, claiming that her concern for other people's feelings sounds like 'a gooey sort of ultra-Christianity'.

LYDIA There isn't any sort of ultra-Christianity. There's just Christianity. And if it's gooey – well, it's gooey.

JOEY I didn't know you were religious.

LYDIA It's wonderful how that word today is made to sound like some curious perversion – permissible of course, like all things, but rather unmentionable...

But Lydia is not a Christian. She maintains the discipline of love and consideration not out of blind belief, but out of self-awareness and rational choice, born of the hardest of experience: Catholic upbringing, Nazi and Stalinist terror.

On another level, Rattigan brings out many of his beliefs about writing in the exchanges between Sebastian, the critic, and Mark, the popular novelist. Sebastian calls Shakespeare: 'That complacent old burgher of Stratford-upon-Avon. God, he's so maddening. With his worship of the Establishment, he makes nonsense of everything we write... Well, Shakespeare *must* infuriate people like us who passionately believe that no man can write well whose heart isn't in the right place.' (By which, as Mark points out, he means 'the left place'.) 'He was both Royal Court and Shaftesbury Avenue, in fact – inconsistent.' At the climax, when he breaks down, Sebastian quotes Shakespeare: 'No Lydia.' 'She'll come no more. Never, never, never, never, never.' 'Oh, damn! I'll never review that bloody man again. I won't review anyone – after all, they all make you blub somewhere – if they're good.'

The extent of Rattigan's self-identification in this play is easy to trace, but it is much more difficult to detect in the second play in the double-bill. As with *The Browning Version* and *Harlequinade*, and the two plays in *Separate Tables*, Rattigan wanted plays which would meld by being the converse of each other. So if the first play was about real love unspoken, the second would have to be about unreal love spoken. In the first play there was plenty of love but too little said about it; in the second there would be no love, but too much would be said about it.

In contrast to *In Praise of Love*, Rattigan wanted the second play to be a purely escapist comedy, but shortly before he had started to write it he had told the film critic Derek Malcolm that he was no longer capable of writing that sort of play. He was too old and if he tried he would probably give way to anger or rage. What he came up with was a crude burlesque on *Tosca*, called *Before Dawn*. In it Baron Scarpia, the wicked head of the secret police, gives Tosca a choice, as in the play and the opera: either she shares his bed, or her lover Mario is shot as a spy. Reluctantly Tosca consents, but then Rattigan invents a new ending. Scarpia proves impotent, and is so embarrassed by the damage his failure will do to his reputation as a villain that he will either have to make good his failure or have Tosca shot too before the night is out. The play is unaccountably feeble, depending for its laughs on obvious double entendres. It is difficult to understand why Rattigan should write such a piece, or, having done so, consent to having it put on in a double-bill with one of his finest plays. Holly Hill has pointed out that not only is it a play unworthy of him but in it he appears to deride both his own playwriting tradition and himself. First, by burlesquing Sardou's most famous play, he is burlesquing the founder of the tradition of the well-made play which he himself was credited, or in some quarters accused, of having carried on and defended, even when it fell out of favour. Second, he pokes fun at one of his own recurring themes – the conflict between physical and spiritual love – the baron representing the former and Tosca's lover the latter. Rattigan actually makes a cheap joke about Tosca's lover being able to offer her only spiritual love because he is a homosexual. Finally, he uses Puccini's opera as a source of cheap gags, yet Puccini was the composer he most liked as background music while he was writing.

It is probably kindest to dismiss *Before Dawn* as an aberration. Yet one begins to suspect, in a dramatist as aware of his theatrical antecedents and his own dramatic intentions as Rattigan, a degree of deliberation. Is it not too complete to be an accident? We have already noticed two elements in the genesis of this double-bill that might support this thesis: the way in which the serious play reads like a testament, a final drawing together of the personal strands of Rattigan's drama; and that even when the plan was only to find a *divertimento* to go with a revival of *The Browning Version*, the play on which he was prepared to let his reputation stand, he was actively considering a send-up of it. May it not be, then, that *Before Dawn*, which was intended to be played second, so closing the evening, was meant as a final cynical pay-off to his whole career? A kind of pulling the building down on top of himself at the end?

After working through the winter in Bermuda on both plays, Rattigan completed them in mid-March 1973, shortly after his return to England. He sent them to Binkie Beaumont, who read them immediately. Early on the morning of 21 March, Beaumont phoned Rattigan, waking him up to tell him that in spite of his aversion to one-act plays, he liked *In Praise of Love* and wanted to present them as a double bill. Beaumont realized that as a result of the main play's genesis it might be a bit difficult to approach Rex Harrison about playing the lead. He suggested to Rattigan that if they could not get Harrison they might try John Gielgud. Rattigan rejected this idea. He was wrong casting, too old and too much the voice beautiful to suggest the outwardly boorish Sebastian. Turning to who should play Lydia, Binkie agreed that Rex Harrison's new wife Rachel Roberts was out of the question – much too tough and down to earth to play someone so essentially frail and vulnerable. He suggested Celia Johnson, who had made a career of playing suffering upper-class English heroines. Rattigan was against her as well, and proposed Joan Greenwood. It mattered to Rattigan, as never before, that the casting for this, his last theatrical testament was right.

The next morning Rattigan was shocked to get another phone call. It was to tell him that Binkie Beaumont was dead. He had died of a heart attack in his bed. Four days later, on 26 March, came another message, this one from Jamaica – Noël Coward was dead. Binkie Beaumont had been out of sympathy with the post-Osborne theatre. Since 1956 and the changes to the entertainment tax, his vice-like grip on the London theatre had been steadily prised lose. Coward had long since retreated to Jamaica, largely confining his forays into the theatre to occasional highly paid cabaret appearances in venues such as Las Vegas. Nevertheless the deaths within days of each other of the two people who had so coloured and dominated the theatre during the early years of Rattigan's career marked the final closing of a door on the theatre that Rattigan had known and understood. Within days of their deaths *The Spectator*, freed of the restraints of the laws of libel, published a devastating attack on both men. They reserved their most deadly venom for Beaumont, recalling his 'private auditions', conducted from the bedroom of his Lord North Street house, clad in black silk pyjamas, and the extent to which his personal sexual preferences had come to be reflected on the London stage. Exaggerated though the attack was, it increased Rattigan's sense that from now on he was on his own.

Once the immediate confusion caused by Beaumont's unexpected and sudden death had subsided, John Perry, who had taken over the reins at H. M. Tennent Ltd, phoned Rattigan and told him that they would still like to proceed with *In Praise of Love*. Perry suggested John Dexter, one of the associate directors of the National Theatre, to direct. Dexter was mainly associated with the Royal Court and the younger dramatists. He had directed the original productions of Arnold Wesker's *Trilogy* and, only a few months previously, Peter Shaffer's *Equus* for the National Theatre at the Old Vic. Although identified with the working-class realism of 'the kitchen sink' school, he was, with Lindsay Anderson, one of the Royal Court directors who in recent years had moved out from pure naturalism towards a more poetic, heightened style of production. He was an interesting choice to direct such a highly condensed work as *In Praise of Love*. Just as rehearsals were about to begin, in mid-August, Dexter wrote to his friend the composer Stephen Sondheim in America: 'You may have heard, I am doing a double bill by Terence Rattigan almost immediately. I can see the disapproving look on your face but I think they are very good and we have a wonderful cast with Joan Greenwood and Donald Sinden...so kindly spare me your expressions of moral disapproval.'[10]

Whatever Rattigan's intentions for the short farce based on *Tosca* which he had written as the second play in the double bill, the effect of *Before Dawn* on the whole evening was disastrous. It was found during the try-out tour that the audience would not accept it after the serious play (which in England was called *After Lydia*). So *Before Dawn* was played first. But it created such antipathy among the audience and critics alike, that many were unready to accept *After Lydia* and became unduly intolerant of its minor faults. When *In Praise of Love* opened at the Duchess Theatre on 27 September 1973, it did not enjoy the success it deserved. In his review for the *Guardian* the next day, Michael Billington, a previous supporter of Rattigan, having sat through

Before Dawn, which he called 'a real stinker', wrote: '*In Praise of Love* is an open attempt to celebrate physical and spiritual passion. Sadly, though, the gap between intention and achievement is cavernous.'[11] On the other hand, Harold Hobson, who had managed to laugh during *Before Dawn* and was in a more receptive mood, said of *After Lydia* '... it is the most piercing exposition of love under great stress that I have ever seen on the stage; it is an experience of such power and beauty as will intensify one's appreciation of what consummate theatre can achieve.'[12]

Rattigan had been anxious that the play might offend Rex Harrison and while it was in rehearsal he had written a long letter to Harrison saying that he hoped he wouldn't mind that he had used Kay Kendall's illness as the basis for the plot of his new play; he apologized for doing so, but said that he had changed so many details and introduced so many other elements that he didn't think anyone would recognize its origins. He added that he was anxious for Harrison to see it and approve. When Harrison went to see the play in London, Rattigan waited for him in the foyer and then sat through the performance with him. Afterwards, when he took Harrison out to dinner, he was still anxious in case it had upset him.

Once he had made sure that Harrison had not been offended he was free to suggest that he should play Sebastian on Broadway. By July 1974, Harrison had been approached by the New York impresario through his agent and had given a qualified yes. Unfortunately, before Rattigan had had a chance to talk to him himself, the *Daily Mail* picked up the story that Harrison might play himself in a play based on his life with Kay Kendall during the months leading up to her death. On 3 August, he wrote Harrison a long anxious letter, ten pages in all. Apologizing that the press had jumped the gun, he said that at least one good thing has come out of it, that Sebastian is *not* Rex Harrison. 'Rex Harrison, to be Sebastian Cruttwell on stage, must play a character part, i.e. he must do everything to avoid any identification by the audience of the two totally dissimilar characters.' He said that there was no danger of the audience identifying Lydia with Kay Kendall, as Kendall was not an Estonian with a rather plodding sense of humour. He told Harrison that far from thinking of him when he was writing Sebastian, he was thinking more of Cyril Connolly or T.C. Worsley. He explained that Sebastian, having married Lydia to save her from the Russians twenty-nine years previously, had found her useful and kept her on and on,

> ... *always* taking her utterly for granted, and assuming that she'd always be there when wanted: [Sebastian] finds out, one day – 6 months before the play opens, and *28¹/₂ years* after they've got married – that in fact he loves her, and doubts if he can ever live without her; but he can't let her know that, or she'll know she's dying... You *do see* how *very, very* different a character that is from my dear friend, who once met a lady, loved her at first sight (as she loved him) and, told by her doctors that she had a mortal disease, married her – not to give her a passport, but for the very highest kind of love...

Rattigan continued, clearly already sensing that there was a danger that Harrison would be tempted to play the part for sympathy from the start,

> ... the play I did write – inspired I admit, by certain *events* that deeply moved me, but not at any time inspired by the characters – relies entirely on the element of surprise. Three-quarters of the way through the evening the audience discovers that a man who has, until that moment, appeared, not only to us but to his wife of 29 years, to his son and to his best friend, to be a selfish, uncaring shit – and most importantly *has been* so for 50 years – suddenly shows that he *does* care – *desperately* – for his wife, quite a bit for his son, and rather a surprising lot for his best friend.

A little further on Rattigan underlined the centrality of his point once more: 'But that "caringness" must – repeat *must* – come as a surprise – or, at the least, creep up on us very belatedly – because if he is shown *early on* as "caring", then we have no play.'

Rex Harrison did agree to play Sebastian Cruttwell on

Broadway, with Julie Harris as Lydia. *After Lydia* was retitled *In Praise of Love* and played on its own. Already over-long in exposition, the play was lengthened to make a full evening in the theatre. This was achieved mainly by restoring cuts from an earlier version which gave· more detail about Lydia's wartime experiences. Rehearsals for the New York production began in October 1974, with Fred Coe taking over the direction from John Dexter. Unfortunately Rattigan was unable to attend them as he had pneumonia, which he had caught while campaigning for the Liberal Party in the second of the 1974 general elections. Rattigan had been a member of the party ever since Puffin Asquith had signed him up after the war. In 1974, Rattigan, like so many other people, found his dormant political idealism rekindled by the fundamental issues raised by the clash between the Prime Minister, Edward Heath, and the striking miners. In October, he put up one of his manuscript copies of *The Deep Blue Sea* for auction to raise money in support of the campaign by the Liberal candidate in Richmond, Alan Watson, who was standing against the left-wing Labour Minister for the Arts, and long-time British Actors' Equity union official, Hugh Jenkins. He also went out on the stump for Watson, making public appearances with him. The pneumonia was so serious that Dr Buky ordered him to hospital. As a result Rattigan was prevented from seeing the American production of *In Praise of Love* until just before the New York opening. What he saw appalled him. Despite all he had said in his ten-page letter, and subsequent conversations with Harrison in Portofino, Harrison was playing Sebastian for sympathy from the moment he came on, thus destroying Rattigan's careful build-up of tension and the dramatic revelation that Sebastian's callousness is a cover for feelings he can hardly bear. Harrison's outburst about not wanting to 'join the brotherhood of buggers' at the time of *Man and Boy* should have provided Rattigan with ample warning, but the fact was that at this advanced stage of his career, Harrison had become a star of the school who believe that the preservation of their own carefully cultivated image with their admirers is more important than the requirements of the part they are supposed to be playing or the integrity of the work they are interpreting. Harrison and Coe had even introduced a piece of business at the start of *In Praise of Love* in which Sebastian sneaks a look at Lydia's latest medical report, the clear intention being that the audience should know of his concern about her condition and recognize Sebastian as a sympathetic character from the outset.[13] Rattigan was also unhappy about the way in which Julie Harris was playing the ending. In the text Rattigan directs that she should smile radiantly at Sebastian, revealing her happiness at the knowledge that her love is returned. Julie Harris seemed unwilling to smile. Rattigan kept telling her that this smile was her 'most important line, it's the most important line in the play'.

Rattigan was very angry, and there was a stand-up row between him and Harrison, followed by an angry exchange of letters. However, the play opened on Broadway substantially as Rattigan had seen it on tour, and the text, as published in America, contains the new lines and the additional business put in by Harrison and Coe. Almost the only American critic to spot what had been done to the play was Holly Hill, herself formerly an actress. Writing in the *Educational Theatre Journal*, she began by declaring that the production illustrated an artistic and critical failure: 'Rex Harrison's performance distorts the character which Rattigan created, and the critics' praise for this distortion exposes their inability to distinguish between acting and writing... Have the critics no ears?' she lamented, echoing the cry of dramatists down the ages. 'Did they not listen to one word Harrison's character said, and feel no contradiction between the callousness of his statements and the oozing charm with which he uttered them?' She concluded that the Broadway presentation was a 'misrepresentation of Rattigan's work'.[14]

Yet the play got generally better reviews in New York than in London, illustrating once again the damage done to it in London by *Before Dawn*. Bolstered by Harrison's name, it ran on Broadway for 199 performances as against 131 in London.

The full power of the play was not realized in production until Anglia Television televised it in 1977. Superbly directed by Alvin Rakoff, who had worked with Rattigan on *Heart to Heart* and understood the full implication of the play, it was done in a version based on the original English script, which was tactfully cut down a little so that it fitted a television slot. This cutting was generally of benefit, tightening the play and increasing the tension in the first and second scenes. The production benefited too from superb performances by Claire Bloom, ideally cast as Lydia, and Kenneth More, giving perhaps the best performance of his career in a part that might have been written for him, as Sebastian. When the recording of the play was complete, Rakoff ran it for Rattigan and one or two other people connected with the production. At the end, all the people in the room sat in tears, unable to speak for a moment. The one with most tears running down his face was Rattigan himself.

Notes

1   *Sunday Express*, 20 June 1971.
2   Holly Hill, op. cit.
3   *Daily Mail*, 4 April 1973.
4   Other provincial revivals included *The Deep Blue Sea* and *Love in Idleness.*
6   *Daily Telegraph*, 28 July 1973.
7   *Guardian*, 28 July 1973.
8   Introductory talk to a season of Rattigan plays on BBC Radio – recorded 17 September 1957.
9   Later, for some reason that Rattigan never explained (although it may have been connected with Rattigan's hopes of inducing Rex Harrison to play Sebastian by changing the precise details of the disease in the play from those of Harrison's wife Kay Kendall), the wife's terminal illness was altered to poly-arteritis caused by prolonged malnutrition during the war years.
10 *The Honourable Beast – A Posthumous Autobiography of John Dexter*, copyright Riggs O'Hara/The estate of John Dexter, Nick Hern Books Ltd, 1993.
11 *Guardian*, 28 September 1973. Subsequently, when Billington saw another production in which *After Lydia* was played on its own, he praised it.
12 *Sunday Times*, 30 September 1973.
13 Harrison's need to be loved by audiences from the moment he appeared in a play had led to a series of clashes with producers. The producers of *My Fair Lady* had had considerable difficulty persuading Harrison not to play Higgins as a loving and sympathetic man from his first entrance.
14 *Educational Theatre Journal*, New York, December 1974.

21

Defiance

In the week before the New York opening of *In Praise of Love* Rattigan had given a long interview to Holly Hill who, against the advice of her tutor, was preparing a postgraduate degree dissertation on his plays. It did not seem an event of much significance to Rattigan at the time, but in giving Holly Hill that interview Rattigan lit a flame that would lead, after his death, to his critical acceptance in the United States and help to fuel further reassessments in Britain.

But these things lay in the future and Rattigan returned to Bermuda deeply disappointed. *In Praise of Love* was to have been the final summation of his life in the theatre, but as a result of the selfish vanity of Rex Harrison, who he had believed was his friend, it had been misunderstood in America. It was a betrayal.

In the year between the London and New York productions of *In Praise of Love* Rattigan had had another of his bursts of restless energy. As well as campaigning for the Liberals in Richmond, he had stayed in hotels in New York, Bournemouth, Edinburgh and in the Martinez in Cannes. During all this Flying Dutchman voyaging he had sorted out many elements of his life. On 30 October he had attended the Churchill Centenary Harrow Songs at the Albert Hall; his guest was Peter Osborn. The two men knew that they were unlikely to meet again, as Osborn was due to sail to Australia to take up an appointment as an Anglican priest. That evening the singing of 'Forty Years On' by the mass of male voices seemed especially charged with emotion.

Another element in his life to be settled in that year was Michael Franklin. He had been instructed to buy a house in Scotland and refurbish it. Rattigan almost certainly never had any intention of living in it. Michael Franklin had chosen it, but Rattigan had not even bothered to see it. When he did visit it in March 1974, he hated it and never spent so much as a single night under its roof. But Franklin lived in it for much of the time when he was not in London or travelling with Rattigan. Rattigan had continued to see Franklin fairly regularly, but Franklin's role in his life remained more or less as it had been, a congenial companion between emotional outbursts, occasional friend and 'service provider'. Just before the New York opening of *In Praise of Love*, Rattigan had made arrangements to dispose of the lease on his Albany chambers. No longer with a base in England where they could be stored, some of his papers went with him to Bermuda, but the bulk of them were divided between the safe-keeping of his London agent Michael Imison of Dr Jan Van Loewen Ltd and Michael Franklin. Some of Rattigan's friends became alarmed by the sometimes careless approach Franklin adopted towards his guardianship of Rattigan's papers. He would get out precious Rattigan manuscripts to show to friends or party guests and leave them on drinks-covered sideboards or at risk of having coffee spilled over them on a kitchen table. Franklin's detractors spread stories of original manuscripts being given away to impress boyfriends or pocketed by visitors. It is possible that the first, homosexual, version of *The Deep Blue Sea* (if it ever existed) disappeared in this way.

Rattigan's most regular travelling companion was Harold French's wife Pegs. She kept house for him, looked after him and did all his secretarial work. After disposing of his Albany chambers he bought a new house in Bermuda, Spanish Grange in Tuckers Town. It was bordered by a golf course so, although he no longer had the stamina to play much, he could watch others.

Amid all his relentless travelling Rattigan had continued to work on other projects, particularly films. He needed the money. He had completed an adaptation of the stage success *Conduct Unbecoming* for British Lion (finally they did not use the screenplay) and in 1973 had done some work on another film about First World War air aces. There was also work on a possible musical for Lerner and Loewe and on the screen adaptation of a French novel called *The Film of Memory* for Liza Minnelli. Work on the latter, however, was held up by his participation in a strike. Rattigan was a member of the Writers' Guild of America, which had called a stoppage against the Hollywood film companies, and even though he was not living in America he did not feel he could break ranks. It is perhaps unsurprising that his long-suffering accountant complained that he was having difficulty in keeping track of all his expenditure, and advised keeping his spending to a minimum. A year or two previously Rattigan had jokingly suggested to his publisher that he ought to write his autobiography while he could still remember things. In the summer of 1974, Roger Machell of Hamish Hamilton agreed a contract with Rattigan for an autobiography of one hundred thousand words, to be delivered by the end of 1975. The tentative title was *Without Tears*.

As his involvement in the Liberal campaign in the 1974 election showed, Rattigan at this period was more active in outside causes than at any time since he was a young man. In October 1974, he was one of eleven leading authors – the others included John Betjeman, J. B. Priestley, Veronica Wedgwood and Rebecca West – who signed a letter to *The Times* in support of the campaign for a Public Lending Right, a long-overdue scheme to compensate authors for the loss of royalties resulting from the drop in their sales because of the increased availability of books on loan through public libraries. He was letter writing as never before. He was particularly prone to sound off at critics whose opinions he disagreed with. His letters to Bernard Levin developed into a full-scale correspondence, but a critic in any medium might suddenly receive a salvo from whatever hotel Rattigan happened to be staying in. They were often written late at night, and apparently under the influence of brandy. Typical, and very revealing of his mood in the years after his sixtieth birthday, was one written shortly before he vacated his chambers in Albany to Elkan Allan of the *Sunday Times*. Allan had previewed a television programme about the McCarthy hearings called *Hollywood on Trial*. Rattigan's letter consisted of six increasingly wildly scrawled postcards. (It should be said that Mr Allan was not aware of ever having had a letter from Rattigan before.) Across the top of the first card was a postscript: 'Answer please, for once, personally... <u>We don't want "ed.s", and "pub"</u> (doubly underlined by Rattigan).

DEAR MR ALLAN,

I don't think you are wont to answer my letters, but please answer this, for I write with a real grievance.

'The Hollywood Ten' (*Omnibus* Rpt)... Why *disappointing?* You nearly stopped me seeing what is surely a really brilliant statement of an ethical – not political – problem: do you betray a friend to The Special Branch when you happen to know he's joined General Walker's private army – in whose aims you once misguidedly believed, and which aims you now consider dangerous to the State?... Your career is at stake. *Do* you, or don't you?

Best, T.R.

PS.   I can't remember the occasion, but I believe that you *do* owe me a letter. Possibly, before I was pleading against your fixed determination to dismiss any film directed by Anthony Asquith (Liberal) written by me (Lib-Lab) and produced by Anatole de Grunwald (Anti-Stalin, pro-Krushchev) as Fascist propaganda... Something of the kind, anyway... Of no importance, of course... Except that 'fascist' doesn't and never did, fit. But *don't* stop your readers watching what we *should* watch – And don't let your political slip show more than it need. An inch is enough. 'King Street' [address of the British Communist Party] would approve this advice – as I *very well know.*

PPS   I repeat: no publication, please. Someday later, perhaps. Not now.

PPPS   If I'd been in Hollywood during those years, instead of being happily employed by Liberals at Shepperton (and I include Alex Korda), it would have been the 'Hollywood Eleven' (which makes a better title than 'Ten' doesn't it?).

But I realize now, that the title of the programme in question was 'Hollywood on Trial'. 'The Hollywood Ten' would have been better (except that it's been used). 'The Hollywood Eleven' best of all. Nudge, nudge, nudge! – make of it what you will. I care no more. T. R. and I don't think King Street does, either.

In fact there had always been more consistency in Rattigan's political attitudes than in his public statement of them in his published work. For instance, in the mid 1950s, when he seemed most out of step with the young, anti-militarist generation, he had raised heated private objections to the jingoistic sentiments and glorification of German civilian deaths in the most popular British film of the period, *The Dam Busters*. Once again it seems a pity he never gave vent to his feelings in public.

Shortly after the London opening of *In Praise of Love*, BBC Television had commissioned Rattigan to write a script about Nijinsky. But no sooner had news of the commission got out than he ran into furious opposition from Romola Nijinska, Nijinsky's widow, who wrote to him insisting that he stop. A few years earlier, there had been talk of Rattigan scripting a film based on Romola Nijinska's own biography of her husband, who had died in 1950 after years of mental disorder. Memories of that project had also coloured his thinking while he had been writing his unproduced script for *Pas de Deux*. Now, however, Rattigan was writing directly about Nijinsky and taking Richard Buckle's biography of the dancer as his starting point. Rattigan was at first willing to accede to Madam Nijinska's demands and was ready to stop work. However, the BBC said she had no case and told him to proceed with the commission, for which he had agreed a contract. As Rattigan wrote an acrimonious correspondence continued between the BBC and Cedric Messina (the producer) on one side and Romola Nijinska and her lawyers on the other. Allegations and counter-allegations mounted, calling into question not only Nijinsky's sexual relations but Rattigan's 'bestial proclivities' as well. Yet in this atmosphere Rattigan produced one of the most sensitive scripts of his career. The nature of Nijinsky's relationships with Diaghilev and Romola had been something that had fascinated him for many years and, as in *In Praise of Love*, his process of creative absorption and distillation had had time to take full effect.

He traced Nijinsky's life from his childhood examination for a place in the St Petersburg Imperial Ballet on to his stardom and through into irrevocable madness. In the script Rattigan squarely confronted the subject he had so often shied away from or concealed in the past: homosexuality. Because one can accept Nijinsky as other-worldly throughout and does not have to believe in him as a man of action, as in the case of Alexander, Lawrence or Nelson, the play works in a way that the previous episodic portraits of real-life heroes do not. There is very little dialogue, much of the significant action being contained in minutely detailed camera instructions. The relationship between Nijinsky and Diaghilev is spelt out with delicacy and precision. There is none of the sexual hypertension in the writing which mars *Bequest to the Nation*, nor the evasiveness that flaws some other plays. Yet the play is not about homosexuality, but about love. After Romola's successful pursuit of Nijinsky and marriage to him, Diaghilev withdraws his love – possessively jealous, he cannot share Nijinsky with anyone. The play ends with Nijinsky locked in madness. Bereft of Diaghilev's love, for which Romola's is an inadequate substitute, Nijinsky becomes trapped in himself, unable to communicate with the real world. During her pursuit of Nijinsky, Romola tells Diaghilev that Nijinsky has no gender. There follows a line which goes far beyond the immediate situation of the play in its significance for Rattigan. Nijinsky says: 'But an artist should have no gender... Art comes directly from God. Has God a gender? Is he male or female? Isn't he both?'

The rows over *Nijinsky* dragged on after it was completed. Rattigan was unwilling to risk having to appear in court to defend his interpretation of Nijinsky's emotional life and so, tragically, asked the BBC not to proceed with the production until after Romola's death. Rattigan regretted this for the rest of his life.

In the summer of 1974, the BBC had commissioned a radio play from Rattigan. It was an arrangement somewhat similar to the international television agreement which had produced *Heart to Heart*. Normally meagre radio fees were bumped up to something like six thousand pounds for a ninety-minute play by the prospect of foreign transmissions. He had started to work on it in the weeks before he went down with pneumonia prior to the New York opening of *In Praise of Love*. He went back to it as soon as he had regained sufficient energy after his return to Bermuda in December 1974. At the time of the revivals of his work following his sixtieth birthday Rattigan had, in his own words, been 'terribly encouraged' that young audiences seemed once again to be in touch with him. But he knew that he was, in a sense, out of touch with them. He had confessed more than once to finding it increasingly difficult to write about modern young people. Frank Marcus had congratulated him on getting the son Joey just right in *In Praise of Love*, which had gratified him, but he knew that if he wanted to write about young people in future it would be safer to make them young people of his own generation or earlier. This is exactly what Rattigan did now. For his new radio commission he went back to an idea he had had thirty-nine years earlier, during the summer of 1935, when he had been busy working with Gielgud on the fated adaptation of *A Tale of Two Cities* – the Rattenbury murder case.

The case had obvious appeal to him. The events had actually occurred in Bournemouth, an archetypal Rattigan setting. Alma Rattenbury, a small-time composer of popular songs, herself middle-aged, was the wife of an older man who could not satisfy her sexually. She had taken as her lover her eighteen-year-old chauffeur–gardener. After taking the young man away with her for a few days of high life in a London hotel she found that he had become jealous of her husband on their return home. When he suspected that Mr and Mrs Rattenbury were having sexual intercourse together, he murdered Mr Rattenbury by beating him over the head with a mallet. Alma Rattenbury and her young lover were jointly charged with the murder. At the time of the trial Alma Rattenbury was the victim of massive popular prejudice. Whether she was really guilty or not, she was held to be guilty for what had happened, because she was the older partner in the affair, a fact which spelt domination in the public mind; having taken a boy for her lover, she was assumed to have led him into a life of depravity, of which murder was the outcome. There was no pity for her, no willingness to try to understand that, 'Out of this unpromising material she had created something that to her was beautiful and made her happy.'[1] In the event, only he was found guilty, with a strong appeal for clemency. Although she had been acquitted, Alma Rattenbury committed suicide. She left a note, in which she spoke of what a beautiful world we live in – 'if only we could let ourselves see it'.

Rattigan does not tell the story in simple chronological narrative but starts, as so often, at a point of crisis and explores what has led up to it during the course of the working-out of the crisis itself. In this case the play opens at the beginning of the trial and, as it proceeds, uses a complex series of flashbacks to build up a composite picture of what has happened. Thus Rattigan shows the way public prejudice places different values on the same events. He heightens this by means of a sub-plot, centred around a sexually repressed lady juror, whose frigidity has driven her husband into the arms of other women, and her adolescent public-schoolboy son. This amounts to a separate play. It is as though instead of creating two separate items to counterpoint each other in a double-bill, as with *The Browning Version* and *Harlequinade* or the two plays in *Separate Tables*, he had interlaced the two together and allowed them to develop side by side in a form of continuous musical counterpoint in which they sometimes touch and affect each other.[2]

The sub-plot comes closer to literal autobiography than anything in Rattigan's work and it is surely no coincidence that the idea of writing an autobiography was much in his mind at the time when he was writing *Cause Célèbre*.[3] Although he had agreed with his publishers to write an autobiography, he never actually got down to it and it seems unlikely that he ever would have done so. It was a form essentially alien to him, a man whose life had been devoted to forms of concealment and role-playing. In any case, almost every play he had ever written had contained elements of autobiography, both literal and, more important, emotional. Rattigan thrived on the disciplined restrictions imposed by playwriting but, even so, the autobiographical elements in the sub-plot of *Cause Célèbre* were explicit and he made no attempt to conceal them. He told the director of the later stage version, Robin Midgley, that the woman, Edith Davenport, was not an exact portrait of his mother because she was more understanding towards him than Mrs Davenport is to her son in the play, but at the same time he made it clear that most of the things that happen to the boy, Tony, had happened to him.

Even the incidental details are correct: she comes from a family of distinguished lawyers who served in India, and now lives not simply in a West Kensington hotel like Aunt Edna, but in Cornwall Gardens, Rattigan's own birthplace. Herself sexually repressed, she finds Alma's willingness to gratify her sexual needs with an adolescent particularly shocking. She loves her son excessively as the only thing she has left from her failed marriage, but will not countenance his adolescent interest in sex. She refuses to have the subject discussed. His only sexual experience so far has been with other boys at his boarding school, but he is avid to 'try it' with a woman. With money from his father, he experiments with a prostitute, but it is a humiliating failure. After this he goes back to an attractive younger boy. During the course of the play he discovers that the picture his mother has painted of his father, who is living apart from the family, is unduly harsh. His flagrant affaires with other women in fact add up to no more than occasional 'medicinal' sexual encounters, without any emotional content, and are the result of his wife's inability to provide sexual satisfaction. The myth of the affaires has been perpetuated principally to save his mother's self-esteem as a 'wronged' woman. This last element in the story may represent Rattigan's re-evaluation of his parents' actual relationship, or be simply a re-evaluation of his own attitude to that relationship. In either case, it had only become possible for him to incorporate such a reassessment in a play after his mother's death.

In the spring of 1975, once the weather had improved

447

sufficiently, he was back in England, travelling around to visit friends. He made two visits to Scotland to see the Midget, although he still stayed in hotels rather than spend a night in any of the six bedrooms of his house at Glenrothes, a visit to the Grand Hotel in Brighton to see friends and a quick dash to the Martinez in Cannes. But all the travelling was too much for him and he was often in pain. By mid-July he was back in the care of Dr Buky in the London Clinic and throughout the autumn kept returning to undergo a series of often painful and exhausting tests. The radio recording of *Cause Célèbre* took place at Broadcasting House in London from 22 to 26 September. The producer, Norman Wright, had engaged a very strong cast, headed by Diana Dors, bringing just the right degree of pent-up sensuality to Alma Rattenbury. Wright's production even incorporated popular songs of the period composed by Alma Rattenbury under her pen name 'Lozzanne'.

Among those who heard *Cause Célèbre* when it was broadcast on 27 October 1975, was a successful young London impresario, an ex-actor called John Gale. He contacted Rattigan and asked if he would consider turning it into a stage play for production in the autumn of 1976. He suggested Dorothy Tutin to play Alma Rattenbury. Rattigan had no idea how the sequence of short scenes, fading in and out of each other from location to location, could be reorganized so that they could be done in the theatre, but agreed to meet Gale, and his suggested director Robert Chetwyn, in Paris. By the time they met Rattigan had come to the conclusion that it would be a good idea to have both of the principal women, Alma Rattenbury and Mrs Davenport, played by the same actress. A strength of *Separate Tables* had been having both contrasting central characters played by the same actors. However this made the already intractable problem of inter-cutting the short scenes even more intractable. The problem was still unresolved when he returned to Bermuda for the winter.

Shortly after Rattigan had returned to Bermuda for Christmas, Dr Buky contacted him with the results of the tests he had undergone in London. The tests confirmed his worst fears, the cancer was now in his bones and was spreading. The prognosis was not good; although it might be slowed down, it seemed irreversible. One of those staying with him in Bermuda when the confirmation came through was his editor at Hamish Hamilton, Roger Machell, a friend since prep-school days at Sandroyd: '...he took the whole thing outwardly very much more lightly than the characters in *In Praise of Love* and with the most extraordinary courage and cheerfulness,' Machell said.[4] His Christmas card to Peter Osborn that year said simply, 'Not too bad.'

When he returned to London and more tests and treatment in January 1976, he refused to stay in hospital when there was no absolute need. Instead, he moved himself into a suite at Claridges. This time he made no attempt to prevent the truth about his condition reaching the newspapers. It was because of newspaper reports that Peter Osborn in Adelaide heard about his terminal cancer. He wrote to Rattigan, telling how much he admired him for having the courage to tell the truth. Telling him that he and members of his congregation were remembering him in their prayers, he reminded him of the summons of Mr Valiant-for-Truth in John Bunyan's *A Pilgrim's Progress* and quoted Barrie's *Peter Pan* – 'To die would be an awfully big adventure.' He assured him that a great many friends would be there to welcome him on the other side. Osborn told him that he still wore the ring that Rattigan had given him when he entered the navy: 'You are very close to my heart and always will be.' He ended by blessing him with the words that end the Church of England service and signed off quoting the final words of the very first letter that Rattigan had written to him forty years earlier: 'Yours, till kingdom come, old chap. Peter.'[5]

Rattigan was resolutely determined not to be sorry for himself. Inviting David Lewin of the *Daily Mail* to share a bottle of champagne with him, he said: 'When this happens you suddenly stop counting the cost of anything. So in the time that's left I shall work harder and indulge myself more.' The earlier leukaemia and burst-appendix scares had prepared him for the idea of death. Even so, he couldn't fail to be moved by the viewing of Alvin Rakoff's television production of *In Praise of Love*.[6] Later that evening, talking to the journalist Philip Oakes back in his suite at Claridges, he said: 'I seemed to spend a great deal of time mopping tears from my face. Not surprising in the circumstances – perhaps, it was not the most ideal entertainment.' It was a question of identification with the heroine dying of leukaemia, he explained. Oakes had a slipped disc and it was typical of Rattigan that, although his own cancer was in his back, he showed more concern about his guest's comfort than his own. 'Don't move,' Rattigan said, getting up to pour drinks. 'Frightful things, backs. Are you sure you're seeing the right man? Is your bed hard enough? I really do sympathize. You must be having an awful time.' Oakes felt a surge of guilt as he remembered the location of Rattigan's cancer. Perhaps Rattigan sensed it, for he pressed on: 'The other thing is not to dwell on it. It's so easy to become a back bore. People don't like it.'[7] The potential embarrassment of the situation was removed by Rattigan's matter-of-fact approach to his illness: 'There's no doubt about the diagnosis. I have to accept it. And, of course, the question arises: how much time do I have left? I would like to complete a couple more plays and write my autobiography. Five years would do it. But there's no guarantee about these things. I'm pushing on as best I can. I actually did some work this morning and I felt rather proud of myself.' All the old discipline had returned, but already it was beginning to become more difficult physically: 'But I still try to do four hours' work a day. If a scene isn't finished I go back to it at night. The excuse of not feeling like it isn't good enough. It's much too obvious.'

He now had two projects in hand: the stage version of *Cause Célèbre* for the impresario John Gale, and a play about the Asquiths. A year earlier, when he was interviewed by her, he had told Holly Hill that he was full of the Asquith play. She asked him how conscious was his repeated use of understatement and emotionally repressed characters in his plays. He told her he found it difficult to know how conscious his choice of subject and style were. To illustrate what he meant he gave her a very complete description of the play he was planning:

It's about the father of a great friend of mine, a Prime Minister called Herbert Asquith. I always wanted to write a play of 1916 because I believe the Battle of the Somme saw the end of a form of Western Civilization, and life was never the same after that. [It will be remembered that the Battle of the Somme had a special significance for the Rattigan family because of the death of Frank's younger brother, Cyril.] Until that moment, life could have gone on – perhaps it wasn't right that it should have gone on in that way, but it could have gone on. And it was in Asquith's power to stop the war... If peace had been settled with Germany – we were not dealing with Nazi Germany – on the basis not of unconditional surrender but a negotiated peace, the holocaust could have been stopped in 1916 – if Asquith were not a sick man.

He was made sicker than he need have been by the death of his favourite son Raymond, who was one of the great leading lights of that generation, the Rupert Brooke generation. He was a brilliant scholar, he had a marvellous future, probably in politics, but quite possibly as a writer. He was killed in the Battle of the Somme, and he chose deliberately to go as a second-lieutenant in the front line when, of course, he could have had what they called 'a cushy job' as the Prime Minister's son.

I found out that during Asquith's visit to General Haig in his headquarters, six weeks after the battle opened, Haig allowed Raymond, this paragon, to come and see his father. A week later Asquith learned the boy had been killed.

It's one of the fascinating 'ifs' of history: what would have happened if Raymond hadn't been killed – and Raymond didn't have to be killed. First of all, he was slightly suicidally inclined himself. Secondly, of course, his father could have saved him. He didn't – with the repressions of the period it wasn't possible. It might have been possible that Margot Asquith, who's a good character to write about, said, 'Henry, your duty is plain. You must save that boy. He's wasted in the front line. Get him into Headquarters or somewhere.' But, by chance, I found out that the Asquiths never touched each other. It used to madden Margot. She said: 'They're unfeeling brutes, these Asquiths. They never even shake hands.' But they loved each other. Of course, Asquith loved his son passionately and the son loved his father. But I, of course, was instantly thinking of the scene with the son and father at opposite ends of the stage, when he's come back from the front line. And from that oddly enough, from just that fact, plus the lucky coincidence really that it should have been right in the middle of the battle that Asquith went to the front, possibly to stop it. Raymond was killed in the second phase of the battle a week later.

Rattigan summed up what he meant by saying to Holly Hill: 'I don't think one ever approaches a subject really consciously. One is apt to say, my God, that would make a marvellous scene, or that is a good theme, or that's something I want to write about. The "how" is a different matter.' He told her he felt like Trigorin, in Chekhov's *The Seagull*, who says that every man writes what he must as well as he can.[8]

Early in 1976 he was still full of the Asquith play. He told Anthony Curtis, who did the first full-scale radio appreciation of his work, that this was the play he was 'engaged in at the moment' and he thought that 1916 was a period he could probably write about better than some of the younger playwrights.[9]

At the time of Rattigan's return to London early in 1976, a revival opened which did even more than other revivals of recent years to jog those who had long since dismissed him into a reassessment of his distinctive genius. At the King's Head, a pub theatre in Islington, normally the home of young radicals and the avant-garde, that seemingly most alien and middle-class of Rattigan characters, the emotionally repressed public school-master, Crocker-Harris, was holding a new and unlikely audience spellbound. Unrecognized among a predominantly young and unkempt audience for *The Browning Version*, Rattigan himself went to a performance in the crowded small backroom in Upper Street, Islington. If any of the hundred or so people squashed on to hard wooden chairs or sitting at small tables noticed the immaculately groomed elderly man who sat among them, they didn't remark on him. His hair was now greying slightly at the temples and receding a little. The chin sagged a little. His face was

452

already puffed, not by old age so much as by cortisone treatment. He would have passed more readily as a successful stockbroker or barrister from nearby Canonbury or newly gentrified Barnsbury than as the author of the evening's entertainment at North London's leading fringe theatre.

The audience was crammed into the hot little room wherever they could find a space or a vantage point, separated from the actors by nothing more than the tacit agreement that creates an invisible boundary between the acting area and the auditorium. It was a very different setting from the one for which Rattigan had created the play almost thirty years earlier. Yet when the lights went down, the effect of the play on the 1976 audience was the same as it had been on the smartly dressed stalls and galleryites of 1948. At the opening they laughed when Taplow surreptitiously took the chocolate from the Crock's box and practised his cruel schoolboy imitation of him for the popular science master. By the end they were frozen, close to tears, as the full tragedy of the Crock's lifelong emotional repression lay revealed in a magisterial performance by Nigel Stock. At one of the tables a group of trainee teachers was openly weeping. So, quietly, was Rattigan, a few tables away.

Afterwards he went backstage to meet the cast. The play's young director, Stewart Trotter, who had asked him to come to a performance recalled: 'We, of course, were all scared stiff and had put on ties to greet the Master. Rattigan, in concession to the Fringe, had come without... the treatment he was having made him pee a lot. So first I took him upstairs to the grotty King's Head loo. Standing outside, I heard a gurgling sound that made me happier than I can say. It was Rattigan singing.'[10]

At the start of the King's Head run, *The Browning Version* had been paired with a play by Frank Marcus, *Carol's Christmas*, but this was found not to work very well and later, at the suggestion of Rattigan's agent Michael Imison, it was coupled with the short television monologue he had written for Margaret Leighton, *All on Her Own*. This was slightly modified and renamed *Duologue*. Played by Barbara Jefford, who also played Millie Crocker Harris, this worked much better as a double bill. That year Stewart

Trotter's King's Head production of *The Browning Version* received the annual H.M. Tennent Award for the best production outside the West End. In the *Daily Telegraph* John Barber referred to Rattigan as 'an old master', saying that the young audience's laughter and appalled silences were a new generation's tribute, 'not only to Rattigan's delicate craftsmanship but to his penetration into the hearts of men and women'.[11] John Elsom in the *Listener* pointed out that Rattigan had always championed the individual against the system – all systems – and thereby expressed 'certain liberal, humane values which we are in danger of forgetting'.[12]

On 30 March, BBC Radio 3 broadcast Anthony Curtis's deeply perceptive *Rattigan's Theatre*, which contained David Rudkin's recognition of Rattigan as '... someone peculiarly haunting and oblique who speaks to me with resonance of existential bleakness and irresoluble carnal solitude...', quoted at the start of this book. As we know, Rattigan heard that broadcast and confirmed to Curtis that Rudkin was right. Roger Machell, Rattigan's editor at Hamish Hamilton, had received nothing from Rattigan towards his autobiography even though the delivery date was now past. Having been interviewed by Curtis for the radio programme, and having listened to it, he began to think about asking Curtis to write a biography instead. Then in April, after conducting more tests, Dr Buky told Rattigan that the cancer was now progressing so fast that he did not think that he had more than a year to live. On 20 April, Machell formally proposed to Anthony Curtis that he should write a commissioned biography of Rattigan. But for the moment Curtis was too tied up with other work to make much progress.

After April 1976, and Dr Buky's forecast of his life expectancy, most of the remainder of Rattigan's life became a race against death, increasing pain and infirmity, to complete the stage version of *Cause Célèbre*. There were occasional distractions. In June there was talk of a production of *The Browning Version* at the National Theatre. Stephen Mitchell wrote him a series of anxious letters about casting and suggested that perhaps Rattigan might cut the Crock's speech about 'two kinds of love' as he feared it might be misunderstood by a modern audience. Rattigan demurred. It was hoped that John Gielgud might at last play the part written for him on the stage, but in the end he was not available. Alec Guinness and Donald Sinden were also considered, but in the end neither of them was ·available either. The production was postponed. When it was mounted, in 1980, the Crock was played, superbly, by Alec McCowen. There was also work on a tentative film script about Baron von Richtofen and another stage musical for Lerner and Loewe. They all came to nothing. Rattigan also busied himself in trying to arrange for an allowance for his elderly Aunt Barbara, who had approached him for help as she was living on her own in straitened circumstances. When he could he saw friends and even went to Lord's to watch cricket.

But most of his energy was devoted to *Cause Célèbre*. He had completed an adaptation of the radio play by the summer, and might have been able to return to his Asquith project, but getting *Cause Célèbre* staged turned out to be fraught with difficulties. The first problem had arisen when he had met Robert Chetwyn, the director. Rattigan was still unsure about how to stage the play. He hoped that Chetwyn would have been able to do some work on it by the time they met and would come up with some solutions. He was disappointed. Chetwyn had apparently been busy with other projects. Rattigan, aware that his time was running out, asked for another director. Rattigan's agent then suggested Peter Coe, a man with a long record of successes with complex, episodic productions, the most notable being the musical *Oliver*. Coe liked the idea, but favoured the documentary elements in the play at the expense of the sub-plot. He was one of a succession of people involved in the production who thought that the sub-plot should be scrapped. Rattigan was now in no doubt that this was his last play — he habitually referred to it as such to those he worked with — and was therefore even more determined than usual that what appeared should be *his* creation rather than someone else's. He said that the various strands represented each of the main preoccupations of his writing, and that by combining them all in one play he was in a sense trying finally to tie them all together. The autobiographical sub-plot was therefore not only very important in his overall design, it was the thing which made the play his own.

Rattigan felt in an increasingly awkward position. The more he worked with Coe, the more convinced he became that he was the wrong director. But he had been suggested by his agent after he had himself asked for a new director, and he was diffident about going to John Gale and asking for yet another change. By the time he had plucked up the courage to have Peter Coe taken off the production and another director had been found, it was the end of the year and Rattigan was back in Bermuda for the winter. Because the production had gone back, missing its intended autumn 1976 production date, Dorothy Tutin was no longer available. Worse to Rattigan, it seemed doubtful that he would ever be strong enough to make the journey to Britain again and so would never see his last play staged. But, as so often with cancer, the disease seemed to progress through alternating ups and downs. Though the pain and the quantities of pain-killing drugs progressively increased, there were still days, even weeks, when he was up on the terrace enjoying the winter sun. The ups, however, were interspersed with longer stays in bed, increasing weakness and continual tiredness. Even the physical act of writing was sometimes difficult. His constant companion was Peggy French. She added to the self-imposed duties of secretary and housekeeper those of nurse. As well as comforting and protecting him, she learnt how to give him his injections. Harold French, a close friend now for forty years, since the first production of *French Without Tears*, was also with him that last winter. Now more or less retired, French had written two volumes of chatty memoirs, one with an affectionate introduction by Rattigan himself. There were occasional visitors from England too: old friends flown out for a week or two, to bring the latest gossip, reminisce and play chess. To the old enthusiasms for cricket and golf, new and seemingly alien obsessions had been added: baseball and American football, which he followed avidly from the radio and the newspapers. Still people brought him projects for new work; two Americans had a scheme for a film about British and American airmen holed up with a woman in a French château during the war. Rattigan himself, after all these years, continued to turn over ideas for a play that would star John Gielgud. The latest was to adapt *The Warden* by Anthony Trollope. But he knew there was no chance of being able to complete it on his own, so he asked the new director found by John Gale for *Cause Célèbre*, Robin Midgley, if he would work on it with him.

Midgley was the Artistic Director of the Haymarket Theatre in Leicester, one of the leading provincial repertory theatres. From there he had launched a number of productions which had gone on to become successes in the West End. Although associated with the new wave in the theatre – he had produced at the Royal Court – he was a long-standing admirer of Rattigan's work. When first approached, Midgley had been keen to do a new Rattigan play, but after reading the version Rattigan had worked on with Peter Coe, he turned it down. It seemed a hybrid – not a play, not a thoroughgoing documentary. But he was interested enough to read both the original radio script and Rattigan's own first stage version. These he liked, and he wrote to Rattigan in Bermuda telling him that the play he would like to do already existed inside those two scripts. This was the news Rattigan had wanted. He cabled Midgley, asking him to compile his own version from the three scripts he had read, and inviting him to fly out to Bermuda for discussions. Midgley found the compilation more difficult than he had expected, as Rattigan had evidently rewritten each script as though from scratch. A lot of scenes were common to each, but the dialogue of these scenes had clearly been rewritten without reference to the earlier versions. Gluing them together into one smooth whole turned out to be a very complex job. Midgley arrived in Bermuda late in January 1977, a very nervous man. When the two men met, Rattigan was also very shy; this was, after all, the third director with whom he had attempted to work on the play. Time was running out, and if this didn't work then the chances of the play being done in his lifetime were slim. Rattigan asked Midgley to read him his version aloud. This was a shrewd move; not only would it preserve his own dwindling reserves of energy, it would break the ice between the two men.

At the end of the reading it was clear that they had a basis for collaboration. Then began two weeks during which they substantially rewrote the play for the final time, and Midgley gained a unique insight into Rattigan's mind and method of working. They worked for two hours each morning and two hours each afternoon. This was now about all that Rattigan had energy for. The additional exertion of actually writing down what they had discussed was too much for him, and this fell almost entirely to Midgley. During the first week they built up Act One scene by scene. When they were satisfied with that, they moved on to Act Two. The importance attached by Rattigan to the sub-plot can be gauged by the fact that he briefly used a new title for the play – *A Woman of Principle*. Although this title could just conceivably apply to Alma Rattenbury, albeit ironically, the character it most obviously fitted was the repressed mother-figure, Mrs Davenport.

As the fortnight progressed, two of the most exciting weeks in Midgley's life, Rattigan seemed to gain strength. He reminisced about his early life, his mistakes, his intentions as a writer and his regrets. His greatest single regret seemed to be that his creation of Aunt Edna had been so misunderstood, and that he had failed, by the joke-trial scene he had written for the third volume of his *Collected Plays*, to get through to people that what he had meant was not that he had written specifically for the popular audience, but that like Shakespeare he knew he had to write what was acceptable to the groundlings before he stood any chance of getting beyond them to make contact with the more discerning audience. It was that audience that mattered to him. His two other regrets were the failure of *Adventure Story* and that *Nijinsky* had not been produced. But not all their talk was serious. Midgley found that Rattigan was still a great giggler and an inveterate gossip.

Early in February, Midgley returned to England, brought together all their work into one clean script and dispatched it to Rattigan in Bermuda. On 15 February, Rattigan replied. He was well satisfied with their work. He asked Midgley to change the placing of one trial scene and detailed a number of changes to individual lines, noting that one in particular would get 'sobs from

Row G aisle seat, or wherever it is they put the author at Leicester anyway!' And signed off, 'Love Terry'.

Rattigan was determined to get to England for the production, which was to open a three-week season in Leicester in mid-May, before transferring to London. It remained doubtful if he would make it. But, he told medical advisers and friends alike, he would rather die in the stalls of a draughty theatre at a rehearsal of his play than in the comfort of his own bed. He set out on 28 April, arriving in the early morning at Heathrow, and was taken, exhausted from the long flight, to a private room in the King Edward VII Hospital, close to London's theatreland.

By then the play was already in rehearsal, but things were not going well. In particular there was difficulty with Glynis Johns, whom Gale had got to replace Dorothy Tutin. Owing to a hormone imbalance she was displaying symptoms similar to hysteria and it began to look as if she would not make the Leicester opening. The rest of the cast were becoming increasingly miserable. Rumours of the production's problems were beginning to leak out to the theatre world, but Midgley and Gale were determined to do all they could to shield Rattigan from what was going on. Rattigan was by now living on borrowed time. The year of life proffered by the doctors was up. In London he was due to have an operation. Although he told people it gave him a slender chance of some sort of recovery in return for a high degree of risk, information given to those around him was that the primary function of the operation would be to reduce the extreme pain in which he now lived. He attended one rehearsal in London, but insisted on delaying the operation until he had at least seen one performance of the play at Leicester. The problem was how to get him to Leicester and back. It would involve at least six hours away from the hospital – a two-hour dash up the motorway, followed by the performance and a further two hours for the return journey. The only feasible performance was a matinée. The first was on Saturday 21 May.

A week before the opening, a further crisis broke: Glynis Johns had to leave the cast. When that happened, Charles Gray, who was holding the production together with a virtuoso performance that wrung every piece of available drama and humour from the pivotal role of Alma Rattenbury's defence lawyer, announced that since his contract specified his appearance opposite Glynis Johns, he was going too. In the event, he was held to his contract, which covered all of his appearances in Leicester. Heather Sears, Midgley's partner, twenty years earlier the virginal young star of British films such as *Room at the Top*, though not quite ideal casting for the sex-starved Alma Rattenbury courageously stepped into the breach to take over from Glynis Johns for the Leicester run.

The packed Leicester first night was an edgy occasion. The cast and the audience contained a number of Rattigan's friends, notably Harold French, who would probably report back to him in his London hospital bed. But no one could honestly say it was a success. The set, although minimal, seemed cumbersome and unattractive, the playing was understandably slow and in places uncertain. Gallantly though Heather Sears tried with Alma Rattenbury, Charles Gray's performance was the highlight of the evening. Without him the prospects for the London production looked grim. Yet Robin Midgley, like Harold French more than forty years previously, kept his nerve. On the Saturday, Rattigan made the journey from London and attended the matinée. Both he and Midgley remained coolly professional, discussing changes to the script and replacements for Glynis Johns and Charles Gray. Returning to London, Rattigan set the date for his operation – 1 June. At the same time he used his veto to prevent the imminent appearance in the West End of a revival from another provincial theatre of *The Deep Blue Sea*. *Separate Tables*, starring John Mills, was already enjoying a successful revival at the Apollo Theatre, and the immediate revival of another of his earlier and most powerful plays might jeopardize the chances of *Cause Célèbre*.

As explained in the Introduction to this book, in December 1976, shortly after rumours of Rattigan's terminal illness had started to circulate in theatrical circles, Gillian Hodson and I had started to compile a television obituary. Most of the work had been done while he was in Bermuda without direct access to him, but although he had not been told it was intended as his obituary, it had been impossible to disguise from him that the

BBC were working on a programme. Shortly after his arrival in London he had expressed a desire to see the programme. So, late on a fine early-summer afternoon one week before his operation, a television engineer and I, with Gillian Hodson, the programme producer Graham Benson and Rattigan's London agent, Michael Imison, climbed to his airy corner room in the King Edward VII Hospital with a colour television set and video playback machine to show him the tape. Although he had not been told that it was his obituary, he must have known. The programme included an outline of his life and extracts from his work, together with statements from friends, foes and critics, some of whom he had not spoken to in years. All had spoken candidly on film in the belief that he himself would never hear their posthumous assessment. Fortunately most of them were favourable, or we would have been more reluctant to agree to his request. John Osborne compared him with Jane Austen and said there had never been any personal animosity between them; Rex Harrison gave no hint of their disagreement over *In Praise of Love* and recalled Rattigan's kindness to him and the first night of *French Without Tears*; critics as varied as Sir Harold Hobson, Michael Billington and E. A. Whitehead were united in recognizing distinctive and unique qualities in his writing. Yet it was an oddly tense cluster of people who surrounded him as he sat up in bed, with Pegs French on a chair beside him, in the small room watching the screen at the foot of his bed. Throughout the hour that the programme ran nurses bustled in and out, changing the flowers, removing trays, making sure he had taken his medicine, seemingly oblivious of what was going on. Rattigan himself, sipping continuously from a glass of brandy and water – a dozen more bottles of brandy were packed in a cardboard box on the floor – made almost no comment, except occasionally to laugh, to say, 'That's true, I'd forgotten', or to sigh nostalgically at the sight of some long-unseen friend, sometimes an actor, sometimes a wartime colleague. The programme reached *Adventure Story*, and Pegs French visibly stiffened. When the dismissive comment came – recalling that '*Adventure Story* was an expensive and tasteless flop' – there was a sharp intake of breath from her, but Rattigan's face didn't change. At the end he seemed drained but pleased. He had laughed, not loudly, but a lot; he had cried silently too. He was shy in his thanks. Michael Imison asked him if Gillian and I could write his biography, and he enthusiastically agreed. If Rattigan knew that Roger Machell had suggested that Anthony Curtis should write his biography he never mentioned it, nor, it seems, had anyone mentioned it to Michael Imison. Perhaps Rattigan did know, and agreed to Gillian Hodson and me doing it as a piece of mischief, in the same way as in the past he had set up situations designed to cause his friends to fall out, so that he could enjoy observing the results. But whatever the truth, he remained unfailingly generous with his time and advice about people to talk to and where to find facts.[13]

On 4 July, five weeks after his operation, he attended the first night of *Cause Célèbre* at Her Majesty's Theatre in London. This time he was in no doubt that this was his last first night; nor were the people in the audience who recognized the figure propped up, but as always immaculately dressed, next to and slightly behind Michael Franklin in the Royal Box. He had been delivered in a limousine in good time for the performance, so there was no awkward last-minute scramble to get him into his seat, nor any ovation as he made his entrance. Glynis Johns was now recovered and back in the cast.[14] Charles Gray's place had been taken by Kenneth Griffith. Griffith, although an equally idiosyncratic actor, was the very opposite of Gray; where Gray was slow-moving and suave, dropping his barbs of wit with effortless aplomb, Griffith promised quicksilver theatricality, giving the play much-needed speed. In the event it turned out a wise choice, because although less subtle than Gray, he served the play better. Although Glynis Johns' performance was a technical *tour de force*, she lacked the power of sexual suggestion and the raw-nerved pain implied by Diana Dors in the original radio production. The pace was swifter, the other actors less uncertain and the set, in Rattigan's opinion at least, better because it was less prominent. But, as the end of the first act approached, the audience seemed to be getting restless. The scene where Alma is confronted with her child who pleads with her to try to save herself by incriminating her lover in court was the only one left before the interval. It was a dangerous moment. The success of the evening seemed suddenly to hang on a child actor called Matthew Ryan. In the event, he gave the most composed and truthful performance of the evening, raising the emotional temperature of the theatre and providing the springboard for Glynis Johns' anguished playing of Alma Rattenbury's decision to give evidence on her own behalf at the trial. The evening was saved.

The final curtain was not the storming success of *French Without Tears*; nor was it the anticlimax of *Man and Boy*. The prolonged clapping and the solid but not over-excited cheers from the back of the circle were in gratitude for an interesting evening in the theatre, and for a long and distinguished career. Although it was by no means his best play, the most important thing at that moment was probably that he had made it – he had survived not only to see it on to the stage, but to see himself fully accepted back into the West End. For the next few months he had two successes – the other was *Separate Tables*, still running after six months – playing simultaneously in London. It was the first time in more than thirty years.

Next day, the reviews were almost uniformly good, the only dose of cold water coming from Milton Shulman in the *Evening Standard*, who found not only the sub-plot contrived but the whole evening lacking in suspense and insight. Bernard Levin summed up the evening best in the *Sunday Times*: 'Rattigan's Act of Defiance' was the headline to his column. It began: 'A critic has a duty to ignore anything happening off stage, and to make no allowances for any shortcomings that may result . . . All the same, I am at any rate partly human, and it would be absurd, as well as impossible, for me to persuade myself that I do not know that Terence Rattigan has for the last couple of years been staring into the eyes of the old gentleman with the scythe . . . So I am doubly delighted to say that *Cause Célèbre* (Her Majesty's) betrays no sign of failing powers; on the contrary it could almost herald a new direction for Sir Terence, and a most interesting one, too.' He concluded: '*Cause Célèbre* is by a man who knows that in every human being there is a capacity to reflect the divine, and that it is love in all its forms, from the noblest to the most tawdry, that is most likely to show the gleam of that reflection. His play is theatrical in the best sense of the word, and I hope he will be spared to write many more such.'[15]

As though buoyed up by such words of praise, two days later Rattigan threw the hospital staff into confusion by getting up and taking himself for a walk round the block without telling anyone. Once outside, he scared himself by finding out how weak he really was. Even so, when Gillian Hodson and I arrived later in the afternoon to talk to him, he was still very pleased with himself; twinkling like a small boy who has played truant and got away with it. The staff told us we were not to stay too long and overtire him, but each time we got up to leave he insisted that we sit down and have another drink and another story. At one point a doctor arrived but, as we were leaving, Rattigan told us on no account to go away, there was more he wanted to say. But even that day, when he seemed so bright, he was still in almost continuous pain. Lying fully dressed on his bed, he could only stay in one position for a few minutes at a time. Every few minutes he would apologize and then laboriously haul himself on to his other side. It was, he said, as if he had two elephants sitting on him alternately. 'I have either Jumbo sitting on my hips, or it's Dumbo. It's very rarely nothing.'

Other friends, from earlier periods in his life came to visit, many consciously to take their final farewell. One was his hostess from the glory days in Sunningdale, the girl his mother had once seemed to hope he would marry, Jean Dawnay. Another was the actor Keith Baxter. Baxter had opened the night before in a Tennessee Williams play to decidedly mixed reviews. Rattigan brushed aside Baxter's expressions of sympathy in an effort to lift the actor's gloom. He told Baxter that Tennessee Williams was the master playwright of the age, and that he must cherish his friendship with him. When Baxter came to leave, his optimism quite restored by Rattigan's infectious enthusiasm, Baxter shook his hand. Rattigan said cheerfully, 'I'm dying, of course.' Baxter replied that he had said that before, when he was in Ischia. 'You told everyone. We all thought how much you were enjoying it.' Rattigan shifted on his bed in a vain attempt to ease his constant pain. 'Why shouldn't a man enjoy his own death? After all, it's the last amusement left.'[16]

Earlier that morning he had given a final radio interview to an old friend, Sheridan Morley. In it, he looked back over his whole career. At only one moment did his voice become bitter – when he recalled the early 1960s: 'I discovered that any play I wrote would get smashed. I just didn't have a chance with anything. But,' he added reflectively, 'perhaps I should have stayed and fought it out. I don't know.' Nevertheless, to be acclaimed again in his own lifetime was very, very gratifying.

I didn't think it would happen to me. I had hoped, though, that it might. I always thought they had been a bit unfair to me – and at a particular time they *were* being a bit unfair to me. It's all very well to dislike one's plays, but they ought to be disliked for a better reason than that they're out of fashion. Out of fashion isn't enough, I think. I always thought that justice would one day be done to me, but whether in my lifetime or not I didn't know. But it is very gratifying that it's happened in my lifetime.[17]

Two weeks later, having made arrangements to have all his plays specially bound and sent as a gift to the Queen, he ordered a car to drive him for a last time through London's theatreland. Down Shaftesbury Avenue past the Apollo, where *Separate Tables* was still playing in the theatre once occupied by *Follow My Leader* and *Flare Path*; past the Globe, the Lyric and the Queen's – the scenes of triumphs and disasters; down the Haymarket, passing Her Majesty's, where the posters for *Cause Célèbre* looked across to the Theatre Royal, once the home of *Ross* and *Bequest to the Nation*; and finally, on the way home, round Piccadilly Circus and past the Criterion, where it had all really started on an inauspicious night just over forty years earlier. He had come a long way since he had queued for the galleries of those same theatres and lain on his hard school bed at Harrow dreaming of saving England in a test match and being kissed simultaneously by Marie Tempest and Gladys Cooper after making speeches to wildly cheering first-night audiences, yet at heart he had remained that small schoolboy. Like so many great writers, behind his worldliness and the façade of sophistication, he had retained a child's innocent enthusiasm and sense of wonder.

In August, a week after arriving back in Bermuda, he collapsed again and was taken to hospital. This time he was reported to have meningitis. Everyone assumed that he could not survive. Michael Franklin rushed over to Bermuda to be with him. But Rattigan recovered, came out of hospital and persuaded Franklin to return to London. In November his lawyer Peter Carter Ruck flew out to Bermuda. Entering Rattigan's room he was shocked to see how much he had diminished in size. He seemed to be wasting away. When Carter Ruck left Rattigan's bedside and went downstairs, he wept.

The end finally came at about midday on Wednesday, 30 November 1977, while Harold French was out playing a round of golf and his nurse was taking a lunchbreak, but with Pegs French sitting beside him. He gave a slight smile and his head dropped on to her shoulder.

Notes

1   *The Trial of Alma Victoria Rattenbury and George Percy Stoner*, edited by F. Tennyson Jesse, William Hodge and Co., London, 1946; one of Rattigan's sources.

2   He had done something similar in the film version of *Separate Tables*, but there the counterpoint is not so effective as the two plays had not been written with this in mind.

3   At various times other titles were suggested including *A Woman of Principle, Come to Judgement* and *Crime Passionelle*.

4   *Rattigan's Theatre*, op. cit.

5   Peter Osborn, op. cit.

6   See previous chapter.

7   Philip Oakes 'Grace Before Going', *Sunday Times*, 4 December 1977.

8   I am indebted to Holly Hill for providing me with a full transcript of her interview with Rattigan.

9   *Rattigan's Theatre*, op. cit.

10 Quoted in B. A. Young, op. cit.

11 *Daily Telegraph*, 9 January 1976.

12 *Listener*, 15 January 1976.

13 A few weeks later, when, as a result of our approaching him, Roger Machell discovered that Gillian Hodson and I were working on a biography, he wrote to Pegs French and Michael Imison in what looked like an attempt to hamper or prevent us.

He told Imison that he feared our book would damage sales of Rattigan's autobiography, ignoring the fact that he had himself discounted this when approaching Anthony Curtis about writing a biography. In his letter to Pegs French he attacked Imison, calling him 'a prize ass', saying that he 'wished to God Terry... hadn't given his permission'. Those around Rattigan then divided into two camps, those who supported a full and candid biography and those who tried to prevent it. While the motives of some were undoubtedly honourable (though in our view misguided and out of line with Rattigan's own wishes as expressed to us), in that they feared the consequences for his reputation if his homosexuality, his love of Kenneth Morgan and other important events in Rattigan's career were brought out into the open, others were motivated by self-interest. It was a scenario typical of so many others that had occurred during his lifetime. If Rattigan became aware of these ructions during the last weeks of his life, he never did anything to withdraw his support for our venture; in fact, rather the reverse, giving us generous amounts of his time and advice during the weeks he remained in London.

14 Rattigan had told Robin Midgley and John Gale that he would be happy for Heather Sears to continue playing Alma, but Gale felt that he needed a more established West End star.

15 *Sunday Times*, 10 July 1977.

16 Told by Keith Baxter in *My Sentiments Exactly*, Oberon Books, London, 1998.

17 Sheridan Morley, *Kaleidoscope*, op. cit.

22

'The Audience is in Front'

Rattigan would have turned eagerly to see what sort of press he had got next morning. He would doubtless have been glad to find that he had been promoted from the arts page to the front page in many of the newspapers, while on the inside pages the space allotted to the obituaries was generous. Whether, however, he would have been quite so pleased by what they said is another matter. True, *The Times* headlined him an 'Enduring influence on the English Theatre', but the familiar, slightly deprecating, emphasis on 'craftsmanship' still predominated in the assessments. 'A prolific writer in the sleek tradition of Pinero, Maugham and Coward', his old friend John Barber called him in the *Daily Telegraph*. Rattigan would doubtless have bowed his head a fraction and, smiling slightly, thanked Barber for the compliment, but secretly he would have been disappointed. He had wanted to be so much more.[1]

It is perplexing that the assessments failed to come to grips with the evidence of the plays themselves. Harold Hobson started his uniquely perceptive obituary in the *Sunday Times* by saying that Rattigan 'had the greatest natural talent for the stage of any man this century'. He thereby asked the question which he set out to answer in the rest of his article – how well had Rattigan put that talent to use in his career? 'Natural talent' would seem the very opposite of the quality with which he was generally credited, craftsmanship, which is essentially something learned and deliberately applied, rather than natural. The implication, therefore, of most critics' assessments was that he had not made good use of his natural talent. At the end of the 1950s, Kenneth Tynan had expressed a widely-felt sense of disappointment in Rattigan, which rapidly escalated into a feeling of betrayal. If Rattigan was, in Tynan's often reiterated phrase, 'the Formosa of the British Theatre', possessed of the geographical potential to become part of the revolution, then he betrayed those who believed in revolution by

468

remaining obstinately occupied by the 'old guard'. The sense of betrayal perhaps accounts for the sustained virulence of the attacks on him in the years after 1956 and the persistent refusal to look beyond the stereotyped image of the calculating craftsman to the actual plays themselves. In his 1970 review of *The Winslow Boy*, Ronald Bryden likened Rattigan to writers working behind the Iron Curtain, a secret dissident whose rebellious cast of mind makes it impossible for him to join the new administration after the liberation. The fact is that he regarded the 1956 Royal Court revolution as only a partial liberation. His most deeply cherished values were neither those of the old guard nor those of the new revolutionary dictatorship. In this respect Rattigan adhered to Graham Greene's dictum that a writer must be prepared to change sides at the drop of a hat because there are always new authorities to challenge and new underdogs who need a voice. Rattigan's values as a writer remained essentially those of his boyhood at Harrow when, behind the authorities' backs, he circulated the works of Huxley and Russell.

In the BBC television obituary of Rattigan, John Osborne, himself a victim of the twin evils of excessive early praise and later critical disappointment, said this about critical reaction to Rattigan:

> The critics do talk a lot of rubbish about craftsmanship because it's something they don't understand at all . . . The fact is that Terence Rattigan's craftsmanship is like a carriage clock. They can see the insides and the workings of it, so it makes them feel more comfortable. They think: 'Oh, yes, I see, that's what he's going to do next – very good!' – And so he gets ten out of ten all the time, quite rightly.[2]

Osborne's observation about craftsmanship seems borne out by the fact that since Rattigan's death perhaps the most obviously well crafted of his plays, *The Winslow Boy*, has been more regularly revived than any other. However, the most significant point about what Osborne says is that he does not find craftsmanship Rattigan's most praiseworthy quality. As we have seen, for one of the playwrights who followed the Osborne generation, David Rudkin,

Rattigan was not at all 'the commercial, middlebrow dramatist his image suggests, but someone peculiarly haunting and oblique, who certainly speaks to me with resonances of existential bleakness and irresoluble carnal solitude'.

The over-concentration on Rattigan's craftsmanship has persisted into the present. In large measure its origins lie in his unprecedented run of successes. To be so consistently successful over the twenty years between 1936 and 1956 implied to his contemporaries a degree of calculating workmanship which could only be put down to exceptional craftsmanship. But the image ignored his failures, both as craftsman and popular entertainer. Two crucial plays, so to speak, disappeared from Rattigan's canon: *Follow My Leader* and *After the Dance*. Rattigan sealed this disappearance by excluding them from his *Collected Plays. After the Dance* is his best serious play before *The Browning Version*, and is in no way the work of a boulevard dramatist. Its commercial failure was, at least in part, due to the accident of timing by which it opened on the eve of the Second World War. The failure of *Follow My Leader* was likewise due to circumstances beyond Rattigan's control. Had it been produced in 1938 amid the controversy surrounding the Munich Crisis, as Rattigan and Goldschmidt had wished, and not been blocked by the Lord Chamberlain's office and the Foreign Office's fear of antagonizing Hitler, *Follow My Leader* would surely have had an impact on Rattigan's reputation, even if it had failed commercially. In 1949, the playwright Ted Willis, reviewing *Adventure Story* for the communist *Daily Worker*, had expressed surprise at the discovery that Rattigan had a conscience. It is hard to believe that Willis would not have noticed Rattigan's conscience earlier had he known of *After the Dance*, *Follow My Leader*, or of the original version of *Love in Idleness*. The failure of *After the Dance* and *Follow My Leader* bit deep with Rattigan and he banished them from memory, along with *First Episode*, until late in his life. It was a weakness that Rattigan allowed himself to be so much influenced by contemporary critics, the demands of commercial managers, of stars and ticket sales. By the time of *Flare Path* there was, as Keith Newman suggested, evidence of his writing sometimes being too much influenced during conception by glances at the box office, with the result that some of his dramatic babies were born with more than a hint of theatrical squint.

As we have seen, until late in life Rattigan all too often failed to stand up for his own work in the face of demands from actors and managers. When he did do so he surprised himself, as he admitted in his letter to Laurence Olivier at the time of *Man and Boy*. Had Rattigan stood up to the Lunts during the production of *Love in Idleness* it might have had a lasting impact on the way in which he developed as a writer and on his reputation. *Less Than Kind*, the play he originally wrote, was a much more politically aware and ambiguous one than the undemanding boulevard comedy he allowed to emerge in its place. Yet, although he bent to the wind of popular expectation, Rattigan still did not deviate so far from his own chosen course. At the core of most of the plays the values still remained consistently his own. Three of his most philosophically uncompromising plays were written at the height of his popularity and were among his most commercially successful: *The Browning Version*, *The Deep Blue Sea* and *Separate Tables*. Set against the commercial pressures of the theatre for which he wrote, his achievement is prodigious.

There is a comment, by an unknown critic, in one of Rattigan's scrapbooks dated about 1954 which reads: 'He chooses lost and confused people who are afraid of life. And in the last act he reclaims them triumphantly through the sympathy of their neighbours. He makes them feel they belong to the human race.' The climaxes of the plays, while often depending on a self-revelation, always involve a decision, a conscious choice on the part of the principal characters. The much-criticized 'happy endings' are never the result of fate; they are the result of a deliberate and hard-come-by decision. They are not really happy endings because while they may lift the heart of the audience through some small act which reasserts human dignity, they nevertheless leave the characters with a lifetime of further, unresolved decisions ahead of them. Their future is in their own hands and depends upon the triumph of the rational over the irrational, courage over cowardice, imagination over pig-headedness, liberalism over prejudice. These

471

are the values of the rational humanist philosophers of Rattigan's youth, men like Huxley and Russell, who so outraged his parents' generation.

At the end of *The Sound Barrier*, Rattigan depicted man as a child alone in a godless and uncaring universe, his fate in his own hands. This Rattigan refused to see as a depressing prospect, but as a challenge in which man has the advantage. He can conquer not only his environment but his pain and fear, if he uses the weapons he has been given – love, imagination, intelligence and courage. In his plays Rattigan set out to show that they offer no easy option, but that they are the only hope that men and women have.

But lack of courage was one of the charges that his critics levelled against Rattigan. They accused him of failing to use his dominant position in the commercial theatre openly to confront the predominantly conservative values and tastes of the ruling social and theatrical élite. That charge was heard again fifteen years after his death, this time in respect of Gay Rights. In his 1992 book *Not in Front of the Audience*,[3] the critic Nicholas de Jongh accused Rattigan of pussy-footing over depicting homosexual characters and gay passion in his plays. De Jongh argued that had Rattigan depicted Major Pollock's offence in *Separate Tables* as a homosexual offence, its positive impact, especially coming from his pen, on the struggle to change the law and lift the persecution of homosexuals, might have been considerable. He dismissed as disingenuous Rattigan's justification: 'If I had written the man as a homosexual the play might have been construed as a thesis drama, begging tolerance specifically of the homosexual. Instead it is a plea for understanding everyone.' De Jongh accused Rattigan of wanting, more than once, to write a 'thesis' drama about homosexuality but then of funking it.

A few years later a contrasting view of Rattigan was advanced by the young critic and theatre director Sean O'Connor. In a brilliant analysis of Rattigan's work in his 1998 book *Straight Acting*,[4] O'Connor suggested that he was dealing with the problem of integrating sex into life, rather than compartmentalising it. Dismissing those who concluded that because Rattigan, like Coward and Tennessee Williams, focused on the dilemmas of women he was committing a form of 'literary transvestism', O'Connor said: 'It's very easy, but not very helpful, to presume that Blanche Dubois is simply Williams in chiffon drag or that Hester in *The Deep Blue Sea* is "really" a gay man just because Rattigan was himself. Such a superficial reading devalues Williams' and Rattigan's imaginative and artistic achievements and smacks of the ingrained misogyny and homophobia of literary studies.'

Edward Albee, another writer who has been charged by critics with dramatic transvestism, dealt with the issue head-on in an article for the *New York Times*:[5] 'It was absolutely preposterous, the notion that gays were writing about gays, but disguising them as straights. Tennessee Williams knew the difference between men and women as well as I do. If you're writing about men, you're writing about men, and if you're writing about women, you're writing about women.'

The fact, surely, is that Gay Rights, however laudable and no matter how much he sympathized with it, was not Rattigan's subject. The struggle for Gay Liberation was the cause of C. H. Rolph, Andrew Halliday Smith, Anthony Grey and the courageous campaigners of the Homosexual Law Reform Society. Rattigan's subject was the difficulty of love, the clash between the persuasion of the mind and the unbidden urgings of the body (Holly Hill's mind-body dichotomy), the failure of people to express their feelings and to meet each other's needs; things common to all men and women. Gender is not the issue here. Had Rattigan allowed *The Deep Blue Sea* to be presented as a homosexual love affair, or the Major's crime in *Separate Tables* to be homosexual soliciting, he might have caused a stir (assuming that he was able to get round the censorship of the Lord Chamberlain's office) and he would almost certainly have drawn attention to himself. In the climate of the time it is possible that this would have led to his arrest (we have noted how the authorities hounded Montagu, Pitt-Rivers and Wildeblood). It would have made Rattigan a martyr, but how much it would have advanced the cause of homosexual rights is questionable. It would certainly have obscured the true subject of both plays. Yes, there may have been an element of lack of personal courage in his decision. But this should not be the basis for damning him as a writer or for ignoring his real virtues as a playwright.

In 1993, a year after the publication of de Jongh's attack on Rattigan for pussy-footing over the issue of homosexuality, *Separate Tables*, using Rattigan's original West End text in which the Major's offence was causing a nuisance to women in a cinema, proved a success when revived in the West End. However, when the text Rattigan had written for the 1956 Broadway production but was talked out of using, in which the Major's offence is importuning men, was revived in 2009 at the Chichester Festival Theatre critical opinion was divided. While some people thought the homosexual text strengthened the play others felt that it weakened it, making the play, as Rattigan himself had argued, simply 'a thesis drama' pleading for understanding for homosexuals. Today, with public attitudes towards homosexuality more tolerant than in Rattigan's lifetime, Rattigan's argument seems more valid than ever. To many members of today's audience the Major's offence of approaching unescorted women in a darkened cinema, 'nudging' them and attempting to 'take other liberties', almost certainly appears more objectionable than the offence of soliciting men for sex.

Back in 1979, the great theatre director Sir Peter Hall, reflecting on Rattigan's talent in his diaries, had appeared to support the charge of dramatic transvestism, but in doing so had revealed the quality in Rattigan that gives his plays particular resonance:

> Perhaps any homosexual dramatist who, during a time of secrecy and blackmail, presented his own emotional life in his work as if he were a woman, suffered some terrible disability . . . I think the problem with Rattigan was that even if he had the opportunity for frankness, his whole repressed class background, the stiff upper lip of Harrow, would have made it impossible for him. Deception and restraint are at the heart of that kind of Englishman. I suppose it's at the heart of me, heterosexual as I am.[6]

The critic Charles Spencer, in a *Daily Telegraph* review of the 1998 revival of *Cause Célèbre* at the Lyric, Hammersmith, pointed to the real importance for Rattigan's work of his homosexuality.

Arguing that his best plays — *The Browning Version* and *The Deep Blue Sea* — are harrowing accounts of 'repressed pain and tumultuous emotion' in which Rattigan reveals himself as the 'champion of the lonely heart in its struggles with English respectability', Spencer concluded: 'The fact that he never felt able to write directly about his own homosexuality, taken by some to be a mark of dishonesty or cowardice, actually adds an extra level of hurt to his work.' Indeed, and it is the deception and restraint which Sir Peter Hall finds at the heart of himself as much as at the heart of Rattigan, that gives the plays their enduring resonance with English audiences.

During his lifetime, although he was respected in some European countries, Rattigan never enjoyed the same critical respect in the United States, even at the height of his fame, as he did in Britain. Yet in the mid-1970s, shortly before Rattigan's death, at a time when feminism and women's rights were at the forefront of public consciousness, it was an American, Holly Hill, who in her thesis and a series of articles and theatre reviews, championed Rattigan. She was perhaps the first person to recognize in Rattigan's writing a unique insight into the feelings and dilemmas of women. One only has to remember Ivor Brown's response in his *Observer* review of *The Deep Blue Sea* — that all that Hester Collyer needed was a good slap and a chat with a marriage-guidance counsellor — to realize how far Rattigan was ahead of his time.

In the early 1980s another American woman, Professor Susan Rusinko (to whom this book is dedicated), took up the torch that Holly Hill had lit. She devoted a whole book, aimed primarily at university students studying literature, to the work of Rattigan. In it she highlighted another important characteristic of Rattigan's work which had until then largely been overlooked. Demolishing the accepted view of Rattigan as a craftsman of the 'well-made play' in the tradition of Pinero, Rusinko compared Rattigan with Chekhov. She analysed the way in which, like Chekhov, Rattigan builds up his scenes and his plays from small, seemingly flat and unrelated details. Writing in 1983, she said that Rattigan's plays are 'characterized by a refinement of mind and style that time is already beginning to prove are more than English public-school virtues and sleek techniques'. Rusinko argued that Rattigan's 'miniaturist elegance of scene construction', particularly in plays such as *The Browning Version* and *In Praise of Love*, 'the ironies and subtle unspoken truths, suggest increasingly the indirectness of Chekhov'. Of Rattigan's often controversial endings, Rusinko wrote:

Rattigan's Chekhovian sense of the continuity of things can be seen particularly in the strong yet deliberately mundane and flat statements made by characters at the conclusions of the plays. These statements are a call to a resumption of life, such as Andrew Crocker Harris's quiet, 'We mustn't let our dinner get cold,' or Sebastian's telling Joey, 'Go on. Move, Joey,' when underneath the routine of the chess game lies the agonizing knowledge of Lydia's impending death. By narrative means, Rattigan's subtextural meanings, like Chekhov's so-called plotless plays, reveal states of being in which internal changes have long since occurred. Characters may be bored, troubled, life-damaged, isolated from communication with others, and alienated from their times, but they do continue to survive and to find some degree of community and communication . . . From self-know-ledge they gather what strength they can, and they endure.[7]

The continuing resonance of Rattigan's work for audiences is borne out by the fact that so many of his plays continue to be successfully produced. In 1980, the National Theatre at last mounted the revival of *The Browning Version*, together with *Harlequinade*, which had been under discussion in the eighteen months before Rattigan's death. The National Theatre's production was a great success, although a 1994 film, starring Albert Finney as the Crock, was less good. In opening out the action it missed the essential Strindbergian claustrophobia of Millie and Crocker Harris's relationship and the stultifying effect of the closed school community, which should act as a metaphor for the wider repression of difference and self-realization in society itself. In the 1951 Anthony Asquith film, which also opened out the action,

Michael Redgrave's astonishing and deeply felt performance managed to internalize and at the same time express the pressure cooker of the Crock's emotions. On stage at Derby Playhouse in 2002, Corin Redgrave emulated his father's memorable screen achievement, with a performance as the Crock which the *Daily Telegraph* critic hailed as a 'masterclass'. Another screen version of the play in 1985, this time by BBC Television using the original Rattigan theatre text and benefiting from superb performances by Ian Holm and Judi Dench as the Crocker Harrises, succeeded in realizing its full Stringbergian power while at the same time bringing out its wider resonances. The production was nominated for a BAFTA award and was shown in America and around the world. Since then further productions have followed at regular intervals.

Another of Rattigan's shortest and most compact plays, *In Praise of Love*, has also continued to resonate with audiences here and in other countries. In 1995 it was staged in both South Africa and in the West End. In 2001, the Theatre Royal in Bath mounted a particularly fine production that released the play's full pent-up emotional power with real-life husband-and-wife team Julian Glover and Isla Blair excellent as Sebastian and Lydia. However, a 2006 production at the Minerva Theatre in Chichester was less well received. The critics detected that by using the expanded version of the text that Rattigan had prepared for the original 1974 Broadway production, the play's explosive emotional power had been diffused and thus weakened. The Minerva production, therefore, served to highlight one of Rattigan's essential characteristics and a major source of his plays' power – their economy.

In the years since his death a number of commentators have likened Rattigan's writing, especially in the shorter plays such as *The Browning Version* and *In Praise of Love*, to that of Strindberg. The other play of similar Strindbergian power, but in three acts, is *The Deep Blue Sea*. In recent years it has received even more major productions than either *The Browning Version* or *In Praise of Love*. There have been revivals in New York and at the National Theatre of Portugal, as well as many in Britain. A 1993 production at the Almeida Theatre in Islington, starring Penelope Wilton as Hester, successfully transferred to the West End. It was directed by Karel Reisz, a director associated with the Royal Court school of dramatists and the revival in British cinema in the late 1950s and early 1960s. Earlier, in 1981, Dorothy Tutin had given a stupendous performance as Hester, surely the best since Peggy Ashcroft in the original, at the Greenwich Theatre. However, this was considerably undermined by the failure of her Freddie to catch the character's charm and seeming nonchalance. One of the difficulties of staging Rattigan plays today is that the new generation of actors, brought up in an age and dramatic tradition more used to the raw expression of emotion, often find it difficult to portray the understated and convention-bound world of Rattigan's generation. In Rattigan's world underlying emotions and repression are slowly revealed through the characters apparent ease and good manners. This surface is not something the characters consciously put on like make-up or brilliantine, but a manner and form of behaviour unconsciously acquired so that it has become an integral part of their character. Happily, this was not a problem in a fine production in 2002 by the young director Thea Sharrock in which Harriet Walter gave a performance as Hester to match that by Dorothy Tutin in 1981. Such productions underline afresh that quality in Rattigan first highlighted by Holly Hill – the extent to which he was ahead of his time in his portrayal of women. *The Deep Blue Sea* had to wait until 2008 before getting its first production in Ireland. Then, when it was produced at the Gate Theatre in Dublin, Helen Meany, writing in the *Guardian*, found herself struck by the play's lack of misogyny and moral judgement. She even went so far as to doubt whether such a play could have been written or staged at all in Ireland at the time when Rattigan was working on it in the early 1950s.

However, since Rattigan's death the play that has received the most regular major revivals has been *The Winslow Boy*. One of Rattigan's least obviously Chekhovian or Strindbergian works, it is perhaps the one which is, in the most obvious way, 'well crafted'. In 1990, a BBC production of the play, starring Emma Thompson, Ian Richardson and Gordon Jackson, was shown coast-to-coast on American television. It seemed to strike a particularly timely chord with Americans. In a country founded on the ideals of individual liberty and independence from the over-mighty state, perhaps this should not be surprising. Reviewing the play in the *Wall Street Journal*, Martha Bayles called it:

> a minor masterpiece, whose virtues show up all the more clearly, now that the dust from the 1950s has settled . . . [it] illustrates the special need to be vigilant against tyranny at home while fighting it abroad. Skeptics keep telling Arthur and Catherine that the troubles of young Ronnie look pretty puny when compared to world events. And Arthur and Catherine keep replying that the individual's right to defend his innocence looks pretty big to them.[8]

Across the country newspapers focused on the play as 'a hymn to individual liberty against despots everywhere' and highlighted Rattigan's vital distinction between the need to do 'right' rather than simply dispense 'justice'. The *Los Angeles Times* called the play a glowing reminder of the universality of Rattigan's 'genteel drama', which remains 'remarkably bracing and timely'.[9]

The ongoing potency for Americans of *The Winslow Boy* and of Rattigan's insistence on ethical questions was strikingly demonstrated in 1999, when, in his closing argument to the Senate's Clinton-impeachment hearings, Congressman Henry Hyde cited Rattigan's treatment of the Archer-Shee case alongside Shakespeare's *Henry V* and Gibbon's *Decline and Fall*. He told senators that he had seen the play and the movie and had a copy of 'the book' and had always been moved by it. He urged senators to follow Arthur Winslow's example in speaking truth to power. He closed his speech by quoting from the play: 'Let Right be done.' Whether or not Rattigan would have been altogether happy to be called to the aid of those seeking to throw out President Clinton does not detract from Hyde's choice of text as a demonstration of Rattigan's universality and power as a dramatist. The point was reinforced by the 1999 release of David Mamet's new film of *The Winslow Boy*, starring Nigel Hawthorne as Arthur Winslow. Mamet, the author of plays such as *Glengarry Glen Ross* and

American Buffalo, and adaptations of *The Three Sisters*, *The Cherry Orchard* and *Uncle Vanya*, proved in many ways the ideal adapter and director for a new big-screen version of *The Winslow Boy*. He told his actors that he believed *The Winslow Boy* to be 'one of the most immaculately written texts in theatre history' and is on record as regarding the play as a masterpiece. In spite of opening out the action to include scenes in the courtroom and the House of Commons to meet the requirements of the cinema, Mamet remained strikingly faithful to the spirit of Rattigan's intentions. He saw Rattigan as exploring a question which is timeless, as resonant at the end of the 1990s when Mamet was working on the film as when Rattigan wrote it. Mamet saw the central question at the play's heart as this: assuming that Ronnie Winslow with his postal order, or a woman accusing Clinton, or anyone else in a similar position is telling the truth – is it worth it?

> At what point are you willing to pursue truth at the chance of either being called a liar or being acknowledged as having told the truth, and having your privacy destroyed? At what point does it cease being courage and become intractability or arrogance? And again, it's an open question. What have you won when you've won? What's the cost of holding a principle?[10]

That central question was posed again with a particularly satisfying clarity in a 2009 production by Stephen Unwin for the English Touring Theatre. Starring Timothy West as an immensely determined, if physically ailing Arthur Winslow, the production succeeded in a way that not all productions do in maintaining the focus securely on that central question. For today's British audiences, faced with a government which often appears dictatorial, is widely accused of attacking civil liberties in the name of combating Islamic terrorism and would seem to be mired mired in corruption, it is a question which has just as much resonance as it did for the post-war audience for whom Rattigan wrote it.

In our original 1979 biography of Rattigan, the first book wholly devoted to his life and work, Gillian Hodson and I were asking, in effect, 'Let Right be done' in the case of the recognition afforded to him as a playwright. Today there is, happily, no longer any need for me to repeat that plea. To reiterate the words of Sean O'Connor in 1998, which I quoted in the Introduction: 'Rattigan seems to have finally confirmed his status as one of the great British dramatists of the·[twentieth] century.' O'Connor went on to explain why it was more than the turn of the wheel of theatrical taste that had enabled his generation to recognize Rattigan's true stature. Even though Rattigan's world and the world inherited by O'Connor's generation are seemingly so different, Rattigan's plays have continued to have a particular resonance for the millennial generation: 'Their great success,' O'Connor says, 'is in articulating the anxieties of difference, of the will to fit in, to be ordinary; and of a corresponding desire to be extraordinary, to be different, to be individual. It is this tension that has enabled these works to transcend the trappings of their period, which had been much of their original attraction for my grandmother in the 1940s and 1950s, and to resonate emotionally for me today.'[11]

Today, more than thirty years since Rattigan's death, hardly a month goes by without one of his plays being on in a theatre somewhere. Over the last twenty years there have probably been more major productions of Rattigan's plays around the world than at any time since his heyday in the 1950s. Not only does this now seem likely to continue but, with the stimulus of the celebrations to mark the centenary of his birth, the number of productions seems set to increase. Not only will there be new productions of many of the plays in theatres in this country and around the world, the National Film Theatre is organizing a retrospective season of his films and an exhibition of his papers is being mounted by the British Library.

Yet the plays which are revived continue to be overwhelmingly those plays which he wrote between the end of the Second World War and his eclipse by the Osborne generation in 1956. The only real exception has been the play from the end of his life in which he returned to his most secure and oblique Chekhovian method, *In Praise of Love*. I have already commented on the 1998 Lyric, Hammersmith, production of that other late play with the potential to release a similar intensity of emotion, *Cause Célèbre*. However, it still cries out for a production that can realize its full potential (realized to some extent in the original radio production but, so far as I know, not since) to be understood as a psychological whole, revealing the two parallel plots as two facets of a single human psyche.

One other play dating from the post-1956 period, a play to which Rattigan himself attached considerable importance, has enjoyed something of a rehabilitation: *Man and Boy*. This has been due mainly to an excellent production by Maria Aitken in 2004–5, which toured Britain and then enjoyed a successful run at London's Duchess Theatre. Not content to rely on the original published text alone, Aitken conducted a thorough search of the Rattigan Papers relating to the play held in the British Library. Working from these, she made a number of judicious cuts and re-introduced various sections from Rattigan's own earlier notes and drafts. Although the result could not totally disguise the play's intrinsically melodramatic nature, the production, greatly helped by a towering performance by David Suchet as Antonescu, was emotionally engaging in a way that the original production with Charles Boyer had never been.

Rattigan's earlier plays have on the whole fared less well. In 1995, to coincide with the fiftieth anniversary of the end of World War II, there were copious revivals outside London of *While the Sun Shines* and *Flare Path*. *Flare Path* was given a particularly good production by the Bristol Old Vic. Far from proving the ultimate piece of period propaganda, relevant only to 1990s audiences as a dose of nostalgia, it was played without self-conscious aping of period mannerisms. As a result its characters' dilemmas and fears came back to life, gripping, moving and as engaging as in 1942. Regrettably, since then there have been only occasional productions and none of particular note. *French Without Tears* has received rather more productions. In 2002 there was a particularly good one at the Northcott Theatre, Exeter, with a young cast throwing themselves into the play without any of the self-conscious aping of what is often caricatured as the 1930s acting style. As a result, the predominantly young audiences at the Northcott (the theatre is in the campus grounds of Exeter University) laughed throughout in sheer delight, much as their great-grandparents had in the 1930s. Sadly, however, a 2007 English Touring Theatre production failed to convince all the critics that the play was anything more than a thin series of riffs on the English male's fear of women and female sexuality.

On the other hand, Rattigan's one 'lost' truly major play dating from the early years, *After the Dance*, at last seems to be making a long overdue return to the recognized canon of his most important and characteristic works. In 1994 the BBC dug out a copy of the text and produced it on television. Although less than perfectly done, the production reawoke interest in it and the following year a new edition of the play was published by Nick Hern Books, with a brilliant Introduction by Dan Rebellato.[12] In 2002 it received its first significant stage production for more than sixty years when Dominic Dromgoole directed it for the Oxford Stage Company and the Salisbury Playhouse. Although the playing of some of the leading parts was less than perfect, the staging of the major scenes was well handled and audiences were left in no doubt as to the play's intrinsic quality and power. To seal *After the Dance's* return to the canon of Rattigan's most important works, the National Theatre has announced a new production opening in June 2010, directed by Thea Sharrock, the director responsible for the fine 2002 production of *The Deep Blue Sea* in which Harriet Walter gave such a powerful performance as Hester. This production of *After the Dance* will mark the launch of the series of major events building up to the centenary of Rattigan's birth in 2011.

In addition, over recent years there have been a number of more formal signifiers of the growing recognition of Rattigan as one of Britain's leading dramatists. In June 2005 an official English Heritage Blue Plaque was unveiled by David Suchet on the wall of the house in Cornwall Gardens, Kensington, where Rattigan was born. Two years later a plaque commemorating Rattigan's many years of residence in Albany was unveiled outside number K5 by Sir Derek Jacobi.

Sadly, the original Hamish Hamilton *Collected Plays of Terence Rattigan* has been out of print for some years, but Nick Hern

Books and Dan Rebellato have continued to work their way steadily through the plays and have to date republished seven of the best known. They are also working on three of his lesser known works. Particularly welcome among these will be *First Episode*, as it will give readers a long overdue opportunity to evaluate Rattigan's development across his whole career.

Among the titles about to be republished by Nick Hern Books is *Love in Idleness*. It is to be hoped that, as well as giving readers a chance to read the text originally performed by Alfred Lunt and Lynn Fontanne, which so distorted Rattigan's original intentions, the new Nick Hern Books and Rebellato edition will direct people back to Rattigan's original, much stronger text, the one accepted by the Lord Chamberlain for production under the title *Less Than Kind*. If not the public perception of Rattigan as an essentially conservative, boulevard dramatist will remain much harder to shake off. Perhaps one day in the not too distant future Nick Hern Books and Dan Rebellato will bring out a complete edition of all of Rattigan's performed plays, possibly together with a few of the most interesting of those that still remain unperformed. Only then will the public be able to gain a real insight into the true extent of Rattigan's achievement and of his importance in British twentieth-century drama.

Susan Rusinko described Rattigan's plays as 'polished without being slick, natural without untidiness'. 'Rattigan's art,' she asserted, 'has given firm shape to the mid-twentieth-century mainstreams of English life, chronicling the sweeping changes in the moods and attitudes of the times, as did Chekhov for his time.' Today, almost three decades after she wrote that, we can see ever more clearly that she was right. Just as we can hear the axe of approaching revolution hacking its way towards us through Chekhov's cherry orchard so, in Rattigan's best plays of the 1930s, 1940s and early 1950s, we can hear the tramp of approaching war, the replacement of the old order by the welfare state and the coming roar of the Angry Young Men in the uncertainties and emotional hesitations of Rattigan's characters. Freddie Page, Hester Collyer and the residents of the Beauregard Hotel in Bournemouth, although they do not talk politics, are as much a reflection of the British middle class of the generation who had, in the phrase of the time, 'lost an Empire but failed to find a role' as Chekhov's three sisters or the characters in *Uncle Vanya* are a reflection of the Russian leisured class of around 1900. Their unease and discontent reflect and prefigure an age of coming change as much as Chekhov's characters reflect and focus the era preceding the Russian Revolution.

In the 'Play of Ideas' debate, James Bridie asked if *Adventure Story* or *The Browning Version* were bereft of ideas, and gave the answer no. The same answer can be given about most of Rattigan's plays, the comedies as much as the dramas. Rattigan fell out of favour because in the 1950s and 1960s his plays were not about contemporary politics or the working class. He wrote about the things that mattered most to him – emotions and ethics. These are timeless. As he made clear in his letter to Elkan Allan, to him all political questions are ethical questions. Even in his least satisfactory plays, such as *Adventure Story* and *Ross*, the central question he poses – is a man great because of what he is or what he does? – is an ethical question.

Rattigan was, in fact, a descendant of that most ancient of all lines of dramatists, a moral dramatist. Although he came from a puritanical background and wrote about repressed characters, the morality of his plays was neither repressive nor puritanical. His philosophy was rational, his values anti-authoritarian and liberal. Writing of the difficulties of love and the inequality of passion, his moral was always affirmative, his plea was for sympathy and tolerance, even though all around him he found intolerance.

When the theatrical revolution of the mid-fifties arrived, Rattigan's image ensured that he would not be recognized for what he was. When he tried to move with the times, he failed. The removal of theatrical taboos coincided with an increased preoccupation in his plays with sex, rather than sex subsumed in love. When he tried to write openly about sex, he found he could not. This was not so much from fear or lingering doubts about the acceptability of homosexuality on the stage, but because, as Sir Peter Hall recognized, his whole personality and quality as a writer was geared to the oblique and the implicit. In *Variation on a Theme*, Sam Duveen says: 'Feelings can't sometimes be helped – but the expression of them can.' In the decade of exuberant taboo-smashing and loud-voiced didactic play-making that followed *Look Back in Anger*, Rattigan lacked not only the instinct and the inclination to write in accordance with the new orthodoxy, but the power of rhetorical language. Verbal aridity, with a sometimes irritating reliance on the kind of slick antithetical word-play that so exasperated Kenneth Tynan, has in the last twenty years been recognized, at its understated best, as one of Rattigan's most enduring strengths.

The critic Michael Billington has argued that few dramatists of the twentieth century wrote 'with more understanding of the human heart than Terence Rattigan'. In order to appreciate the consistent penetration of that understanding one only has to look at two works that no one has thought it worth producing in recent years, one from the very start and one from the end of Rattigan's career – *First Episode* and *Nijinsky*. Both plays deal with homosexual relationships, but both depict with rare sympathy and insight emotions and dilemmas with which the whole audience can identify – unequal love, humiliation and the need to be wanted. That the virtues of neither of these plays was properly recognized was not due to Rattigan. *First Episode* was cut and messed about to meet the needs of its commercial management and the taboos on the presentation of homosexual love during the 1930s. That *Nijinsky* has never been produced was due in the first instance to the objections of Romola Nijinsky. Later attempts to produce it fell foul of a new orthodoxy which interpreted Rattigan's depiction of Romola as 'not sufficiently sympathetic to women'.[13] This is ironic indeed, as the revival in Rattigan's critical reputation was due in large measure to women critics who recognized in his writing a special understanding and sympathy for the position of women.

Two other unperformed Rattigan scripts are certainly worth re-examining and trying out, although both are raw and unpolished. The most difficult is *Pas de Deux*, simply because it needs the addition of songs, music and choreography. But, for the insight it provides into Rattigan's own world and the way in which it depicts people exploring their own sexuality and their feelings of uncertainty and inadequacy about their sexual and emotional identity, it should repay the difficulty of mounting even a small-scale, studio production. *Less Than Kind*, the unperformed but much more penetrating original version of *Love in Idleness*, really ought to be done. It needs care in rehearsal if the comedy is to be as strong as in the version performed by the Lunts, but it is a much more interesting and engrossing play than *Love in Idleness*. It provides a real insight into the concerns of British people towards the end of the Second World War and immediately before the election which ushered in Attlee's government and the welfare state.

Susan Rusinko summed up Rattigan's achievement in these words: 'His comedies, history plays, and moving dramas about flawed or failed characters course their way unerringly down the moral and emotional mainstream of their troubled times.' Rattigan himself, as he repeatedly told his closest friends, wanted to be considered alongside Shakespeare and Shaw among British play-wrights. He is not to be compared with Shakespeare – no one is – and he is different from Shaw. But his best plays endure, as do the best eight or ten plays of Shaw. More than half a century after the period of his greatest popularity, and some ninety years after he lay on his narrow school bed dreaming of winning a test match for England and of being cheered by a first-night audience and hugged by the stars of the day, Rattigan would be pleased to know that, as the stage manager tells Arthur Gosport at the end of *Harlequinade*, 'The audience is in front.' It now seems increasingly certain to go on being there for Terence Rattigan for generations to come.

Notes

1 Rattigan expressed a wish to be cremated, but as this could not be done in Bermuda it was undertaken in Canada. There is a memorial tablet to him in 'the actors' church' – St Paul's, Covent Garden.

2 *Terence Rattigan: A Tribute*, BBC Television, 2 December 1977.

3 *Not in Front of the Audience, Homosexuality on the Stage* by Nicholas de Jongh, Routledge, London, 1992.

4 *Straight Acting: Popular Gay Drama from Wilde to Rattigan* by Sean O'Connor, Cassell, London, 1998.

5 Quoted in *Evening Standard*, London, but undated.

6   *Peter Hall's Diaries – The Story of a Dramatic Battle*, edited by John Goodwin, Hamish Hamilton, London, 1983. Entry for 4 August 1979.

7   *Terence Rattigan* by Susan Rusinko, Twayne Publishers, G. K. Hall & Company, Boston, 1983.

8   *Wall Street Journal*, New York, 5 February 1990.

9   *Los Angeles Times*, Los Angeles, 9 February 1990.

10   The only quibble one might have with Mamet's adaptation is the hint he introduces at the very end of there being some possibility of a future romantic relationship between Catherine and Sir Robert, thus diverting the audience's attention in the film's final moments away from the central question which Mamet himself outlines so clearly. However, in saying that, one also has to admit that Rattigan himself does seem at one time to have sanctioned such an ending, even though he had specifically vetoed the suggestion when the play was first produced on Broadway.

Appendix

Original Casts, Directors, Theatres, Opening Dates and Number of Performances of Principal Productions of Rattigan's Plays in Britain and the United States

Cast lists and directing credits have been compiled and cross-referenced from Rattigan's published plays, *Who's Who* and London and New York reviews.

First Episode (with Philip Heimann)

London: Q Theatre (opened 11 September 1933), transferred to Comedy Theatre
Opening: 26 January 1934
Performances: approximately 80

ALBERT ARNOLD	Max Adrian
PHILIP KAHN	Angus L. MacLeod (Q Theatre: Owen Griffith)
JOHN TAYLOR	Meriel Forbes-Robertson
TONY WODEHOUSE	William Fox (Q Theatre: Noel Dryden)
DAVID LISTER	Patrick Waddington
MARGOT GRESHAM	Barbara Hoffe (Q Theatre: Rosalinde Fuller)
JAMES	Vincent King
A BULLER	Jack Allen (Q Theatre: Robert Syers)

Director: Muriel Pratt

New York: Ritz Theatre
Opening: 17 September 1934
Performances: approximately 40

ALBERT ARNOLD	Max Adrian
PHILIP KAHN	Statts Cotsworth
JOAN TAYLOR	Gerrie Worthing
TONY WODEHOUSE	John Halloran
DAVID LISTER	Patrick Waddington
MARGOT GRESHAM	Leona Maricle
JAMES	Stanley Harrison
A BULLER	T.C. Dunham

Director: Haddon Mason

A Tale of Two Cities (with John Gielgud)

From the novel by Charles Dickens. Written in 1935 but unperformed until 1950
Britain: St Brendan's College Dramatic Society, Clifton
Opening: 23 January 1950
Performances: 6

JARVIS LORRY	Paul Vassalli
JERRY CRUNCHER	Brian Sweet
MADAME DEFARGE	Paul Casling
LUCIE MANETTE	Peter Evans
MISS PROSS	Michael Ryan
ERNEST DEFARGE	Michael Woodley
DR MANETTE	Murray Case
CHARLES DARNAY	Peter Pullin
BARSAD	Peter Hawkins
THE ATTORNEY GENERAL	Colin Culham
SYDNEY CARTON	Derek Crabtree
THE JUDGE	Paddy Love
MR STRYVER	Ralph Tozer
THE SOLICITOR GENERAL	Ronald Smith
GASPARD	John Blake
JACQUES – HIS CHILD	Robin Hallett

JULES	Michael Stewart
GABELLE	John MacDonald
THE MARQUIS DE ST EVREMONDE	Frank Pitt
A ROAD MENDER	Terence Ryan
A VALET	Robert Philpott
CLERK IN TEUSON'S OFFICE	Gordon Baker
AN EMIGRE	J. Tunnard Jackson
A GAOLER IN THE CONCIERGERIE	Peter Blake
A PATRIOT AT THE BARRIER	Terence Walsh
A REVOLUTIONARY	Clive Smith

Director: Hedley Goodall

(First professional production on BBC radio, 1950. Produced by Cleland Finn, with Eric Portman as Sydney Carton.)

Grey Farm (with Hector Bolitho)

(Written in 1935 but not performed until 1940)
New York: Hudson Theatre
Opening: 3 May 1940
Performances: approximately 35

MRS IRON	Evelyn Varden
STEPHEN GRANTHAM	John Cromwell
JUDITH WEAVER	Jane Sterling
JAMES GRANTHAM	Oscar Homolka
MAVIS	Maria Temple
LADY WEAVER	Adrienna Morrison
ELLEN	Vera Mellish

Director: Berthold Viertel

French Without Tears

London: Criterion Theatre
Opening: 6 November 1936
Performances: 1,030

KENNETH LAKE	Trevor Howard

BRIAN CURTIS	Guy Middleton
HON. ALAN HOWARD	Rex Harrison
MARIANNE	Yvonne André
MONSIEUR MAINGOT	Percy Walsh
LT.-CMDR. ROGERS	Roland Culver
DIANA LAKE	Kay Hammond
KIT NEILAN	Robert Flemyng
JACQUELINE MAINGOT	Jessica Tandy
LORD HEYBROOK	William Dear

Director: Harold French

New York: Henry Miller Theatre
Opening: 28 September 1937
Performances: 111

KENNETH LAKE	Philip Friend
BRIAN CURTIS	Guy Middleton
HON. ALAN HOWARD	Frank Lawton
MARIANNE	Simone Petitjean
MONSIEUR MAINGOT	Marcel Valée
LT.-CMDR. ROGERS	Cyril Raymond
DIANA LAKE	Penelope Dudley Ward
JACQUELINE MAINGOT	Jacqueline Porel
LORD HEYBROOK	Edward Ryan, Jr

Director: Harold French

After the Dance

London: St. James's Theatre
Opening: 21 June 1939
Performances: 60

JOHN REID	Martin Walker
PETER SCOTT-FOWLER	Hubert Gregg
WILLIAMS	Gordon Court
JOAN SCOTT-FOWLER	Catherine Lacey
HELEN BANNER	Anne Firth
DR GEORGE BANNER	Robert Kempson

JULIA BROWNE	Viola Lyd
CYRIL CARTER	Leonard Coppins
DAVID SCOTT-FOWLER	Robert Harris
MOVA LEXINGTON	Millicent Wolf
LAWRENCE WALTERS	Osmund Willson
ARTHUR POWER	Henry Caine
MISS POTTER	Lois Heatherley

Director: Michael Macowan

Follow My Leader

(Written 1938 but banned by Lord Chamberlain until 1940)
London: Apollo Theatre
Opening: 16 January 1940
Performances: approximately 15

KARL SLIVOVITZ	Walter Hudd
QUETSCH	Frith Banbury
PAUL	Kenneth Morgan
RISZKI	Erik Chitty
MAJOR OTTO BARATSCH	Francis L. Sullivan
MARIE PILAWA	Eileen Peel
HANS ZEDESI	Reginald Beckwith
ANNOUNCER	Bush Bailey
FIRST PHOTOGRAPHER	Geoffrey Clarke
SECOND PHOTOGRAPHER	Raymond Leigh
CHILD	Odile de Chalus
POLICEMAN	Ronald Fortt
KING STEFAN OF NEURASTHENIA	Athole Stewart
SIR COSMO TATE-JOHNSON	Marcus Barron

Director: Athole Stewart

Flare Path

London: Apollo Theatre
Opening: 13 August 1942

Performances: 679

PETER KYLE	Martin Walker
COUNTESS SKRICZEVINSKY	Adrienne Allen
MRS OAKES	Dora Gregory
SERGEANT MILLER (DUSTY)	Leslie Dwyer
PERCY	George Cole
COUNT SKRICZEVINSKY	Gerard Heinz
FLIGHT-LIEUTENANT GRAHAM	
(TEDDY)	Jack Watling
PATRICIA GRAHAM	Phyllis Calvert
MRS MILLER (MAUDIE)	Kathleen Harrison
SQUADRON-LEADER SWANSON	Ivan Samson
CORPORAL JONES	John Bradley

Director: Anthony Asquith

New York: Henry Miller Theatre
Opening: 23 December 1942
Performances: 14

PETER KYLE	Arthur Margetson
COUNTESS SKRICZEVINSKY	Doris Patston
MRS OAKES	Cynthia Latham
SERGEANT MILLER (DUSTY)	Gerald Savory
PERCY	Bob White
COUNT SKRICZEVINSKY	Alexander Ivo
FLIGHT-LIEUTENANT GRAHAM	
(TEDDY)	Alec Guinness
PATRICIA GRAHAM	Nancy Kelly
MRS MILLER (MAUDIE)	Helena Pickard
SQUADRON-LEADER SWANSON	Reynolds Denniston

Director: Margaret Webster

While the Sun Shines

London: Globe Theatre
Opening: 24 December 1943
Performances: 1,154

HORTON	Douglas Jeffries
THE EARL OF HARPENDEN	Michael Wilding
LIEUTENANT MULVANEY	Hugh McDermott
LADY ELISABETH RANDALL	Jane Baxter
THE DUKE OF AYR AND STIRLING	Ronald Squire
LIEUTENANT COLBERT	Eugene Deckers
MABEL CRUM	Brenda Bruce

Director: Anthony Asquith

New York: Lyceum Theatre
Opening: 19 September 1944
Performances: 39

HORTON	J.P. Wilson
THE EARL OF HARPENDEN	Stanley Bell
LIEUTENANT MULVANEY	Lewis Howard
LADY ELISABETH RANDALL	Anne Burr
THE DUKE OF AYR AND STIRLING	Melville Cooper
LIEUTENANT COLBERT	Alexander Ivo
MABEL CRUM	Cathleen Cordell

Director: George S. Kaufman

Love in Idleness

London: Lyric Theatre
Opening: 20 December 1944
Performances: 213 (limited run)

OLIVIA BROWN	Lynn Fontanne
POLTON	Margaret Murray
MISS DELL	Peggy Dear
SIR JOHN FLETCHER	Alfred Lunt
MICHAEL BROWN	Brian Nissen
DIANA FLETCHER	Kathleen Kent
CELIA WENTWORTH	Mona Harrison
SIR THOMAS MARKHAM	Frank Forder
LADY MARKHAM	Antoinette Keith

Director: Alfred Lunt

Retitled *0 Mistress Mine*

New York: Empire Theatre
Opening: 23 January 1946
Performances: 451

OLIVIA BROWN	Lynn Fontanne
POLTON	Margery Maude
MISS DELL	Esther Mitchell
SIR JOHN FLETCHER	Alfred Lunt
MICHAEL BROWN	Dick Van Patten
DIANA FLETCHER	Ann Lee
CELIA WENTWORTH	Marie Paxton

Director: Alfred Lunt

The Winslow Boy

London: Lyric Theatre
Opening: 23 May 1946
Performances: 476

RONNIE WINSLOW	Michael Newell
VIOLET	Kathleen Harrison
ARTHUR WINSLOW	Frank Cellier
GRACE WINSLOW	Madge Compton
DICKIE WINSLOW	Jack Watling
CATHERINE WINSLOW	Angela Baddeley
JOHN WATHERSTONE	Alastair Bannerman
DESMOND CURRY	Clive Morton
MISS BARNES	Mona Washbourne
FRED	Brian Harding
SIR ROBERT MORTON	Emlyn Williams

Director: Glen Byam Shaw

New York: Empire Theatre
Opening: 29 October 1947
Performances: 218

RONNIE WINSLOW	Michael Newell

VIOLET	Betty Sinclair
ARTHUR WINSLOW	Alan Webb
GRACE WINSLOW	Madge Compton
DICKIE WINSLOW	Owen Holder
CATHERINE WINSLOW	Valerie White
JOHN WATHERSTONE	Michael Kingsley
DESMOND CURRY	George Denson
MISS BARNES	Dorothy Hamilton
FRED	Leonard Michell
SIR ROBERT MORTON	Frank Allenby

Director: Glen Byam Shaw

Playbill

London: Phoenix Theatre
Opening: 8 September 1948
Performances: 245

The Browning Version

JOHN TAPLOW	Peter Scott
FRANK HUNTER	Hector Ross
MILLIE CROCKER-HARRIS	Mary Ellis
ANDREW CROCKER-HARRIS	Eric Portman
DR FROBISHER	Campbell Cotts
PETER GILBERT	Anthony Oliver
MRS GILBERT	Henryetta Edwards

Harlequinade

ARTHUR GOSPORT	Eric Portman
EDNA SELBY	Mary Ellis
DAME MAUD GOSPORT	Marie Lohr
JACK WAKEFIELD	Hector Ross
GEORGE CHUDLEIGH	Kenneth Edwards
FIRST HALBERDIER	Peter Scott
SECOND HALBERDIER	Basil Howes
MISS FISHLOCK	Noel Dyson
FRED INGRAM	Anthony Oliver

JOHNNY	Henry Bryce
MURIEL PALMER	Thelma Ruby
TOM PALMER	Patrick Jordan
MR BURTON	Campbell Cotts
JOYCE LANGLAND	Henryetta Edwards
POLICEMAN	Manville Tarrant

Director: Peter Glenville

New York: Coronet Theatre
Opening: 12 October 1949
Performances: 62

The Browning Version

JOHN TAPLOW	Peter Scott-Smith
FRANK HUNTER	Ron Randell
MILLIE CROCKER-HARRIS	Edna Best
ANDREW CROCKER-HARRIS	Maurice Evans
DR FROBISHER	Louis Hector
PETER GILBERT	Frederick Bradlee
MRS GILBERT	Patricia Wheel

Harlequinade

ARTHUR GOSPORT	Maurice Evans
EDNA SELBY	Edna Best
DAME MAUD GOSPORT	Bertha Belmore
JACK WAKEFIELD	Ron Randell
GEORGE CHUDLEIGH	Harry Sothern
FIRST HALBERDIER	Peter Scott-Smith
SECOND HALBERDIER	Tom Hughes Sand
MISS FISHLOCK	Olive Blakeney
FRED INGRAM	Frederick Bradlee
JOHNNY	Bertram Tanswell
MURIEL PALMER	Eileen Page
TOM PALMER	Peter Martyn
MR BURTON	Louis Hector
JOYCE LANGLAND	Patricia Wheel

Director: Peter Glenville

London: St James's Theatre
Opening: 17 March 1949
Performances: 108

PTOLEMY	Raymond Westwell
PERDICCAS	Antony Baird
MAZARES	Marne Maitland
ALEXANDER	Paul Scofield
PYTHIA OF DELPHI	Veronica Turleigh
HEPHAESTION	Julian Dallas
PHILOTAS	Robert Flemyng
AN ATTENDANT	Natasha Wills
DARIUS, KING OF PERSIA	Noel Willman
BESSUS	William Devlin
QUEEN-MOTHER OF PERSIA	Gwen Ffrangcon-Davies
QUEEN STATIRA OF PERSIA	Hazel Terry
PRINCESS STATIRA OF PERSIA	June Rodney
CLEITUS	Cecil Trouncer
PARMENION	Nicholas Hannen
PALACE OFFICIAL	Walter Gotell
ROXANA	Joy Parker
GREEK SOLDIERS	Stanley Baker, John Van Eyssen
PERSIAN SOLDIERS	Terence Longdon, David Oxley, Frederick Treves

Director: Peter Glenville

Who Is Sylvia?

London: Criterion Theatre
Opening: 24 October 1950
Performances: 381

MARK	Robert Flemyng
WILLIAMS	Esmond Knight
DAPHNE	Diane Hart

SIDNEY	Alan Woolston
ETHEL	Diana Allen
OSCAR	Roland Culver
BUBBLES	Diana Hope
NORA	Diane Hart
DENIS	David Aylmer
WILBERFORCE	Roger Maxwell
DORIS	Diane Hart
CHLOE	Joan Benham
CAROLINE	Athene Seyler

Director: Anthony Quayle

The Deep Blue Sea

London: Duchess Theatre
Opening: 6 March 1952
Performances: 513

PHILIP WELCH	David Aylmer
MRS ELTON	Barbara Leake
ANN WELCH	Ann Walford
HESTER COLLYER	Peggy Ashcroft
MR MILLER	Peter Illing
WILLIAM COLLYER	Roland Culver
FREDDIE PAGE	Kenneth More
JACKIE JACKSON	Raymond Francis

Director: Frith Banbury

New York: Morosco Theatre
Opening: 5 November 1952
Performances: 132

PHILIP WELCH	John Merivale
MRS ELTON	Betty Sinclair
ANN WELCH	Stella Andrew
HESTER COLLYER	Margaret Sullavan
MR MILLER	Herbert Berghof
WILLIAM COLLYER	Alan Webb

FREDDIE PAGE   James Hanley
JACKIE JACKSON   Felix Deebank
Director: Frith Banbury

The Sleeping Prince

London: Phoenix Theatre
Opening: 5 November 1953
Performances: 274

PETER NORTHBROOK	Richard Wattis
MARY	Vivien Leigh
THE MAJOR-DOMO	Paul Hardwick
THE REGENT	Laurence Olivier
THE KING	Jeremy Spenser
THE GRAND DUCHESS	Martita Hunt
THE COUNTESS	Rosamund Greenwood
THE BARONESS	Daphne Newton
THE ARCHDUCHESS	Elaine Inescort
THE PRINCESS	Nicola Delman
FOOTMEN	Peter Barkworth, Angus Mackay, Terence Owen

Director: Laurence Olivier

New York: Coronet Theatre
Opening: 1 November 1956
Performances: 60

PETER NORTHBROOK	Rex O'Malley
MARY	Barbara Bel Geddes
THE MAJOR-DOMO	Ronald Dawson
THE REGENT	Michael Redgrave
THE KING	Johnny Stewart
THE GRAND DUCHESS	Cathleen Nesbitt
THE COUNTESS	Nydia Westman
THE BARONESS	Betty Sinclair
THE ARCHDUCHESS	Neff Jerome
THE PRINCESS	Elwin Stock

BUTLER	Sorrell Booke
FIRST FOOTMAN	William Major
SECOND FOOTMAN	Martin Waldron

Director: Michael Redgrave

Separate Tables

London: St James's Theatre
Opening: 22 September 1954
Performances: 726

Table by the Window

MABEL	Marion Fawcett
LADY MATHESON	Jane Eccles
MRS RAILTON-BELL	Phyllis Neilson-Terry
MISS MEACHAM	May Hallatt
DOREEN	Priscilla Morgan
MR FOWLER	Aubrey Mather
MRS SHANKLAND	Margaret Leighton
MISS COOPER	Beryl Measor
MR MALCOLM	Eric Portman
CHARLES STRATTON	Basil Henson
JEAN TANNER	Patricia Raine

Table Number Seven

JEAN STRATTON	Patricia Raine
CHARLES STRATTON	Basil Henson
MAJOR POLLOCK	Eric Portman
MR FOWLER	Aubrey Mather
MISS COOPER	Beryl Measor
MRS RAILTON-BELL	Phyllis Neilson-Terry
MISS RAILTON-BELL	Margaret Leighton
LADY MATHESON	Jane Eccles
MISS MEACHAM	May Hallatt
MABEL	Marion Fawcett
DOREEN	Priscilla Morgan

Director: Peter Glenville

New York: Music Box Theatre
Opening: 25 October 1956
Performances: 322

Table by the Window

MABEL	Georgia Harvey
LADY MATHESON	Jane Eccles
MRS RAILTON–BELL	Phyllis Neilson-Terry
MISS MEACHAM	May Hallatt
DOREEN	Helena Carroll
MR FOWLER	William Podmore
MRS SHANKLAND	Margaret Leighton
MISS COOPER	Beryl Measor
MR MALCOLM	Eric Portman
CHARLES STRATTON	Donald Harron
JEAN TANNER	Ann Hillary

Table Number Seven

JEAN STRATTON	Ann Hillary
CHARLES STRATTON	Donald Harron
MAJOR POLLOCK	Eric Portman
MR FOWLER	William Podmore
MISS COOPER	Beryl Measor
MRS RAILTON–BELL	Phyllis Neilson-Terry
MISS RAILTON–BELL	Margaret Leighton
LADY MATHESON	Jane Eccles
MISS MEACHAM	May Hallatt
MABEL	Georgia Harvey
DOREEN	Helena Carroll

Director: Peter Glenville

Variation on a Theme

London: Globe Theatre
Opening: 8 May 1958
Performances: 132

ROSE	Margaret Leighton
HETTIE	Jean Anderson
RON	Jeremy Brett
KURT	George Pravda
IFIONA	Felicity Ross
MONA	Mavis Villiers
ADRIAN	Lawrence Dalzell
SAM	Michael Goodliffe

Director: John Gielgud

Ross

London: Theatre Royal, Haymarket
Opening: 12 May 1960
Performances: 762

FLIGHT-LIEUTENANT STOKER	Geoffrey Colvile
FLIGHT-SERGEANT THOMPSON	Dervis Ward
AIRCRAFTMAN PARSONS	Peter Bayliss
AIRCRAFTMAN EVANS	John Southworth
AIRCRAFTMAN DICKINSON	Gerald Harper
AIRCRAFTMAN ROSS	Alec Guinness
FRANKS (THE LECTURER)	James Grout
GENERAL ALLENBY	Harry Andrews
RONALD STORRS	Anthony Nicholls
COLONEL BARRINGTON	Leon Sinden
AUDA ABU TAYI	Mark Dignam
TURKISH MILITARY GOVERNOR	Geoffrey Keen
HAMED	Robert Arnold
RASHID	Charles Laurence
A TURKISH CAPTAIN	Basil Hoskins
A TURKISH SERGEANT	Raymond Adamson
A BRITISH CORPORAL	John Trenaman
ADC	Ian Clark
A PHOTOGRAPHER	Antony Kenway
AN AUSTRALIAN SOLDIER	William Feltham
FLIGHT-LIEUTENANT HIGGINS	Peter Cellier

GROUP-CAPTAIN WOOD   John Stuart
Director: Glen Byam Shaw

Joie de Vivre

London: Queen's Theatre
Opening: 14 July 1960
Performances: 4

KENNETH LAKE	Brook Williams
BRIAN CURTIS	Donald Sinden
HON. ALAN HOWARD	Barry Ingham
MARIANNE	Anna Sharkey
MONSIEUR MAINGOT	Harold Kasket
LIEUTENANT-COMMANDER	Terence Alexander
DIANA LAKE	Joanne Rigby
KIT NEILAN	Robin Hunter
JACQUELINE MAINGOT	Jill Martin
LORD HEYBROOK	James Land
CHI–CHI	Joan Heal
TÉRÈSE	Lilian Mowbray
PIERRE	John Leslie
GASTON	Glenn Wilcox
MAYOR	John Moore

Director: William Chapell
Music by: Robert Stolz
Lyrics by: Paul Dehn

Ross

New York: Eugene O'Neill Theatre
Opening: 26 December 1961
Performances: 159

FLIGHT-LIEUTENANT STOKER	Robert Milli
FLIGHT-SERGEANT THOMPSON	Ted Gunther
AIRCRAFTMAN PARSONS	Bill Glover

AIRCRAFTMAN DICKINSON	Francis Bethencourt
AIRCRAFTMAN ROSS	John Mills
FRANKS (THE LECTURER)	Kenneth Ruta
GENERAL ALLENBY	John Williams
RONALD STORRS	Anthony Nicholls
COLONEL BARRINGTON	Court Benson
AUDA ABU TAYI	Paul Sparer
TURKISH MILITARY GOVERNOR	Geoffrey Keen
HAMED	Cal Bellini
RASHID	Joseph Della Sorte
A TURKISH CAPTAIN	Eric Van Nuys
A TURKISH SERGEANT	Thomas Newman
A BRITISH CORPORAL	Del Tenney
ADC	Nicolas Coster
A PHOTOGRAPHER	Scott Graham
AN AUSTRALIAN SOLDIER	John Hallow
FLIGHT-LIEUTENANT HIGGINS	John Valentine
GROUP-CAPTAIN WOOD	James Craven

Director: Glen Byam Shaw

Man and Boy

London: Queens Theatre
Opening: 4 September 1963
Performances: 69 (limited run)

CAROL PENN	Alice Kennedy Turney
BASIL ANTHONY	Barry Justice
GREGOR ANTONESCU	Charles Boyer
SVEN JOHNSON	Geoffrey Keen
MARK L. HERRIS	Austin Willis
DAVID BEESTON	William Smithers
COUNTESS ANTONESCU	Jane Downs

Director: Michael Benthall

New York: Brooks Atkinson Theatre
Opening: 12 November 1963

Performances: 54

CAROL PENN	Louise Sorel
BASIL ANTHONY	Barry Justice
GREGOR ANTONESCU	Charles Boyer
SVEN JOHNSON	Geoffrey Keen
MARK L. HERRIS	Austin Willis
DAVID BEESTON	William Smithers
COUNTESS ANTONESCU	Jane Downs

Director: Michael Benthall

A Bequest to the Nation

London: Theatre Royal, Haymarket
Opening: 23 September 1970
Performances: 124

GEORGE MATCHAM SNR	Ewan Roberts
KATHERINE MATCHAM	Jean Harvey
BETSY	Deborah Watling
GEORGE MATCHAM JNR	Michael Wardle
EMILY	Una Brandon Jones
FRANCES, LADY NELSON	Leueen MacGrath
NELSON	Ian Holm
LORD BARHAM	A. J. Brown
EMMA HAMILTON	Zoë Caldwell
FRANCESCA	Marisa Merlini
LORD MINTO	Michael Aldridge
CAPTAIN HARDY	Brian Glover
REV. WILLIAM NELSON	Geoffrey Edwards
SARAH NELSON	Eira Griffiths
HORATIO	Stuart Knee
CAPTAIN BLACKWOOD	Geoffrey Deevers
MIDSHIPMAN	Stuart Knee
FOOTMEN, SAILORS, MAIDS	Stanley Lloyd, Conrad Asquith, Graham Edwards, Chris Carbis, Deborah Watling, Alison Coleridge

Director: Peter Glenville

London: Duchess Theatre
Opening: 27 September 1973
Performances: 131
Before Dawn

THE BARON	Donald Sinden
THE LACKEY	Don Fellows
THE CAPTAIN	Richard Warwick
THE DIVA	Joan Greenwood

After Lydia

LYDIA CRUTTWELL	Joan Greenwood
SEBASTIAN CRUTTWELL	Donald Sinden
MARK WALTERS	Don Fellows
JOEY CRUTTWELL	Richard Warwick

Director: John Dexter

New York: Morosco Theatre
Opening: 10 December 1974
Performances: 199

In Praise of Love

LYDIA CRUTTWELL	Julie Harris
SEBASTIAN CRUTTWELL	Rex Harrison
MARK WALTERS	Martin Gabel
JOEY CRUTTWELL	Peter Burnell

Director: Fred Coe

Duologue

Adapted from television play *All on Her Own*
London: King's Head Theatre
Opening: February 1976
Performances: unknown – approximately 15

ROSEMARY	Barbara Jefford

Director: Stewart Trotter

London: Her Majesty's Theatre
Opening: 4 July 1977
Performances: 282

ALMA RATTENBURY	Glynis Johns
FRANCIS RATTENBURY	Anthony Pedley
CHRISTOPHER	Matthew Ryan
IRENE RIGGS	Sheila Grant
GEORGE WOOD	Neil Dalglish
EDITH DAVENPORT	Helen Lindsay
JOHN DAVENPORT	Jeremy Hawk
TONY DAVENPORT	Adam Richardson
STELLA MORRISON	Angela Browne
RANDOLPH BROWN	Kevin Hart
JUDGE	Patrick Barr
O'CONNOR	Kenneth Griffith
CROOM-JOHNSON	Bernard Archard
CASSWELL	Darryl Forbes-Dawson
MONTAGU	Philip Bowen
CLERK OF THE COURT	David Glover
JOAN WEBSTER	Peggy Aitchison
SERGEANT BAGWELL	Anthony Pedley
PORTER	Anthony Howard
WARDER	David Masterman
CORONER	David Glover

Director: Robin Midgley

Rattigan's principal films

Early in his career Rattigan contributed to numerous screenplays uncredited. The following are the principal films he scripted once he became well known:

French Without Tears, 1939. Director: Anthony Asquith.

Quiet Wedding (with Anatole de Grunwald), 1940. Director: Anthony Asquith.

The Day Will Dawn (US: *The Avengers*) (with Anatole de Grunwald and Patrick Kirwan), 1942. Director: Harold French.

Uncensored (with Wolfgang Wilhelm and Rodney Ackland), 1942. Director: Anthony Asquith.

English Without Tears (US: *Her Man Gilbey*) (with Anatole de Grunwald), 1944. Director: Anthony Asquith.

Journey Together, 1945. Director: John Boulting.

The Way to the Stars (US: *Johnny in the Clouds*) (with Anatole de Grunwald), 1945. Director: Anthony Asquith.

Brighton Rock (with Graham Greene), 1947. Director: John Boulting.

While the Sun Shines (with Anatole de Grunwald), 1947. Director: Anthony Asquith.

Bond Street (with Anatole de Grunwald and Rodney Ackland), 1948. Director: Gordon Parry.

The Winslow Boy (with Anatole de Grunwald), 1948. Director: Anthony Asquith.

The Browning Version, 1951. Director: Anthony Asquith. Rattigan won the 1951 Cannes Film Festival award for Best Screenplay.

The Sound Barrier (US: *Breaking the Sound Barrier*), 1952. Director: David Lean.

The Final Test, 1953. Director: Anthony Asquith.

The Man Who Loved Redheads, 1954. Director: Harold French.

The Deep Blue Sea, 1955. Director: Anatole Litvak.

The Prince and the Showgirl, 1957. Director: Laurence Olivier.

Separate Tables (with John Gay), 1958. Director: Delbert Mann.

The VIPs, 1963. Director: Anthony Asquith.

The Yellow Rolls-Royce, 1964. Director: Anthony Asquith.

Goodbye, Mr Chips, 1969. Director: Herbert Ross.

Bequest to the Nation, 1973. Director: James Cellan-Jones.

Rattigan's original television scripts

The Final Test, first transmission, BBC, 29 July 1951. Director: Royston Morley.

Heart to Heart, first transmission, BBC, 6 December 1962. Director: Alvin Rakoff.

Ninety Years On, first transmission BBC, 29 November 1964. Producer: Michael Mills.

Nelson – A Portrait in Miniature, first transmission, ATV, 21 March 1966. Director: Stuart Burge.

All on Her Own, first transmission, BBC 2, 25 September 1968. Director: Hal Burton.

High Summer (adapted from earlier, unperformed stage play), first transmission, Thames Television, 1972. Director: Peter Duguid.

Radio

Cause Célèbre, first broadcast, BBC Radio 4, 27 October 1975. Producer: Norman Wright.

Principal Unperformed Works

Texts held in The Rattigan Papers at the British Library.

Stage

Integer Vitae (*The Pure in Heart*), 1927.
Black Forest, 1935.

Two Dozen Roses, adapted from a play by Aldo Benetii, 1939.
Le Valet Maitre, adapted from a play by Paul Armont and Leopold Marchand, 1939.
Like Father, 1960.
Pas de Deux, 1968.

Films

O Mistress Mine adapted from *Love in Idleness*, 1949.
Crime Wave, 1946.
World Première, 1947.
Burke and Wills, 1969.

Television

Nijinsky, 1974.

Bibliography

Rattigan's works

For the texts of Terence Rattigan's published plays I have used the following (except where otherwise noted in the text or Notes):
The Collected Plays of Terence Rattigan (with prefaces by the author):
Volume I (*French Without Tears, Flare Path, While the Sun Shines, Love in Idleness, The Winslow Boy*), Hamish Hamilton, London, 1953
Volume II (*The Browning Version, Harlequinade, Adventure Story, Who Is Sylvia?, The Deep Blue Sea*), Hamish Hamilton, London, 1953
Volume III (*The Sleeping Prince, Separate Tables, Variation on a Theme, Ross, Heart to Heart*), Hamish Hamilton, London, 1964
Volume IV (*Man and Boy, Bequest to the Nation, In Praise of Love, Before Dawn, Cause Célèbre*), with an introduction by B. A. Young, Hamish Hamilton, London, 1978
After the Dance, Hamish Hamilton, London, 1939, and Nick Hern Books, London, 1995
The Prince and the Showgirl: The Script for the Film, New American Library, New York, 1957
All on Her Own, included in *The Best Short Plays 1970*, edited by Stanley Richards, Chilton, Philadelphia, 1970

For unpublished plays, film, television and radio scripts I am indebted to the late Sir Terence Rattigan, to Peter Carter-Ruck and the Trustees of the Rattigan Trust, to Sally Brown, Curator of Modern Manuscripts at the British Library, to Sir Terence's agent Michael Imison of Michael Imison Playwrights Ltd, to the British Broadcasting Corporation, to Associated Television, to Thames Television and to numerous of Sir Terence's friends and professional colleagues. For other unpublished papers relating to

Terence Rattigan and for unpublished papers and letters written by or about other members of Rattigan's family, in addition to the Rattigan Papers held in the British Library, I sought information from the Theatre Museum, the Foreign Office Papers, the Curzon Papers, the Foreign Office Lists and the Royal Air Force lists in the Public Record Office and the Family Record Office. I have also referred to *The Dictionary of National Biography* and *Who's Who* for relevant years.

Rattigan's many contributions to newspapers, periodicals and radio are acknowledged in the text and Notes, but the following of his contributions to other published works have proved especially useful:

'A Magnificent Pity for Camels' in *Diversion*, edited by John Sutro, Max Parrish, London, 1950

'An Appreciation of his Work in the Theatre', in *The Theatrical Companion to Noël Coward*, Raymond Mander and Joe Mitchenson, Rockliff, London, 1957

I Swore I Never Would (foreword by Terence Rattigan), Harold French, Secker & Warburg, London, 1970

Olivier (contribution by Sir Terence Rattigan), edited by Logan Gourlay, Weidenfeld & Nicolson, London, 1973

Works about Rattigan by other authors

A Critical Analysis of the Plays of Sir Terence Rattigan, Holly Hill, University Microfilms International, New York, 1975

Terence Rattigan; The Man and His Work, Michael Darlow and Gillian Hodson, Quartet Books, London, 1979

Terence Rattigan, Susan Rusinko, Twayne Publishers, G. K. Hall & Company, Boston, 1983

The Rattigan Version, B. A. Young, Hamish Hamilton, London, 1986

Terence Rattigan; A Biography, Geoffrey Wansell, Fourth Estate, London, 1995

Works by other authors quoted or used in preparation of this book

Agate, James, *The Contemporary Theatre, 1944 and 1945*, George Harrap, London, 1946

Annan, Noël (Lord), *Our Age: Portrait Of A Generation*, Weidenfeld & Nicolson, London, 1990

Baxter, Beverley, *First Nights and Noises Off*, Hutchinson, London, 1966

Baxter, Keith, *My Sentiments Exactly*, Oberon Books, London, 1998

Bergler, E., *Homosexuality: Disease or Way of Life*, Hill & Wang, New York, 1956

Billington, Michael, *Peggy Ashcroft*, John Murray, London, 1988

Black, Kitty, *Upper Circle – A Theatrical Chronicle*, Methuen, London, 1984

Bogarde, Dirk, *Snakes and Ladders*, Chatto & Windus, London, 1978

Bolitho, Hector, *My Restless Years*, Parrish, London, 1962

Brandreth, Giles, *John Gielgud – A Celebration*, Pavilion Books, 1994

Byng, Douglas, *As You Were – Reminiscences*, Gerald Duckworth, London, 1970

Carpenter, Humphrey, *OUDS: A Centenary History of Oxford University Dramatic Society*, Oxford University Press, 1985

— *Benjamin Britten*, Faber & Faber, London, 1992

Clark, Colin, *The Colin Clark Diaries: The Prince, The Showgirl and Me*, HarperCollins, London, 1995

Clogg, Richard, *A Concise History of Greece*, Cambridge University Press, 1992

Cotterell, John and Cashin, Fergus, *Richard Burton*, Arthur Barker, London, 1974

Crawley, Aidan, *Look Before You Leap*, Collins, London, 1988

Culver, Roland, *Not Quite a Gentleman*, William Kimber, London, 1979

Dawnay, Jean, *Model Girl*, Weidenfeld & Nicolson, London, 1956

— *How I Became a Fashion Model*, Thomas Nelson, London, 1960 de Jongh, Nicholas, *Not in Front of the Audience: Homosexuality on Stage*, Routledge, London, 1992

Denison, Michael, *Overture and Beginners*, Gollancz, London, 1973

Driberg, Tom, *Ruling Passions*, Jonathan Cape, London, 1977

Duff, Charles, *The Lost Summer: The Heyday of the West End Theatre*, Nick Hern Books, London, 1995

Edwards, Anne, *Vivien Leigh – A Biography*, W. H. Allen, London, 1977

Forbes, Bryan, *Ned's Girl – The Life of Edith Evans*, Hamish Hamilton, London, 1977

— *A Divided Life*, Heinemann, London, 1982

— *That Despicable Race*, Elm Tree Books, London, 1980

— *Notes for a Life*, Collins, London, 1974

Freeman, John, *Face to Face*, BBC Books, London, 1989

French, Harold, *I Swore I Never Would*, Secker & Warburg, London, 1970

— *I Thought I Never Could*, Secker & Warburg, London, 1973

Gielgud, John, *Early Stages*, Macmillan, London, 1939

— *Backward Glances*, Hodder & Stoughton, London, 1989

Grey, Anthony, *Quest for Justice: Towards Homosexual Emancipation*, Sinclair-Stevenson, London, 1992

Griffin, John, *The Winslow Boy: Terence Rattigan*, Longmans, 1989

Hall, Peter, *Peter Hall's Diaries: The Story of a Dramatic Battle*, edited by John Goodwin, Hamish Hamilton, London, 1983

Halliwell, Leslie and Purser, Philip, *Halliwell's Television Companion*, Grafton Books, London, 1986

Hamilton, J. R., *Alexander the Great*, Hutchinson University Library, London, 1973

Harrison, Rex, *Rex – An Autobiography*, Macmillan, London, 1974

— *A Damned Serious Business*, Bantam Press, London, 1990

Hart, Liddell, *T. E. Lawrence: In Arabia and After*, Jonathan Cape, London, 1948

Hartnoll, Phylis (ed.), *The Oxford Companion to the Theatre*, Oxford University Press, 1951

Hayman, Ronald, *John Gielgud*, Heinemann, London, 1971

Hickey, Des and Smith, Gus, *The Prince – The Public and Private Life of Laurence Harvey*, Leslie Frewin, London, 1975

Hickson, Alisdare, *The Poisoned Bowl: Sex, Repression and the Public School*, Constable, London, 1995

Higgins, Patrick, *Hetero-sexual Dictatorship*, Fourth Estate, London, 1996

Holroyd, Michael, *Bernard Shaw* (four volumes), Chatto & Windus, London, 1988–92

Houston, Arthur H., *English Drama – Its Past History and Probable Future*, Royal College of Science, Dublin, 1863

Huggett, Richard, *Binkie Beaumont, Eminence Grise of the West End 1933–73*, Hodder & Stoughton, London, 1989

Hurren, Kenneth, *Theatre Inside Out*, W. H. Allen, London, 1977

James, Robert Rhodes (ed.), *Chips – The Diaries of Sir Henry Channon*, Weidenfeld & Nicolson, London, 1967

Jeffery-Poulter, Stephen, *Peers, Queers And Commons*, Routledge, London, 1991

Jesse, F. Tennyson (ed.), *Rattenbury & Stoner* (Notable British Trials Series), William Hodge, London, 1946

Johnston, John, *The Lord Chamberlain's Blue Pencil*, Hodder & Stoughton, London, 1990

Kitchin, Laurence, *Mid-Century Drama*, Faber & Faber, London, 1960

Lacey, Stephen, *British Realist Theatre: The New Wave in its Context 1956-1965*, Routledge, London, 1995

Lahr, John, *Prick Up Your Ears*, Allen Lane, Penguin, London, 1978

Lawrence, T. E., *Seven Pillars of Wisdom*, Jonathan Cape, London, 1935

Lewes, Kenneth, *The Psychoanalytic Theory of Male Homosexuality*, Quartet Books, London, 1989

Magee, Bryan, *One in Twenty – A Study of Homosexuality in Men and Women*, Secker & Warburg, London, 1966

Marie, Queen of Romania, *The Story of My Life*, Volume 3, Cassell, London, 1935

Meyer, Michael, *Not Prince Hamlet: A Life in Theatrical and Literary London*, Martin Secker & Warburg, London, 1989

Miller, Arthur, *Timebends: A Life*, Methuen, London, 1987

Minney, R. J., *Puffin Asquith – A Biography*, Leslie Frewin, London, 1973

Montagu, Edwin, *The Archer-Shee Case*, David & Charles, Newton Abbot, 1974

More, Kenneth, *Happy Go Lucky – My Life*, Robert Hale, London, 1959

— *More or Less*, Hodder & Stoughton, London, 1978

Newman, K. O., *Mind, Sex and War – Blackouts, Fear of Air Raids and Propaganda*, Pelago, Oxford, 1941

— *Two Hundred and Fifty Times I Saw a Play – or Authors, Actors and Audiences*, Pelago, Oxford, 1944

Nicolson, Sir Harold, *Curzon – Volume 3: The Last Phase 1919–1925*, Ernest Benn, London, 1934

Norwood, Dr Cyril, *The English Tradition in Education*, John Murray, London, 1929

O'Connor, Gary, *Darlings of the Gods: A Year in the Lives of Laurence Olivier and Vivien Leigh*, Hodder & Stoughton, London, 1984

— *The Secret Woman: A Life of Peggy Ashcroft*, Weidenfeld & Nicolson, London, 1997

— *Alec Guinness – Master of Disguise*, Hodder & Stoughton, London, 1995

O'Connor, Sean, *Straight Acting: Popular Gay Drama from Wilde to Rattigan*, Cassell, London, 1998

O'Hara, Riggs, *The Honourable Beast – A Posthumous Autobiography of John Dexter*, Nick Hern Books, London, 1993

Olivier, Laurence, *Confessions of an Actor*, Weidenfeld & Nicolson, London, 1982

Olivier, Tarquin, *My Father Laurence Olivier*, Headline Book Publishing, London, 1992

Oman, Carola, *Nelson*, Hodder & Stoughton, London, 1947

Orton, Joe, *The Orton Diaries*, edited by John Lahr, Methuen, London, 1986

Osborn, Peter, *Exit Praying*, Peacock Publications, Norwood, South Australia, 1995

Osborne, John, *A Better Class of Person*, Faber & Faber, London, 1981

Pakula, Hannah, *The Last Romantic: A Biography of Queen Marie of Roumania*, Weidenfeld & Nicolson, London, 1985

Payn, Graham and Morley, Sheridan, (eds.), *The Noël Coward Diaries*, Little, Brown & Company, London, 1982

Powell, Anthony, *Faces in My Time*, Volume 3 of *To Keep the Ball Rolling: Memoirs of Anthony Powell* (four volumes), Heinemann, London, 1980

Pratley, Gerald, *The Cinema of David Lean*, Tantivy, London, 1974

Pudney, John, *Collected Poems*, Putnam, London, 1957

Press, Truman (ed.), *Somersetshire Country Houses and Villages*, Truman Press, printed by Walker & Co. Ltd, for the Sole Editor – Proprietor, Twickenham, 1931

Rattigan, Frank, *Diversions of a Diplomat*, Chapman and Hall, London, 1924

Rattigan, Sir William Henry, *Events to be Remembered in the History of India from the Invasion of Alexander to the Latest Times*, Punjabee Press, Lahore, 1863

Redgrave, Corin, *Michael Redgrave, My Father*, Richard Cohen Books, London, 1995

Redgrave, Michael, *In My Mind's Eye*, Weidenfeld & Nicolson, London, 1983

Rothschild, Victor (Lord), *Meditations of a Broomstick*, Collins, London, 1977

Russell Taylor, John, *Anger and After*, Methuen, London, 1962

Shaplen, Robert, *Kreuger; Genius and Swindler*, Deutsch, London, 1961

Spoto, Donald, *Laurence Olivier*, HarperCollins, London, 1991

Stone, Paulene, *One Tear is Enough – A Biography of Laurence Harvey*, Michael Joseph, London, 1975

Storr, Anthony, *Sexual Deviation*, Penguin, London, 1964

Symons, Julian, *The Thirties and The Nineties*, Carcanet, 1990

Taylor, A. J. P., *English History 1914–1945*, Oxford University Press, 1965

Tynan, Kenneth, *Curtains*, Longmans, London, 1961

— *A View of the English Stage 1946–63*, Davis Poynter, London, 1975

Ustinov, Peter, *Dear Me*, William Heinemann, London, 1977

Vickers, Hugo, *Cecil Beaton – The Authorised Biography*, Weidenfeld & Nicolson, London, 1985

Wardle, Irving, *The Theatres of George Devine*, Jonathan Cape, London, 1978

Walker, Alexander, *Vivien*, Weidenfeld & Nicolson, London, 1987

Wilcox, Michael, *Benjamin Britten's Operas*, Absolute Press, Bath, 1997

Wilding, Michael, *Apple Sauce as told to Paula Wilcox*, George Allen & Unwin, London, 1982

Williams, Kenneth, *The Diaries of Kenneth Williams*, edited by Russell Davies, HarperCollins, London, 1993

Worsley, T. C., *Fellow Travellers*, London Magazine Editions, London, 1971

— *Flannelled Fool*, Alan Ross Ltd, London, 1966

Zolotow, Maurice, *Stagestruck – Alfred Lunt and Lynn Fontanne*, Heinemann, London, 1965

— *Marilyn Monroe*, W. H. Allen, London, 1961

Quotations and assistance from newspapers, periodicals, radio and television are credited as appropriate in the text.

People interviewed since 1977

Arthur Abeles, Rodney Ackland, Elkan Allan, Dame Peggy Ashcroft, A. J. H. Benn, Michael Billington, John Boulting, Brenda Bruce, Glen Byam Shaw, Peter Carter-Ruck, James Cellan-Jones, Roland Culver, Tony Darnborough, Jean Dawnay, Michael Denison, William Devlin, Peter Duguid, Frank Dunlop, Sheila Dyatt, Robert Flemyng, Michael Franklin, John Gale, Sir John Gielgud, Peter Glenville, Anthony Goldschmidt, Anatole de Grunwald, Rex Harrison, David Heimann, Holly Hill, Sir Harold Hobson, Roger Hunter, Michael Imison, Lady Kaldor, Alfred Lunt, Michael Macowan, Robin Maugham, Cedric Messina, Michael Meyer, Robin Midgeley, Stephen Mitchell, Philip Oakes, John Osborne, John Perry, Alvin Rakoff, Sir Terence Rattigan, Goronwy Rees, Susan Rusinko, Valerie Skardon, Sir John Stow, Jack Watling, A. E. Whitehead, Dorian Williams and Emlyn Williams.

I have also drawn on correspondence with Aidan Crawley, John Montgomery and Peter Osborn.

Index

INTRODUCTORY NOTE: R refers to Terence Rattigan; F to his father, Frank; V to his mother, Vera. Rattigan's major plays and films are listed in the course of the Index; his other writings are placed after the entry for Rattigan, Terence.

conflict with F over career 57; dropped from Harrow cricket team 57–8; character at Oxford 61–2; drag act at OUDS 63, 73; at French crammer's 63–5; Oxford lodgings 65; writes review for *Cherwell* 66–7; in *Romeo and Juliet* (OUDS) 68, 69; meets John Perry 69–70; overawed by Gielgud; 70; sexuality at Oxford 70–4: venereal disease 74; political sympathies 74–5; pacifism and Oxford Union debate 75; writes *First Episode* with Heimann 76, 77–8; at German crammer's 78–9; and Waddington's *First Episode* performance 87; leaves Oxford 88–9; writes six plays in two years 90–1; visits Denmark 91, 94; collaborates with Bolitho 94–5; Dickens adaptation with Gielgud 95–7; reads plays to V 98; interest in Rattenbury case 99; discouraged by rejections 99–100; and Warner Brothers 100, 101–3, 120–1, 122; first visit to Green Room Club 104–5; reaction to success 118–119, 120, 125; letter from Paris hotel manager 120; starts new play 121–2; opinion of Coward 124–5; left-wing politics 126; starts relationship with Osborn 129; takes own flat 129; social life and Osborn 130–1; depression 131; affair with Morgan 132; at Eton v. Harrow match 134; outbreak of World War II 135; struggles to write 137–8; advised by Newman 138; first work with Asquith 138–9; script-writing 139–40; joins RAF 142; wartime sex life 142, 146; RAF training 143–4; RAF service 144–9, 161–2, 163; with Osborn in Southampton 146; promoted 150; voice of acceptable dissent 157; creative processes discussed in Newman's book 159–60; involvement with Newman

161; at New York Waldorf Astoria 162–3; misses Churchill at performance 163; gets script-writing leave 164; in wartime London 164–5; script-writing 171; with RAF Film Unit 172–3; meets Gertrude Lawrence 174–5; working on film scripts and play 175–7; meets Lunt 179; reaction to Lunt's rewriting 182–3, 184–5; seduced by Channon 186–7; success and ambition 189; social life with Channon 192; interest in trials 194; enthusiasm for Archer-Shee case 194–5; fame and fashion 204–5; favours shorter plays 205, 206–7; attitude to critics 207; falls for Morgan 209–10; friendship with Osborn 209; concealing sexuality 210–11; financial state 220–1; and International Screenplays 222–3; and Asquith's drinking 223; hurt by Gielgud 224; interest in Alexander the Great 229–31; at the Stag and Hounds 234; relationship with Morgan 235–6; importance of reputation as writer 235; and *Adventure Story* financing 236; pass at Burton 237, 254; Morgan moves out 238; effect of Morgan's suicide 239, 240–1, 244–5, 247; on marriage 241–2; on film adaptation 245; and F's stroke 246; visits Copenhagen 246; changes agent 247, 260; works on theatrical credo 247–8; Play of Ideas debate 251–2, 255; blocks Ross's career 253; lacks intellectual and creative friends 254–5; relationship with Beaumont 254; writing about F 256–7, 258, 259–60; attitude to criticism 260–1; helps young playwrights 262–3; and English Playwrights Group 263; and television 264–5; Oscar nomination 269; starts relationship with Franklin 269–70; gives up